THE
BEATLES
1963

A YEAR IN THE LIFE

THE BEATLES 1963

A YEAR IN THE LIFE

DAFYDD REES

OMNIBUS PRESS

CONTENTS

*This book is dedicated to those sadly no longer with us,
who graciously gave of their time and their memories
to bring these stories to fruition.*

INTRODUCTION

The idea for this book began as long ago as 2008. I was commuting to Boston from my home on Cape Cod, 150 miles a day, five days a week. I hadn't had a book published for a while and thought it was high time I worked on another one. I chose the Beatles in 1963 because the group started out the year virtually unknown and ended the year six weeks away from being seen on the 'Ed Sullivan Show' before an audience of some 73 million. I initially wrote to as many local newspapers as I could find, asking them to print a letter for people who had seen them in 1963, to get in touch with me. A steady stream of replies arrived and I soon realised that maybe I was on to something. It also dawned on me that talking to people elicited a better response than the written word, so I contacted an old friend, Jan Gammie, and asked whether she would be willing to call people and ask them to recall their 1963 Beatles memories. While she got on with finding stories I worked on the research to find as much as I could about what the group did that year. I wasn't expecting to find that much new information. After fifty years or so I thought little was left to discover – but I was wrong. I hopefully have put to rest some errors that have been out there for years and I will probably be castigated for making some new ones. (Please let me know if I have – beatlesin63@gmail.com). I made several visits to the UK and travelled the length and breadth of England, Scotland and Wales in the process, retracing the short Scottish tour at the beginning of 1963, visiting all the seaside resorts where they had week-long residencies, and the location of several smaller venues, many of which are no more. Countless hours were spent at the British Newspaper Library and the British Library, finding articles in local papers. In all it took about ten years to finish the project and then COVID struck, which put everything on hold.

This is a book for those who remember the 1960s and can wallow in its nostalgia and for the younger generation, who will – hopefully – get a glimpse of what life was like before credit cards, when owning a camera was out of reach for many and making a phone call meant traipsing to the phone box at the end of the road. It's hard to believe that teenagers would sleep on pavements, sometimes in the pouring rain, sometimes for days on end, to buy a ticket to see their favourite pop stars, and an era when people could tell you the first record they bought. All of us, with the passage of time, have memories that fade or change. In Ben MacIntyre's wonderful book *A Foreign Field*, he writes: 'Recollections of a remote time can never be perfectly accurate, but they were offered with simple honesty, and I have tried to record them faithfully.' Close to 300 people provided stories for this book – I cannot thank them enough.

JANUARY
From Hamburg to Birkenhead

TUESDAY 1 JANUARY

Snow had begun falling in the capital on Boxing Day. A weather system had started its move south on Christmas Eve and by New Year's Day, Britain was in the grip of a winter that would turn out to be the worst since 1740. Performers up and down the country were falling foul of the conditions. Nearly 500 miles away and already an hour into the New Year in Hamburg, West Germany, the weather wasn't much better. All New Year's Eve flights from the city had been cancelled. In the midst of all this, the Beatles were playing the last night of a thirteen-night engagement at the Star-Club, sharing a bill with American instrumental act Johnny and the Hurricanes, Tony Sheridan with the Star-Combo, the Strangers, Carol Elvin and fellow Liverpudlians Kingsize Taylor and the Dominoes. This visit to Hamburg, the Beatles' fifth and last, had been taken under much duress. They had signed with EMI's Parlophone label the previous May and had already recorded their first two singles at EMI studios in Abbey Road with producer George Martin. John [Lennon] later said, 'If we'd had our way, we'd have just copped out on the engagement.'

When they had left for Hamburg on 18 December 1962, their first single 'Love Me Do' had risen to number 19 in the *New Record Mirror* (*NRM*) chart, but now stood at number 17. Paul [McCartney] later disparaged the single, saying it was not very good – but 'only a little bit worse than the kind of thing on the hit parade then.' The Beatles were staying in the Hotel Pacific on Neuer Pferdemarkt. Their legacy at the hotel was immortalised in a handwritten message on the wall in one of the rooms, with an arrow pointing to the bed below that read 'John Lennon caught the crabs in this bed.' After snatching a few hours' sleep, the group checked out of the hotel and were driven the 15 miles north to the airport by their friend Icke Braun – appropriately in his VW Beetle, accompanied by Astrid Kirchherr. Although weather conditions had improved overnight, the 12.50pm BEA flight to London was delayed several hours. They spent the night at the Royal Court Hotel in Sloane Square, where they had first stayed the previous June, when they were in London to record at Abbey Road. With a short tour of Scotland scheduled for the coming week, plans were changed and arrangements made for them to fly to Edinburgh the following morning. Thus 1963 began for the Beatles.

> ❛ I was working in a group in Toledo, when the original Johnny and the Hurricanes broke up. They had a difference of opinion as to who was going to run it and how it was going to be run, so the group fell apart, and John had a lot of contracts to fulfil and he needed people to go on the road with him. I had already been playing with a couple of the Hurricanes so I knew he was looking for people. So I went down to his basement, played the chord organ, and went on the road with him. So we went over there in December of 1962. The Star-Club went almost 24/7 – they closed for an hour every day just to clean up. The groups played at different times, running continuously and alternating. Sometimes we weren't even in the club at the same time and sometimes the groups would be out front drinking beer and watching the other groups play. The waitresses were looking up and down

9

those Beatles somethin' else. You could tell somethin' was going on. Waitresses are sometimes pretty smart when it comes to spotting talent.

We stayed at the same hotel. I liked the guys. Paul was very straight, very clean dressed, well mannered. He didn't like German tea. He said it was too weak. So he'd put the tea bag on a spoon and twist the string around to hasten the steeping of the tea. I wonder whether he still does it that way. George [Harrison] liked to party and we'd go down into the basement to drink. John was very much the leader and the straight one, and Ringo [Starr] was just enjoying the fact he was with the group.

After we finished our two weeks at the club we went on to Wiesbaden and played US bases for a while, then I think we went back for another week or so and then we took the train across to the Hook of Holland and went to London for a short tour of England. We stayed in a hotel opposite the Science Museum. Mickey Spillane was making a movie and was staying at the same hotel and I had some fun with him. There was a night club in the hotel and I used to go down there to unwind, being out all night, and one time I was down there and the door flew open and there he was with a valet with some beer and he came up on the stage with me and we partied all night long. He had some of his heavies drive us round England. I remember the weather was really bad.

When we came back to the States we were always talking about the Beatles. I left Johnny and the Hurricanes in January 1964. The following month I watched the Beatles on *The Ed Sullivan Show* with my wife and kids. The Beatles went on to become millionaires and, basically, I just came home, working with local groups. I gave up playing in 1996 when I did my last gig with a group called the Helmsmen. When I talk about what I did and my acquaintance with the Beatles, most of the people round me even to this day don't believe it. That's the way it goes. I do know we were making more money than them at the Star-Club. ❚

EDDIE WAGANFEALD, MUSICIAN, OREGON, OHIO, USA

WEDNESDAY 2 JANUARY

Stepping out into Sloane Square, the group were greeted by more snow before trudging back to London Airport to catch the 1.20pm BEA flight to Edinburgh – where they would meet their ever-reliable roadie Neil Aspinall in the band's Ford Thames 800 Express bus, laden with John and George's Vox amplifiers and Paul's bass cabinet, which had been overhauled and re-covered at Barratt's music shop in Manchester while they were away. After arriving at the airport, the group were informed that their flight was being re-routed to Aberdeen's Dyce Airport because of the bad weather. With the group diverted and Aspinall driving to Edinburgh unaware of the flight change, there was no choice but to cancel their appearance at the Longmore Hall in Keith, Banff.

After they landed in Aberdeen, which was experiencing its coldest temperatures since

MODERN DANCING ENTERPRISES
present
THE "LOVE ME DO" BOYS
THE BEATLES
plus
JOHNNY AND THE COPY CATS
In THE LONGMORE HALL, KEITH,
On WEDNESDAY, JANUARY 2, 1963, 9—1 a.m.
ADMISSION 5/-.
Buses leave Keith via Deskford, Huntly and Dufftown at 8.30 p.m.

1895, the group checked into the Gloucester Hotel in Union Street. John took advantage of the night off and flew back to Liverpool, much to the surprise of his wife Cynthia. In the meantime, Aspinall, discovering that his charges weren't at Edinburgh Airport, was making his way north through the appalling weather to meet up with them. The RAC warned drivers that all roads were treacherous; drizzling rain froze as soon as it hit the ground. Ten roads in Scotland were impassable. Despite snowdrifts preventing travel into Keith from either north or south, the show went ahead with support act Johnny and the Copycats performing throughout the evening. Disappointed fans hoping to see the Beatles could at least enjoy watching Kirk Douglas and Tony Curtis in *The Vikings* at the Keith Playhouse. Two days later, a local teenager attending a 21st birthday party encountered knee-high snow, and rather than ruin her boots, walked home in her stockinged feet.

❝ I was the bass guitarist with Johnny and the Copycats. We were all 16, except rhythm guitarist Ali Ewan, who was 15. We walked through deep snow in Buckie to get to W.F. Johnson (Photographers and Printers) where we stored our equipment in a spare darkroom at the rear of the business. We were picked up by a taxi hired from Gray's Taxis, Portsoy in a two-tone Vauxhall Cresta, with a roof rack. The 12-mile journey took almost an hour due to snowbound roads, but we arrived at the hall at about eight o'clock. A path had been dug from the road to the door by the hall keeper and we started taking in our equipment when we met the dance manager, Ian Falconer, who told us the Beatles weren't going to be able to make it because of the weather. It wasn't unusual for groups coming from the south to be delayed, but we were disappointed with the news as we had heard

them on the radio and really liked them, and we were looking forward to seeing them playing live. We set up our equipment, changed into our 'playing suits' (black trousers, white shirts, red cummerbunds and black 'bolero'-style jackets). As John was our lead singer, he wore a white jacket. We started playing at nine o'clock as the buses arrived, had a fifteen-minute tea break at eleven o'clock then played the Beatles' set as well as ours till 1am. It took us a couple of hours to pack up the equipment and drive home that night. ❞

BILL CAMERON, PHOTOGRAPHER, BUCKIE, SCOTLAND

THURSDAY 3 JANUARY

The first editions of *Disc* and *NRM* of 1963 hit the streets. *Disc* wished Elvis Presley a Happy Birthday on its cover, while page two headlined its Post Bag 'We're Raving Over The Beatles' and gave its Prize Letter to David Smith from Preston, who wondered whether 'the nation's reaction [to the Beatles] will be as enthusiastic as that of the Merseyside public'. The *NRM* featured pictures of Adam Faith, Cliff Richard and Helen Shapiro on its front cover. In the paper's Top 50, Cliff and Elvis took the top two spots. 'Love Me Do' dropped seven places to number 24, sandwiched between hits by Joe Loss and Bernard Cribbins. The *Daily Herald* reported that the first pop discs of 1963 were the 'shabbiest batch for a long time'.

Flights from London to Scotland were getting back on track, albeit delayed. John was up at 5am to catch the 8.15 flight to Glasgow and then to Aberdeen. Even though parts of the A939, A941 and A3 were blocked, Aspinall drove the group to Dyce Airport to pick up John and then on the 60-mile journey to Elgin in Morayshire, heading north-west on the A96, for the evening's show at the Two Red Shoes Ballroom.

THE ELGIN FOLK MUSIC CLUB
Presents
The "Love Me Do" Boys
THE BEATLES
plus
The Alex. Sutherland Sextet
in
THE TWO RED SHOES
on
THURSDAY, 3rd JANUARY
9 p.m. - 1 a.m.   Admission 6/-.
Buses return to Buckie, Forres, Coast, Lossiemouth, etc.

The now four-date Scottish tour earned the group £42 per concert between them (they were on a salary of £30 a week at the time). They were contracted to perform two twenty-minute sets at each venue, but because it had been a block booking of five shows, the initial fee of £250 was reduced to £210. Promoter Albert Bonici had negotiated the Scottish tour with manager Brian Epstein in November 1962 through Jack Fallon at the Cana Variety Agency. Bonici would lose money on the tour, but had a clause in his contract that allowed him first refusal on any further Scottish dates during the year. A canny move that bore fruit later in the year.

The group checked into their lodgings, Myrtle House at 27 Lossie Wynd, a five-minute walk from the venue. The house was owned by 'Ciss' and Jimmy McBean, who regularly boarded groups who performed at the Two Red Shoes. As student nurses Adeline Smith and Joan Allan set off for their shift at Dr Gray's Hospital from their digs next door, they were greeted by John leaning out of a window. 'Nurse, oh nurse,' he called out, 'will you take my pulse, nurse, I'm feeling all faint for having seen you.' Their landlady, Mrs Grossart, appeared at the front door and told him to behave himself.

The weather continued to be a problem, with the temperature close to freezing. Fewer than a hundred people managed to brave the snow and make it to the dance. A complaint about the noise the group were making came from a neighbour. During a break, Bonici took John aside to ask him. 'Can I have a quick word?' John, brushing by to get some coffee, replied, 'Velocity'. The group sat down in the dining area next to the kitchen to have refreshments at Table 1, reserved for all the acts who performed at the club. After the show, they chatted with the Alex Sutherland Sextet's singer Eithne Alexander over a few drinks and some food, before making their way back to Mrs McBean's for the night.

❛ It was a night like any other of my nights as vocalist with the Alex Sutherland Sextet. As the resident group, we backed artists that visited and entertained the huge crowds, which regularly attended the Two Red Shoes – at times stretching four or more deep down the street. I had been in a room over the Two Red Shoes all week after work listening to Lena Horne, Ella Fitzgerald, Sarah Vaughan, etc. No music was read, just my ear and the unfailing faith my mentor and agent Albert Bonici had in my unique quality of tone. Albert cornered me. 'Eithne. The Beatles are the guest group tonight, you'll like them, they're from Liverpool and I have heard great things about them. I want you to listen to what they have to say and what they sing and play – you might pick up some interesting musical tips.' Though Elgin was really a backwoods farming and whisky-distilling town, many new groups who wanted to make it threw themselves into Albert's arms. 'I haven't heard of them, Albert – what is their line-up?' His reply did not fill me with excitement. The Two Red Shoes' biggest crowds turned up for the likes of Acker Bilk and Kenny Ball – clarinets and trumpets, not four guys with just guitars and drums!

No one, it seemed, had been particularly keen to turn out that freezing evening to hear a 'beat group'. The night was bitterly cold I remember – as were relations between the West and the Soviet Union. Everyone had just been traumatised by the Cuban crisis and was still reeling from the possibility that we might be plunged into a Third World War. Talk at home was all related to this and I recall the feeling of fear clouding my teenage brain and heart. Finishing our first stint, Albert burst onto the stage puffing from climbing the five steps from the cafe. 'They're here.' I don't know what I expected. I was hustled towards the cafe and introduced to the Beatles who, to give them their due, jumped up from their haze of smoke and motioned for me to sit with them, commenting on how they liked my singing. I shyly thanked them. I was painfully ill-equipped as a small-town teenager to take on these supremely confident and streetwise individuals determined to enfold me into their company. There was no protestation accepted; I had to sit in the back of the booth, wedged in a Beatle 'bosy' (Scottish word for hug) unable to escape. Thinking back now – how many girls in a few weeks' time would have given their bras and bouffants to be in my position! I did not think this though, and thought them scruffy, loud and overfamiliar. The smoke was heavy and the chat was mainly about Hamburg. Paul, who could see my blushes, deflected some of John's pushy advances towards me and every now and then would raise those soon-to-be familiar eyebrows and widen those boyish eyes.

When they went on the stage to do their stint, the crowd, apart from one or two, viewed them with apathy and disinterest. There was something that excited me about the chords and the harmonies – perhaps also their unkempt appearance, the boyish vulnerability, the devil-may-care attitude to their less than riotous reception. At the end of their slot Albert was full of praise and encouragement and a tad apologetic about the crowd. Back to the cafe, again squashed into the seat and my Beatle bosy. No surreptitious slithering off for coffee and sandwiches for me. I listened with open mouth and innocent disbelief to some of their tales of exploits in Germany and, following some seat rearrangement, made my exit. I had to get home as Mother, I knew, always stayed awake until I was in. Walking home across the railway bridge to where I lived, I felt strangely optimistic about the future. **』**

EITHNE KNEALE, EDUCATIONAL MENTOR, ANDALUSIA, SPAIN

FRIDAY 4 JANUARY

The still jazz-focused *Melody Maker* published its first edition of the year, running the headline 'No Biz Like Snow Biz' with reports of the many artists unable to travel the country because of the severe weather. 'Love Me Do' climbed one place to number 21 in the paper's Top 50. Cliff Richard and the Shadows hit number one with the double A-sided 'The Next Time' and 'Bachelor Boy'. The paper also announced a series of one-nighters for Helen Shapiro, starting in Bradford on 2 February. Danny Williams, Kenny Lynch, the Beatles, the Kestrels and the Red Price Band were to be her support acts. The *New Musical Express*, by far the biggest selling of the four weekly pop newspapers, also put out its first issue of 1963, revealing dates for a forthcoming nationwide UK tour featuring American singers Tommy Roe and Chris Montez, with the Beatles also on the bill, beginning on 9 March at the Granada in East Ham.

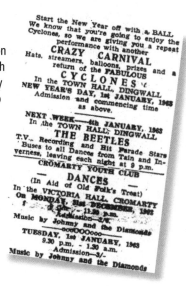

The group set off from Elgin on the A96 west to Inverness and then took the A9 to Dingwall in Ross and Cromarty. The 56-mile trip, which typically took an hour and a half, was considerably longer due to the continuing atrocious weather. The A941, which ran through Elgin north to south, was blocked by snow and stayed that way for another month and a half. Arriving late in the afternoon, the group checked into the National Hotel in the town's High Street. Later they stopped off for a pint at the Commercial Bar, a three-minute walk to their show at the Town Hall, a former Carnegie Library opened in 1903.

Fewer than two dozen turned up to see them, and they performed wearing their coats and scarves because it was so cold inside the hall. Alan Scott, the guitar player for support act the Drumbeats, recalled, 'Over the whole night there were about sixty people who came to the dance. When we were setting up, I went up and asked the Beatles if it would be all right to use their amplification, and in their thick Liverpool accents they said it would be OK. The amplification was very powerful in comparison to what we used. The rest of my group went off to the pub. I was the only one who stayed to listen to them. I thought they were great. Very slick and professional.'

Just 5 miles away, a reported twelve hundred people made their way to the Strathpeffer Pavilion to see local favourites the Melotones open for Irish showband the Chessmen. Part of what meagre proceeds there were from the Beatles' show went to the local fire brigade Old Folks' Appeal.

❛ I was 17 at the time and a live-in waitress from the Black Isle working at the National. I was on a date with my boyfriend Wavell (now my husband). The weather was very cold, not a nice night, and one or two feet of snow lay on the ground. As I was on an early shift the next morning, Wavell dropped me back at the hotel just after ten that evening. As we were arriving, the Beatles' van drew up outside the hotel. I went inside, and shortly afterwards, the boys appeared in the kitchen looking for a cuppa. My fellow waitress, Anne MacAngus, known as 'Big Anne' – I was known as 'Wee Anne' – was also there. We chatted to Paul, George, Ringo and John for over an hour, having a good blether about their music and families. 'Big Anne' was sitting on Paul's knee. She was a huge Beatles fan. However, the cook appeared eventually, and shooed them out and off to their respective rooms. The next morning, I served them a cooked breakfast of bacon and eggs. My sister Jeanette, who also worked at the hotel, remembers the head waitress referring to them as 'scruffs'. Shortly afterwards, they set off on their journey, but not before seeking us out in the reception area to say, 'Cheerio girls, see you soon!' ❜

ANNE GUNN, HOTELIER, DINGWALL, SCOTLAND

SATURDAY **5 JANUARY**

After a hearty cooked breakfast, the group left Dingwall to play their third date of the tour at the Museum Hall on Henderson Street in the Victorian spa town of Bridge of Allan, Stirlingshire. Facing the possibility that parts of the A9 were blocked, they decided to return to Aberdeen and drive to the Bridge of Allan from there. On arriving in Aberdeen, they made a stop at J. T. Forbes on George Street, a music shop that sold guitars, amplifiers and PA systems. Local musician Hamilton Harwood was there at the time and recalled: 'It seems that George Harrison was having problems with his guitar, so he went into the shop to either get a replacement or whatever. I was popping into the shop as I had just left the Strollers to form a new group, the Jaguars, and was meeting the other guys in my new group there, and also my mates from the Strollers. The Strollers were the first group in Scotland to have three white Fenders from America – two Fender Stratocasters and a Fender bass. When I arrived in the shop, the Beatles were there, and although I'd heard of them because they'd been on the radio, I didn't recognise them. I asked who they were, and my rhythm guitarist said, "Oh, they're the Beatles, they're playing at the Beach Ballroom tomorrow." Anyway, they were sitting down playing different instruments, and as I was buying a new guitar, a Fender Jaguar, we all sat jamming together. I did notice that

George's fingernails were a wee bit dirty. When you play guitar, your fingernails on your left hand get a bit grubby.' The manager, Harry Lord, didn't think much of the four young men, but before the end of the year, his shop proudly displayed a banner declaring "The Beatles shopped here."'

The 120-mile trip south-west on the A90 to Perth and then on the A9 through the towns of Auchterarder and Dunblane was a slow process, but the group finally reached the Bridge of Allan where they checked into the Royal Hotel, a short walk from the hall.

❛ I had moved back to Bridge of Allan after spending the summer of 1962 working at my cousin's hotel in Llandudno, the Clovelly. I became friends with one of the waitresses, a Liverpool girl called Valerie McCrimmon, who had a fabulous beehive hairdo, jet black. I was born in Liverpool and had lived there until the family moved north of the border when I was 8. She raved about the group she had seen at the Cavern and was in love with Pete Best.

A few months later, I am back home in Bridge of Allan with no job. The moment I saw that the 'Love Me Do Boys' were to play at the regular Saturday dance at the Museum Hall, I knew I had to go. I reckon I was the only one there who had actually gone to see the Beatles. The Saturday dances were always well attended, and this one was no exception. Possibly 150–200 young people were in the hall, a 50/50 mix of male and female. At the time I was living in Avenue Park, off Henderson Street, the main street that runs through the town. I walked to the hall, over the bridge and down to the other end of Henderson Street. The Museum Hall was laid out as a dance hall. The stage was quite high, and a balcony ran round three sides of the hall, allowing a good view of the stage and the dance floor below. I remember them doing mostly cover versions. The reception when the group came onstage was fabulous. John Lennon in particular had great stage presence – I remember him clearly, holding his guitar high on his chest, parallel to the ground. They were different, exciting and very tight. Everyone had a great time. I joined the Bridge of Allan Holy Trinity Church Youth Club and later in the year when the Beatles were playing in Dundee, the club arranged a coach party trip to see them. I stood on the back balcony. What a difference a few months made. You couldn't hear them play, just the screaming. My cousin's family sold the hotel in Llandudno and moved to Australia and I never did get in touch with Valerie to tell her that I'd seen them. ❜

IAN AINSWORTH, MAINTENANCE ENGINEER, NATIONAL COAL BOARD, CAUSEWAYHEAD, SCOTLAND

SUNDAY 6 JANUARY

The group set off back up the A9 and A90 to play the tour's final date at the Beach Ballroom on the Esplanade in Aberdeen, where they had unexpectedly spent the night four days earlier. The local council had just voted to allow alcoholic drinks to be served at the venue, despite the objections of the St Mark's vicar A. A. Bowyer, who claimed that one of the greatest evils of the present time was drinking. Sundays also meant there was no dancing. The bad weather continued unabated; dynamite was used after an avalanche blocked the railway line between Edinburgh and Carlisle near Galashiels. The night was the coldest yet. Glenlivet, 65 miles to the west of Aberdeen, recorded 34 degrees of frost. Some householders found that when they picked up their milk bottles from their front doorstep, the bottoms remained stuck to the ground. On a far more serious note, there were reports of beer bottles bursting. Roderick Stuart of Westholme Avenue, Aberdeen had too much time on his hands, building a 17 ft 2 in snowman.

When the group arrived at the ballroom in the late afternoon, they found a queue outside the locked doors already lining up to get in. Unaware there was a back door; they chatted with several people in the queue until staff arrived with the keys to open up. Once inside, the group spent time in the upstairs coffee bar, drinking tea and smoking. Introduced by Alfie Wood, they played two forty-five-minute sets and, during their break, they were treated to tea and biscuits by waitresses wearing old-style black-and-white council uniforms. They played 'Love Me Do' and a selection of rock'n'roll classics in the first set, adding 'Please Please Me' for their second. When they asked for requests, audience member Donnie Fraser shouted out 'A Shot Of Rhythm And Blues', which the group duly sang. After the show, they returned to the Gloucester Hotel to spend the night. Gordon Hardie, one of Bonici's assistants, revealed that the box-office take had been just £45, with all but £3 going to the Beatles.

> ' For me, the Beach Ballroom was the best music venue in Aberdeen in the '60s. As a young musician in a local group called the Falcons, the experience was immense. I saw many fabulous groups and singers throughout the decade. In 1962, at the age of 15, I started my first group at the Beehive Youth Club. The club had a Wurlitzer juke box and in it was an exciting new record, 'Love Me Do' by the Beatles, which I played all the time when I was at the club. When I saw the advert in the *Evening Express* for the concert featuring the Johnny Scott Orchestra with special guest group, the Beatles, I just had to go and see this new group I really liked. Tickets were 3/- and it was an all-seated concert. I went with my brother Mike and, as we arrived early, had an opportunity to chat with the Beatles before the show about music, Hamburg and the Liverpool scene. In those days there was no

group security so we knocked on the stage door and were invited in to meet them. They were tuning their guitars and discussing their playlist.

Being a musician myself I was interested in their guitars. John played a Rickenbacker, bought from a GI in Hamburg; George was using a Gretsch Country Gent, on loan from Hessy's Guitar Shop in Liverpool as his own was in for repair; and Paul handed me his Hofner Bass. I noticed their playlist taped to Paul's guitar. I asked whether they would play Chuck Berry's 'Sweet Little Sixteen' as it was a favourite with my group. John dedicated the song especially to the 'lads in the front row'. During the second half of the show they announced their new single, 'Please Please Me'. The audience were enjoying their music very much, judging by their applause and reaction. But there was no screaming, so I could hear every song. I could see how talented and destined for stardom they were. As I was leaving, I asked Tucker Donald, the resident singer with the Johnny Scott Band, what he thought of them. He said 'they were OK' but was not that impressed! Six months later my group the Falcons appeared at the Ballroom on the same stage as the Beatles had. 🕴

BILL COWIE, ROV/PILOT TECHNICIAN, ABERDEEN, SCOTLAND

MONDAY 7 JANUARY

Overnight temperatures in parts of north-east Scotland dropped to 19 degrees of frost. The Moray town of Grantown-on-Spey reached 6 below zero. In the morning, the group made the ten-minute walk from the Gloucester Hotel for breakfast at the Chivas Restaurant. Later in the day, when Bonici and Gordon Hardie were having lunch at the Chivas, they were asked by waitresses, still in a dither from meeting the group, 'Who are these Beatles?' Bonici didn't seem too concerned to have lost money on this short tour; he more than made it back later in the year, even though he had to pay £500 per night for the group's services. Hardie subsequently recalled his memories of the tour. 'I've heard it said they were booed at the Beach Ballroom. That's rubbish. They got a fantastic reception at the Beach Ballroom and at Bridge of Allan. The girls who were there went wild for them. They were a young group trying to make their way in the industry and they were prepared to go to far-flung places and put in the hours.'

The group travelled down the by-now familiar A90 on the 145-mile journey to Glasgow, arriving in the late afternoon for the following day's appearance on Scottish Television. With news that another freeze was on the way, and as several more inches of snow fell in parts of the country, the city was enjoying its first white Christmas since before the Second World War.

TUESDAY 8 JANUARY

The tedium of the weather continued. More than twenty main roads throughout Britain remained blocked because of snow and increasing freezing winds. The forecast was predicting that a thaw might set in in southern parts of England, but for people in Scotland there would be no respite. A further twenty FA Cup ties were called off because of frozen pitches. Some of Blackpool's team took advantage of the conditions at their Bloomfield Road ground and skated instead of playing football.

The group appeared on Scottish Television's children's programme *Roundup* at the Theatre Royal in Hope Street, Glasgow, miming to their forthcoming single 'Please Please Me'. Sound recordist Len Southam was responsible for placing the disc, which the group brought with them, on the turntable. In an effort to get a little extra payment for their appearance, in part because their van – not for the first time, nor the last – was having mechanical troubles, John had asked Southam for more money, but was turned down with a stern "No". They were also interviewed by the hosts, Paul Young and Morag Hood. The programme aired at 5pm.

> ❛ I was at George Heriot's School when I began co-presenting *Roundup* with Morag Hood. The first six were pre-recorded on a Sunday and transmitted the following Tuesday during May 1962, then the first live series started in September. Scottish Television had bought the Theatre Royal back in 1957 and turned it into television studios. The theatre's main studio was basically from the back stalls to the back of the stage. *Roundup* was a magazine-type programme... careers advice, how to look after pets, a schools quiz, a pop spot where young people voted on new releases... a guest star interview and a guest group or singer. We had many famous people on over the years.
>
> In my 1963 diary, I entered the names of the guests who appeared on the show. I had been told in advance that we were to host a group called 'The Beetles'. During the afternoon rehearsal, four neatly dressed young men plus their road manager came quietly into the studio and at the next break were introduced to Morag and myself. 'I'm Paul, that's George, the one with the rings is Ringo and that's John.' So we chatted a bit and they talked about the Scottish dates they had just played. Paul and I chatted about our first names, which were not common in those days, and I remember commenting on the small bass guitar he was using and the fact that he was left-handed and he told me it meant he had to string the guitar differently from the norm. 'My job is to go bdum, bdum, bdom, bdom in the background and John and me have written a few songs.' Masterly understatement!
>
> They rehearsed the song they were going to end our programme with, 'Please Please Me'. They mimed to the track as live music was difficult to balance in those days and there wasn't time to do it properly. The programme was transmitted live and I wonder if the other guests on the programme realised they were in at the beginning of the huge global phenomenon that was about to follow. My diary for the next time they were on the programme in June said simply 'Beatles again'. I had learned how to spell the group's name properly! ❜
>
> **PAUL YOUNG, ACTOR, WRITER, BROADCASTER, GLASGOW, SCOTLAND**

WEDNESDAY 9 JANUARY

After staying a second night in Glasgow, the group drove back to Liverpool. The trip on the A7 took more than six hours. Weather conditions were as bad as they had been north of the border – the highest temperature for the day was 2.2 degrees Celsius. The Liverpool race meeting was abandoned because of frost and snow, but the third-round Cup tie between Liverpool and Wrexham, postponed from Saturday, went ahead. Liverpool came out 3–0 winners. The day's *Liverpool Echo* reported that there was 'No sign of a thaw yet'. Overnight temperatures dropped to minus 4.4 – certainly better than Aberdeen, which had plummeted to minus 11. The AA described driving conditions as 'varied, from treacherous to difficult'. When they finally made it back home, local cinemas were showing *The Bridge On The River Kwai*, *Hatari* and *Five Weeks In A Balloon*, while David Whitfield and Morecambe and Wise were starring in *The Sleeping Beauty* at the Empire Theatre.

After three weeks away from home, the group finally got to sleep in their own beds. Later in the year, George recalled the trip to Scotland. 'It was terrible touring in the snow and the ice. We had some pretty long journeys to cope with and it was darned cold. But we were still hearing 'Love Me Do' on our portable radio – and that warmed us up.'

THURSDAY 10 JANUARY

isc declared that the week had probably gone down 'as one of the greatest-ever in Cliff Richard's career'. Tucked away at the bottom of page nine, below four-star reviews for new singles by Hugo Montenegro and Paula Watson, the Beatles' new record, released the following day, received a three-star review. "Please Please Me' will undoubtedly please the growing band of fans who are following the Beatles. The boys chant this one briskly to a dark twangy background.'

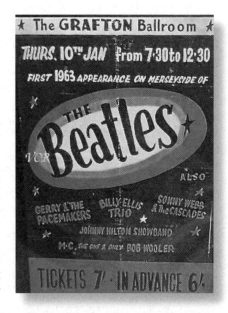

The *NRM*, which had 'Love Me Do' climbing back up seven places to number 17, rated the new single as a 'Top 20 Tip', giving it four stars. 'From the oh-so-successful Beatles comes this follow-up. It's a high-pitched number with plenty of guts, and good tune, vocalising and some off-beat sounds on the disc. The backing verges on great, while the singing is taken by various members of the team. We reckon its chart chances – it would probably make it as even their first disc. Rather bluesy, fast tempo.'

Transglobal Music Co. Inc., acting on behalf of EMI Records in the US, signed a licensing agreement with Chicago-based Vee-Jay Records giving them the rights to release 'Please Please Me', which had already been rejected by Capitol Records' executive Dave Dexter. (EMI had acquired 96 per cent of Capitol's stock in 1955. Dexter, who thought rock'n'roll was 'juvenile and maddeningly repetitive', famously told label president Alan Livingston, 'Alan, they're a bunch of long-haired kids. They're nothing. Forget it'.) The licence was for five years and gave Vee-Jay first refusal on all future recordings.

The Beatles played their first hometown gig of the year at the Grafton Ballroom, where fans queued for two hours before the show. They were supported by Gerry and the Pacemakers, Sonny Webb and the Cascades (Sunday night residents at the Black Cat Club), the Johnny Hilton Show Band and the Billy Ellis Trio with master of ceremonies Bob Wooler. Tickets for the five-hour show, beginning at 7.30pm, cost 7/-, although most had been sold in advance for 6/-. Tickets numbered 504 to 606 had been stolen and weren't valid. The venue issued a stern warning that the police had been notified.

Following their performance, the Beatles were interviewed by the *Evening Standard*'s Maureen Cleave, who had been urged by Liverpool journalist Gillian Reynolds to see them. 'The Beatles made me laugh immediately,' she wrote, 'their wit was just so keen and sharp – John Lennon, especially. They all had this wonderful quality. It wasn't innocent, but everything was new to them.'

By the time the group returned to their respective homes, temperatures were dropping to their lowest in Liverpool since 29 December, falling to minus 5 with 9 degrees of frost.

❝ The first time I heard the Beatles was when they were doing a show at Hambleton Hall, in what was considered a rough area of Liverpool in those days. They were wearing leather jackets with their hair brushed back and it was definitely once seen, never forgotten. We then started investigating other clubs they played at, and that's how we heard of the Cavern. I was an apprentice hairdresser at Ellison Lea's, a salon over the original NEMS shop and Mike McCartney [Paul's brother] worked in the Andre Bernard shop opposite. None of us had any money and so we'd nip downstairs to the record shop and go into the booths and listen to the records.

My friends and I were regular Cavern dwellers. Practically everyone had their own seats as it were. I always used to sit in the corner, in the alcove to the left of the stage. The Beatles at that stage were known to chat to all the girls. We used to hang about at the coffee bar at the back hoping that one of them would come and chat with us. They used to occasionally give the girls lifts home – a lot of the groups did in those days – and on one particular night we got a lift home from Paul. He'd just got his car – a green classic. I was dropped off last and as I was about to get out of the car John suddenly said, 'Paul will be round to pick you up tomorrow night.' I said something like, 'That'll be no good. I work until 6 o'clock.' He came out with the classic line, 'He's not asking you to marry him.' Paul, being the gentleman that he was, got out and walked me up to the door and made a proper arrangement.

So, the next night we had a date. I remember it was just before they left for Hamburg for the final time. We went to the Forum cinema on the corner of Lime Street. After the film he took me back to Rory Storm's house. When I got there George was there. Paul vanished for a while and George got very chatty. Then it was time to go and I remember it was a very snowy night. I was walking down the path and George came running up behind me as if to pick me up for some reason. He slipped and fell flat on his back. Paul stood there looking a bit more grown-up, and then he drove me home. I didn't go out with Paul again, but soon began dating George. I got home one night and found a note he had put through my door saying, 'Please ring me'. He had been giving me the odd lift home from the Cavern so he knew where I lived. I remember when they got a silver disc for 'Please Please Me' and he brought it round to show me; my mum asked whether she could play it.

After that was a hit, things really began to change. I arranged to meet him at the Floral Hall in Southport when they were doing a show. Tony Bramwell, who had just started working for them, got George out of the back of the theatre and into his car with George's mother and me. That was the first experience I had of Beatlemania. It was rather frightening. George picked me up from the salon a couple of times. I had to do night school on Tuesday nights so he came round to pick me up in his Ford Anglia. One time a hairstyle I had became fashionable and my boss made me go and have a photograph taken to go outside the shop. Bill Harry saw it and asked if he could use it in *Mersey Beat*. They were doing this series every month called 'The Face of Beauty'. One day George came back from somewhere a little earlier than I had expected and I was getting ready with rollers in my hair and a dressing gown. He walked in and said, 'So this is the Face of Beauty!'

I met my husband Mike in the Kardomah coffee bar. At this point I swore I wouldn't go out with any more musicians. I thought they were a load of layabouts! Anyway, we got married in 1967 and I continued hairdressing until the '70s. Then I became a Beatles tour guide. Mike and I opened The Beatles Story in 1990. I thought it could last up to ten years because there were always going to be anniversaries every year. We foresaw how the market could develop. I don't think we ever thought that it would be the success it has become though! The last time I saw George was when he came to Liverpool with the Delaney and Bonnie tour. We were having a drink in the Lord Nelson when he came in with his entourage. He summoned me over with a crook of his finger and we engaged in some small talk. I met Paul at LIPA in the 1990s and more recently had a nice surprise from him. My daughter is a friend of the DJ Matt Everitt who was interviewing Paul on his radio show when she celebrated her birthday and he asked whether Paul would do him a favour and sing 'Happy Birthday' for her. He said, 'You might know her mum. Her name was Bernadette Farrell.' Paul said, 'Yeah, I remember her. I often say that but I do remember her.' He then sang 'Happy Birthday' for her and sent me his best wishes. ❞

BERNADETTE BYRNE, TOUR GUIDE AND CO-FOUNDER OF THE
BEATLES STORY LIVERPOOL, FORMBY, MERSEYSIDE

FRIDAY 11 JANUARY

'Please Please Me' was released. The EMI press release accompanying the new single trumpeted, 'Here's the first big chart-bustin' bombshell of '63!!!! The Beatles have made The Record of the Year.' In the *NME*, DJ Keith Fordyce wrote, 'This vocal and instrumental quartet has turned out a really enjoyable platter, full of beat, vigour and vitality – and what's more, it's different. I can't think of any other group currently recording in this style.' The trade paper *Record Retailer* felt that the single had 'chart written all over it and seems sure to do well'. *Saturday Club* host Brian Matthew said, 'Visually and musically the Beatles are the most exciting and accomplished group to emerge since the Shadows. In the next few months, they will become one of the hottest properties in the music industry.' *Melody Maker* featured a

cover story on Duke Ellington's forthcoming UK tour and was the one paper not to review the single. 'Love Me Do' stayed at number 21 in the paper's Top 50.

With the *Liverpool Daily Post* blasting the headline 'Another Ice Age Week-End Ahead', the group played a lunchtime show at the Cavern Club, for which they were paid £20, with Kingsize Taylor and the Dominoes in support. The show's ad stated: 'This date coincides with the release of the Beatles' record 'Please Please Me'. COME AND HEAR THEM PLAY IT'. They then drove to Halesowen Road in Old Hill, near Dudley, Staffordshire, for a show at the Plaza Ballroom. It was one of four Black Country venues run by Mary and Joe Regan, affectionately known as Ma and Pa Regan. Seventeen-year-old Carol Law, for whom Friday night was Plaza night, recalled: 'Dad would drop me and my boyfriend Alan off on the way to his fishing club, and pick us up on the way home. I got such a surprise when the Beatles came onstage. I knew who they were, but didn't know they were playing that evening. I can still remember them vividly, standing on the stage, Paul on the right, with all of them wearing dark suits. It was a wonderful evening and at the end, there was Dad, waiting in the foyer. He never let me go home on my own, even if I was with Alan! He would stand chatting to Mrs Regan's husband while he waited. Mr Regan was always dressed in a dinner jacket with a black bow tie. The Plaza was a fantastic venue, a great place for young people to go. Refreshments were sold downstairs, and there was a staircase leading up to the ballroom, with the stage on the right. They used to have this alcove where you could sit. In those days, you would have several groups playing in one evening. The great thing about the Plaza was that it had a revolving stage, so as each group finished their set, it would go round, and the next group would appear, already playing.' A later show that evening at the Ritz Ballroom (formerly a snooker hall) in King's Heath, Birmingham, a little over 10 miles away, was postponed until 15 February. The unrelenting weather made it impossible for the group to get to the venue. They spent the night at the Regans' in Woodbourne Road, Edgbaston, where they were greeted by the couple's three Alsatians.

‘ I grew up in Liverpool, and when I left school in the early '60s I went to work as a typist for a shipping company down by the docks. The office was in the Tower Building in Water Street, only a five-minute walk to Mathew Street. I can't remember exactly when we started to go to the Cavern, but it was very early on. We had two lunch hours – one was from ten to twelve until one, and the second from ten to one until two. The girls on the first lunch break would dive down to get front-row seats when the Beatles were on, then would take it in turns to go out one by one, holding the seats for the girls on the second lunch break, and dash back to work. The Beatles were on Monday, Wednesday and Friday, then they would do Tuesday and Thursday the following week. Once we had some photographs of them and took them into the little side room by the stage which they used as a dressing room and got them to sign them for us. They were actually quite shy about it! John put 'From John Lennon', he didn't bother with 'Lennon' later

on. When we got back to work – we were sometimes a little late and would smell absolutely awful. The boss used to say, 'You've been there again, haven't you?' It was a dead giveaway! It was a very strong disinfectant-y smell, oh it was horrible, but we thought it was fantastic.

Most of the people who went there were the same age as me – about 16 or 17. All the girls from the office would go, and I used to meet up with my friend Margaret, who worked in a photographer's up the road. We knew each other through our boyfriends who were friends and did everything together. Four of us went to the Cavern the day the group were filmed for television – it was the only day they were ever filmed there. We were standing by the arches at the side, it was packed and the television people were telling us what to do. They said one thing we mustn't do is whistle, and of course we all did. They did things over and over again with the cameras and the Beatles were very excited, they were brilliant, it was a fabulous day! We wanted them to be famous and do well, but we wanted to keep them as well. We knew we were losing them about that time, but it was good to have been there that day.

We used to go to the Aintree Institute on a Saturday night, all the Liverpool groups would be on, but it was the Beatles we all went to see. I remember once going there and George was on the same bus! His car must have broken down. He had an old Ford Anglia and used to park it by my husband Arthur's car (who was my boyfriend at that time). One night Arthur and his friend Eric helped the group unload their kit from their old van. That's their claim to fame – they were the Beatles' roadie for one night! Pete Best was still in the line-up, and we all just loved him, just loved him. My favourite was always George though. He didn't sing very much though; all he would sing was 'I'm Henry The Eighth I Am' and 'The Sheik Of Araby'. I remember he used to call Brian Epstein 'Mr Frankenstein!' We were very upset when Pete left. People would say he was too quiet, but he was so nice. He was also gorgeous and would look down his eyes at you.

It was a great time to be young in Liverpool. Everyone seemed to have a few bob spare in those days. I earned £4 10s a week as a typist, but we had money to spare. I was clothes mad, shoes mad, music mad. Margaret and I are still great friends. Recently we went to the fiftieth anniversary of the Cavern. Margaret was invited as a guest for all the help she had given the guys who took it over. It was a brilliant evening, and the club is very like the original. The original was a death trap to be honest. All the stone steps were very worn, no such thing as Health and Safety! I have three grown-up sons now, and they say, 'Mum, you were so lucky to have been in Liverpool at that time.' They live all over the world, but I tell them all the stories. They think Liverpool is the centre of the universe! ’

PAT PETERS, TYPIST AND HOUSEWIFE, BILLINGE, MERSEYSIDE

SATURDAY 12 JANUARY

The group set off on the nearly 200-mile drive south to play their southernmost gig yet at the Invicta Ballroom in Fullagers Yard, just off the High Street next to Woolworth's in Chatham, Kent. Once again, they had to drive through fog (visibility at Liverpool Airport was down to 10 yards), heavy snow and gale-force winds. The docks in the Chatham harbour were frozen and the Royal Navy was called upon to use an icebreaker to keep them open; the River Medway to Rochester froze for the first time ever with ice 2 inches thick, and on the south coast of Kent, the Channel froze from Dover to Eastbourne. The *Chatham Observer & Kent Messenger* reported that the weather conditions were the worst in eighty years.

As a warm welcome that night, the group played to a ballroom packed to the rafters with adoring fans and maybe a few souls simply looking to shelter from the cold. The Jaybirds opened and the Beatles were introduced by the hall's manager and bingo caller, Ray Wade. One audience member, Alan Cackett, recalled the evening. 'At the time we weren't into groups – except for the Shadows. Apart from school concerts, I'd never seen a live pop music show and had no idea what to expect. To be brutally honest, the sound that night was awful. It was muddy and far removed from the clear-cut sound of the pop records of the time. But from the opening strains of 'I Saw Her Standing There', I was mesmerised.'

It was the last time Ringo used his bass-drum head with his own name on it – the following day when they made their *Thank Your Lucky Stars* appearance it had been removed. On their return to Liverpool, they got in touch with artist Terry 'Tex' O'Hara, whose brother Brian was a member of the Fourmost. They asked him to take a drawing Paul had made the previous year and fashion a logo for the group. 'I did about five to ten drawings, which I've still got, and showed them to the group,' he recalled. 'They settled on one logo, which was put on a piece of linen and stretched across the front of the drum.'

> ❝ I had my 16th birthday in November of 1962 and the same weekend met my boyfriend. He was in the Royal Navy and on leave before going to sea the following week for a year. I wrote to him and kept him informed about all the news from home. He was sorry to have missed the opportunity of actually seeing the Beatles perform in Chatham, the only time they ever came to our little corner of Kent. The weather was so bad that winter, the snow started late Boxing Day afternoon and didn't disappear until March. I went to a friend's party that night but caught a bus as it was so cold. By the time the party finished there was at least 6 inches of snow and a crowd of us all had to walk home, having great fun throwing snowballs and even making snowmen. My new white leather pixie boots were full of snow but they did survive! I lived in Gillingham then, but my friends and I would have crawled to get to the theatre so we could see and hear our idols! Not that there was much to be heard as obviously there were so many screaming girls wherever they went. I think we had to pay about 7/6 for tickets, but got there early to make sure we'd get in. We spoke of that night for months afterwards.
>
> When my boyfriend returned the following Christmas, he came loaded with LPs that he had bought while abroad, and we still have them to this day. The three Medway towns then had a marvellous amount of places to go for entertainment. Numerous dance halls, coffee bars, bowling alleys as well as the proverbial pubs; we often couldn't decide quite where to go on Friday and Saturday nights. We had most of the big groups here. Sadly these great places are now no more, mostly car parks or apartments and houses built on the land. I feel lucky to have been a teenager in that marvellous decade. These days young people don't have anywhere to go and we had so much. ❞
>
> **MERILYN LATIMER, SCHOOL HOUSEKEEPER, ROCHESTER, KENT**

SUNDAY 13 JANUARY

The group drove to Aston near Birmingham to record their first appearance on Associated-Rediffusion's *Thank Your Lucky Stars* at Alpha Television Studios. They appeared on a nine-act bill with Frankie Vaughan, Alma Cogan, Mr Acker Bilk (who performed 'A Taste Of Honey', a song the Beatles would feature in their set for the forthcoming Helen Shapiro tour), Mark Wynter, Chris Barber's Jazz Band, the Brook Brothers, David Macbeth and Mike Berry. Later in the year Vaughan told the *Liverpool Echo* that he recognised their great promise. 'I thought they were great. Exciting, Terrific.' They were introduced by host Brian Matthew and mimed to 'Please Please Me', closing the first half of the show.

Music publisher Dick James had secured them the slot through his friendship with the show's producer Philip Jones. He had called Jones the previous November, the day after 'Please Please Me' and 'Ask Me Why' had been recorded – while he was in a meeting with Brian Epstein. Jones recalled that he had no idea how to present them. 'We decided to put each one of them inside a big metal heart. It was obvious that the song, not our set, would be the thing that sold them.'

Andrew Loog Oldham, who was Wynter's press agent and would soon be hired by Epstein to assist the group's press representative Tony Calder, remembered his first encounter, describing it as a pop epiphany. 'The Beatles didn't look that different from the other acts – they were all wearing suits and ties – but they exuded an attitude that was blunt and honest as they mimed to the soundtrack of their single. The sound was familiar but this was no mere copy of the American music we all loved – it took it to another level and injected pentecostal joy back into rock'n'roll.' He asked John who their manager was. John pointed in the direction of Epstein. According to Oldham, 'He radiated success in his expensive overcoat, paisley scarf and haughty demeanour.' Oldham's first job, at a meagre £5 a week, was to take the Beatles to *Boyfriend* magazine's office for a photo session, but he soon found himself doing PR for Gerry and the Pacemakers and Billy J. Kramer with the Dakotas as well. In April, he and Calder, both 19-year-olds, joined forces to create IMAGE, the first independent pop music PR company and became managers of the Rolling Stones.

The programme was broadcast the following Saturday at 5.50pm. Earning £45 for each of the two dates on the days before and after, this appearance was a £104 windfall. After the recording, the Beatles drove back to London, where they stayed the night. Power outages, ice and severe frost saw many people go without their traditional Sunday dinner. Manchester was named the coldest place in Britain. The following day about two thousand children were sent home from schools because of frozen outside toilets.

❝ I first met the Beatles at the Cavern when Mike Berry and the Outlaws topped the bill there in August 1962. We were seen as this London group, who'd had a hit record and been on the telly. Brian Epstein was flogging the Beatles to us as soon as we arrived in Liverpool. We met him, and we were invited back to his flat to listen to a tape of theirs. The quality wasn't great, and I don't remember what I thought, but Chas Hodges, who was one of the Outlaws, remembers he liked the harmonies. But other than that, we weren't overwhelmed by this tape. Brian said to me, 'Listen, if you get my boys on TV, I'll get you a load of work up here.' Lovely guy, but so naive.

Paul McCartney gave me a lift back to my grotty hotel (12/6 a night) in Mount Pleasant in his car. Anyway, they liked us as a group, and in particular our 'Tribute To Buddy Holly' record, as they were great fans of the Crickets. Then in October we performed at the Preston Grasshoppers Rugby Club gig. We were billed as 'Mike Berry and the Outlaws supported by new group the Beatles'. Paul has reminded me of that once or twice. My manager Robert Stigwood got me on the 'Bobby Vee Meets The Crickets' tour in late '62. He wangled it that I was able to actually sing a couple of songs with the Crickets. So right in the middle of that awful British winter, I bumped into the Beatles again when we both appeared on *Thank Your Lucky Stars*. My diary entry recalls that the night before I played a gig at the Matrix Hall in Coventry, backed by the Elektrons. I stayed at the Brandon Hall Hotel and drove to the TV studios in Birmingham the next morning in my misty green VW. The Beatles and I were in the canteen talking about songs, and John said to me, 'We'll write you a song!', almost grabbing my lapels. I didn't think much of it at the time, as in those days, you didn't write your own songs, you were either a writer or a singer. I was signed to Joe Meek, who thought he could do it all himself with people he had full control over. So I pooh-poohed the idea of someone else writing a song for us because John was just another guy in another group. But John knew my voice. They knew my records and would have come up with a song that totally suited my voice, with a great tune and lyrics, and I have no doubt that it would have been a hit. I thought no more of it as they weren't known for their writing and that was the end of that. Looking back, I hadn't been that impressed with 'Love Me Do'. Of course I love it now, but back then, I just didn't realise what I was turning down. The light dawned on me rather too late and it's been one of my biggest regrets ever since!

Anyway I told them that the Crickets loved their single and then soon afterwards they wrote a letter to them thanking them. It meant a lot to them, but I suspect Brian would have been behind the letter, and probably had it typed up by his secretary, and got the boys to sign it. For the recording of *Thank Your Lucky Stars*, they'd mark it all out, where you were going to stand, if you were going to move, where you would move to, but it was all pretty static in those days. Then they'd just run through, playing the record that you would mime to – on this occasion it was 'Don't You Think It's Time' – and they would film it. Sometimes we would watch the other acts and sometimes we would just stay in our dressing rooms till we were called.

I'd become really disillusioned with Joe by this time. Before I'd signed with him, I'd seen Jack Good. He'd heard this demo of mine and wanted to see me. So we met up and he said to me, 'I want to make you the new Adam Faith.' Then I saw Joe the next week and he said to me, 'I'm going to make you the British Buddy Holly.' That appealed to me much more, so in my naivety, I signed with Joe. 'We'll bring out an LP, with a ghostly picture of Buddy in the background.' I liked Joe's vision for me if it had come to fruition. It would have been great, but at the time I didn't know he was a pretty screwed-up sort of guy. He had this persecution complex and fear of people nicking his ideas, and I think signing with him instead of Jack Good was probably the second biggest mistake of my career: signed with the wrong bloke and turned down John Lennon's song! **'**

MIKE BERRY, ACTOR AND SINGER, WANDSWORTH, LONDON

MONDAY 14 JANUARY

In the morning, the group made their way from their hotel to Covent Garden and the first-floor photographic studio of Angus McBean at 53-55 Endell Street. McBean was a renowned portrait photographer and the official photographer for the Old Vic, Glyndebourne, the Royal Opera House and Sadler's Wells Theatre. He took a series of photos of the group. Unhappy with the results, he took another

series of shots at EMI House the following week. McBean remembered them as 'a gangling group of four young men in mole-coloured velveteen performing suits of terrible cut'. Two of the images appeared on *The Beatles' Hits* EP and the 1982 reissue of 'Please Please Me'. On their way out, they signed McBean's visitors' book; playwright Terence Rattigan had been the first signatory of the year. They wrote, 'Paul McCartney - a Beatle! John Lennon - another Beatle, George Harrison - likewise, Ringo Starr - same again?'

Teen magazine *Valentine* mentioned the group for the first time. Its 'Red-Hot Low' column reported that while eating out in London and pretending to be the Shadows, the group were approached by a fellow diner who said, 'Excuse me - my girlfriend said is it really true you are the Tornados?'

Although their first £100 show was not until 4 March, Epstein signed a deal for that figure with promoter Albert Kinder for an August date at the Grafton Ballroom. A clause in the contract stated that the group would not play 'within a radius of 10 miles of any of the venues mentioned herein for two weeks prior to this engagement'. Kinder failed to make any contingency for the group playing after the date - which they did, making their final appearance at the Cavern the following night, much to Kinder's displeasure.

They then set off on the four-hour drive for the evening's show at the Civic Hall on Whitby Road in Ellesmere Port on the Wirral, for the Wolverham Welfare Association Dance. 700 people crammed into the hall for the 8pm show, which ran to midnight and saw the Four Hits & A Miss and the Whitby Ward Trio open for the group. Malcolm Powell, the Trio's drummer, chatted with Ringo, who said that if their next single didn't do as well as 'Love Me Do', he was going to 'jack it all in'. Denise Parrott, the 5-year-old sister of their keyboard player, met the Beatles backstage but found it 'all very boring!'

TUESDAY 15 JANUARY

The group finally had their first day off since returning from Hamburg. The forecast for Liverpool included mist and a touch of rain or sleet, with snow thrown in. Much of the rest of Britain had to cope with further blizzards. The roads continued to be hazardous to drive on and travel across the country was disrupted, with British Railways cancelling several trains from both Euston and Liverpool. The Cambridge University boat crew took to the River Ouse to train - it was the only strip of water within 50 miles of the university which was not frozen. Doris Bernhard, whose cottage in Earith sat at the edge of the river, commented, 'Their arrival was a bit of a shock to me. They asked my husband if they could use the garden. Poor dears had nowhere to go. And it was so cold and icy. They got the boats under my trellis fence with the roses on, and down on to the lawn by the water.'

One Liverpool record shop reported that it had sold thirteen hundred copies of 'Please Please Me' in its first three days on sale. Touts in Manchester clubs were selling the single for 2/- over the recommended retail price.

'At my secondary school – the King John School in Thundersley, Essex – we had a record club where we paid 3d to listen to the latest records for half an hour on Monday lunchtimes. The money went to the swimming-pool fund, as we were trying to get an outdoor pool. We could take new records in to be played, but many were provided by the two teachers who ran it. It was here I first heard 'Please Please Me'. I already knew who the Beatles were, remembering hearing 'Love Me Do' played as a new single on *Pick Of The Pops* with Alan Freeman in late 1962 and writing it down in my notebook. (I was the sad type that wrote down singles I liked and saved for whatever I could afford.) I had to wait until late November and went to our local shop, Croisettes. They sold TVs, washing machines, record players and stereograms. They also sold a few singles and albums, mostly our parents' and grandparents' type of music. They didn't have it in stock, not even in the bargain bin – a source of many of my records, as I got more for my money. I also looked in Southend in Boots and in a musical instrument shop without any luck. So I ended up ordering it from Croisettes and waited for several weeks. When it arrived, the weather was really bad with snow and ice everywhere, so I waited until it got better, because I didn't want to fall over and break the single on my way home. **)**

MARILYN LAZELL, SCHOOLTEACHER, WITHAM, ESSEX

WEDNESDAY 16 JANUARY

Overnight rain and sleet and freezing temperatures caused mayhem in Liverpool, with forty-seven corporation buses involved in collisions, some of them serious. Car drivers struggled to maintain control of their vehicles. Professor Andrew Semple, the City Medical Officer of Health, reported that more than thirty ambulances had been called out during a three-hour period in the morning. By midday, sixty-five people had been treated at Broadgreen and Walton Hospitals. Less than a mile from John's Menlove Road home, buses were unable to negotiate the gradient at King's Drive and the road had to be closed. Snowdrifts continued to blow across the north-west.

Neil Aspinall managed to negotiate his van the 35-mile journey to Manchester for a TV show and a radio show. Rehearsals for *People And Places* began in Studio Four at the Granada TV Centre in Quay Street at 3pm. The Beatles had made their debut on the show the previous October when they performed 'Some Other Guy' and 'Love Me Do'. The group then had half an hour to get from the TV studio to the Playhouse Theatre on the corner of Warwick Street and Chichester Street in the suburb of Hulme to begin a 4.30pm rehearsal for the BBC Light Programme show *Here We Go*. It was here that they had made their radio debut, on the same programme, on 7 March 1962. Producer Peter Pilbeam, commenting on their audition before their debut, wrote, 'Paul McCartney – no, John Lennon – yes. An unusual group, not as rocky as most. More country and western with a tendency to play music. Overall – yes.'

At 6.35pm, the twenty-five-minute live transmission of *People And Places* aired, with the group – making their fourth appearance on the show – miming to 'Ask Me Why' and 'Please Please Me'. They returned to the Playhouse, where the recording of *Here We Go* took place at 8.45pm in front of a live studio audience. They performed 'Chains' (a US hit written by Gerry Goffin and Carole King for the Cookies), 'Please Please Me', 'Three Cool Cats' and 'Ask Me Why', which they had played for their second *Here We Go* appearance in June 1962. At the end of the recording, fans refused to leave their seats, shouting and stamping for the group to perform more numbers. The drive home to Liverpool was somewhat easier as it began to thaw on Merseyside.

THURSDAY 17 JANUARY

The front page of the *Liverpool Echo* reported 'Freezing Again But City Roads Clear' and 'Snow And Ice On Many Roads'. 'The 26th day of Britain's "little ice age" opened with a blast of phenomenal frost,' the paper commented, 'producing a grim picture of road weather conditions. All roads throughout the country were affected by snow or ice or both. Many drivers left their vehicles at home, with the result that trains and buses were crowded.' An AA spokesman reported that roads had been affected by snow or ice or both and many had glacier surfaces like Alpine passes.

'Please Please Me' made its national chart debut, entering the *NRM* Top 50 at number 45, while 'Love

Me Do' dropped to number 28. In an article headlined 'Not Everybody's Cup, But These Clubs Are Here To Stay', *The Guardian* reported that 'most of the clubs (in the north) have twist or jazz groups, the Beatles for instance, or Bee Bumble and the Stingers, playing on some nights.'

The group played a noontime gig with Kingsize Taylor and the Dominoes at the Cavern Club. Making the 3-mile journey by way of the Mersey Tunnel, they then drove to Conway Street in Birkenhead, where they gave an evening performance at the Majestic Ballroom ('The Unbeatable Beatles – Please Come Early to Avoid Disappointment') with fellow Liverpudlians the Chants in support. Police were called to restore order when some five hundred fans were left outside without tickets, standing in freezing temperatures. Despite 'Please Please Me' making its chart debut, they closed their set with 'Love Me Do'. It was the first of four appearances at the venue – part of the Top Rank chain – they made during the year. The previous month they had performed there at the *Mersey Beat* awards, winning Best Group. The Ballroom had re-opened on 30 March 1962 after a £40,000 re-fit.

❛ I grew up in Moreton in the Wirral and went to school locally, leaving in 1960 when I turned 15. I worked for a few months as a trainee window dresser but was made redundant. I then went to art college before getting a job at Johnson's Cleaners in Liscard and Moreton. I stayed there for a few years until I got married and had my first child. I had a friend who was an office worker in Liverpool, and she would spend her lunchtimes in the Cavern. I couldn't get there on a regular basis, as I only had one half-day a week – Wednesdays – and even then, I didn't finish until one o'clock. The lunchtime shows were over by two o'clock, 2.15, although I did manage to get away early a few times, travelling on the Mersey rail train, which took about fifteen minutes into town. I'd seen the group in '61, '62 in quite a few places – the Tower Ballroom in New Brighton, Hulme Hall in Port Sunlight, Liscard, Wallasey, the Hoylake YMCA, and later with Roy Orbison at the Empire, and at the Majestic in Birkenhead. The Majestic was our favourite. I think I only missed one of their appearances there. An old Victorian dance hall, they would hold dances in the evenings, and an afternoon dance on Saturday afternoons for the young ones.

One night in particular stands out in my memory. It was the freezing cold winter of early '63, and my school-friend Ann and I had to queue round the side of the ballroom for tickets. There was ice on the ground, and I slipped, falling backwards and cracked my head. It was so cold, I didn't feel the pain! The day before I'd gone on my half-day to Birkenhead market. I didn't have much money but paid a lot for this pair of black leather shoes. The next night, I wore them for the first time, with my jeans.

The Majestic had a white wrought-iron balcony going round the whole ballroom, with little tables to sit at. We were right at the front of the balcony, looking over the left-hand side, almost over the top of the stage. Whilst I was tapping my foot to the music, my shoe slipped off, over the balcony and onto the stage, hitting John Lennon on the head! There was no alcohol in those days, just bottles of Coke, and he poured his Coca-Cola from this bottle into one of my shoes and proceeded to drink from it! I'd just paid 29/11 for them! I went out one week nearly every single night to see them. My mum said, 'When are you going to wash your hair?' and I said, 'It won't be getting washed this week!' No hairdryers in those days, and I had long black hair which took hours in front of the fire to dry. I just didn't have time that week. Amazing really.

At Johnson's we offered on-the-spot cleaning. We had a Hoffman presser and it was done on the premises. The lady who used to work the presser had a sister who worked at Beno Dorn, the tailors who made the Beatles suits in the early days. Every time the group had a suit made, I'd get a square of material from them, and a button. I kept them all and catalogued them. Mum wouldn't let me put anything on the walls, so I bought a cheap roll of wallpaper to put all my bits and pieces on, record sleeves and stuff, and when it got full, I just rolled it up, and then started again. When we got married, me Mam threw the whole lot in the bin! Autographs and everything. The night they did 'Love Me Do' at the Majestic, I got the record, and sleeve in plain white, and all four signed it. It all went.

I remember seeing them on *Scene At 6.30* on Granada. I said to Ann, 'We've lost them. They're not ours anymore. They'll never come back now,' tears running down my cheeks. I'm still a fan after all these years. I always say our teenage years were the best ever – the teenage years we had, in the '60s. **❜**

JUNE ASHLEY, BRITISH TELECOM ENGINEER, WALLASEY, MERSEYSIDE

FRIDAY 18 JANUARY

'**P**lease Please Me' entered the *Melody Maker* chart at number 47, along with singles from Del Shannon, the Four Seasons, Chris Montez, Marty Robbins, Rick Nelson and the Orlons. 'Love Me Do' dropped to number 26. The Beatles and the Four Seasons had the distinction of being the only two acts to have two singles each in the Top 50.

The group received their weekly wage of £30. Ringo paid 17/- for three copies of 'Please Please Me', receiving a 10 per cent discount. Billed as 'The Beetles', they played at the Floral Hall Ballroom on Morecambe Promenade, an hour and a half's drive north of Liverpool. Gerry and the Pacemakers' roadie Les Hurst filled in for a flu-stricken Neil Aspinall.

Although the weather was nowhere near as bad as in other parts of the country, the River Lune was almost frozen over in some parts. People played ice hockey on the canal, sledged on the shore and someone used a pickaxe to break through the ice in the Super Swimming Stadium. The *Morecambe Visitor* reported that temperatures had brought fishing to a standstill and caused the biggest setback in the building trade since 1947 at a time when unemployment was at its highest for five years.

There was a small mention of the group's appearance in the *Morecambe Guardian*. 'Tonight The Beatles, described as Britain's newest television sensation featured in *People And Places* on ITV this week – will provide the beat. Almost certainly they will feature their hit single 'Love Me Do'.'

❛ In the early '60s there was plenty to do in Morecambe. There were two dance halls – the Floral Hall and the Central Pier. During the summer season they used to have something called 'Live Jive and Record Hop', which cost about a shilling to get in. On Tuesday nights they'd have local groups playing, and Friday and Saturday groups from Liverpool, Manchester and the surrounding area. I would go along to the Floral on a Friday night as a matter of course, usually meeting up with friends beforehand for a drink or two in the railway station bar. They sold proper beer there, not like the 'ditchwater' they sold at the Floral like Watneys Red Barrel – pale ale didn't go down too well up North! Even though we were too young to drink, nobody bothered those days. We'd always buy a ticket on the door at the Floral Hall, nobody bought tickets in advance then. The boys dressed very smartly – we'd all wear a shirt and tie with a

jacket. The girls would arrive with scarves on their heads with their rollers still on, then go into the Ladies' and take out their curlers!

So, Friday nights were a regular thing, and I didn't think any more about it the evening the Beatles came. They'd played there before – I hadn't seen them, but I knew the song 'Love Me Do' and that was it. It wasn't packed that evening, and I was standing down at the front beside Alan Birdshall, the Floral's manager, who I knew quite well. One thing that struck me that evening was that everyone actually stood watching and listening – that wasn't what usually happened. Usually everyone would be dancing and not listening too much to the group. Alan had booked lots of groups for various venues – he used to be a redcoat at Butlin's and knew his stuff. It was brilliant, although I was just 15 and didn't realise what I was witnessing at the time. I remember they played 'Please Please Me', introducing it as their new single. Of course, I went out and bought it after seeing them. **〕**

NEVILLE KENNEDY, PLASTERER, MORECAMBE, LANCASHIRE

SATURDAY 19 JANUARY

The bitter cold continued. Householders in areas of Liverpool awoke to find themselves without water because of frozen pipes. All southbound vehicles on the A66 were being stopped or re-directed to prevent further chaos. Shane Fenton and the Fentones got stuck on the Derbyshire moors and weren't rescued until four o'clock in the morning. For the first time since 1929, several lakes in the Lake District were frozen over and skaters took advantage of the situation. Liverpool Corporation posted notices at Calderstone, Greenbank, Sefton and Walton parks saying that the ice was safe for skating – at the skater's own risk, however.

Merseyside escaped the brunt of the continuing bad weather. Leaving the city in the early afternoon, with Hurst once again filling in for Aspinall, the group set off through the Mersey tunnel and then south on the A41 for Whitchurch in Shropshire for the evening's show at the Town Hall on the High Street. Classes for the spring term of the Joan Whiting School of Stage Dancing had taken place earlier in the day at the hall. As they drove up to the venue, the previous Sunday's recording of *Thank Your Lucky Stars* was coming to an end on TV. Despite the cold weather, the hall was filled to capacity (as it always was on Saturday nights). The show began at 8pm with support act the Marauders, after which the Beatles played their first set. During the interval, while local group the Savages played, the group went across the road to the Victoria Hotel for a drink and chatted with the locals. After about twenty minutes they returned to the hall, disappearing into their dressing room while the Dakotas played. They came back for their second set, which ended just before midnight.

❛ The rock'n'roll dances at the Town Hall Ballroom were promoted by Keith Fisher, who ran an agency in Stoke-on-Trent. He used to 'block book' acts for up to six nights and would put them on 'the circuit' which covered the Midlands and the north-west. He would arrange for coaches to bring people in from surrounding areas such as Wem, Shrewsbury and Wrexham.

One evening a disturbance broke out near the Town Hall, which involved the local police and local youths. A few weeks later, he asked me if I would be interested in taking over the running of the dances. After giving it some consideration, I decided to give it a try. This meant that I would have to employ local staff for security, ticket office, cloakroom and the snack bar. My parents ran the snack bar, which sold mainly soft drinks

and crisps, as we had no licence to sell alcohol. The remainder of the staff were friends or friends of the family. Keith would telephone me on a Wednesday and advise me on the acts that would be appearing the following Saturday. We had regular supporting acts as well as a local group playing during the intervals. Keith supplied an amplifier for them as a reward.

You can imagine my amazement when Keith telephoned me on Wednesday 16 January and told me that the Beatles would be playing at the Town Hall three days later. This meant that I had to hastily arrange for advertising posters to be printed and to be displayed in the local shop windows. On the night of the 19th, I arrived at the Town Hall at about 6pm and helped with all the equipment set-up, assisted by the hall's caretaker. The Beatles' roadie arrived in an old van at about 6.15pm, followed a short while later by the Beatles themselves. Soon afterwards, a gentleman by the name of Tudor Fisher appeared at the rear of the stage. He owned the local electrical store in the High Street. He informed me that the overhead stage lighting, which was various colours, was not to be used as it belonged to the Whitchurch Theatre and Operatic Group. This would have left us with only the white stage lights, which would have been ineffective. After some discussion, it was agreed that we could use them on this occasion. I believe that someone had tipped him off and that was the reason for his presence.

At about 6.50pm Keith and Brian Epstein arrived in a Jaguar. Epstein was immaculately dressed in a suit and officer-style camel-haired overcoat. I took them upstairs to the dressing rooms. The Beatles carried their own suits and by this time the support acts, the Marauders and the Dakotas, had arrived and were setting up. The show began at 8pm and ended at about 11.50 and the audience started to leave. Keith and Brian Epstein came across the dance floor to thank me for a successful event and both left, leaving the Beatles in the hall.

There were three Liverpudlian girls who were left stranded after the dance (I believe that they had arrived with the Beatles). They had been advised by the group's roadie that they would not be returning to Liverpool with the group. Two local girls heard of their plight and offered to accommodate them for the night and then put them on a train to Liverpool the next day. The locally hired staff and I helped the roadies to load the equipment onto the various vehicles of the various groups who had performed. It was now about 12.40am and we didn't realise whilst loading that the fog had started to come down very thick. Their roadie said that he would take a chance and drive back to Liverpool and then left with the equipment. However, the group were less keen on venturing home in the fog. They were in a jovial mood after playing such a good gig. I suggested that they might like to come to my parents' house for a drink and something to eat, to which they gratefully accepted.

When we got to our house in Smallbrook Road we went into the sitting room, which was saved for special occasions. I went to advise my parents that we had guests and my mother was delighted to hear that it was the Beatles. She then produced drinks and spam sandwiches with tomato sauce. After we had all eaten, the group started to tap on the coffee table, throw the cushions around and generally became a little rowdy. I remember my mother requesting us all to keep the noise down as we had elderly neighbours next door and my two younger brothers, Ray and Stewart, were fast asleep upstairs. At about 1.40am I looked outside and noticed that the fog had begun to clear and so they decided that they would take a chance and head for home. They weren't sure of the way to get back onto the main road, so I travelled with them until we stopped outside the Hollies Hotel on Chester Road, and that was the last time that I had any personal contact with them. I did not appreciate at the time how globally well known they would become and cherish the opportunity of having met them and getting to know them a little. In the morning I gave my brother Stewart a pink-coloured ticket from the show with their autographs signed 'To Stewart'. He took the autographs to school the next morning, handed them around for people to see. He never saw them again. 🎵

**MICHAEL DALE, PRODUCTIVE AT GM PLANT AND COACH AND
HGV DRIVER, WHITCHURCH, SHROPSHIRE**

SUNDAY 20 JANUARY

Liverpool's City Engineer's Department was called out at 3am and worked through the day, trying to keep the city's streets and pavements safe. Some one thousand men, including parks and gardens staff, cleared the pavements, while four hundred men and twenty-six gritters dealt with the roads. With Les Hurst unavailable, a still-sick Aspinall hauled himself out of bed for the group's Cavern Club performance in the evening. The group headed a bill which also featured Pete Hartigan's Jazzmen, the Dennisons (residents at the Jive Hive in Crosby every Wednesday), the Merseybeats and the Bluegenes. Aspinall recalled, 'I don't remember much of that night. I was all feverish, sweating and a sort of funny yellow colour.' He informed Epstein that he would be unable to drive the group down to London the following day, but then bumped into GPO telephone engineer Mal Evans, a regular at the Cavern, and asked him, 'Mal, can you run the boys to London and back for me?' To which Evans replied, 'Yeah, OK.'

The Cavern had been founded as a traditional jazz venue in January 1957. The Beatles had first played there on 9 February 1961 and it was exactly nine months later that Brian Epstein first saw them. Gerry Marsden of Gerry and the Pacemakers later said the venue 'stank of disinfectant and stale onions. It was hot, sweaty and oppressive. It was a nightmare to get in and out of; struggling down the stairs from Mathew Street to the cellar with all our gear was tough, but it was the only entrance because there was no backstage – and no backstage toilet, either. I shudder to think of the effect of a fire down there, had there ever been one.' Paid £20 for their appearance three days earlier, for this performance, the Beatles earned £45.

> ❛ We played the Sunday lunchtime sessions regularly at the Cavern but I don't think we realised that the session in January 1963 would be one of the last times the Beatles played there at lunchtime. We often shared the same gear with them. When we played night-time shows with them we usually went on after them because the Cavern closed about eleven o'clock, and by the time everyone got out, you'd missed your bus or train or ferry. If you were on that last spot from half ten to half eleven, people would have to leave in the middle of your set. So top of the bill didn't want to be onstage when people were leaving. Consequently, if we were on before the Beatles, they would use our equipment. If it was the other way round, we would use theirs. We'd get it back to each other the next day.
>
> During one lunchtime session at the Cavern, I went there to see Bob Wooler, just me and Bob going through the diary – and believe it or not, I've still got the diary – with Bob's initials in. 'BE', which of course referred to Brian Epstein, was written on quite a lot of the pages. So, when I went in for this meeting before one of the lunchtime sessions, a friend of mine, Chris Wharton, came with me. He was also a friend of Epstein's. His dad had a coach-spraying business. John's beloved Rickenbacker was looking very tarnished, and Chris said to John, 'I could have it sprayed black for you.' So John had said, 'Oh great, yeah.' Chris walked in and I noticed the guitar case was old and tattered, black, ripped a bit, and had Star-Club stickers all over it. I knew it was either the Beatles' or the Big Three's. I had a good look at it, and it was the Beatles'. I asked, 'What's this?' Chris said, 'It's John's Rickenbacker, it's been sprayed black.' I said, 'Can I have a look?' It was on a bench, so I just played the strings. I said, 'It's slightly flat toppy.' So he asked me if I could tune it. I was engrossed, absolutely engrossed. The Beatles were doing the lunchtime session that day, and we heard someone coming down the steps, and it was George and John. They said, 'Oh is this the guitar?' So they opened it up, and it was like Christmas morning. John was like a 10-year-old. He thought it looked great. I'll never forget that.
>
> In May of 1963, we took part in the Lancashire and Cheshire Beat Group Contest. They had all the groups on, then they voted, and the ten best groups did the second half. There must have been about twenty or twenty-five groups. So we were in the top ten, and we went on to do the second half, and we were going to do the same two songs, as we had just gone down an absolute storm. Everyone was saying, 'Oh they're gonna win it, they're gonna win it.' Then the Escorts went on, and did one of the

songs that we had just done! We thought, we can't do it again. They were so-called mates, they still are actually. Luckily, we had a big repertoire, so we had no problem doing another song. They won and we came second. George and Ringo gave the awards out. I think we got a very little cup. The winner was going to win a recording contract with Decca. Actually it didn't work out, and they ended up on the same label as us, Fontana.

On the August Bank Holiday 1963, if you recall it always used to fall at the beginning of the month, and it was the last time the Beatles played the Cavern. We were going to go on immediately before them and it was roasting hot outside. The Cavern never bothered to count how many people came in, it was just so cramped it wasn't true. There were just so many people in there, there wasn't room to dance. The condensation was running down the walls. There was only one socket on the stage at the Cavern – a five-amp socket, just the one, that's all, so the plug boards would go into the one socket. So we went on immediately before the Beatles, and when we came off, we were absolutely saturated. There was only one little band room at the side, and they were waiting for us. We all had a chat, and Paul was pretty cheesed off. The power had gone off because of the damp. The conditions really were horrendous. There was just one light on the stage and all the power was off. So eventually they went onstage, went into their show, and all the girls were screaming. To be honest, we hadn't seen girls screaming before, but of course they had been touring by then and the screaming had started. It was unbearable. I was standing at the back just wanting to go home. Me, the biggest Beatles fan you will find in the world, and I just thought 'I can't watch this.' It was awful and embarrassing.

So the power went off completely after they had done about three or four songs, the amplification went off, and the Beatles, being the Beatles, improvised. Paul went over to the upright piano, John picked up his acoustic which you could hear, but that's all, and Paul went into an old-fashioned song that no one had ever heard. It sounded like a song from the 1920s, one that his dad would have played in the Jim Mac band. I will never ever forget seeing that. In 1967, when *Sgt. Pepper's* came out, there was a song on it – 'When I'm Sixty-Four'. It was the song he had played on the piano that night when the power went out. I could not believe it. I thought, 'I've heard this song before!' Paul said he wrote the song when he was 14. The Cavern sounded awful, the heat and the sweat and the smell, but it was great! **❜**

BILLY KINSLEY, MUSICIAN, SINGER, LIVERPOOL, MERSEYSIDE

MONDAY 21 JANUARY

All major roads between Scotland and England were cut off. There were blockages and breakdowns on nearly all major roads in Lancashire and most minor roads were impassable. In some places, drifts were so deep that snowploughs gave up the battle.

Mal Evans drove the group to London for a recording of Radio Luxembourg's *The Friday Spectacular* – their third – at EMI House's ground floor studio in Manchester Square. Evans picked George up around 10.45am, then John, Paul and Ringo, before heading south. They stopped off at the Grindley Brook petrol station outside Whitchurch to fill up the van and have some lunch, which comprised cups of tea and bacon sandwiches. Shortly thereafter, they continued driving to London with George taking over at the wheel. When they reached EMI House, they reported to the office of EMI's general promotion manager Arthur Muxlow for the recording of the show. They played 'Please Please Me' and 'Ask Me Why'. Co-host Muriel Young was drowned out by the screams of the hundred or so teenagers in the audience.

The group were interviewed by Young and her fellow host Shaw Taylor. Paul later told *Boyfriend*, 'We had only made one record, 'Love Me Do', and Muriel Young introduced us by our Christian names only. She got as far as John, Paul... and then, suddenly, the place went wild. Usually it takes a couple of years for a group to be recognised by their first names, but, boy! That really knocked us out!' Also present at EMI during the day was Vee-Jay's head of its international department Barbara Gardner, who put pen to paper signing the Beatles to the label in the US. She was in London to supervise the recording of the LP *Pop Gospel Live In London* by the Chris Barber Sextet and the Alex Bradford Singers. Following the recording of *The Friday Spectacular*, the group spent the night at the Cavendish Hotel in Gower Street, across the road from the Royal Academy of Dramatic Art, where Brian Epstein had trained in the late 1950s.

❛ What turned out to be a typical Saturday night out pub crawl with the lads – which always ended up at the local dance at Whitchurch Town Hall – turned out to be one that was memorable for me. I was wearing a nifty jacket that had been given to me by Charles Lewis, the owner of the racing stables where I worked. I was drinking in the Victoria Hall when the Beatles came into the bar area. John Lennon came up to me and asked, 'Where d'you get the drape mate?' admiring the oatmeal-coloured jacket with its silk lining and no lapels. I was probably the only person in the area that had such a jacket. Having explained how I obtained 'the drape', we parted company and he went off to rejoin his bandmates for a drink and subsequently perform their second set.

Two days later, I was waiting for my work colleague at the Grindley Brook petrol station, on the outskirts of town, and having a cup of tea from the kiosk, when a dormobile pulled up with scrawled writing along the side of it which spelt 'The Beatles', among other things. Out got five lads, one of whom started filling up the tank. The other four approached the kiosk and while I was standing there we made eye contact. John said, 'You're the one with the drape we saw the other night.' They got their food and drink, climbed back into their van and were on their way down the A41 into town and beyond. ❜

SNOWY BETTANEY, JOCKEY, WHITCHURCH, CHESHIRE

TUESDAY 22 JANUARY

After a morning of shopping, the group arrived at the Paris Studio in the basement of Rex House at 12 Regent Street in London, just before noon. They appeared live on the Light Programme show *Pop Inn*, chatting with host Keith Fordyce before he played 'Please Please Me'. The forty-five-minute show, in front of an audience of around four hundred, also featured actor (and future Dr Who) Jon Pertwee and fellow singers Joan Regan and Shane Fenton. Following their segment, the group made the five-minute journey to the Playhouse Theatre on Northumberland Avenue near the Embankment, to record their debut on the upcoming edition of *Saturday Club*. Rehearsals began at 2.30pm for the 4pm hour-long recording. The group performed 'Some Other Guy' (a 1962 Richard Barrett song written with Jerry Leiber and Mike Stoller), 'Love Me Do', 'Please Please Me', 'Keep Your Hands Off My Baby' (a Gerry Goffin/Carole King tune then in the Top 50 for Little Eva) and 'Beautiful Dreamer' (a Stephen Foster song penned nearly one hundred years earlier, recently updated by Gerry Goffin and Jack Keller for Tony Orlando). They found time to do an interview in the theatre's tea bar with Gordon Williams, whose subsequent article in *Scene* was headed 'Anatomy Of A Hot Property'.

Afterwards, the group returned to the Paris Theatre for a 5.30pm rehearsal of *The Talent Spot*, another appearance arranged for them by Dick James. Introduced by host Gary Marshal, they performed 'Please Please Me', 'Ask Me Why' and 'Some Other Guy' at the 7pm recording in front of a live audience. The group also found time during the day to take part in a series of round-robin interviews. As they left for an interview at the Mayfair Hotel in Stratton Street with *Daily Mail* journalist Adrian Mitchell, fans tried to tear the door off their taxi. They set off home around 10pm, unaware of the morning's headlines in Liverpool – '1,700 Men Clear City Pavements – Thousands Of Tons Of Snow Being Removed'. Snow was cleared and dumped into the city's Canning Dock. They stopped off for dinner in Fortes restaurant at Newport Pagnell services.

> ❛ *The Talent Spot* was a show where artists would come in and play their latest singles and my job was to talk with them about when they recorded them, who wrote them, simple questions like that. I talked to Paul briefly while they were setting up their equipment – they had more gear than anybody had ever had on the show. They were so busy tuning up, running through numbers and even writing new material, so I ran up to the control room to tell my producer Brian Willey that I wasn't getting anywhere and then went to my dressing room behind the backstage area to write my script for the show. I was walking down the long-carpeted corridor and coming towards me was this forlorn figure, slight in build and stature, staring at the carpet. As we neared each other I said, 'Hi' and he said, 'Can I ask you a question? My name is Brian Epstein – what do I do?' I took him up to the control room and said, 'Brian, this is Brian.' When they launched into 'Please Please Me' in front of the audience it was like World War III. There was one portly uniformed commissionaire from central casting, well past the age of being physically able to hold anyone back if they'd tried to rush the stage. The thing that struck me – and it was the same when I first saw Sinatra live and heard Oscar Peterson and Count Basie – their tempi was incredible. It never varied. Seeing them that day, I knew that they would be incredibly huge. ❜
>
> **GARY MARSHAL, SINGER AND ACTOR, LAS VEGAS, NEVADA, USA**

WEDNESDAY 23 JANUARY

Following dinner, the group continued their journey home. The freezing cold, heavy snow, and a blanket of fog presented problems for Evans. The windscreen shattered, causing him to knock the rest of the broken glass so he could continue driving. Not for the first time, the group took it in turns to lie on top of each other in the back to stay warm, while Evans fashioned a balaclava from a paper bag with holes in it to see through. The second leg of the trip took some five hours, including a stop for an early morning cuppa at a transport cafe. At about 5am, they arrived in Liverpool, despite frozen snow causing hazardous conditions on the city's outskirts. They spent much of the day sleeping off their ordeal.

There was no sign of a let up in the weather through the weekend. Hundreds of families in Liverpool were without water because of frozen pipes and mains. Ice floes formed on the Mersey for first time since 1947. Roads in the suburbs were still badly affected by hard-packed snow while in the city centre it was still treacherous underfoot and drivers were using extreme care. The 12.25am train from Euston Station, which was scheduled to arrive at 4.52am, finally limped into Lime Street at 8.57am.

The group were scheduled to play the Emporium Ballroom in Doncaster in the evening, but the show was postponed – maybe because of the weather – and never rescheduled. Instead, the group made their way in minus 7 degree temperatures to perform at the Cavern again, this time with the Four Mosts (soon to change their name to the Fourmost). Ken Dallas and the Silhouettes and Freddie Starr and the Midnighters in support.

' I was studying at the Liverpool College of Art along with John Lennon. He was in the Silver Beetles and shared a flat on Gambier Terrace with fellow student Stuart Sutcliffe. They had promised to play at the college's dances so the Students' Union bought them an amplifier and a bass. They invited me up to the library at college one day to have a rehearsal with them but the music they were into was just alien to me. I just didn't like it at all. John asked me if I would join them, but I was already with the Silhouettes, who were very musical, very technical, and the Silver Beetles were very raw, and I just didn't like the music they were playing. So I said, 'No!' They were also about to go to Germany and John said Stuart was prepared to go with them to play bass but wasn't a bass player, so would I teach him? I agreed, saying that in return I'd like to measure the bass the Students' Union had bought them – a Hofner President – as I wanted to try and make one. So off I went to their flat, measured every inch of the bass and showed Stuart how to play 'C'mon Everybody', 'Summertime Blues' and the twelve-bar boogie in E. I made the bass guitar with the help of my dad who was a joiner and eventually sold it to Pete [Mackey], the bass player with the Roadrunners. I got fifteen quid for it.

When the Silver Beetles came home from Hamburg they played at St John's Hall in Bootle and we were on the same bill. As soon as I heard them, I just knew. They were just phenomenal. They had been playing ten hours a night in Germany, so if you don't get good after that, you might as well pack it in. We played with them again at the Cavern in January 1963. We were sitting in the dressing room chatting while the other groups were on. Paul was sitting with a piece of paper writing things down. He was asking me for words that rhymed with other words, like 'city', and I'd say 'pretty'. What he was actually doing was writing songs. I often wonder how many of my words got into any of them. Paul's bass amp had blown and he asked Rod [McClelland] if he could borrow his single Vox for their slot. When we got it back, the speakers were all crackly, so he had blown that one as well!

The dressing room in the Cavern was tiny. It was like a little band room really just to the left of the stage. You would step up onto the stage and it was just like a little square, sweaty room. When there were multiple groups on, we used to take our own amps down the narrow stairs and wait to set them up. Bob Wooler would give us a couple of minutes whilst playing recorded music. There may have been amps there but I always remember using my own. I used to hate carrying it down the stairs. Sometimes we did what they'd call 'Marathons'. We'd do a lunchtime session at the Cavern, then say, Blair Hall in the afternoon, then we'd go back to the Cavern in the evening and be on at eleven o'clock at night. It was quite normal to do that. There was an event at the Rialto Theatre where record producer John Schroeder was looking for local talent to sign up to his Oriole label. There was so much talent in Liverpool at the time that he ended up with two albums – *Merseybeat Number One* and *Merseybeat Number Two*. We managed to get on the first LP with 'Someday', and from that we got signed to Oriole, and made our first single in London with John producing.

After many memorable shows and a residency at the Kingsway in Southport, we eventually split up in 1965 and I joined Rory Storm and the Hurricanes for a while. I only stayed for about nine months. I'm still gigging and do lots of charity events, Shadows' tributes, all good fun. I'll play until I drop. I recall seeing an interview with the Beatles when they came back from America. They were asked where they had all gone and they said, 'Nowhere. We were stuck in our hotel room all the time. We couldn't go out.' I think that life would never have done me at all, I would have hated it. So maybe it's not such a bad thing that I turned them down back in the late '50s! I've had a very happy career, and I wouldn't swap it for anything. I can go to the shops and buy things, Paul McCartney can't do that. '

DAVID L. MAY, MUSICIAN, MAGHULL, MERSEYSIDE

THURSDAY 24 JANUARY

On the first anniversary of signing a management deal with Brian Epstein, the group were featured in the national press for the first time. Under the heading 'Popland Goes British' in his *Daily Mirror* 'On The Record' column, Patrick Doncaster wrote, 'Watch the Beatles, a guitar-based instrumental quartet from Liverpool with a style of their own.'

After experiencing the coldest night since 1941, with 19 degrees of frost, the group made a personal appearance at Epstein's NEMS record store at 12–14 Whitechapel in Liverpool. They signed copies of 'Please Please Me', which climbed to number 33 in the week's *NRM* chart as 'Love Me Do' dropped to number 37. They treated shoppers to an impromptu performance, with George sitting at the bottom of the stairs on a stool, Ringo standing next to him playing a single snare drum and John and Paul on the stairs leading from the pop department on the ground floor to the television, radio and tape recorders and classical records on the first floor. Epstein's management offices were on the third floor above the shop.

Afterwards, they drove through the Mersey Tunnel and took the A41 south-west into Wales for a sold-out performance at the Assembly Hall in the High Street in Mold, Flintshire – a concert booked by the Mold Urban District Council the previous October. The severe weather was affecting Wales as well. Water was being rationed as the Water Board struggled to get supplies from reservoirs. Arriving a couple of hours early, they stopped off for a pint (or two) at the Cross Keys pub on the outskirts of Mold. When they got to the hall, Wally Rees, the rhythm guitarist of support group the Chariots, was playing the piano. 'It's good, that', complimented Paul. Bob Wooler travelled from Liverpool to compère the night, as did Brian Epstein, wearing brown-and-white leather shoes – a definite first for North Wales. Paul's younger brother Mike also attended, taking a series of photos backstage.

Before their performance, the *Wrexham Leader*'s 'Off Beat' columnist David Sandison conducted a lengthy interview with the group in their dressing room. Asked what he disliked about popularity, Paul said, 'The long journey to dates. Once you've arrived it's fine, but the hours wasted in cars and trains are enough to drive you round the bend.' On the subject of their hobbies and tastes, John and Paul responded in unison, 'Girls, songwriting, eating and sleeping.' They were paid £50 for the show. Rhona Jardine-Phillips, who was involved with booking the Thursday night dances, thought it was money well spent.

Afterwards, George made a quick getaway, driving to nearby Broughton to spend the night with his aunt Janey. The rest of the group accepted an invitation from Moya Brown and her brother Ian to go back to their father's pub at the Talbot Hotel in Holywell. Brown later recalled, 'My sister was friends with the tour manager for Gerry and the Pacemakers, who were friends with the Beatles. After the concert, she persuaded them to come back to the pub. I was Paul McCartney's passenger, showing him the way. I was a really big fan, so it was quite daunting. However, when we got there, Dad had closed the pub. We knocked on the door and I said he had to let me in because the Beatles were with us. He replied, "I don't care who they are, they're not coming in." After a bit of persuasion, he let us in. We ate sandwiches and drank beer and John Lennon banged out a tune on the pub's upright piano.'

> ‘ During the autumn of 1962, I began attending the weekly dances each Thursday night in the Assembly Hall in Mold (thirty-five miles from Liverpool, just over the border in Wales). Mold is the county town of Flintshire and as such was the place that teenagers from the surrounding towns and villages gravitated towards for entertainment, boasting not only a dance hall but a cinema too. Teenagers were bussed in – no one had cars then – in fact, I was one of the few whose father owned a car. I would travel down with my friend Jacky, but there would be lots of teenagers there who attended

our school. The dance hall was rather spartan. There was no licence but a soft drinks counter in the corner. All the older boys would be in the Cross Keys pub around the back and would not arrive until later. I think 10pm was the cut-off time for entry – presumably to ensure that they were not too drunk and caused trouble. There would always be bouncers on the door to look after us.

On Christmas Eve 1962 I recall attending a Christmas dance. An announcement was made that the Beatles would be playing on 24 January and we were advised to buy tickets in advance as there was likely to be a great demand. We quickly bought our tickets and sure enough it was a sell-out and people were turned away. I can still recall the atmosphere that night and the excitement building up as the supporting group played. Boys were coming in from the Cross Keys and reported that the Beatles were in there and had bought a bottle of whiskey – that denoted real wealth to us then. The roar as they entered the hall was electric. They related so well to the audience, particularly John Lennon with his dry scouse wit. However, my favourite then was Paul McCartney although that changed over the years as their own personal styles of music developed. The feeling I had was that they were special and different from any other groups we had seen. They sang old favourites and songs they had composed. Everyone was on the floor. The heat was unbelievable – no air con then. I think that they had really enjoyed themselves and I recall John saying that they would love to come again but because 'Please Please Me' was heading for number one, the fee would have to increase from £50 to £500. It was clear then that they were out of our league and would not perform in Mold again. The Beatles' visit often comes up in conversation with young people and they are amazed that this happened. I will treasure that evening for the rest of my life. **]**

MARGARET LYSAGHT, COMPANY DIRECTOR, MOLD, FLINTSHIRE, WALES

FRIDAY **25 JANUARY**

I n the new *Melody Maker*, 'Please Please Me' climbed eight places to number 39, as 'Love Me Do' dropped to number 34. Hidden away on page 10, Janice Nicholls reviewed 'Please Please Me' in her 'Oi'll Give It Foive' column, writing that she thought it better than their previous record. 'I think it should do a lot better than 'Love Me Do'. A lot of people don't like it, but I do.' *Here We Go*, recorded on 16 January, aired on the Light Programme at 5pm, presented by Ray Peters and featuring regulars Bernard Herrmann and the NDO, with guests the Trad Lads and Ken Kirkham. The Beatles were bottom of the bill; the track 'Three Cool Cats' was not broadcast.

A dance promoted by the local Baptist church youth club.

BAPTIST YOUTH CLUB
PRESENTS
The Greatest Teenage Dance
FEATURING —
THE BEATLES
Supported By — THE ELECTONES THE MIKE TAYLOR
COMBO   THE MUSTANGS WITH RICKY DAY
IN THE CO-OPERATIVE HALL,
FRIDAY NEXT, JANUARY 25th
Non-Stop Dancing 7.30 to 11.30 p.m.
Tickets 6/.   Buffet

At long last there was some good news on the weather front, as warmer air moved in from the Atlantic and with it a resultant thaw. Just after 6pm, the group set off for the Co-operative Hall in Market Street, Darwen, Lancashire. John and Ringo travelled with Neil Aspinall in the group van, while George drove in his Ford Anglia, bought from the Hawthorne Engineering Company in Warrington, with Paul as his passenger. Aspinall stopped near the British Queen pub and had to ask where the Co-op was. Fog had made them late. The hall's David Yates met them on their arrival and showed them up to their dressing room. A sold-out crowd of 450 paid 6/- (including a buffet) to see the Electones, the Mike Taylor Combo and the Mustangs with Ricky Day, before the Beatles went onstage at around 9.30pm. Tom Proudfoot, who promoted the show for the Bolton Road Baptist Youth Club, had booked them after seeing them on *People And Places* the previous October. One Co-op regular, affectionately known as Bubbles, grabbed hold of one of Paul's legs and refused to let go. Only after he inadvertently kicked her in the breasts did he manage to free himself from her grip. Bubbles didn't seem unduly concerned. During their set at 10pm, Monday's recording of *The Friday Spectacular* aired on Radio Luxembourg. The group signed autographs after the show. Paul asked David Yates, 'Do you know the way to Southport?' He told them it was down the main road and asked whether they would give him a lift as he was going that way. As they drove towards Blackburn, George dropped him off at the corner of the Birch Hall Estate.

❛The Mustangs got together in 1960 and we were going to be the next Shadows. We got our first break playing at our local church Youth Club dance. We were one of the four good-ish groups in Darwen, but decided we needed a singer, so we hired Sammy McNally, who had just left the group the Shotguns. On the day we supported the Beatles in 1963, we arrived at the Co-op Hall at around 6.30pm. We were early as we were the first group onstage and needed to set up our equipment early. I remember lugging amplifiers up the fifty or so steps to the hall which was situated above the Menswear and Furniture Departments. Just as we had finished unloading, the Beatles arrived and began to unload their kit. Sammy helped carry some of Ringo's drum kit and Jim Hickey, our drummer's dad, offered to help carry Paul's speaker cabinet upstairs. He got a shock when he tried to pick it up as it was a custom-made cabinet that had several layers of bricks in the bottom to hold it down and give a better sound. He nearly put his back out!

It was the biggest audience we had ever had and we loved it. The Beatles came on and the whole room was completely blown away by them. They played the loudest, harshest rock'n'roll that we had ever heard. It dawned on all of us there that night that the face of live music was about to change for ever. Little did we all realise the impact that they would make on world music. We spoke to them afterwards. It was a brilliant night and one that will remain in the memory for ever.❜

JOHN BENTLEY, SENIOR PROCUREMENT MANAGER, BRITISH TELECOM, DARWEN, LANCASHIRE

SATURDAY 26 JANUARY

The *Liverpool Echo*'s front-page headline read 'Thaw Brings Burst-Pipe Saturday' with news that pensioners had been flooded out of their flats. The city's Water Engineer, J. W. T. Stilgoe, warned that without economising, supplies would fail. Temperatures reached 3.2 degrees – the highest since 22 December. In the south-east, the thaw had an even greater impact. An Eastern Electricity spokesman said that the power cut was 'the longest spell without electricity we have ever heard of'. Luton and Dunstable Hospital borrowed a US Army generator to keep running. Four ice cream vans in Derby used their generators to keep hospital incubators working.

Tuesday's recording of *Saturday Club* was broadcast on the Light Programme from 10am to 12pm. Host Brian Matthew, in his introduction to 'Love Me Do', said, 'At the moment, the majority of the Beatles' fans are in their hometown of Liverpool, and I have a very strong suspicion it won't be long before they're all over the country.' A small *Radio Times* feature on the group's appearance said, 'Any group with so uncompromising a name as the Beatles has much to overcome to win recognition from those who have little interest in Hit Parade music.' A fan recorded the programme on several 5-inch reel-to-reel tapes, subsequently storing them in his attic – the recording of 'Keep Your Hands Off My Baby' would be included on *The Beatles Live At The BBC*.

> KING'S HALL, STOKE
> SATURDAY, JAN., 26TH   No   64
> Midland Entertainments and Rockstar Enterprises present
> ★★★ Hit Recorders of "LOVE ME DO" ★★★
> **THE BEATLES**
> 7-45—11-45 p.m.
> Licensed Bar   Buffet   Late Buses   TICKETS : 6/-
> No admission after 10 p.m.

The group drove approximately 50 miles to Macclesfield in Cheshire for a show starting at 7.45pm at the El Rio Club in the Brocklehurst Memorial Hall on Queen Victoria Street, with local group Wayne Fontana and the Jets in support. On arrival, they had a meal at the Cavendish coffee bar across the road. When they began their set people stood on tables and chairs to see them. As many as 500 squeezed into the hall, which had a considerably smaller capacity. Some clung on to ropes that hung across the ceiling. Backstage, John and Paul began writing the song 'Misery', which they finished the following day during a break from rehearsal at the Cavern. John still had time to let fan Patricia Lowe sit on his knee. She got the group's autographs, signed on her arm.

Once they finished their set, they stopped off for some fish and chips on Mill Lane – once again signing autographs, on this occasion on a pea container lid and Andrew Kidd's driving licence – before heading south on the A536 to Stoke-on-Trent, Staffordshire, where they performed a second show at the King's Hall in Glebe Street, this time promoted as 'Hit Recorders of 'Love Me Do''.

❛ I was a 15-year-old working as a live-in kennel maid on a farm in the hills outside Macclesfield. That winter was particularly bad. The road to the farm was closed with snow for weeks at a time, with only a narrow path for a horse or motorbike to get through. I knew the Beatles were playing in the town and decided to walk the seven miles to see them. I was refused entry as they saw I was too young and I suspect my Wellington boots and winter attire didn't help. I walked up the side street by the El Rio and as I was passing a side door, I saw them. I stopped and said hello and explained I wanted to see them but was refused entry. They led me to their dressing room (a small room downstairs), gave me their autographs and had a chat for a couple of minutes before they were called onstage. I walked up the stairs and out onto the street listening to the screams of the girls inside as they went on. I never got to see the group though. I kept the autographs safe for a few years and then I discovered Bob Dylan and the autographs went into the bin. What would they be worth now? ❜

JOAN DUGGAN, CHEMICAL PROCESS OPERATOR, BIDDULPH, STAFFORDSHIRE

SUNDAY 27 JANUARY

During the day the group rehearsed at the Cavern in preparation for their upcoming nationwide package tour with Helen Shapiro. Mike McCartney took photographs and they took a break from rehearsing to be interviewed by *NME* scribe Alan Smith.

In the evening, they drove down the East Lancs Road to Manchester, to perform at the Three Coins at 64a Fountain Street, where they were described as 'Britain's Newest TV Sensations'. The club was located in the basement of the building, which also housed a chartered accountant, a paper merchants and a tailor. Manchester newspapers were full of gloom and doom with headlines such as 'Thaw Brings Flood Chaos'. A total of 170,290 pipe bursts had been reported to Manchester Corporation since Christmas, and there were dire warnings that as many as fifty thousand homes could be flooded if the thaw continued. Concert promoter Danny Betesh, who booked the group this night, remembered: 'Even before they broke nationally, that excitement in the north-west was special, it really was. I remember people queueing from about 1pm, and the club opened at 6.30pm. The queues went right down Fountain Street to Lewis's. Brian was always terrific to deal with. I booked the first headline tour they ever did in this country with Brian, and we had Roy Orbison and Gerry and the Pacemakers on the bill. You'd be in theatres where the sound wasn't as sophisticated as now, so the screaming would almost drown out the vocals. Perhaps people were better behaved in those days, but you wouldn't get trouble, just screaming and girls fainting.' The crowd paid 4/- (or 5/- at the door) and refused to leave until the group did an encore. One of the group's cars had its mirrors and aerial pulled off and a window smashed.

MONDAY 28 JANUARY

The group headed north on a near 200-mile trip to Newcastle-upon-Tyne, Northumberland, which had also fallen victim to flooding and burst pipes. A Water Board official said that two million gallons were being lost every day. Thawing continued as temperatures reached 5 degrees. They arrived at the Majestic Ballroom on the corner of Clayton Street and Westgate Road in the early afternoon. Peter O'Donnell, who was already a fan, wandered into the building to find them setting up their equipment for a sound check. 'Hello lads,' he said, 'welcome to Newcastle,' as he shook hands with them. Before he had a chance to chat with them, they fled to their dressing room to avoid hordes of young girls who had also come into the ballroom. The stage was only inches higher than the dance floor, so only those at the front could have a decent view of the group.

Ray Marshall, a reporter for the *Evening Chronicle*, who had seen flyers for the show in the Majestic's foyer a couple of weeks earlier, hoisted a young girl onto his shoulders so she could see the group. He recalled later: 'When the Beatles came on, everyone stopped and went to the stage. This really was a group with a difference. The sound was raw, special, exciting. There was Paul McCartney, sweating, pounding away on his bass guitar, George Harrison, smiling and picking his strings, Ringo, head from side to side and providing the steady beat. But on the right, standing there, looking menacingly at the crowd, full-voiced, smashing his hand through the strings of his guitar was John Lennon. The amplifiers may have been tiny but the sound was big. Everyone there knew this was different, this was special. The Beatles went through their repertoire and wound up their performance with 'Twist And Shout', and Lennon just about ripped his throat out doing it.' After the show, they drove the short journey to the Imperial Hotel on Jesmond Road, where they spent the night.

'I was in the Percy Main Social Club in North Shields that December, when a group appeared on the television which grabbed the attention of me and my mates. They were totally different to anything we had seen before. The two-minute footage is still vivid in my memory and I still get a tingle when I see the same or similar black-and-white image of the Beatles singing 'Love Me Do'. It was the main topic of conversation between the gang over the Christmas holidays.

As part of the engineering apprenticeship, it was virtually compulsory to attend day release college to achieve qualifications. Our day was Friday and our gang of four budding engineers attended Bath Lane College of Further Education in Newcastle. There was a bonus though – the Majestic, where I had been many times to see the recording artistes of the day, held a Friday lunchtime bop. It was excellent and we couldn't wait for the bell to go. We would go in with our haversacks with our draughtsman's T-squares sticking out the back. The place was heaving with office and shop girls twisting and bopping their lunch breaks away. Lads were often in short supply so we usually managed to get a dance and were taught to twist and bop at the 'Maj'. On our next visit to the lunchtime session I noticed a poster in the foyer advertising the Beatles, featuring their chart single 'Love Me Do', appearing on 28 January. I bought two tickets which I seem to remember were 10/9 each, which was quite expensive at the time.

Well, the day arrived which would change my life forever. I travelled the 10 miles from the coast on the bus. It was freezing cold but we would soon warm up when the music started. Everyone started dancing but would soon stop and move to the stage to watch the group. This is the first time I can remember this happening, it truly was amazing. Even though there was nobody dancing, the floor was actually moving up and down with the beat of the music. It was a fantastic concert and one I never forgot. Within a few weeks I would be wearing Beatle suits, Chelsea boots, a black polo-necked sweater and a new Beatle hair cut that took a while to grow in. A few years ago I had a message on Friends Reunited from a lady asking if I was the same Micky Saunders that took her to see the Beatles. We fell out when they sang 'I Saw Her Standing There' to her. She was stunning and 17 and I couldn't really blame them. Still a fan of them and my children John and Julia are named after Lennon and his mum. '

**MICK SAUNDERS, ENGINEERING QUALITY INSPECTOR, SHIREMOOR,
NEWCASTLE-UPON-TYNE, TYNE AND WEAR**

TUESDAY 29 JANUARY

A proposed concert at the Astoria Ballroom in Middlesbrough never materialised, allowing the group to make the long trek back home to Liverpool. Eden Kane, a year on from his Top 3 hit 'Forget Me Not', performed in their place. After a weekend of milder weather, temperatures once again plunged to freezing and blizzards swept across the country. In Liverpool, however, a slow thaw began, which continued for a couple of days. Local roads were now nearly all clear of ice and slush. When they got back home, Paul took his girlfriend Thelma Pickles into town. He bought a large writing pad, ostensibly to practise his signature. The previous Tuesday's recording of *The Talent Spot* was broadcast on the Light Programme at 5pm, with fellow guests Patsy Ann Noble, Col James, Rog Whittaker and resident group the Ted Taylor Four.

WEDNESDAY 30 JANUARY

The *Liverpool Daily Post* reported that six main roads remained blocked, with more scattered snow showers and freezing temperatures expected during the day. The group played a lunchtime show at the Cavern Club with the Dakotas and Johnny Sandon and the Remo Four also on the bill. Sandon had been a member of the Searchers about eighteen months earlier – when the Remo Four were booked for a tour of US military bases, they asked him to become their lead singer.

‘ The first time I saw the Beatles was in a church hall in Knotty Ash. I was still at school and lived in nearby West Derby. It was back in the days of Pete Best and Stu Sutcliffe. I met my friend Linda at Blackmore Park County Primary School. We were in the same class at school as Rory Best, Pete Best's younger brother. We both passed our Eleven Plus but went to different grammar schools – me to Aigburth Vale in Aigburth, and Linda to Holly Lodge in West Derby, where she lived. The Casbah was in Haymans Green and within walking distance of where we both lived. I left school in the summer of 1961 and started work in September of that year for the Inland Revenue in the Liver Buildings. My district was Liverpool 10. Linda started working in 1963 for the Inland Revenue in Liverpool 2 district in Wellington Buildings.

We were both 18 by then and our offices were quite close to each other, so it was then that we started going up to the Cavern for the lunchtime sessions. It only took five or ten minutes, mostly uphill! We'd eat our butties at our desks to give ourselves more time, and of course there was no alcohol or anything. If you wanted a drink, it was only Coke or orange squash, but most of us only went to listen to the music and dance. It was great. The atmosphere was amazing, but it wasn't a particularly nice place. The condensation from all the people packed in there would run down off the arches, and the whole place smelled of disinfectant. You'd get down to the bottom of the stairs, and it would waft up. It was quite small, and the stage was just one step up off the ground, so you could get really close up to the groups. It was brilliant, and always packed.

We would go there in the evenings sometimes, and we also started going to other clubs then and would get the bus into Liverpool and other places to the Mardi Gras, the Iron Door, Aintree Institute and the Blue Angel, etc. A girl I worked with at the Liver Buildings, called Carol, lived in Bebington on the Wirral. One evening I went home to her house and we went to see the Beatles at the Tower Ballroom in New Brighton. It was quite different to seeing them at the Cavern. I stayed overnight, and the next morning we went back in to work together. Someone had given my mother a signed photograph of the Beatles which I still have. Recently, when *The Antiques Roadshow* came nearby, I took it along, just out of interest. They looked at it and said although it was very good, it wasn't genuine, so obviously it was just a very good fake! Linda and I are still friends and go on holiday together each summer. ’

ANGELA POWELL, PERSONAL ASSISTANT, BARNSTON, WIRRAL, CHESHIRE

THURSDAY 31 JANUARY

Morning broke with icy roads, but as the day wore on temperatures in Liverpool finally inched above freezing. The headline in the week's edition of *Disc* read 'Beatles Come Crashing In' – 'Sensational Merseyside group, the Beatles, have crashed into the charts at number 9' with 'Please Please Me'. It jumped seventeen places to number 16 in the *NRM* chart, and 'Love Me Do' climbed back up one place to number 36. In an article, Wesley Laine wrote: 'Whether you like them or not, you've got to admit that the Beatles are just about the most talked-about group on the British beat scene.' Fellow artists were jumping on the wagon. Kenny Lynch, who was about to tour with them, said, 'One reason I think they'll succeed is because they manage to reproduce their record sounds onstage. Apart from that their sound is so great they can't miss.'

The group played another lunchtime gig at the Cavern. In the evening they made a return visit to the Majestic Ballroom in Birkenhead. Learning their lesson from the show two weeks earlier, the venue's management put on two shows to cope with demand, at 6pm and 9pm. Also on the bill were Freddie Starr and the Midnighters and Tommy Quickly and the Challengers (incorrectly credited on the poster as Johnny Quickly and the Challengers). Quickly became another one of Epstein's signings but, despite having an estimated £20,000 spent on launching him with the Lennon/McCartney song 'Tip Of My Tongue' in July, would be one of Epstein's few failures.

❝ The local church in West Kirby organised a Harvest Festival every year, and in 1957, the contribution from our smaller parish in Newton was me getting a group together to do half a dozen numbers. We called ourselves the Rocking Six, just for that evening, and I'd put the group together with a friend from my school, Calday Grammar, and a couple of lads from Birkenhead Grammar. We played skiffle behind the bike sheds, but when it came to getting in front of a microphone, we went straight into rock'n'roll. Later that year we became Gus and the Thundercaps, taking the name from my

Gus Travis

nickname – Gus – and Gene Vincent's Blue Caps. We'd seen some in a shop in Liverpool, black-and-white striped caps, Ivy League style, and the idea was that our group would wear black-and-white vertical striped shirts, and the black-and-white caps, which I thought looked absolutely fabulous. The only problem was, we kept being billed as Gus and the ThunderCLAPS, so eventually had to change the name. I liked the name Travis, I thought it sounded a bit rockabilly, a bit country, and was also a fan of a rhythm and blues group called Hank Ballard and the Midnighters. So we took on the name the Midnighters. Sometime in late 1962, Freddie Starr started tagging on to our pianist Alan Watts, who would pick him up at his house, and he'd come onstage when I was having a break and do a couple of numbers and his impressions. He was good, but totally off the wall and totally unreliable.

We were doing bigger venues by this time, and on the bill with other notable groups of the time. We played at the Cavern one evening in January 1963 with the Fourmost, the Silhouettes and the Beatles. I was sitting strumming my guitar before we went on – it was an acoustic guitar – I never went electric. John Lennon said to me, 'Get yourself a set of Black Diamond strings and you might be able to keep it in tune!' He grabbed it from me and played it for a while before handing it back. I actually hated the Cavern, as a singer that is, because it was like singing into a vacuum. In those days monitors didn't exist, so it was literally like singing into a void. There was no bounce back from the brick walls. For the young people who were just down there to have a bop and a dance, it was a great atmosphere, but as a singer, no. It was so cramped in the dressing room, you just had to do the best you could. Thankfully we didn't have much gear in those days, just an amp and our guitars. One thing we did like about playing at the Cavern was that it had its own PA. I knew that Bob Wooler liked 'When My Blue Moon Turns To Gold Again' by Slim Whitman. One evening I said over the mic, 'This is for Bob Wooler' and the group launched into it at twice the speed it should have been played at. He wasn't happy about it to say the least, and neither was I! But he was a good man, Bob. He gave me a tip that I always remembered – he said when you introduce a song, try not to say 'Now I'd like to do ...', and I've never done that since. Everybody else still does it, but I haven't since the day Bob said that to me. We didn't play the Cavern very often, maybe three or four times. A week after playing with the Beatles at the Cavern, we were on the bill with them at the Majestic in Birkenhead. I loved the Majestic! It had a balcony round the top, and a really good dancefloor. There were tables round the edge of the floor, with lots of room for dancing, and a good high stage. If you were doing a gig, everyone would just stand on the dance floor watching and dancing. Backstage it was really just pegs to hang your clothes on because there weren't 'His' and 'Hers' dressing rooms at that time.

Around April 1963, a few months after Freddie joined, I decided to leave. The other Midnighters stayed with Freddie as lead vocalist for a while. They went down to London to record with Joe Meek, bringing out a couple of singles on the Decca label later that year. I was still working for Cunard during the day, and joined a local instrumental group called the Four Dymonds for around eighteen months, and after that a West Kirby group called Johnny Rocco and the Jets, whose lead singer Steve Day had just left. They asked me to join them as they had lots of gigs lined up in the Midlands. It was good money, so I joined them for a while. In 1964 we changed our name to Gus Travis and the Rain Checks. I carried on gigging for fun throughout the '60s and '70s, and still keep the name Gus Travis and the Midnighters going to this day with the odd charity gig. Looking back to the early '60s on Merseyside, well, it was just one big ball. 🥁

GUS TRAVIS, SHIPPING CLERK, BURTON, SOUTH WIRRAL, CHESHIRE

FEBRUARY

A Day at Abbey Road

FRIDAY 1 FEBRUARY

The brand-new *NME* revealed that 'Please Please Me' had entered the chart at number 17, the week's highest new entry. In an article headed 'You've Pleased – Pleased Us! Say The Beatles', Alan Smith described the group as 'r-and-b styled'. Paul told him, 'We've got nearly a hundred [songs] up our sleeves, and we're writing all the time! I suppose "writing" is the wrong word, really. John and I just hammer out a number on our instruments. If we want anyone to hear it we record it, then send them a tape.' The single climbed another eighteen places to number 21 in the *Melody Maker* chart, while 'Love Me Do' dropped to number 37.

The *Daily Mail*'s Adrian Mitchell, who had interviewed the Beatles at the Mayfair Hotel on 22 January, became the first Fleet Street journalist to write a piece on the group. He asked John how the Beatles got their name. 'It came in a vision – a man appeared on a flaming pie and said unto them "From this day on you are Beatles with an A."' Mitchell also wrote, 'And here comes the Beatles, crawling up the charts with 'Please Please Me', a record which is almost incoherent except for its solid, battering beat.'

With George celebrating the fifth anniversary of his joining the Quarrymen, the group travelled to Sutton Coldfield to perform at St Peter's Church Hall on Maney Hill Road before a sold-out audience of one hundred. Leaving local group Gerry Day and the Dukes to close the show in their wake, they drove 8 miles to the Assembly Rooms on Corporation Street in Tamworth, Staffordshire. Promoted by K.D.S. Enterprises as a 'rock and twist sensational dance and show', rumours had circulated that the Beatles were not going to appear. The doors were shut before 9.30pm with hundreds of fans being turned away, including several coachloads from Birmingham and its environs. Bill Jones, in his 'Record Spin' column in that morning's *Tamworth Herald*, wrote that, 'This is a rare treat for local pop fans, for as a follow up to their big selling record debut *Love Me Do*, the lads make a very strong bid for Top 10 honours with 'Please Please Me''. He went on to describe the foursome as having 'a distinctive fringe hair-style and they explain their odd name in an odd way: It came to us in a meat pie – which being translated means – in a dream'. During Gerry Levene and the Avengers' set – Ringo, standing behind the curtains – pulled drummer Graeme Edge's stool towards him, forcing Edge to lean forward to reach his drum kit. The Beatles finally played for half an hour from 11.45pm to 12.15am. One of a group of female students training to be secretaries at Tamworth College asked John (her favourite) to play 'Please Please Me'. Paul replied, 'We have just sung that one Missus!'

ASSEMBLY ROOMS, TAMWORTH

FEB. 1st   TO-NIGHT (FRIDAY)   FEB. 1st

ROCK AND TWIST SENSATIONAL
DANCE AND SHOW
to Stars of T.V., Radio and Stage

THE BEATLES
Hit Recorders of "Love Me Do," direct from T.V.'s "Thank Your Lucky Stars" with their new release, "Please Please Me."

PLUS THE MIDLANDS TOP PROFESSIONAL GROUP
GERRY LEVENE AND THE AVENGERS
ALSO FULL SUPPORTING GROUP
THE REBELS
DANCE 8 p.m. till 1 a.m.   LICENSED BAR.   ADMISSION 6/6 (2)

❛The Rebels were one of the original groups around in the area at the time and started off as a skiffle group. We only played around the local area – the working men's clubs and pubs, Drayton Manor Ballroom. We had an old Morris J2 van, in which we used to carry our equipment around. There wasn't enough room for all of us to travel in it as well, so one of us would drive, one of us would be in the passenger seat, and the other two would follow on behind in our own cars. Promoter Vince Baker wanted to manage us, but he didn't have a very good reputation for looking after groups – in fact, after the gig at the Assembly Rooms, we had to go knocking on his door to get paid! So we turned him down. We were getting towards the end of our musical days by then anyway – we all had apprenticeships, and were in our final year, so had exams coming up. We wanted to concentrate on getting our qualifications.

Anyway, we knew that the Beatles were going to be playing that night, but they really weren't that well known at the time. We knew 'Love Me Do', but it hadn't made a huge impact on the charts. They had a big local following around Liverpool, but this gig was as 'Please Please Me' was climbing up the charts. Vince Baker couldn't afford the £150 the Beatles wanted that night, so he split the venue between Sutton Coldfield and Tamworth. That was the reason they were late turning up.

The Assembly Rooms were mostly used as a dance and music hall. It's a tall building, with a large dance floor, stage, and balcony upstairs looking down over the hall. There was a bar under the stage – a sort of basement area, which you got to from steps at the side of the stage. The entry to the dressing rooms was at the side of the stage, which you could access from the back of building as well. The dressing rooms were shared and were behind the stage. Baker said he didn't want anyone in the backstage area when the Beatles arrived. There was no screaming or hysteria, just the usual enthusiasm for the groups. We were sent out from the dressing room by Baker, still in our stage suits, into the main dance area, and watched the Beatles from there. We waited and waited. People began to get restless and everyone started thinking they weren't going to appear. Then all of a sudden, the curtains opened and so began a magical half hour. It was fairly obvious there was something different and dynamic about them, but who would have known at that point that they would go on to be the most phenomenal pop group ever?❜

**DON STEVENSON, ROCKET ENGINE DESIGN ENGINEER,
WILNECOTE, TAMWORTH, STAFFORDSHIRE**

SATURDAY 2 FEBRUARY

As the group prepared for their first date on a fourteen-date Helen Shapiro-headed package tour, the early morning temperature in Bradford – where the evening's two concerts were to take place at the Gaumont Cinema on New Victoria Street – was 4.4 degrees. The tour bus left the Allsop Place bus depot in London and headed north, with Shapiro, Kenny Lynch (who had just finished a cabaret season at the Jack of Clubs in London), the Kestrels, the Honeys, the Red Price Band, compère Dave Allen, and special guest star Danny Williams on board. The journey took the better part of five hours. Snowmen built on Boxing Day were still standing. The group had not gone to bed until after 3am, and got off to a late start from their homes in Liverpool. Driven directly to Bradford by Neil Aspinall, the journey was slow going because of white-out conditions.

Maureen Cleave's 10 January interview was published in the *Evening Standard*. 'The Beatles are the darlings of Merseyside... But I think it's their looks that really get people going, that start the girls queuing outside the Liverpool Grafton at 5.30 for 8pm. Their average age is 20, and they have what their manager likes to call "exceptional taste in clothes." They look scruffy, but scruffy on purpose. They wear bell-bottom suits of a rich Burgundy colour with black velvet collars. Boots of course. Shoes seems to have died out altogether. Their shirts are pink and their hairstyles are French. Liverpool lads of 12 and upwards now have small bouffant Beatle heads with the fringe brushed forwards. On the stage, there's none of this humble bowing of the head or self-effacing trips over the microphone leads. They stand there, bursting with self-confidence and professional polish – as well they might, for they have been at this game since 1958. They know exactly what they can get away with, and their inter-song patter is in the Max Miller-music hall tradition, with slightly bawdy schoolboy overtones. John Lennon has an upper lip which is brutal in a devastating way. George Harrison is handsome, whimsical and untidy. Paul McCartney has a round baby face, while

Ringo Starr is ugly but cute... Their physical appearance inspires frenzy. They look beat-up and depraved in the nicest way. It takes you back, doesn't it? To the early days of rock'n'roll.'

Arriving in Bradford, the group met bill-topper Shapiro for the first time. 'Paul, who was always the spokesman and diplomat, introduced me, one by one, to the rest of the group,' she recalled. 'I used to watch them at every show and, although sometimes they were very loud, and some things used to go wrong with their amplifiers, they still had this magnetic quality, you just had to watch them, because you didn't know what they were going to do next.' Ringo remembered Shapiro as the star of the tour. 'Helen had the telly in her dressing room and we didn't have one. We had to ask her if we could watch hers. We weren't getting packed houses, but we were on the boards, man.' The continuing bad weather had its effect, and neither of the houses at 6pm and 8.30pm in the 3,318-capacity cinema were more than half full. Tickets for the tour ranged from 3/6 to 8/6. The Beatles followed the Honeys and sang six numbers. By the time the tour closed on 3 March at the Gaumont in Hanley, Staffordshire, the group were closing the first half. Their payment for the tour was £80 a week. Ringo later told *NRM* journalist Peter Jones that the tour 'meant we'd able to get to work before lots of different audiences all over the country. So we had another task on our hands – to get together the strongest possible act to sell ourselves on a theatre stage instead of on a dance-hall rostrum.'

> ❛ As an arts and entertainment journalist, I have attended many opening nights over the years. But the one which stands out for me was that historic evening in Bradford when the Beatles were part of a new package show – their first nationwide tour. The Gaumont was a popular venue for concerts, as well as being a cinema, and I had seen the likes of Buddy Holly, Eddie Cochran, Gene Vincent, Cliff Richard and the Shadows there. So, when the *New Musical Express* asked me to review a programme headlined by Helen Shapiro, plus Kenny Lynch, special guest star Danny Williams and other support, including the Beatles, I didn't hesitate. Television was black and white in those days, so there was a real buzz in going to a big auditorium like the Gaumont, where everything came alive in full colour. And inside there was a real warm atmosphere, contrasting with the freezing conditions outside when winters were really winters!
>
> All the performers came up to expectations but, with no disrespect to the others, it was the Beatles who created the major talking point, and rightly so, although media interest was limited to start with. That provided a great opportunity for a face-to-face meeting with the Liverpool lads and Brian Epstein after interviews with the sparkling Helen and the others. Back then, packages were usually

of two houses at each theatre, limiting the spots performers were allotted. The Beatles managed to pack in six numbers in the early house. What you saw was what you got then, long before modern technology. So the sounds could be quite raw, that only adding to the appeal as the smartly dressed quartet bounced their way through 'Love Me Do', 'A Taste of Honey', 'Beautiful Dreamer', 'Chains', 'Keep Your Hands Off My Baby' and then closing with 'Please Please Me'. A bonus of being there before Beatlemania took off was the chance to hear all the words, which were drowned out by noise and screaming on most of the other occasions when I saw them before they stopped touring.

In between shows, out came my *NME* Press card and I was soon in the small dressing room given to the Beatles, standing there alone chatting to Paul and John, who had plenty to say, the quieter George, and Ringo, who chipped in with some quips of his own from time to time, while manager Brian made sure that the information given about future plans was correct. They were all very polite and helpful. When I met up with them again backstage at Sheffield City Hall towards the end of the tour, I was made to feel very welcome. John commented on how well my opening night review in the *NME* had been received by the group and, as a thank you, they signed a photograph and gave it to me. **"**

GORDON SAMPSON, JOURNALIST, BRIGHOUSE, WEST RIDING OF YORKSHIRE

SUNDAY 3 FEBRUARY

With a two-day break before the next tour date, the group took part in an eight-hour 'Rhythm & Blues Marathon' at the Cavern, appearing on a bill with the Four Mosts, Kingsize Taylor and the Dominoes with guest singer Cilla Black, up-and-coming Mancunian group the Hollies, Earl Preston and the T. T.'s, the Merseybeats, the Swinging Bluegenes (yet to change the spelling to Blue Jeans) and the Roadrunners. Regular Cavern attendee Sue Evans wrote in her diary, 'Danced with four gorgeous beat types. Sat on one's shoulders to see the Beatles. They are the most FAB fellows – heavenly time.'

After the show, Paul invited Epstein out for dinner. Epstein, recently described by the *NRM* as 'The dapper dictator of Merseyside,' replied, 'That's very sweet of you. Of course, I should love it. I can't remember when I was invited to dinner last – not by someone I like.'

" With hindsight I suppose 1963 was rather an extraordinary year for me. I started it as a 17-year-old schoolboy at Birkenhead School, receiving ten bob a week pocket money and living at home with my mum and dad, all expenses paid, and finished it as an 18-year-old professional drummer with the Roadrunners at the Star-Club in Hamburg on £30 a week, living in the Pacific Hotel, all expenses paid. Not a career trajectory which went down well with my folks as it was a fee-paying school and I hadn't shown up for most of the Lent term. I left at Easter on the understanding that I would complete my A Levels at the Liverpool College of Commerce. I enrolled but didn't show up much there either! Until we went to Hamburg in December, four of us were students and  the fifth was holding down a steady job. We also had a residency at Hope Hall which was where we met up with Paul McCartney's brother Mike, becoming, with him, components of assorted events and happenings organised by Adrian Henri, poet, painter and all-purpose anarchic spirit. As far as I can remember, Cavern DJ Bob Wooler liked us because our repertoire was a bit different from the then Liverpool norm (more Chicago blues covers, Muddy Waters, etc.). We auditioned for him sometime in November 1962, having played our first paid gig at the Liverpool College of Art the previous month. So he booked us for the eight-hour 'Rhythm & Blues Marathon', which the Beatles headlined. George Harrison thought we were quite good so I suspect that's how we came to be on the bill of two subsequent Beatles' Cavern appearances including their last on 3 August. I recall becoming quite friendly with Paul and Mike's dad Jim, who invited me to his house in Forthlin Road and it being stuffed with gifts from fans and unopened mail. **J**

DAVID BOYCE, ACTOR, DRUMMER AND SINGER, WIRRAL, MERSEYSIDE

MONDAY 4 FEBRUARY

The appalling weather continued with main roads blocked and another burst of heavy snow causing motorists to abandon their cars. The group played what was to be their 152nd and last lunchtime date at the Cavern, which was packed to the hilt despite temperatures of 1 degree – and for which they had a pay rise, now earning £30. Afterwards, John and Paul were interviewed by *Melody Maker*'s Chris Roberts in Brian Epstein's office. They told him of their varied musical tastes. 'We like a bit of classical music, a bit of modern jazz, a bit of everything.' They mentioned Ray Charles, the Isley Brothers and Arthur Alexander in particular.

❝ In 1959 I started working in my father's tailor and outfitters shop about hundred yards from the Cavern. I used to go to the lunchtime sessions virtually every day. It cost a shilling to get in. Three years later Granada TV filmed the Beatles there after Brian Epstein started managing them. He wanted to smarten them up and told them to stop looking scruffy onstage. On the day of the filming Paul rushed into the shop and said, 'Eh Mike, have you got any black sweaters? We need them for the TV.' I got him black slipovers which you see them wearing on that show. I don't know if we ever got paid. I had four years working with my dad wearing a suit and a stiff collar every day, going round to the Cavern at lunchtime and coming back stinking of the place. My dad would say, 'Go and get changed, Michael.'

In February 1961, the group I was in did a gig with the Beatles at the Aintree Institute and we were the first group on. We'd seen them many times at the Cavern, but they were amazing that night. It was, 'Oh hang on. Rory Storm was the best group in Liverpool, but now it's the Beatles.' With all the excitement I forgot to get my fee. The next day the Beatles played at the Cavern and afterwards I went down to the Grapes where they were drinking. I was sitting with Paul and I told him I'd forgotten to pick up my fee. John was at the next table and turned around and said, 'That's the last effing chance you'll see that.'

In April 1963 I entered Mike and the Thunderbirds in the Lancashire and Cheshire Beat Contest after seeing an ad in *Mersey Beat*. I don't remember much about the competition but I do recall turning around at some point and seeing George and Ringo and one of them was wearing a purple jacket. I moved into a flat in Falkner Street in 1964 after my dad had said, 'I've had enough of you coming home at four o'clock in the morning.' It was the same one where John and Cynthia spent their honeymoon in August of 1962. One day after a Cavern session, our drummer, Pete Clarke, said he was going down to the Kardomah for a coffee with his girlfriend and asked whether I wanted to come with him. It was there I met Bernadette, my wife of fifty-plus years. While I was away working in Switzerland, she decided to redecorate the flat. She pasted one wall with cuttings from newspapers and magazines and painted another purple, orange and black gloss. It was a psychedelic nightmare.

By the end of the '70s I decided to have another go at getting a proper job, so I went to work for a free newspaper called *Mersey Mart*. In 1981 we had the Toxteth riots and, for me, that was the catalyst for what changed in the city. Margaret Thatcher sent Michael Heseltine to Liverpool to find out how this could have happened in one of England's major cities. The first thing that came out of that was the International Garden Festival and the re-generation of the derelict Albert Dock.

Beatle City and Cavern Walks both began in 1984. Beatle City hadn't done particularly well and was bought out by a company called Transworld Leisure in 1986. They advertised for an events manager and I got the job. At the end of our season my boss asked whether any of us wanted to run Beatle City. I raised my hand and was put in charge. It went through another change of hands and I then travelled to Dallas with it. I came back to England on Christmas Eve in 1987 without a job. Liverpool had lost its Beatles museum. Bernie and I went to the head of the Tourism Board in Liverpool and said there should be a Beatles exhibit. He really didn't want to know, no doubt in part because he didn't like the Beatles. Anyway, he gave us some money, basically to shut us up. He gave us sixteen hundred quid and said, 'Go and do a feasibility study on a Beatles exhibition.' I was happy to have the money to keep us going for a few months. I didn't even know what a feasibility study was. I went to as many people as I could to advise me.

About halfway through doing this I thought I didn't want to work for someone else again and decided we should do it ourselves. So we sat down and drew up a business plan on the back of a brown envelope. It took two years to raise the £750,000 to build the exhibition because very few people in Liverpool believed that the Beatles would be a draw for the city. I needed the blessing of Apple to proceed and I nearly gave up, but being stubborn, refused to take no for an answer. My first approach to Apple was to meet Derek Taylor, its legendary publicity guru and friend of the Beatles. He told me to meet him in the crypt of St Martin-in-the-Fields Church in London. He said I would recognise him because he would be reading *The Guardian*. He also asked me to bring an Apple 'wish list' and he would grade them one to five. Once vetted by Derek I had a meeting with Neil Aspinall, whose first comment was, 'I don't want you to open this museum.' His reason for this was that if it failed, he would get all the stick from the press as well as from his sometimes-difficult masters. We never had a formal agreement with Apple, ultimately just a nod in the dark from Neil. The Albert Dock was the perfect place for the exhibit because the first time we went into the basement the vaulted ceiling and smell of damp reminded us of the Cavern. One of the eighteen features had to be a perfect replica of the Cavern because the original had been knocked down by the Council for an underground railway ventilation shaft that was never built. The Beatles Story opened on the first of May 1990 during a recession and it was a critical success from day one. I stayed with it until it was sold to Mersey Travel in 2008. **J**

**MIKE BYRNE, MUSICIAN AND FOUNDER CO-FOUNDER OF THE
BEATLES STORY EXHIBITION, FORMBY, MERSEYSIDE**

TUESDAY 5 FEBRUARY

Blizzards struck many parts of the country and there was still no end in sight for the Arctic spell, now in its forty-first day. The group set off for Doncaster, a two-hour drive east, to continue the Helen Shapiro tour with two shows at 6.15pm and 8.30pm at the 2,020-seater Gaumont on Hallgate. Advertisements in local newspapers had begun listing the Beatles second on the bill. Carol Roope, a local reporter and DJ at RAF Finningley, interviewed the group for the Foto News Agency. Photographer

Charlie Worsdale snapped the group in their dressing room while they listened to music on their record player. 'I was lucky enough to photograph them, standing in the wings at the side and I also had a backstage pass,' he recalled. 'It was amazing to see them at such close quarters. I remember they were all very funny and always making jokes. They had a very dry sense of humour, especially John. I went into their dressing room where they had a Dansette record player and I was quite pleased because the music they were playing was by some of my favourite acts, like Ray Charles, Fats Domino and Chuck Berry. I was actually quite a jazz fan and when they came back later in the year I went to see Tubby Hayes at the Two Palfreys at Cantley.' Concert promoter Arthur Howes congratulated the recently appointed Gaumont manager John Gaukrodger on a 'marvellous show'. The group spent the night at the nearby Regent Hotel.

❝ The day after my 17th birthday in 1963 I was on day release at college. I was a music fan, so I knew the Beatles were coming to play at the Gaumont. As a student apprentice, I couldn't afford to buy a ticket, and in any case, I wasn't a particular fan at that time. It was still early on in their career before they really broke big and we only knew that one song, 'Love Me Do'. In our break, about four or five of us decided to wander down – the college was only about 150 yards up from the Gaumont corner. We knew roughly what time they would get there, and sure enough, there were hundreds of girls outside. We were just hanging around when some cars came by, one had guitar cases fastened to the top. They drove round to the stage door entrance and all the girls screamed and ran round the corner. There was only about half a dozen or so of us left at the front when a van pulled up outside. The doors opened, and out came the Beatles! It was a brief encounter as they ran straight into the theatre. Needless to say, when the girls heard they had missed them they weren't too pleased.

Owen Jennings, a friend from work, met the Beatles a few weeks later when they played at the swimming baths. In the winter months, they used to drain the pool and cover it with a sprung dance floor, and they'd have groups on and hold dances. He was with half a dozen colleagues having a drink in the Leopard pub in town. They'd already bought their tickets for the show and made their way up to the baths. Owen decided to finish his drink and went to the Baths on his own. He put his coat into the cloak room and had a white square ticket with two and sixpence in the middle and in each corner was the name of each Beatle. Apparently as he walked in, the Beatles were stood at a table in the foyer. They said, 'Would you like us to sign your ticket for you?' and he just turned round and said, 'No, it doesn't matter.' He thought they were just another group. Now of course he regrets it bitterly as he could have sold them for a fortune.

Owen and I both met our future wives at Burton's, and my wife Wendy and I had our first date at a Burton's dance in the Co-op Ballroom. At the factory they used to have a knitting hub at the side where we spent our lunch hours. We had records playing and they had a bit of dancing, table tennis and darts. We used to go to Barker and Wigfall's a lot. It was an electrical shop in town where they sold records. The first record I ever bought was 'Glad All Over' by the Dave Clark Five which I'd listen to over and over again on the Dansette record player. When the Beatles became really popular, we used to get hundreds of requests for Beatle jackets and collarless suits! The orders would come through and we had to hand-cut so many suits a day. They had a bonus scheme where you got so many points for every suit you made. Burton's won the contract to make the Beatles jackets and James Bond's jacket for one of the films. About fifteen of us were apprentices, and the rest were older men. We still have a reunion every year! ❞

JOHN BURKE, CLOTHING MANUFACTURER MANAGER, DONCASTER, SOUTH YORKSHIRE

WEDNESDAY 6 FEBRUARY

As they enjoyed breakfast, the group signed autographs on Parlophone promotional cards for staff at the Regent. Soon afterwards the tour bus set off on the 120-mile drive south down the A1 to the 1,690-capacity Granada on St Peter's Street in Bedford, Bedfordshire. Snow and icy road conditions had returned to the town after the recent thaw. Snow drifts were being reported as high as 7 feet. Bus driver Franklyn Campbell was stranded in nearby Lavendon. Rescuers couldn't find him at first, but he was discovered on the top deck with several loose seats as his bedding for the night.

At the 7pm show, the Beatles created such a stir that Ivan Morgan, the Granada's manager, asked Shapiro whether the group could top the bill at the 9.10pm performance. The *Bedford Record & Circular* commented that the Beatles were 'only one group of so many, and are touring in "one-nighters" purely on the strength of one hit record'. The reviewer went on to write, 'It's a fine song, well delivered, but they had better get their pens out once again and find another hit to qualify a continued success. We don't think 'Please Please Me' will provide the answer'. The *Bedfordshire Times & Advertiser* sent their reviewer off to see the Bradgate Players' production of *Lady Windermere's Fan* at the Civic Theatre. Not for the last time, players from the local rugby team acted as bouncers.

Andrew Loog Oldham attended the gig, remembering, "The kids broke all the backstage windows. It was pandemonium. Onstage, you could not hear the Beatles for the roar of the crowd, and the roar I heard was the roar of the whole world. You can hear something without seeing it, in the same way as you can have an experience that is beyond anything you've had before. You don't have to be clever, you only have to be a member of the public. The noise that night hit me emotionally, like a blow to the chest. The audience that evening expressed something beyond repressed adolescent sexuality. The noise they made was the sound of the future. Even though I hadn't seen the world, I heard the whole world screaming. The power of the Beatles touched and changed minds and bodies all over the world. I didn't see it – I heard and felt it. When I looked at Brian, he had the same lump in his throat and tear in his eye as I."

❛ When my parents married, we all lived at the Regent Hotel – Grandma Nellie, Dad Colin, Mum Peggy, me, my brother Dave and later younger brother Andy. Over the years, many stars of the day would stay. The first one I remember was Lonnie Donegan – he actually recorded 'My Old Man's a Dustman' at the Gaumont.

I was 14 years old in February 1963 and a pupil at Doncaster Grammar School, when I returned home one day to find about ten or twelve girls on the corner of the square. When I got in, I said to Mum, 'What's with all the girls outside?' She said, 'Oh, there's a group who've booked in who're playing at the Gaumont tonight, but I've told the girls that they're not here, they're at the Danum.' I asked her the name of the group, getting excited at this point, and she said, 'Oh, it's somebody called the Beatles.' I said, 'You what?! They're fantastic! They're the most fantastic group in the world!' 'Oh well,' she said, 'they're upstairs.'

So I went upstairs and there they were in the television lounge, strumming their guitars! I didn't go in – that was not done; you didn't disturb guests. But I went near the glass doors and heard them. I had a ticket for the show later that evening though. We were good friends with the manager of the cinema, and it was never any problem getting hold of tickets. When they came onstage, they were just awesome! We had this thing at the time called an early morning call. Essentially it meant someone going up to a guest's room and knocking on the door with a cup of tea. Like all good teenagers I had a paper round, so I called in the previous evening to cancel my round the next morning so I could join my brother Dave in taking their tea up. The lads had two twin rooms between them. One pair was in 33 and I think the other was in 19. We knocked on their doors and there was no answer, but we went in anyway and left it on their bedside tables! We were disappointed not to meet them, but of course by now it was time for us to go to school.

We headed round the corner to our school in Thorne Road, and coincidentally, both emerged from the front door half an hour later. Dave asked me what was wrong and I told him I just felt ill, and he said so did he. We'd both been so excited about the Beatles staying that it had made us poorly! So we returned home to the hotel to find they had gone, but they had left some signed promotion cards for us with the breakfast cook Mrs Bowes. I still have one. They had signed the register the previous day – on the left-hand page it read: Date, Name, Address, Nationality – 5/2/63, Mr G. Hetherington, 56 Kennersdene, Tynemouth, British; G Harrison, 174 Mackets Lane, Liverpool 25, British, Great Britain; and on the right: 5/2/62, R Starkey, 10 Admiral Grove, Liverpool, British; 5/2/62, John Lennon, 251 Menlove Avenue, Liverpool, White Man; Paul McCartney, 20 Forthlin Road, Liverpool, Green Man. Six further people put dittos under the incorrect date, until Mr B. Bootle of Whitley Bay realised the year was wrong and corrected it to '63.

I recall the crowds round the back of the Gaumont the second time they came and the group came to the window and all the girls were screaming. There was screaming at the February show, but not as bad as when they returned later in the year. People were sleeping on the pavements to get tickets. We had a bar downstairs which was originally called the Archives. As homage to the Beatles, we renamed it Abbey Road in 2002. My brother had come up with the idea. It's in the cellars of the original building, where Grandma Nellie used to cook the dinners. It has brick arches and looks kind of like the Cavern. I spoke to a designer, and he came up with the idea. He designed a Beatles bar, with function suite called the Studio. It's full of Beatles memorabilia, stuff we've collected over the years. My sister-in-law claims that on their second visit to Doncaster, she met George in the bar at the Danum, and kissed him on the cheek and got his autograph. **)**

MIKE LONGWORTH, HOSPITALITY BUSINESS CONSULTANT, HARWELL, SOUTH YORKSHIRE

THURSDAY 7 FEBRUARY

"**B**eatles Shake The 30!' declared *Disc* on its front page, accompanied by a picture of the group. Inside, an article written by June Harris, headed 'Liverpool Group Takes Britain By Storm', gave a breakdown of the four individuals. Harris quoted Brian Epstein, 'they have been prepared for this success. When you work in the rough and tumble of Liverpool clubs, you can be kicked around and treated like dirt. If you get over this, as the Beatles did, you can face ANY audience.' 'Please Please Me' climbed two places to number 7. *NRM*'s chart page was headed 'The Beatle Challenge "Wow" It's the Beatles All The Way', and 'Please Please Me' jumped 13 places to number 3, while 'Love Me Do' dropped to number 44.

Rather than endure the three-hour journey on the tour bus back up the A1 to the 1,594-seater ABC Cinema in Wakefield, the group travelled with Aspinall in the Ford Thames bus. The A1 was single-file traffic in some places, with gale force winds and a reported 6 inches of snow in the Lake District. The A55 from Merseyside to North Wales was cut off for the first time ever. They arrived at the cinema, on the corner of Kirkgate and Sun Lane in the middle of the afternoon. After a soundcheck, they sent out for fish and chips across the road at Sammy Herbert's before the first show at 6.10pm. The second began at 8.25pm.

'Please Please Me' was released on the Vee-Jay label (VJ 498) in the US, coupled with 'Ask Me Why' – incorrectly credited to the Beattles. Ewart Abner, president of Chicago-based label, took a copy of the single to Art Roberts, the music director of local radio station *WLS*. Roberts recalled, 'I listened to his story about a group, and looked at pictures in teen magazines he brought back from England. I figured, what if this group would get as popular in the United States as they were in England and Europe? So I added the record to the list.' Dick Biondi, host of the station's *Silver Dollar Survey*, played it. Fewer than eight thousand copies were pressed and even fewer were sold. Alan Livingston had told their producer George Martin that the record was not suitable for the US market.

❝ I was 15 back in February 1963. I was avoiding school, frequenting the Black Horse pub and a bohemian coffee bar – espresso coffee, frothy and exotic. You had to try and make one last at least a couple of hours and there was great excitement when... a boutique opened! Not that I could afford to buy anything. I couldn't understand why Helen Shapiro and the rest were on with the Beatles. I just wanted to see THEM. I went with my friend Jill Robinson, I think, and maybe Jane Eckersley. It was a short bus ride into Wakefield town centre from where I lived on Bradford Road. Neither Jane nor Jill lived nearby; we had scholarships to the posho Wakefield Girls High School. I got expelled and Jane got sent away to a boarding school in Filey. Our lovely Jill was the most sensible of the Terrible Trio. I bought all the Beatles records – funded by my Saturday job in a coffee bar. I had a little Dansette record player, turquoise and white. I also went to the Mecca a few times – very exciting. I'd also seen the new-look hair – the bob with a bit of back-combing to give height. 'Long at the sides and shorter at the back,' I said to the hairdresser. 'Don't be daft,' she said and chopped off my long black hair so it was just short black hair. I'd never been to a hairdresser's before and never went again. I just let it grow and ironed it straight – with an iron, on the ironing board. Quite difficult. I also sellotaped my fringe flat every night. I remember all the girls in the Ladies' Toilets backcombing their hair and the place stunk of hair lacquer.

I was too young to go really but I had an older boyfriend. I also had discovered stiletto heels, American Tan stockings, and based my eye make-up on Elizabeth Taylor in the film *Cleopatra*! Prescription shades hid my extravagant make-up, eyeliner stolen from Woolies or Boots. That was basically my make-up sorted for the next forty years, until I got ill in my fifties and was suddenly allergic to make-up. It was a look that carried me through my beatnik era – narrow jeans that you had to take in yourself, plus baggy Sloppy Joe jumper, and the Beatles period – discovering aforementioned high-heels, black polo-neck, tight skirts. I say skirts – I only had one. It cost me 19/11.

A short time after I saw the Beatles I remember running away to London for a while and living rough, stealing food, getting a bit of money from tourists having their photo taken with me – they must have thought I was the archetypal swinging '60s chick. I knew I had to go to Art College, although I had no idea what an art college was or how to go to one, but I felt instinctively I would at last find somewhere I fitted in. But I was told I needed at least five O levels. Then I got pregnant and got put in a home laughably called 'the Haven', but I managed to keep my baby (she was supposed to be adopted, it's what they did in those days). I eventually got my O levels and did two years at Wakefield School of Art. In 1968 I got into Cardiff College of Art with my little daughter, who was three by then. I was allowed to bring her in with me, so she also had loads of artwork by the end of the three years and had her own exhibition next to mine! We got a First Class Honours Degree! I'm now the director of the Queens Hall Studio in Widnes where the Beatles played a few times. We did a Community Heritage funded project on the Queens Hall, but the building was demolished for a block of flats. ❞

JAKI FLOREK, ARTIST, RUNCORN, CHESHIRE

FRIDAY 8 FEBRUARY

'Please Please Me' jumped to number 5 in the week's *NME* chart. A headline read, 'Beatles Head Package Show', reporting that after the Helen Shapiro and Tommy Roe and Chris Montez tours, the group would go on another tour with an unnamed US artist for three weeks, beginning 18 May. The article reported that the group were soon going to be recording their first LP – which George Martin had revealed might be called *Off The Beatle Track*.

Melody Maker, meanwhile, featured its first article on the group, headlined 'It's All Happening Beatlewise'. John told Chris Roberts, 'It's true we've written about a hundred songs – some of them are rubbish of course.' Brian Epstein described them as 'the biggest thing to happen to the music scene since Elvis Presley'. Roberts presciently ended his article with the sentence, 'A hefty shot of their exciting music is just what the meandering pop scene needed.' In the paper's Top 50, 'Please Please Me' climbed twelve places to number 9 while 'Love Me Do' dropped to number 41.

At approximately 10am, the tour bus wound north on the A66 from Wakefield in the snow, on what should have been a three-hour journey to the 1,880-seater ABC in Warwick Road in Carlisle. When they reached Scotch Corner just south of Darlington, they found the road blocked. Their only option was to continue north on the A1 to Newcastle-upon-Tyne and then take the A69 reaching Carlisle from the east. Some eight hours after setting out from Wakefield, they arrived in Carlisle. It was just before the 6.15pm start of the show. The Sands Car Park was filled with long-distance lorries unable to travel through snow-blocked roads north or south out of the town.

Prior to the show, Kenny Lynch asked John what he was hoping to get out of the music business. As they stood either side of a grand piano, John said, 'All we want to do is earn a million quid and then piss off.' The ABC's manager Norman Scott-Buccleuch described the group as 'just another act' and one that 'did not attract any attention'. At least not until later.

After the second show at 8.30pm, the group returned to the four-star Crown and Mitre Hotel on English Street. Sitting in the hotel lounge at midnight, the group, Shapiro and Lynch were invited into the Carlisle Golf Club annual dance by a golf club committee member. Taking advantage of the opportunity for free food, they tucked into the buffet and then hit the dance floor, before golf club chairman Bill Berry saw the leather-jacketed quartet and took umbrage at their presence. Lynch recalled the six of them sitting in the bar at the hotel. 'Ringo was dressed from head to toe in leather. He looked like Gene Vincent on acid! The huntsmen were all dressed in their red jackets and suits, and this guy came up and shouted, "How did you people get in here?" Ringo said, "Who the bloody hell are you talking to? We were invited!" The head of the hunt came over when he heard the commotion, and said, "I invited them, this is Helen Shapiro, the Beatles, and Kenny Lynch!", but the other guy had never heard of any of them.' The hotel's assistant manager David Auty recalled them being 'very annoyed and upset', escorting them out through a side-door 'to avoid any embarrassment'.

The incident received national coverage – the *Daily Mail* reported 'Helen Shapiro Barred From Dance'. The paper proved that Fleet Street knew little of this exciting new group, describing them as Kenny Lynch's instrumental group. Shapiro subsequently described the experience as 'unpleasant'.

‘ I left school when I was 15 and got a job as a shorthand typist for a local motor engineers in Carlisle – Dias and Company, who were Austin dealers – and ended up staying there for ten years. I loved the job so much I would have worked there for nothing! I met my friend Ruth and we were both great fans of the pop music of the era. We bought every record that came out – I think I must have bought them all. We would buy the records at E. T. Roberts on a place called the Crescent. If you liked a particular record, you would go to the lady behind the counter and ask to listen to it in the booths, and they would put it on for you. The Beatles were favourites of ours, and we would go to each other's houses and listen to their records non-stop. We knew every single word to every single song. I used to drive my Dad mad playing them all the time.

Ruth and I would either go to one of the five cinemas in Carlisle or we would spend the whole evening in a coffee shop in town called Pieri's. It had a juke box and we would get a coffee in a glass cup on a glass saucer, and just sit there all night playing records on the juke box. We would go there from Monday to Saturday if there wasn't a film on at the cinema we wanted to see. It was run by an Italian couple, Henry and Tina. They were lovely people and were happy for us to sit there all night, in fact they encouraged us to do so. They also sold delicious ice creams from the front of the shop. There were a couple of dance halls in the town, but I wasn't allowed to go to them until I was older. The only one I could go to when I was younger was Bond's. They used to teach people to dance there as well. We went there not because we wanted to learn to dance but because they played all these good records. Of course, there was no drink in any of these places. You would get a glass of orange squash and that was about it!

It was announced in the evening paper that tickets were going on sale for a show featuring the Beatles. We were unbelievably excited! We kept screaming 'The Beatles are coming to Carlisle!' I don't recall there being a queue at all, we just went down to the box office the next day and got the tickets. When the evening came, we got the bus into town, which was about a mile, and joined everyone else walking towards the cinema. People were just looking at each other and screaming! There was no trouble at all, it was all just good harmless fun. There was a bit of screaming when they came onstage but nothing like it was when we returned to see them in November. This time you could hear the first few words of each song and after that you would have to lip read to work out what they were singing! In those days the last bus home was half past ten. The shows finished about ten o'clock and my mother used to say 'Don't get the last bus, get the one before that,' because she always thought the last bus would be full of drunks, so I was never able to wait outside the stage door in the hope of getting autographs. In those days you did as your parents told you! I've still got my *Please Please Me* LP I bought in E. T. Roberts. It's in the loft, and nobody's allowed to touch it! ’

LEXIE COLLIER, SECRETARY, CARLISLE, CUMBRIA

SATURDAY 9 FEBRUARY

The entourage set off for Sunderland – a two-hour journey due east on the A69. Driving through a blizzard, it took considerably longer. The weather conditions were officially recorded as being the worst since 1947. Without a break from Arctic weather for seven weeks, roads throughout the country were still blocked by snow. Now fog and ice had to be contended with.

The Beatles arrived at the 2,220-seater Empire Theatre in the High Street in mid-afternoon. After the usual soundcheck, they took part in a press call. Tony Colling, a photographer for the *Sunderland*

Echo, remembered them being happy to pose for photos. 'The group were chatty with no pretence and joked and laughed with the press. In recent years, I was posing some pictures with a young group who were being difficult and I told them... The Beatles were less bother to photograph. Of course, they didn't believe me.' Also there was Ian Wright, a 16-year-old darkroom boy on the *Northern Echo*. 'In those early days there were no backstage passes so I just left my old rusty school bike with Don the Doorman and wandered around backstage photographing everyone on the bill. I photographed the Beatles with my flash the size of a Bentley headlamp, which when it went off temporally blinded them. As they began to move away rubbing their eyes, I shouted, "Stop, stop, I need your names." How naive. There were fifteen hundred working men's clubs in the Northeast of England coupled with about twenty nightclubs with gambling, and then you had the dance halls and venues for the actual bus touring shows, the variety shows. My editor, Harry Evans, said to me, "Photograph everyone because you don't know who's going to be famous."'

Once again, atrocious weather made for two poorly attended houses. Wright reckoned only about five hundred were in the audience for each show. Helen Shapiro recalled waking in her hotel room and seeing John, ever the mischief-maker, standing in virtual darkness with a hat and raincoat on. She later described her feelings for him. 'I had a special feeling for John. He probably realised I had a crush on him. He called me "Helly" and was incredibly protective. I was mad on him, really mad. I had the biggest crush on him any 16-year-old could have on a guy.'

❝ If only I'd been able to hear them above the pandemonium that erupted as soon as they stepped onstage at Sunderland Empire, I may well have become a Beatles fan immediately. But then I wouldn't have almost written them off in a review that has passed into local legend – and which has caused great hilarity among friends since then. It was one of the first reviews of the Beatles outside Liverpool and I used to joke that they'd improved after reading it. It appeared in the *Sunderland Echo* and I might have been even more dismissive, but for the fact that I liked them so much when I met them. Yes, I met the Beatles and was quite nonchalant about it at the time – in fact most of my attention was taken up by Helen Shapiro who was, after all, top of the bill. I was a teenage reporter at the paper, sent to interview Shapiro who was big news at the time – and very nice despite the mega-stardom. It was also the first time I wrote a review for a show at the Empire, and I was told by one of older hands on the paper, 'Make sure you mention everybody on the bill.' But while we were there, my photographer colleague Tony Colling and I met some of the other acts – including the Beatles, of whom neither of us had heard at the time. They chatted away, chaffing each other and I remember thinking they were really canny lads. I also thought that the lads, not much older than me, were quite fanciable, especially George who was wearing a polo neck sweater.

My boyfriend at the time, David James, and I took our free Press seats in the front stalls – 8/6 (just over 40p) to paying customers. The cheapest seats were 3/-. Part of the problem was that other artists I'd seen controlled the enthusiasm of their audience. Not so the Beatles who, to be fair, didn't stand much of a chance to be heard above the mega-decibel high-pitched screams which greeted them when they appeared onstage. And what a strange sight they seemed, in their ultra-slimline, slightly shiny suits and yet-to-become-fashionable Beatle haircuts. Likely lads about Sunderland at the time tended to sport short back-and-sides haircuts with parting, and wear sports jackets, twill trousers and suede shoes. Seeing the Beatles soundlessly mouthing words and strumming notes we never heard and jigging about furiously all the while to a rhythm imperceptible to us was really like watching a comic silent film. A screaming girl, on her feet like most of the rest of the audience, hit Dave on the shoulder. I did become a Beatles fan later, but why on earth did I not get their signatures in my notebook? All four of them, with the date, 9 February 1963, would be worth a pretty penny now. Or better still, I could have got my mate Tony to take my picture with them. Still, my dismissal of the Fab Four has been a great tale to tell over the years. ❞

CAROL ROBERTON, JOURNALIST, SUNDERLAND, TYNE AND WEAR

SUNDAY 10 FEBRUARY

Booked for their fourth recording session at EMI Studios the following day, the group drove almost the length of the country from Sunderland to London – a six-hour drive on the A1, much of it in a snowstorm. After their early evening arrival at the Royal Court Hotel, where they were staying the night, they posed for photographer Cyrus Andrews in Sloane Square and its environs. Although they were scheduled to spend a long day in the studio the following day, they still enjoyed a night out on the town. Peter Jay and the Jaywalkers filled in for them on the Helen Shapiro tour at the Embassy Cinema in Peterborough. The tour resumed on the 23rd after Shapiro completed a three-day recording session in Nashville, Tennessee.

❝ It all started with 'Nellie The Elephant', 'The Runaway Train' and 'The Ugly Duckling', songs that I absolutely loved listening to as a child in the late 1950s. As well as hearing them played regularly on the BBC's *Children's Favourites* programme on Saturday mornings, we also had 78 rpm records of many of them at home in Stanmore, a smart leafy suburb of north-west London, situated at the end of the Bakerloo line. My younger brother Nigel and I loved playing the brittle 10" discs on our old wind-up record player. That is, until we eventually discovered the joy of using them as early frisbees and ended up smashing many of the discs upstairs in the attic where our parents couldn't hear us. Sacrilege indeed! Luckily however, the sturdier 45 was a lot harder to break, and I still have my copy of the first single I ever bought at the tender age of 8 in March 1961 – the King Brothers' '76 Trombones'. Meanwhile my favourite artists in those early '60s days included Cliff Richard and the Shadows, Adam Faith and Frank Ifield, along with a dark-haired teenage heart-throb who I'd fallen madly in love with – the siren from Stepney otherwise known as Helen Shapiro, a nice Jewish girl with a deep sultry voice who was definitely wobbling the collies of this young and equally Jewish fan as soon as I came across her photo or saw her on television.

But as much as I swooned over Helen there was another sound which suddenly hit me for six in January 1963. I can still remember the very moment that I first heard the group that was destined to dominate my musical life from that day onwards: standing at the foot of the stairs in our hall lounge, aged 10 and listening to an amazingly vibrant new song with a harmonica intro, unique-sounding harmonies and an overall energy which I'd never heard the likes of before. It was shortly before 5pm on a Sunday when Alan Freeman announced a record climbing the nation's charts on his weekly *Pick Of The Pops* show on the BBC's Light Programme. The song was entitled 'Please Please Me' and my world was suddenly transformed forever. The following week it entered the Top 20 at number 16 and then the next week when Alan Freeman played Brenda Lee's 'All Alone Am I' at Number 10, I thought it might have dropped out of the chart. Next came The Shadows' 'Dance On' at number 9, Maureen Evans' 'Like I Do' at number 8 and Mike Berry's 'Don't You Think It's Time' at number 7. Then over the airwaves came that familiar harmonica sound. They had made the Top 10 for the first time ever – at number 6! It climbed to number one the following week, before enjoying a three-week run at the top. I don't think anyone had any idea how they were going to change our lives in the coming months and years.

Half a century on in my role as Editor/Publisher of the acclaimed industry resource SongLink International, I present the annual SongLink Prizes for songwriting at the Liverpool Institute for Performing Arts (LIPA) in the presence of Sir Paul McCartney, who inducted me as a Companion of LIPA back in 2006. It's true to say that this schoolboy, when 10 years old, was north-west London's biggest Fab Four fan despite my father's assurance at the time that 'these Beatles will never last.' **7**

DAVID STARK, EDITOR AND PUBLISHER OF SONGLINK INTERNATIONAL, DRUMMER WITH THE TREMBLING WILBURYS, BELSIZE PARK, LONDON

MONDAY 11 FEBRUARY

The group arrived at EMI's Abbey Road Studio Two to begin recording their debut LP at 10am. George Martin had made the suggestion to make an LP at a meeting at EMI House on 16 November 1962, the day after the group had returned from their penultimate trip to Hamburg. At that stage, the plan was to record them live at the Cavern.

In the three-hour morning session, they recorded ten takes of 'There's A Place' and nine of 'Seventeen' (subsequently retitled 'I Saw Her Standing There'). When Martin and engineers Norman Smith and Richard Langham took a lunch break at the Heroes of Alma pub, the group stayed behind in the studio and continued working, keeping themselves going with just milk.

During the afternoon session from 2.30pm to 6pm, five takes and two overdubs of 'A Taste Of Honey', six takes and two overdubs of 'Do You Want To Know A Secret' (written by John the previous August when he was staying at Brian Epstein's Liverpool flat just after he'd got married), three overdubs of 'There's A Place', three overdubs of 'Seventeen' and eleven takes of 'Misery' were recorded. After an hour-and-a-half dinner break, they returned to the studio at 7.30pm, recording thirteen takes of 'Hold Me Tight', three takes of 'Anna (Go To Him)', one take of 'Boys', four takes of 'Chains' and three takes of 'Baby It's You', a cover of the Shirelles' 1961 US hit, written by Burt Bacharach, Mack David and Luther Dixon. At about 10pm, the group took a break for coffee and biscuits, before returning to record one of the highlights of their live show, 'Twist And Shout'. It was cut in two takes. Paul later said, 'We did 'Twist And Shout' last because if we'd done it first we couldn't have done any of the others.' When all was said and done, the entire LP had taken 585 minutes to record.

Martin said of the remarkable day, 'There wasn't a lot of money at Parlophone. I was working to an annual budget of £55,000 and I could spend it however I wished, but I had to produce a certain amount of records a year. So, I wanted to get the Beatles' first album recorded in a day and released very quickly, because once we'd made the first single, my commercial mind told me that I had to have an album out very soon. So I got the boys together and asked them, "What have you got? What can we record quickly?" They replied by telling me, "Only the stuff we can do in our act!"'

With their equipment packed into Neil Aspinall's van, they were driven back to the Royal Court Hotel, where they spent a second night. The next day they were to head up to Lancashire for another series of one-night stands. Paul later described making the album as 'one of the main ambitions in our lives. We felt that it would be a showcase for the group and it was tremendously important for us that it sounded bang on the button. As it happened, we were pleased.' John described his performance on 'Twist And Shout' as 'a frantic guy, doing his best. That record was the nearest thing that tried to capture us live, you know, and the nearest thing to what we might have sounded like to the audience in Hamburg and Liverpool.'

'It was February 1962. Norman Smith, Peter Brown, Malcolm Addy (Cliff's engineer) and Stuart Eltham were the big engineers on the pop side. You had to be a people person as a second engineer, making sure the artists were comfortable, whether they wanted a cup of tea or anything, really. You would set the tape machines up, clean all the recording heads on them with cotton buds and amyl acetate and clean the pinch rollers, making sure there was no dirt on the heads so the tapes could run smoothly. We kept logs of exactly what happened on the sessions. I had always kept immaculate

records. If you didn't, it would come back to bite you. The producer may say something like, 'Just mark that, the middle eight was good,' which had to be logged.

A year after joining, Norman mentioned to me that they'd had the Beatles in for a session and I was asked if I would I do a three-session day the following week. You always had to be asked if you wanted to do overtime. The producer would then book the studio and allocate the engineers. I didn't have any plans so I said, 'Yes, I'll do it.' George Martin was to produce with Norman as first engineer and me as second engineer. Norman introduced me to everyone – the four Beatles and Neil Aspinall. We brought them in through the side exit – the one that people didn't know about, past the air raid shelter, which is now used as an echo chamber – and straight into Number Two from the garage side and helped them unload the van and set up their equipment. It was all rather shabby and there were no backs on the amplifiers. When we checked for dirt inside, there were lots of bits of paper girls had thrown up from dance floors with telephone numbers on them.

We knew all the songs we were going to record. They had performed them hundreds of times, and knew them well, it was just a question of adapting the live show for a studio setting. Ten songs in thirteen hours, we just recorded one song after another. Most of what I was doing was making notes – if George said, 'We're going to do that afterwards,' or 'Mark this on the master,' 'That's the best,' etc.

The group were down on the floor and we were upstairs in the control room. The studio management were quite insistent on staff having a break. During the course of a long session Bob Beckett would come in and ask, 'How much longer are you going on for? My boys have got to have their break.' You would sometimes be asked if you didn't mind missing your break but on this day we went down to the Heroes of Alma pub, George, Norman and myself, whilst the group stayed behind. We'd never seen this before, artists would generally go to the canteen, but they wanted to go on rehearsing. When you look back, it's rather strange considering they'd just come down from playing a concert and were more or less playing every day and we were basically recording their stage show, but it shows their dedication.

During the afternoon when the group were upstairs listening and we were downstairs adjusting the microphones, Norman and I helped ourselves to a couple of Ringo's cigarettes he'd left on the drum kit so we had a quick smoke.

'Twist And Shout' was the last track we recorded, and there's been a lot of erroneous talk about how that came about. We had always planned to record it, it was just a matter of whether John could do it, so it was a case of George saying, 'Well, let's give it a try and see how we get on.' Neil supplied him with some milk and throat lozenges. He did it in two full recordings and a breakdown.

Halfway through the evening, Brian Epstein and Dick James turned up together. It was the first time I had met Brian. He was a perfect gentleman. He was a lovely man. They turned up just to listen and of course wanted to hear what we had done. I played the tapes back and then they wanted to hear them again. I looked at the clock and looked at Norman and said, 'Well, I've got a session in the morning.' In those days EMI didn't pay for taxis or anything like that and the tube had stopped. Although home wasn't far away, it was a meaty walk, so I said, 'Well, how am I going to get home?' Brian asked where I lived and said, 'Well I'll drive you home, if that's all right?' I said as long as somebody drives me home, that's all right. So I played the tapes again and Brian drove me home in his car. These days you would call it a Harry Potter type car – a Ford Anglia with the sloped window at the back. Whether it was his or whether he had borrowed it, I don't know, but that's what he drove me back in. The overtime rates at EMI were actually very generous, they were very good like that. 〕

RICHARD LANGHAM, PURVEYOR OF QUALITY SOAP, PALMERS GREEN, LONDON

TUESDAY 12 FEBRUARY

Despite spending more than twelve hours in the studio the day before, the group had to be up bright and early for a photo shoot for weekly teen magazine *Valentine*, which had just run its first article on them. They arrived late at the magazine's offices in Farringdon Street. At nine o'clock they took a taxi to the University of London Union in Malet Street with photographer Derek Berwin. He took photos of the group in the University's swimming pool. After shots of them on the diving board were taken, they all took the plunge – except Ringo, who couldn't swim. Also featured were *Valentine* staffers, Valerie Bridgestock, 'Davy' and 'Clancy T. Smith' – the latter two pseudonyms. Sid Hayden, who was 'Davy', recalled the day. 'I'm holding a beach ball in one of the shots, while Valerie was wearing a swimming cap and holding a rubber ring. Like Ringo, I was also a non-swimmer. After the shoot I recall seeing them outside waiting to hail a taxi and nobody knew who they were. Every time we featured the Beatles in the magazine, sales went up.' Shortly after 11am, Berwin drove the group to London Airport in his Volkswagen Beetle. They boarded flight number STW134 arriving in Liverpool in the early afternoon. There was little respite as they then had to make the hour-long drive to Oldham for the regular Tuesday 'Teenbeat Special' at the Astoria Ballroom at the intersection of King Street and Union Street.

A two thousand-strong crowd, many of whom had waited for over two hours, snaked down the road towards the Duke of Wellington pub, blocking the pavement. Police called in reinforcements after fans pushed down a steel guard rail at the Star Inn crossing, spilling dozens into the road junction and holding up traffic. They asked the management to open the doors early because of the mass outside. Fifteen-year-old apprentice fitter John Williams was on his way home from Platt Brothers on the bus and saw people already queuing. 'I dashed home, got changed and rushed back to the Astoria as quickly as I could. By this time the queue was very long. After about an hour, the doors opened and people started to go inside. As I passed the doorman, he put his arm across and said "That's it, sorry. It's full."' An estimated twelve hundred fans were turned away.

Arriving at the ballroom's Chaucer Street entrance, the group unloaded their van with the help of two local boys, Bobby Leach and Rick Turton. The group played two half-hour spots. Paul and George performed the bulk of the vocals, as John's already weakened voice was made worse by his performance of 'Twist And Shout' the night before. Among the mayhem one girl almost lost her dress, despite the efforts of bodyguards trying to prevent fans reaching the stage, who also stood on chairs and sat on each other's shoulders.

Between sets, the group met John McCann, a business acquaintance of Paul's father Jim. He passed a message from Jim McCartney to Paul and invited them to his house after the show to have dinner and meet his children. Following the performance, he drove his Vauxhall Victor estate up to the side door. The group made a dash for it and McCann drove them to his house in Windsor Road. Neil Aspinall followed in the van, tossing promotional post cards out of the window as he went. Fans eagerly picked them up. When the group walked into the McCann's front room, they found a spread of tea and sandwiches had been laid on for them. Ringo sat down on the coal scuttle near the fireplace and dozed off. One of McCann's daughters phoned her friend, Pat Costello, who came round and ended up having her hand kissed by Paul.

' I started my career in photography when I was very young and by the age of 16 was Fleet Street's youngest staff photographer. I was offered a job as staff photographer by Fleetway Publications – the magnificent sum of £1,600 a year, a key to the executive toilet, and a parking space! They had a big photographic studio where they did room sets and food and fashion. I did virtually everything else. One day when I arrived at work, they said, 'Oh we have another pop group coming in, they're called the Beatles.' I'd never heard of them. I asked what had been organised, and they said we'd rented the pool in the basement of the University of London Union for an hour. They arrived at the studio, just a bunch of ordinary lads really, and we all jumped in a taxi to Malet Street. There was a writer with us called Valerie, who did a lot of pop stuff. The boys got changed and we took the pictures. They had funny hair, which got all wet. I didn't take any pics of them in their trunks in the shower afterwards (imagine!), but I took some of them having their hair blow-dried. Time was short and by the time they'd got changed, we were rushing to get back to the studio. We did some more photos and mucked around for a while, then John suddenly said, 'Oh fuck, we're going to miss our fucking flight!' They said, 'Where's our car?' Apparently, a car should have arrived at the studio to take them to the airport. At first, I thought we'd messed up and were supposed to order this car, but they said no, it should have been organised by their side. So I said, 'Well, I'll run you to the airport.' I had just bought an old white VW Beetle, which was parked in a little alleyway at the side of the studio. We all piled into the Beetle and drove off. As soon as we got to the airport, they jumped out and ran away. It wasn't until about two or three weeks later when the Beatles explosion happened that I realised what a photo opportunity I had missed! I stayed with Fleetway for about three or four years, then left to work as an advertising photographer. I had clients such as Rolls-Royce, Ford, Jaguar and Martini, and competed in the World Championships for Underwater Photography, holding the title for three years. I was privileged to be asked by King Hussein of Jordan to photograph his family on many occasions, and I go back in my mind and think, 'If only I'd got the Beatles to autograph the top of my white Beetle and shrink-wrapped it, I'd probably be a millionaire by now!' '

DEREK BERWIN, PHOTOGRAPHER, EPPING, ESSEX

WEDNESDAY 13 FEBRUARY

The group drove the 130-mile plus trip across country to Hull to perform at the Majestic Ballroom, in the suburb of Witham. Arctic weather had returned the previous evening, followed by snow and icy conditions in the morning, although Anfield was declared fit to play, allowing Liverpool fans to see their first home game since before Christmas.

The group had previously appeared at the Majestic on 20 October 1962. Tickets for the 7.30 show sold for 3/6. Johnny Paterson, the leader of support group the Aces, recalled, 'Every girl who came in put her coat and handbag in the cloakroom. There were so many that the bags were in a big pile. The Beatles came on and the screaming started. Girls were still coming in, getting their ticket and throwing their bags and coats over the cloakroom counter to rush inside. The manager asked how many people were inside and the lady who gave out the tickets replied, 'Only room for two more and we are at capacity of 732.' He shut the main doors for a bit. The people already inside had pink tickets. He opened a new roll of green tickets and reopened the doors to let more people in. They were like sardines – it was dangerous.' An estimated sixteen hundred were in the venue that night.

Driving home from the concert, the group's Ford Thames bus – with George at the wheel – crashed into a roadside fence on the A614 Rawcliffe Road near the Burton's factory in Goole at 1am. Police Constable Kershaw, located at Greenawn Corner, spotted the van travelling from Boothferry Bridge towards Paragon corner. After the van disappeared from view, Kershaw heard the crash. As he reached the scene, he saw the Beatles and Neil Aspinall pushing the vehicle back on to the road. George claimed that ice on the road caused him to lose control. The *Goole Times* reporting the story, headlined its front-page article, 'A Hit, But Not In The Top 20.'

> ❝ I had first seen the Beatles on *People And Places* back in late 1962 and became a fan immediately – I had never heard such a refreshing sound. I was given '*Love Me Do*' for my 21st birthday in December of that year. At the time I was working as a shorthand typist for a trawler owner on St Andrew's Dock in Hull. One of my colleagues, Gordon Findlay, was a local pianist and through him I knew a few others on the music scene. We were great fans of Brian Matthew who introduced *Saturday Club* on the Light Programme. The girls who made the nets for the trawlers were off on a Saturday and when we were working, Gordon and I used to sneak off for half an hour and listen to their radio in the net store. We loved the music and Brian really promoted the Beatles and all the other groups. We loved him. Gordon and I and another colleague went to see them when they came to the Majestic Ballroom and I took my precious record with me. We couldn't believe how many had come, all due to 'Please Please Me' making the charts. Leon Riley, who was a popular ballad singer in Hull at the time, was the compère that night and asked if I would like to go backstage to meet them. Needless to say I did. Ringo was really friendly, John had a girl sitting on his knee, Paul commented that he wished that they were on a percentage of the takings (as they had been booked for a nominal fee before they were famous) and I can't even remember anything about George. They signed my record on both sides and also a promotion photo. Several years ago I sold them at a Christies' Rock & Roll Auction. It was a very exciting day – the record sold for £10,000 and the promotion photo for £1,800. I'm in my seventies now and it's flattering to know that I was told, quite often, that I was the first girl to wear a mini skirt in Hull! ❞
>
> **PAT NICHOLS, PAYROLL CLERK, KINGSTON-UPON-HULL, EAST RIDING OF YORKSHIRE**

THURSDAY 14 FEBRUARY

*D*isc reported, incorrectly as it turned out, that the Beatles were going to tour with Duane Eddy and Ben E. King. 'Please Please Me' jumped four places to number 3 in the paper's Top 30 and stayed at number 3 in the *NRM* chart, behind Jet Harris and Tony Meehan's 'Diamonds' and Frank Ifield's 'The Wayward Wind'. The group were featured on the paper's front page; inside Norman Jopling wrote about their forthcoming LP.

Love was obviously in the air as the temperature in Liverpool soared to 10 degrees – and with it another thaw and some rain. The group played at a St Valentine's Day Dance ('We present your Valentines The Beatles plus Free Gifts for the First Five Hundred Ladies – All Pay at Door 3/6 – 7.30-11.30' – although some ads had 'Four Hundred Ladies') at Mecca's Locarno Ballroom, part of the Mecca chain, on West Derby Road in Liverpool, next door to the Grafton Ballroom. Resident groups the Nat Allen Showband and the Delemeres supported them. Ringo announced that each Beatle received over thirty Valentine cards. After the show, Ringo told his girlfriend Maureen Cox, an assistant hairdresser at Ashley Du Pre's near the Cotton Exchange, to wait outside in the car so no one would see them together. A girl came up to her and asked whether she was going out with Ringo. Cox told her 'No' at which point the girl scratched her face. The group went to the Blue Angel club on Seel Street following the show.

❛ In the late 1950s the company I was working for in Newcastle sent me to art college on day release two days a week to study photography. It was there that I met Dave Shipley, who was doing the same course, and we became friends. We discovered that we were both into music and used to sing and play guitar together. We started doing some local gigs, and during a trip to the Isle of Man, we visited a place called Villa Marina where Ivy Benson's band were playing. They held talent competitions there, so we entered one and won a prize, just singing harmonies with our guitars. We were staying at a place called the Delamere Hotel in Douglas,

and flushed with our success, we decided when we got back home to form a group, calling ourselves the Delemeres, although incorrectly spelt. We started doing gigs all over the north-east, working men's clubs and the like – quite hard going, but managed to make a name for ourselves. I was singing as well as playing the guitar and piano.

Our big break came in 1960 when we were spotted by Mecca, who offered us a two-week relief job at the Palais de Danse in Edinburgh. The management were impressed enough to offer us a full-time contract as resident group at one of their ballrooms – the Locarno in Liverpool. It was too good an opportunity to miss, so we packed in our day jobs on Tyneside and headed for Merseyside. It was the beginning of a fantastic couple of years. I rented a flat in Sefton Park and various people would stay over there. We used to hold parties there every Saturday night, and everyone would come along. I loved Paul McCartney. He was fab. We both had searchlights on our cars – Paul's was a Cortina convertible, and mine a Vauxhall Velux, and we'd drive around Liverpool with those searchlights on late at night.

Things were really taking off at the time and we backed so many artistes of the day. We were doing four nights a week at the Locarno, and on the other nights we'd go out and check out our competition. One night we went down to the Cavern when the Beatles were playing. Pete Best was on drums – he was good, sang and was handsome. John Lennon shouted, 'Oh I see the Geordie lads are in.' We got the best booking you see, we got forty-five quid for three or four nights a week at the Locarno. The Locarno was a massive ballroom with a revolving stage. There was a huge orchestra – Nat Allen and His Orchestra were the permanent group and we were the small five-piece. The button would be pressed on the revolving stage and Nat Allen would end his set playing 'Blue Moon' in the same key as our first number, and we'd go straight into it. Nat and the group were moved to Belfast as Mecca wanted groups, but we stayed on.

It was a 'dry' ballroom, which meant they only sold soft drinks and snacks upstairs, so we'd go to the pub across the road for a drink beforehand. It was a beautiful ballroom though and being a photographer I kept a camera in my locker. I'd say to anyone who was around, 'Come on, photograph time!' I had photographs of the Beatles and the Stones, who were in the dressing room before the show passing round a bottle of whisky! I didn't keep the negatives unfortunately and lost the album the pictures were in some years later.

We played with the Beatles twice in 1963, the first at a Valentine's Day dance at the Locarno. The first five hundred girls to arrive that evening were given a present. The lads hadn't played there before and shared the dressing room with us. Paul was nice as ever, I didn't like John, he was a bit bolshy, Ringo, nice simple man, and George, quiet. The second time we played with them was at the Grafton Ballroom later that year at a charity gig. Our singer Colin Wemyss left the group that December to get married and was replaced by Karl Terry on lead vocals.

When our two years in Liverpool had finished we went up to Glasgow to do a three-month residency at the Dennison Palais. We got the 'Liverpool treatment' when we were there because we were classed as a Liverpool group! I found the music world a bit up and down, and finally decided I had had enough. We all headed back to Tyneside and I went back to the job I trained to do before I joined the group – photography. I started my own business and we did really well. I moved to the Algarve ten years ago and keep myself busy running a photographic group down here. **❞**

GORDON RAILION, PHOTOGRAPHER, SÃO BRÁS de ALPORTEL, PORTUGAL

FRIDAY 15 FEBRUARY

The front page of the week's *NME* revealed that the group's 'Life-lines' were inside. For their professional ambitions they wrote, 'To be rich and famous' (John), 'to popularise our sound' (Paul), 'to fulfil all group's hopes' (George) and 'to get to the top' (Ringo). George's birth date was inaccurately listed as 1942. Ringo's revelation of his dislike of Donald Duck saw him subsequently inundated with Donald Ducks. Paul, George and Ringo all admitted that Brigitte Bardot was their favourite actress. Their favourites drinks were whisky and tea (John), milk (Paul), tea (George) and whisky (Ringo). On page two, in an article headed 'Groups Are In', Derek Johnson wrote that almost half the week's Top 30 were by groups or duos. The paper ran an article headed 'Beatles–Eddy Package Starts Tour In May', which reported that Duane Eddy was confirmed for the tour, with a possibility that the Four Seasons would be added, rather than Ben E. King. A Swedish tour between 10 May and 17 May for TV and personal appearances was also mentioned. 'Please Please Me' moved up to number 3 in the chart.

Melody Maker devoted most of its week's issue to the annual Readers' Jazz Poll, but mentioned that the 'Beatles cut [their] first LP', recording fourteen tracks in twelve hours. 'Please Please Me' stood at number 2 behind 'Diamonds', as 'Love Me Do' dropped to number 43.

Kenny Lynch recorded a version of 'Misery', with guitar ace Bert Weedon playing on the track. The song had been written by John and Paul at the request of Shapiro's producer Norrie Paramor, but rejected.

In the evening, the Beatles played at the Plaza (formerly the Rookery Cinema) in Handsworth, Birmingham, with local acts the Cheetahs, the Blue Stars, Dave Lacey and the Corvettes, and the Redcaps in support. The group left during the Blue Stars' performance. Bob Bowman, the Blue Stars' guitarist, recalled, 'They did their set fairly early on and we went on and while we were onstage, I watched all four of them as they walked across the front of the stage from the dressing room which was onstage left across to the other side and down the fire escape, which was where the groups and the gear actually came in. Rather embarrassingly we had quite a few Beatles songs in our repertoire at the time and we were probably playing one of them as they walked across.'

The group than drove to the Ritz Ballroom in York Road, King's Heath, arriving in time to take the stage at 10pm – the rescheduled 11 January show. Club owner Joe Regan made them tea and sandwiches, after they came in from the pouring rain. After the concert, the group stayed at the Norfolk Hotel in Hagley Road, Birmingham.

❝ It was a cold winter afternoon in 1963. We, the Cheetahs, were actually rehearsing up on the stage when [the Beatles] arrived. Black Country group the Redcaps were there too; Mick Walker patted John Lennon on the back as he entered the ballroom behind Paul McCartney. They came in via the fire escape, which doubled as the main route for groups to bring their gear in. All four Beatles wore black leather jackets and they walked in a line like that classic 'Abbey Road' picture; an upright Paul with three stooping-over followers. Ringo brought up the rear. From my perch behind the drum kit I was reminded of Snow White's merry line of dwarfs with daft but adorable Dozy bringing up the rear.

We finished rehearsing and sat and talked to John mostly about the Star-Club, where they were legends and where we'd played recently too. We had a good laugh about a diet of sauerkraut and pork chops at the Seaman's Mission where all the groups used to meet and eat. Ringo admired my drum kit; it was a three-day-old, champagne pearl Ludwig. In fact, the very first set of Ludwig in the UK. Ringo asked if he could use them for their session. I was of course delighted. It was a story I would tell for the next half century – 'How Ringo used MY drums.' At the Plaza we all shared one dressing room. It was right by the side of the dance floor, with a door and stairs leading up to the stage.

The owner of the Plazas Handsworth and Old Hill, the Ritz King's Heath and the Gary Owen Irish Club in Digbeth was Mary (Ma or Mrs – Mrs to her face, Ma behind her back) Regan. She was also our personal manager and, as Robert Plant reminded me recently, 'her favourites', much to the annoyance of other groups. She treated us to a big American car as our tour bus. We were pageboys in our 'Cheetah' gear at her daughter Carmel's wedding. When we weren't playing, we spent many a happy day feasting in the kitchen at Ma Regan's enormous house in Woodbourne Road, Edgbaston. It used to belong to the famous journalist and actor Godfrey Winn. However, all the beautiful gardens he created were neglected and became a jungle where her three Alsatians patrolled ready to pounce on anyone who had no business being there. I remember an upstairs room where silver coins from the box-office doors were wheelbarrowed in to form a mini-mountain of money. Joe Regan would literally shovel it from there into coal sacks.

Mrs Regan was an ex-headmistress from Ireland; though no one knew how she made the transition from teaching to ballroom owner. She used the same strict principals though; if there was a fight on the dance floor she would haul her large frame up onto the stage and point out to the bouncers those to be evicted. 'Ma' would make a point of coming into the dressing room to talk to all the groups before the night started in earnest. Musos in underpants just continued to get dressed obliviously and this included the Beatles that night, to whom we simply said, 'Play well.' It was indeed like a royal visit. The screaming girls shook the building and the Beatles were nigh on impossible to hear but it was fabulous to be part of it. It was the only time I asked for autographs, so glad I did. ❞

EUAN ROSE, SCRIPTWRITER AND MUSICIAN, BROMSGROVE, WORCESTERSHIRE

SATURDAY 16 FEBRUARY

The group drove to Oxford, where they performed in front of a three hundred-strong sold-out audience at the Carfax Assembly Rooms in Cornmarket Street. The show was promoted by Billy Forrest with the Madisons in support. Will Jarvis and Neil Robinson of the Madisons jammed with John and Paul at the soundcheck. Jarvis recalled, 'We arrived in the afternoon and ended up rehearsing with them. Paul on the piano playing old Chuck Berry numbers.' After the soundcheck, John, Paul and Jarvis went out for a Chinese meal around the corner in Ship Street. Backstage, 14-year-old Syd Kearney got the group's autographs, signed on a Morris Motors radiators branch document – the only piece of paper he had at hand. He recalled it being 'just an ordinary dance... The reason I was there was that a friend knew the Beatles after having seen them at the Cavern. It was a great night but nobody thought they were going to be the phenomenon they ended up being.'

The show lasted from 8pm to 11.45pm with advance tickets selling for 6/-. Girls in the crowd stood on tables to get a better view and screamed and shouted, now customary wherever the group appeared. The Madisons normally adjourned to the Crown pub around the corner after their set, but stayed to watch the Beatles. 'It was obvious to us that they were something special,' recalled Jarvis. 'The packed audience had to be kept away from the stage with an arrangement of tables and chairs, something we had never seen before.' Following the show, the Beatles drove back to the Hotel President in Russell Square, the group's new London home from home.

❛ The Madisons were a fairly well-established local group. They'd had some sort of row and broke up. The singer left the group and a new one came in. I knew the guitarist, Will Jarvis, who suggested me as the pianist, so that was how I came to join them. We were one of the better groups around Oxford at the time and had an exceptionally good guitarist in Will. We had played at the Carfax Assembly Rooms many times, supporting the likes of Adam Faith, Cliff Richard and Screaming Lord Sutch. They had regular music nights there and we perhaps played every five or six weeks or so. The Carfax was originally a ballroom and had a sprung dance floor. It was owned by the Co-operative Society and occupied the upper floor of a building on the Corn Market, the ground floor of which was a municipal restaurant. When we got the call to support the Beatles, we knew who they were. The only thing that was different initially was that we were asked to be there early to set up. Normally, you would turn up at about half six to set up your gear and have a quick run through for a 7.30 start, but we were told that particular day to be there in the afternoon. We didn't own a van at the time and had to call on a friend to take us in. It wasn't all of the group, just myself and Will, and we arrived about three in the afternoon to set up. In the hall were John and Paul, no George nor Ringo. We spent the afternoon with them, setting up the stuff, and did the odd bit of rehearsing with them. They were playing all the old stuff, 'Roll Over Beethoven', etc. About half four, either John or Paul said to Will and I that they hadn't eaten all day and did we know anywhere they could go to eat? Will said 'Yes, there was a cafe in the local market, or a Chinese down on Ship Street.' They asked us to join them and for some reason I declined, saying I had to be home, and went to get the bus instead! Will went with them to the Chinese.

Our set was around forty-five minutes, an hour at the most. There were no other support acts that evening, it was just us and the Beatles on the bill. It was sold out, about three hundred people, and although it was a memorable occasion, it wasn't 'stand out' if you know what I mean, but it was the first time girls actually stood on the tables to get a better view, and the first time we stayed after our set to watch the main group rather than go to the Crown pub across the road! The Beatles had borrowed quite a lot of our equipment that evening, so they didn't have to unload all of their stuff. After they finished, they went into the dressing room and quickly buzzed off. The building that holds all these memories is still there, landlocked by other buildings. The top floor is locked, with no one knowing who has the key, and the lower half is a branch of HSBC bank. **'**

NEIL ROBINSON, INSURANCE AGENT, LITTLEMORE, OXFORDSHIRE

SUNDAY 17 FEBRUARY

*D*isc writer David Pearson arrived early to interview the group at the Hotel President and was greeted by a sleepy foursome. He tried to get some sensible answers to his questions as they got ready to travel to Teddington for a recording of *Thank Your Lucky Stars*. They made the 15-mile journey through west London, with Pearson on board, stopping for petrol on the way. Aspinall had to ask the petrol attendant for directions. He demonstrated with excessive arm movements, causing John to quip, 'Just a moment, sir, you can't do Billy Fury's act here.'

The group arrived at the Teddington Studio Centre on Broom Road in Teddington Lock, Middlesex, for an 11am rehearsal. They made a beeline for the canteen for some strong coffee, initially attempting to eat a vase of flowers in the middle of the table. They told Pearson their plans for a holiday in the Canary Islands – without Paul, who said he would be taking a bus tour of Chester. He didn't. Asked their personal ambitions, John said, 'I'd like to record in English'; Paul, 'I'd like for us to be in a big TV show with lots of sketches – only none of us can draw'; George 'I'd like to sing an instrumental'; and Ringo 'To play lead drums'. John was also asked what he would have been if he hadn't left school to take up rock'n'roll. 'The biggest boy in school,' was his reply.

They were the third act on a seven-act bill with Billy Fury, Jet Harris and Tony Meehan, Carol Deene, Duffy Power, Billie Davis, and the Clyde Valley Stompers, along with guest DJ Jimmy Savile and host Brian Matthew. They mimed to 'Please Please Me' at the afternoon recording, which aired the following Saturday. Artist Peter Blake, who later designed the *Sgt. Pepper's Lonely Hearts Club Band* sleeve, met the group for the first time. 'The very first time I met the Beatles was at a rehearsal for a television programme in 1963. It was the first one they did in London. I sat where the audience would have been all by myself and watched the show. After the Beatles did their song, they came into the seats and did an interview. They sat right in front of me, I suppose, because I was the only person sitting there and they were drawn toward me. I listened to the interview and they turned around, smiled and waved.' They signed autographs for cameraman John Rees, who was an avid collector of artists' signatures when they appeared on the show. In time, Rees, who had a habit of running up debts at a nearby cafe, provided his autographs as collateral. The group returned to Liverpool after the recording.

70

❛I had a phone call from Ian Menzies, leader of the Clyde Valley Stompers, Scotland's premier jazz band. Ian explained that the Stompers were about to move their base from Glasgow to London, and since their current clarinettist had decided not to go, would I consider taking his place? My response was, 'Let me grab a toothbrush – I'm ready to leave right now!' Some nine months after I joined the Clydes, Ian retired to Jersey, but not without asserting his ownership of the Clyde Valley Stompers name and stipulating that he, despite abdicating all creative involvement, would retain control of the group's finances. Although still only 20 years old, I was asked to take over 'leadership' of a band suddenly thrown into turmoil. The termination of our recording contract with Pye and a spate of personnel defections would prove to be just the first of many new setbacks I'd have to cope with. And there were occasions when the very future of the Clyde Valley Stompers seemed in serious doubt. But the boys and I dug in, worked hard at creating a fresh new sound, and not only managed to maintain the group's existing fan base, but actually started to build on it. Our jazzed-up arrangement of Prokofiev's 'Peter And The Wolf' caught the ear of George Martin, who duly invited us to EMI Studios to record what would turn out to be the Clyde Valley Stompers' first ever hit single. At a stroke, the Clydes were launched into the glitzy world of mainstream popular music.

I recall playing the Cavern in Liverpool one Sunday night. Originally a jazz club when it opened in 1957, the Cavern had yielded to skiffle during the height of the washboard-and-tea-chest craze, but by the early '60s was actively promoting jazz again. Ominously, however, the interval band on this occasion was to be what the poster outside described merely as a 'Support Group'. Of all the venues I knew in Britain, the Cavern was probably the most uncomfortable to play in, but one of the most exhilarating too. Low and vaulted like a miniature underground station, it was a veritable sweat box when packed to capacity with upwards of five hundred pumped-up clubbers. Condensation glistening on the walls when the joint was jumping was testament to that, and there was always a risk of your trombone player having his slide whipped away by the flailing arm of an overenthusiastic jive monkey. At the end of our first set, it was a relief to get out of that Turkish bath and into the group room at the side of the stage, cramped and airless though it was.

Yet the four lads in the interval group seemed as keen to get onstage as we were to get off – and it immediately became apparent why. Although they had been un-billed on the poster outside, the audience were well aware of who they were and made their delight at seeing them, obvious the moment they emerged onstage. The screaming and shouting was so loud it drowned out whatever sounds were blasting from the group's amplification gear. To a purveyor of acoustic music like me, this was a disquieting new phenomenon indeed. 'Nah, don't worry about it, man,' said our piano player, who had been around the scene much longer than I had. 'Ten a penny round here these so-called beat combos. Electric skiffle groups, I call 'em. Seven-day wonders. Here today, gone tomorrow.' Who was I to argue, and what did it matter, anyway? In a few days' time, we'd have forgotten about this dingy backstreet cellar and would be appearing at London's Royal Albert Hall, in a festival featuring the foremost jazz bands in Britain.

Less than a year later, we were booked to tape *Thank Your Lucky Stars*. A middle-aged studio hand who'd buttonholed me during rehearsals said, 'Lucky stars? Loada crap the lotta them, cock. Flashes in the pan. Yeah, gimme David Whitfield, Joan Regan, Pearl Carr an' Teddy Johnson. Them's real stars for ya!' After the recording, the Beatles, unnoticed and alone, loaded their gear into a little delivery van. 'Imagine havin' to travel all the way back from London to Liverpool cooped up in a windowless tin can like that,' said our trombone player from the comparative opulence of our new minibus. 'No wonder the poor buggers look cheesed off.'

Fast forward twelve months, and the cheese was on the other plate, so to speak. The boys and I, now calling ourselves Pete Kerr's Scottish All-Stars, were sitting in a pub after group rehearsals on 7

February 1964, when the evening news came up on the telly behind the bar. The main item showed the Beatles arriving at New York's John F. Kennedy Airport for the start of their first American tour. There were shots of the estimated four thousand hysterical fans who had turned up to meet them, before the camera panned to a motorcade of four limos heading for the city centre. 'No sign of their wee delivery van now,' said our trombone player, gobsmacked. 'It's the end of the world,' gulped our drummer. 'As we know it,' said our guitarist, stoically. I didn't say anything. But I knew that, although the world would continue to spin, I had finally come the end of that long and winding road. Or at least this stretch of it. I went on to enjoy a successful career as a record producer, hitting the jackpot in 1972 with the Royal Scots Dragoon Guards' 'Amazing Grace', which sold thirteen million copies worldwide, to become the biggest-selling instrumental single of all time. More recently, I turned my hand to writing books, including the award-winning *Snowball Oranges* series of humorous travelogues set in Mallorca. ❜

PETER KERR, MUSICIAN AND AUTHOR, HADDINGTON, EAST LOTHIAN, SCOTLAND

MONDAY 18 FEBRUARY

The *Liverpool Echo* announced, 'Fog Blanket After Another Cold Night,' as temperatures dropped to their lowest since late January. Mersey ferry services were operating by radar because of fog, with visibility down to about 30 yards. Visibility at Liverpool Airport was even worse, resulting in flights being rerouted to Manchester.

The group drove south along the Speke Road, the short distance to Widnes. As they reached Moor Lane, they were greeted by snow banked 4 feet high on the side of the road – as well as potholes. They were to play two NEMS-promoted dates at the Queen's Hall with Buddy Britten and the Regents and the Mersey Beats. Only a few months earlier, the Beatles had supported the Regents at more than one gig.

The hall had opened in 1957, an imposing building that was once a Wesleyan Methodist Chapel, built almost a century earlier. It was the group's fifth appearance at the venue, the previous four having been in September and October 1962, and was promoted as a 'Sensational Farewell Showdance' – a particularly prescient announcement. The group appeared onstage at 8pm and 9.30pm. The nearby La Scala Ballroom, which had presented Freddie Starr and the Midnighters the previous Saturday and saw Mike Berry perform on the 20th, wisely decided not to compete and had a bingo night instead. Both houses were sell-outs, accounting for some five thousand fans. Those who couldn't get in had the opportunity to go and see Elvis Presley in *Kid Galahad* at the Plaza cinema – or play bingo of course.

While the Beatles were raising the roof, the Town Council appointed William Wycherley as the venue's new manager. His soon-to-be

SENSATIONAL FAREWELL
"Showdance"
NEMS ENTERPRISES PRESENT
at the Queens Hall, WIDNES
Monday, 18th February, 1963

6.30 TWO SEPARATE SHOWS 8.45
Your Own Famous, Fabulous Fantastic
Sensational, Magnificent, Superb

BEATLES
Stars of TV., B.B.C. & Parlophone Records
PLUS
BUDDY BRITTEN
& The Regents
(Decca Recording Artistes)
AND
THE MERSEY BEATS

TICKETS (which MUST be purchased in advance)
For the 6-30 p.m. Show 4/-
For the 8-45 p.m. Show 5/6
From DAWSONS (Widnes & Runcorn) & THE MUSIC SHOP

Note . . . THE BEATLES
will appear on Stage at 8-0 p.m. & 9-30 p.m.
The Date again . . Monday 18th February, 1963

predecessor George Marsh left at the end of the month, his last two bookings being the Beatles and the Royal Philharmonic Orchestra. Like so many other local newspapers in early 1963, the *Widnes Weekly News* ignored the Beatles' visit – instead the paper reviewed the Widnes Boys' Brigade production of *Snow White And The Seven Dwarfs* at St Ambrose Parish Church Hall and showed their excitement at the first sighting of spring rhubarb.

' I can remember four lads singing some skiffle songs at an evening at the Church Hall at the Ball O' Ditton. This could have been one of the regular Scout Dances run by the 10th Widnes (Hough Green) scouts, of which they and me were all members. I was already hooked on the Shadows and desperately wanted to be Hank Marvin. I approached them to see if they would be interested in getting together to play Shadows-style numbers. The answer was obviously yes, and that's how it started. I can remember practising at Hough Green youth club, and at each other's homes and we played a few Scout Dances to gain experience and build our repertoire.

The Gang Show was announced and we thought we were good enough to take part. It was held at the Queen's Hall and was the first big gig we played. We kept going and got more professional. We tried out a few vocalists once we realised that we couldn't keep going just playing instrumentals – even the Shadows had Cliff! John Turner came for an audition with us at Hough Green School, and once we found the right key for him to sing in, we never looked back. That must have been late 1962, and now calling ourselves the Cheetahs, we were still playing quite a few instrumentals and it was a gradual change to doing all vocal numbers.

We played mainly in the Widnes area in youth clubs, then moved to dance halls a bit further afield. We played a number of times at the Queen's Hall, and that's where I first saw the Beatles. That was probably the point at which we changed our playlist into all vocals, missing out the instrumentals! Our drummer, Dave Preece, had seen the Beatles the first time they played at the Queen's Hall. I didn't know he had gone, but he told me afterwards that he'd seen a great group. I asked him half-jokingly, 'Were they as good as the Shadows?' He looked rather sheepish and said, 'I think they were better.' And I thought how can a member of my group say something like that? Detrimental against the Shadows! So I thought I'd go and watch this group when they next played here.

It was the day before my 20th birthday. I stood at the back, and was thinking, 'I'm not going to like this group'. Hank Marvin was, after all, my hero. However, I found myself getting closer and closer to the stage. They just drew me in. At the end of each number, there was very enthusiastic clapping, but then the audience went quiet. People from the audience would shout up to the stage, 'John, play this number', or 'play that number,' amidst perfect quiet, so you could hear every word, and obviously you heard every word back, and my impression was, 'How do these kids know, how do they know all of these tunes?' But of course the Beatles had an enormous following in Liverpool and Merseyside, and we were only about 10 miles from Liverpool, but in our own little cocoon in Widnes. I thought they were absolutely fabulous. The thing that really impressed me – if ever I broke a string onstage, we went into a routine – we went into an old jazz number, 'Big Noise From Winnetka', which was mainly a bass and drum solo, and the drummer would play it on the strings of the bass guitar. So we would quickly go into this while I would go off and change the string, put it on, and tune it up. But George Harrison broke a string on this particular evening, and it never threw him one little bit, he just carried on. Nobody would have known he'd broken a string. He just leaned to one side and handed his guitar to someone in the wings, they passed him another guitar, which was readily strung, and off they went. And I thought, 'Wow, that's a polished performance!' There was something magical about them. When we saw them, I thought, 'They're definitely something else.' We had a separate singer whose job it was just to sing, but they did everything themselves. They wrote their own music, and their musicianship was just brilliant compared to anybody else who was around at that time. I was just blown away. **"**

RAY JONES, MOTOR TRADE COST ENGINEER, WESHAM, LANCASHIRE

TUESDAY 19 FEBRUARY

At lunchtime, the group met with photographer Michael Ward, who had just driven up from London after being commissioned by teen magazine *Honey* to snap the group. After a quick pint, they went around Liverpool together, shooting in front of the stone steps of the Pier Head and the balustrades of the Victoria Monument. With the weather getting colder by the minute, they got fed up and Ward called it a day. Ward later said, 'I'd never heard of them, and they weren't remotely interested in me.'

The group left for Brian Epstein's office to warm up before heading over to the Cavern, where they rehearsed for the evening's show. Fans had been queuing for two days, no doubt taking note of the poster which read 'Be early! Tell Your Friends.' Rescheduled from two days earlier, the group were now being paid £60 for a Cavern appearance.

Headlining a bill which also featured Lee Curtis and the All Stars, Freddie Starr and the Midnighters and the Pathfinders, they received a telegram from Epstein congratulating the group on reaching number one with 'Please Please Me' in the new *NME* chart: 'To a great group from a happy guy, congratulations on a wonderful achievement – Brian.' DJ Bob Wooler announced the news from the stage. At the side of the stage, John and Cynthia celebrated with several drinks. The gig was the last time any of the group ever saw Pete Best – he was now drumming in Lee Curtis's group. Following the show, at about 11pm, the Beatles drove down to London.

"I was the bass player with the Pathfinders when we played with the Beatles at the Cavern. We were one of the original '60s Birkenhead beat groups on the Liverpool music scene. We played at the Cavern and all the notable city venues – the Iron Door, Downbeat, Mardi Gras as well as across the Mersey in Birkenhead, and the Kraal Club in New Brighton on the Wirral. Recording for Decca and Parlophone and with radio and television appearances (one of our records was featured on *Juke Box Jury*), we introduced our unique style to the Liverpool groups' sound, in what would come to be known as 'Merseybeat'.

When we played with the Beatles at the Cavern, I remember speaking to Paul McCartney in the changing room to the left of stage. He had just been presented with a wooden replica of his famous Hofner violin-shaped bass guitar by some Liverpool schoolgirls, which had been signed by many of the girls from the school. Needless to say, the club was full to capacity. So much so we had trouble getting our gear in past the long queue outside the door and down the steps. When the Cavern was full, condensation used to drip from the ceiling and because the club was sprayed with some form of disinfectant to clean it from the previous night's gig, your clothes smelled. That evening was no exception. We were on before them so you can imagine the atmosphere that night.

After the Cavern experience and by the time we made our recordings, the group had changed personnel again. We had a number of changes over the six years we were formed but this was typical of the Merseybeat scene at time – many of the local group members interchanged between the different groups and all the groups knew each other, as many of them played on the Liverpool circuit, which included venues such as Litherland Town Hall, Orrell Park Ballroom and of course the Cavern Club. I particularly remember playing with Ringo Starr, Freddie Starr as singer and the lead guitarist from the Remo Four at the Downbeat Club in Liverpool one night in 1963. In Mathew Street opposite the Cavern Club is a wall where each brick has the name of a '60s Merseybeat group on it (a very popular tourist spot). The Beatles' name is in the centre of the bricks. **❞**

ROY BROCKHURST, TEACHER, CHESTER, CHESHIRE

WEDNESDAY **20 FEBRUARY**

While George Martin and engineers Stuart Eltham and Geoff Emerick worked on overdubs for 'Misery' and 'Baby It's You' – Martin added piano and celeste, respectively – at Abbey Road from 10.30am to 1pm, the Beatles had another photo session with Angus McBean, this time at EMI House. Among the photos taken was the now-famous image of the group leaning over the railings at 20 Manchester Square, used for the sleeve of their debut LP.

The group then dashed across town to get to the Playhouse Theatre for an 11.15am rehearsal for a live appearance on the Light Programme's *Parade Of The Pops*, singing 'Love Me Do' and 'Please Please Me'. The programme was hosted by Denny Piercy, the former drummer for Dickie Valentine. The Beatles played alongside Lynn Collins, Dougie Arthur, Gordon Somers, the Milltones, Vince Hill and regulars Bob Miller and the Millermen. *Parade Of The Pops* first aired in January 1960 and had a listenership of about eight million – the highest for any weekday pop show. One 50-year-old had attended all but one show since its inception, but the majority of its listeners were office workers taking an extended lunch hour.

Following the hour-long show, which was broadcast from 12.31pm to 1.30pm, the group set off on the 160-mile journey to Doncaster, West Riding, where they performed before a sold-out crowd of eleven hundred at the St James Street Swimming Baths. Wednesday was 'Beat Night' at the baths, with Len Boot's resident group playing. The staff were basically council workers – gardeners, plumbers, builders, park keepers – who worked there in the evenings. There was a hole in the wall near the stage door, where artists would go for coffee. The pool was boarded over to create a dance floor and Baths Superintendent William Pearson confessed to a feeling of slight seasickness when he walked over it on occasion. Teenager Bernard Warner was turned away at the door, but when he mentioned his name to promoter Robin Eldridge, was let in. His father, in his position as concert secretary of the Yarborough Social Club in Bentley, had beforehand tried to book the group to play five spots on a Sunday for £45, but the committee turned the group down for being too expensive.

The *Doncaster Chronicle* reported the show briefly under the heading 'Beatles' played to large audience'. After the show, the group stopped off for a quick pint at the Old Barrel cafe in French Gate before driving back to Liverpool.

> ❛ I was a teacher, starting off doing PE and games, then moved on to Craft, and then French. I spent some time teaching at a camp school in Itchingfield, Sussex, before going back to Doncaster, starting with Junior and then Secondary. My husband Bill managed the St James' Swimming Baths and we lived together in a flat on the premises, which allowed us to swim and dance and have plenty of company. I used to give Bill a hand on Wednesdays and Saturdays when there were concerts there. Robin Eldridge, a local agent, booked all the groups so we basically took what he sent. Queues would snake all the way round most nights. Once they got in there was no spirits. They had to go out with a pass and if they lost it they couldn't get back in. They would come to the Baths to find a boyfriend or a girlfriend and then they'd rise above the Baths and go

to the Co-op. It was rather elegant there – the Baths was the breeding ground. As you went inside, the pool was in front of you. At the very back was the stage. We would empty the pool from the shallow end first and then the Works Department would come in and fill in the pool from the bottom up and screw everything together before putting this maple floor on top. It was a work of art and it covered the entire pool. And then of course once the dancing started, with the springs underneath, the floor would bounce up and down.

The Beatles had been booked months earlier for £40 and although I hadn't really heard of them at the time, people were wondering whether they would honour their commitment because they were becoming quite successful. After they arrived, they set up their instruments and played a couple of numbers and then they spotted the sign that said, 'Slipper Baths'. We asked if they'd like one. 'Yes please,' was the reply. After they all had one they swanned off into town and then they turned up at night and played their little hearts out. I was serving soft drinks, teas and coffees in my white overalls at the other end of the hall, but we weren't all that busy because everyone was listening to them. I should have invited them upstairs for a bite to eat. They would have come, you know. Why didn't I get a lock of their hair or an autograph? It was my job to pick up all the empty bottles of orangeade and limeade that ended up on the floor. Poor old Len Boot and his group didn't get a look in. We were watching showbiz history but didn't realise it. I can still see the faces of the young people just staring as The Beatles played. It was amazing.

It was a lovely time – you could swim at the Baths in the summer, and in the winter it was a dance hall. Different people would work there at the different times of the year, lots of people coming and going. It was a beautiful building, sadly no more. We had Turkish baths, a laundry, and a large area below stairs where they would cook. There were windows where you could look up from down below and see people swimming, but they did away with those in the end. Bill passed away in 2004 and when I was going through his things I found a medal in a wooden case. It was for representing Great Britain in the Men's 400 metres Freestyle at the 1936 Olympic Games in Berlin. He was a very modest man. ❜

BETTY PEARSON, TEACHER, DONCASTER, SOUTH YORKSHIRE

THURSDAY 21 FEBRUARY

B ack on home turf, the group woke to frost and patches of fog – and the news that 'Please Please Me' had become the group's first number one, knocking 'The Wayward Wind' off the top in the *Disc* chart, whilst climbing one place to number 2 in *NRM*, as 'Love Me Do' dropped out of the chart after eighteen weeks in the Top 50. The *Liverpool Echo*'s 'Over The Mersey Wall' columnist George Harrison wrote his first article on the group, reporting that fans had begun queuing the previous weekend for Tuesday's performance at the Cavern. He wrote that the group were 'slightly surprised' about their new-found fame, noting that they no longer wore leather jackets and had become more dress conscious. He quite rightly commented that, 'very rarely indeed does a hitherto "unknown" group hit the record jack-pot twice with their first two discs. It means that the Beatles are now heading for big money.' Signs

that Fleet Street was beginning to take notice came in a Vicky cartoon in the *Evening Standard*. Foreign Secretary Alec Douglas-Home, and soon-to-be Prime Minister, had stated that the Soviet Union could be subverted with pop records, and the cartoon featured several record sleeves flying over the Iron Curtain, including one by the Beatles. It was captioned, 'We're lost, Tovarich, Here Comes The British Deterrent!'

In the evening the group, variously billed as 'Britain's No. 1 Vocal/Instrumental Group' and 'Those Chart-Topping Heart-Stopping Beatles', played two shows at 7.30pm and 11.30pm at the Majestic Ballroom in Conway Street, Birkenhead, with Freddie Starr and the Midnighters in support.

❝ I grew up on the Wirral and formed a group along with some friends I met at a local youth club. We called ourselves Gus Travis and the Thundercaps. We listened to American records before they were played on national radio, mainly rhythm and blues, and that's the sort of music we played. Freddie Starr was around on the scene with a guy called Derry Wilkie, working as a duo with various groups in the area whenever they could. Our manager at the time, Alan Watts, saw Freddie singing in a club and thought he had potential. He started doing gigs with us in late 1962, and by spring 1963, Gus had left to join another group, with Freddie taking over on lead vocals and including a bit of comedy in the act. Freddie's surname was Fowell, which wasn't a particularly rock'n'roll name, so I suggested he call himself 'Star' because the group were called the Midnighters. It wasn't anything to do with Ringo Starr, it was to do with midnight!

Back then all the groups mostly did covers, it was only when the Beatles came along and started to write their own songs that anybody thought about it. They didn't start performing their own stuff for quite a while after they formed because people wanted to hear the popular songs of the time, they didn't want to hear new stuff because they couldn't relate to it. But the Beatles wanted to sound different and began writing their own songs. We were playing quite a lot at the Cavern in early 1963, and other larger local venues like the Majestic Ballroom in Birkenhead. The Maj was a nice place to play. It was originally a cinema converted into a ballroom, and we played there a few times, and supported the Beatles there that year. I remember that date specifically as they had just gone to number one that week with 'Please Please Me' and were on a real high.

We never saw any money from our recordings, but if you were playing five or six nights a week, you got paid anything between £12 and £15 a night, so if there were five of you, you got between two and three quid. Sometimes you would do double bookings – first group on at one venue, then travel on to the next to close the show. It wasn't bad money. I was earning more from the group than my day-time job as an insurance clerk! We weren't really thinking about the royalties from record sales, we wanted the cash in our pockets so to speak. We were buying expensive gear on HP [hire purchase], but still made a profit! I suppose we were lucky in a sense that there were so many venues in the local area, but we were travelling a lot and working six or seven nights a week, so I left the group in August, and formed a trio with Dave Georgson on lead guitar and John Cochrane on drums. We all had day jobs, so only played at weekends.

Gus and I still play together with a couple of other guys, Pete Watson on lead guitar, and Dave Jones on drums. We do a few charity shows, still calling ourselves the Midnighters! **❜**

IAN McQUAIR, INSURANCE BROKER, BURTON, SOUTH WIRRAL, CHESHIRE

FRIDAY 22 FEBRUARY

Arthur Howes took out a front-page ad in the *NME*, announcing several forthcoming tours, under the heading 'Arthur Howes Presents: Stars From The Hit Parade', including the Beatles' with both Helen Shapiro and Tommy Roe and Chris Montez. The paper also reported that the tour with Duane Eddy was to open at the Walthamstow Granada on 18 May. 'Please Please Me', after three weeks on the chart, climbing from number 17 to number 5 to number 3, hit the top, tying with 'The Wayward Wind'. An ad on the back page read 'Congratulations The Beatles – No. 1 In The Charts With Please Please Me'. Under the heading 'Beatles Wax Nine Of Their Titles', the newspaper erroneously reported that 'Keep Your Hands Off My Baby' had been recorded during the 11 February sessions for their debut LP.

The single remained at number 2 behind 'Diamonds' in *Melody Maker*'s weekly chart, as 'Love Me Do' dropped out of the Top 50. Two weeks after the paper's first coverage on the group, the paper printed the article 'Don't copy – and keep it simple! The Beatles tell Jerry Dawson'. Interviewed in Brian Epstein's Liverpool office, they told Dawson, 'Please, please don't copy. Try to be original, as we have done. Play what you like and don't try to be too clever. Keep it simple.' Talking about their current hit, Paul said, 'It was a bit fussy, and he [George Martin] advised us to smooth it out a bit. Simplify it. We did – and the result speaks for itself.'

In the morning, Paul drove John to Epstein's flat at 36 Falkner Street in Liverpool, where they signed a contract for the creation of the publishing company Northern Songs. The terms of the contract saw them share 49 per cent with Epstein, while music publisher Dick James and his accountant Charles Silver took the remaining 51 per cent. The contract ran until 10 February 1973. 'Brian was at the house with a lawyer-type guy,' recalled Paul, 'but nobody said to us, "This is your lawyer and he's representing your interests in this thing." We just showed up, got out the car, went into this dark little house, and we just signed this thing, not really knowing what it was all about, that we were signing rights away for our songs... John and I didn't know you could own songs. We thought they just existed in the air.'

The group were scheduled to play a performance that evening in Manchester at the Oasis Club on Lloyd Street, the group's third trip to the city since the New Year. Arriving mid-afternoon, it was discovered their microphones had been left in Liverpool. A quick phone call was made to Barratts, the local musical instruments shop.

The club was located in a former textile warehouse, in the shadow of the city's Town Hall. The venue had opened in November 1961 as 'Manchester's Most Fab Club For Young People', under the ownership of John Orr, Rick Dixon and Hugh Goodwin. It served as a coffee and snack bar between 10am and 2pm.

Support act Chris Nava's Combo probably played in front of their largest ever audience. Dixon recalled, 'The first time the Beatles played the Oasis there were thirty-seven people there.' On this occasion, however, 'We crammed about twelve hundred into the place, and the capacity was about five hundred. There were about five thousand queuing, four or five deep, right round the block and in the surrounding streets.' After the show, Paul sat on the edge of the stage, signing autographs.

❛ My father was a dance band leader in the 1950s. Phil Edge and the Boys played at the Levenshulme Palais for many years, finishing in 1961 when music was changing and all the groups were becoming more popular. I was running a cafe on Stockport Road at the time called '700.' It was my own business although the premises were rented. We were always busy, and Glyn Ellis, later to become Wayne Fontana, would come in to wash the pots and pans for me. In 1961, I was thinking of moving on, and someone suggested I go and see Hugh Goodwin. I don't know how he got my name or knew about me, but he was very interested in me joining them. Initially he just wanted me to go in and sort out the cafe side of the business, which I agreed to do. The [Oasis] club had a long history, starting off as a jazz club. It had evolved into a coffee/dance club, and was managed by Ricky. He wasn't really suitable for the job and wanted to be get more involved in agency work, so Hugh had this idea that I buy Ricky out, and take on the agency side, booking the groups, etc. My husband Graham used to come and pick me up after work. He had been in the police force but left when we got married, and the idea was that we would run it together. There were so many groups around at the time. The very first time the Hollies performed together was at the Oasis. We didn't have an age limit because no alcohol was served, so it was mostly 15- to 16-year-olds who had to be home at a certain time. We opened at lunchtimes, and the employees at Kendals [department store] used to come in on their lunch hour for a buttie. Dave Lee Travis did the window displays there and was always asking if he could have a go at DJing, so in the end we let him, and he was very good.

The Beatles came to the club a lot in the early days. Whenever they were at the Granada Studios, they used it like a pop-in centre! I'd go down to the studios to watch them when Johnnie Hamp was producing the shows. Nobody thought they were going to be as famous as they were, goodness me, I would have had them singing all sort of things if I'd known. They played tricks on me all the time. They'd creep down the stairs to the box office, and suddenly pop up, making me jump. They'd shout 'Mrs Cloggy? Mrs Cloggy?' They never had any money and were always hungry. They'd have egg and chips and ice cream. The only Beatle I didn't know particularly well was Ringo. He was really nice though. He'd come in and stick his head in the freezer to see if we had any ice cream, and he liked his eggs upside down. I remember that. The others were lovely, just ordinary lads.

I don't remember the first time they played there, but I certainly remember when they came to play after they had had their first hit. The place was packed. The kids had been queuing from early morning, and it was a freezing cold day. They were queuing round the block. Security wise, it wasn't just four lads nipping down the stairs and in, nothing like that. During the day, I'd had the police there, I'd had the fire brigade there, all asking for free tickets! But they were just making sure everything was going to be all right. After the show had finished, I couldn't get out of the office. The phone rang, and when I answered, it was George's girlfriend, who wanted to talk to him. I said it was impossible, but she said, 'Oh please try, I really need to speak to him.' In the end, I asked the doorman if he could see if he could get George to the office. Incredibly, he managed to get him from one side of the club to the other without anybody recognising him. It was only when he actually got into my office that they cottoned on. The pair of us were stuck in there for the rest of the evening! We paid them £30 for that night. ❜

PAULINE CLEGG, SALES MANAGER, DOUGLAS, ISLE OF MAN

SATURDAY 23 FEBRUARY

The group returned to the Helen Shapiro package tour, with two dates at 6.15pm and 8.30pm at the 1,582-seater Granada Cinema in West Gate, Mansfield. They had moved up the bill, with Kenny Lynch being put in the slot before the group by Arthur Howes, who told him, 'Look, you'd better go on just before the Beatles. You're the only one who doesn't care how badly you go down.' When faced with the ordeal, Lynch told the audiences, 'I'm not bringing them on until you're quiet.'

On their arrival in town, the group checked into the Swan Hotel in Church Street and – despite their lack of interest in sport – joined several other members of the troupe to watch the England versus France rugby union international in the Granada TV shop next door to the cinema. Full back John Wilcox's two penalties were enough to give England a 6-5 victory. Afterwards, they had a bite to eat. The previous Sunday's recording of *Thank Your Lucky Stars* aired between 5.50pm and 6.30pm, which the group watched on the television in Shapiro's dressing room. She recalled John being 'fascinated but rather put off by the way he looked, because he used to have this stance with the guitar across his chest and the legs rather bowed, going up and down. He was quite horrified. But he was excited at seeing himself on the screen.' Shapiro had just returned from three days of recording in Nashville and was suffering from laryngitis, so fans at the two shows were treated to the Beatles singing a couple of extra songs.

> ❝ I left school at 15 and joined the staff of the Swan Hotel in Mansfield as a 16-year-old commis chef. It was my first job, and I was there working for Mansfield Brewery for a number of years. Many of the groups who played at the Granada stayed at the Swan. It was just off Market Place, and only about 200 yards down Church Street to the cinema on West Gate. There was a real buzz going round the place the night the Beatles were booked in to stay. I'd been aware of them from my friend Eric Mussom, who was a fellow commis chef. He played in a local group and knew all about them and stirred up the excitement. My shifts started in the morning at eight, and we'd work till about half past two, then return back to work about six o'clock to feed the residents and anyone else who came in wanting a meal. Last orders were at nine, but if there was no one in the restaurant, we could just go home. Arthur Price, the Head Chef, had asked Eric and I to be on standby and said he trusted us to look after them that evening.
>
>
>
> I think [the Beatles] performance finished at about ten, and they came back to the hotel wanting a meal. I can't remember exactly what we served them, but it was pretty basic. They had their instruments with them and Paul strummed along with Eric and me. We asked all sorts of questions. They were a fantastic group of lads. I could walk home from the hotel in approximately eight minutes, but that night, I caught the last bus. Of course, when I got in, my father said, 'You're home late lad!' I excitedly told him I was late because I stayed behind to meet the Beatles. I sat with them, spoke to them, I strummed a guitar with them! If it was anyone else, it wouldn't have seemed like much, but this was the Beatles! It was a magical moment. Of course, I got all their autographs that evening which I later gave to my girlfriend. They were signed on one of our menus. After we split up, she moved to South Africa and I presume my autographs went with her. ❞
>
> **DOUGIE COLTON LEE, CHEF, MANSFIELD, NOTTINGHAMSHIRE**

SUNDAY 24 FEBRUARY

Three of the group took advantage of Kenny Lynch's offer of a ride to their next venue, an hour and a half south to Coventry, where they were scheduled to play two shows at 6pm and 8.30pm at the 2,136-seater Coventry Theatre – where Frankie Howerd and Sidney James were starring in the pantomime *Puss In Boots*. Lynch wanted to get there early to visit the newly consecrated Cathedral and had rented a car for the occasion; afterwards, they made the five-minute trip to the theatre in Hales Street. They sat in the parked car behind it to listen to the end of *Pick Of The Pops*, hearing the group had knocked 'Diamonds' off the top spot.

Once inside they did a quick soundcheck before going up to the dress circle for publicity shots. While there, Shapiro wandered over to Ringo's drum kit and started playing. She asked, 'Why do drummers always make faces?' Ringo replied, 'Because they concentrate.' A thaw in the weather had allowed Coventry City to play its first game since 29 December the day before. However, a new freezing spell was about to start.

❝ I'd made my chart debut in 1960 and at the beginning of 1963 was on my way to a Top 10 hit with 'Up On The Roof'. There were lots of tours going on around that time, and I joined the Helen Shapiro one at the beginning of February. We'd be arriving in one town, just as another tour was leaving. We travelled around together on the tour coach, and I was always sitting next to John. If they were writing, Paul and John would go down to the back of the coach, and someone would come up and take their place. I remember John and Paul saying they were thinking of running up to the microphone together and shaking their heads and singing 'Whoooo!' I said, 'You can't do that. They'll think you're a bunch of poofs.' When I was on the coach, I preferred to look out of the window.

I was standing up in the aisle of the coach next to Helen when I first heard 'Misery', with John playing it on the guitar. The boys had written it for Helen and although she liked it, she felt it was a bit too manly for her. I joked with them 'Well, don't waste it, I'll record it!' I was about halfway through recording an album at the time. I'd record for a couple of days, then be back on the tour again. I recorded 'Misery' in Studio Number One at Abbey Road and put it on the album. Unfortunately, John didn't appreciate Bert Weedon's guitar playing. I bumped into him at Dick James' office shortly after, and he said, 'Who's that on guitar? He's crap!' He said, 'Why didn't you get me to play guitar?' I told him it was because I thought he'd be too busy, and never told him that I had picked Bert specially!

During the tour, we were due to play at 'Newsome's' Theatre in Coventry. We all called it 'Newsome's' after the guy who owned it, Sam Newsome. He'd get all the big acts to play there. It was like an out-of-town London Palladium. On this occasion I decided to hire a car, as I wanted to visit the cathedral to see the giant tapestry. I'd met Graham Sutherland, the artist, at a cocktail party, and had told him I'd go and see it when I was in town. Three of the Beatles joined me, Paul and George, and either John or Ringo. Anyway, there was just the four of us. We parked in the car park next to the cathedral and went inside. After a while, one of them nudged me and said, 'Come on, we've got to get out of here and listen to the radio!' They wanted to hear if 'Please Please Me' had gone to number one. So we crowded round the car radio, and let out a huge cheer when we heard on *Pick Of The Pops* that they had reached the top slot. They played their hearts out on that tour, like everyone else, but it would have taken a blowtorch to get those audiences to warm to us. **"**

KENNY LYNCH, SINGER AND ENTERTAINER, HENLEY-ON-THAMES, OXFORDSHIRE

MONDAY 25 FEBRUARY

George celebrated his 20th birthday, enjoying a day off from the tour. Brian Epstein gave him a gold cigarette lighter. At 10am, George Martin and engineers Norman Smith and A. B. Lincoln began mixing and making mono and stereo masters of the group's debut LP.

The group drove from Coventry to Leigh for a show at the Casino Ballroom in Lord Street. This night heralded the first of the club's 'It's NEMS Enterprises' Fabulous "Showdance"' events. Epstein had approached Joe and Winnie Brierley, who ran the club, about booking the venue for four consecutive weeks to feature artists on his roster. The Brierleys agreed even though they had never heard of the Beatles. Tickets were 5/- and fans were advised – 'Jiving From 7.30pm – Be Early!' Printers Collins & Darwell were responsible for printing the tickets. The owner's son printed off some extra and sold them in a nearby pub. Despite a newspaper ad proclaiming, 'They are all sold. Therefore there will be no admission at the door without a ticket,' many arrived ticketless to encounter doormen Peter Hume and Vinnie Hilton standing behind locked glass entrance doors. Epstein made it more difficult for local fans, laying on coaches to bring fans from Merseyside, parking along Lord Street and into nearby Silk Street in front of the entrance. Rows of seats were put up to keep fans from reaching the stage.

While Johnny Prior's resident group were performing, Epstein took the Beatles to the Ellesmere on East Lancashire Road for dinner. The group performed 'Please Please Me' at the end of their second half-hour set, and Paul thanked the crowd for making it number one. They put on their leather and corduroy overcoats, signed autographs and drove home to Liverpool in two cars.

The following day Joe Brierley visited Winnie, suffering from diabetes, in hospital in nearby Wigan. Asked what he thought of the Beatles, Joe said, 'Bloody awful.' The *Leigh Chronicle* reported that, 'The balconies were packed solid with fans. Some girls faked fainting spells to try to get backstage to see their idols. Others sat on friends' shoulders to get a better view.' Winnie recalled the night 'was really the start of the rock'n'roll era at the Casino. At first we wouldn't allow modern dancing but we had to give way and move with the times.'

❛ My career in music started off in 1956 when I formed the skiffle group the Dominoes with Clive Powell, Johnny Hodgkinson, Kenny Fillingham, Eric Eastham and on tea chest, Bill Jones. By 1957 we were playing around the country at American air force bases. I worked down the pit during the day at Bedford Colliery and played music by night. The last week in May and first week in June each year were known as 'Wake's Weeks', when the pits and cotton mills closed down, and everyone had a holiday.

During the Wake's Weeks of 1959, I went on holiday to Butlins in Pwllheli, North Wales. The resident group was Rory Blackwell and the Blackjacks. Rory was a friend of mine, and when he had to sack two of the group for misbehaving, he asked me if I could help him out. I felt I really needed the time off, I was on holiday after all, so I declined, but recommended my groupmate Clive, who was playing at the camp's Pig and Whistle pub that week. We went along to see him that night, and Rory was knocked out by him. Clive agreed to join the group for the rest of the week, which also meant that he wouldn't be able to join me in the camp's annual People's National Talent Contest. I was going to go it alone, but in the end asked another friend to join me. Wigan had just won the rugby league Challenge Cup final down at Wembley, so I decided to sing a song Clive had, that I had set to the tune of Lonnie Donegan's 'The Grand Coulee Dam'. It went 'Wigan have thirteen wonders...' and told the story of the match. It went down a storm! The only person who didn't approve was my mate Rory Storm. He and his group the Hurricanes had also entered the competition. Rory thought it wasn't really the right thing to do in the competition, different lyrics set to someone else's song. I pointed out that he spent his time doing cover versions, so what was the difference! I beat him though, like I always did – he was a great mover but couldn't sing much! His drummer at the time was a lad from Liverpool called Ritchie Starkey. Clive was offered a full-time job with the other Rory and ended up moving down to London and gaining fame as Georgie Fame.

The Dominoes continued to play around the local pubs and clubs in the north-west and by 1963 changed their name to the Beat Boys. We signed a contract with Decca and brought out a single produced by Joe Meek called 'That's My Plan'. My wife June ran the bars at the Casino. The week before the Beatles' performance, the Beat Boys were the featured act, but on this particular night I was out watching a local group, so June asked Joe Brierley if she could bring our 3-year-old son Paul to the show. Afterwards June told me that they had gone backstage to meet the group. They asked after me and Paul McCartney sat my Paul on his lap and they all signed a photo of themselves on which Paul wrote 'To Little Paul, from Grandad Paul.' Sadly, in the intervening years the photo got lost. June told me they sat in the front row and Ringo kept looking at Paul moving his head from side to side. ❜

RONNIE CARR, MUSICIAN, LEIGH, GREATER MANCHESTER

TUESDAY 26 FEBRUARY

The package tour resumed with two shows at 6.25pm and 8.40pm at the 1,487-seater Gaumont Palace in Corporation Street, Taunton, Somerset. The shows were in competition with Modern Dancing for absolute beginners at the Taunton School of Ballroom Dancing, a weekly whist drive at the Old Folks' Rest Centre and a plea to come 'Courting!... and join the Young Conservatives at the Shire Hall.'

Shapiro, still suffering from laryngitis, missed the shows, with current 'Tell Him' chart maker Billie Davis filling in for her and Danny Williams, promoting his new single 'My Own True Love', a vocal version of Max Steinar's *Gone With The Wind* theme, topping the bill. Davis recalled her experience. 'I remember the

Beatles sitting in the front row watching me rehearse. I was having terrible trouble with them as they'd been on the road a few weeks and I was having to lock my dressing-room door.'

The *Somerset County Gazette*'s reviewer wrote, 'The Beatles, a vocal-instrumental quartet whose style is reminiscent of the Tex/Mex originals, the long-standing Crickets, came over well aurally, but in parts their act was rather amateurish. Their 'Beautiful Dreamer' and 'Please Please Me' did them justice, as did most of their punchy numbers, such as 'Long Tall Sally' and a Cookies' original 'Chains'. But as soon as they relaxed the pace to vocalise Acker Bilk's 'A Taste Of Honey' their co-ordination fell to pieces.' The *Somerset County Herald* commented, 'The audience received with most enthusiasm an orgy of dissonant electronic noises from the Beatles, who have crashed the Top 20 like a space-ship to the moon with 'Please Please Me'. Vocally nasal and instrumentally catarrhal-sounding, these four Liverpudlians made heavy weather of 'A Taste Of Honey' but blew up a storm of excitement with 'Long Tall Sally' and 'Keep Your Hands Off My Baby.'

> ❛ It was 1962 I was 15 years old and working in an office. One day a friend of mine told me a neighbour of hers had told her about a new group by the name of the Beatles. She said that they were very good and very different and if we had a chance to go and see them we must do so. Great news when we heard that the Helen Shapiro show was coming to the Gaumont in Taunton and the Beatles were performing. Taunton was only a short distance from us. We managed to get tickets and transport, with the little money we had saved. We had no idea what to expect but were very excited. The Beatles were the supporting act and came on as the last act of the first half. We were amazed at their hair, their clothes and their cheeky banter. They were so full of fun and when they started to play we were mesmerised.
>
>
>
> We just wanted more of them. We saved for their records and tried to keep up with all the up-to-date news. We heard that they were performing in Weston that July and they were headlining. We had to get some tickets. We were so lucky we managed to be in the front row. I will never forget that day. I was facing Paul and I fell in love with him. When the show finished, we rushed to the back door to see if we could catch them coming out but our coach was due to leave so we weren't able to stay any longer. We were very disappointed.
>
> Records, photographs or any memorabilia which I could get hold of I would cherish. Posters went up on the bedroom wall. I saved like mad so that I could keep up with the single and LP records which they produced. The *Hard's Day Night* movie was sat through many times. In November 1964 they came to Bristol and played at the Colston Hall – I had to go. As we had problems finding transport I asked my parents if they would take us. They agreed and decided that they would like to see the show. Although they sat at the back I am sure they had a shock when all the girls started screaming (including me). My parents said after it was an experience they probably would not repeat, but they sort of enjoyed it (well Mum did if not Dad). It was impossible not to get caught up in the mania but I was glad that I had seen them at the beginning of their career. Unfortunately, that was the last time I saw them live. What a privilege to have been there at the beginning. I will always be grateful that the Beatles came to the West Country, which is a place that is usually forgotten. ❜
>
> **JENNY PONSILLO, OFFICE ADMINISTRATOR, STREET, SOMERSET**

WEDNESDAY 27 FEBRUARY

The tour bus set off on one of its longest journeys, travelling close to 300 miles to the eighteen hundred-seater Rialto Theatre in Fishergate, York, Yorkshire, with a slight detour to Bristol to pick up the Kestrels, local boys who had spent the night in their own beds. Snow still lay on the ground in York. The night before, the Rialto had hosted a Pancake Tuesday Bingo night with hundreds of lucky charms given away, including one of solid gold, along with a giant box of chocolates and 4lb of Best Steak, two ladies' handbags and, as always, the guaranteed prize money.

The two shows – at 6.40pm and 8.45pm – were the second in a package of five concerts at the venue, with Brian Hyland and Little Eva having appeared two weeks earlier. The Beatles returned on 13 March, two further shows were scheduled for 27 March with Joe Brown, the Tornados and Susan Maughan and as well as a final 3 April show with Cliff Richard and the Shadows. John Hattersley-Colson, who managed the Rialto with Derek Lacy, remembered the Beatles as 'nice young lads. There were no airs and graces with them. They were ordinary Lancashire lads like me. The show was fantastic. It went very well indeed. People who went never forgot it. When they became really famous I thought, "I had a mug of tea with those lads and a laugh and a joke and a giggle with them."'

Between the two shows, fans went round to the side of the theatre, where photos rained down on them, thrown from their dressing room by the group. *The Yorkshire Evening Press* reported that, 'In the absence of Helen Shapiro – a flu victim – last night's York Rialto package show was a little like Hamlet without the Prince of Denmark... Screams of delight greeted the Beatles, a Liverpudlian quartet who obliged with, among others, the songs they wrote themselves and which have taken them into the Hit Parade – 'Love Me Do' and 'Please Please Me'. The paper's Stacey Brewer had already reviewed 'Please Please Me'. 'Their first release was so unusual that some people didn't quite know how to take them. But talent is one thing that shows even more than detergent whiteness. And the Beatles have plenty of talent.' Following the second show, they walked across the road to spend the night at the Edinburgh Arms, a four-room B&B run by Merrik and Muriel Bousfield.

> ❝ I first saw the Beatles on TV, just after the six o'clock news with Bill Grundy. They did two numbers I think, one of them was definitely 'Love Me Do' and I think the other might have been 'A Taste of Honey'. From that day on I was totally a Beatles fan. In February 1963 I saw an advert in *The Yorkshire Evening Press* for tickets for a Helen Shapiro show with the Beatles at the bottom of the bill. I was 20 at the time and took my 12-year-old cousin Lyn Tatterton with me. They came back the following month, but I couldn't get to see them. I wasn't too upset after I found that John, my favourite, didn't appear because he was ill. They came back for a third visit, this time with Roy Orbison. I went with a friend from work by the name of Gerald Harrison. Gerry was a fan of Roy Orbison and wanted to go and see him, and I of course wanted to see the Beatles, so we decided to go together. Later Gerry became known as Dustin Gee, the comedian and impressionist. Anyway, it was a great show, even though you couldn't hear anything for screaming girls. I began cutting out every article and picture of the Beatles I could find and would stick them on the walls of my print room at Shepherd's, where I worked. After a while my boss

thought it was time I stopped but, totally ignoring him, I carried on until every bit of wall was covered in photos of the Fab Four. My room was put on the tourist trail for visiting dignitaries, which I thought was hilarious. The next year I made a trip to London to go to the *NME* Poll-Winners' Concert at the Empire Pool, Wembley. I went with two friends and we crammed into a little two-tone blue Austin Metropolitan, and headed down the old A1 to the Empire Pool. We must have left really early, because we were the first ones in the car park. I can't remember anything specific about the show, but I know we headed back the same day, feeling exhilarated. **"**

AVERIL ADDISON, PRINT OFFICE ASSISTANT, YORK, WEST YORKSHIRE

THURSDAY 28 FEBRUARY

'**P**lease Please Me' stayed at number one on the week's *Disc* chart and number 2 in the *NRM* for a second week. The tour continued, heading south-west to the 1,525-seater Granada in Castle Gates, Shrewsbury, Shropshire. On the three-hour trip, John and Paul wrote 'From Me To You', subsequently described by Dick James as a 'perfect Tin Pan Alley song'.

When they arrived at the venue for the 6.15pm and 8.30pm shows, they played the song to the returning Helen Shapiro, with Paul on piano while John stood by his side singing. John later told the *NME*, 'There we were, not taking ourselves seriously. Just fooling about on the guitar. This went on for a while. Then we began to get a good melody line and we really started to work at it. Before that journey was over, we'd completed the lyric, everything.' Later in the year, Helen Shapiro took some credit for the writing of the song in an interview with *Hit Parade*. 'We were travelling in the coach one day, from one town to another, and John and Paul got out their guitars. I had my banjo and we all played around for a little while. Suddenly John and Paul got the inspiration for a melody, and before you could say 'Beatle' they were off to a little musical world of their own! Within minutes they'd got the first outline of 'From Me To You' and they asked me what I thought of it. I told them the truth – it was great!'

Unbeknownst to the group, they received their second royalty statement from EMI.

" By 1963, the Kestrels had been together for about five years. We'd had a fair amount of success as a live act, and made plenty of appearances on TV and radio, including *Six-Five Special*, *Workers Playtime*, *Saturday Club*, *Easy Beat* and were regulars on an Adam Faith TV series in late '62. We'd released a handful of singles on Pye, Decca and Piccadilly, but hadn't had a hit.

When we were booked on that January 1963 tour, no one had really heard of the Beatles. We thought everyone would come to see bill-topper Helen Shapiro who had had a couple of number one hits to her credit. We were all travelling to a gig by coach and John and Paul were seated near the back of the bus and using the time to work on a song. I was sitting towards the middle of the coach and could hear what was going on. Suddenly I heard the recognisable voice of Kenny Lynch saying, 'I can't listen to any more of this crap' and he came towards me to find a seat nearer the front. Kenny had had hit records and also wrote songs and thought that what Paul and John were working on was, in his book, 'crap.'

Months went by and we were booked to tour with the Beatles again, but this time they were the bill-toppers. We would go on before them and it was quite a struggle. The fans had been working up to a fever pitch for the Fab Four – not us. They screamed and shouted for them and frankly didn't want to know us. I suppose were we keeping them from their idols. To be honest, 1963 was a bit of a blur and I can't remember that much about it. So the month after we finished our second tour with the Beatles, Roger Cook came up to London, and spent a week learning his part for the Kestrels, and we were back on the road. However, soon after we decided to split, so he was only in the group for about three or four months. We completed all the bookings we had at that stage, one of which was a tour with Herman's Hermits, and it was on that tour that Roger and I wrote our first song together, 'You've Got Your Troubles'. We wrote it in a dressing room. We didn't know at the time it was going to be so big, but we did think we had something not bad.

During a break in that tour, we came back down to London and made a demo of the song. We'd been signed to Mills Music by Tony Hiller, who was also a big songwriter, and he played it to Noel Walker, who went on to produce the song for the Fortunes, but it was Cyril Gee who played the demo to George Martin. Although George loved it, he was more interested in the sound that we made. He was in the process of leaving EMI and forming his own company, AIR London, and was looking for acts to sign to his new label, and Cyril asked us if we'd care to meet him. We were the first signing on his new label, and the first single we cut for him was Paul McCartney's 'Michelle' as David and Jonathan. The name was given to us by George's wife Judy, from the biblical connection. We had a Top 20 hit with 'Michelle' in the US and when we toured the radio stations over there, hundreds of girls would be there after rumours spread that we were John and Paul promoting the single incognito. From the time that Roger joined the Kestrels and we wrote 'You've Got Your Troubles' we really haven't looked back.

Around the mid-'70s, when we had been writing together for about twelve years, Roger had had enough. The final straw was when we were banned from *Top Of The Pops*. Tony Burrows, Roger and I, along with Johnny Goodison had recorded a song called 'Lady Pearl' for Decca under the name Currant Kraze. As we were the producers of the song, Stanley Dorfman, who used to be the producer of the programme, rang me. It wasn't long after we'd had the situation where Tony sang three songs on the show one night, and I had done a couple. Dorfman said, 'We want them on *Top of The Pops* next week, could you give me the name of the group?' So I said, 'Yes, of course. Tony Burrows...' He interrupted and said, 'Wait a minute. It's not another...?' I said, 'Yes, it's our usual studio group.' He wouldn't use us. We were effectively banned. He said, 'We are promoting you, it's not appropriate.' When that happened, that was it for Roger. He said, 'That's it. If we can't have success and people accept it, then I'm going to America where success is embraced not envied.' He begged me to go, but I said no. Roger and I are still in touch. He went on to write hits for other people, and so did I, so it worked out pretty well. 🟥

ROGER GREENAWAY, SINGER/SONGWRITER, COMPOSER AND PRODUCER, WALTON-ON-THAMES, SURREY

MARCH
And the screaming begins

FRIDAY 1 MARCH

'Please Please Me' enjoyed its second week at number one in the *NME* chart – with Frank Ifield dropping to number 2. By way of a thank you to their fans, an ad in the paper read, 'You've PLEASED PLEASED Us! – Thank You, Folks – Paul, John, George, Ringo'. The single replaced 'Diamonds' at the top of the *Melody Maker* chart as well. The paper announced a 'Radio series and tour for Beatles', listing appearances on *Side By Side*, *Saturday Club*, *On The Scene* and *Easy Beat*. Epstein revealed that 'they will possibly be doing three or four of the new series, which will be transmitted between April and June.' A string of upcoming live appearances were also mentioned: at the Royal Albert Hall, the Pigalle

Club, a week in Sweden, a package tour with Duane Eddy from 18 May to 9 June, a Merseybeat showcase headlining twelve dates during April, May and June. The paper also revealed the group had planned a holiday in the Canary Islands in April and May.

The tour continued with two performances at the 2,120-seater Odeon in Lord Street, Southport, Lancashire at 6.25pm and 8.40pm. The weather was still shocking – visibility in parts of the north-west was down to 25 yards, resulting in a spate of accidents. Fans phoned the cinema after rumours began circulating that Helen Shapiro wouldn't be performing. Queues stretched into Lord Street and Post Office Avenue and scores of police were deployed to control the fans. The first house, which was by no means a sell-out, left through a rear exit – things had become chaotic out front as fans waited to get into the second show. The *Southport Visiter* covered the show, commenting that the people of the town had 'no lack of enthusiasm' and that 'mothers and fathers, even grandfathers, and teenagers bobbed to the music as the curtains parted.' The paper also felt that the Beatles 'were as robust as ever'.

❝ At school I had a very keen interest in photography and I started off by photographing our class football team and taking two or three pictures during the sports days. I joined the Litherland Photographic Society and got a lot of encouragement from them. In my spare time I used to sail dinghies up at Southport and by chance met a gentleman who was the senior photographer for the local newspaper, the *Southport Visiter*. We got chatting and he asked, 'Do you really want to be a photographer?' and I said, 'Yes.' I was just coming up to 16 and he said, 'Finish your schooling and then give me a ring.' Twelve months later he said if I still wanted to be a photographer I should turn up at their office the next Monday and show him what I knew. Well, it turned out I couldn't really do as much as I thought! Luckily they had an opening for an Article Pupil and when he asked if I'd be interested, I jumped at the opportunity.

My parents had made sure I had a decent suit for my first day at work and, after some introductions, I was taken into the dark room. The chief photographer, a rather gruff gentleman called Mr Sadler, said, 'Ah, the new man, right, let's not get that new suit ruined. Take your jacket off and put these overalls on, your first job is to scrub down these benches!' So from thinking I was going to be clicking and snapping from day one, I was cleaning the darkroom, learning about the chemicals, and what could go wrong etc. It turned out to be a very good grounding.

They put me through a course at Wednesbury College of Technology for two block release courses. I was given a five by four plate camera for training, and there was great excitement when the girls in the office heard the Beatles were coming to play at the Odeon. I managed to tag along and get onto the stage behind the curtains before the group came on. They appeared by the side of the stage and were waiting to be introduced for their slot in the first house when a policeman approached John Lennon and asked for an autograph. He had a piece of paper but no pencil. John responded in typical fashion saying, 'Ho ho ho, an officer without a pencil.' Someone came up with one and I quickly took a picture. I was preparing to take a second shot when two security guys grabbed me and threw me off the stage! I landed in the area between the organ and the seats and was told I wouldn't work with the Beatles again. I was standing where I landed staring up at the stage and remember all the girls jumping up and down and screaming.

The night I was thrown off stage for taking a photograph of the Beatles has stuck with me, although the photograph I took that evening has disappeared – we had a whole file of Beatles photographs that was put out on loan from our Liverpool office which subsequently went missing and has never turned up again sadly. 🟊

JOHN DALY, PHOTOGRAPHER, THORNTON, MERSEYSIDE

SATURDAY 2 MARCH

The tour crossed over the Pennines to the 2,271-seater City Hall in Barker's Pool, Sheffield, Yorkshire, with two shows at 6.10pm and 8.40pm. The *Sheffield Star* review was headlined 'Beatles Deserve The Top Billing', saying that 'Halfway down the bill – in small letters – are a group called the Beatles. But don't let the fact that they are not top of the bill mislead you. The Beatles are NEWS... Now their latest disc 'Please Please Me' stands at the top of the hit parade and they are currently the hottest new property on the pop scene. And although this is their first stage tour, they proved that they deserve every bit of praise heaped upon them – they write most of their own tunes, and are first-class instrumentalists and sing extremely well. They were the hit of the show.'

City (Oval) Hall, Sheffield
ARTHUR HOWES
presents
THE HELEN SHAPIRO
SHOW
Saturday, 2nd March, 1963
FIRST HOUSE
at **6.10** p.m.
Doors open at 5.50 p.m.
PLATFORM - 3/6
(UNRESERVED)
(Front Entrance)
Booking Agents: Wilson Peck Ltd.

The moment the group finished the second show, they headed back west again, taking the A628 to Didsbury, a suburb south of Manchester. There they made a live appearance on TV show *ABC At Large* in Studio Two of the Studio Centre on Parrs Wood Road at 11pm. The clip of their appearance on *Thank Your Lucky Stars* from 17 February was shown. Gerry Marsden was also featured on the show; he had recently announced that a John Lennon song called 'Pretty Little Girl' was being considered for his follow-up to 'How Do You Do It?'

Presenter David Hamilton later recalled passing the group and Epstein on the way to the announcers' booth and hearing Epstein castigate one of them for not going to the dentist. He recalled Epstein as charming and articulate, but 'Messrs Lennon, McCartney, Harrison and Starr were a different story. They acted as though they were above it all. Other groups were pleased to be on TV to advertise their wares, the Beatles' attitude was clearly that they didn't need it.' Following the interview, the group drove back to Sheffield, arriving at their hotel around 1am.

> ❛ I was born in 1935 and have lived in Sheffield all my life. When we were married, my husband Bryan and I moved to a house in Gleadless, on the outskirts of the city. One of my special memories is of my 28th birthday. Bryan and I didn't have much money at the time, we had a little daughter, Lindsay, who was four, and I had given up my job as a wages clerk at Moore & Wright. But Bryan was determined to give me a birthday treat. He knew I liked Helen Shapiro, so he bought two tickets to see her at the City Hall. We packed Lindsay off to her grandmother Ida and set off into town on the bus. Looking towards the stage, there were two big lion statues. Between the lions were steps that lead up to the stage from the dressing rooms. At either side of the lions were seats. They were cheap, because obviously you were looking at the back of the stars! Helen Shapiro came on, and she was good, but... then came the Beatles. They were wearing full-drape burgundy suits, with shoelace ties. They were just up and coming at the time, but they were absolutely fantastic, and what was so nice about them, they turned round, and played to the audience that they would normally have their backs to! They hadn't forgotten about the poor people behind them. The atmosphere was magical. Not far from where I live in Gleadless, there was a ballroom called the Azena. It was a dance hall and was open mostly on a Saturday evening, and a few weeks later, they came back to play there. I couldn't go because I was ill, but the whole area was packed with cars and youngsters going to the show. ❜
>
> **SHIRLEY GROUCUTT, OFFICE WORKER, GLEADLESS, YORKSHIRE**

SUNDAY 3 MARCH

The Beatles' stint on the Helen Shapiro-headlining tour came to an end at the 2,151-seater Gaumont in Piccadilly, Hanley, Staffordshire, with two shows at 6.15pm and 8.40pm. After the second show, the group popped into the Honeys' dressing room to say a fond farewell. John then asked *The Evening Sentinel* reporter Derek Adams, who was there to review the concert, where they could get some fish and chips. Adams recalled the evening, 'I watched both houses from the wings and recall the group larking around and pushing each other before they actually appeared before the screaming hordes that had solidly packed the venue. When they finished their act they were all bathed in perspiration and both John and Paul dunked their heads beneath the dressing room's cold water tap. We chatted in the dressing room for about three quarters of an hour, which included the official interval, while girls screamed at the dressing room window from the outside pavement below us. Ringo actually chucked a glass of water through the open dressing room window to the delight of the screamers.' After the show, hundreds of teenagers gathered outside the stage door hoping to catch a glimpse of the artists. When asked by the *Staffordshire Weekly Sentinel* about being mobbed, the group said, 'You get used to it. The time to start worrying is when it doesn't happen.'

At 11.30pm, Adams drove to Kelly's fish and chip shop in nearby Etruria, with the group following him in their van. They sat down at a table and had fish and chips with bread and butter and tea – and after much argument Ringo paid. At about half past midnight, they went their separate ways – Adams back to his bedsit in Basford and the Beatles to their digs at 6 Adventure Place at a theatrical landlady's. The Gaumont's manager Mr J. A. E. Ramsden commented that the gig was 'one of the most successful shows ever produced here! Adams, in his *Sentinel* review, headed 'Teenagers Give 'Pop Star' Helen A Great Welcome', wrote that, 'at times the enthusiasm of the audience was so great that compère Dave Allen had a difficult time restoring order before the show could continue.' Later in the year, Paul told journalist Peter Jones, 'That's why it was so important to do well on the Helen Shapiro tour. We knew the southerners were starting to buy our records and we [had] to prove ourselves to them. Till then, it really had been the Shadows. And we were a completely different sort of group to them.'

❛I grew up with my sisters, Anita and Pearl, the daughters of Jay Liddell, who was a drummer and band leader. Our father had Pearl take piano lessons while I learnt to play the drums. We began performing in our teens as the Liddell Triplets and appeared live in the Portsmouth area. Eve Taylor became our agent – she was also Adam Faith's agent and we toured with him in 1960.

We then toured with Cliff and the Shadows in Israel. We joined the Helen Shapiro tour in Bradford at the Gaumont [now performing as the Honeys]. Everyone travelled together by coach and there would be a van following with the Beatles' gear. We all had quite a laugh and the Beatles would pass around the words to half-written songs to see what we all thought. If someone started singing a popular song then we would all join in. The boys also enjoyed playing cards at the back of the coach. One song we used to sing onstage was 'Manyana' and the boys used to take the mickey and have a singalong on the bus. My sisters and I remember getting off the coach and fans asking if we were part of the Beatles. Although they had released 'Please Please Me', no one knew who made up the group. It was interesting watching their act from the side of the stage, but they certainly looked different with those haircuts. As the tour went on their popularity grew with fans screaming and queueing at the stage door and we realised something was happening. At the Gaumont in Hanley, the four of them came into our dressing-room after the show to say goodbye. They appeared to be excited but also sad to be leaving the show as I believe they were really enjoying the tour. John said, 'I'm sure we will meet up again', but unfortunately we never did. **❜**

VILMA HARVEY, SINGER AND ARTIST, FARLINGTON, HAMPSHIRE

MONDAY 4 MARCH

The group earned their first three-figure sum, being paid £100 for their sold-out performance at the Plaza Ballroom on the corner of Duke Street and Crab Street in St Helens, Lancashire. For their previous four visits, on consecutive Mondays in June and July the previous year, they earned a total of £100. It was their fifth appearance at the venue, part of the sixteen-venue Whetstone Circuit, and turned out to be their last. Once again, the local newspaper chose to ignore the visit - other than a classified advertisement that said the show was sold out. Instead, the paper wrote about Petula Clark ('Pet Is Now A Star In Paris') and reviewed the Newtown Players' thriller *Search By Night*. Following their performance, the group drove to London through the night before reaching the Hotel President in the early hours of the morning.

TUESDAY 5 MARCH

The group awoke in time to begin a series of photo shoots with EMI staffers John Dove and Edgar Brind. They went to EMI House, where they were snapped outside the building with George Martin and Dick James. Once inside, they went to Martin's fourth floor office and changed into suits, while Dove and Brind took photos of James and Brian Epstein. After changing, they were snapped outside the building on the spiral staircase that led down to the basement level. The entourage left for Abbey Road with Martin in tow – on the way, they drove to Montague Place and Malet Street, where they were shot standing around a parking meter, on which John placed his glasses.

Arriving at Abbey Road, Dove took a series of shots outside the front entrance. The group then gave a fifteen-minute interview to *Boyfriend*, published in its 11 May edition. Asked whether they got nervous at the recording studio, John replied, 'Well, everyone gets nerves, but we've found that the best way to get ourselves completely relaxed and make ourselves at home is with everyone in the studio.' George explained that they ran through the music for about ten minutes on their own, while Ringo added, 'We think that the results we get on record are more vital and live because we believe in doing the singing and playing together, and not recording them separately.' Paul was asked whether the relaxed manner in which they recorded had anything to do with their success. 'Yes,' he replied, 'It's our magic formula for making hits, and it's worked wonderfully so far. And we're going to keep it this way as long as the hits keep coming.'

The session began at 2.30pm with thirteen takes of 'From Me To You', the number written five days beforehand on the tour bus to Shrewsbury. Lennon recalled, 'We nearly didn't record it because we thought it was too bluesy at first, but when we'd finished it and George Martin had scored it with harmonica it was all right.' They also recorded thirteen takes of 'Thank You Little Girl', subsequently titled 'Thank You Girl'. They took an hour-and-a-half break at 5.30pm, adjourning to the canteen, before returning to record five takes of 'The One After 909'. Photographer Dezo Hoffmann took pictures of the group while they recorded. (Hoffmann was a staff photographer at the *NRM*. At an editorial meeting in 1962, he picked up a letter to the editor and a photo of the Beatles fell out. He asked the editor about doing a photo feature in Liverpool on the group, but was told it was too expensive to go to Liverpool. Hoffmann recalled, 'It took me three months to convince him to send me.')

> ❝ I started dancing at the age of three at Winnie Mac's Broadgreen School of Dance and Drama – in my opinion the best dance school in all of Liverpool (maybe in the world). I passed my Eleven Plus and had a place at Queen Mary Grammar School, but when they told me I had to stay until I was 16, I decided to go to Highfield in Broadgreen instead, as I knew I wanted to be dancing by then. By the age of 12, I was semi-pro in a double act called the Slick Chicks with my best friend Ann Harvey. During that time, up until I was 15, George Harrison was my first boyfriend. I left school at 15 and joined a circus with Digger Pugh's Aerial Ballet. At 16, I was part of the Ballet Montparnasse can-can troupe and met and fell in love with Paul McCartney. We had a fun teenage relationship.
>
> My brother, Alan Caldwell, was Rory Storm, aka 'Mr Showmanship', 'The Golden Boy', because of his charisma and talent. Our mum's chip butties, cheese barm cakes and constant kettle on in our house at 'Stormsville' in Broadgreen Road meant it was always full of music and musicians well into the early hours. My mum loved Paul, and I believe vice versa. On 5 March, the group were in London recording. Paul had called me and said he and Ringo were sharing the driving and would get back

to my house pretty late; that didn't matter 'cos we were a 'late house'. Mum, Rory and I waited for them – they arrived in the early hours tired out from the journey. Ringo had driven the last leg and he said they were so knackered that when coming through Old Swan, they'd run over a dog but were too tired to stop. I was horrified, I threw them out of the house in shock and Rory and I went walking all round the area to look for the dog. Of course, there wasn't one, it had been a joke! The end result of this was that Paul and I split up. My mum was most upset; one – because of how she felt about him, and two – because I never got my birthday present the next day.

Although Paul and I saw each other occasionally during the next summer season, it just wasn't the same, as I'd met and fallen in love with my future husband, Shane Fenton. We married a year later in 1964 and performed as a double act called Shane Fenton and Iris – The Personality Pair, which was a song and dance act and absolutely brilliant because I couldn't sing and he couldn't dance! Then we started a show group when show groups were all the rage and travelled all over the world. I've been so lucky to have such a wonderful family, and I've had a fabulous life. My time with Paul was one of many highlights of my teenage life and if he and Ringo hadn't made that silly remark, which wasn't true, about the dog, maybe, just maybe, my life would have turned out differently. 🔳

IRIS CALDWELL, DANCE AND DRAMA TEACHER, REIGATE, SURREY

WEDNESDAY 6 MARCH

After a morning off, the group drove to the Playhouse Theatre in Manchester to make a fifth and final appearance on *Here We Go*. Rehearsals began at 4pm, with the recording between 8pm and 8.45pm. They performed 'I Saw Her Standing There', 'Misery', 'Do You Want To Know A Secret' (the first of six performances of the song on radio in 1963) and 'Please Please Me'. Fellow guests were regulars Bernard Herrmann and the NDO, with the Trad Lads and Paul Andrews. Host Ray Peters congratulated the group on topping the chart with 'Please Please Me'.

THURSDAY 7 MARCH

The week's *Disc* reported that the Beatles had recorded their follow-up to 'Please Please Me' – which slipped a place in the Top 30, giving way to Cliff Richard and the Shadows' double A-side, 'Summer Holiday'/'Dancing Shoes'. The single dropped to number 3 in the *NRM* chart. The group joined Gerry and the Pacemakers, the Big Three, Billy J. Kramer with the Dakotas and DJ Bob Wooler for a one-night stand package, 'Mersey Beat Showcase', on the fourth floor of the Elizabethan Ballroom in Upper Parliament Street, Nottingham, now luxuriating in 50 degree weather. There were five more of these showcases through to 16 June, whenever all the acts were available at the same time.

Bob Sturgeon, a regional sales rep for Princes Foods, promoted the show after hearing 'Love Me Do'. He asked his friend Keith Gordon, a local schoolteacher at Ellis School, to compère the evening. Gordon recalled that Fan Club application forms were handed out at the door – one of which he got all four Beatles to sign on the back.

NEMS Enterprises organised two coaches to take eighty fans from Liverpool to the 7.30pm gig at a cost of £1.25 each. The coaches parked nearby in Wollaton Street, while the equipment van came down Parliament Terrace to the ballroom, which was situated above the Co-operative House. The Co-op proclaimed, 'You can obtain any of the top ten this week and every week in the luxurious record bar on the lower ground floor.' Stuart Dixon, who was working in the display department of the Co-op at the time, operated the lift to load the equipment up to the ballroom. He also had the group as his passengers but had no idea who they were.

Rob Taylor recalled that after the show ended, he 'nipped off quickly to the loo before me and my mates left for home. After a while wandering around, realised I was lost. One of the doors I randomly tried led into a sitting area where I could see some people chatting. When they heard the door open, they turned around and I could see that it was the Beatles. It could have been very awkward, me walking in on them like that, but they were very nice about it. They directed me to the toilet and I went on my way.' After the shows, the group took the hour-long trip north on the A60 to Mansfield, where they spent the night at the Swan Hotel.

❝ I was working at the Land Registry department of the Civil Service when I saw an advertisement for the 'Mersey Beat Showcase' coming to the Elizabethan Ballroom. I'd heard 'Love Me Do' on Radio Luxembourg. I asked a colleague, Alan Benjamin, if he would like to go, and he said, 'Yes', so I offered to get the tickets. They were being sold at Kenton Coopers, the music shop 50 yards or so down from the Ballroom. I went along probably two or three days after reading about the show and without any rushing around or queuing, managed to get two tickets, one of which was ticket number one! The tickets said 'Rock and Roll Concert Dance, starring the Beatles All Star Show', priced 6/6, including a buffet – I don't remember that bit!

On the night of the show, I went to Alan's house for tea and his dad ran us in to town. During the show, there was no hysteria, certainly no screaming. The stage where the groups were playing wasn't raised up that much from the dance floor, perhaps no more than about a foot, and the only thing protecting the groups from the audience was a couple of ropes between some chrome posts. I thought all of the groups were good in their own way, but for me the Big Three were the group that for us musically were the most impressive. Probably they were slightly older than the Beatles, by a year or two and had also been to Hamburg. They were only a trio, but my goodness couldn't they shift it! They were more a driving rock'n'roll group. The Beatles were equally driving but they were starting to be more melodic and put their own stamp on things, which of course became the secret for their success. They certainly stood out because of their appearance – the cutaway Beatles suit collars, cuban heels, and haircuts.

The following year, I was the bassist with the Farran Kristy Big Six and we were down at Abbey Road auditioning. I was chatting with Mal Evans outside the studio and he let me sit inside Paul McCartney's newly delivered Aston Martin DB5, which had an in-car record player for vinyl 45s! I then met the man himself when I found myself in the Gents' loo with him. We talked briefly and he showed interest in the fact that Bendix, known mainly for washing machines, were making amps as well. Later he came to look at my amp and played on my Fender Jazz Bass. Unfortunately, I wasn't in the studio when he popped in so I never got the opportunity of seeing Paul McCartney play my bass guitar, but he did invite me down to Studio Two – they were recording 'Every Little Thing'. George Martin and Ringo were experimenting with various sounds and Ringo was beating a tea chest with a microphone stuffed underneath it. Nothing came of the audition though. **❞**

BOB WHITE, PUBLIC RELATIONS EXECUTIVE, MAPPERLEY, NOTTINGHAMSHIRE

FRIDAY 8 MARCH

Readers of *Melody Maker* were greeted with the front-page news that country singer Patsy Cline had been killed in a plane crash. The paper also revealed that the Beatles were to give a charity concert in Liverpool on 12 June, with the proceeds going to the NSPCC, 'as a token of their appreciation of the young people of the city, who made their success possible.'

'Please Please Me' was also knocked off the top spot in the *NME* chart by 'Summer Holiday' – though remained at number one in the *Melody Maker* chart. In an article headed 'Beatles Almost Threw 'Please Please Me' Away', John told the *NME*'s Alan Smith that 'we almost abandoned it as the B-side of 'Love Me Do!' Imagine that – a number that could get us to the top, just tucked away!' The paper also incorrectly reported that the 'Beatles wax three more'. If being toppled by Cliff wasn't bad enough, Paul was fined £5 by Liverpool City Magistrates for speeding; it wouldn't be for the last time that year.

The group travelled on the A1 north to Harrogate, Yorkshire, for a performance at the Royal Hall in Ripon Road. Local promoter Derek Arnold had booked them for a dance at the venue having seen them in Liverpool in 1962. With an estimated one thousand crammed onto the dance floor, there was little room for dancing. After setting up their gear in the hall, George and Ringo wandered through the town. During the group's two sets, Ringo discarded some broken sticks. Ricky Fenton and the Apaches closed the show; afterwards, while clearing up, lead guitarist Bob Mason's father saw Ringo's sticks and took them as a souvenir. Mason later commented that the group looked 'quite different to any other musos we had seen – quite long hair for that time, although not really long – but just for those times. They had leather coats on and looked like French art students.' They were paid £75 for their two half-hour sets.

'In 1962 I met up with this local quartet called the Apaches who were looking for a singer. Bob Mason was the lead guitarist, Dennis Wardman the bassist, with Dave Reed on keyboards and John Cowley on drums. We only played local gigs, youth clubs, etc., but we had to step very quickly from a fun, pastime type of group to semi-professional status. We had started playing further afield, so buying a van and hiring a manager cum driver was essential. So Bob's father was elected. He had met Derek Arnold who was booking us for town halls throughout Yorkshire. Early in 1963 we were told we were to play our own Royal Hall with a group called the Beatles, who had just returned from Hamburg. We'd already heard 'Love Me Do' but didn't make the connection at the time. Normally we would have at least an hour or so journey to a gig but this was different as it was in our own home town. We had got to the Royal Hall early evening and set up our gear onstage.

When the Beatles turned up they had to carry their own equipment in and on to the stage with the help of one roadie. I remember them being very humorous. Later in the dressing room, we were talking guitars as we prepared to go onstage. At the time I had a Hagstrom Jumbo semi-acoustic electric guitar, which cost me about £80. I still have it! George was showing interest because it looked similar to the Gibsons they used, which cost about £200. George, John and Paul all had a strum and were impressed. After the show I invited them down to my parents' house to a buffet and a beer, but John declined the offer as they were recording in London the next day (apparently that wasn't true) and playing a gig the same night. Soon it was to be over but memories still linger. What an honour to go onstage before and after the Beatles – never to be forgotten. When we played with them, I was two weeks shy of my 20th birthday. We played a fiftieth anniversary concert at the Royal Hall in March 2013 with a Beatles tribute band and I was 70. **J**

GEORGE McCORMICK, DRIVER, HARROGATE, NORTH YORKSHIRE

SATURDAY 9 MARCH

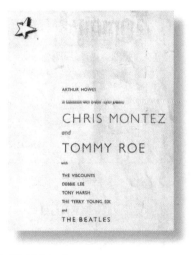

The group headed back down the A1, a four-hour journey through a snowbound countryside, to begin another nationwide tour – only five days since the previous one had ended. They opened at the 2,468-seater Granada in Barking Road, East Ham, London, supporting 'America's Exciting' Chris Montez and 'America's Fabulous' Tommy Roe (the group had been performing Roe's hit 'Sheila' on and off since the previous September). Montez wondered, 'Who are these guys the Beatles? I try to keep up to date with the British scene but I don't know their work.' He soon did. The twenty-one-date, twice-nightly tour, with tickets priced from 5/- to 9/6, also featured the Viscounts, Debbie Lee, the Terry Young Six, compère Tony Marsh, a local lad from Chingford, and on this one date, local group the Foresters, who performed before the show started and at the interval.

Their set for the tour featured 'Love Me Do', 'Misery', 'A Taste Of Honey', 'Do You Want To Know A Secret', 'Please Please Me' and 'I Saw Her Standing There'. The *NME*'s Andy Gray, under the headline 'Screams Acclaim Beatles, Montez, Roe', described Montez as 'eel-wriggling' and Roe as a 'sedate twister', but wrote that the Beatles 'stole top honours for entertainment and audience reaction... This all-action quartet from Liverpool has everything - exciting new sound, terrific instrumental attack, exhilarating solo and group vocal effects, and a fresh energy that leaves them (they told me later) limp at the end of each act. Admitted they still need better production, and a good choreographer, tailor and barber, but this apart, they are the most exciting newcomers in Britain today.' In *Melody Maker*, Chris Roberts didn't think much of either Roe or Montez, writing that 'Roe seemed to forget he was holding a microphone; Chris Montez just sang weakly. Neither had the semblance of a stage act.' He thought that the Beatles, described as 'The Merseyside marvels', 'could take it to the Americans, and that's about the highest compliment you could pay a British R&B-style group.' The audience included Shadows Hank Marvin and Bruce Welch and rocker Wee Willie Harris. The tour bus returned to the West End after the second show.

' I was born and bred in Poplar, East London, where in 1962 I met my future wife, Lynda. We were both still at school. At that time 'package tours' of pop stars would do the rounds of provincial theatres and cinemas. The tours presented a great opportunity to see your favourite stars of the day at an affordable price. Early in 1963 one such tour was advertised at my wife's local venue, the East Ham Granada, and it featured two American singers, Chris Montez and Tommy Roe. We both liked these artists so bought tickets for the show for the princely sum of 6/6 each. Not mentioned on the ticket was a supporting act called the Beatles. Their performance was impressive, a mixture of rock standards and some of their own compositions. John Lennon belting out 'Twist And Shout' is a standout memory. There wasn't the adulation and hysteria at that time but they were certainly the stars of that particular show. They were certainly different, as pop music in those days was dominated by solo artists and some instrumental groups.

Shortly after, the Beatles released their first album which everyone seemed to buy (we still have our copy). Then they had one hit after another, which led to Beatlemania, which we experienced in November 1963 when they returned to the Granada. We bought tickets, which were more expensive at 7/6, but I was working by then earning £5 per week so I could afford it. The atmosphere and noise on the night of the concert was amazing, surpassing that of West Ham football ground just down the road. The queue outside the cinema was mainly female and every time a door or window opened in the building it generated hysteria. The concert itself was a non-event for entertainment because you couldn't hear a thing for girls screaming. No elaborate sound systems and video screens in those days. Girls were getting hysterical and passing out, my younger sister amongst them. I'm sure my wife would have joined them if I hadn't been there! We remained Beatles fans for the rest of their career, but never got to another concert. **'**

JIM ROLLINSON, QUANTITY SURVEYOR, ROMFORD, ESSEX

SUNDAY 10 MARCH

The tour continued with two performances at 5.30pm and 8pm at the 1,935-seater Hippodrome in Hurst Street, Birmingham, Warwickshire. Roy Hayes recalled the evening: 'I was working at Chamberlain and Hookham (long gone now) in Park Street in the middle of Birmingham. We made industrial and domestic gas and electrical meters. My friends and I loved music. We were around at the birth of rock'n'roll in the 1950s, and loved Elvis, Chuck Berry, Little Richard, Buddy Holly, Fats Domino, Jerry Lee Lewis, the list goes on and on, buying all their singles. These stars had a big influence on Lennon and McCartney when the Beatles started, so in early 1963 we had heard of the group but really went to see Tommy Roe and Chris Montez. So my mates and I took the 32 bus from Hall Green into the city and the Hippodrome. The Beatles were on

in the first half. They were fantastic. We had not heard these songs played by a group before and the sound was great. They were solid with plenty of bass. When Chris Montez came on after the interval the audience started booing and chanting "We Want The Beatles!" I felt sorry for the guy. He really hadn't got a chance after the Beatles nor Tommy Roe for that matter, but the Beatles stole the show, they were just magic.' The company drove back to London in the coach after the second show.

I attended Stourbridge Girls High School and was part of a group of girls who all noticed this new group the Beatles. 'Which one do you like best?' etc. Somebody would like John, and somebody would like George, and so on. We collected all the photographs – anything that was in the paper, and we recorded *Saturday Club* from the radio if the Beatles were on. We'd cut out newspaper articles and stick them into scrap books. I bought 'Love Me Do,' and loved the B-side, 'P.S. I Love You'. Then a boyfriend bought me the *Please Please Me* LP.

Our local music shop was called Mark and Moody's, which was an old Stourbridge firm. There were two shops together, one sold stationery and the shop next door was dedicated solely towards records and music. I had a little blue-and-white Dansette record player, and a portable Dansette radio. I would record *Pick Of The Pops* on my brown-and-white tape recorder, and woe betide anyone who came into my bedroom when I was recording. I didn't have a socket in my bedroom, so I used to plug it into the light! I wasn't allowed to put pictures on my bedroom walls. I had pink wallpaper with roses on it. Instead, I had scrapbooks and would stick them all in there. We went through this craze of writing down the words to songs – I had notebooks, not just for the Beatles, but other songs as well. I used to get the *NME* at Mark and Moody's, but we would also get information on local gigs in the *Stourbridge Express*, the local newspaper. Our school was very strict, and the teachers certainly wouldn't have approved at all if they thought we were clammering to see the Beatles!

I saw them five times in total – four times in 1963, and once in 1964. The first time was at the Plaza in Old Hill. It was a freezing cold winter, and I don't recollect there being too many people there. I was as close to Paul McCartney as makes no difference. I can't even remember if there was a stage, I'm sure we were all on the one level. We were all dancing so close to them. I have a feeling my dad dropped me off and picked me up after the show, as although it was only a few miles away, it was difficult to get to by bus.

The next time we saw them was in March at the Hippodrome. I don't recall how we got there, but we all bought programmes, and after the show, went round to the back of the theatre hoping the Beatles would come out to sign autographs, or at least to catch a glimpse of them. After a while, we handed our programmes over the big wooden gate – it was very high, you couldn't see over it at all, and waited and waited. We were about to give up, when suddenly they came flying over the top of the gate! We all quickly grabbed what we could – some had been signed by all four Beatles, some only two or three, and all of them by Chris Montez, mine twice for some reason! Some signed photographs of Chris Montez then came flying over. It was raining and everything got a bit soggy. I'm still in touch with the same group of girls from school, and I'm the only one who still has her programmes from the Hippodrome and the Town Hall.

ANGELA GAULD, LANGUAGE TEACHER, KINVER, WORCESTERSHIRE

MONDAY 11 MARCH

On a day off from the tour, the group made their fourth and final appearance on Radio Luxembourg's *The Friday Spectacular* from EMI House's ground floor studio. After the show, on which 'Please Please Me' and 'Ask Me Why' were played, Dick James presented the group, Brian Epstein and George Martin with gold cufflinks. A scheduled appearance to tape a slot for *Saturday Club* from 5.30pm to 6.30pm was cancelled, with John under the weather and confined to his hotel room.

TUESDAY 12 MARCH

Fifteen-year-olds Pamela Black and Carol Lloyd started queuing outside the Cavern to buy tickets for the group's Good Friday performance on 12 April. 'The Beatles are fabulous and have marvellous personalities,' the girls professed, 'and they're not married.' Their parents didn't believe they'd stay in line for the month and they were proved to be right when the girls admitted that they left at 10pm every night and got back at 7.30 every morning.

The group continued the tour as a three-piece with John suffering from a heavy cold, returning to the Granada in Bedford, with shows at 7pm and 9.10pm. While on their way, the previous Wednesday's session of *Here We Go* was broadcast on the Light Programme, with 'I Saw Her Standing There' edited out, at 5pm. During the show, one girl in the audience shouted out for 'Love Me Do'. Paul stepped up to the mic and said, 'We can't,' no doubt because John wasn't on hand to play the harmonica solo. Paul sang 'Long Tall Sally' instead.

The *Bedford Record & Circular* was obviously less impressed, not even mentioning them in their review of the show. It was headlined 'Chris Montez Knocks Them At The Granada' and described him as 'a beat-bouncing bundle of energy' who 'took the stage in his grasp'. The only other two acts on the bill to get a mention were the Viscounts and Tommy Roe. Once again, the *Bedfordshire Times & Advertiser* didn't see fit to review the show. After the concert, the group had to be smuggled out of the cinema to get to their vehicle, which was waiting in Midland Road, before being driven to the Bridge Hotel where they spent the night.

> ❝ I went to Elstow's Abbey School just outside Bedford but couldn't wait to leave and get a job. I started as an apprentice compositor at local printing company Sidney Press which gave me a really good grounding. As soon as I was earning money, I started buying records – Cliff and the Shadows, Joe Brown, Billy Fury, etc. There was a stage show each month at the Granada in Bedford and we used to go along to whatever was on. We'd usually get in early to get our tickets ahead of time. It was a monthly outing along with my friend Dave Lack whom I'd grown up with; we saw all the big acts of

the day – the Beatles were just an incidental addition to the programme! As there were several dance halls in the area, we were regulars at the Saturday night dance at the Corn Exchange. Sunday night it was the Conservative 'Con' Club. We also went to see Ike and Tina Turner at the California Ballroom in Dunstable, so Bedfordshire was quite well served for shows and touring groups. But the Granada was the big one – the one all the big American acts would turn up at.

At the time it seemed that if you could pick up a guitar and you came from Liverpool or Manchester, you'd be a star! It was a 'pre-drinking' age for us so we'd hang out at Pascal's Coffee Bar, a popular meeting place for local youngsters. It occupied two floors above Glenfield Lawrence Motor Scooter shop in Mill Street. It was the early days of 'frothy' coffee, which was all new and rather American. Then a Wimpy Bar opened down the road – everything was sort of changing at that point and everything from across the Atlantic seemed to be hip. That was the big thing, hence all the American artists came over at the time. Almost every top of the bill was an American artist. You'd have a few British groups second or third down the bill. It's crazy to say, but I really only ended up seeing the Beatles because they were appearing on the bill one evening when we went on our regular monthly outing. I didn't know much about them, although I liked 'Love Me Do', but I didn't think it was anything special. I recall a bit of screaming and shouting, but that was getting pretty normal for all the groups by then. To be honest, it was just another night out at the Granada, with a good time had by all. After that, things really took off for the Beatles but it was still the early days. My nephew is always saying to me, 'The freedom you had was incredible, to be able to go off for the day and nobody bothered.' We just had to be back by teatime. They were innocent times. 🎵

ALAN WOODING, JOURNALIST, BEDFORD, BEDFORDSHIRE

WEDNESDAY 13 MARCH

The group – still a trio – set off on a 208-mile trip to York to the Rialto Theatre, where they had appeared only two weeks earlier. They played two shows at 6.40pm and 8.45pm, with tickets selling from 4/6 to 8/6. An ailing John showed up at Abbey Road to overdub his harmonica part on 'Thank You Girl'. Forgetting his instrument, he borrowed engineer Malcolm Davies', at the suggestion of Geoff Emerick, who was engineering the session. When he returned it, John told Davies that it 'tasted like a sack of potatoes'.

Arriving in York in pouring rain, the group signed autographs at the stage door for hundreds of waiting fans for nearly half an hour. During the interval, two fans left and went round to the stage door, shouting for the Beatles. George and Paul hung out of the top window and shouted, 'What do you want?' to which the girls replied, 'Come down.' They did not, but they did drop down signed photographs for them. The girls cried all the way home, later saying, 'It was the best day of our lives.' They later wrote to Paul, through the fan club, and he wrote back. They took turns holding on to the letter.

After the second house, manager Don McCallion put a stop to another autograph session when overeager fans tried to get through the stage door, an image captured by a *Yorkshire Evening Press* photographer. 'I've had enough,' McCallion told the newspaper. 'I warned them that if they didn't behave and form orderly queues I'd stop the session. Well they wouldn't play fair, so I'm having no more. I can't spare the staff to control them.'

The *Evening Press* reporter Stacey Brewer wrote that 'the boys struggled admirably with their hit number 'Please Please Me', while 'the rest of their programme was re-jigged for two-part singing'. After the show Brewer sat in the empty theatre with Paul and George chatting until the small hours. George told him that the group's next single had been written as they travelled from York to Shrewsbury after the last time they appeared at the Rialto.

❝ My parents, Merrik and Muriel Bousfield, ran the Edinburgh Arms pub on Fishergate in York from 1958 to 1967. I was 10 when we arrived there and had the excitement of many stars of the time staying with us when they were playing at the Rialto opposite. Even if they weren't staying, many would pop in for a drink before the show. I was a pupil at Queen Anne Grammar School for Girls, just off Bootham, and had been a fan of the Beatles from when I first heard 'Love Me Do' on the radio.

I was really excited when they were booked into the pub to stay in February 1963. I already had a ticket for the show – I recall the tickets going on sale at lunch time, and I had to miss school to stand in the queue, which was quite daring in those days! I have had polio since I was 4 and walked with a caliper, so I was lucky that we lived opposite the theatre and I didn't have to walk very far. When the group arrived, we asked them to come through to sign the book and I asked them for their autographs. They were so friendly and asked me if I was going to the show. They were really lovely, they weren't rude, they didn't think they were better than anyone else, they were just like one of us, very down to earth. John was perhaps a bit more outspoken than the other three, but not in your face as he was later on.

I went to the show with my younger brother, Merrick. He kept putting his hand over my mouth to stop me screaming. It was frustrating to say the least – I wanted so badly to scream! We had great seats, just three rows from the front. I recall the group had a full English breakfast the next morning, served by my brother – sadly I couldn't carry meals upstairs, so I missed out there! They stayed in two of our twin rooms at the end of a corridor, George sharing with Paul, and John with Ringo.

When they came the following month they stayed at the White Swan Hotel. It seemed that security issues meant they couldn't stay with us. But my dad got a letter from them apologising for not staying with us. Unfortunately, he didn't keep the letter! We were lucky enough to be friends with the manager of the Rialto, so on subsequent visits that year from the Beatles, he gave us tickets, as I would have been unable to queue overnight. I went to all of their shows in York that year, I wouldn't have missed any of them. I had become an obsessive fan and belonged to the Beatles Fan Club, had Beatles posters, Beatles buttons, Beatles everything! I thought they were the most fantastic group ever. I still have the treasured autograph book and wouldn't part with it for the world. ❞

GILL THOMPSON, HOTELIER, WOODTHORPE, NORTH YORKSHIRE

THURSDAY 14 MARCH

*D*isc announced that before the week was out the group would be awarded a Silver Disc for 'Please Please Me', which stayed at number 2 in the Top 30 chart. The paper reviewed Kenny Lynch's version of 'Misery', citing its 'crisp beat and an out-of-the-rut attack', feeling it 'catchy enough to send Kenny up on the roof of sales once more'. Later in the month, Lynch became the owner of a bloodhound he named Misery.

'Please Please Me' climbed back up one place to number 2 in the *NRM*. The group were featured on the front cover of the paper along with news of a Beatles exclusive ('Picture Round-up of their latest recording session – See Centre Pages'). Under the headline 'A Beatles Recording Session', there were four photos of the group in the studio taken by Dezo Hoffmann on the 5th, as well as one in the Abbey Road canteen having tea with George Martin. Kenny Lynch's single was also reviewed, described as a 'fastish tuneful effort that looks like being another hit for [Lynch]. We reckon it will make the 20 pretty soon'. It also mentioned that it was 'penned by two of the Beatles', and was one of the week's 'Top 20 Tips'.

That day, Northern Songs Limited was incorporated by the Performing Rights Society and registered its first five songs – 'Misery', 'I Saw Her Standing There', 'There's A Place', 'Hold Me Tight' and 'Do You Want To Know A Secret'. In its first six months, the company made £17,000.

In the morning, George Martin edited and mixed their new single 'From Me To You'. The moment Ringo got hold of a promotional copy, he took it down to the Saddle Club one night and gave the attendant clubbers a preview. That day, Billy J. Kramer was also at Abbey Road with the Dakotas. They cut 'Do You Want To Know A Secret' and 'I'll Be On My Way'.

With John still absent, the tour travelled from York to the 1,992-seater Gaumont at the junction of St George's Parade and Snow Hill in Wolverhampton, Staffordshire, for two shows at 6.30pm and 8.40pm. The *Express & Star* commented that 'The Beatles, with their unusual haircuts, did well to emerge from a particularly ill-mannered audience buffeting with credit'. The *Wolverhampton Chronicle* was unimpressed with Montez and Roe and wrote that it was the rest of the bill, all British, who 'saved the show'. 'Then there was the refreshing sound of the Beatles. These characters have a lot of ground to make up too, but at least they managed to perform their act with enthusiasm, and their own numbers'.

❛ In 1963 I was 15 years old. Like all teenagers at the time I loved the pop music of the day and had just started buying the *NME* and *Melody Maker*. My favourite acts at the time were Chris Montez and Tommy Roe. So when it was announced that they were going to tour the UK, I wanted to go and see them. I can't remember where I first heard about it, but my friend and I got tickets for their show at the Gaumont. We were very excited to be seeing these two pop idols. One of the acts on the tour was a group called the Beatles. They played their set which was OK, but most people like us were waiting to see Chris and Tommy, so did not really take too much notice.

Little did we know at the time that within six months we would join an all-night queue at the Gaumont to get tickets to see the Beatles again. This time they were top of the bill. The Beatles had arrived! Within a few weeks of our first concert, everyone – including us – were Beatles mad. Friends were envious because we had already seen them. It was a real tussle with my parents to get them to let me queue all night. However, my friend, who was two years older, was going so they relented. I remember catching the bus to the Gaumont feeling excited and scared to queue outside all night, but I need not have worried because after getting off it and walking towards the cinema we were shocked to see this enormous queue all preparing to spend the night there. The police walked around several times making sure that there was no trouble and that everyone was safe. The next morning the box office opened and we got crushed in the rush to get our tickets. Can I remember the concert? Well not much, as I, like everyone else, just screamed. Looking back now it makes me smile. I saw them twice, once before they were famous and once after. Not really listening at the first concert when I could have heard them, and not being able to hear them if I wanted to at the second. ❜

ESMEE WARD, LOCAL AUTHORITY WORKER, PAIGNTON, DEVON

FRIDAY 15 MARCH

'Please Please Me' stayed at number 2 on the *NME* chart and dropped to number 2 in the *Melody Maker* chart. Both papers reviewed Kenny Lynch's new single. The *NME* thought that it didn't 'sound an encouraging title' but that 'much more depressing numbers [have] turned out to be successful'. *Melody Maker* wrote that 'Kenny Lynch's important follow-up to his first hit is just not good enough for the singer. Kenny makes the best of the song but needs something better to show his considerable style. But it has a teen beat attraction which could click.'

The tour group checked out of the Queen Victoria Hotel and headed to Bristol for two shows, at 6.30pm and 8.45pm, at the 1,834-seater Colston Hall. John made his way there after missing three dates. Arriving late afternoon, they enjoyed a drink in the hall's cafe, where actors from the Rapier Players were taking a break from rehearsing their next production, Frank Lonsdale's *On Approval*. Whether their evening performance, an adaptation of Jane Austen's *Emma*, at the adjoining Little Theatre, was affected by the noise coming from the Colston Hall is unknown. The tour party spent the night at the Grand Hotel in Broad Street.

The *Bristol Evening Post* review was headlined, 'It's The Latest Craze... Pop Star Strip'. Reviewer David Elias commented that Roe ripped off his jacket not once, but twice, while Montez's act comprised the singer throwing off his jacket, followed by his tie and finally after 'a bit of jigging about, mostly on his knees', unbuttoned his shirt and pulled out his shirt tails. Elias praised the Viscounts for redeeming the show and said the Beatles, 'compared with the stars, didn't too badly at all'. Monday's recording of Radio Luxembourg's *The Friday Spectacular* aired from 10pm to 11pm.

❝ I turned 16 in June 1963 and was studying for my O levels at Newport High School in South Wales. Unfortunately, I was rather distracted – my friends and I had all become mad Beatles fans, so how I managed to pass all seven exams is remarkable. We saw them four times that year and chose shows that we could travel to by train.

The first one we saw was at the Colston Hall in Bristol. Our little group were me, Ruth, Kathryn, Susan and Glenys and we'd just finished doing our mock exams. We travelled from Newport down to Bristol on the train, which we thought was a wonderful place. My diary notes: 'Great show. Tommy Roe very good looking, nice too, and the Beatles are great too. All nice, George is gorgeous, and all of them funny too. That swine Chris Montez, he was vile! Crude and vulgar and disgusting. He took his shirt off (underlined) and he is all fat. We nearly died when he sang 'You're The One'.

After the show finished it was pouring with rain and we hung around for autographs. Our obsession with the Beatles was pretty innocent. All we wanted to do was meet them and get their autographs. I seem to recall we first became aware of them when 'Love Me Do' came out. Then we watched all the pop programmes and listened to every *Saturday Club* of course. We were into it all greatly, and sad to say, not much else! There wasn't much to do in Newport for teenagers back then.

There was a dance hall called the Majestic with a coffee bar above it. We'd go there on a Saturday with our trannies to listen to *Saturday Club* and drink our frothy coffees!

That summer when we were thinking what we were going to do with our lives, we went to see [the Beatles] in Weston-super-Mare. We had front row seats, which cost us 8/6. The tickets were for the first house. We went down for the day and swanned about looking for them. We spoke to some lads on the pedal boats who told us where they were staying – the Old Pier Hotel. We went up there and there were lots of girls hanging around. Their van was parked outside with messages written all over it, but we didn't do anything like that. We thought we were older and more mature! We went down to the beach, caught the sun, and ate our sandwiches before we went to see the first show. When we went in to see the show, there was a lot of screaming and you were just waiting for THEM. Then THEY were there. Susan took some photographs of them onstage. It was all excitement, thinking of course that they were looking right at us! They were wearing velvet jackets and horrible striped trousers! You could tell that John couldn't see anything as he was short-sighted. I'm sure George was staring at me! Our misspent youth – it's quite depressing really!

After the show we went outside and somebody gave us a ticket for the second house. As there were five of us, we asked the manager if we could go in one by one. I wrote in my diary, 'We asked the manager if we could go in one by one with the spare ticket but he was horrible and said no. He asked us to leave. We tried to give the ticket away but no one would believe us!' We then set off for the station. Susan cut down a little alley way at the back of the cinema. We met two girls who said they had met the Beatles and we were annoyed about that. So we decided to wait for them. There were steps that led up into the cinema. I then recorded in my diary, 'Then the most unbelievable thing happened – George was suddenly standing at the top of the steps!' He'd come out for a breath of air. Susan was at the top. She then passed all of our autograph books to him, and he used her pen to sign them all but he wasn't all nice and chatty! He didn't say a word, except when we asked him if he could get the others to come out. He said, 'Oh they won't come out now.' Of course, they had another show to do. Kathryn was behind me and wanted to touch him but couldn't quite reach. My diary also says, 'He seemed a bit dopey.' I have no idea what I meant by that! Then we had to go. We talked about it all the way home – we had to wait two hours at Bristol Station to catch the connection to Newport. It was quite safe of course and Ruth's father was waiting for us. We didn't get home till two o'clock! Of course, my mother was still awake waiting, and I had to tell her all about it. ❜

SHEILA MILLAR, RETAIL ASSISTANT, TWEEDBANK, GALASHIELS, SELKIRKSHIRE, SCOTLAND

SATURDAY 16 MARCH

Driving up to London following their two concerts in Bristol, the group arrived at 9am at Broadcasting House in Portland Place, London – their first time in the building – for a 10am live recording of *Saturday Club*. *Disc*'s Peter Thomson was of the opinion that it was the best *Saturday Club* in ages, mainly because the Beatles performed live with only a brief rehearsal. The show should have been recorded the previous Monday but postponed because of John's cold. Recording in Studio 3A, they performed 'I Saw Her Standing There', 'Misery', two Chuck Berry songs – 'Too Much Monkey Business' and 'I'm Talking About You' (a regular in their Hamburg repertoire), 'Please Please Me' and 'The Hippy Hippy Shake' (originally recorded by its writer Chan Romero in 1959). Fellow guests were Susan Maughan, the Karl Denver Trio, the Brook Brothers, the Jeff Rowena Six, Bob Wallis and His

Storyville Jazzmen and Tommy Sanderson and the Sandmen. The show was hosted Brian Matthew, who mentioned John's illness.

After the recording, they set off on a three-hour plus drive to the City Hall in Sheffield, Yorkshire, for two shows at 6.10pm and 8.40pm. Fifteen-year-old Julie Barnett later recalled, 'We originally booked to see Chris Montez, who was quite famous at the time, but by the time the show arrived everyone was excited about the Beatles. I got backstage thanks to a friend who was acting as an usher that night. I got Chris Montez's autograph in his dressing room and I bumped into George Harrison and Paul McCartney in a corridor, so I got them to sign as well.' The group spent the night at the Grand Hotel in Leopold Street.

❛ In March 1963, I was a 16-year-old apprentice bricklayer, working for a local building firm called Ackroyd & Abbott. I had a number of friends who lived close by, most of them like me having moved into the area when the estate had been built just after the war. Two of them, Alan Theaker and Maurice Downing, accompanied me to both [Beatles'] shows at the City Hall in March and May. We traveled into town on the 49 bus, a distance of about 5 miles, and I was talking about having heard the Beatles on Brian Matthew's 'Saturday Club' that morning. Saturday mornings were part of the working week back then, but my foreman on the building site, John Fletcher, liked music, and didn't mind me taking my Perdio Park Lane transistor radio to work.

We had bought tickets to the first house to alleviate any problems about getting the last bus home, because if you missed that it was a long walk. I knew having done it on more than one occasion and getting a taxi was out of the question, because we just couldn't afford them. The Beatles played a vibrant set, belting out 'I Saw Her Standing There' and they received great applause for 'Please Please Me', but they didn't get anything like the constant screaming that was to blight many of their future shows. It was good to be able to hear them sing and play, giving some indication that maybe they had a decent future ahead of them. On the way home, talk was naturally about the concert and it having been a good night out, but there were certainly no thoughts from any of us that we had just witnessed the beginning of what would be the greatest phenomenon that the British music industry had ever seen. What a difference a few weeks can make!

Roy Orbison had been top of the bill when his tour with the Beatles had started, and rightly so. However, the Beatles had struck a chord with thousands of teenage girls and as the tour started, reports started of mass hysteria taking place at their concerts and the reporting of this fanned the flames for future shows. This prompted a change to the running order, in that instead of Roy Orbison closing the show, after all the screaming for the Beatles, he would close the first part, after Gerry and the Pacemakers, with the Beatles ending the show. There was some hubbub during the interval with occasional screams as girls caught sight of roadies preparing the stage, but as soon as it was obvious the moptops were about to make an appearance, the screams grew louder and more persistent with the decibel level raising to a crescendo. They came on laughing and waving, but when they launched into their first song they might just as well have not bothered. The noise generated by the hundreds of young girls screaming as loud and as long as their lungs would allow, totally drowned out the music. I thought it would subside after the first song or two, then hopefully three or four, but no, it continued all the way through the set and the feeling at the end was one of relief. I would have left before the end but Alan seemed determined to endure it, and now I suppose I can say I was there at the start of Beatlemania, although I would much rather have heard the group. I vowed after that I would never attend another Beatles concert. ❜

MIKE LAWTON, FUEL OIL SALESMAN, GRENOSIDE, SHEFFIELD, SOUTH YORKSHIRE

SUNDAY 17 MARCH

The group travelled south-east on the A1, a two-hour trip for the evening's performance at the 1,484-seater Embassy Cinema on Broadway in Peterborough. Before the show, Carol Barrett and some friends went to the stage door and told the stage-door keeper that they were members of the Beatles' fan club. 'They let us backstage and the group were in there practising and drinking tea,' Barrett recalled. 'John Lennon didn't say a great deal, but the other three were still very relaxed considering Beatlemania had just struck. They had just bought a small record player but didn't have any records. So, they paid for me to get a cab back to my house to pick up some of my records. We were really annoyed with ourselves afterwards that we didn't get any photos.'

When they had played at the venue the previous December supporting Frank Ifield, the *Telegraph*'s Colin Bostock-Smith was somewhat dismissive of their performance. This time around he was more positive, writing, 'With a vigorous and lively programme of close-harmony singing, goon humour, and piercing guitar playing, they carried the crowd with them all the way. Their performance of their hit 'Please Please Me' won the greatest ovation the theatre has heard in some months. As far as musical ability goes, their act gave them little chance to display any. But presentation wise, they are home and dry. The Beatles are right at the top – and they deserve to be there.' He liked Chris Montez considerably less – 'Discarding jacket and tie in simulated "wild abandon", he spent most his act getting splinters in his knees.'

I was the keyboard player with the Dynatones, the premier instrumental group in East Anglia at the time. Arthur Howes, the impresario who booked the tour, contacted our manager Arthur Lemon three weeks before the show. Howes thought it would be great PR for us. He allotted ten minutes to us at the start of both shows. I spent a few minutes before the show, jamming with Paul and Ringo, just playing some blues and since our bassist Colin Hodgkinson and Paul were both left-handed players, Paul was trying out Colin's Fender. The Beatles looked different with their flop-top hair, Beatles trademark suits and Beatle boots, incredible personalities who projected themselves as real people. John did most of the announcing of the songs. Paul introduced 'Till There Was You'. During Chris Montez's slot I spent five minutes with John on the side of the stage and he said, 'Adrian, you guys have got to get off the Shadows' shit – get into the blues like we've done.' I told him that Colin and I were already listening to Oscar Peterson, Thelonious Monk, Charlie Mingus and Jimmy Smith. He said, 'Good.' The instruments that the Beatles were using were so totally different to any other group's we had seen. John was playing a Rickenbacker 325 Capri, Paul a Hofner 500/1 violin bass guitar and George had recently purchased his first Gibson. By comparison, the Dynatones line-up was two red-and-white Fender Strats, a left-handed Fender Precision bass, an English Premier drum kit, plus my little Univox keyboard and the cinema's Steinway concert grand piano. Both Rickenbacker and Hofner later admitted that if it hadn't have been for the Beatles, both companies would have had financial problems. It was terribly unfortunate for Montez and Roe to tour with, unbeknownst to everybody, the greatest commercial musical outfit of the 20th century. **ʼ**

**ADRIAN TITMAN KING, MUSICIAN, KELOWNA, BRITISH
COLUMBIA, CANADA AND DALLAS, TEXAS, USA**

MONDAY 18 MARCH

Setting off from the Bull Hotel, the tour continued with a three-hour journey on the A47, travelling to the 1,468-seater Regal in St Aldate Street, Gloucester, Gloucestershire for two more shows. Three fans spotted the group walking down Eastgate Street but were too nervous to cross the road and chat with them. Sally Burge of Leighterton, Tetbury, rushed towards the stage when Chris Montez was singing 'You're The One' and threw a package that contained a box of chocolates and a letter. For her efforts, she fell into the orchestra pit. Montez's manager Jim Lee remembered seeing it happen. 'She banged her teeth. It still hurts just thinking about it.' She was carried out of the theatre by members of the St John Ambulance Brigade. The letter revealed that she had gone without three school lunches to buy the chocolates and had travelled to Bristol the previous week to see the show there as well.

ʻIn March 1963, I was the 17-year-old bass guitarist in the Gloucester rock group, the Beatniks. Our manager was Paul Davies, and we were both trainee reporters on the city's evening newspaper, the *Citizen*. We thought we were pretty well versed in the music scene and, on the Friday before the sell-out Monday, 18 March show at the twelve hundred-seat Regal Theatre, the paper carried a preview which pondered whether the up-and-coming Beatles were going to upstage the top-of-the-bill American stars, Chris Montez and Tommy Roe. For me, the Beatles did just that, despite John Lennon's sore throat. By this time, they were sporting their moptop haircuts but not their round collar suits. The group closed the first half of the show in sensational style to deafening screams from the mainly female audience. There was more sensational copy to come.

So, we set off to the nearby New County Hotel in Southgate Street, where we knew the tour party was staying. In the ballroom the stars of the show were having dinner. As our interview with Chris Montez continued I noticed that John and Paul were approaching from an adjoining table. They asked if I knew that their new LP was coming out and that sales of 'Please Please Me' were going very well. They could do with any publicity they could get. Yes, this was the Beatles asking me for publicity! I told them I was very impressed with their set because I was in a group and we were already rehearsing 'Please Please Me'. The Beatles were not household names at this time, so I asked them to write down their names in my notebook to make sure I got the spelling right – and they did. Back at the office again we produced two reports – one about the girl who'd fallen into the orchestra pit and the other about the Beatles. As we expected, only the story about the girl appeared in the next day's paper. Subeditor Bill Handover told me in response to a mild protest: 'Who are these Beatles – I've never heard of them?' Within weeks even Bill knew who they were, as Beatlemania began to sweep the country.

What happened to the Beatles signatures in my notebook? Unfortunately, reporters have to file their notebooks for at least six months in case of legal action or disputes about who said what and when. After six months the notebook was thrown in the rubbish bin during a routine clear out. I had forgotten it had been signed by what became the greatest group in pop music history. **」**

HUGH WORSNIP, JOURNALIST, GLOUCESTER, GLOUCESTERSHIRE

TUESDAY **19 MARCH**

The entourage travelled back east, a 150-mile trip to the 1,869-seater Regal in St Andrew's Street, Cambridge, Cambridgeshire for two shows at 6.15pm and 8.30pm. Not for the first time, players from Great Shelford Football Club were on hand to provide crowd control. Club secretary Jim Dean took John's dirty shirt to the boiler room and scrubbed it clean. He remembered John being 'well pleased'. At the end of Tommy Roe and Chris Montez's sets, the crowd began calling out, 'We Want The Beatles!' Despite the curtains being closed the chants continued. In the audience that night was Michael Howard, then president of the Cambridge Union. 'My most abiding memory of the concert was that it was impossible to hear any of the music because of the screaming of the fans. I don't suppose that was unique later on, but I imagine that was one of the earliest examples of that phenomenon.'

After the show several fans went down the passageway that led to Downing Place. The chants of 'We Want The Beatles!' continued when a fan threw a stone up at a small window at the side of the Regal which turned out to be the group's dressing room. There was the sound of glass crashing and then quiet. The window opened and John came to the window and shouted out, 'Who threw that fucking stone? You've cut Paul's face.' The window shut and the crowd dispersed.

The *Cambridge News*, despite feeling that the Viscounts were the most versatile group of the evening, wrote, 'The Beatles, a four-man "rock" group with weird hairstyles as a gimmick, sang and played their current hits, 'Love Me Do' and 'Please, Please' [sic].' Commenting on the entire show, the paper went on to say, 'This fast-moving show was not the best Cambridge audiences have seen, but enthusiastic teenagers who saw both houses, agreed that the flying visit of the stars was well worthwhile.'

' I had left school by 1963, having only done one year of sixth form as I was going to finish off outside, and was just about to start my nurse's training a year early with the May intake at Addenbrooke's Hospital. I was working on a temporary basis in the library of Trinity College, and was one of four – me, my sister Judith, and two brothers. We went to the same school as Pink Floyd. Syd Barrett was in the same class as me at Morley Memorial Junior School and later went off to the boy's high school and I went on to the grammar school. Later he got together with Roger Waters, and the rest is history. It was all that sort of mix at the time when we were younger.

It was my brother Nick Barraclough who was the musical one. He had been to Miller & Sons, the go-to place in Cambridge to buy records. We would play them at home on the record player my parents had bought, a Pye Black Box. The record shop had been in the Robinson family for quite some time. They would have parties in the basement, which were wonderful. The music was loud and you would just dance. You just didn't stop dancing, it was fabulous. We all had those net petticoats. I only had one, but friends had lots more than I did. You would go downstairs and say, 'Can I listen to this before I buy it?' and they would put it on in the booth. After about an hour or so, they would realise you weren't going to buy it, and you would be turfed out! This was the job of 'Mr Miller's' son, who worked down there.

Judith was still at school and had queued for tickets to see the Beatles at the Regal. She didn't have to queue overnight – she wouldn't have been allowed to by our parents anyway and my brother was too young to come with us. We caught the 106 bus to the early show, having had something to eat beforehand. We lived quite close to Cambridge city centre, just off Hills Road. I can just remember all the girls getting up and screaming, but I didn't! I'm a bit more reserved and it took a lot for me to do something like that! Towards the end I thought, 'Oh gosh, I can't be the only one sitting down.' So we did – we screamed. I had a friend called Julie at school, who then went on to do nurse's training at Addenbrooke's with me. When we'd qualified, she got engaged and it was then I realised she was marrying Barry Robinson, 'Mr Miller's' son, who was the chap who had turfed us out of the basement! He was the great, great grandson of the founder of the shop. Apparently in 1963, he bought all the copies of the Beatles' LPs from other retailers in the city so Millers were the only shop selling them. ❞

ALISON BARRELL, MIDWIFE, CAMBRIDGE, CAMBRIDGESHIRE

WEDNESDAY 20 MARCH

The eleventh date of the twenty-one-date tour was in Romford in Essex, a 60-mile drive south on the A10. Before they left Cambridge, the group bumped into local housewife Brenda Downham, who was doing her shopping with her 2-year-old son Donald and infant daughter Susan. The group came running round a corner, one of them careening into Susan's push chair. Downham recalled, 'I was just concerned that the children hadn't got hurt, so I turned round and shouted at them, and told them they were big enough to look where they were going. They asked if the children were hurt, one of them spoke to both of them, and I said they were all right. One of them offered Susan sixpence, but she pushed it away and it dropped onto the pavement as she said, 'Don't want.' I said, 'We don't want nothing of yours, just get out of the way and let us get on!' Afterwards I thought I had been rather nasty to them, but it was just all of a sudden and I only wanted to protect my children. I always noticed them on television after that, and still feel guilty that I shouted at the Beatles!'

The short distance to the 2,019-seater ABC allowed the group to visit James and Louisa Graves in nearby George Street – the parents of Ringo's stepfather Harry. They had bought Ringo his first drum kit for Christmas in 1956, and travelled with it on several trains from Romford to Liverpool. The group closed the first half of the 6.45pm and 9pm shows. Afterwards, they drove back to London.

❝ In those days 'package tours' used to go from town to town and the pop stars of the time would all be on the same bill at local cinemas. My friend Pip and I were 14 years old at the time and attended Chase Cross Girls' School. On this particular day, we decided to catch a bus into Romford after school and wait outside the ABC to try and get a glimpse of some of the stars and, as they usually arrived by coach, maybe some autographs. We weren't allowed to go to the show, however, as our parents thought we were too young! So we duly waited outside the cinema dressed in our school uniforms, and were joined by two other girls from another local girls' school.

When the coach arrived, the four of us were allowed to board with our autograph books. We went from seat to seat and everyone kindly signed our books. I asked one young man, 'Are you one of them?' He replied, 'No – I'm not one of them but I'll sign for you.' It was Ringo. I also got

John's and I was so confused I got Paul's autograph twice. I missed George somehow or I would have had the whole set! I still have the autographs in my autograph book, which I treasure. We got off the coach with Paul and he let us carry his bags to the stage door. We were smitten! We asked him if we could come in and he said he didn't think the doorman would allow it!

The next time the Beatles came to Romford was a totally different matter. I queued outside the Odeon from 5.30am for tickets. We had front row seats and I remember Ringo nodding and smiling at us, which of course sent us into fits of screaming! In those days, there were numerous tours featuring all the pop groups performing at the same gig. I think we saw just about everyone who was popular in the '60s. Pip and I both still live in Romford and meet up regularly. We clearly remember that afternoon after school when we met the Beatles and I think we both secretly were annoyed we were in our school uniforms! **"**

VALERIE TAYLOR, HUMAN RESOURCES MANAGER, ROMFORD, ESSEX

THURSDAY 21 MARCH

'**P**lease Please Me' dropped to number 5 in both the *Disc* and *NRM* charts – the latter included a photo of the group outside Abbey Road on its front page under the heading 'Names And Faces...', along with the Cougars, Ruby and the Romantics, the Cascades, and the Tornados' George Bellamy on his wedding day. The group began rehearsing at 10am in the BBC's Piccadilly Studios at 201 Piccadilly in London for the Light Programme's weekly show *On The Scene*. Their first time in Studio One, they recorded 'Misery', 'Do You Want To Know A Secret' and 'Please Please Me' between 1pm and 2pm.

After the session the group drove to Croydon for the next date on the tour, two shows at 6.45pm and 9pm at the 2,118-seater ABC in London Road, West Croydon, Surrey. Dawn James, a writer for weekly teen magazine *Mirabelle*, met them for the first time, asking for them at the stage door. 'I don't know them,' said the stage doorman, 'They must be a new group, go in and ask someone else.'

Writing in the *Times-Herald*, Peter Watson commented, 'I am not a 'square.' I like 80 per cent of the pop records released in Britain today – and I am going to try and be very kind in reviewing the package show at the ABC Croydon last Thursday which featured American stars Tommy Roe and Chris Montez. But believe you me, it's not going to be easy... I was disappointed with the Beatles – probably because I was able to hear very little of them... Montez undid his shirt buttons down to the waist... I hadn't come to see his chest.' The *Croydon Advertiser* didn't even bother to mention the Beatles in its review.

" During 1961 I became the producer in charge of BBC Radio's 'Pop' auditions and to my disgust I found none of those who had been accepted had ever been used. A new schedule was planned for 1962 so I suggested a slot featuring recent audition passes would be a welcome showcase for a whole heap of young talent. 'OK,' was the answer. 'You can have six weeks.' So it launched under the ghastly title *Teenagers' Turn*. The first recording venue was Studio One, Piccadilly – in a building about 200 yards from Piccadilly Circus. My initial audiences were very small in number, maybe only thirty or forty people plus a few publishers' song pluggers who loyally came to my rescue to help support the new show. After the first few programmes had been aired my run was extended to a thirteen-week duration and then to an indefinite run under my original title *The Talent Spot*. We were also in a more grand venue, a three hundred-seater auditorium known as 'The Paris', a converted news cinema in London's Lower Regent Street.

And so we ran throughout 1962 without a stop and, with four acts per week, as you can probably guess, I had long ago used up all the audition passes. Many agencies helped me out with their acts and it was inevitable that I would sooner or later meet Brian Epstein and become aware of his very extensive collection of great groups and soloists. In early November, he called and told me of a group he had working in Hamburg. They were due back home in a few weeks and he asked if I would like them on the show. I would have to accept them unseen, but he did have a good tape recording of one of their shows to which I listened and was most happy to give them a date.

And so it was that the Beatles made their broadcasting debut on BBC national radio on Tuesday 4 December 1962. The three other acts on that show had all appeared before, but the Beatles were new, so they were placed at the bottom of the bill. Well, the great day came – these four lads about whom we knew very little, looking immaculate in their 'Edwardian' suits duly arrived and rehearsed their two numbers. The audience loved them and, after the show, Epstein asked me if I would have them back some time. I told him I would be very happy to have them return – let's say in six or seven weeks' time. The rest is history.

By the time they returned in January 1963, everyone in the audience knew about them and were eager to see and hear them; they were 'Top of the Bill' and it was the turning point for my previously sparse audience figures which suddenly blossomed to full houses from then on. During 1963 I had another 5pm radio slot running concurrently with *The Talent Spot*. Quite the other end of the 'pop' spectrum, it was titled *On The Scene* with its host Craig Douglas, and that was my next meeting with them.

It was some twenty-one months later before I got them again for a session. By then I was producing *Saturday Club* and, apart from them dropping into the show for a chat now and then with Brian Matthew, they were always too busy elsewhere. But the time came when they weren't too far away for a recording session while appearing at the Odeon, Hammersmith, in 'Another Beatles' Christmas Show'. That session was heard in *Saturday Club* at 10am on Boxing Day, 1964. Thereafter they didn't do sessions any more for it was no longer practical. It was much more preferable to have them just pop in for a chat and play their records. *The Talent Spot* finally ended on 28 June 1963 after seventy editions and having presented hundreds of potential new stars to the pop world. But its greatest triumph was having played an important role in the history of the Beatles. **❞**

BRIAN WILLEY, BBC RADIO PRODUCER, ESHER, SURREY

FRIDAY 22 MARCH

*P*lease Please Me was released. Thousands of teenage fans across the country parted company with 30s 11d to buy the group's debut LP, initially in mono form only. 'Please Please Me' dropped to number 4 in both the week's *NME* and the *Melody Maker* charts. The *NME* reported that Roy Orbison was being lined up to replace Duane Eddy on the group's forthcoming tour and that Petula Clark was cutting 'Please Please Me' in French.

The group featured on the front cover of the *Melody Maker* for the first time, with a photo headlined 'Beatles Eye-View!' Inside Chris Roberts wrote a piece titled 'The Beat Boys!' about the burgeoning Merseybeat boom, discovering 'the Scouse Sound in Britain's Nashville', describing the group – one of somewhere between two hundred and fifty and three hundred Merseybeat groups – as 'those sombrely dressed swingers'. He reported that since the weekend, four girls had been sitting outside the Cavern, huddled in blankets - during the evenings at least - waiting for the Beatles to come home.

The group left the Hotel President and headed north to Doncaster, for the evening's two performances at the Gaumont at 6.15pm and 8.30pm. Billed as 'Britain's Great Dynamic Beatles', they closed the first half of the 8.30 show, singing 'Love Me Do', 'Ask Me Why', 'Misery', 'A Taste Of Honey', 'Do You Want To Know A Secret', 'Please Please Me' and 'Long Tall Sally' – a long-time favourite of the group's and the song with which they closed their last-ever concert, at Candlestick Park in San Francisco on 29 August, 1966. They spent the night at the Danum Hotel.

❛ I went to Dovedale Road County Primary School in Liverpool and for most of that time I was in the same class as George Harrison. George was living in Speke at the time and I remember he was best friends with a lad by the name of Ronnie Forshaw. Also at the school two years ahead of me was John Lennon. I have a recollection of him giving me a bloody nose in Herondale Road, which was the road that ran down the front of Dovedale. In 1954 I passed my Eleven Plus and went to Quarry Bank High School. Ahead of me again by two years was John Lennon. By this time he had teamed up with a chap called Pete Shotton and they were both notorious for getting up to mischief around the school. In those days the students of Liverpool University used to have a Rag Day which they called Panto Day, which would take place in late winter, early spring. The students used to get up to all sorts of pranks. One year the statues outside the Harthill Road entrance to Calderstones Park were covered in paint. This was attributed to the University students. As it turned out, it was said that it was Lennon and his pals that carried out this act of vandalism.

I first heard the Beatles on the radio during my first week at University in Manchester in October 1962. We listened to Radio Luxembourg on the top floor of the Unitarian College. I heard 'Love Me Do'. It sounded quite strange, but rather jazzy compared with a lot of what was going around at the time. At that time, I didn't realise Lennon and Harrison were in the group. I was reading their 'Life-Lines' in the *NME* in early 1963 and saw that Lennon went to Quarry Bank High School. In fact I didn't realise Harrison had been at Dovedale until an old school friend by the name of George Taylor told me in the summer of 1963, despite having seen them perform onstage.

It was in March 1963 that I actually spent some money on a Beatles record. I bought their first LP. I had read the reviews of it in the *NME*. It had a track-by-track account of the recording session. It told how 'Twist And Shout' had been done in two takes. It convinced me what an amazing talent they were. I bought the record from a shop in Manchester just off Oxford Road. It was a small music shop and I popped in there the day before it was released and I said to the man behind the counter, 'Have you got the new Beatles LP in?' He said, 'Yes. Do you want a copy?' Obviously I said 'Yes'. I didn't get a chance to play it that night, but that Friday was the last day of the University term and I was going home back to Liverpool. I played it when I got home and thought, 'This is amazing.' I graduated from Manchester University in June 1965 and two months later I joined Midland Bank, starting at their Overseas Branch in Castle Street, Liverpool, which is now the Viva Brazil restaurant. It was that summer I went to the Cavern the one and only time to see Millie. I look back now at 1963 and think we saw the Beatles at their best. They were still a gigging band and I think the *Please Please Me* LP is an amazing record. ❜

RICHARD BANYARD, BANK OFFICIAL, HESWALL, WIRRAL, MERSEYSIDE

SATURDAY 23 MARCH

The tour bus left the Danum Hotel and headed north on the A1, a two-hour plus trip to Newcastle-upon-Tyne – the northernmost town on the tour – for two shows at the 2,135-seater City Hall in Northumberland Road. Because the shows were sold out, fans sat in the orchestra stalls behind the group. Billy Mitchell, a 15-year-old in a local group called the Triffids, remembered, 'It wasn't the best idea of seating as the PA was obviously pointing outwards towards the audience so we had to guess quite a lot of what going on. It didn't matter though, because we could see how fantastic they were. It was Dolly Mixture and Jelly Babies time as well so they were coming flying up onto the stage. They did turn round a few times to sing and acknowledge that we were there. They did half a dozen songs, finished the first half, and blew everybody else off the stage. It was just ridiculous that Tommy Roe and Chris Montez should have to follow them.' The Jelly Babies craze had started after John and George had told some fans at a stage door that they liked the confection. 'If only we had realised what we were starting,' said John, 'What began as a trickle of Jelly Babies being sent to us, soon grew into an avalanche. We had to pass most of them on to children's organisations.'

Photographer Ian Wright, who had met the group at their show in Sunderland on 9 February, cycled to the venue with his trusty camera. John asked him to take more photos of the group so he could send them to his aunt Mimi. He told Wright, 'There's a Mexican guy on the bill tonight called Chris Montez. He's crap.' Now two-thirds into the tour, tempers were beginning to fray and ongoing contention between John and Montez resulted in the Beatle pouring a pint of beer over the singer at a post-show party to celebrate the release of the *Please Please Me* LP. Ringo was late getting on the tour bus and ended up stuck at the stage door signing autographs for the attendant fans. He told them that if they stood in an orderly queue, he would sign for everyone. The tour party stayed at the Royal Turks Head Hotel on Grey Street, but the Beatles hired a car to take them back to Liverpool. They slept in their own beds for the first time in almost three weeks.

The Journal wrote, 'The best acts on the bill were, without doubt, the top-class supporting acts – which never seem to be given their own chance right at the top – the British-produced Viscounts Trio, and the exciting new group the Beatles. They were the climax of the first half with their song, 'Please Please Me.' Most of the *Evening Chronicle*'s review was devoted to Montez's antics. John, sipping a whisky and ginger, talked to the paper's Harold Brough about their reception. 'Honestly, I've never known anything like it outside Liverpool. The fans were tremendous. We were absolutely staggered. They just went wild.' The paper added, 'It was the British group, the Beatles, who stole the show.'

> ❝ Some school mates and I were members of our local Boys Club back in '62, where the main activities were boxing, football and the like. We weren't much into sport, but it was somewhere to hang out. Frankie Vaughan was President of Youth Clubs of Great Britain at the time, and was running a competition to find new talent, hence our group the Bits 'N Pieces were formed, with me on drums. We played together in our spare time, as we all had apprenticeships after leaving school. We were in the habit of looking up what groups were playing at the Maj in the *Evening Chronicle* and saw that on 28 January there was a group called the
> Beatles. We thought 'what a silly name for a group' and went to the cinema instead to see Ray Milland in *The Man With The X-Ray Eyes*. On our way home, we passed by the Maj and heard this wonderful music coming out of the hall. We realised then that we had made the wrong decision!
>
> So when I heard that they were coming back to Newcastle in March, Alan and I made sure that we got tickets. We were dead excited as we travelled into town on the number 14 bus. We had fantastic seats, right in the middle of the front row. As we sat down, we were approached by two girls. They

asked us if we would do them a 'huge favour.' One of them said she was Paul McCartney's girlfriend, and they had seats at the end of the row. Would we swap with them? Being decent young lads, we agreed, and sure enough, when the group came on, Paul looked down and sang a song to her. At the end of the set, the girls thanked us and disappeared, and we took up our original seats. I remember the group wearing brown suits and pink shirts, really unusual in those days. I noticed these things, being in a group, and followed all the latest trends. They had a style of their own. I'd been bitten by the Beatles bug and made sure I saw then again when they came back in June.

As part of my apprenticeship, I had to attend a day release course with apprentices from other companies. One of them, who worked for Ward Brothers, which was next door to the Royal Turks Head Hotel, told me that he had been asked to take some rubbish out to the courtyard at the back of the printers, which they shared with the hotel. He opened the door, and startled three blokes, standing smoking on the fire escape. They were John, Paul and George. They quickly stubbed out their ciggies and went back inside. **❞**

KEN SMILES, NEWSAGENT, GATESHEAD, TYNE AND WEAR

SUNDAY **24 MARCH**

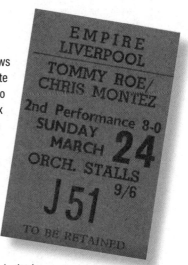

The group returned home to a wet and rainy Liverpool for two shows at the 2,381-seater Empire Theatre in Lime Street, the fifteenth date of the tour. Jimmy Watson, the *NRM*'s editor, came to the city to write a major feature on the Liverpool music scene. He described 'Six thousand ardent fans packing into every available corner of the venue for the two shows. Hundreds, possibly thousands, more crammed the streets around the theatre to be satisfied with mere glimpses of their idols as they entered and left the theatre.' The police forbade the group from going outside in case they caused a stampede. Because of this, Watson commented, fans might think they were becoming big-headed – but, he wrote, 'I am convinced that is one thing which will never, never happen to these boys.' One veteran police sergeant proudly showed Watson an autographed picture of the group he got in their dressing room between shows. Paul also invited Watson to tea the following day. As they were performing in their home city, it was decided the Beatles would close the two shows, taking place at 5.40pm and 8pm. Mike McCartney and Dezo Hoffmann took photos of the group backstage.

They had previously played at the venue in June 1957, when, as the Quarrymen, they auditioned for the Carroll Levis' 'Search For The Stars' talent show. They auditioned again in 1959, that time as Johnny and the Moondogs. Although they didn't win, they got through to the final, which was held in Manchester. They made their first appearance at the venue as the Beatles in October 1962, on a bill with the Breakaways, Craig Douglas, Jet Harris, Kenny Lynch and Sounds Incorporated. They performed four numbers and also provided backup for Craig Douglas.

The *NRM* reported that, 'These fans could have been forgiven for being impatient for the Beatles to appear but no, like true Northerners, every act was generously applauded by an attentive audience and then a veritable storm broke loose when the local lads were finally announced. It was good to see the interest taken by usually blasé theatre staff and the policemen called in to control the crowds.'

❝ I grew up in a village called Bromborough on the Wirral. My first exposure to music was in the early '60s when we used to go to a youth club in a hall in nearby Eastham. There wasn't a bar there, so we used to sneak into the Stanley Arms, the pub down the road, for a drink beforehand – you could only get orange squash in the hall. A lot of the groups who played there went on to become some of the famous Mersey groups, but to us at the time it was just another night out.

We used to go to the Hulme Hall as well and it was there that I first saw the Beatles. It must have been in 1962 as I was still at school. I was in the sixth form and although I never did it, some of the girls from school would take a change of clothes into school with them, and get the train from West Kirby to Liverpool at the end of the morning lessons to go and see the Beatles at a lunch time session. There wasn't a particular time when we started liking them, they were just around. I remember seeing John Lennon in his underpants one night at Hulme Hall! We had all rushed the stage, and the dressing room was round the back.

By 1963 they were playing much bigger venues, and I saw them at the Grafton just after they came back from Hamburg. It was early January, and I'd just ended my relationship with my boyfriend Dave. He rang me up and said, 'I've got two tickets to see the Beatles at the Grafton, I thought you'd like to come.' I didn't really want to rekindle the relationship, but I did want to go and see the Beatles, so I went. I spent most of the evening on his shoulders, with my back against a pillar watching them perform.

It was only a week later when my friend Linda Williams and I went to see them at the Majestic. We took along our copies of 'Love Me Do', and after the show we went round the back and found a door and flight of stairs. It would have been Linda who dared us to go up the stairs, because I would have dreaded being caught and thrown out! So on we went and halfway up the stairs John and George came down. We stopped them and they signed the record, both on one side, and then we carried on up the stairs to find the dressing room. I ended up sitting in between Paul and Ringo, who were there with the Chants, the support group that evening. We had to leave to catch the last bus home to Bromborough at quarter to twelve. The next time I saw them was the following March at the Empire in Liverpool. It was easy to get to because it is right next to Lime Street Station, in fact you could walk out of one exit right by the theatre. I'd gone with a group of friends this time, but don't recall much about it. Looking back, everything just seems to merge into another memory. ❞

JENNY DAVIES, NUMERACY CONSULTANT, NESTON, SOUTH WIRRAL, CHESHIRE

MONDAY 25 MARCH

On a rare day off, the group spent the morning doing a photo session with Dezo Hoffmann for the *NRM*. They first visited the barber shop in the basement of Horne Brothers on Lord Street, where they had their hair cut by barber Jim Cannon, who gave Ringo his first Beatle haircut. They then travelled to Allerton Golf Course, Paul in his recently purchased four-door Ford Consul Classic in Goodwood Green, George in his Ford Anglia and Hoffmann driving his more stately Austin Cambridge A60. He took several shots of them and was himself filmed on an 8mm camera, first by Paul and then George, putting new film in his camera. They then went to Paul's house a half-mile away, Ringo riding as Paul's passenger, with John in the back filming the journey.

In the evening, Paul, Brian Epstein, Bob Wooler and promoter Danny Betesh, amongst others, attended the opening night of Mister Smith's, a new nightclub in Manchester which saw Frankie Howerd top the bill. Hoffmann travelled with Paul and snapped a photo of the pair together. He later recalled, 'I asked the editor about doing a photo feature in Liverpool on these boys. He said it was too expensive to go to Liverpool. It took me three months to convince him to send me. When I arrived, I went to see Brian Epstein, and we had the most fantastic type of rapport straight away. Maybe that was because I didn't want to take the kind of pictures he expected, you know, the sort where people are shaking hands in the office. I stayed there for three days, and that's how the Beatles and I became friends.'

> ❛ I came over from Los Angeles for that tour in 1963 because I was Chris Montez's manager at the time and had written 'Let's Dance'. One day early in the tour the promoter knocked on Chris' dressing room door and told him that he wanted to change the billing and put the Beatles at the top. I told him, 'That's not going to happen or if it does happen, we're out of here – no more shows. We'll go back to the States. That's the way it's going to be. We're not going to change it,' and it wasn't changed. They backed off and let it go on as planned. Chris and Tommy Roe were the stars of the show. If you think back at that time no English artist had ever been big in America. Once in a while, someone would come along and have a hit, but did I think the Beatles would have a hit in America? At that time, it didn't even occur to me.
>
> We pretty much spent twenty-four hours a day with them – we slept in the same hotels, travelled on the bus with them. I recall them writing on the bus once. Paul was sitting on the arm of a seat while John was sitting on the arm across the aisle and they both had a guitar and were writing. There was another time when I was already on the bus and they came on and they were walking down the aisle toward me and I'm trying to get a picture of some scenery. I had this camera – and back then, they weren't that user friendly. You had to know what you were doing and I didn't, but I had this Yashica movie camera that was very good, but you had to set apertures and do this and that and so forth and I was trying to use the damn thing and I'm trying to get pictures of the scenery and they got in the way and I was trying to get them to move. So I still have this double exposure of them walking down the aisle of the bus.
>
> They wore pink shirts onstage and after each show they'd roll them up in a ball and put them in a suitcase and then the next night they'd undo the ball and the shirts would have thousands of wrinkles in them from the sweat that had dried, but you couldn't see that from the audience. During one of the shows we were waiting back in our area and John had a little record player he carried with him everywhere and he kept playing [the Miracles'] 'You Really Got A Hold On Me'. We would always have to eat late – by this time everything had closed – we would often be in the kitchen of one of these hotels and eating odds and ends. Anyway, we were in this mezzanine-style room at a hotel and we were all goofing off and people started going to bed because it was late and John got up and he walked across the floor and when he got to about the centre of the floor his pants fell down around his ankles. He did it on purpose, of course.
>
> When we got to Liverpool, Ringo and I went out and got drunk together. What I remember clearly is both of us in a rest room at a urinal, drunk taking a pee. That's all I can remember about that night – after all I was drunk. We spent two days in Liverpool and I remember meeting Brian Epstein at his record store. I remember when the bus returned to London after the final show on that Beatles tour and we were all going our separate ways. It was very foggy and I have this picture in my mind of the four of them kind of walking off into the fog and disappearing. It was like the ending of a film where they walk off into the distance and you don't see them anymore. ❜
>
> **JIM LEE, SONGWRITER, BOULDER CREEK, CALIFORNIA, USA**

TUESDAY 26 MARCH

The tour continued with two dates at the Granada in Mansfield, where they had previously performed on 23 February. Unlike then, fans began assembling outside the cinema once they knew the group had arrived. Local singer Shane Fenton recalled the day. 'There were hundreds of girls blocking off the streets nearby – but being in the business I knew that if you went through the shop of the local chippie, through his back room, and then up over the roof of the cinema dressing-room and down a fire escape, you could get into the cinema backstage. I'd already worked with them a few times, so I went over the roof and found them trapped in their dressing room. They said they were starving, so I went back home... and told my mother all about it and she made them up a picnic basket full of food, with containers full of hot soup and piles of salmon sandwiches, which I took to them backstage, again going over the roof, and they were absolutely knocked out.' They stayed overnight at the Clifton Hotel on Terrace Road. Like so many other towns, the Mansfield media was yet to be enthused with the Beatles, sending a reviewer to the Opera For All's production of *La Traviata* at the Civic Hall. They also covered the presentation of a silver medal of the National Operatic and Dramatic Association to Ronald Smith, known as Mansfield's Singing Painter.

<blockquote>

❛ My friend Diane Bradley and I were only 15 in 1963, so too young really to be going to dance halls, but a group of us used to go on a Saturday night to a youth club at the Parochial Hall on Brunt Street, commonly known as 'The Proc'. They used to have groups on there and even though we were still at school, everybody used to go. It was mostly just local groups, although once or twice they had more well-known groups there. Mostly the bigger groups came to the Granada.

We didn't really know of the Beatles because they hadn't really taken off when they came, and it was a school night so I wouldn't have been allowed to go anyway. Diane and I always cut through the alley at the side of the theatre on our way home from Queen Elizabeth Grammar School. On this particular afternoon, we bumped into Ringo and began chatting to him. John was in the nearby chip shop and while Ringo was signing his autograph for us, Paul and George came by. They hung back but not in a standoffish sort of way. It just seemed like Ringo was more relaxed and sociable somehow. They all had five o'clock shadows but no way were they scruffy. They wore identical long, brown suede coats the likes of which were unseen in Mansfield in those days, as well as Chelsea boots.

Diane recalls them coming across the road from Marks & Spencer, carrying M&S carrier bags. I don't have any memory of that, but I do remember looking at his signature after they left and saying to Diane, 'Who's Bingo Starr?' Of course we hadn't heard of Ringo then. Little did we know that very soon everyone would know of him. I wish we had realised who we were talking to and that we had got the rest of the autographs.

There was plenty to do for teenagers in Mansfield. We had our own specialist record shop called Syd Booth's on Queen Street. This was the place everybody used to go for records and radiograms. There was also another shop on Leeming Street called Vallance's. I remember going to the cinema with Diane and dropping in to listen to records in the booths there, but the shop didn't last for very long. Just off the Market Square there was a coffee bar called the Bentinck and a jazz club at the Eight Bells, a pub in town. We had a Dorothy Perkins in the town where I would spend my pocket money on the standard teenage uniform of hipster trousers and Matalo sweaters. ❜

HILARY PARSONS, LIBRARY ASSISTANT, MANSFIELD, NOTTINGHAMSHIRE

</blockquote>

WEDNESDAY 27 MARCH

The group headed south, a half-hour drive on the A60 to Northampton for the evening's two shows at 6.30 and 8.45 at the 1,954-seater ABC in Abington Square, arriving in time for lunch at the Angel Hotel. Before the shows, they had a drink at the Bantam Cock pub next door and were invited to eat at the Chicken & Grill Restaurant – across the roundabout from the ABC – after the evening's performances by owner and local concert promotor Ron Stanley. After the show, one teenage fan spotted Paul and George on their way there, offered them some of her Maltesers and in exchange got them to autograph the wrapper. They had chicken and chips during their two-hour stay and played the spoons. They were observed leapfrogging down the road as they wound their way down Abington Street to the Westone Hotel in the early hours. In the alleyway beside the restaurant lay the Gayeway Dancing Club, run by

Stanley – one of the top night clubs in the area, and also a dance studio and hairstylists ('Go Gay – Go To The Gayeway').

The *Northampton Chronicle & Echo* were mightily impressed with this first appearance by the group, headlining its review, 'The Shadows Must Beware Of Lads From Lancashire'. 'It was Britain's own dynamic Beatles who swept aside these Stateside snipers with a torrid, talented act which found the target and stole the show', the reviewer wrote. 'As they showed last night it will not be long before they acquire world-wide acclaim... the Beatles took the stage by storm – and saved last night's show from mediocrity... in stage-presence the long-haired Lancashire lads left the Yanks out in the cold'.

❛ I left school at 15. This is how it worked with the so-called careers officers: 'You've got long fingers, you can be a sewing machine mechanic.' I am the worst sort of person to be a mechanic, but went into it for a while and survived it, leaving to take up a couple of jobs in warehouses, etc. A friend of mine who was a projectionist – there were many cinemas in Northampton at the time – told me they were looking for one at the ABC. I thought it sounded interesting, so I went along and had an interview, and got the job. On show days, although we didn't have to, we got there early. We had the stage to get ready, and I just liked hanging about. It meant a late night, as after the show finished we had to put the stage back together again ready for cinema the next day.

By this time, wherever [the Beatles] went Jelly Babies were thrown on the stage. I collected some of them up, and it was my excuse to go up to their dressing room. Someone said, 'Oh, they're only Jelly Babies,' but I said, 'Oh, I have to go up there anyway.' I didn't really but I popped into their dressing room and they said, 'Oh, chuck 'em in the corner,' and had a bit of a laugh. Of course, when they came back in November, it was completely different. It was phenomenal really for Northampton, the town did go quite mad really – we all wanted a bit of Beatlemania. I heard afterwards that a lot of the local restaurants had offered to send in takeaway food for them. Everyone wanted a piece of the action!

That night the area around the cinema was teeming with teenagers. I remember at the sound check, they swapped instruments. Paul got behind the drum kit, Ringo played a little bit of bass guitar, they were just fooling around a bit. After they had gone to the dressing room, I had a little tap on Ringo's drums! I was backstage for the shows. One of my jobs was, when the curtains closed, to stop them knocking over the very expensive microphones, we had to walk out of view of the audience with the curtains. They were motorised and we had to walk along and guide them away from the microphones. So my job was to stand in the wings, and after the act, they would close again. I was doing this after one of the acts when I received a tap on the shoulder. 'Excuse me mate,' and it was John Lennon. When the show had finished, they had to get them safely out of the theatre – there were fans everywhere. The plan was to walk them out of the stage door, through the ABC car park, up a ladder, and along a wall leading into a factory. Then through the factory, which was about three streets away from the theatre. My instructions from the manager were to walk across the tarmac of the car park and help point them in the right direction. So there I was, still a teenager, walking through a car park with the Beatles!

On a recent family occasion, we had a look round the old theatre. It is somewhat condensed down now, but I stood on the stage for the first time in fifty-odd years. My cousin was with me and I was able to show him backstage, and showed him the Beatles dressing room, which was quite nice. It doesn't seem like over fifty years ago when I had my encounter with the Beatles, and when I hear Paul McCartney being interviewed, I think, 'Wow, I was really there'. ❜

PHILIP HANZLIK, CHEMICAL MANUFACTURING WORKER,
HIGHAM FERRERS, NORTHAMPTONSHIRE

THURSDAY 28 MARCH

'Please Please Me' dropped to number 7 in *Disc*, which also confirmed that the group were going to tour with Roy Orbison. The record also dropped to number 7 in the *NRM* charts. Norman Jopling broke down *Please Please Me* in the paper, writing that 'for a debut LP it's surprisingly good and up to standard – a goodly number of the tracks on this could be issued as singles and maintain the boys' chart standard. A good cover pic and excellent sleeve

notes make this a worthwhile LP in all senses of the word.' The previous week's recording of *On The Scene* aired on the Light Programme at 5pm, hosted by Craig Douglas, who introduced the group, with guests Mark Wynter, Mike Berry, Shane Fenton and the Les Reed Combo.

Fans were waiting outside the 1,958-seater ABC in London Inn Square, Exeter, Devonshire, when the tour bus arrived for the evening's two concerts. After a soundcheck, the group took in the sights, going into the Left Bank record shop opposite the cinema in Paris Street. Paul asked whether they had *Please Please Me* in stock. A fan asked them for their autographs and produced the only thing at hand – a paper bag. Following the second show, as the groups were clearing the stage, Paul chatted to Tony Osborne, a member of support act the Corvettes. 'We were talking about their hit 'Please Please Me' and we got to the piano and he said to me, 'What part do you want to sing?' and we sang the whole song together with him tinkling the ivories. He just lifted up the lid and we played it all the way through together – we were playing as if we were mates from the same group. George Harrison was showing our guitarist John Greenslade the chords of their next single and backstage they passed round their cigarettes. When we had our photo taken with them John Lennon said, 'Don't say cheese, say crap.' After the second show, the group stayed overnight at the Royal Hotel.

❝ The day we [the Corvettes] appeared with the Beatles, we arrived early to set up our gear, and were still there when they turned up. George Harrison came up to me and said, "'Ave you got a ciggie mate?' So we disappeared behind the stage, and we sat there chatting about what all guitarists talk about – 'What guitar do you play? Why do you play it? Who's your favourite?' It just went on and on. 'What strings do you use? You have two guitarists in the group?' They'd arrived to set up and be ready, and I had all that time with George. They were just another group to us to be honest. The Beatles were in a dressing room on their own, but most of the evening I was sitting

down on the left-hand side of the stage with George. We sat there smoking. The cinema's stage manager was a bloke called Chiefy Pasternak. He caught us, and said, 'Get out of here! And if I catch you smoking anywhere near my stage again, you won't live.' So George shot off to join the other Beatles, and I just sat there taking in the show.

We did our set, mostly Shadows stuff, as that was what the kids wanted. The kids just screamed and screamed. They screamed at anything back in those days. It didn't matter whether it was a village hall, or a local pub, they screamed. As soon as you went onstage, they screamed. They did it because they were excited. When we were all packed up and due to go home, there were so many people outside, fans of all the groups who had been on, including the Beatles, that they thought it better that the Beatles didn't go. We went upstairs into their dressing room, and we were locked in there with them with sandwiches, coffee and tea for about three hours, just the Beatles and the Corvettes. Ringo sat at the back of the dressing room, sulking. When I asked George about it, he said, 'Oh, he gets in a sulk about anything. You don't want to talk to him, miserable old sod he is. Today it's because he thought John was playing too loud.' He was sitting up at the window, right at the back, over-looking the main street, and he did that for three hours! I don't remember him talking to anyone. Lennon just walked around taking the piss out of anyone and everyone. When anyone talked to him, he was better than them, he had an answer for everything. The word arrogant comes to mind! As soon as I realised what he was like, I decided not to talk to him anyway. I spent a while talking to Paul about songwriting – how he got his ideas, as I was a songwriter as well. Most of the time I spent with George, we just smoked ciggies and chatted the night away. If you put two guitarists together, they'll find something to talk about. No matter how good or bad they are. **❯**

JOHN GREENSLADE, GUITARIST, SONGWRITER, EXMOUTH, DEVON

FRIDAY 29 MARCH

'Please Please Me' dropped to number 9 in the *NME* chart and number 7 in the *Melody Maker* chart, while the *Please Please Me* LP entered the *NME* album chart at number 9. The *NME* also printed its charts point table for the first three months of the year. Unsurprisingly Cliff Richard topped the list with 584 points, followed by Frank Ifield and the Shadows. Elvis Presley was sixth with 246 points, and eleven points behind him, in seventh place, were the Beatles.

The group left the Royal Hotel for the long 200-mile-plus journey back to London for two shows at 7pm and 9.15pm at the 3,050-seater Odeon in Loampit Vale, Lewisham. Billed as 'The most commercial sounding Rhythm and Blues group' in the *Advertiser & News*, they arrived at 4.30pm and immediately talked to local reporter Paula Gracey from the *Lewisham Journal & Borough News*, who called them 'easy-to-talk-to with plenty of individual personality'. The newspaper's Bret Arliss, who reviewed new singles each week in his 'Spinning Tops' column, was given a preview of the group's new single 'From Me To You', playing it on their battery-operated record player. Arliss asked DJ Brian Matthew his opinion of the record – 'Mate, I'll put my shirt on it, and my suit, and my shoes, and certainly my best gramophone needle'.

During their performances, the group were bombarded with toys and chocolates, even a hand-made beetle. After the shows, they obliged fans, dropping signed photos and cards from their dressing room high above the stage door. Following the concert, they drove up the A40 to Headstone Lane in North Harrow to the home of Shadows' guitarist Bruce Welch, who was throwing a party to celebrate Cliff Richard and the Shadows' six-week British tour, which was to close in Brighton on 7 April. They performed at the party doing a passable impression of the Shadows, presumably with the bespectacled John playing the role of Hank Marvin, before Cliff joined in. On meeting Cliff for the first time, John said, 'Oh, wait till I tell the girls back home! Marvin played them Cliff's forthcoming single 'Your Eyes Tell On Me' – which ended up on the flipside of 'It's All In The Game'. Welch later told Billy J. Kramer that he thought they'd written a few catchy songs. 'Nothing special. Once they dry up that'll be the end of them.' When they said their farewells, milkmen were already on their rounds.

❛ Some fifty years on, it seems strange that we saw the concert from the first row of the stalls because a friend had given us tickets to see Tommy Roe – with a supporting role appearance by the Beatles, a group scarcely known in the UK. At the time I was in my third year of grammar school and, at almost 14 years old, was fast discovering that pop music, boys and youth club dances were much more interesting than the life I had hitherto led, which was mostly focused on daily swimming training sessions. I kept a rather untidy diary, where for the day of the concert I made a note saying 'Red Cross and then Beatles, Tommy Roe and Chris Montez – marvellous!!' – a far cry from the entry later that year, for 8 December, which said 'BEATLES, BEATLES, went to see the BEATLES ... screamed myself sick, worth it ... got a very sore throat.'

In 1963 the world was a very different place, even in London young teenage girls could go to concerts unaccompanied and provided they were home by 11pm or midnight there was no reason to worry. As in this case, I usually went with my sister Jan, a couple of years my senior, but more because we were close friends and enjoyed the same music than to ensure I came home safely. That first concert featuring the Beatles introduced me to a new world, a new concept of music and rock'n'roll. I already loved all pop music and regularly listened to Radio Luxembourg – the only radio station of its kind in the days before 'pirate' radio. I had seen the Beatles on UK television, where they were described as a Liverpool group who had performed mostly in Hamburg, Germany, during the 1960–62 period, largely because of the very high number of up and coming groups in the UK and particularly in Liverpool in the early '60s. I remember the concert as a memorable evening of great music, but did not realise the immense importance of the event I had just witnessed and when our friend who worked at the theatre offered us a chance of a personal introduction to the Beatles in the coffee bar next door after the show, we actually turned down the opportunity! I personally feel privileged and fortunate to have lived my teenage years during a period that would later be seen as an unquestionable turning point in the history of British and international pop music. ❜

BARBARA POTTON, TRANSLATOR, CARONNO PERTUSELLA, ITALY

SATURDAY 30 MARCH

With the icy weather finally easing and the sun shining on the south coast, the group set off from the Royal Court Hotel in Sloane Square for the penultimate night of the tour at the 2,228-seater Guildhall in the Square, Portsmouth. They played two shows at 6.30pm and 8.50pm. The previous evening had seen a concert by Mantovani and His Orchestra. After the show, the group stayed the night at the Keppels Head Hotel. The *Portsmouth Evening News*, under the heading, 'Britain Wins Pop Tussle At Guildhall', reported that the evening was an 'opportunity to judge the state of pop singing on both sides of the Atlantic'. The *Hampshire Telegraph* commented that, 'The Beatles, a fiercely singing group from Liverpool, jerked the audience into life with their current hit 'Please Please Me' and 'Love Me Do'. Brian Epstein signed a £1,000 contract for five nights on the Channel Islands in August.

❝ The Beatles may have travelled to Hamburg on their road to success but they hardly ever came to the south of England. My home city of Portsmouth was enhanced in the post-war decades by a busy seaside industry. In 1959 the civic authorities finally completed the re-building of the city's Guildhall, which had been bombed to a shell in 1941. Immediately top stars began to appear in the concert hall. I was 9 years old in 1959 and growing up with delightful parents who had no fondness for anything 'pop' or American, despite which it became a major part of my life from the early '60s. It seems in retrospect that it all fell into place in one week in October 1962, when the Beatles released 'Love Me Do' and I celebrated my first teenage birthday. Within a matter of months, I was sold completely on the new sounds of the beat and rhythm'n'blues groups, I was reading about them in *Melody Maker* and other publications, their records were on Radio Luxembourg and then the Beatles appeared on *Thank Your Lucky Stars*. I loved them. I'd never seen a live performance by any kind of pop act when I discovered that the Beatles were due at the Guildhall in March 1963.

So that Saturday evening was the first gig I ever saw. I can tell you that I went alone to the first house, that I walked there on a sunny spring evening and I recall eating a large bar of chocolate, which left me feeling a bit queasy. I've no idea what I wore but I won't have looked too cool. Neither have I any idea how I got the ticket but I guess I walked up from school to the box office and bought one. The Beatles were not yet 'superstars'. I remember them finishing the first half and sounding very exciting; I know now that their set was largely tracks from the first album but the only song I recall from that night was Chris Montez singing 'La Bamba' – and removing his shirt while he did so. So there we are – the first act I ever saw was the Beatles. I loved them but I can hardly recall a thing. Nonetheless, I had now embarked on a lifetime of gigs as a fan – and eventually a performer.

Eight days later the Beatles appeared at Southsea seafront's Savoy Ballroom and I wasn't going. The Savoy was a licensed ballroom, which attracted older punters, Teddy Boys, sailors and anyway it was a Sunday. I don't think I even bothered asking my folks, but with some pals I cycled to a nearby park for a kickabout and then went to the Savoy where we saw the Beatles arrive. Then it was off home. By November, when they came for the third and last time my preferences were already shifting towards the Stones and the rhythm'n'blues scene but when a school pal said his mum was willing to queue for tickets I bought two – the second for my younger sister Liz. We caught the number 17 bus from Albert Road – just six months earlier and it would have been one of the city's now obsolete trolley-buses – but on arrival we just milled about outside the Guildhall, disappointed to learn that they were not playing because Paul was ill. I think my sister was more upset than I was, but we went back on 3 December and there they were. We had good seats – about a dozen rows back – and could see everything clearly but it's absolutely true that the dominant sound was screaming – it was an event to see but not one to hear! My life was changed. ❞

DAVE ALLEN, LECTURER IN VISUAL ARTS, PORTSMOUTH, HAMPSHIRE

SUNDAY 31 MARCH

Losing an hour's sleep as clocks changed to British Summer Time, the group travelled from Portsmouth to Leicester for the final two shows of the tour. They were scheduled to perform at 5.40pm and 8pm at the two thousand-seater De Montfort Hall in Granville Road, Leicester, promoted by Arthur Kimbrell. The *Leicester Mercury* described the group as 'another act which set the girls screeching madly'. Apparently, the only Beatles' number the reviewer enjoyed was 'A Taste Of Honey'. The newspaper didn't see the importance of sending a photographer to either of the shows. Instead, they covered a jazz concert, the opening of a Scout hut and a boys' brigade annual inspection. And so, the Beatles' second major tour of the year came to an end. The group drove back to London where they stayed at the Royal Court Hotel again.

DE MONTFORT HALL — LEICESTER
Big All-Star Shows presented by Arthur Kimbrell

SUNDAY, MARCH 24th, at 7 p.m.
MANTOVANI AND HIS ORCHESTRA
Balcony 9/6; Gallery 6/6; Stalls 9/6, 8/6, 6/6, 5/-.

SUNDAY, MARCH 31st, 5.40 p.m. and 8.0 p.m.
FIRST TIME HERE — DIRECT FROM AMERICA
CHRIS MONTEZ ● TOMMY ROE
Plus Britain's Sensational BEATLES and other Top Star Acts.
Balcony 9/6, 8/6; Gallery 6/6; Stalls 8/6, 7/6, 6/6, 5/-

EASTER SUNDAY, APRIL 14th, 5.40 p.m. and 8.0 p.m.
WOOLF PHILLIPS CONCERT ORCHESTRA.
SHIRLEY BASSEY ● MATT MONRO
Balcony 12/6, 10/6; Gallery 8/6, 7/6; Stalls 12/6, 10/6, 8/6, 7/6, 6/-
From Arthur Kimbrell, 38, Rugby Road, Hinckley (Tel. 3563), or Municipal Box Office, Charles Street, Leicester. Postal bookings enclose remittance and s.a.e. Enquire at Godiva Coaches, Ford Street, re transport and tickets.

Although the group's relationship with Chris Montez had been somewhat fraught, they got on well with Tommy Roe. He recalled, 'John let me borrow his Gibson guitar on the bus to write songs. I started my song 'Everybody' then, and that became a Top 5 hit for me. I could tell that the Beatles were special, and I tried to get my label ABC Paramount to sign them, but was turned down. When they came to the US in 1964, they invited me to perform with them in Washington, DC, at the Coliseum. It was an exciting time, and I was very pleased by that invitation.' Roe's abiding memory of the tour was the weather. 'It was very cold. The hotel rooms had heaters on the wall that you put shillings in, so you'd be up all night putting shillings in the meter. In the States we had hot running water and air-conditioning, but in England they were just starting to refurbish their society. It was kind of raw sometimes.'

‘ During the autumn of 1962, my sister – who at 14 was six years younger than me – bought a copy of 'Love Me Do'. While I thought the record was OK, I was more into American artists, namely Roy Orbison, the Everly Brothers and, of course, Elvis – who could do no wrong.

The following March, my friend and I booked tickets for a concert at the De Montfort Hall. By this time the Beatles had reached number one with 'Please Please Me', but I still wasn't really interested and didn't realise that they were also on the bill. The compère announced that the next act was causing a stir around the country, especially with a number one single. He then announced 'The Beatles'. They walked onto the stage in what were to become their trademark suits and haircuts. Paul McCartney launched into an amazing performance of 'Long Tall Sally' and they continued with several songs from their

first album, together with a couple of Chuck Berry classics. I was by now completely sold on this new group to the extent that my sister was placed in the background where the purchasing of singles and albums were concerned. Strangely enough, although there was some screaming, I could hear them quite well, which was fortunate, as later in the year bedlam reigned and the music seemed secondary.

When the group came to Leicester again, I thought I would try and obtain some tickets as they were going on sale one Sunday morning. I set off on the Vespa I had bought with a loan. When

I approached the ticket office in the centre of town, the queue was probably a quarter of a mile-long right down Charles Street to the clock tower. I decided not to bother. I probably wouldn't have heard a note in any case. Unfortunately, I didn't keep either the programme or my ticket from that memorable evening when we saw the Beatles, which I regret to this day, but I at least can say I saw them and heard them. **❞**

ROBIN WHAIT, FINANCIER, LEICESTER, LEICESTERSHIRE

APRIL

We're All Going On A Summer Holiday

MONDAY 1 APRIL

*M*irabelle made mention of the Beatles for the first time since its 16 February issue, in a picture spread of the hottest current acts. The group began a three-hour recording session for the Light Programme's *Side By Side* at the BBC's Studio One in Piccadilly at 2.30pm. The twenty-three-part series was hosted by Karl Denver and ran through 23 September. The Beatles performed 'I Saw Her Standing There', 'Do You Want To Know A Secret', 'Baby It's You' (the first time they performed the song), 'Please Please Me', 'From Me To You' and 'Misery'. After an hour-long break, they recorded a further session, this time four hours long, playing 'From Me To You', 'Long Tall Sally', 'A Taste Of Honey' (which Paul described to host John Dunn as one of his aunt Jin's favourite songs), 'Chains', 'Thank You Girl' and 'Boys' (Ringo's first featured vocals on another Shirelles song, written by Luther Dixon and Wes Farrell, and performed a half dozen times on the radio during 1963). They also performed 'Side By Side' with the Karl Denver Trio. The two shows aired on 22 April and 13 May.

TUESDAY 2 APRIL

*T*he group set off on yet another trip up the M1 – this time to Gleadless, a Sheffield suburb about 5 miles south of the city centre. They had originally been booked to perform at the Black Cat Club, a venue run by brothers Peter and Geoff Stringfellow in St Aidan's Church Hall on City Road. Peter Stringfellow recalled that he first approached Brian Epstein to book the group in November 1962. 'As we didn't have a telephone at home, I did all my bookings from a public call box on the council estate where Mum lived.' Epstein initially offered him the group for £50, but as the weeks passed, by the time Stringfellow finally decided to book them, the fee had risen to £100. They eventually agreed on £85. 'I came out of the telephone box in a sweat because I never paid that amount of money to a band before,' Stringfellow remembered.

More tickets were sold than the Black Cat could accommodate for the planned 12 February date, so Stringfellow booked the larger Azena Ballroom in White Lane for £28. It is believed that Stringfellow sold two thousand tickets for the show, despite the venue having a capacity of five hundred. He told a local newspaper, 'The demand is so terrific that we have decided to move the whole show to another venue to give more youngsters the chance of seeing the group.' Opened in 1957, the ballroom was owned by husband and wife Arnold and Zena Fidler, built on a piece of farmland they owned. As demand increased, Stringfellow upped the prices for the night from 4/- to 6/- – for many fans a prohibitive increase. An advertisement was placed in the day's *Star* newspaper and a further thousand fans showed up on the night. A fire door was opened from inside, allowing even more people into an already packed-to-the-rafters building. People stood on chairs, which in turn had been placed on tables. The police were called. The long-forgotten support acts were Mark Stone and the Aidens and Count Linsey III and the Skeletons, also known as the Screaming Howling Horror of Fitzalan Square.

❝ In 1963 I was 19 and working at Edgar Allan Steelworks on Sheffield Road in Tinsley, only a minute's walk from Sheffield Wednesday's football ground. On the evening of 2 March, the band I was in, Dean Marshall and the Deputies, were booked to play at a dance at the Newton Hall in Chapeltown. My friend Mick Marshall and I had also got tickets to see Helen Shapiro at the City Hall that night. Mick had got the tickets and booked them for the earlier show so that I'd have enough time to get to our gig. The Beatles were on in the first half of the show, and when they had finished I said to Mick, 'C'mon, let's see if we can get backstage to see them.' There was no security to stop us and finding a door at the end of a corridor, I knocked, then opened it. The Beatles were there, relaxing after their set onstage. I explained that I played guitar and liked their music, so they invited us in. John Lennon handed me a guitar and asked me to play along with them in the dressing room. I don't know how long we played together, but all too soon Mick was reminding me that I had a gig to go to. When we were about to leave, I noticed that John had laid his plectrum on his guitar. I had been using my own, that I carried in my pocket, so I asked John if he would swap. He readily agreed, and so that night at the gig I played using John Lennon's plectrum. I still don't know to this day if Lennon played their second show using mine.

As we made to leave, I mentioned that I would be seeing them in a month's time at the Azena. John then told me I was welcome to come backstage again next time. So when the Azena show came round, they had already been back to Sheffield for another date at the City Hall. I was there with some other mates, and when I said I had got an invitation to go backstage afterwards, they didn't believe me. I almost didn't make it, because when the show finished and I tried to get backstage, a massive security guy wouldn't let me in. I said they asked me to come. He said, 'No, go away. They don't want anybody in there. Go away.' Then John Lennon opened a door to see what the fuss was, saw me, then said, 'He's all right, let him in.' Once again, I was handed a guitar to play with, and had a chat with them. They were just ordinary blokes, who, like me, had a great enthusiasm for music, and it's incredible to think that a short while later the world would become engulfed in Beatlemania. Thinking back, I don't know what happened to Lennon's plectrum. I did use it for about five years, then probably mislaid and lost it. I remember there was a message over the PA that night. 'Will Diane Frost please go to reception.' My brother Roger ran her back to her house, where she found out her father had died. My wife doesn't like it when I tell my Beatles story because it reminds her of that night. ❞

PETE JACKSON, MUSICIAN, SHEFFIELD, SOUTH YORKSHIRE

WEDNESDAY 3 APRIL

The Beatles drove back to London in time to meet up with Dezo Hoffmann at Westminster Photographic at 58 Old Compton Street. Hoffmann wanted to show the pictures and the 8mm film he had taken in Liverpool the previous week. Later, they made their way over to the Playhouse Theatre for a 5.30pm rehearsal for *Easy Beat*. They conducted several interviews set up by their press officer Tony Barrow. The recording took place at 8.30pm and they performed 'Please Please Me', 'Misery' and 'From Me To You' in front of a packed studio. This was the first – but by no means the last – time that radio listeners heard 'From Me To You'. It became their most recorded song for the BBC – fourteen times in total. John and Paul also took part in the programme's record-review panel segment 'Going Up!' with Laura Lee and Clare

O'Rourke, expressing their views on Bert Weedon's 'Night Cry', Cleo Laine's 'It Looks Like They're In Love', the Vernons Girls' 'Do The Bird' and Tommy Roe's 'The Folk Singer'. They received the additional princely sum of a guinea each for the segment. Fellow guests included Beverley Jones, Wout Steenhuis, Tony Steven, Terry Lightfoot's Jazzmen and the Johnny Howard Band with Laura Lee. Gerry Marsden was in the audience and introduced 'From Me To You'. The show aired the following Sunday.

❝ Producer Bernie Andrews, who joined the BBC on the same day I did, was canny enough to specialise in operating the new mobile tape machines then coming into use. They were thought to be beyond the skills of Studio Managers, so he rapidly became a 'Tape Op', someone who could record and edit very quickly on the EMI TR90 machines. He was a wizard on these and soon established a reputation and was much in demand. I, on the other hand, applied for a transfer to the role of studio manager. Someone higher up had enough sense to realise that some of us TOs could actually exhibit some artistic talents. Because of this common love of popular music Bernie and I started to follow the activities of a producer friend, Jimmy Grant, to see how he went about immersing himself in the music scene. At that time skiffle was becoming all the rage and Jimmy had persuaded the controller of the Light Programme to give him thirty minutes from 10am to 10.30am on Saturday mornings for a programme called *Skiffle Club*. There was a vogue at that time for several 'Club' programmes so there was *Guitar Club* and *Jazz Club*. Naturally Bernie was chosen by Jimmy to help in the studio production of *Skiffle Club*. This programme was so popular that within a fairly short time – by BBC standards – it was extended to two hours and renamed *Saturday Club*. For *Saturday Club* we would gather in the studio about 8am with Jimmy and presenter Brian Matthew to go through everything before transmission. Such was the popularity of the show that exposure on Saturday morning frequently led to chart success. *Easy Beat* went out on Sunday mornings. This was recorded live in the Playhouse Theatre before a live audience, all good fun which the young audience enjoyed very much, especially when the Beatles turned up to play live on the show for the first time.

Later in 1963, I obtained my first job as a BBC Producer. A busy and fun time as I learned the ropes and I devised a new fast-moving programme, *Where It's At*, modelled on the style which was being heard on pirate radio, with jingles, interviews and up-to-date music. One of the best editions was made in June 1967 when the Beatles issued *Sgt. Pepper*. Kenny Everett was working for me doing bits and pieces in the show and because he was a close friend of the Beatles, he was able to go to Abbey Road and talk to all of them about the different tracks. It was a brilliant, exclusive piece and won acclaim for every one of us. In 1967 in response to the growing popularity of pirate radio, the BBC decided on a reorganisation of its radio networks into four generically structured ones, Radios 1, 2, 3 and 4 replacing the old Home, Light and Third. Those of us with a bent for pop obviously chose to work on the new Radio 1 and I was chosen to launch it with the *Breakfast Show* presented by Tony Blackburn on Radio 1. That was to be my life for the next twenty-six years.

In 1985 they made me Network Controller. In that position, at the top of the pile, I was responsible for just about everything. A lot of fun, blood, sweat and tears twenty-four hours a day, but better than working for a living! That was it really until John Birt came into the BBC as Director General. His ideas and mine about how to run the biggest popular radio station in the UK were very different and, in any case, I had been there too long. I departed in 1993 and since then I have worked as a consultant on radio in various capacities and eventually in 2004 found a new career entertaining passengers on cruise liners with stories about various aspects of life in the BBC and stories of some of the great musical acts, 'Singing Legends' as I call them, which is a wonderful way to see the world and share my enthusiasm.

Around 1970 the BBC purchased *The Elvis Presley Story*. We heard that they were planning to make *The Beatles Story* next and my boss, Mark White, thought it unacceptable for an American company to write the story of Britain's greatest group. As I had edited *The Elvis Presley Story* for UK transmission I was offered the chance to produce *The Beatles Story*. It was a massive task, but although I had the full cooperation of Derek Taylor in the Apple office, none of the Beatles was prepared to actually contribute to the series at the initial stage. So I spent nearly a year travelling the world collecting material and unheard interviews with the four as well as most of their former friends and colleagues. Eventually what emerged was thirteen one-hour episodes for the initial transmission in 1972 and a year later it was extended to fourteen one-hours as I updated it. That interview with John was done by me, with Charlie Gillett, in November 1973 for a major series Radio 1 was making called *The Story Of Pop*. It was a typical Los Angeles sunny afternoon when we were invited to go to Lou Adler's house in Bel Air where John was living with May Pang. He and Yoko were going through their separation at that time. During the chat John insisted that we stop to watch TV where he had booked a commercial to promote his album, *Mind Games*. It was very funny as Tony King, John's promotion manager, had 'dragged' up as Her Majesty the Queen and was seen and heard promoting the album 'by John Lennon, who sent his MBE back!' It was a very happy afternoon with lots of reminiscences about England and John made some very kind comments about Bernie Andrews and the fun the Beatles had on *Easy Beat* and *Saturday Club*. I'll always remember John's quote in response to a question about the American government's attempts to deport him, 'No way am I going to allow them to take me away from all this great music!' **"**

JOHNNY BEERLING, CRUISE LECTURER, SKIPTON, NORTH YORKSHIRE

THURSDAY **4 APRIL**

*P*lease Please Me entered the *NRM* LP chart at number 8, while the 'Please Please Me' single had dropped to number 11. It also dropped on the *Disc* chart, to number 13, as Gerry and the Pacemakers' 'How Do You Do It' went to number one.

George was suffering from a sore throat. The group were driven to the BBC's Paris Studio, arriving in time for an 11am recording of a second episode of the *Side By Side* show. They performed 'Too Much Monkey Business', 'Love Me Do', 'Boys', 'I'll Be On My Way' (the only occasion they performed the Paul-written song, which appeared on the B-side of Billy J. Kramer with the Dakotas' 'Do You Want To Know A Secret') and 'From Me To You'. The programme was broadcast on 24 June. At the end of the three-hour session, they stepped out onto Lower Regent Street, captured on film by Karl Denver Trio guitarist Kevin Neill. A further *Side By Side* appearance had been pencilled in for taping from 2pm to 6pm, but was cancelled so the group could honour a commitment to perform an early evening concert at Stowe School. They found time to visit the Cecil Gee menswear store at 39 Shaftesbury Avenue, where they were photographed both outside and in by Dezo Hoffmann and his assistant David Magnus.

At about 3pm, the *NRM*'s Jimmy Watson drove them to Stowe in Buckinghamshire, about one hour and forty-five minutes away. Schoolboy Dave Moores – a native Liverpudlian, and nephew of Littlewoods empire boss, John Moores – had written to Brian Epstein asking whether he could book the group to perform at the school. Correspondence went back and forth between Epstein and Moores until a fee of £100 was agreed on. 'It would be a great pleasure for the boys to appear at Stowe,' Epstein wrote, 'There are four Beatles, a road manager and myself ... With the regard to the lighting I will arrange that with those concerned more or less immediately before the performance.' He added 'I am delighted that you are arranging a meal for us after ... Is there a good hotel in the district?' On arrival, they performed two half-hour sets of fourteen numbers. Following the concert in the school's Roxburgh Hall, they had a meal with the boys, visited the headmaster's study and had plenty of photographs taken before driving to the Green Man hotel, in the village of Syresham, Buckinghamshire, where they stayed the night.

❝ In the early '60s, I had a guitar group at Stowe playing lame versions of the Shadows and some instrumental skiffle favourites: we played every year during the Easter term in the big school hall as a kind of concert. Although we didn't sing in our band, a bloke called David Moores, who we occasionally had singing for us, said there was a group in his hometown called the Beatles who ought to come and play instead of us at the Easter concert. I was not happy. Some load of schmucks from a town which NOBODY had ever been to were going to have our slot.

On the day, a reception party stood outside the hall in the pale spring sunlight. We had NO idea what to expect as none of us had ever met a pop star. You could say unprepared was our collective adjective. Two Ford saloon cars scrunched up to the gravel in front of the theatre and out got a collection of thin, pale, small youths – none other than the Fab Four and their roadie. As a team we took the equipment into the hall, three amplifiers and four drum boxes and some suits on hangers which went to one of the music practice rooms near the stage that was their dressing room. They asked if they could see the school, our assumption being they had never been to a school, and after a very brief tour ended up at the tuck shop. Mr Tom who ran this public school version of a roadside caff asked if they would like anything to eat and as they wolfed down a meal for ten, I realised I had witnessed one of the more common after effects of the use of speed. You can't blame them really.

By seven, the hall was full and some light jazz music was playing over the PA system to set the mood. I was in the fourth row of the audience so I waited as the lights dimmed. An ear shattering wall of screams roared up from the back of the hall as the teachers' daughters stood, jumped and yelled at the opening curtains. By George – Paul, John and even Ringo – I was in the middle of Beatlemania. The curtains swung back, that deep Scouse voice counted 'Won, two, three, foah...' and my life changed forever. So, the Fabs had got as far as the fifth word of the opening number 'I Saw Her Standing There', which if you count it out on your fingers is 'seventeen'. That instant was the pivotal moment I grew up. In my ears was the loudest, fastest, clearest, sexiest noise I had ever heard. In front of me four incandescent singers with tight, TIGHT, trousers and guitars were all singing something magical in harmony and laughing and dancing and we hadn't even got to the end of the first verse yet.

We now know the lads' history of hundreds of hours playing in clubs and years of writing and playing their own music but at that unimaginable moment ten seconds into their performance, it was exactly like being hit in the face with a huge multi-coloured and loud fist. And it went on through all the songs from their just-released first LP including 'Twist And Shout' or, looking at the audience of sweaty, red-faced rich kids, smoking incredibly thin and very surreptitious Woodbines ('Twits and Snout' no less). I staggered out into the night and at that decisive moment didn't want to be a rock star: I knew I'd never get to be that thin. ❞

JOHN BLOOMFIELD, 'TEMPLE 64', LIGHTING DESIGNER, MARLBOROUGH, WILTSHIRE

FRIDAY 5 APRIL

'Please Please Me' dropped six places to number 13 in both the week's *NME* and *Melody Maker* charts, while the LP climbed three places to number 6 in the *NME* chart and entered the *Melody Maker* chart at number 10. Gerry Marsden, whose 'How Do You Do It' went to number one, told Alan Smith in an *NME* interview, 'The Beatles and ourselves – we let go when we get on stage. I'm not being detrimental, but in the south I think, the groups have let themselves act a bit formal. On Merseyside it's beat, beat all the way. We go on and really have a ball.' He also said that their follow-up might be "Hello Little Girl" by John Beatle' or a number called 'It's Happened To Me'. The *Daily Mail* reviewed 'From Me To You', saying, 'The Beatles have let loose a flood-tide of good will. This is a hit.'

Allen Evans reviewed the group's LP for the *NME*, commenting, 'Fourteen exciting tracks, with the vocal-instrumental drive that has put this Liverpool group way up on top in a very short time. The title tune and 'Love Me Do' are well known, but there are twelve other thrillers, including John Lennon's singing of a torrid 'Twist And Shout', and the Shirelles' 'Baby It's You'; 'Boys', with drummer Ringo Starr shining, and a pippin of a duet of 'Misery' by John and Paul McCartney; and lead guitarist George Harrison is powerfully evident throughout.'

The group visited EMI House for a lunchtime ceremony, appearing before label executives, journalists and photographers. They were also presented with a silver disc for two hundred and fifty thousand sales of 'Please Please Me' by George Martin on behalf of *Disc*. To celebrate the achievement, Brian Epstein gave them all blue glass beetle cufflinks set in gold. They performed a short set and posed for photographs with Martin taken by Philip Gotlop. After the event they made their first visit to the Mayfair offices of their accounting firm, Bryce Hanmer and Isherwood, at 23 Albemarle Street, forgoing a planned photography shoot on boats on the Serpentine. Afterwards, they returned to the Royal Court Hotel, where they signed autographs and took photos with waiting fans.

SATURDAY 6 APRIL

Tony Barrow, writing under his *Liverpool Echo* pseudonym 'Disker', reviewed 'From Me To You'. He wrote that the group 'invented, perfected and pioneered fresh pop ideas which are revitalising and revolutionising the British Top 20 scene.'

The group travelled to Buxton for an 8pm show at the Pavilion Ballroom in St John's Road. Trevor Auty, the son of the Pavilion Gardens' Entertainments and Publicity Manager, recalled his father being 'over the moon to be able to secure their booking in April 1963 and although they were a big name, their worldwide success was still to happen, so it turned out to be a real scoop.' Dennis Brooke Auty was one of the more forward-thinking theatre managers. He had incorporated a 'Twist/Jive Record Club' in 1962 and increased admission to 1/6 because of its popularity, as well as roller skating four times a week, wrestling on Monday evenings, bingo on Tuesdays and Fridays and old-time dancing on Thursdays.

On arrival, the group checked into the Grove Hotel opposite the venue. However, a contretemps with the owner saw them return to Liverpool rather than stay the night. A rumour going round Buxton for years was that owner Clifford Brunt was upset to find cigarettes had been stubbed out on the carpet in one of the rooms they were staying in. They had a drink, believed to be draught Bass, at the George Hotel, before Paul asked local teen John Goodwin where the stage entrance to the Pavilion was. The previous Wednesday, seven hundred advance bookings had already been taken and there were queues outside the ballroom as early as 8.30 in the morning to buy the 6/- tickets. The usual Saturday afternoon roller-skating session ended at 4.30pm. It was the largest attendance for a Saturday night dance at the Pavilion that year. Local band the Trixons opened the show at 8pm and the Beatles performed two half-hour sets. The concert ended at 11.45pm.

❝ My parents, Clifford and Beryl Brunt, were managers at the Grove Hotel in Buxton. We had twenty-six letting bedrooms, with only one bathroom on each floor, and were always busy, especially on Bank Holidays. They were awful because all the day-trippers would come in as there was only one cafe, Collinson's, in the town at the time. The rooms cost £1 2/6 for bed and breakfast, and 7/6 for high tea. It was my job to run the kitchen, and although they were good times, we never had a minute to spare. One Christmas I wasn't even able to open my presents until a couple of days after Boxing Day when we had quietened down a bit. We all had to muck in, my parents only earned about £7 joint wages between them, so my sisters and I were all expected to help out. We lived in two rooms in the hotel, numbers 17 and 18, and had a record player in one of them.

The hotel was just across the road from the Pavilion Gardens Ballroom, where they'd hold dances every Saturday night. There were always different acts coming to play, and usually they would stay at the Grove as we were so close to the venue. The Beatles had booked two rooms in the hotel to do a gig one Saturday night. They'd booked in early, around four o'clock, and went upstairs and were messing about and smoking. There was no central heating in the hotel, if you wanted any heat, you had to put a shilling in the electric fire. When it was time for them to go across the road to the gig, they said to my father that they had decided they were going to go back to Liverpool after the show and wouldn't be staying after all. My father said, 'Well you've got to pay for the rooms because they will have to be cleaned again and the towels changed,' and John Lennon said, 'Do you know who we are?' to which my father replied that he didn't. John said, 'We're the Beatles!' My father said, 'I don't care if you're the bloody cockroaches, get out!' and that was it. They didn't pay! When the work was done, I could go across to the dances at the Pavilion.

I worked at the hotel until I was 25, seven years in total, and spent the rest of my career in catering. Unfortunately, the hotel building is empty now and a bit of an eye sore. It belongs to Robinson's the brewers and is falling into disrepair. Hopefully someone will buy it and bring it back to life. 🥖

SUSAN HUTCHINSON, CATERER, BUXTON, DERBYSHIRE

SUNDAY 7 APRIL

Wednesday's recording of *Easy Beat*, introduced by Brian Matthew aired on the Light Programme at 10.31am. The group left Liverpool for the long drive to the south coast, where they were playing at the Savoy Ballroom on South Parade in Southsea between 7.30pm and 11.45pm. As they arrived, a crowd was already beginning to assemble and the group had to negotiate their way through to get into the building. When the Savoy Ballroom manager George Turner, who had paid £50 for the group's appearance, realised the demand to see them, he raised the usual 3/6d ticket price to 5/-.

Paul made a beeline for the piano with a new tune he'd come up with on the journey down. Support act Mike Devon and the Diplomats showed up a little later. George sat with band members Keith Francis and Colin Wilkinson, showing them how he played certain chords. The Beatles had to ask whether they could use drummer Terry Wiseman's kit, as Ringo's had been waylaid on the journey down to Southsea due to van troubles. This created a problem as two stages had been set up about 30 feet apart. After the Diplomats' first set, Wiseman helped Ringo and Neil Aspinall carry his drums, cymbals and stands across the hall, then carrying them back again when the Diplomats played a second set.

Mike Devon recalled the evening, 'There were no fire regulations like there are today. People were milling about in Clarendon Road, South Parade, on the beach and esplanade. The crowds then went into the foyer and up the stairs. It was just chock-a-block with people wanting to see the Beatles.' Even then, not everyone managed to get in. The stairs leading to the dance floor were packed with fans. While they were onstage, selections from *Please Please Me* aired on *Alan Dell's Showcase* on Radio Luxembourg. Keith Francis asked the Beatles to sign his gold label *Please Please Me* LP after the show, when the two bands shared some Cokes. The group spent the night at the Pendragon Hotel.

❛ 7 April 1963 is a night I will always remember. It was the time Mike Devon and the Diplomats supported the Beatles when they played at the Savoy Ballroom in Southsea. The gig was booked weeks before, but it was only a short time beforehand that we found out that we were on the bill with the Beatles. We had a copy of the *Please Please Me* LP and included about half a dozen songs from it in our set. We didn't play any of those songs that night. I remember John saying he didn't want us to. We got to the ballroom at about 7pm, after playing the night before in Weymouth. All the group were tired, but soon forgot about it as we knew it was

going to be a big night for us. The Beatles were already there, so it was just us and them in an empty dance hall. A roadie was setting up their equipment on the centre stage. There were two stages there which made things easier.

The first thing I noticed about the Beatles? Long black leather overcoats, with roll neck black jumpers and cuban-heeled short boot shoes with elastic sides. Paul was playing the grand piano. John and George were sat on the edge of the stage tuning their guitars. I had never seen a Rickenbacker before. It seemed a bit strange at the time that Paul played a cheaper Hofner violin bass, but it must have had a good sound as he has played it ever since! He stopped playing the piano and went to tune up his bass. He came over to me and said he had broken one of the tuning pegs, so I was able to lend him a pair of pliers from our small case of essential spares. Ringo was really the only Beatle who spent time chatting to us. He seemed unaffected by sudden stardom at the time.

At last, it was time for the Beatles to come onstage and play their one-hour set. They started off with 'Some Other Guy', then they played most of the numbers from the *Please Please Me* album and also some old rock'n'roll songs. This was a bit of a shock to me. We hadn't been playing these songs since the '50s, but their versions seemed to have brought new life into them. The 'Mersey Beat' no doubt. The highlight of their set was when John said, 'This is our new record' and they played 'From Me To You'. It was fantastic hearing it for the first time. Crowds clambered onto our stage to get a better view. After they finished, the group were rushed away through the crowd and out of the building. George Turner paid them £50 and we got £15. More than two thousand people, well beyond the legal limit, paid 5/- to get in. ❜

COLIN WILKINSON, PLUMBER, PORTSMOUTH, HAMPSHIRE

MONDAY 8 APRIL

John became a father for the first time. John Charles Julian Lennon was born at Sefton General Hospital in Smithdown Road, Sefton, Liverpool. The 6lb 11oz baby was born with his umbilical chord around his neck. Godfather Brian Epstein arranged for John's wife Cynthia to have a private room at a cost of 25/- a day. He also told his assistant Alistair Taylor to buy a Silver Cross pram for the new mother. John telephoned Aunt Mimi nightly to see how the pair was doing. John, George and Ringo headed back to London, while Paul took the ferry over to the Isle of Wight to visit his cousin Bett and her husband Mike Robbins, who ran the Bow Bars pub on Union Street in Ryde.

LEYTON SUPER BATHS, - LEYTON, E.10

MONDAY 8th APRIL, 1963

The Fabulous

Beatles

Bus Routes, 35, 38, 38a, 69, 249, 257, 234, 70, 170, 26 .

NEAREST UNDERGROUND: LEYTON (CENTRAL)

Once back in London, they made the 10-mile journey through the city and the East End for the evening's performance at the Leyton Baths on the High Road in Leyton. During the winter months, the pool was boarded over and turned into a dance hall. Peter Jay had been performing nearby and came to see the end of the show. Asked whether there was a good place they could have a meal at that time of night, he took them to a cafe on Old Compton Street in Soho.

❝ I had started my DJ career playing records in my local youth club in Chingford, Essex, in the 1950s. First off just in the canteen area and then in the school hall that had a large stage area and more room for dancing. Sometimes I would just DJ on my own on the stage and other times share the evening with a group. This gave me confidence to answer an ad in the *New Musical Express* placed by a company called Galaxy Entertainments who were looking for DJs. I had an audition and got the job. One of the venues run by Galaxy was Leyton Baths where I became resident DJ. Singers and groups of the time would regularly appear, including of course the Beatles. Brian Epstein had insisted that they still appear at the remaining outstanding dance hall dates that had been previously made.

In front of a packed crowd of dancing, screaming fans, they played most of the tracks featured on the *Please Please Me* LP and gave a preview of their forthcoming single, 'From Me To You'. After the show I went backstage, complete with camera, to congratulate the boys. I introduced myself, and as it was a teen night no alcohol was served, so I asked if they wanted a drink, which meant I had to go to the pub opposite to get them a beer each. As there were no glasses backstage they drank their beers from teacups. We had a good chat, talking mostly about music and their favourite artists. They went out of their way to be jovial, obliging and friendly. I asked if I could take a photo of them. 'Of course,' they replied. 'Just a minute,' said Paul, 'I must clean my teeth first.' After a while Paul was ready and John positioned the group for their photo. 'Right,' John said. 'When I say three, we'll all smile and you take the picture.' John began counting 'one, two, THREE' – literally yelling 'THREE' and making the other Beatles and myself nearly jump out of skins. I wasn't able to take the picture, but Paul was the worst casualty. He had still been holding the open tube of toothpaste and when John had shouted, he squeezed the tube and a long length of toothpaste shot down his trouser leg. After much laughter I finally got my photo with Paul keeping his hand over the embarrassing stain on his trousers. ❞

NORMAN SCOTT, DISC JOCKEY, ENFIELD, MIDDLESEX

TUESDAY 9 APRIL

Teen magazine *Romeo* featured the Beatles for the first time in an article titled, 'These Beatles Aren't Bugging Anybody!' It noted that Ringo 'dislikes Donald Duck and Chinese food,' John 'thick strings of chunky beads and traditional jazz,' and Paul 'phoney people and shaving.' It also reported that George enjoyed driving around in his Ford Anglia, which probably explained why one of his pet hates was 'travelling on buses' along with getting his hair cut.

The group began Pop Inn rehearsals at 12.30pm in the Paris Studio. The show aired live at 1pm on the Light Programme. They were interviewed and their forthcoming single 'From Me To You' was played. Also featured on the bill were David Jacobs, Arthur Askey, Winifred Atwell, Shani Wallis, Paul and Paula and Keith Fordyce.

Afterwards, the group drove across town to Wembley TV Studios in Wembley Park Drive for a 2pm rehearsal for a live appearance on Associated-Rediffusion's *Tuesday Rendezvous*. After a three-hour rehearsal, the show aired live at 5pm. The group mimed to 'From Me To You' and a shortened version of 'Please Please Me' over the closing credits. Fellow guests were puppets Ollie Beak and Fred Barker, naturalist Grahame Dangerfield and chefs Fanny and Johnnie Craddock.

After the show's 5.55pm finish, the group made the 5-mile trip to the Gaumont State on the Kilburn High Road – the largest cinema in Europe when it opened in 1937 – for the evening's 'Teen Beat' 8pm show. Many fans were turned away at the door. Stevenage group the Sinners played a short set in between the Beatles' two half-hour performances. The cinema's manager Ron Stoten was captured holding back fans during near-riot scenes under the headline 'Screaming Teenagers Flock To Hear The Beatles'. He said, 'Fantastic. I've never known anything like it'. Compère Vic Sutcliffe as well as staff members John Cansick and Peter Fallows helped Stoten keep the fans at bay. The *Kilburn Times* commented that the four of them were probably more exhausted than the Beatles after their efforts.

❝ In the summer of 1962, as a member of Cliff Bennett and the Rebel Rousers, I headed out to Hamburg to the Star-Club. It was a pretty big club, in a tiny little street in the St Pauli red light district. It was a converted cinema, so it was quite spacious inside, really well set up. Best equipment, best Fender amplifiers – they had a Hammond organ onstage – and they got all the best groups from the UK. That's where we met all the groups from Liverpool. We didn't know anything about Liverpool and we'd never heard of these groups – they were totally unknown out of their environment. The great thing about the Star-Club was we worked with American artists

as well. I backed Bo Diddley on bass while I was out there.

I first met the Beatles on the last two nights they ever did there. It was covered in snow. I remember when we left England that time, London Airport was shut for a while. We didn't think any of the planes were going to take off. Eventually we did, so we actually missed our first night in Hamburg as we arrived late. We were picked up at the airport by Horst Fascher and taken to our hotel and on to the club. I saw the Beatles perform that night for the first time. There really was something a bit more special about them than the other people. They had attitude, the music was heavy and driving, they had a personality about themselves, which I think was one of the major factors in them becoming as big as they were. The only one I met in those two days was John Lennon. It was the night after I'd seen them, and I was going backstage. Lennon was coming out, so I introduced myself and said, 'I really enjoyed the show last night and I hear you've got a new record coming out, I wish you all the best with it.' He said, 'Oh yes, Frank isn't it? Yeah, I liked your show as well, and I've been talking to people in the club and it seems that next to Cliff in the group you're the most popular member – I can't think why, your harmonies are fucking ridiculous.' He was always nice to me after that, whenever I ran into him.

We stood around backstage and they played these things over the tannoy and we listened, and that's when Horst Fascher actually came into the club and played the demo that John had left with him – it was an acetate of 'Please Please Me'. When the Rebel Rousers got back from Hamburg, the Beatles had really been making waves. I'd been telling all my friends about them – no one had actually seen them at this point. Three of my friends came with me to see them at the Gaumont State in Kilburn in my little Ford Anglia and Cliff came up with another couple of the Rebel Rousers. They did two sets, and we watched the first one, then I went backstage with Cliff and the other Rebel Rousers just to say 'Hi'. I remember talking to George backstage that night. They had just recorded their follow-up to 'Please Please Me' but had been offered 'I Like It' [written by Mitch Murray]. I distinctly remember George saying, 'We were offered this song and it's called 'I Like Your Shoes, I Like Your Coat, I Like Your Hat' or something like that. We don't like it, Gerry can have that one too.'

We left them after the interval, I went back to my friends, and they had actually decided they didn't like the Beatles! They said they were a bit fed up and didn't want to stay, so we left, and went off in my car to have a hamburger, and I never saw the second set!'

While I was in Hamburg, I had made friends with the Searchers. Just palled up with them for no other reason other than they were very nice guys, very moderate living, didn't abuse themselves, get drunk or pilled up or anything like that, which happened to everyone at the Star-Club, so they were my kind of people, they were funny, I got to know them well. Chris Curtis was very funny and great socially. He was always in London, so we used to hang around together. We were out having dinner one night in a little restaurant in Cranbourn Street called Antonio's, which featured flamenco dancing – not a great thing when you're having dinner, it's very noisy – he was telling me about the trouble they were having with Tony Jackson and that they were going to have a change in the group. I think he was waiting for me to say something, which I didn't, so he actually said, 'But I suppose you're happy with Cliff?' I said, 'Well, we've just been signed up by Brian Epstein and I'd feel really bad if I was the one to rock the boat.' Anyway, I was touring Ireland when I decided to call Chris to tell him I wanted to join the group. My first gig with them was on the 3 August at the Coventry Theatre. I hadn't had a rehearsal with the group, I was just learning their songs from the records, and suddenly we were going to start in a week's time. They said we would have a rehearsal in the afternoon – there was a six o'clock show. 'We'll meet at the theatre at one o'clock and have a rehearsal.' So I took the train up from London and got there for one o'clock. The Searchers arrived at four-thirty! We ran through some songs back stage and that was that! Here I am nearly sixty years on, still touring as a member of the Searchers. 🥇

FRANK ALLEN, MUSICIAN AND WRITER, HILLINGDON, MIDDLESEX

WEDNESDAY 10 APRIL

The group headed back north, yet again, for the evening's show at the Majestic Ballroom in Birkenhead, supported by Dee Young and the Pontiacs. It was the seventeenth and last time they played at the venue. The performance began at 7.30pm, with tickets selling at 6/-. About thirty female fans began queuing at 4.30am, through pouring rain. Seventeen-year-old Vera Maher said that she and her friend Rosa Preston, had taken the day off from work. 'There are only two rows of seats near the group and we came early to make sure of getting in them.' The Majestic's manager, Bill Marsden, said, 'It's amazing that a queue should start at such an unearthly hour – particularly so as they have all got tickets. I don't understand it.' During the show John was grabbed by his tie by an overzealous fan. He went to bed still wearing it, unable to take it off after soaking in sweat from the show. 'Matched my pyjamas a treat,' he later said. When he woke in the morning, still unable to remove it, he cut it off with a pair of scissors.

‘ When I was 17, I started work as a junior teller at the Bank of Scotland, based in Liverpool. I went for my interview and I met the managing director who gave me a lecture up in his office. He said, 'You will not wear suede shoes and you will not wear coloured shirts.' Woe betide you if you came into work in a sheepskin coat. So I wore a suit and white shirt to work every day. They were a very conservative bank. During my lunch breaks my friend Bill and I would go to the Cavern. We were keen dancers, keen drinkers – albeit the Cavern wasn't licensed at that time. We used to go at lunchtime and then at the weekend, we'd go of an evening. We saw a couple of lunchtime Beatles' gigs, and we certainly saw them at weekends. After a while of course, we were pressured by the management to become members, because we'd tried to get in as cheaply as we could – by the time I became a member I'd already been going there for two or three years. Of a weekend it would be pretty much open all night I think because from memory we'd stay and have an early morning breakfast for 2/6. Nobody knew what you were eating because the lighting was so dim, but if you'd been there dancing all night you were looking forward to the breakfast.

The Cavern was quite a dingy place. You'd go down the narrow stairs from Mathew Street into what seemed like the hold of a ship. It was dark and there were dim lights. It wasn't a very big place. It was deceptive in that it looked bigger than you thought. The volume was always deafening. Whenever there was a break I was grateful to let my ears have a rest. Despite being dingy, the Cavern was part of the scene and I think many went there not to see a particular group but just to go there. It was what youngsters wanted, including myself. I hadn't got a car. I had a motor bike, so quite often if the weather looked to be half decent, Bill and I would go on my bike. We'd have fairly warm clothes on during the winter, so we'd have to go to the cloakroom, which was a little tiny counter, and Cilla Black would sometimes be there to take your coats. I used to chat her up – at least try to. So when I got my membership card on 10 April 1963, little did I know that the Beatles would only appear there a couple more times, but I remember going many times that year.

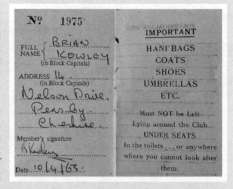

I still went clubbing through the '60s, but then the Cavern got a license and people started getting drunk and causing trouble and there would be fights outside. I went on going there until I started courting in around 1967 and then I got married in 1969. I worked for the bank and joined a marine company. After a while they were bought out by another company and this happened another three times and then finally I was made redundant. I needed another few years of employment before pensions kicked in. So I bought my local post office. I got four and a bit years out of it before the Labour government shut some twenty-five hundred post offices of which mine was going to be one. Mike McCartney, who lives in the street next to me, used to come in and we'd chew the fat and moan about this and that. One day I told him, 'I think I could do with getting your Paul involved.' He's got a house up the road and I wanted him to help me. Mike obviously spoke with Paul, because I found out he had written some letters to some high ups, but even if the Pope had got involved it wouldn't have made any difference. But the name McCartney does get things done and I had phone calls from TV stations in Canada and Japan and they came and interviewed me. **]**

BRIAN KEWLEY, COMPANY DIRECTOR, HESWALL, WIRRAL, MERSEYSIDE

THURSDAY 11 APRIL

The group's third single, 'From Me To You' coupled with 'Thank You Girl', was released. The EMI press release stated: 'In defiance of the tiresome trend towards weepie lost-love wailers, 'From Me To You' is a rip-rockin' up-tempo ballad which has a happy-go-lucky romantic story-line. Ear-catching High-spot: Those unexpected falsetto-voice high-kicks on the line 'If there's anything I can do.' Off-beat Finale: Sudden switch of speed and rhythm for that end-of-the-track instrumental climax. Unanimous Verdict: The sturdy beat plus the unique Beatle-blending of harmonica, guitars and voices plus the thoroughly infectious tune must make 'From Me To You' another dead-cert number one chart-smasher!'

Don Nicholl, reviewing the group's new single in *Disc*, commented, 'The Top 20 seems a pure formality so far as the Merseyside marvels are concerned at the present time. The Beatles' own song-writing members, John Lennon and Paul McCartney, are responsible for both the numbers on the latest release. 'From Me To You' is a lusty beater. A ballad on the up-tempo with a simple set of words, and some surprising falsetto phrases. These mouth-organs, guitars and voices are almost certain to send it to the top.' 'Please

Please Me' dropped to number 20 in the paper's chart and dates for the group's tour with Roy Orbison and Gerry and the Pacemakers were announced, as was an appearance on BBC-TV's *Pops And Lenny* series.

The *NRM*'s cover featured photos of the Beatles and Gerry and the Pacemakers taken by Dezo Hoffmann, headed 'The Big Beat', alongside ads of the group's two singles. The paper commented, 'Latest from the Beatles is opened by some smooth group wordless vocalising. Then they begin the plaintive fast-ish number with plenty of their distinctive high-pitched sounds and perhaps better vocal work than on their last two discs. It's got a good catchy tune and some decent lyrics to hold it up. The boys supply themselves with a good beat backing on the number – it should be a number one.' 'Please Please Me' dropped six places to number 17, while the LP jumped five places to number 3.

With Good Friday the following day, the week's *NME* and *Melody Maker* both published early. 'Please Please Me' dropped to number 22 in the *NME* chart and number 17 in the *Melody Maker* chart. The LP climbed one place to number 5 in the *NME* chart and three places to number 7 in *Melody Maker*, which – under the heading 'Below par Beatles...' – felt that 'The Beatles have a certain follow-up hit with 'From Me To You' – but if this average song was done by a less prominent group it would mean little. An up-tempo beat number with a just so-so melody, it is not nearly so outstanding in originality as 'Please Please Me'. It's a best-seller, inevitably – but the group ought to be able to do something better than this as a follow-up to an initial hit.' Keith Fordyce in his *NME* review titled 'Beatles Sparkle Again' wrote, 'That lively group from Liverpool, the Beatles, have a new one on Parlophone called 'From Me To You'. Singing and harmonising are good, and there's plenty of sparkle. Lyric is commercial, but I don't rate the tune as being anything like as good as on the last two discs from this group. 'Thank You Girl' is a steady beat number, a little bit on the slow side. I think you can safely expect to see this disc in the charts very quickly.' Not a man to mince words, Bunny Lewis in weekly tabloid magazine *Reveille* found it 'a little dull'.

With the remainder of his tie removed and replaced by another, John travelled to Sefton General to see his newborn son for the first time. During the visit, he told Cynthia he was intending go on holiday to Spain with Epstein. John signed autographs and then left for an interview with the *NME*'s Alan Smith. He commented on the effect of the recording of the group's LP on his voice: 'Just lately things have been getting better. But my voice wasn't the same for a long time after. Every time I swallowed it was like sandpaper. We sang for twelve hours, almost non-stop. We had colds and we were concerned how it would affect the record. And by the end of the day, all we wanted to do was drink pints of milk.'

The group travelled 40 miles north-east to Middleton, playing at the Co-operative Hall in Long Street from 7.30pm to 11pm. Three hundred fans, paying 7/6, crammed into the venue, built in 1871. It never celebrated its centenary, closing down soon after the Beatles' appearance – ostensibly because of structural damage done to the floor and brickwork by many of those Three hundred fans.

After performing for more than an hour, the group came off stage, changed out of their maroon suits, packed up their gear and signed autographs, while local group Shaun and Sum People played to the packed house. Within half an hour, the group were on their way back to Liverpool.

❛ Myself, Tony Duckworth, David Tierney and Jimmy Eckersly used to hang around Middleton Gardens during the week after we'd got home from school. The night the Beatles were playing at the Co-op, the four of us decided to walk from the gardens near the picture house up to the Co-op at the Assheton Arms gardens to see if any groups were on. You had to be 16 to get in. We were all 13 and skint.

That night we'd arrived at the back of the Co-op Hall at the stage door entrance. At the front of the Co-op were two doors, one took you into the Co-op Store which was on the left-hand side and the other up to the dance hall. We were waiting for a good opportunity to sneak into the dance hall. We knew something was on as we could hear music from outside. We were stood at the back by the stage door when a van pulled up, and when I looked towards it, I was looking at Paul McCartney, although at the time he was just another bloke. I had no idea who he was.

The four of them got out of the van and started to unload their equipment. We stood watching them and I asked if they needed any help and one of them said, 'Yeah come on.' So me and my mates helped them up the stairs with their equipment. When the van had been unloaded the four of us were stood upstairs with the Beatles in the Co-op Hall at the back of the stage. They were having a laugh with us and were calling the four of us 'scallywags'. Paul had a box of photographs of the group. He'd taken some of them out of the box and was holding them in his hand when I asked him if I could have one. He said yes and I asked him if he would sign it, which he did and then he passed it to John, Ringo and George and they also signed it. Then one of the staff in the Co-op dance hall came along and told us we'd have to leave as we were underage. 'Come on you lot. Out!' we were told.

So, we left the dance hall and the four of us began to make our way home up Wood Street onto Langley Estate. We all lived on Fairfield Road. As we were walking up Wood Street, Duckie [Tony Duckworth] asked me to show him the signed photograph. I took it out of my pocket and TT [David Tierney] took it off me, looked at it then gave it to Duckie. He looked at it and said, 'That's great.' Then asked, 'Can I have it?' and I said, 'No, it's mine' to which he replied, 'No it's for all of us' and ripped it up. The photograph was left to be blown away and we carried on walking up the road. **❞**

ANTHONY FITZPATRICK, LONG DISTANCE LORRY DRIVER, MIDDLETON, GREATER MANCHESTER

FRIDAY 12 APRIL

Taking the poster heeding 'Please Please Be Early' quite literally, two girls had started queuing a month earlier, working in shifts to ensure front row seats, finally gained admittance to an eight-hour marathon at the Cavern – no doubt happy to be indoors after early morning snow and sleet showers. Advertised in *Mersey Beat* as a 'Good Friday Great Shot Of Rhythm And Blues Marathon No. 2', the show began at 4pm. Members paid 7/6 to see the Beatles, the Four Mosts, the Dennisons, the Nomads, the Panthers, Faron's Flamingos, the Flintstones, the Roadrunners and Group One. While back in Liverpool, John was chatting with local musician Steve Day, when Gerry Marsden – then sitting at the top with 'How Do You Do It?' – approached him and said, 'How does it feel to be Brian's number two group, then?' John's response was to give Marsden two fingers.

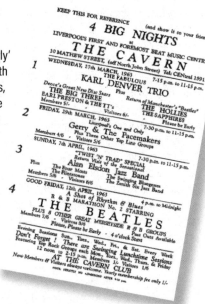

The Dennisons' lead singer Eddie Parry remembered the day, 'You had to wait about five hours before you went onstage but I didn't mind as I was watching my idol, John Lennon. Our lead guitarist Steve McLaren and I got the idea for a song that night and that was our first single 'Be My Girl'. The Beatles performed at 9.50, playing a forty-five-minute set, followed by Faron's Flamingos, who closed the almost eight-hour show.

❝ My father was a professional musician who had his own jazz band and played with the Ted Heath Orchestra for a while. Mum was a wonderful pianist and met my father when she was playing with the Ivy Benson Orchestra during the war. I was born in 1942 and remember all the bombing, but, as a family, we always had our music. Dad would drag the piano out into the street on a Saturday night and the local pub would provide crates of beer. When I was 7, there was a competition in Stanley Park to advertise Smith's Crisps. I sang 'Mammy' and won! My prize was a red and yellow push scooter. I'll never forget walking home with my dad, holding it.

Johnny Tempest invited me to come along to one of their rehearsals one night and I thought they were tremendous. Initially I played rhythm guitar and sang lead vocals when Johnny got tired, which he did a lot. We didn't know why. Sadly, it turned out he had a brain tumour and died on his 21st birthday. I took over the lead vocals and changed my name from Billy Ruffley to my middle name Faron.

I first saw the Beatles at the Jacaranda. They'd just got back from a stint in Germany and were painting the walls of the coffee bar. They weren't highly regarded at the time. Allan Williams owned the place, and wanted Bob Wooler to compère there, and said, 'Could you take them off my hands?' Bob said he might be able to get them booked at Litherland Town Hall for £4 a night, and so it was arranged. We didn't play with them the first week, but the second week, we did. Stu [Sutcliffe] was wearing a leather jacket with a fur collar, and it stank! They were all wearing jeans, and John's had a big rip down the side. John had a Gibson valve amp which he turned on with a hammer, and his Rickenbacker guitar, Paul had his solid red Rosetti with three strings. I was standing outside signing autographs when Bob went into one of his big announcements – 'DIRECT FROM HAMBURG... THE BEATLES!' They went straight into Little Richard's 'Ooh! My Soul'. Paul's voice was amazing. Every hair on my head stood up. I'd never heard anything like it. They did [Elvis's] 'Wooden Heart' with the German bit in the middle. But it was the way they interacted with the audience. They talked to them. They chatted to each other onstage, all laughing and joking. 'Gis a ciggie!' 'Shut yer gob and buy yer own!' They would eat butties onstage, and Paul would shout to George, 'What've you got on yours?' 'I'll swap you for an egg one.' It was just sheer brilliance. I said, 'What's going on?' and Bob said, 'What do you think?' I jokingly replied that they'd never last, that's how green with envy I was.

Easter weekend 1963 we played one of the Rhythm and Blues Marathons at the Cavern. The marathons would start in the middle of the afternoon, some finished around midnight, and others went right through to the following morning. The place was always really chocka. They tended to be on holiday weekends, so people weren't having to rush to get back to work. I was wearing a long corduroy coat I'd got in France and Paul came up to me and said, 'Wow, that coat's amazing. Where did you get it?' Eppy was down there, and he said, 'Come and look at this Brian.' They were wearing their white shirts and blue velvet waistcoats instead of the jeans and leather jackets. When they went on, they were just amazing, so far ahead with their ideas. We'd sometimes mix it up a bit, different members of different groups, and we always had to share the same gear for the marathons. We played the final night the Beatles played the Cavern as well. It was another holiday weekend in August. They were getting big by then and the place was heaving. It was so hot in there that the condensation was running down the walls. They had to stop the show a couple of times to mop up the floor of the stage and they wouldn't let us plug in our amplifiers in. There were far too many people in there and it was complete chaos. ❞

FARON RUFFLEY, MUSICIAN, AUGHTON, LANCASHIRE

SATURDAY 13 APRIL

The group took an early morning flight to London to make their BBC-TV debut on *The 625 Show*. Following a band call at 10.30am in Studio E at the BBC's Lime Grove Studios in Shepherd's Bush, camera rehearsals began at 11.30am with a final rehearsal taking place at 4.30pm. The taping took place from 7.30pm to 8.15pm. They performed 'From Me To You', 'Thank You Girl' and 'Please Please Me'.

The show was compèred by Jimmy Young and also featured Rolf and Tino, Bobbi Carrol, Hank Locklin, Wout Steenhuis, Johnny Pearson, Edwin Braben and a four-piece band led by Micky Greeve. It aired the following Tuesday.

SUNDAY 14 APRIL

Easter morning, the group drove down to Teddington, and despite a late night, arrived in time for an 11am rehearsal for *Thank Your Lucky Stars* at Teddington Studio Centre. Their third appearance on the show, they mimed to 'From Me To You' at the 5.50pm recording. Hosted by Brian Matthew, also on the bill were Del Shannon, Bert Weedon, Mike Berry, the Vernons Girls, the Dave Clark Five and Kent Walton. The show aired the following Saturday.

During a break in rehearsals the group met photographer Fiona Adams for the first time and renaissance man Giorgio Gomelsky, who approached Brian Epstein about making a Beatles' movie. Although nothing came of Gomelsky's suggestion, he did persuade the group to go to his Crawdaddy Club in nearby Richmond after the recording, where the Rolling Stones were performing. They stopped off for a pint at the nearby Anglers pub before Aspinall drove them to the club. They arrived during the Stones' first set. The two groups met in the bar in between sets and, duly impressed, they stayed for the second. At the end of the evening, they adjourned to 102 Edith Grove in West Brompton, where Stones Mick Jagger, Keith Richard and Brian Jones shared a flat and talked into the small hours of the morning. Brian asked for an autographed photo which he subsequently hung on a wall. He later recalled the encounter, 'We talked about our hopes halfway through the night. We could hardly believe that our kind of music would catch on.' Inviting the Stones to their upcoming concert at the Royal Albert Hall, the group left around 4am. George and Ringo were driven back to the Hotel President by the Stones' piano player Ian Stewart.

❝ I had joined the Vernons Girls in 1962 along with Fran Lea and Mo [Maureen] Kennedy. We were wrapping up a long tour with Cliff Richard and the Shadows and I remember being on the coach with Cliff and Bruce Welch. I was the youngest of the Vernons Girls, so therefore the hippest! Bruce asked me whether I'd heard of the Beatles. I said, 'Of course I have.' He said, 'Well, we're having a party and the Beatles are going to be there. You should come.' So off we headed on said date to Bruce's house. We were standing there chatting, when Mo suddenly said, 'Who's THAT?' and four – what we thought were – very long-haired lads walked through the door. I said, 'Oh my God, that's the Beatles, they're fantastic!' Mo just went, 'Ugh,' and turned away. We were a little mouthy in those days.

A little later John came over, of course we didn't really know him as John Lennon then, and he introduced himself, and said, 'You're the Vernons aren't you?' and Mo looked at him like he was a piece of dirt on her shoe. I answered everything, as she clearly wasn't going to say anything. We'd done a B-side of a Liverpool thing called 'You Know What I Mean'. John said, 'I love that song. Actually, we've got a song you might be interested in.' Mo, still unimpressed, just looked at him and said, 'No thanks,' and turned away.

We must have done two or three *Thank Your Lucky Stars* with the Beatles. It was a whole day thing at Teddington and you just went on and did your bit and went back to the dressing room. I remember Del Shannon was chatting me up all the time when we did the show in April 1963. We had our photographs taken all together, me on Paul's knee, with Del looking down at me from behind! We did another show with him at the Albert Hall that year and went out for dinner afterwards.

When we toured with the Beatles later on, Mo went up to John and said, 'Ya alright John? You know that song you wrote for us?' He said, 'You can bugger off. You didn't want it when ya didn't know us, did ya?!' He was really only joking because they got on really well, in fact they had a bit of a thing going on. One day Cynthia turned up at Mo's Regent's Park flat. She was waiting at the bottom of the steps for John with a cab waiting. Mo and John were up to something at the top of the stairs and I was in the middle trying to hurry them up

When we did the November tour with them we were all messing around one day, and John said to me, 'It's your birthday today, isn't it?' Ringo had told me the previous week that he was going to teach me the drums, so he said, 'Come on, I'll show you a paradiddle,' so I got behind Richie's drums and he was showing me what to do, and John said, 'I'll bet if I told that lot down there that Ringo got you these drums as a birthday present, they'd believe me!' gesturing towards the press gathered below. So he stood on the apron of the stage, and said, 'Fellas, I don't know if you want to hear this, but Ringo has bought Jean a set of drums for her birthday!' So they're writing it down and taking photographs, and went away, feeling that they'd got a good story. The next day, in the papers, there was a picture of Mo sitting at the drums, and I was peeved off that it wasn't me! On the last night of the tour I was singing 'Tomorrow's Another Day' and my mic started moving. I turned around and one of the Beatles was at the piano with a coat over his head with something hooked around the mic stand, pulling it. I left the group in 1964 before beginning a solo career as Samantha Jones. ❞

JEAN GOUMAL, SINGER, HENLEY-ON-THAMES, OXFORDSHIRE

MONDAY 15 APRIL

The group made the two and a half hour drive to the market town of Tenbury Wells in Worcestershire for a show booked by the Riverside Dancing Club committee, in a room at the back of the Bridge Hotel in Teme Street. They arrived mid-afternoon and wandered round the town, before being treated to dinner by the landlord of the hotel.

Pat Lambert was part of the committee who booked the group for £100. 'I was running a hairdressing salon called Top Style and remember them showing up and walking past the shop. Several of my customers ran into the street their hair still in rollers. I remember Ringo eating an ice-cream even though it was really cold that day, and apparently John asked passersby whether they could give him a cigarette.' A fan took a photo of the group outside the sweet shop at 8 Teme Street.

Jim Tompkins, who had earlier gone looking for them at the Oak pub and been told by landlord Jack Knowles that he didn't want 'any long-haired scruffy beggars' in his pub, was bought a pint of Wrekin bitter by George while they chatted. Crowds started forming at 7pm. Fans came from nearby Ludlow and Cleehill by bus. Members paid 3/6 admittance. El Riot and the Rebels opened; the Beatles followed and played to a packed crowd. Edwina Bishop remembered the atmosphere being great and that 'the music was very loud, but at that age any noise was good.' Lambert recalled, 'It was just like the records. It was loud and raucous and all the girls were screaming. They were very good. I took my autograph book along and I asked them all to sign it, which they did.' Committee members Tony Lambert – Pat's husband – and Ernie Davies introduced the group. After the show, the Beatles headed south-east to Worcester, spending the night at the Star Hotel.

> ❛ Monday 15 April at the Riverside Club. Dancing from 9pm till 1am, 8/- on the door. I remember it well. I was 22 years old and lead guitarist in a group called El Riot and the Rebels. Ray Thomas was El Riot the singer, John Lodge was the bass player, Mike Heard was rhythm and Ricky Wade was our drummer. Ray and John later became part of the Moody Blues. We did numerous gigs at the Riverside Club, working for Jean Morton of TV fame. She rang us and said she had a special gig for us, to support an up-and-coming group called the Beatles. They had already had chart success with 'Please Please Me'. Jean had booked them some time earlier and they had to honour their contract.
>
> On the night, we arrived much earlier than we needed so we could get a chance to chat with them before the show. There were posters and drawings of the Beatles all over the dance hall. I got to say a quick 'Hello' and set up my gear. We did our first spot and went down a storm. Ray had tinted his hair silver and the girls loved it. They were chanting for more. Then it was the Beatles turn – they were OK, but I think El Riot and the Rebels stole the show! At the end of the evening, we had a good old chat with the Beatles – great lads and good fun. People were sending autograph books to the dressing room for us all to sign. We then had our photograph taken with the group. A great night was had by all. I did meet them again at Abbey Road Studios when I was another group called the Vogues. We had a chat and I jogged their memory of the Riverside Club. Great memories. ❜
>
> **BRYAN BETTERIDGE, MUSICIAN, SUTTON COLDFIELD, WEST MIDLANDS**

TUESDAY 16 APRIL

The group travelled to Granada TV Centre's Studio Four in Manchester to rehearse for the evening's broadcast of *Scene At 6.30*, arriving around 3pm. The group mimed to 'From Me To You'. They had been booked by producer Johnny Hamp, who in the 1970s was responsible for popular TV shows *The Comedians* and *The Wheeltappers And Shunters Social Club*. It was not their first appearance on the show – a *Scene At 6.30* crew had filmed them at the Cavern on 22 August 1962, when the show was known as *People And Places*.

Saturday's recording of *The 625 Show* aired at the same time on the BBC. In his review of the show the *Daily Mirror*'s TV critic Richard Sear wrote 'One other person deserves credit – the Beatles' barber. He has a talent for straight comedy.' In response, 'Two Angry Fans' from Bromley in Kent suggested that Sear 'should get with it and style his hair the same way', while Miss T. Wright of London SE9 supposed that Sear was 'dead gone on Beethoven.'

❝ I wasn't much into pop music. The first 45 rpm disc I ever bought was a comedy number – Bernard Cribbins's 'Gossip Calypso' – and my first LP was similar – Flanders and Swann doing animal songs. So the Beatles might well have passed me by had not my boarding school buddy been a keen student of the charts. I was only mildly interested in his obsessional tracking of who was up and who was down from the pages of the *New Musical Express*, but when he came to stay in the holidays I found myself caught up in a sort of Beatlemania.

We were boy choristers at Canterbury Cathedral. Home for me was in Barnes in south-west London, but I only got to spend half the school holidays there. The first half of the Easter break had been spent in Canterbury as 'Boarder Choir', singing the Passiontide and Easter music. We were allowed home only on Easter Monday and my friend was coming to stay. My father worked for the BBC External Services at Bush House. At the time he was posted to the Arabic Service. I used to visit Bush House, meet the characters and eccentrics (Dad included) and stuff my face in the famous canteen with its more or less international cuisine. One also got to visit the studios and pretend to read the news. The studios, of course, had tape decks and turntables. The Arabs were used to different music and their taste in singing with its strange quarter tones was a startling contrast to the church music we choristers sang or the Hit Parade that I caught on my illicit transistor radio after lights out. But it was on the turntable of a Bush House radio studio, with Arab production staff in attendance, that we first heard 'From Me To You', purchased on our way from Barnes to Bush House. We also took along *Please Please Me* the first LP released a month earlier. I remember admiring the coloured photo of the Fab Four posing down a stair well as we crossed Barnes Common on the way to the station. ❞

CHRISTOPHER GRAHAM, FORMER UK INFORMATION COMMISSIONER,
LAY PREACHER DIOCESE OF CHESTER, HALE, CHESHIRE

WEDNESDAY 17 APRIL

The group drove 180 miles to Luton, Bedfordshire, to perform at the Majestic Ballroom in Mill Street, where Gene Vincent had performed the previous Sunday. Described as 'The most luxurious ballroom in the district', the venue had recently been converted to the Ballroom from the Gaumont, opening its doors the previous October. It also served as a Top Rank Bingo and Social Club.

An ad had recently been placed in the *Luton News'* Situations Vacant column for a disc-jockey at the venue. The job called for someone with 'personality-plus' and would include hosting the ballroom's record session most evenings of the week, as well as to 'engage and introduce' visiting pop stars to the venue. Twenty-seven people applied for the job, which then current disc jockey Bob Mitchell described as 'a job with great prospects'. The town had yet to jump on the Beatles' bandwagon: the show was not sold out. Only two hundred and fifty fans paid 6/6 to see the show and the group were able walk in and out the building without any fuss. Ringo ate crisps while signing autographs. Following the show, the group returned to London and spent the night at the Royal Court Hotel.

THURSDAY 18 APRIL

'The Beatles Come In At Number 10!' blared the front page of *Disc*. Brian Epstein told the paper that the single was selling 'at the rate of thousands a day, so great is the demand'. Only 'Please Please Me', which dropped to number 28, had entered the Top 30 higher in the year. In the *NRM* chart, 'From Me To You' entered at number 23, one place below the falling 'Please Please Me'. In the LP chart *Please Please Me* stayed at number 3.

In the morning, the group drove to the Royal Albert Hall on Kensington Gore for an all-day rehearsal for the evening's 'Swinging Sound '63' concert, part of which was broadcast live on the Light Programme at 9.10pm – the second of three music programmes, broadcast on 14 March and 2 May. Backstage in dressing room 5A, between rehearsals and the 8pm concert, Roger Henning, an Australian DJ living in London, interviewed the group – albeit briefly. The thirty-two-second interview included the group singing the Australian bush ballad 'Waltzing Matilda', accompanied by harmonica and ukulele.

The bill also featured Del Shannon, the Springfields, Rolf Harris, the Vernons Girls, Kenny Lynch, Robin Hall and Jimmie MacGregor, George Melly, Susan Maughan, Shane Fenton and the Fentones, the Chris Barber Band with Ottilie Patterson, the Eric Delaney Band, the BBC Jazz Club All Stars and Lance Percival, filling in for Matt Monro, who had burst a blood vessel in his throat. Shannon told John that he planned to record 'From Me To You' for the American market, particularly taken with the use of the A-minor chord in the middle of the bridge. George spent much of the afternoon in the dressing room playing Tom Springfield's twelve-string guitar.

In the first half of the concert, the Beatles, introduced by Melly, sang 'Please Please Me' and 'Misery', and in the second 'Twist And Shout' – despite rehearsing 'Thank You Girl' and not telling the producers about the change – and 'From Me To You'. The show ended with the assembled company performing 'Mack The Knife' as the Light Programme faded the broadcast at 10.15pm.

Mick Jagger, Brian Jones and Keith Richard attended, given front-row tickets and backstage passes by the Beatles, as did *Radio Times*' assistant editor Tony Aspler, who brought actress Jane Asher with him as part of a celebrity piece he was writing for the magazine. During the interval, Asher was taken to meet the Beatles in the hall's Green Room, where she was invited by Ringo to attend a party afterwards.

Following the show, Brian Jones helped Neil Aspinall and Mal Evans carry the group's equipment to their van. The Beatles had originally planned to go to the Ad Lib club, but instead accepted journalist Chris Hutchins' invite to his flat at 398 King's Road. They first drove to the Royal Court Hotel, hitching a ride with Shane Fenton, with Asher also on board. Hutchins recalled that, 'the old Regency furniture in the cramped living room was hastily pushed aside to make space for the unexpected guests, and they squatted on the dark green pile carpet. As the only woman, Jane was in the centre. She was pale-faced and suitably thin for the period that spawned Twiggy. When she spoke, her voice reflected her Wimpole Street background, singling her out as upper-middle-class, yet her kindly smile made the rest of us feel comfortable. I raised my glass of Mateus Rosé, then the sophisticated drink for young Chelsea trendies. 'To The Beatles.' The group went with Fenton to Jack Isow's, a well-known club on Soho's Brewer Street, leaving Paul alone with Asher.

❛In the early '60s when I was performing as Shane Fenton, I'd already done a gig with the Beatles in 1962 and a couple of radio shows earlier in 1963 – as well as seeing them when I was back home in Mansfield the previous month. I met them again when we both took part in the 'Swinging Sound '63' concert at the Royal Albert Hall. I had been given a guitar by my father in 1955 which through the years had been signed by Buddy Holly and the Crickets, Bill Haley, Chuck Berry, Eddie Cochran, Gene Vincent and Cliff Richard and decided that this might be my best chance to get the Beatles to add their signatures. I was a bit embarrassed to go up and ask them to sign my guitar, so one of the backstage workers by the name of Len said, 'Give it to me I'll do it for you son.' He nipped off with the guitar and sure enough came back five minutes later. They'd all signed it. They didn't even know it was my guitar.

Towards the end of the evening, I think it was Paul and John who came up to me and said, 'Listen, you live in London. You must know the best place to go out and meet some birds. Where can we go? And when can you take us?' So later that night I took them down to a place called Jack Isow's. It was a bit of a clip joint where the girls would come down and encourage young men who went in there to buy a bottle of champagne at an exorbitant price. But of course the Beatles knew about all this because we'd all been playing in Hamburg and Frankfurt which had been full of clip joints. So we went in anyway, the boys sat down and ordered three Cokes. Not all four of them went – I don't think Paul was there, but the boys sat there with their Coca-Colas. Suddenly three girls came over, sat next to them and tried to encourage them to buy some champagne. They soon realised it wasn't going to happen and they disappeared to the powder room and never returned.

I went back to Isow's some time later and the minute I walked in these three girls came over and said, 'Hey, where are those nice three boys from Liverpool?' I said, 'Wait a minute, they're number 1 in the charts now. How come you want to know them now when you didn't want to know them three weeks ago? I doubt whether you'll ever see them again.' Later in the year, the BBC threw another Pop Proms and this time, dream of dreams, they had the Rolling Stones on and the Beatles and some of the British pop stars that were around. So then again of course I bumped into Len who very quickly took my guitar up the Stones dressing room and got them to sign it. Five minutes later he was back and I had these wonderful autographs on my guitar. ❜

ALVIN STARDUST, ACTOR, MUSICIAN, IFOLD, WEST SUSSEX

FRIDAY 19 APRIL

As 'Please Please Me' dropped out of the *NME* Top 30 and down six places to number 23 in *Melody Maker*, 'From Me To You' crashed into both charts at numbers 6 and 19, respectively – tying with the Temperance Seven and the Shadows as the highest chart entry by a group in the history of the *NME*. The LP climbed two places in both the *NME* and *Melody Maker* charts, to numbers 3 and 5, respectively.

The *NME* revealed that the group had been added to the line-up of its annual Poll-Winners' Concert and announced a series a new dates, in an article titled 'Pacemakers and Beatles: Many Big Pop Shows'. Eleven days were scheduled at the Paris Olympia in September, some dates in support of Orbison were switched, and Hanley (24 May) and Kingston (30 May) were cancelled. John's interview with Alan Smith conducted on 11 April was printed under the heading, 'Throat Sweets Keep Us Going – Say Beatles!' *Melody*

Maker ran with the headline 'Beatles Back With A Bang!' on the front page, reporting that 'The Beatles have made it again! Today, the beat boys from Liverpool have smashed their own disc sales record – and leapt into the Hit Parade at No. 19. The song? 'From Me To You', another composition by hit-writing Beatles John Lennon and Paul McCartney. By today, sales of the smash hit single will have reached two hundred thousand in the seven days since its release – setting up a bigger sales register than their first chart-topper, 'Please Please Me.'

An EMI Records spokesman said: 'Altogether, it looks like being a much bigger record for the Beatles than 'Please Please Me' – they are going from strength to strength. In the best-selling LP chart, too, the vocal-instrumental unit is gaining ground – their debut LP rose two spots today to No. 5. The spectacular success of 'From Me To You' means a hat-trick of hits for them. Their first single, 'Love Me Do', was a heavy seller. McCartney and Lennon are consolidating their position as two of Britain's most prolific new songwriters. Next week, Parlophone issues the first single by another Merseyside group, Billy J. Kramer and [sic] the Dakotas. Title: 'Do You Want To Know A Secret?' penned by Paul and John. They have another song for recording soon – Duffy Power's 'I Saw Her Standing There.'

The second 'Mersey Beat Showcase' concert took place that evening at the King's Hall in Stoke-on-Trent, where the group had previously performed on 26 January. Admittance for the 7.30pm to 1am show was 10/-.

> ❛ I remember the day the Beatles came to the King's Hall in Stoke very well. I used to go there regularly in the early '60s. One of the main reasons to go to dance halls back then was to see how many young ladies were there! That evening stuck in my mind in particular because in those days the lads used to stand on one side and the girls on the other, and you would talk about who you were going to go and ask to dance. Then you would dance around handbags and things, sticky-out dresses and all that sort of thing. This was the first evening that I had ever seen people standing still in front of the stage, watching the group play. Prior to that, everybody danced. There were just rows and rows of people, just standing looking at the stage. I had never seen that before.
>
>
>
> I went every week to the King's Hall because I knew people and got in for nothing. I was a 20-year-old policeman at the time – that's why I got in for nothing. I stayed in the force until 1966 and the following year I became a professional entertainer. Peter Williams is my real name, and from that, I became Pete Conway, which is my stage name and has been since 1967. I went to work in an office, English Electric, which eventually became part of ICL, when I left the police force. In the evenings and weekends I appeared in the clubs. The first time I appeared I was billed as 'Peter Williams' and my boss on the Monday morning said, 'I saw your name in the paper advertising Saturday night and you need a showbiz name.' So we put Pete in front of everyone's name who I worked with. One of whom was Colin Conway and we had a vote and I became 'Pete Conway' that morning. After I had had some success, people would say to my mum and dad, 'Oh hello Mr Conway, hello Mrs Conway.' I started as a comic and I did all right for myself. I was doing the clubs and won a few talent competitions, including 'New Faces' in 1973 and got the entertainment bug. I was a comedian for a long time, so rather than become a singer, I became a comic. I was doing an hour and the group would leave me on my own. They were wonderful days. I've survived more than fifty years now. I must retire soon. I've just done two years on the road with my lad Robbie. We've done two world tours. I pop on and do ten minutes with him and leave him to do the next two hours! I've really enjoyed it and I'm still active and I've never left Stoke. ❜
>
> **PETE CONWAY, COMEDIAN AND BROADCASTER, STOKE-ON-TRENT, STAFFORDSHIRE**

SATURDAY 20 APRIL

The group left Liverpool in the afternoon, heading for the small Cheshire town of Frodsham. On arrival, they drove to the top of Overton Hill, to the Mersey View Pleasure Ground. Built at the turn of the century, the helter skelter stood tall in an area that had become a favourite place for picnics and Sunday School outings through the 1920s and 1930s. William Comaish, the venue's general manager, had written to Brian Epstein as early as the previous November to book the group. The agreement reached was for a £75 fee, although if in the meantime 'Please Please Me' made the Top 5 in the *NRM* chart, there would be an additional payment of £25.

The ballroom was the only venue in the area where local pop fans could see their favourite acts. Dilys O'Neill, a regular, recalled, 'Once inside with the beat of the music, the lights, the laughter and the camaraderie, the magic began. All the boys stood on one side of the dancefloor and the girls sat on forms at the other end. When the group struck up, the boys would dash across and invite the girls to dance. We were hardly ever wallflowers then! By the end of the evening our poor feet were killing us. In the interval pop and Lawless' famous meat pies were served for those who were hungry.'

The previous Sunday's recording of *Thank Your Lucky Stars* aired at 5.50pm, while fans began arriving for the 8pm show. Support act Bill Gorman and His Orchestra, with vocalists Jimmy Nolan and Veronica Moore, opened the concert. Screams from the packed house greeted the Beatles as they took to the stage. Around midnight, the group drove back to Liverpool.

> ❝ My family became involved with the Mersey View Pleasure Grounds just after the Second World War. They had been involved before then, with several others, but eventually it was just my father Kenneth, his brother Percy and a chap called Mr Comaish who had shares in the place. On Saturdays through the summer season, it was a big attraction for Sunday School outings for children from Liverpool and the surrounding area. On a Saturday afternoon, you could have around three or four hundred children arriving on double decker buses. Along with the ballroom, there was a helter skelter, swing boats, a big playground with swings and see-saws, and a small nine-hole putting green on the other side. I remember suggesting that we have some dodgems, but the idea was never taken up. The view was magnificent, it really is a great location.
>
> When I was around 14, I had a weekend job working in the car park and on the helter skelter, which the venue was famous for. We just used to sell Coke, squash, crisps and pies from our bakery. When the dance bands lost favour to the groups in the early '60s was when I really started to go up there. Believe it or not, the place was not licensed! Of course, a lot of people used to drink in Frodsham then get a taxi up about half past nine at night. The main group were always on from 10/10.30pm till 11.30 – quite late. They switched to three groups on a Saturday night – there would be the beginners on early evening from about eight o'clock for an hour, and the star act would come on last.
>
> I had a ticket to get in through the door, which cost 6/6, but I didn't have to buy it – I'm afraid it was a case of who you knew! I remember they had to put men on the gate to stop people coming into the venue without a ticket. They had about three or four fellows on the gates and I remember I couldn't believe it when they told me how many people they had to turn away without tickets. There would have been close to a thousand people there in total. There weren't any police there, it was just people that we knew who had been asked to come in and help on the evening.
>
> I went with a local friend called Clive. We were able to stand near the front, behind the counter selling teas and coffees, which was more or less next to the stage. Of course, I knew most of the

ladies who were working there and serving behind the counter. It was something that I really hadn't experienced before. There was a bit of screaming, although it didn't affect the music, and the atmosphere was electric! A lot of the set was early Beatles stuff, quite up tempo, and they played 'Twist And Shout' at the end, which was my absolute favourite. Clive and I both got their autographs – not that we met them. My father got them for us, and I believe Clive later sold his for around £700. I have no idea where mine are! The family bakery business was started by my grandfather in the early 1900s, and we are in our third generation now, still on the same premises. I am still living over the shop! People who come into the shop still mention the grand old days of the Mersey View and all the groups who played there. **"**

JOHN LAWLESS, MASTER BAKER, FRODSHAM, CHESHIRE

SUNDAY 21 APRIL

The group appeared at the annual 'New Musical Express Annual Poll-Winners' All-Star Concert' at the Empire Pool and Sports Arena in Wembley at 2.30pm, playing to an audience of eight thousand. The bill also featured Joe Loss Orchestra, the Springfields, Mark Wynter, the Jet Harris Tony Meehan Group, Frank Ifield, Gerry and the Pacemakers, Kenny Ball and His Jazzmen, Adam Faith, the Shadows, Mike Berry, the Tornados, the Brook Brothers, Joe Brown and the Bruvvers, Billy Fury, and Cliff Richard. Alan Smith wrote in the *NME*, 'They crashed into the throbbing beat of its first number, 'Please Please Me', to the delight of the audience who were seeing them at a Poll Concert for the first time. 'Please Please Me' was followed by the Beatles' current hit, 'From Me To You', and then their dynamic version of the Isley Brothers' 'Twist And Shout'. Before their pulsating climax 'Long Tall Sally', bass guitarist Paul McCartney cracked, 'Here's a song immortalised by that great gospel singer Victor Silvester!' The Beatles

look like being Poll Concert residents for many years to come.'

In the evening the group, billed as 'The most sensational group in England', gave a private concert at the Pigalle night club in Piccadilly from 8pm to 11.30pm, supported by the Castaways and Dave Antony and the Druids. Promoter Barry Clayman recalled paying them £100 for two forty-five-minute sets. 'We used to hire the Pigalle on Sundays. Brian Epstein phoned and said, 'We are doing the *NME* Poll-Winners' Concert. It's on a Sunday, we want to do a gig and someone said you are doing some concerts at this nightclub.' I think we had twelve hundred people in there, and the licence was about seven hundred, so we were probably pushing it a bit. It was a great atmosphere, plenty of sweat.'

I was living in Willesden in north-west London in the early '60s, and a pupil at John Kelly Boy's Technical College in Neasden. A big Buddy Holly and Shadows fan, I'd bought myself a guitar in about 1961. I had a Saturday job in a little grocer's shop in Willesden, and in late '62, a lad I was working with said, 'Oh, there's this group called the Beatles, they've got a new record out called 'Love Me Do'. It's really good!' I hadn't heard of them at that point. Then I heard it. The first record I ever bought of theirs though was their first album. I was a massive Rolling Stones fan. I saw them in 1963 in Richmond when they were just starting out, but my wife Anne was a huge Beatles fan, and we had a bit of rivalry between us! I was sort of a reluctant closet Beatles fan, but of course I loved them, and it started a lifelong obsession. I bought everything that came out, watched them every time they appeared on television. I remember when they first appeared on *Thank Your Lucky Stars*. I took some photographs of the screen on our black-and-white TV at home

and wrote on the back: 'The Beatles' first appearance on *Thank Your Lucky Stars*. The Beatles are, left to right Paul McCartney, Ringo Starr, John Lennon and George Harrison doing 'Please Please Me'.' I still have it! The pictures came out surprisingly well! Our local record shop was in Harlesden, where we'd buy our records. When the family moved from there to New Malden in Surrey – which is how I met my wife Anne, we lived in the same street – we would go down to a little record shop there. After moving to New Malden, I went to school at Twickenham Technical College. I was playing in a little group then, and Anne would come and watch us play, and she still comes to watch me play, bless her! I went to all the NME Poll-Winners' concerts at the Empire Pool, Wembley with Anne. I was still living in Willesden the first time I went, and it was only about ten minutes on the tube to Wembley. I've kept all the programmes and still remember a quote from John Lennon in one of them saying, 'Our aim is to popularise Merseyside rhythm and blues,' and I remember thinking, 'What does that mean?' We didn't manage to see the group in concert other than the Poll-Winners' shows until 1964, and we saw them again in 1965.

As well as playing guitar, in the early '70s I started DJing with Stuart Colman. We used to have a residency at a pub in the Old Kent Road in London. There was a bit of a rock'n'roll/rockabilly revival going on then and there wasn't a dedicated rock'n'roll show on national radio. We decided it needed one, and we organised a thing called 'The Rock and Roll Radio Campaign,' which was an idea to try and persuade Radio 1 to have such a show. We organised a march on the BBC in 1976, and had about six or seven thousand Teddy Boys and Girls come to London. We had groups playing on trucks - Screaming Lord Sutch was one of them, and marched from Marble Arch to Broadcasting House. We handed in a petition to the boss, and gave him a cassette of us doing a rock'n'roll show, not to say 'Hire us' but more 'This is the sort of show you should be doing.' A few months later I had a call from Radio 1 asking if Stuart and I could go up. The upshot of it was that they had decided they were going to do a rock'n'roll show, and that they'd like us to present it! We were expecting them to give it to Emperor Rosko or someone known like that. So we went from playing a pub in the Old Kent Road to Radio 1! It ran as a three-month series initially called 'It's Rock and Roll,' and came back the next year, running for three or four series. It became quite a cult show, and that was really the beginning of my broadcasting career. In the late '80s we moved to Bournemouth, where I carried on DJing and approached the local commercial radio station suggesting a '50s/'60s show. I was initially hired to do one show a week, ending up being there for about fifteen years, doing everything from the breakfast show to drive time. I later went back to the BBC in Wiltshire, networking all of the South and West, and do a lot of documentaries on people like the Beatles and Elvis. It was whilst doing a programme for the World Service in 1999 that I got to meet Paul McCartney. In recent years, I have been producing and presenting a radio show which goes out on the BBC West and Southwest area network every Saturday night called 'Saturday Night Rock and Roll Party.' My mum and dad were never the sort of parents who said, 'Turn that music down!' or anything, in fact they absolutely loved the Beatles as well. Dad loved 'She Loves You,' which he referred to as 'That Yeah Yeah Yeah Song'! **"**

GEOFF BARKER, BBC RADIO PRESENTER, PRODUCER, PLYMOUTH, DEVON

MONDAY 22 APRIL

On a rare day off, the group visited Dezo Hoffmann's studio in Wardour Street, the first of four sessions between April and July. They had photos taken in their new Dougie Millings-designed grey collarless suits, worn for the first time the day before at the *NME* Poll-Winners' Concert. The 1 April recording of *Side By Side* aired on the Light Programme at 5pm, as they were making their way home to Liverpool.

" I first became aware of the Beatles when I was at Broadgreen Primary School in Liverpool in late '62, early '63. I can remember hearing them on the radio, on a show called *Here We Go*. I would rush home from school to try and catch them. It would have been on at about four or five in the afternoon. I remember telling people at school, 'They're going to be very big!' and my classmates would say, 'Oh, they're never going to get anywhere with a name like that.' From then on, I listened whenever they were on the radio – there was one show called *Talent Spot*, and another one called *On The Scene*. I remember the two series they did – *Side By Side* and *Pop Go The Beatles*. I heard 'From Me To You' for the first time when they appeared on *Side By Side*.

My brother Geoff worked at the Woolton Village branch of Martins bank where John Lennon's aunt Mimi banked. I remember him coming home from work one day in mid-'63 and saying, 'John

Lennon's auntie's just been in, and she said that their next record is going to be the biggest of all time.' And it was 'She Loves You'.

There was a lad who lived in our road and his father was the brother of the comedian Tommy Trinder. He got us tickets for Liverpool versus Fulham at Anfield sometime in November 1963. The tickets he got us were in the directors' box, sitting next to Tommy Trinder, who at the time was chairman of Fulham! Liverpool won 2-0. He was also the chief electrician at the Empire Theatre and managed to get us tickets to see the Beatles' show at the Empire the following month. I found my dad's 1963 diary, and it's strange that the assassination of President Kennedy, the Beatles, and me and my brother Geoff going to see them, are all in capital letters. The build-up to the crescendo was amazing. I was just pinned to the back of my seat with the noise. It was like standing behind a jet. I was only 11 at the time, and my brother was 19. Being a few years older, he'd seen them loads of times at the Cavern. It was a great night, but I can only say that I saw them, but I certainly didn't hear them! I have their autographs from that evening in a little book, which I still have. I've got the ticket stubs as well! They were 10/6, in the Royal Stalls.

I was at the same school that John Lennon went to, and it was quite common by that time for the group's autographs to be forged. I started there in September '63, and even then people were writing his name in the books as if he was there, when he hadn't been there since '57. I can remember coming home on the bus from Quarry Bank School a couple of months after I'd started there and talking to this lad about the Beatles. This girl sitting opposite, who was at Aigburth Vale said, 'The Beatles are dead. It's the Rattles now.' The Rattles were German and had been performing in Liverpool around this time, including the Cavern. After I left school, I did have a flirtation with becoming a teacher, but I wasn't very good at it, so went to work for the City Council. I was working there during the Toxteth Riots. In the early 2000s, I was on the quiz show *15 to 1* and managed to get to the grand final. A few years ago I was travelling around America and Canada on a Greyhound Bus, and everywhere I went it was 'Beatles, Beatles, Beatles,' and one night I was in Vancouver, checking into my hotel. I was expecting the usual Beatles thing from the receptionist, but he said, 'Liverpool, that's where that crazy goalkeeper went, wasn't it?' He was talking about Bruce Grobbelaar! ❚

PAUL TAYLOR, COUNCIL WORKER, LIVERPOOL, MERSEYSIDE

TUESDAY **23 APRIL**

I n the morning the group attended a photo shoot at Liverpool's African Chambers in Old Hall Street for a Lybro Jeans print ad. Photographer Richard Cooper recalled, 'They looked moody but they were very relaxed and amused about the whole business. It was at the shoot that John announced to the other members of the group that they would be number one by the end of the week, a fact they took completely in their stride. They stayed until the pictures were developed and made their comments about each one.'

In the late afternoon the group drove to Southport to perform at the Floral Hall on the Promenade, with Johnny Templer and the Hi-Cats and Denny Curtis and the Renegades in support. The *Southport Visiter* reported that, 'The corporation's policy of bringing the top stars to Southport paid off again last night when the Beatles attracted a capacity crowd at the Floral Hall with hundreds of other being turned away at the door. It was undoubtedly the best and most enthusiastic crowd ever to attend one of these shows and the group were given a rousing welcome as they started out on a repertoire of hit songs which have brought them fame in only a few short months.'

❝ I started going to the Floral Hall in my father's Crombie overcoat when I was 14. I actually met my wife at the Floral one Christmas, underneath the clock and I've been with her ever since – over fifty years. One day a chap across the road from me who was a taxi driver and was aware that I was in a group came over and said, 'You know, I've seen this fantastic group at a place called the Casbah Club.' I said, 'Where the hell is that?' He said, 'It's in Eamons Green, Liverpool.' And I never thought anymore about it because we were so involved with our own music at which we were rubbish.

The Kingsway, which was called the Marine Club at the time, started doing a rock night on Monday nights. It was situated on the first floor with a restaurant below on the ground floor. So, we went there one night, and we'd had a drink or two and as we walked up the stairs into the room the bass sound hit you right in the gut. From the back of the room, I saw what I thought was my cousin Ged – but it turned out to be Paul McCartney. Then I realised it was this group the taxi driver had told me about. We'd heard things like this on record but never live. I was drawn towards the stage and a lot of the guys there weren't dancing but just watching the Beatles.

Our bass guitarist's girlfriend's mother was the chief usherette at the Odeon and she managed to wangle it so we could do the Minors' Saturday morning show. So, we'd go in and rehearse then they let all the horrible kids in and we'd bash away and they'd pelt us with all sorts of bloody stuff and scream and shout. The Odeon was where the Beatles played on the Helen Shapiro tour. There was a huge local interest with them being on that tour. They were the magnets. All the locals were waiting for the Beatles. I had a Bedford van and took the rest of the group, who were called the Toledo Four.

The cinema had what was known as a cottage. It was a two up, two down on the street that ran parallel with Lord Street and they ran a rest and recreation room where staff could make a cup of tea, hang up their clothes or whatever. Two of the usherettes I worked with at ICT told me the Beatles did an acoustic show for the staff in the cottage that night.

I saw them for the last time at the Floral Hall. It was packed out, but I don't recall there being any screaming. Southport people don't do things like that. It was a wealthy town. You could say Southport was a dormitory town for people who had businesses in Liverpool and Manchester. Obviously, the girls near the front of the stage were getting their underwear in an uproar which is about normal, but I don't recall there being anything the media would class as mass hysteria. ❞

ALEX PATON, AUTHOR, HISTORIAN, MUSICOLOGIST, SOUTHPORT, LANCASHIRE

WEDNESDAY 24 APRIL

Returning south as soon as they had driven back up north, the Beatles headlined the third 'Mersey Beat Showcase' at the Majestic Ballroom on Seven Sisters Road, Finsbury Park. Two thousand fans filled the hall to see the group, Gerry and the Pacemakers, Billy J. Kramer with the Dakotas and the Big Three. June Harris reviewed the concert for *Disc:* 'Wow – what a scene! Liverpool blitzed London with a resounding crack! The Merseybeat Showcase package just couldn't miss making their mark south of the Mersey. But they did more than that. In a field day for Liverpool the four groups brought their sound to London with an ear-splitting crash that left two thousand fans screaming for more.'

In the afternoon, the group had met with Giorgio Gomelsky and *Jazz Beat* columnist Peter Clayton at Gomelsky's flat in Lexham Gardens, near the West London Air Terminal. Clayton recalled the meeting, 'I went into a living room where four young men were sitting around eating omelettes off their laps. I suppose I should remember some of those tart witticisms which became such a feature of Beatles press conferences, but all I can recall are the omelettes, each in the centre of a big plate, like a stranded yellow fish, and the Beatles' pale faces and grey suits and prolific hair (by today's standards, of course, they were short-haired; you could see their ears).' Gomelsky's idea was to make a day-in-the-life film about the group. 'They are fabulous. So hip. Part of a new culture. They are going to be enormous and we are going to write a film for them,' he told Clayton. A detailed synopsis of a story was written but Epstein, in Clayton's opinion, 'probably mistook Giorgio's explosive enthusiasm for just another attempt to stampede him into something.'

❝ I was a 20-year-old promoter in 1963, doing really well, and earning more money than I knew what to do with! What really happened was that as a promoter, we always used to book all the groups that I thought were worthy of doing a promotion of several nights. The Beatles were one of those groups. These were the days when it was 3/6 to pay to come in on the door, and the groups were earning anything from £17 to £35 a night. I went to Liverpool in early 1963 to meet Brian Epstein. He was a charming man, but he was very green in terms of the business, not in terms of business acumen, because he was a very clever guy,

but his knowledge of the music industry at that time was very small. I suggested to him that we put together what I called 'The Mersey Beat Showcase'. It included the Beatles, Gerry and the Pacemakers, Billy J. Kramer and the Dakotas, the Big Three and Bob Wooler. It has never been mentioned over the years that I came up with the name, but Brian and I agreed to call it that, and the fee for the four groups and Bob Wooler was £200 per night – for the lot. Brian, who was a lovely guy, saw and realised the huge potential of the Beatles. He was very shrewd and would do whatever it took.

Keith Wainwright Fisher and I promoted two dates – Stoke and Finsbury Park – on our own and co-promoted the other dates. I remember Brian Epstein coming up to me at the Stoke show and saying, 'This is never going to happen again.' What he meant was that he had just seen the enormous response that Mersey Beat had on the audiences, and '£200 a night – this will never happen again!' What happened was that from then onwards, group's fees went up dramatically and I can always remember paying Tom Jones £450 for a night at the King's Hall, thinking that I was going to lose my trousers really.

I remember going down to London for the Finsbury Park show. It was all very early days Beatle-wise, before the massive explosion. It was a great night – London was always a difficult one to promote in. I had Led Zeppelin, would you believe, placed them at Hanley and Trentham Gardens, and it was 3/6! I opened my own club, the Golden Torch, in Stoke-on-Trent in 1965, which I ran for eight years, and had acts like Black Sabbath, T. Rex, Uriah Heep, Edgar Broughton, Billy J. Kramer, the list of artists was just enormous, but that was normal then. It's sad that the small clubs can no longer afford these groups, but that's show business. It's an industry now, not a business. The glory days of the early '60s will never be repeated. In those days if you were a top group, and you had a roadie, you would turn up in a transit, with four Vox amplifiers and a Ludwig drum kit! But they had someone to carry it and set it up. **❞**

CHRIS BURTON, PROMOTER, MEIR PARK, STOKE-ON-TRENT, STAFFORDSHIRE

THURSDAY 25 APRIL

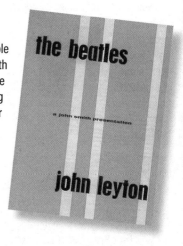

'From Me To You' jumped to number 2 in the *Disc* chart – unable to topple 'How Do You Do It?', which was enjoying its fourth week at the top. 'Please Please Me' finally dropped out of the Top 30. The paper's back page reported on the group's forthcoming holiday, under the headline 'The Truth About That Beatles Hair Style!' The group regaled interviewer Chris Hutchins with tales of previous holidays they had enjoyed and gave more than one version of how the Beatle haircut came to be. In the *NRM*, 'From Me To You' jumped twenty places to number 3, while 'Please Please Me' dropped to number 30. The paper reported that touts in some Manchester clubs were selling the single 2/- over the retail price – and not for the first time. In the LP chart, *Please Please Me* climbed one place to number 2.

The group met journalist Maureen O'Grady at *Boyfriend*'s offices in Regent Street. She took them to Fiona Adams' photographic studio at 21 Kingly Street. After taking a series of shots, Adams, O'Grady and the group piled into a taxi and drove to the crossroads of Gower Street and the Euston Road, which was in the process of being widened. Using war-time demolition as her background, Adams shot a further three rolls of film. One of the images ended up as the cover for the *Twist And Shout* EP, released on 12 July that year.

In the evening, the 'Mersey Beat Showcase' caravan gave two performances at 5.30pm and 8pm in the Concert Hall at Croydon's Fairfield Halls. John Leyton, who had been booked as a guest star, pulled out on the day, due to illness. Ringo used Tony Mansfield of the Dakotas' drum kit. Mayor Councillor John Aston and Jane Asher were both at the show. The *Croydon Advertiser* reviewer wrote, 'that ushers deployed themselves in a serried rank to guard the stage from the teenage mob, gives you some idea what kind of an evening it was. Either you like beat, or you don't. I don't.' Richard Green felt differently in the *Times-Herald*. 'To say that the Beatles were terrific would be an understatement. They projected an electric wave of excitement which gripped every single person at the concert and earned them the kind of reception usually reserved for Royal occasions.'

❛ I was a pupil at Woodcote Secondary School in Coulsdon in Surrey, and a keen amateur photographer. I had a pre-war Rolleiflex camera – a neighbour had found it in their loft and didn't want it, so my mother lent me the £10 to buy it from him. I also bought a professional electronic flash unit, a Mecablitz 502, which had a lead you plugged into the camera. When you pressed the shutter, the flash would go off. I'd already been processing my own films, with a much lesser quality camera, in a little dark room I had a constructed in the corner of my bedroom.

At the Fairfield Halls, they ran a thing called the Corps of Stewards. It basically meant they got people in who they didn't pay to show people to their seats. In return, they would get to see the shows. My father John was one of those, and as a lover of classical music, got to see lots of concerts. The manager of the hall was a chap called Colonel Piper, and my father asked the Colonel if I would be able to go backstage to take photographs of the various acts appearing at the venue. I was only 15 at the time, and as I wanted to work in photography, it was a great opportunity. I was probably a bit awestruck but the Beatles had not attained their real fame and there was no real Beatlemania. To me, they were just a group playing at a venue in the town where I lived.

I arrived in time for the second show, and said at the door, 'Colonel Piper has said I can go backstage and take some photographs' and was waved through. There was no security in those days! I wandered backstage and managed to get a few photographs. I took one of Ringo and John being interviewed by a lady called Mrs Kirby, who was from a local hospital radio station and had a tape recorder and microphone with her, and then went out into the hall. I enjoyed the show and took a few pictures of the group onstage. I went backstage again afterwards and took a photograph of the Beatles sitting under a line of coat hooks. They seemed knackered but were very pleasant and helpful to me. I only had twelve pictures on my roll of film. Film was expensive back then. The backstage photo I took was the last shot I had.

I went home on the bus, developed the film, and proudly took the prints into school with me the next day. Everyone wanted to see them, I was very popular that day, rather showing off a little! At home, I got into terrible trouble – when I got home the night before, I'd put the flash gun down on the sofa, and headed up to my 'darkroom' to develop the pictures. The flash had a little battery in it that was like a mini car battery, and you had to top it up with distilled water, and it was acid. It had leaked out onto my mother's sofa, and it had to be re-covered! However, I couldn't have taken the photograph of the Beatles backstage without it.

I bought the *Please Please Me* LP shortly after, and still have it full of scratches in the loft! I left school and had a job for a while with a local photo agency based in Croydon. I still have the Rollie camera I took the pictures of the Beatles with. ❜

ANDY WRIGHT, PHOTOGRAPHER, CODICOTE, HERTFORDSHIRE

FRIDAY 26 APRIL

The *NME* was the first paper to have 'From Me To You' reach number one – it leapt six places after its chart entry the previous week. In the *Melody Maker* chart, it jumped sixteen places to number 3, while 'Please Please Me' dropped to number 28. The LP climbed one place to number 2 in the *NME* chart and two places to number 3 in *Melody Maker*, as it was released in stereo.

Billy J. Kramer with the Dakotas' debut single, 'Do You Want To Know A Secret', was also released. The *NRM* thought it would be a big hit but described it as 'a fair-old song, and the boys sing it in a very Beatle-ish way'. However, Keith Fordyce's review in the *NME* was effusive in its praise. 'Yet again a new group with a first time hit? Yes I reckon so... Incidentally, the first-class commercial quality of these two songs may be due to the fact that they were both written by Messrs McCartney and Lennon of the Beatles.'

In an article headed 'Bouncing Beatles Make No. 3' in *Melody Maker*, George told the paper, 'Don't mention work. We're off on holiday, and that's all we can think of at the moment. The record? We're all knocked out over it. We didn't think it would go so fast. It's fab.'

Around noon, the group drove back up north to Shrewsbury for a show at the Music Hall, where they had previously played on 14 December 1962, arriving in the late afternoon. Before the show, they had dinner at Cressage Old Hall, the home of local doctors Herbert 'Dusty' Miller and his wife Mabel, and their children. Their son, Shrewsbury School pupil Andrew Miller, persuaded the group to sign their autographs in his copy of *The Cynic's Autograph Book*. (Miller went on to become one of Britain's most successful concert promoters and a major force in the creation of the Nordoff Robbins Music Therapy charity).

Located in the Square, the venue was a Victorian music hall, standing three stories high with pillars on the facade. The place was packed with close to seven hundred people – over capacity for the venue. Tickets had been sold in advance, but more were sold on the night – even causing concern that the balconies might collapse. The group returned home to Liverpool after the show.

❝ My friend Sid Cummings and I used to do amateur radio together. He went to the Tech in Shrewsbury, and I went on to the Secondary Modern. We were mates since we were 13, and we used to listen to Duane Eddy, the Shadows and the like. 'If you played bass, and I played lead...' and we'd work out how we would play it if we had a group. My first guitar was a stick with two pieces nailed on the end with one string, and a pickup which was an earpiece from an old World War Two headset. We didn't have an amplifier in the early days, we just used my radio. It was an old Ultra, brown bakelite case, with white bakelite on the front. There was a two-pronged output at the back of the old radios, that said 'PU' [Pick Up], which meant you could play through the amplifier of the radio.

We used to rehearse at the Belle Vue Youth Club on Rocke Street. The club asked us if we would do a proper gig, and I remember the first time I was petrified. I had to ask permission from my father to take the radio with me to use as an amp that night. As I was walking down Potts Way, I stopped, and thought, 'I can't do this.' Anyway, we played the six songs we had rehearsed, with me singing 'Blue Moon', and the rest were instrumentals, mostly Shadows. We got some more gigs after that and had settled on the name Andre and the Electrons. We'd been going for a while, playing village halls etc., touring round the different parts of Shropshire, and had quite a local following.

Someone told me that Lewis Buckley, an agent from Manchester, was booking in support acts for the Music Hall, so I phoned him up and told him what we did, and he booked us – bless him. In April, we were booked to play at the Music Hall. We arrived to find the Beatles' equipment already set up. We shared a dressing room with them on the second floor, and they were all very friendly. They were taking the mick out of me because I had dressed in semi-darkness at home and was wearing odd socks. John said to me, 'Always wear black socks lad, then you'll always have a pair.' I've worn black socks ever since! Ringo spent most of the time in the dressing room sitting by the big window, with a radio listening to Radio Luxembourg. The reception was coming and going. Paul was showing

John the lyrics of a song he had started to write on the way there on the back of a cigarette packet. He asked me if I wrote songs as well, and I said I did, so we chatted about that for a while. The girls were going crazy waiting for the Beatles. We played our usual repertoire of Shadows' songs that night. I jumped off the stage at the end of our set – it was only about a foot high – and had my jacket ripped off by some girls!

We stayed to watch. They were the first group I had heard who sounded just like they did on record. You could tell John was the leader, he had a look somehow, a bit of a hard case, but I actually think it was Paul who was in charge. **"**

ANDRE WHEELDON, MUSICIAN, SHREWSBURY, SHROPSHIRE

SATURDAY 27 APRIL

The group travelled to Northwich, an hour away from Liverpool, for a performance at the Memorial Hall in Chester Way. Tickets cost 7/6 at the door and the evening's event lasted from 7.45pm to 11.45pm. It was the fourth of six performances they gave at the venue. Denny Curtis and the Renegades and the Cruisers with Karl Terry in supported. Billy J. Kramer's debut on *Thank Your Lucky Stars* was broadcast – he performed 'Do You Want To Know A Secret'.

" My memories of the gig that night are that we all did two spots and I still have the playing timetable. The Beatles were in one dressing room and Denny Curtis and the Renegades and my group in the other. The playing times for all were pinned on the doors. Our first three numbers were the same as the Beatles and after the show Ringo came back to the Blue Angel club in our van as I had played in Rory Storm's Hurricanes. When I got into the club George and I were standing on the landing. You could see all the local musicians looking at George from the bar. I offered him a drink which he refused, explaining he could buy everybody in the club a drink but they would think he was bigheaded and if he didn't buy a drink they would all think he was a skinflint so he couldn't win. I asked him how things were going, and he said he couldn't hear himself playing with all the screaming. **"**

KARL TERRY, MUSICIAN, LIVERPOOL, MERSEYSIDE

SUNDAY 28 APRIL–THURSDAY 9 MAY

After ninety-four dates since the start of the year, the group took a well-earned rest. Epstein felt they had 'worked so hard in the past year [that he] decided they were going to have a holiday no matter what came up.' George, Paul and Ringo flew to Barcelona, where they ended up staying the night, as bad weather meant a further flight to the island of Tenerife was cancelled.

The following day they flew to the island's Los Rodeos Airport, then took the half-hour journey to the villa La Montañeta in Los Realejos to stay with Klaus Voormann at his parents' house. To get around the island, the group had a red Austin Healey Sprite at their disposal, owned by Voormann's father. Both Paul and George had mishaps. Paul was almost carried out to sea off Martiánez beach, while George had a scare when he went for a swim and got his foot stuck in a rock. He eventually broke free, later saying, 'Add to this the fact that we had a spell of lousy weather and you'll understand that we were quite glad to get back to a few noisy audiences in Britain.'

During the trip, they attended a bullfight in Santa Cruz. They also visited Mount Teide National Park, took a trip to the town of La Orotava, and spent time with other tourists at the Taoro Hotel, the Rancho Grande and the Lido San Telmo, where they asked British owner David Gilbert if they could perform. He declined, most likely because of strict rules that were in place under the Franco regime. Paul bought some shirts, George a washable suede coat and Ringo thirty-six china bulls, a dozen swords and some toreador miniatures, which he brought home as souvenirs.

John also flew to Barcelona, staying there with Brian Epstein. Together they spent a few days at the Avenida Palace Hotel, before flying to Torremolinos on the southern coast of Spain. John recalled, 'I went on holiday to Spain, which started all the rumours that he and I were having a love affair, but not quite. It was never consummated, but we did have a pretty intense relationship. It was my first experience with someone I knew was homosexual.' Paul suspected the trip was 'a power play on John's part because John was a very political animal.' Cynthia, busy setting up home with Julian at Mendips, thought nothing of it. 'John said he'd been working very hard, with the concert tours and the album. He needed a break.'

John wrote the song 'Bad To Me' on the holiday, though Paul later claimed that he had a hand in it, writing it with John in the back of their van driving from Manchester to London. 'Amenities in van (or lack of!), hard floor, no windows, pitch darkness all around. One guitar between us, a pen and paper we couldn't see to use, and George and Ringo singing 'Southend-on-Sea.'

On 30 April, BBC Studio Manager Vernon Lawrence wrote a letter to his assistant head of department, Donald MacLean, suggesting a radio series called *Beatle Time*. Imagined as a fifty or sixty-minute evening or weekend broadcast on the Light Programme, he suggested that a group of seven to nine musicians should back a guest vocalist each week, such as Susan Maughan or Mark Wynter, with a group such as Brian Poole and the Tremeloes (the Dagenham-based group who had been signed to Decca Records in favour of the Beatles, ostensibly because of their closer geographical location to London), or Russ Sainty and the Nu-Notes providing a 'rock' element. With John and Paul acting as compères, he suggested a budget of approximately £250.

Record Retailer revealed that 'Tony Barrow is leaving Decca to become Press and Public Relations Officer for NEMS Enterprises and will be handling all the Brian Epstein Liverpool groups from next Monday. His offices will be at 13 Monmouth Street, W.C. 2 (Covent Garden 2332).' Barrow had agreed to take the job over lunch with Brian Epstein at Wheeler's, a seafood restaurant in London. Earning £15 a week at Decca, his new salary was £32. Barrow hired an assistant, Jo Bergman, and a secretary, Valerie Sumpter. His office also became the home to the official Beatles Fan Club. By year's end, the office was receiving in excess of a thousand letters a week, some of them with strange requests, perhaps the strangest was a package containing four small cakes of chewing gum. Included was a note requesting that the Beatles were to chew each piece and then return in four carefully marked envelopes supplied.

On the same page of *Record Retailer* as the Barrow announcement was the advertisement, 'SECRETARY/TYPIST 18–21 years, required by small Press Office which handles publicity for top recording artists. 10–6pm Mon–Fri. For interview appointment telephone COV 2332 next Monday after 10am.'

Del Shannon, on a day off from his ongoing UK tour, spent an evening at West End Studios in London, where he recorded 'From Me To You', Linda Scott's 'Town Crier' and two news self-penned songs, 'Little Sandy' and 'Walk Like An Angel.' Shannon produced the session with arranger Ivor Raymonde. One of the takes of 'From Me To You' included Johnny Tillotson duetting with Shannon, though this version was never released as they were on different labels. Two days after the session, 'Town Crier' aired on BBC radio's *Go Man Go* show. Shannon's manager Irving Micahnik took possession of the master tapes and later lost them. Luckily his version of 'From Me To You' survived and became the A-side of Shannon's next and last single for the Bigtop label. Shannon and Tillotson also sang the song together at the Liverpool Empire.

All four pop papers for the week ending 4 May had 'From Me To You' knocking 'How Do You Do It' off the top spot, while 'Please Please Me' dropped one place to number 31 in the *NRM* and from number 28 to number 41 in *Melody Maker*. *Please Please Me* toppled *Summer Holiday* from number one in both the *Melody Maker* and *NME* LP charts, but had to wait patiently at number 2 in the *NRM*.

Disc ran the front-page headline 'Beatles Take Over Again!' with the news that 'From Me To You' had gone to number one, earning them a second Silver Disc. *NRM* featured the headline 'Beatles No. 1!' on its front page along with a photo taken of the group at the recent Fairfield Halls concert in Croydon, and *Melody Maker* ran the headline 'Scouse Sound Takes Over the Charts!' on page three.

The *Liverpool Echo* published a letter from a mother about her 14-year-old daughter. '[She] had rather lost interest in her schoolwork, and her reports were gradually deteriorating until recently, when she seemed suddenly to regain interest, even taking longer over her homework than the syllabus demanded. Greatly relieved at this I congratulated her and said how pleased we all were, &c. 'Well you see, Mum,' she said quite seriously, '[My teacher] told us all that the Beatles all got umpteen passes in their G.C.E!' That teacher is certainly 'with it.'

❛ I had joined EMI's Columbia Records in late '59 and worked in the sales office for a year or so. I noticed that all the A&R managers at the time started to have assistants, so I asked the managing director, L.G. Wood, if any of the others were going to have one, and he said he would send me up for an interview with Norrie Paramor. Norrie taught me everything I know about the music industry.

Gradually he started getting more into the film writing side of things, and I was looking after the office and the artistes. One of these artistes was Helen Shapiro. Norrie asked me if I'd like to try and write a song for her. I asked my friend Mike Hawker, who I had done some writing with, about it. He said the main thing to get right was the title and came up with 'Don't Treat Me Like A Child'. So he wrote the lyrics and I wrote the music. Norrie heard it and thought it was fantastic, so we recorded it.

I always used to play the piano late at night. I was living with my parents in north London, and I used to play until one, two o'clock in the morning. My mother was particularly fond of a certain tune that I played and would ask me to play it every evening when I came in from work. When we had to come up with a follow-up, I remembered this tune and took it to Mike. It became Helen's first number one hit, 'You Don't Know'. It is a song that stands out to me as the most important of my career, although we followed that up with 'Walking Back To Happiness', which won an Ivor Novello award for Best Song Of The Year [in 1961] and shot me to fame, so to speak. Norrie teased me that I was taking over his job!

It was when 'Walking Back To Happiness' was still at number one that I felt it was time to move on. I had two or three offers, one from Philips, which was a big record company at the time, and the one from Oriole. Oriole had a studio in New Bond Street. I was worried that we wouldn't be able to produce the sounds from there I knew we would need, as I was used to Abbey Road, but my fears were unfounded when I met one of the engineers, Geoff Frost. He was a brilliant man, and he felt that together we could make some wonderful records. One of the major things that happened during my time at Oriole was having the idea to take a mobile recording unit up to Liverpool. I'd had a call from Bill Harry, who wanted to tell me about all the wonderful groups playing in Liverpool at the time. He said he'd take me around and introduce me to Brian Epstein and all the groups. I spent a weekend up there, and he took me all over the place. I was amazed at how many groups there were. I said to Bill, 'we have to do something about recording this stuff.' I didn't know how I was going to do it, but as I was driving back down from Liverpool to London, I came up with the idea of going up with a mobile recording unit and recording all of those groups.

Mobile recording wasn't in existence at the time, it was just an idea I had come up with, so I put it to Geoff. 'If Liverpool can produce the Beatles, then maybe there are some other great groups playing the clubs there, just waiting to be discovered?' Bill had managed to hire the Rialto, where we were able to set up the recording unit in the control room. He had put the word out around Liverpool that we were looking to record groups to be part of a live album. It went out in the press and the word went out like wildfire. You would not believe how many groups lined up for us to record! We set up the instruments and all the groups were to use the same ones. I was then faced with the mammoth task of going through all of this wonderful stuff back home in the studio in London.

In the end, we had enough to fill two albums, which became *This Is Mersey Beat*. The albums were released simultaneously by Oriole on 5 July 1963, and both made it into the album charts. It was great for the label and I was thrilled with the outcome, and I think we were the first company to take the studio to the artiste, quite an achievement really. While we were up there we went to all the clubs. The Cavern was an unbelievable place. It would have been impossible to record anything down there! But seeing these groups perform, not just in the evening, but also at lunchtime. It was extraordinary. After the night sessions, all the groups would meet at an 'after hours' club, the Blue Angel. On one occasion I was there when Bill Harry introduced me to John Lennon, Brian Epstein and Cilla Black. I was sitting next to John and he said to me, 'You see that guy sitting up there by the bar? He owns the place. His name is Allan Williams. Doesn't his face have great character?' He got hold of a serviette, sketched a quick picture of this guy and gave it to me. After he left I stayed for another hour or so, and as I left, without thinking, I threw the serviette in the wastepaper basket! 🥲

JOHN SCHROEDER, PRODUCER, COMPOSER, WEYBRIDGE, SURREY

MAY

Pop Go The Beatles

FRIDAY 10 MAY

'From Me To You' remained at number one in the *NME* and *Melody Maker* charts. 'Please Please Me' climbed one place to number 40 in the *Melody Maker* chart. 'From Me To You' also stayed at number one in the previous day's *NRM*, with 'Please Please Me' dropping ten places to number 41. *Please Please Me* finally made

it to number one in the *NRM*. The *NME* revealed that 'From Me To You' was inspired by its 'From You To Us' letters column. In an interview with Alan Smith, Paul said that they hadn't really splashed out on anything since their new-found wealth. 'We got a record player for our van, but I can't think of anything else.' Better late than never, Smith also revealed that he had just received a card from the Beatles while they were on holiday, which read, 'Dear Everybody, we have never felt so healthy as now – swimming and eating and breathing all day! It's a great place, with palms, natives, and bananas to eat. Matumba is also very fine. We hope 'From Me To You' is still (er... pardon) in your chart. All the best from The Beatles (a band).'

Paul accompanied Jane Asher to the BBC Television Centre, where she appeared as a panellist on the show *Let's Imagine - Writing A Top Pop*. The panellists were provided with a free buffet; as he was only a guest, Paul was refused entry into the lunchroom.

In the evening, George and Ringo, back home in Liverpool, went to the second night of Harry Lowe's 'Lancashire and Cheshire Beat Group Contest' at the Philharmonic Hall. Judges Peter Pilbeam, Franklyn Boyd, Peter Sullivan, Jerry Dawson, Tony Osborne and Jimmy Watson declared the Escorts the winners – with the prize an audition with Decca. The Merseybeats and Derry Wilkie and the Pressmen took second and third place, respectively. At the show, George told Dick Rowe – Decca's A&R chief, who would be forever known as the man who turned down the Beatles – that he should sign the Rolling Stones (Rowe saw the group at the Crawdaddy Club two days later).

In an interview with *The Bootle Times*, George said, 'Before we signed our record contract we would have thought a contest like this would have been marvellous – a truly big thing.' However, he noted that 'The Liverpool sound has been flogged to death. Letters in the musical press have already made it clear that the public is now fed up to the back teeth with the so-called Liverpool sound.'

❛ Three of us from Morrison's School for Boys in Rose Street, Allerton – me, Terry Sylvester and John Kinrade, used to congregate in the shed at Greenbank Park, not far from Penny Lane. We'd sit there in the shed, singing and playing guitars. Our instruments were very basic, but John and Terry had a good knowledge of chords. When we got together as a group we called ourselves the Mexicans, after a record that the Fentones did and started off just playing instrumentals; we never thought about singing. Terry and John were more accomplished than I was at the guitar, so I had the ultimatum – play bass or you're out! I went down with my mum to Frank Hessy's where she signed the HP agreement for my first bass guitar. A guy called Mickey Hacket lived just down the road from

John, and he joined us with his snare drum to make up the group. He was just in it for fun so didn't stay long. Later he was replaced by Ringo Starr's cousin, John Foster, also known as Johnny Sticks. We went to our first real rehearsal with our gear in a wheelbarrow. It was in a local church hall (St Anthony of Padua), and we thought we were just going there to rehearse, but we'd been tricked – Father Ignatius didn't tell us we'd be going there on a youth club night, so all the kids were there! By 1962 we'd all left school.

We impressed Bob Wooler at a gig at the Majestic Ballroom in Birkenhead, and he asked us if we'd like to play the Cavern regularly, which of course we did! By this time we'd changed our name to the Escorts, after the Ford car. Somehow we ended up with a residency at the Blue Angel, possibly because John was Ringo's cousin. Maybe the connection helped, but we shouldn't really have been there as it was a licensed premises and we were still only 15 and 16 years of age. We were doing really well in all the local polls run by *Mersey Beat* magazine and winning a few contests.

One night I was walking back home after a rehearsal at John's house and was passing a garage called the Blue Star on Smithdown Road when someone in a blue Ford Classic called out, 'Hey mate, give us a push!' It was Paul McCartney! His starting motor had jammed, so I pushed him and got him going. I ran home that night with a beating heart just like a fan. He was one of my idols then and still is.

In 1963 we were voted the second most popular group by the readers of *Mersey Beat* magazine. We entered the Lancashire and Cheshire Beat Contest at the Philharmonic Hall in May. The others were all established groups, we were the upstarts, the young whippersnappers. You could tell by our haircuts, and we had shiny blue lurex suits. The groups with the most votes went on to the second half, and at the end of the evening, we won the main category – 'Most Promising Group'. George and Ringo presented us with a little cup, and we were all given little individual ones as well, rather cheap and nasty things. We were then whisked off to Granada Studios to sing the winning song, live on a news show and then all ended up in the Blue Angel to celebrate. ❚

MIKE GREGORY, MUSICIAN, BRYNCOCH, WEST GLAMORGAN, WALES

SATURDAY 11 MAY

Two days after returning from their holiday, the group played their first concert since 27 April, leaving their homes in Liverpool and driving the 60 miles plus trip north-east to the Imperial Ballroom in Carr Road, Nelson. Known locally as 'The Imp', the ballroom had been a roller-skating rink which had played host to the likes of Bill Haley and His Comets, Jerry Lee Lewis and Little Richard, among others. The venue's stage manager Alan Wilson, who also ran the Multi-Relays record shop in town, recommended the Beatles to the Imp's general manager Bob Caine - despite never having seen them. The Imp's co-owner, Alec Holt, booked them for £20.

Arriving in Nelson, the group and Brian Epstein visited Holt's offices above his shoe shop. Glen South, who was also on the bill, subsequently claimed that 'Brian Epstein hired a flat-top lorry and loaded it with about thirty screaming teenage girls who, in exchange for free entry, would stand at the front and whip the rest of the audience into a frenzy.' A queue began forming shortly after 4pm, causing traffic jams outside. Tickets were 6/6; the two thousand-capacity standing-room only venue sold out. The evening started at 7.30pm, with Eddie G. Martin and the Sabres and fellow Liverpudlians the Fourmost making their professional debut (Brian Epstein had just changed their name from the Four Mosts). When the Beatles went on at close to 10.30, fans had to be held back – Caine, in his trademark white dinner jacket, helped police in the line of duty.

The *Nelson Leader* published an article headlined 'Beatles On The Battlefield' by Leigh Morrissey. 'What a Saturday night! The night I was trapped for twenty minutes behind the stage of the Imperial Ballroom, as police, ballroom staff and anyone else willing to help formed a human chain to prevent the practically two thousand excited young people from clambering on to the stage. The night around fifty girls were carried backstage, where they lay in a dazed condition after fainting. In other words, the night the Beatles visited Nelson… I saw hysterical girls drop like nine-pins for one reason or another; partly because of excitement and, no doubt, partly as a result of the packed atmosphere. They – I counted fifty or thereabouts – were picked up and carried over the stage, the only means of escape from the excited crowd, to the back of the ballroom. The girls, many of whom were shaking from head to toe and crying, were laid on the floor. It looked like a battlefield. It is a sight I never want to see again.'

❛ My girlfriend at the time collected the bus adverts for all the groups appearing at the Imp and, as she didn't catch the school bus home but I did, I used to pinch the adverts (usually from halfway down the stairs of the double decker as I could slip them into my satchel). On the occasion of the Beatles coming, I thought I'd have an extra copy! I still have it and it's proudly displayed in my living room. My mother didn't like me going 'down the Imp' as she was rather protective of this innocent 18-year-old and it was a bus ride from my home in Colne so would have meant leaving early. However, on this occasion I got permission to go.

I don't remember too much of any of the supporting groups but got right to the front for the Beatles. It was all standing and at 6 ft 2 in I had a good view. I particularly remember George singing 'Roll Over Beethoven' and the microphone kept swinging away from him and he was constantly having to grab it back. Early on, a young girl at the side of me fainted and the crowd was saying just leave her there. They were all treading on her, so being a well-behaved teenager I picked her up and took her to the back where the main door was. Unfortunately, I banged her head as I tried to manoeuvre her through the rather small door. If she hadn't been unconscious before, well she probably was now! I never did manage to get back to the front again.

Later that evening as I was going, I met two girls who asked me who was on that night. I told them and they seemed peeved that they'd missed it. They had been on a mystery tour from Rochdale and ended up at a working men's club a couple of streets away. They asked me if I could get tickets for the next week's show (which I think was for the Searchers). I gave them my address and one of them called Dilys posted me the money with a note saying, 'I trust you.' We had agreed to meet the next week outside and when we did, I gave them the tickets. She asked me if I was going in with them but I said I was going for a walk in the local park. (My mother hadn't approved of anyone called Dilys from Rochdale but I was allowed to take them the tickets.) I caught an early bus home. Eighteen years old and still at school and thoroughly under the control of my mother, I reckon I should have gone down the Imp a bit more often and maybe made a date of it with Dilys. Who knows where it would have led? ❜

DAVID LYONS, ARTIST, BARLEY, LANCASHIRE

SUNDAY 12 MAY

The group got an early start from Liverpool, making the 100-mile trip south to Birmingham to record a segment for *Thank Your Lucky Stars* at Alpha's TV Studios in Aston. At the recording, they mimed to 'From Me To You' and 'I Saw Her Standing There.' The show aired the following Saturday.

Between the afternoon rehearsal and the evening recording, Ringo's new Ludwig drum kit and Swiss-made Paiste cymbals arrived, brought up from London by Drum City's manager Gerry Evans. Ringo had visited the shop in Shaftesbury Avenue with Brian Epstein the previous month and traded his Premier kit for the Ludwig. Drum City's owner Ivor Arbiter recalled the visit: 'I'd had a phone call from the shop to say that someone called Brian Epstein was there with a drummer. Here was this drummer, Ringo, Schmingo, whatever his name was. At that time I certainly hadn't heard of the

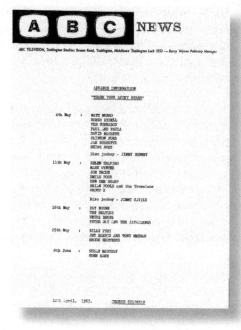

Beatles. I remember Ringo was looking at my desk, and on the desk I had a swatch of colours. We didn't talk about which brand at this point. Ringo said, 'I like this colour.' We didn't get too heavily into what the drums were or what they sounded like. They chose Ludwig because of the colour, and I made some sort of deal with Brian. I have a feeling that they paid a bit of money for the drums... we had the kit in stock.' On one occasion Arbiter said it was a £238 Ludwig Downbeat. Arbiter, who designed the logo, asked Eddie Stokes, a local sign painter, to paint it on the bass drum head. As Ringo was buying the kit, the salesman went to the Ludwig logo to rip it off. Ringo said, 'No, you gotta leave that on. It's American.'

Evans took the Premier kit back to London with him. 'We renovated it in our workshop, and then sold it.' Arbiter was obviously particularly proud of the transaction, placing an ad in the next *Melody Maker*, 'Have just delivered new Ludwig kit to the Fabulous Beatles.' Fellow drummer Peter Jay, who was also on the show, bought Ringo's old ride cymbal for £5 and used it for the rest of his career.

MONDAY 13 MAY

Disc's June Harris interviewed the group at NEMS' Monmouth Street offices. They told Harris about their holidays, specifically the weather. 'We didn't take coats or anything, because everyone said the weather would be just great,' George recalled. 'When we got out at Barcelona airport we had to start searching for the sun. Then we were told our flight to Tenerife had been cancelled because of bad weather.' They also talked about a bullfight they went to. 'They make this big production scene, when the most frightened of amateur matadors comes on,' Ringo said. 'The trumpets play, everyone shouts 'olé!' and if the matador shows a yellow streak, they start throwing Coca-Cola bottles at him.' Paul mentioned his brush with death while swimming. 'When I got past a reef the waves started looking murderous, so I turned back but got washed out. I started waving frantically to the boys, but they just grinned back. Here was everything just happening and no Paul McCartney to share in the benefits. I whacked the hell out of them when I eventually got back on the beach.'

At 5pm the second 1 April recording of *Side By Side* was broadcast on the Light Programme.

TUESDAY 14 MAY

The group drove to the north-east for a 7pm concert at the Rink Ballroom in Park Lane, Sunderland. People began queuing for the 5/- tickets as soon as they got out of work, with the line soon stretching round the nearby car park and about 200 yards into the town centre. Two fans walking up Holmeside to join the queue were convinced the Beatles, with Paul at the wheel, stopped in a red Renault Dauphine to let them cross the road. To cope with the exuberant crowd, a barricade of benches was set up between the group and the fans. The walkway behind the stage was also sealed off so the

group could use it as a dressing room. Between their two sets, the Rink's manager William Longstaff pleaded with fans to move back because some of those at the front were in danger of being crushed.

After the group finished their second set with 'Twist And Shout', they made their escape, as fans knocked over the benches in a frenzy. Paul had to fend off an overzealous fan, hitting her on the head with his guitar. They were chased through the ballroom's kitchen and over a 6-foot wall. As they tried to reach their van, they were mobbed and only the efforts of the police enabled their getaway. The *Newcastle Journal* reported that 'Girls fainted and had to be carried out; others who were unable to see climbed on to each other's shoulders.' John said, 'We were really worried. The crowd were pushing up close to the stage that we couldn't play.'

❝ The Rink was a dance hall, with a little stage at the end where for years Bill Sowerby and his band played old-fashioned songs we didn't know, like 'My Mother's Arms'. The older people would get up and dance and we'd sit around and watch until they started playing records. It was starting to change with the older people moving out and us teenagers coming in with our music. Usually, the resident dance band would support the main act but this night the Beatles were the only group. It was packed. Full of teenagers and everyone was screaming at them. It was a natural reaction. Silly, really. Just to see them in the flesh. We didn't  scream when we went to see Cliff Richard. The Beatles were completely different to everybody else. Cliff was easy-going. You sat there and enjoyed it and clapped at the end. There was no screaming. It was difficult to tell how good the Beatles were because of the screaming. You could hear them but hearing them wasn't the thing. It was seeing them! Everyone was screaming all the time. You just lapped it up. John Lennon just stood there. You couldn't take your eyes off him. ❞

**IAN AND ANN FINDLAY, MARINE ENGINEER AND LEGAL
SECRETARY, SUNDERLAND, TYNE AND WEAR**

WEDNESDAY 15 MAY

Paul drove the group to the Roman city of Chester, arriving at the Royalty Theatre on City Road just after lunchtime. The group ventured across the road to eat at Yeng Hong, a Chinese restaurant at number 27. Afternoon became evening. Traffic came to a standstill as fans congregated outside the theatre, gazing up at the dressing room windows in the hope of seeing their idols. Police were called in to clear the way for traffic. The group played two shows - at 6.30pm and 8.40pm - with Gerry and the Pacemakers in support.

Tony Glanville commented in his 'Beatin' Around' column in the *Chester Chronicle*, 'Before I went to Chester's Royalty Theatre on Wednesday to see Gerry and the Pacemakers and the Beatles, I must admit I was rather sceptical as to how they would fill the bill. I came away pleasantly surprised - and a little deaf... but... the show was spoilt by the audience themselves. The girls in particular were the worst offenders, for I don't think they stopped screaming from the time each group went on until it came off. It seems to be the custom nowadays to spoil a show by screaming.' Glanville also chatted with Neil Aspinall backstage, who told him that working in Germany had enabled the group to develop their own style.

On the way home at 11.40pm, Paul was stopped by PC Powell in Birkenhead for driving at 60 miles per hour down New Chester Road. With a prior previous speeding conviction and lacking his driving licence or insurance, he agreed to produce them at Allerton Police Station within five days. He didn't.

❛ I spent most of my younger days going to the Mersey View in Frodsham when my mum went dancing there. As a teenager I think I spent more time there than at home. My dad was in the local Fire Service and they held dances there for the Fire Service Charity. I had my 21st birthday party there and worked behind the bar for a while. I saw the Beatles on several occasions, but my best memory of seeing them was in Chester. On the evening before, I met up with some friends who told me that they were going to the Royalty to see the Beatles and they asked me to join them. I worked for Merseyside and North Wales Electricity Board at the time and recall going into work the next morning and asking my boss, Mr Ellams, a dear old-fashioned man who wore a trilby hat each day, if I could have the afternoon off to go and see the Beatles. He said, 'Who are they?' bless him.

Anyway, he gave me the afternoon off and I met the girls and we went to Chester. We headed for City Road and stood around for a time but the girls decided to go for a walk around the town. I didn't go. I had noticed that there was a Chinese restaurant across the road from the theatre and I remember saying to the others, 'I bet the Beatles will go in there.' I stood at the stage door and eventually it opened and out walked the boys. Paul was the nearest to me and I grabbed hold of his hand and kept holding it whilst I asked for their autographs. We laughed and joked together and then they said that if I let them go and have a meal in peace across the road and didn't tell anyone where they were that they would gladly sign autographs for me. Still holding Paul's hand, which by now he had put in his pocket and mine went in there too, we all crossed the road.

I marched up and down the street and anyone that stopped me to ask or stood near the theatre I told a lie to and told them I had spoken to their manager and they wouldn't be here until the evening. Each time I passed the restaurant I could see the boys near the back of the restaurant watching me. When they came out, they kept their promise and all signed a promotion card for me. Paul said to me, 'You're the best security we've ever had.' I then pushed my luck further and I asked if just Paul and John would sign another one for me. They asked why and I set them off in fits of laughter when I said, 'Because you are my favourite ones!' But they did as I asked. I then spent the night screaming my head off with the rest of the audience and my friends could not believe my luck. **J**

JILL FELL, ACCOUNTS CLERK, FRODSHAM, CHESHIRE

THURSDAY 16 MAY

'From Me To You' continued its run at number one in the *Disc* and *NRM* charts, 'Please Please Me' dropped one place to number 42 in the latter and *Please Please Me* settled into what became a long tenure at the top of the LP charts. *Disc*'s centre spread featured the headline, 'It's Liverpool All The Way As Bookings Pile Up', listing a series of twelve Sunday dates during the summer as well as several radio and TV slots and upcoming one-night stands.

At 1.30pm, rehearsals began at BBC Television Theatre in Shepherd's Bush, London, for the evening's live appearance on *Pops And Lenny*. For the group's second appearance on national BBC television, they performed 'From Me To You', a short version of 'Please Please Me' and – with the rest of the company – 'After You've Gone'. The show aired from 5pm to 5.30pm. Ringo used his new Ludwig drum kit in a live performance for the first time.

Bronwen Walsh, who was in the audience, walked down the side of the theatre after the performance and found an open door. 'We went in – and straight afterwards security locked the door. The Beatles were waiting to make their getaway but couldn't get out until the van came round. A lot of girls were banging on the doors, but we were inside – and for an hour, so were the Beatles. They were so friendly and nice, and once they knew we weren't hysterical they were happy to have us. They were very ordinary guys, very friendly. Cynthia Lennon was there, standing in the background with a cape on. John kept saying to her, 'Did you get that?' Nobody realised he was married – he was pretending she was a reporter. You can imagine what it was like the next day in school. My friends were incredibly jealous.'

It's 1963. I am 14 and, like almost every girl in England, I am head over heels in love with a Beatle. The Beatles are about to make one of their appearances on television, and my sister and I are beside ourselves with anticipation, breathlessly planting ourselves in front of the TV set hours before the time they are scheduled to appear, squabbling as usual over which one is the best. There are no recording devices, no way of replaying these precious Beatle moments over and over again. No, if you miss them on TV, then you miss them – end of story; hence our frantic preparations for every appearance on the small screen, even intently watching every minute of '*Pops and Lenny*'. 'My' Beatle was George. I fell in love with him after studying a grainy photograph in the *NME* and deciding he was the one for me. He had the best cheekbones, dark, expressive eyes and a cool expression that hinted at both distance and slight amusement. When I saw the Fab Four interviewed on TV (usually wreathed in cigarette smoke), sitting in a bored line, flanked by a watchful Brian Epstein, answering stupid press questions with laconic Scouse wit, it seemed to me that George had the dryest sense of humour, came out with the best one-

liners. He rarely smiled, even when he was being funny, and this made him all the more mysterious and enticing. And of course, in my naive teenage head, he was also unthreatening: a black-and-white TV version of what I thought boys ought to be like, but also so out of reach that I could only admire and adore him helplessly from the outer reaches of the planet – or Norfolk, as it was actually called.

My family had moved to Norfolk, so my sister and I were still a little lost, bombarded by impenetrable Norfolk dialect and regarded as outsiders, with our Essex accents. The Beatles were our safe haven in this difficult and lonely transition to a new home and a new life, the familiar and loved heroes that gave us comfort. When we first arrived in this alien county, we had missed a Beatles concert in Norwich by a few weeks; but a girl in my class at school had attended and had mysteriously obtained all the Beatles' home addresses and was selling them at break time for half-a-crown each. I handed over my 2/6 eagerly, clutching the precious paper bearing George's address to my adolescent bosom. One Hundred and Seventy Four, Mackets Lane, Liverpool – suddenly the Mecca of my imagination.

I hurried home to compose my very first (and last) fan letter to George. What did I say? I can't remember, but I was a budding writer, so it would be a masterpiece of a letter, surely, brimming with wit and beauty... No. It was an incoherent outpouring of cliched adoration and loyalty, along the lines of 'I think you're fab' and 'I much prefer 'Please Please Me' to 'Come On' by the Stones...' I don't know if I expected a reply, but one day a letter did come, and it had a Liverpool postmark, addressed to me in unfamiliar handwriting. My heart skipped a beat. I opened it with trembling fingers and found – a letter from George's mum, Louise. It started much as you might expect, along the lines of 'Sorry George hasn't got time to write because he's busy touring.' I was astonished – George's mum had bothered to write back! And then a question suddenly leapt off the page. 'Are you by any chance related to a writer called Ivy Ferrari, who writes doctor and nurse romances?' And now my heart skipped even more beats – because my mother was the writer called Ivy Ferrari, a romantic novelist churning out Mills and Boon paperbacks with titles like *Nurse At Ryminster, Doctor At Ryminster, Almoner At Ryminster*. I couldn't believe it. Mrs Harrison was a fan of my mother! Of course, I replied. The word eager doesn't quite cover it. I WAS WRITING TO THE MOTHER OF A BEATLE – MY BEATLE! And thus began a correspondence that lasted for several years.

I sent her signed copies of my mother's novels, illustrated with lurid couples embracing on their red and green covers. She sent me notes from George ('Dear Mum, get me up at 3, love George') written on the backs of old envelopes. She sent me pictures cut out of newspapers that she had managed to get all four of them to sign (John Lennon drawing a big lipstick mouth on one, I recall). She sent a piece of a suit that George had worn when he played in Hamburg. And most exciting of all, she sent snippets of their life, small secrets that I felt privileged to receive. She told me John was her favourite because he danced the tango with her in the kitchen and made her laugh. She told me when George phoned her from hotel rooms for a chat. I asked her about Liverpool, about her life as a girl, and she shared tales of her life in a city I had never seen. I don't know why she always replied. We were from different planets, but reply she always did. Imagine then, my astonishment when I received a Harrison missive telling me that she 'always' read my letters to George over the phone. I felt faint. George knew who I was! I had a name! I had an identity! I was in George's head!

Mrs Harrison was intrigued by the romantic heroes of Ryminster Hospital: 'Does your mum know any real doctors like Doctor David Callender? ('He was fairly tall and tough-looking, with tawny-brown hair and a lean, intent face. His eyes were dark and compelling, so full of fire and life they drew me like a magnet...' Wry answer from my mother: 'If only...!' Private thought from me: Sounds just like George.)

I will always treasure the memory of those letters from Liverpool. George's mother made me feel special, interesting. We wrote to each other for several years, although gradually the correspondence faded as I moved to London and started my working life. I fortuitously landed a job in an advertising agency on Baker Street, which just happened to be across the road from the original Apple building – the one with a giant psychedelic Indian figure painted on it. Needless to say, I haunted the place, breathlessly noting every time John Lennon's psychedelic Rolls-Royce appeared in the street, or Mick Jagger was spotted arriving with his entourage.

One day, I found myself standing a few feet away from George himself, in the Apple boutique in the basement, where exotic, expensive hippie clothes twinkled and gleamed. I stood frozen behind my Beatle, imagining our encounter. I would say 'Hello George – I'm the girl from Norfolk.' And he would turn and smile at me – one of those rare, beautiful smiles – and Patti Boyd (his then wife and object of my churning jealousy) would be instantly forgotten, to be replaced by me. After all, I already knew and loved my future mother-in-law. What better fairy-tale ending to my years of yearning could there be? Instead, I stood rooted to the spot, too cowardly to speak, and George disappeared through a door at the back of the shop.

Mrs Harrison died in 1970. I remember reading about it in the papers, and wishing somehow I could attend her funeral. But I already knew that there would be a horde of fans rubbernecking at the churchyard gates – and somehow I didn't want to be one of them. George's mum had made me feel special, different, touched by a small handful of stardust – whether she meant to or not. George married and had a son. So did I. After years travelling, I went back to live in a Norfolk cottage, while George retired to Henley, to an outrageous gothic mansion called Friar Park, the restoration of the house and gardens becoming his life's work until he died. In the later years, when asked, he would call himself a gardener. In the same way that he found peace and pleasure from the plants that he grew, I am now doing the same. In 1996, I fictionalised this story in my novel *The Girl from Norfolk With The Flying Table*. These days I can watch the Beatles whenever I want: on television, on my tablet, on my laptop, even on my phone. And these days, as I focus in on those grainy early images of George, so solemn and self-contained as he plays his guitar, coolly oblivious to the studio cameras, I still wonder about one thing connected to those early teenage years: what happened to all those signed copies of Mills and Boon romances that once adorned the parental Harrison home? Somehow I don't imagine that the Doctor at Ryminster ever made it to Friar Park. **❜**

LILIE FERRARI, WRITER, AYLSHAM, NORFOLK

FRIDAY 17 MAY

The front page of the week's *NME* featured photos of Elvis, Jet Harris and Tony Meehan, Cliff Richard, Ray Charles, Billy J. Kramer and the Beatles, captioned 'The Beatles continue to occupy the top place in the *NME* Charts with 'From Me To You''. 'From Me To You' began a third week at number one in the *Melody Maker* chart, as 'Please Please Me' dropped to number 49.

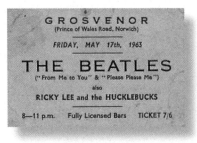

John and Paul had a working lunch at accountancy firm Bryce, Hanmer and Isherwood. Paul arrived late, only to discover that in his absence it had been decided to change the songwriting credit from McCartney/Lennon to Lennon/McCartney. Harry Pinsker was assigned the role of their accountant and when he first met them in his office, he thought they were 'four scruffy boys'. Jaep Music Limited, a music publishing company comprising the rest of the NEMS roster, with Brian Epstein and Dick James as its directors, was incorporated.

The group made their first foray into East Anglia, a two-and-a-half hour journey to Norwich, for an appearance at the Grosvenor Rooms on Prince of Wales Road. Local promoters Ray Aldous and Peter Holmes, who had met as 4-year-olds at St Augustine Primary School, had signed the deal with Brian Epstein on 19 April, paying the group £250. They hiked the ticket price from the usual 2/6 to 7/6 to meet the cost of the high fee. Neil Aspinall arrived with George and Ringo in the group's van in the early afternoon. Because of their lunch meeting, John and Paul travelled by train.

After a soundcheck, the group went out to get some food and then watched the films *Sparrows Can't Sing* and *The Set Up* at the ABC Cinema two doors away from the Grosvenor. On their return, they met with support act Ricky Lee and the Hucklebucks, who were setting up their gear around theirs. Lee's group included a couple of Beatles' numbers in their act. Their rhythm guitarist Mick Hague asked George what the chord was in the chorus. As the time for the show drew close, the seventeen hundred fans found themselves amongst the queue for the evening's performance. The group played two twenty-minute spots. Promoter Aldous recalled that 'Paul was jolly. Ringo was the comedian, George never said a dickie-bird. And John was quiet. You didn't get much out of John. He was the quiet man in the corner.'

The group packed up their equipment in their van and went to Valori's fish and chip shop in Rose Lane, where they were served cod and chips by Jimmy Hughes. John's choice of fish – haddock, was not on the menu. Two teens from Yarmouth, Mick Fisher and John Talbot, passed them the salt and vinegar and had a brief chat, mentioning how many girls from Yarmouth had come to the show.

❛ I was at the Grosvenor Ballroom, Norwich, when the Beatles visited our fine city. I went with two friends, meeting them at their respective homes, en route to the venue. This walk would probably have taken about an hour from my home. I expect we purchased the tickets on the door, which you were able to do in those days and managed to wedge ourselves against the left-hand side of the stage, close to where George was standing. We shouted and screamed our way through all their numbers, always trying to touch any trouser leg that came close. I cannot remember much about the actual performance, except that at the end of this historic evening our ears were ringing with the vibration from being so close to the amplifiers, but who cared, we had just witnessed our heroes.

After the Beatles left the stage, we dashed around to the side alley to wait patiently against the gates to see them depart. I was fortunate to have them sign the back of my admission ticket. However, to make my evening, I took along a large photograph of the group, which I had sent away for from the *Daily Mail* and after shouting their names and holding up the photograph through the tall railings, John, George and Paul emerged from their travelling van, to sign the photo, all addressed, 'To Jan', accompanied by kisses. Both of these souvenirs I still possess and am unlikely to part with. My evening was completed when Paul wrote his signature on the inside of my left wrist, which I duly covered with cellophane and did not wash for two weeks, much to the amusement of my parents. I certainly was the envy of all my school friends. Oh for those wonderful heady days again. Great, great memories and historic times, not that I realised they were historic at the time, but certainly never to be witnessed again. I was so very, very lucky to have had the opportunity to be at the Grosvenor that Friday night in 1963 and also very proud too. ❜

JAN BOUNDEN, PERSONAL BANKER, NORWICH, NORFOLK

SATURDAY 18 MAY

The Beatles travelled to the Adelphi on the Bath Road in Slough to begin their third UK tour – twenty-one twice-nightly dates presented by Peter Walsh, who ran Starlite Artistes, and Kennedy Street Enterprises in association with Tito Burns. Headlined by Roy Orbison, the bill also featured Gerry and the Pacemakers, Louise Cordet (who had already met the group at her mother Helene's Saddle Room club on Hamilton Place, Westminster), Ian Crawford, Erkey Grant, David Macbeth, the Terry Young Six and compère Tony Marsh. The original plan had been for the tour to feature Duane Eddy, but when that fell through, Ben E. King and the Four Seasons had also been mentioned. Finally Orbison, making his first appearances in the UK, agreed to headline the package. These two shows broke the Adelphi's box office record; tickets cost between 5/6 and 10/6 and sold out within five days of going on sale. Manager Nigel Lockyer said, 'I could have sold them three times over!'

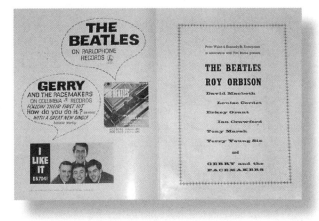

The previous Sunday's recording of *Thank Your Lucky Stars* aired at 5.55pm, five minutes before the first of the evening's two shows. The second followed at 8.30pm. The group performed 'Some Other Guy', 'Do You Want To Know A Secret', 'Love Me Do', 'From Me To You', 'Please Please Me', 'I Saw Her Standing There' and 'Twist And Shout'. During their performance, Gerry Marsden walked onstage and presented them with a silver disc for two hundred and fifty thousand sales of 'From Me To You', saying, 'From me to you for 'From Me To You'. Fan Liz Taylor recalled her experience. 'We sat nicely in our seats until [they] came onstage, when we stood and screamed our heads off and could hear hardly anything! I was fan number 114 in the original fan club. I was 14 at the time and it seems another world away.'

While Orbison was booked as the headliner, the increasing ascendancy of the Beatles resulted in him going onstage immediately before them. He recalled a discussion with Brian Epstein and John in his dressing room about who should close the show, where John said, 'You're getting all the money, so why don't we close it?' Earning three times what the Beatles were for the tour, he agreed.

The day's *Liverpool Echo* reported that people with the same names as the Beatles were being bombarded with phone calls. John Lennon of Scotland Road, whose number was NOR 1649, had been pestered day and night by teenage girls. 'Some of the girls who ring up are a real nuisance. They just will not believe that they have the wrong person's home and they keep insisting on talking to John Lennon. They really get rude at times.' Apparently several George Harrisons and P. McCartneys had experienced the same, as did Mrs P. Presley from Childwall. 'I am weary of answering the phone only to have some giggling girl to ask, 'Is Elvis there?' or 'Will you get Elvis to sing for me?' It's all so funny for them, but so tedious for us.'

❛ Even after more than fifty years, the memory is sharp. The Beatles came to a packed Adelphi in Slough only six months after first appearing on children's television. Their impact had been immediate and universal among teenagers of the day – strange British accents from ordinary kids making extraordinary sounds. And it was as if their words had flown straight out of your own head – so close to life as we were experiencing it. In the early days they wore sharp suits and haircuts – the Beatle fringe aside – that were pretty clean cut. I was in the fourth form at Windsor Boys Grammar School. And I had discovered girls, love, etc.

We booked tickets to see them as part of the Roy Orbison tour – the Americans still dominated the pop scene. By the time they reached Slough all that had changed. We all loved Roy, but the waiting was unbearable. When they did finally appear, the place went absolutely bonkers. That said, we were pretty well behaved by modern standards – all seated – so the only thing the girls could do was scream and shriek their heads off. Typical of the boys' reaction, I sat at first

---

dumb in disbelief to see and hear these four lads with their fantastic fashions and funny Merseyside patter. I was transfixed, then transported into the magical world of their distinctive new sounds and emotions. Everyone knew all the words to the songs and we all twisted and shouted along with them – one mind and feeling like we were onstage ourselves. It was a massive emotional experience, with many girls in hysterical tears – none of us had experienced highs like this before. It just left us Beatle addicts craving more. ❞

BRYCE MARTIN, JOURNALIST, HOLYPORT, BERKSHIRE

SUNDAY 19 MAY

The tour bus left London and headed north to Hanley. Jane Asher saw Paul off as he got on the coach. The evening's two shows at the 2,151-seater Gaumont in Piccadilly were at 6.10pm and 8.30pm – a further four thousand fans had tried to get tickets. That figure paled into insignificance, however, against the 33,644 fans who watched Stoke City beat Luton Town to gain promotion to the First Division the day before at the Victoria Ground. The 48-year-old legend Stanley Matthews, who had made his debut for Stoke thirty years earlier, scored City's second goal.

This was the group's fourth visit to Stoke-on-Trent – and the best, according to George. Three girls used a fire escape to reach the group's dressing room 100 feet above the ground. They were taken into police custody, but later released. They managed to get the group's autographs for their troubles. One of them later recalled her story. 'I got a ladder, climbed it and knocked on the dressing room window, that was subsequently opened by George. Showing his concern that a 12-year-old might fall, he offered me a ciggie from a packet of ten Gold Leaf. John said, 'Do you come here often?' I started climbing down the ladder when I saw a policeman come into view telling me to get down. George said, 'You'd better do as he says. Have a nice life.' 'Thank you,' I said, 'and you.''

The *Evening Sentinel*'s review boasted 'Four thousand Pop Fans Have Big Night', reporting that box office records were broken for the two shows. As much as they enjoyed Orbison's performance, the *Sentinel* wrote that the fans' 'enthusiasm reached frenzy pitch with the appearance of the Beatles.'

MONDAY 20 MAY

Mirabelle featured the group on its front cover for the first time since February in its 'Boys! Boys! Boys!' issue, which also featured love problems discussed by Adam Faith and disc queries by Billy Fury. In this edition, however, they afforded the group more than just the cover. It asked the question 'Who Wants To Be A Lady Beatle?' as they cornered 'The Newest "Mod" Boys in Show-Biz!'

The tour bus headed south to Southampton for two performances at 6.15pm and 8.40pm at the

2,289-seater Gaumont on Commercial Road. During one of the shows, George raised his hands had to quiet the audience, saying, 'We are very flattered by the screams. Thank you for that, but we would appreciate it if you could save them for in-between the songs because we want you to hear our music.'

A reviewer for the *Southampton Echo* wrote, 'The young pop stars of today are in grave danger of becoming deaf old men. This thought struck me... when a combined attack of over-amplification and feminine hysteria left my critical faculties in a weakened state... I must confess that the quality of Mersey strained me considerably on this occasion. The Beatles received the loudest screams, so I really couldn't tell just what they were like... Forgive me girls, if I appear harsh, but that terrible screaming does blunt the judgement.' The reviewer may have been the first journalist to make a pun from a line in *The Merchant Of Venice* – but he certainly wasn't the last.

❝ The first thing that comes to mind thinking back to seeing the Beatles was that we went as a family, which would seem odd nowadays. My brother Barry was ten years older than me and working at British American Tobacco in Southampton. He cycled the 2 or 3 miles down to the Gaumont in his lunch hour to get the tickets. It's quite surprising that he didn't have to queue, but the tickets he got were for 'the gods', which is why he thinks he was lucky. We lived close to the centre of Southampton and were able to walk to the show. It only took about ten minutes to get there. We went with friends of the family. They had a son who was the same age as me. They lived out in the New Forest and drove in from there to our house and left the car there, and we all walked down together.

I was only 10, but remember it was almost impossible to hear anything for the screaming. I remember the atmosphere to this day. The Upper Circle, where we were sitting, was the furthest away from the stage. It was the first time in my life that I was part of an occasion. Being part of the atmosphere was really exciting. I had combed my hair forward to make it look like the Beatles! I remember that there was a Beatles wig that you could buy, which was plastic. Either myself or a friend bought one, and I do remember wearing it at some point!

My brother was quite instrumental in me getting involved in music and the Beatles. He had saved up to go on a school trip but wasn't selected, so he bought his first record player with the money. He showed it off by playing his new records to the whole family in the living room. So he is responsible for my interest in music, if not my taste. My late wife Wendy was a huge Beatles fan, and in fact was at that same gig in 1963. We didn't know each other at the time, she went with a girlfriend from school. I'm still in touch with her friends from school days, we enjoy getting together and talking about the old days over a cup of tea. My wife was very keen on Paul McCartney and when our son was born, I didn't really have a say in it – he was to be called Paul! ❞

RAY LE RAY, QUALITY ANALYST, SOUTHAMPTON, HAMPSHIRE

TUESDAY **21 MAY**

Back in London, the group began rehearsals for *Saturday Club* and their first bill-topping appearance at the Playhouse Theatre at 2.30pm. Paul, sitting by the side of the stage, told fellow guest Mike Berry, 'Listen to this, this is Billy J.'s new song.' He played 'Bad To Me.' Berry recalled Paul playing it on an acoustic guitar, thinking it could have been his: 'The string of hits they wrote for Billy J. and the like could have been mine. I missed out, but there you go.' At the 5.30pm to 6.30pm recording, they were interviewed by host Brian Matthew and performed 'I Saw Her Standing There', 'Do You Want To Know A

Secret', 'Boys', 'Long Tall Sally', 'From Me To You' and 'Money'. The programme aired the following Saturday.

After a forty-five-minute dinner break in the theatre canteen, during which Ringo perused the current edition of *Private Eye*, they began rehearsals for another Light Programme show, *Steppin' Out*, which aired on 3 June. At the 10pm recording, in front of a studio audience, they were introduced by host Diz Disley: 'We have here four young fellas who, since they emerged from the trackless interior of Merseyside a mere matter of months ago, have been laying 'em in the aisles all over the Isles – from Land's End to John O' Groats – so mind your backs, wacks, for it's the earth-shaking sounds of the Beatles!' They performed 'Please Please Me', 'I Saw Her Standing There', 'Roll Over Beethoven', 'Twist And Shout', which was edited out when broadcast, 'Thank You Girl' and 'From Me To You'.

❝ 1963 was a very exciting time to be in the music business and I was lucky enough to be in the middle of it all. I'd started in the business at an early age. A pupil at Grafton Road Infant School in Dagenham, I played the lead in *Goldilocks* and got the entertainment bug. So my parents enrolled me at the Windsorettes Dance School at the age of 6, then later at the Pat Dwyer Dancing School in Rainham, which I attended in the evenings after school. We did lots of events during 1953 for the Coronation, street parties and the like, and even ended up doing a show at the Royal Albert Hall when I was 13. I left school at 16 and went to work in an office. I hated it, so one day I rang a friend who had also been at the dance school. I asked her if she'd like to team up and we managed to get ourselves an agent, who sent us out on the road to theatres in Scotland and the north of England. It was a good grounding and although we loved it, after a year or so we both ended up getting married, and shortly afterwards my daughter Karen was born. I made the decision at the time to quit the business and focus on family life.

After a while though, my husband and I decided we needed some extra income. All I wanted to do was sing, so I made some phone calls and ended up auditioning for John Schroeder, the A&R manager at Oriole Records. My first single was a John D. Loudermilk song called 'Does My Heartache Show' released in the summer of 1962. I spent much of that year performing in Germany. Back in the UK the following year, I appeared on all the main television and radio shows of the day. I just went from one show to another. We were all however swept away by Beatlemania, which took hold that year. All you heard everywhere you went was 'Beatles, Beatles, Beatles'; 'Have you met the Beatles?'; 'Do you know the Beatles?' You were totally aware of it and it was impossible to escape from. For me, to be mentioned on the same show as the Beatles, well, that was quite an accolade in itself.

In May 1963, I recorded a spot for *Saturday Club* on the same bill as the Beatles. We didn't meet though – we all had different recording times, so you just turned up at your specified time and did your thing, but it was exciting just to have appeared on the same bill as them. It seemed we kept missing each other throughout the year. I was on *Thank Your Lucky Stars* two weeks before one of their appearances; I appeared at the Royal Albert Hall a month after they performed there as well as performing at the London Palladium a couple of months before they did. I even did a concert in Llandudno a week before they were there. I never experienced superstardom but feel to a certain extent I touched the edge of it. I knew what it was like to be chased for an autograph! It's amazing how many people are still interested in those heady days back in the early '60s. I talk for three quarters of an hour, then sing some of the old songs, and if they want me back, I talk about how I became one of the first lady Toastmasters and then do an encore – just like the old days. ❞

**JAN BURNETTE, MEMBER OF THE TOASTMASTERS AND MASTERS
OF CEREMONIES FEDERATION, FLIXTON, SUFFOLK**

WEDNESDAY 22 MAY

Less than a week after their first East Anglian appearance in Norwich, the group returned to the area, playing two shows at 6.30pm and 8.45pm at the Gaumont in St Helen's Street, Ipswich. On arrival in the town, they checked into the Great White Horse Hotel in Tavern Street and took time for some window shopping, pausing outside Footman's department store on Westgate Street, before taking the short walk along Carr Street to the Gaumont.

Fourteen-year-old Carole Howes recalled, 'I used to spend a lot of time watching pop shows at the Gaumont and hanging round the stage door in the hopes of getting autographs and seeing the stars. As usual, I had been around the backstage entrance the day the Beatles were appearing. I hadn't seen them but was heading towards my bus stop when who should be walking towards me but John Lennon and George Harrison! I stopped them and got their autographs. I have still got them to this day, along with many others. I can't remember much – I think I was a bit shell-shocked.'

The Gaumont's manager David Lowe introduced himself and invited the group into his office, telling them he had a soft spot for people from Liverpool. The Beatles had their photo taken with winners of the Gaumont's regular talent competition – the prize was meeting the stars of the next show. Eleven-year-old Margaret Sewell was one of the lucky winners. 'You can tell by the look on my face in that picture that I'm thinking, 'I can't really believe I'm here.' For some reason I only got two Beatle autographs – John and Ringo. I don't know why I didn't get all four.' Sixteen-year-old Ipswich factory worker Pat Hands found her way backstage, only to be roughly dealt with by a doorman. Paul McCartney came to her rescue and signed her autograph book – as did John.

The local press continued to show its disinterest in 'pop' music – the *East Anglian Times* ran an ad saying the shows were the following Wednesday and sent a reviewer to the Felixstowe Drama Festival for the Early Stagers' production of Arthur Miller's *Death Of A Salesman* instead.

❝ My plan was always to go to sea and travel, and I decided the best way to do this was to do an apprenticeship in catering and then join the Merchant Navy. After leaving Kesgrave School, I joined the Great White Horse Hotel, starting off as a waiter. The hotel was close to the Gaumont, where I would go on a regular basis to see all the up-and-coming pop groups that were around in the early '60s. Most of the groups would stay at the White Horse, and when the Beatles came to town in May 1963, I was told they were booked in. I was on duty that day and was asked if I would work late, as they were providing a buffet for them and their entourage after the show. In return, I was allowed time off to go to the concert! As I was straight back on duty afterwards, I was the only one attending the concert wearing a suit and tie! I couldn't hang around afterwards because I had to dash back to the hotel.

We'd laid on a buffet in the restaurant area. The group and their entourage arrived and sat in the lounge area. They came through, picked up some bits and pieces from the buffet, and took them back to the bar area, where they were all having a few beers. They were very matey, very ordinary, lots of jokes and banter. They stayed up really late, quite a large crowd of them, drinking and smoking. I was so tired after working such a long shift, but they were such friendly lads, I didn't mind. The next morning, they played a joke on one of the chambermaids. She had gone in to clean the room, and they were all in one bed! She was quite shocked! That morning there was a group of fans outside, and we were told by the management to keep our mouths shut, and not to reveal any details of the group's stay. The Beatles were a breath of fresh air, somebody with a different accent, very polite. ❞

CHARLES FINCH, RESTAURATEUR, COCKFIELD, SUFFOLK

THURSDAY 23 MAY

'From Me To You' remained at number one in the *Disc* and *NRM* charts for the fourth week, while 'Please Please Me' dropped out of the latter's Top 50 after eighteen weeks. *NRM* reviewed the rerelease of 'My Bonnie' – 'It doesn't sound much like the Beatles do now... good rock well performed but unlikely to be another 'From Me To You'.' *Disc* announced that John would be writing his own account of the tour with Roy Orbison in the paper the following week and that the group would appear in their own radio series *Pop Go The Beatles* – the first episode due to air on the Light Programme on 4 June.

The tour continued with a three-hour drive up the A1 for two shows at 6.15pm and 8.30pm at the twenty-five hundred-capacity Odeon in Angel Row, Nottingham. John, Paul and George stopped off for lunch at the Willow Cafe in Stamford, Rutland (Paul ordered a knickerbocker glory with a fried egg on top), while Ringo ate with Terry Young Six bassist John Rostill at the nearby Olde Barn Restaurant.

At the venue, PC Peter Gibson was assigned to stand by the door of the group's dressing room, while his colleagues were outside holding back the crowd. Several fans lay down in the aisles during the performance, exhausted from screaming too much. At the end of the evening, several fans made their way to the back entrance of the cinema in the hope of catching a glimpse of the Beatles. They were not to be disappointed – the group appeared through a door at the top of the fire escape and waved. John balanced a pile of autograph books and LPs on the railing, throwing them down to the fans. Many of the LPs and books were ruined. One fan remembered, 'The fab four thought it was very funny and went back inside laughing, leaving scenes of mayhem below. I've been a bit ambivalent about them since.'

Following the second show, the group were whisked off to the Shakespeare Street police station where they enjoyed a smoke and a drink with the local constabulary. Gibson remembered them sitting in a corner in comfy chairs and chatting among themselves. 'They were as good as gold,' he recalled. Afterwards, they made their way to Mansfield, where they spent the night at the Swan Hotel.

> ❛ Nottingham in those days was a very industrial city, a very British city. We had plenty of employment, with all the pits around the city of course; Player's Cigarettes and Raleigh Bicycles, where my dad worked, employing ten thousand people. That's all gone now. It's a very different place now than it was in 1963. Everyone was happy, and there was lots of work about. I'd had an interest in photography since I was at school. I had a Box Brownie and would develop the photographs myself in the attic. I was 19 years old in 1963 and had been working for the *Nottingham Post* since I was 15. I had a big heavy camera from the 1930s, with a wide screen and no auto-focus. The shutter speed was 250 to the second and was all a bit hit and miss! If a picture came out OK you were really pleased! I was assigned to take photographs of many of the shows that came to town. You had to get there early to take photographs because you couldn't use a flash during the show, so I'd turn up and hang around backstage waiting for an opportunity.

I was a fan of Roy Orbison, so was pleased to be sent to cover his tour show at the Odeon. As usual I got there early, looking for an opportunity for a good photograph. I'd been asked to get a picture of the Beatles, who were appearing on the same bill. We'd set up the camera in the manager's office. It was called a VN plate camera and you had to set it at either 2, 3 or 4 yards – you had to get the distance absolutely correct because there was hardly any depth of focus. It was only a little square room, and when the Beatles came in, I had to press my back right against the wall and set the camera on '2 yards'. I'd attached the flash already and opened the blind to attach another flash – there was a flash at the front of the camera as well. I had to put the plate in, take the sheath out, take the photograph, put the sheath back in, and do it all again for the second picture.

After I had taken the second picture, I asked them to sit still for a moment longer so I could take all their names in order! They just smiled and said their names out loud. I should probably have known them but it's something you do automatically as a photographer, to make sure you get the names down. They chatted happily, after all we were all about the same age! There used to be a saying, 'A picture says a thousand words,' and I think it is true, there is a lot more to it than just snapping. My all-time favourite picture, taken with the Nikon I used in the pre-digital era, is of a permed Peter Shilton kissing the European Cup. In my wardrobe I have a memento – Brian Clough's blazer after one of Forest's Wembley outings. It is a size too big for me, but it will never, ever be sold. If I had my time again, I would not do anything else. It's better than working for a living. ❜

TREVOR BARTLETT, PHOTOGRAPHER, BEESTON, NOTTINGHAMSHIRE

FRIDAY 24 MAY

'From Me To You' remained at the top of the singles' chart for a fifth week in the *NME* and began a fourth week at number one in *Melody Maker*, while 'Please Please Me' dropped out of the Top 50 after eighteen weeks. The paper also reviewed 'My Bonnie' disparagingly, writing that it 'sounds like it's straight from a Surrey dance hall with everybody trying to be so original and ending up corny.'

The group drove to London to record the first episode of *Pop Go The Beatles* in number 2 studio at BBC's Aeolian Hall at 135–137 New Bond Street, broadcast on 4 June. Four programmes had been commissioned, with a further eleven optioned. The Beatles were paid £42 per show. Beginning at 2pm, they recorded 'From Me To You', 'Everybody's Trying To Be My Baby' (a track from Carl Perkins' 1959 LP *Dance Album Of Carl Perkins*, which had been in the group's live set since 1961), 'Do You Want To Know A Secret', 'You Really Got A Hold On Me' (the Miracles' US hit earlier in the year), 'Misery' and 'The Hippy Hippy Shake'. The Lorne Gibson Trio were the first guests on the show and together the two groups recorded 'Pop Go The Beatles', based on the nursery rhyme 'Pop Goes The Weasel', which opened and closed each week's broadcast. Jane Asher sat in the control room during the recording.

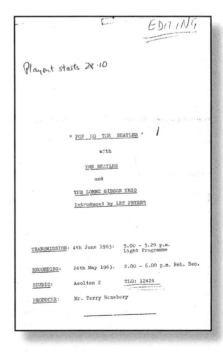

183

As the recording extended beyond its scheduled 6pm, the group had to borrow Gerry and the Pacemakers' minibus to get to Walthamstow in time for the 7pm show at the Granada on Hoe Street. The *Walthamstow Guardian* wrote, 'Top tenners, the Beatles, strongly supported by Gerry and the Pacemakers, produced a near riot among the Walthamstow teenagers. Girls rushed the stage and ended up in bear hugs with the hardy St John Ambulance Brigade men who were acting as a blockade. Most acts were drowned out by the girls, giving vent to their emotions, despite pleas from compère Tony Marsh not to scream until the end of each number. The only respect paid was to American bill topper Roy Orbison.'

❛ I was walking through the streets of Soho when I first heard 'Love Me Do'. It was coming out of a bar or a record store, and I remember thinking 'that's a little bit different', although it never occurred to me that it was anything special, it was just another pop song. By late '62 I was touring with Chubby Checker with a group called the Gary Edwards Combo, and was looking for something new, so I put an advert in the *Melody Maker*: 'Bass player looking for a group' or something like that. One of the replies I got was from Lorne Gibson. He was sharing a flat with a BBC producer called Ian Grant, in Cleveland Square, Bayswater. A large Victorian house in a garden square, it had been split up into three flats. It was dubbed the 'Rock and Roll House'. On the top floor was Billy Fury, the floor below was Gerry Dorsey, in his pre-Engelbert Humperdinck days, and Lorne and Ian on the ground floor. Lorne was looking for a couple of musicians to join him, with the idea of calling the group 'the Lorne Gibson Trio'.

I got off the tube at Lancaster Gate, and headed up to the flat for an interview, and got the job. I was about 18 at the time, and we were joined by Steve Vaughan on guitar. Lorne already had a record deal with Decca. By 1963, we were well ensconced with the BBC, doing a couple of radio broadcasts a week. Initially *Saturday Club* and *Easy Beat* and then we got a call to be on the first episode of a new series called *Pop Go The Beatles*. We arrived at the studio – in those days the studios were primarily being used for drama, so there were lots of heavy-duty curtains hanging around to help adjust the room acoustics. We pushed our way through the curtain and there on the other side were the Beatles. It was the first time we had met them. The idea for the show was that each week they'd do a version of 'Pop Goes The Weasel' with that week's guest. George decided to go and have a cup of tea so Steve ended up playing lead guitar, I played bass, Ringo played drums, John played harmonica and Paul stood in front of the microphone and screamed. It ended up that our version was used throughout the series as the opening song. I don't know why George didn't play on the recording – maybe he didn't like 'Pop Goes The Weasel'. ❜

VIC ARNOLD, MUSICIAN, NEAR HAVERFORDWEST, PEMBROKESHIRE, WALES

SATURDAY 25 MAY

The previous Tuesday's recording of *Saturday Club* aired at 10am, while the Beatles headed north for two shows at the City Hall in Sheffield, at 6.10pm and 8.40pm. As the group walked onstage, uniformed commissionaires rushed to prevent teenagers from mobbing them. The theatre's centre staircase was lined with officers throughout their set. Fans hurled autograph books, streamers and pieces of paper at the group – as well as the obligatory Jelly Babies. Tony Marsh was forced to tell the crowd, 'Simmer down or the concert is off.'

In between shows, a reporter with the *Sheffield Telegraph* had tea and biscuits with Paul. Commenting on the fans' reaction to the group, Paul said, 'It gets up your back sometimes when they start but the point is if they stop screaming you know something's wrong and you are slipping. So, in a way, you accept it.' Ten minutes before the second show started, Paul hurled a bag of Jelly Babies at Orbison as he was being interviewed by Chris Hutchins, saying, 'That's the ninth bag we've had given us tonight and it's only 8.30.' In the interview, Orbison commented, 'These boys have enough originality to storm our charts in the US with the same effect as they have already done here, but it will need some careful handling. You see they have something that's entirely new even to us Americans and although we have an influx of hit groups at home at the present time I really do believe your own boys could top our charts as frequently as they seem to be doing here.'

After the show, officials rushed eight attendants to stand guard at the stage door. One burly attendant said, 'For a while I was worried. I thought we wouldn't be able to hold them,' while audience member, Brian Clay, wrote in his diary that it was 'like a Roman orgy with screaming twisting girls'. From this point on the group always received a police escort.

When the group finally got out of the hall, they were driven the short distance to the Grand Hotel, where they stayed the night, smuggled in through the rear entrance. The *Sheffield Star* reviewed the show: 'Their presentation was top-notch, but their numbers were drowned by continual screaming from their fans. It was impossible to distinguish any words, except in their present number one recording, 'From Me To You' (which everyone knows by heart anyway).'

❝ Pete Stringfellow used to have a few clubs in Sheffield, and one of them was the Black Cat Club. He was originally going to have the Beatles there, but it wasn't big enough, so he had to find another venue which was called the Azena, so I went to see them there. I was only 14 at the time and screaming idiot-like. I had been a Beatles fan from the first time I heard 'Love Me Do' on Radio Luxembourg. I went with four school friends, Hilary, Frances, and another Susan. My dad took us there because we were only young. Hilary fainted, and was taken backstage. She actually got to meet Ringo, who was her favourite, which was more than we managed! It happened again, the second time at the City Hall. Either she really passed out or she faked it the second time, but she did very well out of it!

We would always arrive early to queue for tickets, and after the shows we'd wait outside to catch a glimpse of our heroes. We got the autographs one morning outside their hotel. We'd travel down early and wait outside the Grand Hotel, and just wait, hoping. This particular time, we got invited inside – I think the management felt a bit sorry for us. So we went inside and waited for quite a while. Then the group came down, and signed our autographs, before being driven away. We counted ourselves pretty lucky to be honest. It was even exciting just being inside the Grand. When you are still at school, these things are.

I'm still a Beatles fan, and still have all my old LPs stowed away, but now have all the old records on CD, and am still dedicated to George! I was looking at my shabby old autograph book a few years ago, and when I heard that the BBC-TV show *Flog It* was coming to Sheffield, I just knew it was the right time to sell it. I was upset at the time, and wish I had photocopied it, but you have to go with your gut feeling, and the proceeds paid for a wonderful holiday for me and my husband. I still have all the wonderful memories in my mind. I visited Liverpool recently, and finally made it to the Cavern Club, which I was really pleased about, and visited the Beatles Experience down at Albert Docks. I got a bit emotional seeing John's statue outside the Cavern, it really brought it all back. ❞

SUSAN TURTON, HOUSEWIFE, SHEFFIELD, SOUTH YORKSHIRE

SUNDAY 26 MAY

The group returned home to play two shows at 5.40pm and 8pm at the Empire Theatre in Lime Street – their first Liverpool dates since 12 April. They were greeted by fans holding 'Welcome Home Beatles' banners. The Empire had been showing the musical *Enrico* since Wednesday, featuring 'Italy's Top Comedy Personality,' Renato Rascel. A try-out before a West End run, billed as 'The World Premiere of the £80,000 English Comedy Musical Production', it never made it to the capital.

On arrival, Ringo bought some Butterkist popcorn from one of the ice cream ladies. The other Beatles chose ice creams. Mike McCartney and Dezo Hoffmann were both there capturing this scene on film. A NEMS worker recalled, 'We were seeing our Beatles in a completely different light. They were still our Beatles so far as the music was concerned, but we were in a vast theatre, a far more formal atmosphere than the Cavern, and we were a long way away from John, Paul, George and Ringo. We could feel the change in them as they returned to Liverpool. They were touring celebrities now. We didn't feel they were letting us down by leaving Liverpool but things would never be the same.' Paul, tired of travelling on the tour bus, drove his own car for the remaining dates of the tour. Neither the *Echo* nor the *Post* saw fit to review the show; the *Post* ran a story on its front page that film star William Holden had been bitten by a python while on location.

❛ I was born a couple of weeks before the end of the second World War in Europe. When I was quite small I went to Canada with my mother, returning in 1948 when my father had been able to get housing for us in the Newcastle area. The house was always full of music and I was brought up on Glenn Miller and the big bands. The first record I had was a 78 of Tennessee Ernie Ford's 'Sixteen Tons.' The real change came however when my parents bought me 'Hound Dog' and 'Don't Be Cruel' by Elvis and my dad bought a powerful radio that I could tune in to American Forces Network. When I was 13 my dad got a major promotion and we moved from the north east to Formby and I went to the nearby Waterloo Grammar School. I left school after I took my O levels and went to work for Canadian Pacific in the Passenger Department. Working there meant I could go to all the lunch time sessions in the Cavern, where I saw the Beatles during 1961–1962 on over ninety occasions and at other Merseyside venues. Most of what you read about their personalities are pretty much correct in the sense that Paul was the PR man, John was often dismissive and aggressive, George was often serious and Pete Best kept himself to himself. I would often chat to George during the lunch-time break and he always seemed to have time to talk about the music. They were as popular with both sexes and in their own way were fashion icons – not only through the black leather jackets and jeans, but also the original Cuban heel boots which they bought in Paris and which were not actually the same as the boots that later became famous, but also in things like corduroy suits and different American style shirts. I remember the first time they wore the boots; George, in particular, got quite annoyed when with typical Merseyside humour someone shouted out, 'Why are you wearing girls' high heels?'

I well recall the first time Brian Epstein came down to the Cavern which was when things started to change somewhat as he put the group in suits, but to be fair also tidied up their performances and made them sharper and more focused. Pete Best was very popular and I would from time to time carry his drums up the stairs of the Kingsway Club in Southport. When he was replaced by Ringo, it really did create a storm – and I still recall the black eye that George got from a disgruntled fan.

I would say they were at their peak as a rock and roll group in 1962 and I saw them a half dozen times plus at evening shows that they played at the Kingsway Club in Southport where they were outstanding. Once they started to gain success particularly after 'Please Please Me' there is no doubt that things changed and when I saw them for the last time at the Liverpool Empire in May I think I came to the view that it wasn't worth paying 45p to be present for twenty-eight minutes of screaming when I had been used to two hours of music for 12½p! At the end of the day, those of us who saw the Beatles in 1961 to early '63 saw what the rest of the world never saw and it's a great shame that no live recordings with the exception of the poorly recorded Hamburg tapes have ever been found, but we all still live in hope. To be honest, someone in 1963 who saw the Beatles hadn't really seen the Beatles at all. **⌡**

SIR RON WATSON CBE, POLITICIAN, SOUTHPORT, LANCASHIRE

MONDAY 27 MAY

The Beatles travelled to Wales for the ninth date of the Roy Orbison tour, performing two sold-out shows at 6.15pm and 8.30pm at the Capitol Theatre on Dock Street in Cardiff. Before they performed, Dave Edmunds, a shop assistant at Barratts music shop, was sent to the venue by his manager. He later recalled, 'The shop manager said, 'Why don't you take this stuff around, sticks, strings, bass strings whatever, for the Beatles and see if they need anything and give them a deal so they remember Barratts of Manchester.' So we went around and sure enough they were setting up, going for a soundcheck in the afternoon and we rolled in. There was no security in those days. I stayed for the whole day. In the evening, I was just standing on the side of the stage watching the Beatles. We were too nervous to charge them so we just gave them everything, all the sticks and strings. I gave Paul McCartney a set of bass strings.' (Within a decade, Edmunds had topped the charts with his cover version of 'I Hear You Knocking.')

Philip Walker of the *South Wales Echo* went to the group's dressing room, a couple of flights up a spiral staircase, during the interval of the first show. 'I went upstairs to talk to them – and walked into a crazy world. Girls, Beatles and baggage crowded their dressing room in chaos. Two girls sat at a table taking notes. The Beatles could be picked out by their polo sweaters, denim shirts and long hair. George Harrison was sitting on a dressing room table. 'See those girls,' he said, 'they come from Austria. Penarth, Austria.' 'No, Australia,' said Paul McCartney. 'That's right, Australia.' The girls kept on writing. Another girl walked in. Paul went up to her, 'Hello, my dear, I'm from the *South Wales Echo*. Would you care to give me a few details about yourself.' In his article, headed 'Philip Walker Visits... The World Of The Beatles,' he described them as 'real 'whackers'... meaning they are the boys from Liverpool, talk with ugly, flat, accents, and are proud of it. Anyone who has the Liverpool accent in the North or Midlands has a status symbol. For if you come from Liverpool, you are in with the Beatles and their music. And that's as good as you can get.'

The *Cardiff & Suburban News'* reporter Derek Wayland and the *Western Mail'*s Garrod Whatley also interviewed them in their dressing room. They invited Wayland to have dinner with them after the second show, bidding him farewell just after midnight. Afterwards, they returned to the Angel Hotel, where they spent the night. Wayland said, 'They are the nicest bunch of guys I've dined with for many a day.' Paul, George and Ringo re-enacted their visit to a bullfight in Tenerife for him, taking the roles of matador, picador and bull.

'From Me To You,' coupled with 'Thank You Girl,' was released in the US on Vee-Jay (catalogue number VJ 522). *Cash Box* named the single as its Pick of the Week in its 'Newcomers' section, describing it as 'a real catchy cha cha twist romantic novelty that the fellas deliver in attention-getting manner.' The single did considerably better than 'Please Please Me', garnering airplay in the Los Angeles area – courtesy of Dick Biondi, by then working for KRLA – and selling just over twenty thousand copies by the time it charted in March 1964.

❛In 1962 I went to Cardiff Art College to study Graphic Design – although in those days it was known as Advertising Art or Commercial Art. And one day in 1963 a girl called Sally Ferguson was canvassing amongst the students in our group. 'Would you like to go and see this group from Liverpool? They're playing at the Capitol.' We all said, 'I don't know.' You know, as students, you don't want to part with your money too easily. Anyway, there was a bit of a hoo-hah and we said, 'Is there anybody else on with them?' She said, 'There's some American guy called Roy Orbison.' So, I said, 'Yeah, we'll definitely go and see him.' So that's how it came about. Front row of the circle. It was 10 bob or 10/6, which was a lot of money to us in those days. I think about five of us went.

While we were queuing outside in the sunshine, a little guy in a very sharp Italian suit just walked by and into the foyer. It was Gerry Marsden. I remember before the Beatles came on the curtains were closed and they parted and they literally exploded with 'Twist And Shout'. No introduction, no nothing, just straight into it. That was it. There was a lot of screaming going on, but you could hear the music in parts. The girls were screaming and jumping up and down though. We had a great view and they were charismatic. I seem to recall they also sang 'I Saw Her Standing There' and I remember John Lennon playing the harmonica. I've read since that the Beatles got top billing, but I'm sure Roy Orbison closed the show. The compère came on before him and said, 'People in Wales can sing, but this guy can sing too.' At one point, they turned all the PA system off apart from one microphone. He sang 'In Dreams' into this microphone and you could hear the back of the auditorium upstairs rattling. I had never experienced such a powerful voice. The thing that struck me more than anything else was that he hardly opened his mouth. He had tremendous range and power. It was staggering.❜

STUART PEREIRA, AUTHOR, TINGLEY, WEST YORKSHIRE

TUESDAY 28 MAY

EMI Records exercised its option on the group, extending their contract a further year and increasing their royalty from 1d to 2d. The tour continued with one of its shorter trips, from Cardiff to Worcester for two shows at 6pm and 8.30pm at the Gaumont on Foregate Street.

The cathedral city had just experienced its hottest day of the year and was looking forward to the Leadon Vale Sheep Shearing Society, a Garden Fête at the Ronkswood Hospital, Billy Watkins' Mammoth Fun Fair and the annual Worcester Regatta. The King's School headmaster Mr David Annett had recently placed the continental-style coffee bar El Flamingo on New Street 'out of bounds' to its six hundred pupils, some of whom no doubt were Beatles' fans.

Chatting with *Worcester Evening News*' music writer Antony Willard, John said that the group had been 'on holiday and were now facing a hectic summer.' He also said that the group had been booked for another visit to Hamburg. Willard reviewed the gig, commenting, 'The Liverpoplians, who have brought the first new sound to British pop music since the Shadows, were trying to relax between houses. But it was difficult. Outside a crowd of girls bayed for them as they waded through a shoal of autograph books.' One fan dashed home to fetch a hard-boiled egg for a forlorn George, while Paul filmed the screaming hordes on his cine camera.

‘ My then boyfriend, subsequent husband, and no longer with me, John, loved the same sort of music. I was up in the town posting the letters from the shop I worked in, and John came running out of the shop he worked in and said, 'You'll never believe this – Roy Orbison is coming to Worcester!' He gave me the money for the tickets, I think it was 19/-, and I went straight back to the post office and got the postal orders. So we sent away for the tickets – they were front row seats. I would have worn a dress to the show, although I don't remember which one. You only wore trousers in those days if you were going

pea picking. I know I wore my three-quarter length Mac, which I got in Russell and Dorrell's in Worcester, stockings with seams, and flat shoes. At that time we didn't know much about the Beatles and certainly didn't know they were on the bill until we got there that evening. So I had to work out the bus schedule – I was concerned that I wouldn't get home in reasonable time, and to our delight, when we saw the programme, we discovered that the Beatles were on the bill.

We got off at the old bus stop where the new library now is, and then walked up. I've heard people mention the queue, and yes there was a long queue, and a lot of excitement. After we had seen in the programme that the Beatles were on, I remember thinking to myself, I hope I've enough energy left to scream for them! Really, from that moment, you knew that they were something new, something different, and it would go on for a long, long time. Right from the moment you heard John Lennon, it was just never ending, and every song seemed better than the one you heard before. It was just coming at you from every angle, and it was all so new, it was the best you'd ever heard. We had to rush out the minute the Beatles had finished to catch the last bus, otherwise there would have been hell to pay. I hadn't even told my parents where I was going, I wasn't even allowed to have a boyfriend!

I got back safely and in reasonable time. I didn't talk to my parents at all when I got back. I just went in and went straight upstairs to bed! My ears were still ringing, I was buzzing with excitement, and had to switch it all off, and come back down to earth. It was so hard! I didn't tell them where I'd been till years later. My parents were not into pop music at all, but my mother loved all the oldies before then, so she was very musical. They knew of John's existence but didn't really approve. I worked in the outfitters, Gerrards, and John in a home and handyman shop. The shops were close enough for us to meet for lunch. John listened to the wireless all the time and it was him who started taking an interest in the Beatles. He would record the records, and play me John Lennon's voice... 'If I Fell In Love With You' ...all the songs. They just got to you. We left the shops about a year before we got married and went to work in a local factory called Jackson's Fibre and Millboard Company. They would put 'Workers Playtime' on in the morning and we would all sing along. We sang along to the Beatles. They were all everybody was talking about at the time. When they had a new record out, everybody in the factory wanted to go and buy it. We'd all talk about what we thought of it. ❜

JANET TAYLOR, HOUSEWIFE, DRAKES BROUGHTON, WORCESTERSHIRE

WEDNESDAY 29 MAY

The tour bus headed north to York for two dates at 6.40pm and 8.45pm at the Rialto – the group's third visit to the venue in three months. Manager Don McCallion had been upset with fans who wanted autographs the last time the Beatles played there and found himself in an equally bad-tempered frame of mind, as he was inundated with ticket requests even though the two shows had sold out weeks earlier.

Stacey Brewer reviewed the show for *The Yorkshire Evening Press*, headlined, 'A Great Night For The Fan At York "Pop" Show'. He wrote that the Beatles 'could have sung a Liverpool bus timetable and scored a hit! After the show, they attended a backstage party where some girls requested the group carve their autographs in their shoes. They stayed the night at the Royal Station Hotel.

❛ I was in my fourth year at Nunthorpe Grammar School for boys in York [in 1963], having passed my Eleven Plus and started back in 1959, the year my music hero, Buddy Holly, tragically died. I remember we were put into classes according to alphabet for the first year and these remained our 'form' classes for the five years. Hence my new pals made that first year were Mal Sims, Baz Starkey and Dave Sutcliffe – all the Ss along with myself. Mal, Baz, Dave and myself were all music mad and formed our first group together in 1961 – naturally enough called the Four Ss! We did all the usual stuff, the Shadows, Duane Eddy, the Spotnicks etc. and played in youth clubs and school dances. Our tastes were varied and we liked to watch other live acts as often as possible, getting into pubs and

Working Men's Clubs whenever we could to watch the 'turn'. But the best venue in York in those days was the Rialto, where all the package tours were to be seen.

Then, one day in 1963, Baz rolled up to us in class and said that Roy Orbison was on a package tour and it was coming to the Rialto. Great excitement! We all loved the Big 'O' and resolved to get tickets when the booking office opened later in the week. Problem was, we would have to go during the lunch break at school, a bit of a tall order with only an hour allotted. We all mounted our bikes and cycled across York to the theatre with our 'sarnies' tucked into saddlebags, intending to munch on them whilst queuing. Imagine our dismay on arrival at seeing a queue, which seemed like a mile long around the block. We hadn't realised that one of the supporting acts was the Beatles! Anyway, we weren't about to give up at that point so we locked our bikes and joined the queue – eventually leaving with tickets two hours later!

On return to Nunthorpe we were in big trouble and when we joined the physics class the teacher (Mr Dawson as I recall) sent us to the Deputy Headmaster, a tyrant named Mr Jewell – the pupils called him 'Jimmy' but 'Adolf' would have been nearer the mark. He had little sympathy for our tale. He kindly opted not to administer corporal punishment but put all four of us into detention that week and gave us one hundred lines apiece.

We arrived at the concert some weeks later and were very near the front in the more expensive seats. I remember by that time, because of the mayhem around the Beatles every performance, Roy Orbison closed the first half and the group closed the show although he was top-billing. When he came on they had a single spotlight on him as he sang and you could hear a pin drop in the auditorium. I swear the hairs on the back of my neck stood up as I watched him. The audience were mesmerised as he performed all the hits, but not only them, I could see George Harrison standing in the wings watching him throughout, and John Lennon joined him for quite a while. When we whistled and clapped, so did they – magic!

The MC finally introduced the Beatles over a cacophony of screaming girls and shouting, whistling boys, us four wondered what the fuss was about. We soon found out. The group were absolutely brilliant and we were hooked from start to finish. I'm not claiming that we heard the songs clearly as we did when Roy was on – people were standing on seats screaming and shouting, a nearby girl was carried aloft and out after fainting. The poor lass missed the 'Fab Four'. So, we joined them all, carried along on the euphoria. What a tale we had to tell at school next day. It was worth every one of the hundred lines and being in detention for an hour after school. We were converted Beatles fans (but didn't think any less of Roy Orbison!). We needed to rethink our repertoire for the group with immediate effect – fewer Shadows numbers and much more 'Twist And Shout'! ❜

CLIVE 'ALFIE' SHEPHERD, BIOMEDICAL SCIENTIST, MIDDLESBROUGH, NORTH YORKSHIRE

THURSDAY 30 MAY

Beatles' fans were treated to a front-page special in the week's edition of *Disc*. In a new weekly column, John wrote about his experiences on the tour, revealing that a fan had given them a kitten – although they wanted to have travelled with it as a mascot, they decided against it. 'If Ringo had his way he'd insist on bringing a complete menagerie into the act!' John added. 'From Me To You' stayed at the top of the paper's Top 30, as it did in the *NRM* – for a fifth week.

The group set off on the two-hour trip south-west to Manchester, for two shows at 6.15pm and 8.45pm at the Odeon on Oxford Street. They stopped off for lunch at the Norfolk Hotel on the way. After they arrived, the group – obviously still hungry – had a meal in the cinema's empty restaurant. A reporter approached them and asked whether they were from Liverpool, and if so, which record of theirs was in the charts. She was told that it was 'From Me To You' and then she remarked that another Liverpool group – the Beatles – were also in the charts! She apologised when she realised that was them. Backstage, they pleaded with a reporter to tell girls to stop sending them Jelly Babies. 'We've got two tons of them now,' said John, 'Tell them to send us E-Type Jaguars or button-down shirts.'

Police held back some three hundred fans as the group left by the stage door an hour after the second house. The fans ran after the tour bus as it drove up Oxford Street towards St Peter's Square. The traffic lights at the corner changed to green as the bus approached. Odeon manager Brian Bint said, 'It went straight through. Another few seconds and the coach might have been halted for good.'

The following morning, workmen were called to repair a swing door at the front entrance – pulled off its hinges by fans. Derek Taylor, working as a theatre critic and columnist for the northern edition of the *Daily Express*, saw the show – buying his own tickets. His review, dictated without notes and headlined 'Derek Taylor Crashes Gaily Through The Liverpool Sound Barrier' read, 'The Liverpool Sound came to Manchester last night and I thought it was magnificent... Indecipherable, meaningless nonsense, of course, but as beneficial and invigorating as a week on a beach at the pierhead overlooking the Mersey. The spectacle of these fresh, cheeky, sharp, young entertainers in apposition to the shiny-eyed teenage idolaters is as good as a rejuvenating drug for the jaded adult. I suppose there is not-yet-a-first-class musician among them. Last night's audience of screamers gave the ear little chance of picking up two consecutive notes... Their stage manner has little polish but limitless energy, and they have in abundance the fundamental rough good humour of their native city... Nobody could hear themselves trying to think. The act was largely drowned, but it didn't matter at all. It was marvellous, meaningless, impertinent, exhilarating stuff.'

Barry Croft was less complimentary in the *Manchester Chronicle*. 'I regret to say that the Mersey Beat, which we have all waited anxiously to hear live, was beaten into the stage by the Mancunian killer-scream... I wonder why people pay half a guinea just to blow their little tops?'

❛ I was on my way to watch Manchester City take on Spurs at Maine Road and I thought I'd pick up some tickets for the Beatles/Roy Orbison show later that month. I breezed into the Odeon box office and was surprised to find that all the tickets had sold out, not realising that folk had been queuing up all night in the hope of securing the precious tickets. I did manage to get tickets for the show through Sue's (my then girlfriend, and now wife of fifty years) brother Denys's mate Derek.

So to 30 May (by which time City had been relegated!). After a few minor acts, Gerry and the Pacemakers closed the first half brilliantly with 'You'll Never Walk Alone'. In the second half Roy Orbison came on third and introduced himself as having just flown in from America, and his arms

were still aching. His singing would be better than his jokes. Could he really perform live as he did on his records we wondered? Roy absolutely smashed it, soaring through his repertoire of 'Only The Lonely', 'Running Scared', 'Crying', 'Dream Baby' and others, whilst the audience watched and listened enraptured in silent awe and you could hear a pin drop.

That same audience incredibly, then exploded into a crescendo of Beatlemania, mainly the girls, screaming, shouting, and leaping up and down – particularly when George came out with the immortal line, 'Any girls fancy coming round the back with me after the show?' We were buzzing, knowing that we'd seen something very special. I didn't buy a programme on the night but managed to pick one up years later in an auction, for a 'premium price' (the wife knows). Perusing the write up on the Beatles, which was mainly a brief history, there was no real indication of just how big the boys were going to become, concluding with the line 'From Me to You has hit the jackpot once again'. Not even a prophetic – 'and a great future beckons.' The abiding memory of the concert was the contrast between the reception that the Big O and the Beatles received. Indeed it was difficult to believe that it was the same audience for both acts. Wonderful, phenomenal and astounding. ❞

DAVE WALLACE, MECHANICAL ENGINEERING PROJECT ENGINEER, LEIGH, LANCASHIRE

FRIDAY 31 MAY

'From Me To You' and 'Do You Want To Know A Secret' shared the number one spot in the *NME* chart, while 'From Me To You' began its fifth week at number one in the *Melody Maker* chart. The *Daily Express* printed a list of politicians' favourite records, with Labour's Shadow Minister of Education Frederick Willey choosing 'From Me To You'.

Before the group headed off to Southend-on-Sea, John and Paul recorded a demo of 'Bad To Me'. They played two evening shows at the 2,286-seater Odeon on the High Street at 6.35pm and 8.50pm. The *Southend Standard* reviewed the show, under the two-part headline, 'Take These Lads From Liverpool … And Show Really Packs Punch', giving the town's 'screamagers' yet another chance to exercise their undeniably strong vocal powers, wrote that the Beatles 'had the unenviable job of following this great act (Roy Orbison), but came through with their reputation still intact'. The reviewer was most taken with Gerry and the Pacemakers (describing Marsden as 'the pint-sized Merseysider'), who stole 'a great deal of the limelight'.

❝ It was a lovely life, growing up in an English seaside town. You couldn't beat it. Southend was fantastic. We lived a minute from the beach, and only a ten-minute walk from the Odeon in town. I hated school. I was a pupil at Dowsett High School for Girls, and one parents' evening the headmistress told my mother that I'd never hold a job down, would go from factory to factory, and that I was basically unemployable. Luckily back then you could leave school at 15, which I did, taking up a three-year apprenticeship at Betty's hairdressers on York Road. It was only a five-minute walk to work, and I loved it. There was a chap in town called Denny Knott, who owned two hugely popular coffee bars. He was the big man in Southend. The Capri on Weston Road was the first underground coffee bar, and the other one was called the Jacobean. There was also a place called the Zanzibar.

We'd buy one coffee and stay there all day! Mum didn't like me going to the coffee bars, and although I thought she never knew, in hindsight, she did. She preferred it if I had friends round, which she encouraged, so I was lucky in that way. I'd have parties every other Saturday, and she would cook for everyone, and they'd stay over. There was a little shop down Clarence Road where we would buy our records. It used to be a big post office, which turned into a hairdresser's and the little record shop. You could listen to the new releases in the booths.

At Betty's, I used to do about seventy-five heads of hair on Christmas Eve. Everything from setting, hair up, French buns. We had a client who worked at the Odeon, and she would give us tickets for all the shows. We heard the Beatles were coming to town. Me and my school friends loved them, and my bedroom walls were covered in pictures of them. My favourite was George – oh yes. My friend's – Paul. There was a competition in a local magazine to win tickets to see the show. Second prize was a signed photograph of the group. I entered, didn't win first prize, but I did win second – the signed photograph! It was properly signed, not printed, and we were so lucky that our client gave us some tickets to see the show; me, my friend Hazel from the hairdresser's, and two school friends. It was an amazing evening, but you couldn't hear a thing. The noise was unbelievable, like nothing I had ever heard before. ,

VAL MILLER, HAIRDRESSER AND HOUSEWIFE, LEIGH-ON-SEA, ESSEX

JUNE
Back to the one-night stands

SATURDAY 1 JUNE

Despite arriving back in London after midnight, the group arrived at the BBC Paris Studio by 9.30am to record the first of two four-hour sessions for *Pop Go The Beatles*. In the morning, they recorded 'A Shot Of Rhythm And Blues', 'Memphis Tennessee', 'A Taste Of Honey', 'Sure To Fall (In Love With You)', 'Money' (which they had performed on *Saturday Club* on 21 May) and 'From Me To You'. After an hour's break, they began recording a second episode, performing 'Too Much Monkey Business', 'I Got To Find My Baby', 'Youngblood', 'Baby It's You' (the second and last time they performed it on radio), 'Till There Was You' (Paul had learnt the song from Peggy Lee's version, which his cousin Bett had given to him), and 'Love Me Do', finishing at 5.30pm. The morning session aired on 18 June, featuring guests Carter-Lewis and the Southerners, and the afternoon session on 11 June, with the Countrymen. Aware that the first show was going to air on Paul's birthday, the rest of the group sang a raucous version of 'Happy Birthday To You' between 'Memphis, Tennessee' and 'A Taste Of Honey'.

Epstein, ever present, introduced the group to the publisher of monthly magazine *Beat Instrumental*, Sean O'Mahony, who planned to start a monthly Beatles' magazine. The pair had previously met for drinks at the Westbury Hotel in February, with Epstein telling him, 'The Beatles are going to be very, very big.' O'Mahony later recalled, 'As soon as I shook hands with John, Paul, George and Ringo, I realised this wasn't going to be one of their jokey encounters with the press. Editing their magazine meant that they would have to admit someone new to their inner circle and put up with me in their dressing rooms, recording studios, homes – in fact, virtually everywhere they went... Paul McCartney asked most of the questions. His main concern was what I was going to put into the magazine to fill it every month.'

As soon as the session finished, the group drove south through rush hour traffic over the Vauxhall Bridge to Mitcham Road in Tooting, arriving just in time for the 6.45pm performance at the 3,104-seater Granada. Interviewed for the 'Newsman's Diary' column in the *Balham & Tooting News & Mercury*, George said, 'I've got 'eadache after that. This audience is one of the best we have had.' Paul, named as 'McArtney', commented, 'We don't mind the screams though, because we know the show's going down well.' Following the 9pm show, they returned to the West End.

❝ I was fortunate to go to a really good school, Waverley Grammar, in Birmingham, which was very enlightened at the time. They had a jazz and blues society, and a couple of the teachers organised operas every year. It was there that I met Ken Hawker. We formed a skiffle group together, much to the disapproval of the headmaster! Ken played piano and I played guitar. We managed to get a concert organised at school, featuring the group, which was quite a feat. We thought, 'Why not start writing songs together?' which is what we did. I left school and went to work for ICI in Birmingham as a lab assistant while Ken joined the Civil Service.

But I had it in my head that I wanted to work in the music business, so we would write in the evenings and at weekends. One day we decided 'OK, come on, let's go down to London.' We bought a return ticket by coach – the cheaper option! We knocked on the doors of all the publishers in Denmark Street and they mostly said, 'No, no, go away,' but one of them at Noel Gay's, Terry Kennedy, at last said, 'Come on in, you've brought your guitars, so play something.' We'd brought perhaps five or six songs, but only played a couple, and Terry said,

'Yeah, I'll get the boss down.' He listened, and said, 'Yes, we may have to do something. I'll let you know.' We had just got back to Birmingham when Terry rang. He said, 'You've got a deal.' It was a songwriting contract, with Terry acting as our manager.

We moved down to London more or less immediately and stayed at Terry's house. After a while, Terry left Noel Gay and went to work for Southern Music, taking us with him. In our early days down in London, we were given an audition by the BBC. When we passed, we were so delighted. We started doing shows like *Easy Beat* and *Saturday Club* which were really big shows at the time. We always tried to put a group together to play, so Terry said, 'Well let's call you a group now. You can be Carter-Lewis and the Southerners.' It sounded better than Hawker-Shakespeare (my real name) and the Southerners so we said, 'OK!' We would do these shows for the BBC, and sort of became known as the 'weird' group. Nobody knew what we were going to do. We'd take old songs and do them in a Buddy Holly style, we'd take folk songs and do them in a rock style, we just wanted to experiment.

We were then asked to guest on *Pop Go The Beatles*. We were aware of the Beatles – and thought they were brilliant. We didn't see them in the light of the stars they became, and say, 'Oh it's so nice to meet you' etc. It was just all musicians together, and that was it. For the *Pop Go The Beatles* sessions, you were more or less on your own – they just recorded you doing your own stuff, but I remember this day particularly, because the Beatles came out to listen to us. They were obviously going to do their bit later, and they came out and sat down and listened to us, and said, 'Great fellows, that's really good!' We chatted for a while, just about music – George was definitely the nicest.

I hated live performances, and once we'd formed Carter-Lewis and the Southerners we were getting lots of radio exposure, and the money was there to go and tour. Terry said, 'You must go and do this.' In Tin Pan Alley there was a cafe where everyone hung out who wanted work. So if we had a gig, we would go there and say, 'Do you fancy doing a show tonight?' We'd bump into Jimmy Page a lot in the studios and got to know him quite well. We'd always go for a beer after the session, and one day we asked him if he'd like to come out on the road with us and he said, 'Yeah, I'd love to.' We had a lot of fun, but I thought, 'This is not for me. I'd rather be at home writing in the studio and recording.' That's why we disbanded really. We were getting more and more offers for session work, and for me it meant good money, without having to be out on the road.

Terry suggested getting another voice in and doing really good three-part harmonies. We approached Perry Ford, had a little practice to see if it worked, and it did. So Terry said, 'Fantastic. We'll make some records with the three of you,' and he thought of the name the Ivy League. We made a record which wasn't a success at all, so I thought, 'Well that's that out of the way,' but then Ken and I wrote 'Funny How Love Can Be,' and Terry said, 'This is great; I think you should record this yourselves.' We'd get three, maybe four sessions a day in London, and from that, we found we really sang well together. We sang with Mick Jagger on Chris Farlowe's 'Out of Time,' and backing vocals on Jeff Beck's 'Hi Ho Silver Lining.' Mickie Most called me up and said that Jeff couldn't reach some of the high notes and I just went along and helped out. By 1967 we were recording as the Flowerpot Men, and we'd had a hit with 'Let's Go To San Francisco.' I sang the lead vocals but didn't want to go out on the road again, so Tony Burrows came in and took over. He was going around from one group to another at the time, all hugely successful. The Flowerpot Men wanted to go on to more poppy stuff, so they became White Plains, recorded by Roger Greenaway, and that was fine by us. In 1970, I wrote 'Knock Knock Who's There?' with Geoff Stephens which Mary Hopkin sang in the Eurovision Song Contest. He'd write great songs, but he didn't know how to demo them – he didn't know the chords, so I sorted out a lot of his songs, and I did the demo of 'Winchester Cathedral.' He thought it was either absolute rubbish or could be a Top 10 hit. I thought it was quite unusual, and we ended up recording it ourselves, with me doing the vocal, just as I had done it on the demo. It was released under the name the New Vaudeville Band. He couldn't afford to pay me as the budget for the recording had run out, so he asked if I'd accept £10 and a share of the royalties, and I agreed. It turned out to be a good decision! My wife Gill and I also wrote 'Beach Baby,' which was a big hit for First Class, which was me, Tony Burrows and Chas Mills. I've never given away records, just licensed songs, so they've always come back to me. I have been lucky to make a living out of writing for fifty or so years, but they were the glory years. ∎

JOHN CARTER, SINGER, SONGWRITER AND PRODUCER, RICHMOND-UPON-THAMES, SURREY

SUNDAY **2 JUNE**

The Beatles headed to the south coast for two shows at the Hippodrome in Brighton at 6.15 and 8.30, the fourteenth date of the tour. On the drive down, the group heard that 'From Me To You', in its sixth week at number one on *Pick Of The Pops*, now shared the top spot with 'Do You Want To Know A Secret' – the only time in chart history that joint number ones were written by the same songwriters. As they approached the town for the 6.15pm show, they stopped by the fountain outside the Black Lion Pub in Patcham Village to change cars. A group of youngsters spotted them, including Mike Wenham who recalled, 'We had to go to church on Sundays so we could attend the Youth Club. We would normally turn up ten minutes early, sit at the very back and suffer in silence whilst the vicar delivered his sermon and hymns were sung. On this particular Sunday we all decided that we wouldn't go to church and hope that nobody would notice we were missing. Our plan was to mess about for a while and then go up to the church when they all came out and make it look as though we had been there all the time. A very large car with blacked out windows pulled up next to the fountain. About five minutes later an even bigger car turned up, also with blacked out windows, and both rear doors opened. One after the other, four blokes jumped out and started to transfer to the first car. My mates didn't have a clue what was going on, but I was mad about the pop groups of the day, and I soon recognized the four blokes as John, Paul, George and Ringo. I stood with gob wide open, wanting to say something but nothing came out. The last one to get in the car was Ringo and he scruffed up my hair and gave us a wave before being driven off at high speed towards Brighton.'

The group's car had to negotiate a throng of fans as it drove along the seafront onto Middle Street. The first show was not without incident – seconds into their set, the power went out. Despite being fixed, it happened again. It turned out that a bass drum was resting on a mains supply point. Screaming fans were probably oblivious to the fact that no music was coming from the stage.

❝ In the early '60s I was working as a photojournalist for the *Mid-Sussex Times*, an old-fashioned newspaper based in Haywards Heath. One of the reporters, called Alan Jones, talked the editor, a very crusty old gent, into starting a pop music column. Alan and I would go to gigs for pictures and interviews. We had been to the Brighton Hippodrome a few times and would go backstage for pictures. But on the evening of 2 June for the Beatles' concert, we were told no interviews, no cameras, no backstage passes. Outside hundreds of screaming girls with bobbed hair, black eyeliner and mini dresses were held back by white-helmeted and gloved police (in the '60s they were all very smart).

We did get into the Hippodrome, but right at the back with my camera under my coat. The girls were already screaming, but when the Beatles came onstage it was deafening. I managed to get my camera out and with a telephoto lens, resting on Alan's shoulder to steady it, and with the crowds jumping and screaming, I managed to fire off a roll of film. As for the music, I know it sounds a cliche and everybody said it, but you could not hear a thing for screaming. You'd catch a first chord of a song then the screams would start again. I believe I was the only one to get pictures that night. As a postscript, I was in New York working for the *Daily Express*. On 8 December 1980, I was in a Chinese restaurant with an *Express* journalist when he got a call telling him that John Lennon had been shot outside the Dakota Building. I dashed over to the building and began taking pictures of hundreds of Beatles fans, holding candles, singing, crying and chanting 'Give Peace A Chance' in the road outside the building. "

COLIN PAYNE, PHOTOGRAPHER, EAST HOATHLY, EAST SUSSEX

MONDAY 3 JUNE

Fleet Street was beginning to take notice of the Beatles. In the morning's *Guardian*, Stanley Reynolds wrote about graffiti on the front of St George's Hall in Liverpool that declared 'I Love The Beatles', in an article titled 'Big Time'. He commented, 'There is hardly anything cryptic about this declaration to anyone who has ever viewed *Juke Box Jury*, listened to *Pick Of The Pops*, or fathered a teenage daughter, for in the last six months the Beatles have become the most popular vocal-instrumental group in Britain, and, as everyone with any pretension towards mass culture should know, the Beatles are from Liverpool.' At 10.31am, the episode of *Steppin' Out* recorded on 21 May aired.

In the US, Del Shannon's version of 'From Me To You' was released on the Big Top label. *Cash Box* reviewed the single, calling it 'an infectious, thump-a-twist version of the tune that's currently riding in the number one slot in England – via the Beatles stand,' although very few in the US knew anything about the group.

Cloudy skies greeted those in the south-east on the last day of the Whitsun weekend. The group performed two sets at 6.45pm and 9pm at the 2,434-seater Granada in Powis Street, Woolwich. The cinema was showing the film *Pure Hell Of St Trinian's* – no doubt a case of screaming girls both on and off the screen. After the first show, fans brought the area to a standstill, pouring out onto the street, milling around the cinema hoping for a glimpse of their heroes. At one point, John opened a window, leant out and waved at the increasingly hysterical girls down below.

❝1963 seems another world when I look through a small diary, written in pencil by a 14-year-old from London suburbia. It is hard to believe more than fifty years on, that this was me noting down daily events (including the weather) and feelings which encapsulated everyday life at that time when the Beatles were going to emerge onto the group scene and remain part of our lives. On the back page of the yellow *Mirabelle* and *Marty* diary, a spin off from the must have magazines for every aspiring teenager of the day, I wrote the words 'I Love' and then many names of groups and singers. Adam Faith and Eden Kane feature and in larger letters was Elvis, but at the top and underlined was the Beatles.

From my diary, the first few months of 1963 seem to be a blur of snow, school and meeting up with friends with an eclectic mix of comments such as on Friday 18 January 'Mr Gaitskell died today' and going to 'Wimpy for dinner'. On 20 January I noted 'recorded *Pick Of The Pops*. Physics and Arith tests tomorrow.' Several times I listened to Radio Luxembourg (once in the bath!) and on 23 February noted I was stopped watching *That Was The Week That Was* by my father. Clearly unsuitable viewing.

However, Friday 10 May was an important day. I noted I rang up my friend Anne and 'she has got the tickets to see the Beatles.' So Whit Monday 3 June was going to be my first introduction to the Beatles, who were playing live in Woolwich, a few miles from where I lived in Welling. It was a few weeks before the day. I recorded days at school, family visits and watching a Charlton v Southampton match on 18 May at the Valley when 'Charlton would have got chucked out but they won 2-1.' On 25 May, I 'bought material for a shift dress 17/6 (75p)' and on Saturday 1 June I went to a Lords Cricket Match with a group of school friends in the boiling heat. I remember that outing well – not the cricket but fooling around with the boys. Monday 3 June was, as I noted, a cloudy day. We were off to Woolwich Odeon. My diary confirms this and notes 'I went to see the Beatles, Gerry and the Pacemakers, Roy Orbison. GREAT! Everyone screaming. Had a fab time.' I remember the crowds. I remember the screaming. I remember the excitement of being 14 and part of the music scene. I knew the Beatles were great. I said so but could not have imagined how great they would become. The start of years of listening to Beatles music as we went from teenagers to mothers and grandmothers. We were there. They were great. It was fab. However, after 3 June, we were back to the world of school tests, crushes and the world of growing up in the '60s. ❞

GAYNOR WINGHAM, SOCIAL WORK CONSULTANT, ELTHAM, KENT

TUESDAY **4 JUNE**

*B*oyfriend's Maureen O'Grady spoke with Tony Barrow about organising a competition prize of 'Lunch With The Beatles.' Brian Epstein had not been informed and was more than a little upset when he read about the competition in the magazine the following month.

After a free morning, the group headed north on the M1, by now a familiar route, for the final five dates of the Roy Orbison tour. The first episode of *Pop Go The Beatles* aired at 5pm while the group were on the road. It was recorded on 24 May and hosted by Lee Peters, with guests the Lorne Gibson Trio. In its report published on 2 August, the BBC's Audience Research Department, estimated that 5.3 per cent of the population listened to the show, equal to around 2.8 million people. The Appreciation Index was a below-average 52 out of 100, with audience reactions ranging from the delighted to 'they make an obnoxious noise.'

The group arrived at the 1,960-seater Town Hall on Congreve Street in Birmingham for two further sold-out gigs, at 6.30pm and 8.45pm. John, George and Ringo rushed into the theatre through a side door, but Paul momentarily got stuck in the tour coach after being spotted by fans. The *Evening Mail & Despatch* noted in its review of the show, 'This was the Beatle Drive - 1963 version. The drive came from four young Merseysiders known as the Beatles. Their mere appearance onstage, before a note was played, was sufficient to drive two capacity houses into a frenzy of hysterical squeals, hand-clapping and feet-stamping. The music, by any standard, was rough-hewn, stamped out with the slogging subtlety of an imprecise steam hammer. But to the four thousand listeners it was, by excessive demonstration, ecstasy.'

❝ I used to read the *NME* and would scour the American charts for new releases. When anything came up that sounded interesting, I'd head to Dugmore's, the record shop in Smethwick, where I grew up. It was run by two sisters. To myself at the time, a guy in his early twenties, they seemed like old women, but they were probably only about 40. They seemed very hip for their respective ages. I never used to buy British records, because generally they were total rip-offs – covers of American classics.

When I read that the Beatles wrote their own material, I was intrigued, and went along with two or three mates to Thimblemill Baths in Smethwick when they came to play there. It was November 1962, and a regular thing to put a dance floor over the pool in the winter. It wasn't particularly full that evening. They didn't go down very well, with shouts of 'Mug heads!' and 'Gits!' I really enjoyed them though, and at the end of their set I went down to the front and said, 'That was great, I really enjoyed it!' John Lennon said, 'Oh thanks, wack.' George said, 'Very kind,' and Paul said, 'It was all right for a laugh!' They didn't have that much original material at this time, so they did an incredible amount of covers, good covers of stuff which weren't in the British charts and would never make the British charts. I had the originals of these records at home, so I deduced that I must have been buying the same stuff as the Beatles as soon as they were released. The next time I saw them was at the Plaza in Handsworth. My diary entry for the day read, 'Went to the Plaza from the Farcroft (which was the pub next door.) Got inside the door to see the Beatles. They were terrific.'

4 June was the evening they played the Town Hall in Birmingham. It's a beautiful ornate building. It's built in the style of the Colosseum in Rome, with pillars outside, and very beautiful inside. A curved balcony runs down the side of the stage, the very balcony that I saw Buddy Holly and the Crickets from. I went with my mates Ned and Steve – we were quite near the front, in the stalls, about seven or eight rows back. The Beatles came on after Orbison, and you just couldn't hear them. It surely must have been at the point in time when they thought, 'we can't go on much longer doing live shows like this.'

My diary entry for 29 June records, 'Set out for Old Hill with Ned, Moss and Steve. Couldn't get in to see the Beatles. We were too late and it was rammed. Rose and Crown. Plaza side door.' What this means is that we'd spent too long in the pub, and the gig was sold out by the time we got there! My then girlfriend Carol was a regular at the Plaza and was already inside. We snuck round the side when the gig finished, and met up with Carol, who told me not to be disappointed that we didn't get in because there had been an announcement made that they were coming back the following week. I found it hard to believe that they would be coming back so soon but come back they did. We'd made a mental note to get there earlier on 5 July, and all got in to see the show. I'm not sure if it was this evening, or one of the others, but John Lennon would sometimes ad-lib when singing 'Twist And Shout' and sing 'Pissed on stout'. This was the last time I saw them live. I'd lost my enthusiasm somewhat after the Town Hall gig. It wasn't so bad on the Plaza evenings as the venue was so much smaller, so even though there was screaming going on, you were close enough to get involved in the atmosphere, and also to read their lips! ❞

GEOFF POOLE, FINANCE MANAGER, SMETHWICK, WEST MIDLANDS

WEDNESDAY 5 JUNE

E MI's Len Wood wrote to George Martin in reply to the producer thanking the company for giving the Beatles a royalty increase. 'Surely we have given the manager of the Beatles just the ammunition he requires to secure an additional term contract from the Beatles for himself and in turn to give us further options. I should be glad if you pursue the subject vigorously on these lines and let me know how things develop because if we do not get further options all we have done is to give away a fair chunk of Company money.'

The next stop of the tour was Leeds, an almost three-hour drive through Nottingham, Mansfield and Doncaster. They were met by police on the A1, who escorted them to the 2,556-seater Odeon in the Headrow for two shows at 6.10pm and 8.40pm. Noel Hall, one of the policemen on duty, asked for the group's autographs backstage for his daughter Jennifer. Following the second house, they returned to the Metropole Hotel on King Street, where they spent the night.

Ronald Wilkinson reviewed the show in the *Yorkshire Evening Post*, 'Their set was drowned out for the whole of its duration by one ear-splitting shriek which whistled with maniacal fury like some weird wind machine worked by a mad stage hand' and described the evening as 'bedlam'. *The Yorkshire Evening News* reviewer was 'breathless', among the three thousand teenagers who went 'wild with enthusiasm'. Caught up in the fervour, the reviewer wrote, 'I came away with their screams, cries, cheers and clapping still ringing in my ears, never have I heard the like of it before... in the true tradition of show business the group kept on singing not even being put off by the various missiles which kept arriving on the stage, thrown by their more adventurous fans.'

> ❝ I grew up in St Helens and spent my childhood living at number 56, Graham Street. About a dozen houses further down the road lived a young lad by the name of Geoff Taggart. He was two years younger than me and you know how when you're younger, you don't play with kids who are two years younger. It must have been 1957, I was in the street talking about 'Whole Lotta Shakin' Goin' On' and I invited him into my house to listen to it. Then as the weeks went by I'd go round to his house and he'd come to mine and we'd sing together. Geoff took up the guitar and we started writing songs together. We used to have exercise books at school in which you used to do your homework and Geoff says he still has one with the first song we ever wrote called 'Rockin' At The Zoo'.
>
> We were Roy Orbison fans so we went to Liverpool in May 1963 to try and get to see him and give him some songs. We couldn't get backstage but bumped into a guy outside called David Macbeth. He was on the tour and said, 'If you can come to Leeds I'll try and get you in.' So we travelled to Leeds which is about 60 miles away – and it was a long 60 because there was no motorway back then – and we get there, thinking we wouldn't get in, but Macbeth was there and he got us backstage. So we go in and we get taken to Roy Orbison's dressing room.
>
> There he is, real nice Southern gentleman with jet black hair and we tell him, 'We've got some songs for you.' He said, 'OK, let me hear them,' and we had with us a Grundig reel-to-reel that weighed fifty pounds probably and put it on the dressing room table. So we start playing the songs to him, and then in come the Beatles, which annoyed us a little bit because we wanted Roy to listen to us. They were clowning around for a while but then they all disappeared next door which I guess was their dressing room. I remember standing next to John in the corridor and he was tuning his guitar. Ringo had shown me his hands full of rings. I don't recall much about George. I said to Geoff, 'Shall we take a photo of the Beatles?' He said, 'No. They're just a load of Scousers. We don't want them.' One by one they drifted away, but Paul stayed and asked, 'Are those your songs on that tape recorder?' And he started listening to them and said, 'They're pretty good.' So Paul says to me, 'Sing me one of your songs.' Now I'm not the best singer in the world, but anyhow I sang a song called 'If I Really Knew'. He said, 'I like that, but why don't you change the title to 'I'd Be In Paradise?'' We left a bit after

that and they'd given us free tickets to see the show. Well, we didn't hear the Beatles because there were two thousand girls screaming. I remember everyone was sitting down, then everybody stood up and then everybody stood on their seats. It was chaos.

Some years later I went to Liverpool to guest on Spencer Leigh's show on Radio Merseyside and it was like a *Juke Box Jury*. I can't remember who else was on the panel, but I think it was one of the Swinging Blue Jeans, someone from the Mojos, and Mike McCartney, who was in the Scaffold at the time. After the show was over I chatted to Mike and told him the story about when I met Paul and he'd told me to change the lyric to 'I'd Be In Paradise', and Mike said, 'I believe every word. We lived near Paradise Street and he always tried to put the word paradise in his songs.' Then in the late '80s, Shakin' Stevens cut the song. He didn't do any of the rockers he said he liked but did 'If I Really Knew' the one I'd sung to Paul. The song was on a CD *Country Blues* by Shaky a few years back and if I remember right I got a royalty cheque for a couple of pounds! Soon after we met the Beatles in June 1963, I went to Nashville after a magazine called *Opry* offered two weeks in Nashville – flight and hotel for a hundred quid. I saw Johnny Cash, Marty Robbins, Wanda Jackson and Jerry Lee Lewis, and was invited to a George Jones recording session. His backing vocalists that night were the Jordanaires. I met them all and Gordon Stoker and I got on really well. He said to me, 'Hey man, what's all this Beatles business?' When I got home I sent him the *Please Please Me* album. Just before he died a few years ago, I called him and he told me that his son still had it. **]**

JIM NEWCOMBE, SONGWRITER, MOULD ENGINEER, BURLINGTON, ONTARIO, CANADA

THURSDAY 6 JUNE

Billy J. Kramer's 'Do You Want To Know A Secret' knocked 'From Me To You' off the top of the week's *Disc* chart. John, in his second column for the paper, revealed that Paul used green toothpaste as shaving soap. He commented on a drawing of the group by two fans. 'The portraits were very good, except for the one of Ringo. But let's face it, no one could capture his mug in charcoal.' His comment so upset people that he had to explain what he meant in an open letter to *Mersey Beat*. 'I had been discussing some charcoal drawings of members of the group which had been sent by a fan. I mentioned that Ringo Starr was ugly – I was, of course, only referring to the charcoal drawings and not Ringo himself.' 'From Me To You' remained at number one in the *NRM* and 'My Bonnie' charted at number 48.

Since the first episode of *Pop Go The Beatles* aired, producer Terry Henebery received more than one hundred cards from listeners expressing their delight that the Beatles now had their own radio programme. One less happy listener, Erica Clandon from Lydiate in Lancashire, was featured under the headline 'Bad Time' in *Disc*'s post bag, 'The Beatles are my favourite group and I read with interest that they are to be given their own radio series. Now I find that the programme is transmitted at 5pm on Tuesday, when I, and thousands more of their fans, are working. Why can't the BBC put such programmes on when more people are likely to be able to tune in?' Henebery later recalled that getting the 'Pop Goes The Weasel' theme down on tape took as long as their own songs. 'Not because of any incompetence on the Beatles' part but because they were just fooling about. Remember, they were very much younger, they were very inexperienced and they'd come to the studio and horse about. You had to crack the whip and get on the loudspeaker talk-back key quite a lot and say, 'Come on, chaps!' They'd be lying all over the floor giggling. I can remember just looking at the clock, throwing your hands up in horror, thinking will they ever settle down? Stop horsing about? I mean people would go and get locked in the toilets and fool about.'

It was a day off for the group. They travelled north of the border to attend a party hosted by a Scottish businessman.

FRIDAY 7 JUNE

In the new issue of the *NME*, 'From Me To You' dropped to number 2, while 'Do You Want To Know A Secret' enjoyed the top spot on its own. In *Melody Maker* the positions were reversed. The group drove to the Theatre Royal in Glasgow to make a second appearance on STV's *Roundup*, alongside Gerry and the Pacemakers. After John tried to make Gerry laugh, the show's floor manager was heard to say, 'You won't get anywhere in show business if you don't get a more professional attitude.' Co-host Paul Young drove Ringo and George to the Odeon in his MG Midget after the recording.

Police arrived at midday for the group's two evening shows at 6.40pm and 9pm at the 2,784-seater Odeon on the corner of Renfield and West Regent streets in Glasgow's city centre. Fans began assembling soon after, many of whom didn't have tickets. Chief Constable James Robertson had to bring in reinforcements. Police Sergeant Irene Livingstone was caught up in the hysteria, being jostled as the crowd numbers increased as the afternoon wore on. Once the show started, she found her way into the Odeon. 'I met one of the girls from the St Andrew's Ambulance Society and she was just bringing out an endless procession of bodies into the foyer. These young girls were collapsing with hysteria. This is what I imagine hell was like. It was just wall-to-wall screaming.'

Bruce Baxter, guitarist for the Terry Young Six, remembered the evening: 'Girls had filled the orchestra pit at the front and then they surged up onto the stage. The bouncers were throwing them off but one girl got hold of Roy's glasses. He got them back and was unhurt, but he was shocked.' The stage curtains had to be brought down.

Ringo also had memories of the shows in Glasgow. 'It was terrible, following Roy. He'd slay them and they'd scream for more. In Glasgow we were all backstage, listening to the tremendous applause he was getting. He was doing it just by his voice. Just standing there singing, not moving or anything. He was knocking them out. As it got near our turn, we would hide behind the curtains whispering to each other, 'Guess who's next folks. It's your favourite rave!' But once we got onstage it was always OK.'

Under the headline 'Six thousand Pop Fans Go Wild' the *Glasgow Herald* commented, 'Teenagers made attempts to storm the stage when the Beatles and Roy Orbison were on, but specially-drafted attendants kept them at bay as programmes and soft drink cartons were thrown on to the stage. It was one of the most riotous receptions for any show since Cliff Richard and the Shadows visited the same theatre a few months ago. After the second show, about two thousand fans stood outside the stage door chanting, 'We want the Beatles.' Police dispersed them.'

> ❝ My first recollection of the Beatles was when they topped the charts with 'Please Please Me' in February 1963, although they didn't feature hugely in our household although my mother, of course, thought their hair was too long. It was through Hugh, one of my friends at school, in late 1962, that I met his cousin, the lovely Margaret. She was my first girlfriend. It was she who bought the tickets for us to go and see Roy Orbison. It was a treat from her to me. She was a very kind person, a very indulgent person. Although still at school, she was soon to become a trainee nurse. Why was it so special to see someone like Roy Orbison? Going to the Odeon in itself was an event, going to the Odeon to see Roy Orbison, was 'oh my goodness,' and going with my 'girlfriend'! It was quite a big thing. I felt pretty grown up and sophisticated.

We met outside, I remember Margaret had a very happy, excited face. When we got inside, I was surprised at just how big it was. We had seats halfway up the front stalls, a lovely view. I don't recall even knowing in advance that the Beatles were to appear on the same bill. It was Roy we had gone to see. But it was a great evening! All the acts were wonderful. I enjoyed the Beatles, and remember thinking, 'Ah yes, this is what my sister was going on about!' I recall some girls getting excited, but not to the point of hysteria. There was certainly some screaming, but it wasn't constant. Dare I say it, Roy Orbison was still the highlight of the evening for me. For some months after the concert, and indeed to this day, when I tell people I saw the Beatles live, they say 'What? You saw the Beatles?' and I know that I experienced something special, even though I didn't realise it at the time. The evening was special, but for all the aforementioned reasons – the excitement of going to the Odeon, being with Margaret, going to a 'pop' concert – all of this made it a moment in time for me.

Margaret and I saw each other for a while afterwards, at least until I went to university, but then we drifted apart. Margaret went on to become a nurse. Some five or so years later, my father was stabbed by a thug in Glasgow, and ended up in hospital in a serious condition. By remarkable coincidence his nurse was Margaret. Some years ago when I was living in Wimbledon, I used to go running in the park. One particular day, this huge helicopter landed close to where I was running. A couple of limousines appeared, and out of one of them came Pope John Paul who was being transported to his next 'gig'! He had been staying overnight with the Papal Legate, the Vatican's ambassador to Britain, who lived nearby. Only a clutch of priests and nuns, myself, a couple of policemen, a man and his dog were around. He got out – he was quite small and serene I remember – and gave us all a Papal blessing. When I tell people this papal story, and that I saw the Beatles live in 1963, generally they're more impressed that I saw the Beatles. **"**

LAURENCE FRYER, LAWYER, DULWICH, LONDON

SATURDAY **8 JUNE**

Arriving in Newcastle, for two shows at the City Hall, the tour coach drove by teens with sleeping bags on the pavements. After the shows, at 6.30pm and 8.40pm, local boy David Macbeth arranged for the group to relax at La Dolce Vita night club on Low Friar Street, where chemin de fer and dice were on offer for those who wanted a flutter. Los Andinos, Teddy Foster, Julie Rolls, the Bob Stephenson Sextet and La Dolce Vita Girls provided the evening's cabaret. Louise Cordet had her first alcoholic drink – a gin and orange. The group then returned to the Royal Turks Head Hotel.

' I lived in North Shields and still do. The Hit Parade was very much our hobby in those days. We used to have a little shop that sold records, and we'd go down when new songs came out and listen to them in the booths. You never heard the records before the release date and it was always exciting to find out when a new record was coming out and you would race down to the shop with your six and thruppence. We'd hear about the new releases through word of mouth at school or on Radio Luxembourg. I'd curl up in front of the fire at night with a blanket wrapped round me and put the radio on. I had posters all over my bedroom wall. There was *Girl* and *Princess* magazines, and they used to have centrefold pages of the pop stars. I didn't want to leave pin holes in the posters, so I used to leave corners of the magazine, the white bits, and put the pins through there! My parents didn't seem to mind. Dad was a bit Victorian and couldn't really make head nor tail of the '60s. I shared a bedroom with my brother, who was eight years younger than me.

I had a friend, Jackie, who lived in Maidenhead and she used to go to Reading every week to see five or six groups all at once. She used to write to me about this group called the Beatles. I hadn't a clue who they were really. Of course, they started to get more popular, and that was it, I was off! When we found out that they were coming to the City Hall, we went up after school on the bus to Newcastle to get the tickets.

The City Hall is an iconic building in the centre of Newcastle. It is a theatre rather than a dance hall. The Majestic was a dance hall, and you would just stand on the dance floor, but the City Hall was THE place. The sound is good and you can see from everywhere. On the stage, they had seats, and you could sit behind the groups on big risers, maybe three tiers. We just went to the box office and got the tickets. We didn't have to queue. We knew the Beatles were playing with Roy Orbison, and that was why we bought the tickets. On the ticket it said, 'the Beatles with Roy Orbison and full support', so they had joint double billing. I remember being in my seat in the balcony and looking down on them. But it wasn't full and it wasn't mania. People weren't screaming and screaming. It wasn't like you see them on the telly now, when everyone is crying their eyes out. It was amazing really, we just took it in our stride, that we could go and see them. When we went to try and get tickets for the next concert at the City Hall, the queues went around the building, we just couldn't get any. It was a sell-out, and we just couldn't get a ticket. **⟩**

HEATHER PAGE, SECRETARY, HOUSEWIFE, NORTH SHIELDS, TYNE AND WEAR

SUNDAY 9 JUNE

Another long drive was in store for the tour party – a three-hour drive south to Blackburn through Harrogate, circumventing the Yorkshire Dales in temperatures soaring into the 80s. And so, the twenty-one-date tour with Roy Orbison came to an end, with two shows at the thirty-five-hundred-seater King Georges Hall in Northgate, Blackburn, at 6pm and 8.10pm. During the second house, a group of girls got past the police cordon and rushed the stage. Eileen Trippier, a pupil at Rhyddings Secondary school, was intercepted before she could reach her favourite Beatle, John. One male teen climbed on to the ledge of the balcony. Only the intervention of his friends holding onto his legs. Another teen shouted out 'Up the Rolling Stones' and was duly thumped with an umbrella by a girl nearby.

Between shows, the group chatted with journalists from the *Blackburn Times* and the *Evening Telegraph*. John told them that the night's audience was 'the best crowd we have had yet, the next being Glasgow'. After the second show, with fans queuing outside the stage door seeking autographs, the group made a break for it and into a waiting car. *Telegraph* photographer Milton Howarth was mistaken for Ringo and barely escaped the mob. He did, however, end up joining the group at a party at the Imp, 10 miles away in Nelson. He was even given a ride back home to Blackburn.

The *Blackburn Times*' front-page headline read, 'They SCREAMED, They TWISTED, They FAINTED As The Beatles Sang'. The article reported, 'A seething mass of fans made it to the stage at the end of the first house, but their passions had nothing on the second. Then, even a barrier of policemen failed to quench their enthusiasm, and a few succeeded in mounting the stage – almost delirious when they had actually touched a Beatle! But many more were dragged unceremoniously away, to be pitched back into the rabble.'

❛ In 1959 our parents bought my sister Barbara and I our first record player. At that time our favourite singer was Cliff Richard and the first record we bought was 'Living Doll'. I left school in 1960 when I was 15 and started work in a solicitor's office. Every Saturday night I went dancing with Barbara and my friends. There were two main dance halls in Blackburn – the Locarno Ballroom (a former cinema) and King Georges Hall (the Civic Centre in which all the touring shows, roller skating and boxing and wrestling matches were held).

We lived about an hour's drive from Blackpool and went there on day trips and holidays. It was a great place in those days. In 1963 I met my husband David at a Saturday night dance at the Locarno. The following evening he took me to see Cliff in *Summer Holiday* – that could not have been a better date. David didn't appreciate it as he was a Jerry Lee Lewis and Elvis fan. We used to go to the Wimpy Bar which had just opened. That was the first time we had burgers and thought they were great.

A couple of months later David bought tickets for us to see the Beatles and Roy Orbison show at the King Georges Hall. In those days you remained seated during a show. Not this time. We were all on our feet singing, screaming and cheering. One girl in the audience managed to climb onto the stage and take Roy Orbison's glasses. It was a fabulous show and David and I enjoyed it so much. From that night, Cliff always took second place to the Beatles. I had been converted. My favourite was Paul.

The '60s were such a good time in my life. It is a privilege to me that I was a teenager during that time. Life was good as the austerities in the aftermath of war had disappeared. People were content and could afford holidays and had money to spend. The lyrics of the Beatles and other artists' songs in the '60s reflected this in their happiness and optimism. I had kept my ticket and programme from the show in a box in the loft. There was an advert in the *Lancashire Telegraph* asking if anyone wanted to sell tickets or programmes from the show. I decided to sell. ❜

CAROLE DONNELLY, SOLICITOR'S LEGAL ASSISTANT, DARWEN, LANCASHIRE

MONDAY 10 JUNE

Although the tour had come to an end, there was no respite for the group. They had a full slate of concerts scheduled until the end of June. For the evening's concert in Bath, George rented a car to drive more than 200 miles for the show at the Pavilion on North Parade, Bridge Road in the evening. Neil Aspinall arrived in the Ford Thames at around 5pm, shortly before the group. Chris Cryer, lead guitarist of support act the Colin Anthony Combo, saw fans vandalising George's rental. Headlamps, mirrors and window wipers were all being removed, so he ran inside to tell them. George replied with a four-letter word followed by, 'I only hired that car in Liverpool this morning.'

Scheduled to start at 7.30pm, the show began an hour earlier because of the size of the crowd assembling outside. Chet and the Triumphs began the show, after which the Beatles played

a forty-five-minute set. The Colin Anthony Combo followed, with the Beatles finishing off the evening with another forty-five-minute set. Maggie Randall and Yvonne Buck met the group backstage and were allowed to watch the show from the wings. Randall got their autographs on the back of a cigarette packet, which she duly sent to her German pen friend. The group limped back to Liverpool after the show, with various car parts missing, most importantly headlights.

❝ Sometime in early 1963, my group [the Colin Anthony Combo]'s manager Brian K. Jones gave me the list of dates we had coming up, and one was at the Pavilion (our hometown), sharing a bill with the Beatles. I'd seen them on television and thought 'they're not bad.' What a surprise we were in for! Situated in the centre of city, next to a Convent School for Girls, the Pavilion opened in 1910 as a skating rink, then later had a wide range of uses, including being an assembly point for aircraft wings in the Second World War. On the day, I went to work as usual and had the afternoon off so that we could organise ourselves for the gig. When we arrived, we found the place swarming with hundreds of people, mainly girls! I said to the other guys in the group, 'I think this gig is going to be something else!'

The Beatles arrived around half past five and navigated their way through the throng of fans down the side of the hall towards the stage door. I didn't know all the names of the guys at the time, but Ringo came up to me and asked where the dressing rooms were. Now in those days there was a small dressing room for the 'star' plus a big band room. When I showed him where the 'stars' went he remarked, 'It's like a rabbit hutch!' – except his choice of language was more colourful. So I suggested we all 'muck-in' together. John, who I found to be a typical Scouser, was playing up to the convent girls over the wall. Paul seemed to be the leader of the group who knew exactly what they wanted and needed and George was quite quiet although later we got on very well.

When they did their first set there was an incredible volume of noise. Then, of course it was our turn – sandwiched between them. So I warned the 'Combo' that we'd better be good because they're going to be screaming for the Beatles all the way through our set, which actually wasn't the case. They clapped and screamed for us as well which made it a very enjoyable evening for us, like we'd never experienced before – or probably since! The following month we met up again, when we went to see them in Weston-super-Mare. It was like meeting old mates. I really liked them as people. The history of what happened after is well documented but their appearance in Bath that night went almost unnoticed and with the lack of media attention a lot of people don't realise they ever played there. But for those who were there, they tell a very different story. ❞

COLIN ANTHONY, SINGER, LONDON

TUESDAY 11 JUNE

The second episode of *Pop Go The Beatles*, recorded on 1 June, was broadcast at 5pm on the Light Programme, while Friday's recording of *Roundup* aired on STV. The group had a well-earned day off.

WEDNESDAY 12 JUNE

Roger Bratt and Roger Cox, two 17-year-olds from Coseley appeared before Mr H. Fellows, the Chairman of Bilston Magistrates. Their offence was walking around town singing 'From Me To You' very loudly. When stopped by a police officer, who described the noise as 'terrible', Bratt replied, 'It's top of the pops.' They admitted disorderly behaviour and were both fined £2 by Mr Fellows, who admonished them. 'There is a time and place to sing the top of the pops.'

The group gave a charity performance for the National Society for Prevention of Cruelty to Children (NSPCC) at the Grafton Rooms in Liverpool. John Cashford, the NSPCC organiser for the Liverpool and Bootle area, said the Beatles had agreed to donate their fee 'as a gesture of gratitude and appreciation to the young people of Merseyside for their wonderful support. It is gratifying to know that these talented young people, at the most dazzling and demanding time of their career, can take time to remember those less fortunate than themselves.' Tickets for the show cost 6/-. It ran from 7.30pm to 11.30pm, and also featured Gerry and the Pacemakers, the Delemeres and Paul Francis plus the Dominant Four.

One fan described the Grafton as 'a relatively intimate place, big but much more friendly than the Empire and no orchestra pit keeping people away from the stage.' He and his pals found themselves a place right in the front of the stage. 'Bob Wooler spoke but his voice floated over our minds. Nothing mattered until they came on the stage. All of a sudden, the four were ambling towards us. George said "hello" and the others nodded in our direction. I wondered if they were really glad to see old friends after so long away from the Cavern crowd. They just did their forty-minute set and left. Instantly, the withdrawal symptoms set in. There was no way we could have a natter with them as we always did at the Cavern.'

❝ I went to Greycoats but left incapable of doing anything, so I went to Cripplegate Secretarial College in the City of London where I did company law, English law, etc. etc. but even then all I could do was type eighty words a minute, shorthand twenty-five. And every day I'd been given a little bit of money by my parents to go and find a job. But I'd always go to Soho to the coffee bars and come back home and always be asked, 'Did you get a job?' 'No, nobody wanted me. I can't understand it.' Then one day just so I could honestly say I'd tried I went to an Alfred Marks Bureau near Soho Square. It was about five o'clock as they were about to close and I said, 'I don't suppose you've got anything?' And they said, 'Yes. It's some typing and a little bit of shorthand for a magazine just around the corner in Regent Street. It's called *Boyfriend*.' So they phoned them and said, 'They'll wait for you.'

So I go round there and there's two members of staff – Penny Valentine and Maggie Koumi – and Ken Walmsley, who was deaf, so it did seem strange that he was in charge of a magazine to do with music. I had to do this typing test where he dictated to me and he spoke really slowly in a Scottish accent. So I wrote it down and then typed it out, took it out of the typewriter and said to Penny and Maggie, 'I couldn't understand what he was saying. It's hopeless.' They said, 'Stay there.' They went into his office and they came back with him and said, 'You've got the job.' And I said, 'Why?' They later told me that he hadn't liked anyone who'd come in and it was getting particularly urgent and the next person who walked through the door would get the job. So that's how I got it. Then one day, Penny decided to get married and wanted a three-week honeymoon, but Ken said she could only have two weeks like everybody else. She was always quite militant and she put her foot down, and he put his foot down and that was it, she went. So he said to me, who used to blush when anyone famous came into the office, 'You're going to have to fill in until we find someone.' I said, 'I don't know about that,' and he said, 'You'll be all right.'

I didn't know he had any intention of finding anyone for £10 a week, which was my princely wage. So I used to have to go and interview people and ask them what their favourite colour, favourite food, favourite film was. This would have been around September 1962 and then towards the end of that year we started getting postcards from people about this group from Liverpool. There was a press launch at EMI in Manchester Square for the *Please Please Me* LP. Leslie Thomas, who went on to become a very successful novelist and who was on the newsdesk at the *Evening News*, didn't have a clue who they were. I said to him, 'Haven't you heard of them?' In fact I might have been the only person there who had heard of them, because George came up to me and told me I was the only person he recognised. Fiona Adams, *Boyfriend*'s photographer was there, and I arranged for them to do a photo session and we were going to do it at the Serpentine with them on the boats and John said, 'No. We can't. We have to go and see our accountant.'

Anyway, we did get to do a session with them the following month at *Boyfriend*'s offices which were at 168 Regent Street and all four of them arrived together. We all met up in the offices and then we went down in the lift and into an alleyway to Kingly Street. It was at number 21 and we had to go up these rickety wooden stairs to the studio which I think was on the top floor. The woman below kept budgerigars so there was this awful smell when you went by her door. We did the session and then Fiona, who was very good at finding locations, said she wanted to go somewhere else outside. So we all took a taxi to Euston Road and I carried their coats. We did a whole bunch of photos there. Then about 3.30pm, we finished so they could get to perform in Croydon that night.

The next time I saw them was up in Liverpool. It had all been arranged with Tony Barrow, so Fiona and I took the train up there, which was a five-hour journey back in those days. We stayed at the Adelphi Hotel – we always stayed at the nicest hotels. We were mainly up there to do pieces on several of the Liverpool acts the following day. We got to the stage door and there were all these girls outside. We knocked on the door and these big bouncers opened it and we said, 'We're up here to see the Beatles. Our names have been left.' They looked at the sheet and said, 'No – they're not here.' So we went over the road to the pub and had a drink. We then went back and I said, 'Can you get a message through to the dressing room?' But they said, 'We can't leave the door, love.' So we went back to the pub and by now I was getting really mad. We went back again and I asked, 'Is Mr Epstein here?' They found him and came back and said, 'Sorry love, he doesn't know anything about it.' So we went back to the pub again. We went back across to the stage door and I banged on it, and they said, 'Oh, not you again.' I saw Brian walk by in the background and I said, 'Brian! What's going on? I'm very annoyed. We arranged with Tony to come here tonight and then to spend tomorrow with several of your other acts. We travelled five hours on a train from London and you're saying you know nothing about it?' So he said, 'You better come in.'

We went into the dressing room and the boys couldn't have been more surprised and delighted. John said, 'What are you doing here?' 'I said, What are we doing here? We've been outside and been across to the pub, sent a message to Brian, who said he didn't know anything about it.' So Brian was now trying to take control and he said, 'What's the order of songs tonight? What shall we do?' And John turned around and said, 'You mind your own effing business. You just take your cut and don't interfere with things that have nothing to do with you.' Anyway, it all worked out in the end because after the show John and George invited us over to the Blue Angel. George drove us there and showed us around Liverpool in his car. How we survived the night I'll never know? Later Tony called me and warned me and said I needed to call Brian in Liverpool. So I called him, and said, 'Hello Brian.' He said, 'I've just seen the latest edition of *Boyfriend*. How dare you offer my boys as prizes. They're not prizes to be won.' I told him, 'We've done lots of these 'Win A Date With' lunches.' I felt terrible about it, so I said, 'If you feel so strongly about it we can print a retraction.' 'Oh, that would make the boys look really good, wouldn't it?' he said. I knew I couldn't win, so I said, 'Brian, what do you want me to do? He said, 'I suppose we'll have to go ahead with it.' So that's what happened and I think I'm the only person who's ever given them away as prizes.

In November, I attended a reception at EMI for them and I spoke with George and asked, 'Would it be all right to join the tour?' He said, 'Yes, that's fine, but you'll have to check with Arthur.' So I went to see the promoter Arthur Howes and he had a crewcut, a snakeskin overcoat and a big Jag car. He said it was OK to join the tour, so that's what we did for a few dates. The following month, I went to EMI's Christmas party at Abbey Road. I remember having a little too much to drink, so Ringo asked Robert Freeman to give me a lift home. And I think much against his better judgement, he did. 〞

MAUREEN O'GRADY, JOURNALIST AND PRESS AGENT, LONDON

THURSDAY 13 JUNE

'From Me To You' dropped to number 4 in the *Disc* chart, but stayed at number one in *NRM*. George had to make the 100-mile drive to Goole to appear in court, stemming from the traffic incident in February when the group were returning from Hull. Described as a musician of 174 Mackets Lane, Woolton, Liverpool, he was fined £10 after pleading not guilty to a charge of driving a van without due care and attention. PC Kershaw, when questioned by Chief Inspector C.E. Clipston, said that the van George was driving had mounted a grass verge and knocked down seven concrete posts outside Burton's factory, and there were tyre marks on the road for a distance of 56 feet. George's solicitor Mr M. A. Atkin submitted that the police evidence had not indicated any negligence by his client. Despite the Beatle telling PC Kershaw at the scene that the cause was the icy road, presiding magistrate Mr T. C. Kettlewell, the Mayor Alderman F. W. Gosney, Mrs A. E. Smith and Mrs M. Broderick found George guilty. The *Goole Times* headline read, 'This Beatle Was Careless And Crashed At Road Bend.'

He left the court with Brian Epstein, making their way through a gaggle of teenagers in search of an autograph, before heading back to Liverpool. In the late afternoon, the group made the hour-long drive to the Stockport district of Offerton and the Palace Theatre Club on Turncroft Lane, where they performed a thirty-minute set before a sold-out crowd of more than three hundred fans, with the Pete Marsh Trio in support.

After finishing their performance, the Beatles headed north on the B6178, a 10-mile drive to the Southern Sporting Club in Birch Street, Gorton, to perform a second show. Doorman Eddie Chorlton recalled, 'We didn't get in to see the show as we were busy keeping an eye on the door and the street. I do remember them rushing right out past us when the show ended and a car was waiting. They jumped in and took right off. When the car got up towards the corner of Hyde Road it pulled over and I saw a couple of girls jump in with them.'

❛ I was a 20-year-old living a double life. By day, an insurance clerk at the head office of Refuge Assurance in Manchester. By night, a barman at one of the many cabaret clubs in the area in the '60s, the popular Offerton Palace Theatre Club. Along with my mate, Brian, I had taken the four-night weekly work to supplement our modest daytime salaries. The evening 'work' turned out to be my social life for an unforgettable five years! Even on our nights off we could not keep away from the place and we would watch the acts that we only caught snatches of while working. As I did not get much time to spend money, my weekly night wage was tossed into a shoebox unopened which I kept under the bed at home at Mum and Dad's. It would accumulate until I needed something special.

I had been an avid record collector since Elvis came on the scene so it is no surprise that I had Beatles 45s in my collection. Imagine the excitement I felt when the club booked the Beatles for one of their recently introduced Thursday Night Specials. Sid Elgar, the owner had booked them for two appearances, one at the Palace to close the first half, and the other at the Southern Sporting Club. I finished work early at the Refuge on the day, and after a quick tea, I made my way to the Palace in good time. As I turned the corner into Turncroft Lane, I could not believe my eyes. The street was heaving with screaming girls through whom I had to fight my way to the heavily guarded entrance to prepare the bar for what promised to be a hectic night. The Palace audience were of a more mature nature but that did not dampen the electric atmosphere of anticipation. Mike Sullivan, the club manager and ex-wrestler, told me the Beatles had requested twelve bottles of Coke to be taken down to their dressing room. This I jumped at. The dressing room seemed as busy as the club audience and I had no real time for a chat. I do regret not asking for their autographs, but I was used to seeing celebrities and never gave it a thought at the time. Little did I realise what lay ahead for these four lads.

They performed a thirty-minute act. Continuous screaming could be heard from outside in the street. The place was alive. The highlight for me was John Lennon singing 'Twist And Shout'. He belted it out. It was raw. We had seen nothing like it. We were used to crooners. What was happening? The hairs on the back of my neck stood on end. An evening everybody there will never forget. On a personal level it was an end of one era and the beginning of another. My appearance went from the 'Billy Fury' look to the 'mop head fringe' look. The following year I dipped into my shoebox and, along with four mates from the Palace, we took our first ever trip abroad to the sunshine island of Majorca. One evening the hotel manager assumed that as we were lads from England, 'Could we sing,' he asked. Naturally we lied and said yes. And what did they want to hear? – the Beatles' 'Can't Buy Me Love'. We sang it – they loved it. But at the time it was great to be English and we lapped it up – living in the reflected glory of the Beatles! ❜

TONY PHILBIN, ASSURANCE ADMIN MANAGER, MARPLE BRIDGE, CHESHIRE

FRIDAY 14 JUNE

'From Me To You' dropped to number 3 in the *Melody Maker* chart, replaced at the top by 'Do You Want To Know A Secret', while 'My Bonnie' charted at number 38. Acts managed by Brian Epstein occupied the top three places in the *NME* singles chart, with Gerry and the Pacemakers' 'I Like It' at number one, Billy J. Kramer with the Dakotas at number 2 and 'From Me To You' at number 3. In a *Melody Maker* story headlined 'Beatles Nix Palladium, Film Offers', John told the paper, 'There have been offers of a spot in the Palladium show. But we don't feel that we are ready. We have seen others go on and be torn to pieces, and we don't want it to happen to us. We know it means money, but we would rather wait till we feel we are ready.' He also discussed potential film appearances. 'We have been offered scene parts in a package show sort of film where about twenty different pop stars all appear with no story and no meaning. We prefer to wait until we find a film with a good plot that will hold the interest of the teenagers. Otherwise it might do us more harm than good.'

At 7.30pm, the last Mersey Beat Showcase took place at the Tower Ballroom in New Brighton, Wallasey, with the Beatles, Gerry and the Pacemakers, the Fourmost, Ian Crawford and the Boomerangs, Earl Preston and the T. T.'s, Deke Rivers and the Big Sound and the Nomads. The combination of a high temperature and overexcitement saw a steady stream of girls being carried across the stage to a team of first-aid workers. Sipping ice-cold drinks in the dressing room after their performance, the Beatles expressed mild annoyance at the fainting fans to Chris Hutchins. The group's performance was their twenty-seventh and last appearance at the venue. (In the 1930s, George's grandfather had been a commissionaire at the ballroom.)

Shortly after 11.30pm, they headed off in Paul's car for the Blue Angel with Hutchins in tow. As they drove down Seabank Road in Wallasey, Paul was stopped for speeding – again. Hutchins interviewed them once they arrived at the club. They told him about a male fan at a recent show who jumped onstage and danced the Cavern Stomp, while at another two boys hid in one of their hotel rooms for seven hours. In his review of the concert earlier in the evening, Hutchins wrote, 'Girls were plucked from the front row in a state of collapse and carried across the stage to a team of first-aid workers who had more on their hands than they could tackle. It was a fantastic night and one that echoed the success of these hit makers.' At the club, the group spent some time with Lord Woodbine, a highly regarded Trinidian calypso singer, who had driven the Beatles to Hamburg when they played there in 1960, opening for them at their first performance.

SATURDAY 15 JUNE

Five days after their show down in Bath, the group had to make their way south again, driving more than four hours to perform at the City Hall in Fisherton Street, Salisbury. Jaybee Clubs promoters Jack Fallon and Bill Reid, who were paying the group £300 for their appearance, were offered £200 by Brian Epstein to cancel the gig. Previously, Fallon and Reid had booked the Beatles for a show at McIlroy's Ballroom in Swindon on 17 July 1962, for a fee of £27 10s. Reid remembered their 1962 gig: they were 'a very unusual band. They just turned up in a van, got out and got up onstage. They were entirely different to the other bands around at the time, who were playing in gold lamé costumes. People kept telling us they were going to have a hit record, but we heard this all the time.' Even though only 360 people saw them in a venue which had a capacity of more than fifteen hundred, Reid spotted their potential and booked them again. The City Hall had only recently been renovated, closing down as a cinema at the end of December 1961 and only reopening on 30 January.

Advertised with the line 'Dancing 7.45 to 11.45. Admission 7/6. No admittance after 10', fans began queuing at 3pm for the fifteen hundred tickets on sale. In a review headed 'Big Welcome For Beatles', the *Salisbury Journal* commented, 'As the opening number struck up, hundreds of youngsters flocked on to the floor... It was the first appearance in Salisbury of a group who shot to fame last year and have been called the most exciting group since the Shadows – the Beatles.' The sold-out show, also featuring the Dale Stevens Group Five, Mike Shayne and the Deltas, was the largest-attended event in the area. One over-zealous fan climbed a drainpipe at the back of the theatre and got Ringo's autograph as a reward.

❝ In 1963 I was 18 years old and working five-and-a-half days a week in Woolworth's. We only had two weeks holiday a year. Life was about having a great time and I was – concerts, dancing, cinema, socialising, lots of friends and boys! I lived in a village called Downton, on the edge of the New Forest. I spent a lot of time staying at friend's houses in Salisbury as this was better than catching the last bus home at night and meant I could stay out later. Salisbury had a lot going on. The City Hall was used for concerts; groups touring and local groups. It had, and still has, a dance floor and tiered seats. Also in Salisbury was the Playhouse Theatre and I can remember a very good jazz club, coffee bars and lots of pubs. Two great coffee bars were the Man Friday and the Bath Bun. I loved standing and playing the juke box, also dancing to the music – just having a great time.

In Salisbury, new shops were opening with all the new fashions. I loved the changing fashions and the beehive hairdos – all that back-combing! It was all very exciting and changes were happening very fast. We had three cinemas – the Odeon, the Gaumont and the ABC. One of my favourite night spots was the Palais. It opened three nights a week; Monday, Friday and Saturday from about 7pm–11pm. It got very crowded and sweaty, which was all part of the atmosphere. It was positioned on the second floor of a building and you had to go upstairs to get in. There were two bouncers on the door even then. The stage was at the end of the room. During the interval the latest records would be played but my friends and I would nip out to the pubs instead as there was one each side of the Palais.

On 15 June, the Beatles came to Salisbury. I was with a friend and we went inside an hour before the doors opened as we knew the backstage manager. We had the privilege of sitting in the seating area listening to them practising before the concert started (even though the curtains were drawn so we couldn't see the Beatles themselves). At the interval we were lucky enough to be able to go backstage where George Harrison was putting his guitar into his case. I asked him for his autograph and if there was any chance of meeting the other three. He said 'sure' and took us into the dressing room. We were in there for about twenty minutes chatting to them. John Lennon was washing the makeup off of his shirt collar. Ringo and George were sat on a bench cracking jokes and Paul was stood talking with Brian Epstein and us. We knew that they were going to be a phenomenon and we felt very lucky that day! 🎵

DIANA HANHAM, PHARMACY ASSISTANT, AMESBURY, WILTSHIRE

SUNDAY 16 JUNE

A s 'From Me To You' held off Gerry and the Pacemakers' 'I Like It' at number 2, and Billy J. Kramer's version of 'Do You Want To Know A Secret' at number 3 in the *NRM* chart, the three Liverpool groups played two John Smith-promoted shows at 6pm and 8.30pm at the Odeon in Romford. The remaining act on the bill – the Vikings, from Birmingham – never invaded the charts. Number 4 on the chart was fellow Liverpudlian Billy Fury with 'When Will You Say I Love You'.

The group's vehicle was spotted travelling down Eastern Road as they arrived in Romford. Hundreds of girls surrounded the van and tried to wrench the doors open, ripping the aerial off and badly denting the doors and bonnet. Several girls tried to get onto the roof and scrawled lipstick over the bodywork. Originally planning to visit James and Louisa Graves again, Neil Aspinall instead reversed the car through the crowd and sought refuge in the police station further down South Street. Later, when the group finally arrived at the cinema, police linked arms to clear a path through the heaving crowd at the stage door.

In between shows, Sandra Goodrich – who had sung at the Odeon's Saturday morning cinema show the previous week and was to become Sandie Shaw – met the group backstage with her best friend Janet Llewellyn and watched the show from the wings. She later recalled, 'As Paul went on he kissed my cheek and said, "This one's for you, la." I couldn't have cared less. John was the only man for me, but he completely ignored me. I couldn't understand it. When he came close I could feel my whole being shudder with anticipation. Surely he felt it too? Later, in the dressing room, Ringo tried to put his hands up Janet's blouse, and we both marched out indignantly. It's a good job he didn't try that on with me or he would have discovered the cotton wool padding in my otherwise empty bra.' Rosetta Hartigan, Christine Samways and Lesley Townsend, who had queued overnight to buy tickets, also got to meet them.

After the show, unable to leave the cinema by the stage door because of the crowd outside, Billy J. Kramer, the Dakotas and Gerry and the Pacemakers piled into the now lipstick-smeared van parked at a side exit, while the Beatles made a dash for a taxi waiting out front. Teens on the other side of the street rushed towards the cab – one policeman was hit in the eye by a coin and struck on the head. The taxi driver managed to get away and took the group to the Parkside Hotel on North Street. The group switched back into their own car and headed back to London.

The *Romford Times* headline read, 'Rock Boys Flee Screaming Mob As Teenagers Go Wild'. The paper described how 'a taxi load of pop stars ploughed through hundreds of screaming teenagers during some of the wildest scenes Romford has even seen'. The *Romford Recorder* reported that, 'During the two performances, girls pelted the stage with cards and gifts for Beatle Paul MacKenzie [sic] who was 21 last week.'

❝ The Beatles were our favourite group of the time, so my friends Rosetta, Lesley and I really wanted to see them. We thought the best way to get front row tickets was to queue up all night before the box office opened in the morning. We got to the Romford Odeon before dark and it was light and probably around 6am before anybody else arrived. I remember at some point speaking to reporters from the *Romford Recorder* and asking if it could be arranged to meet the Beatles to get their autographs as we had queued all night for tickets. The newspaper honoured its promise and on the day of the concert we were taken to the group's dressing room to get autographs and have photos taken. Paul wasn't
there. It was John, George, Ringo, Rosetta, Lesley and myself. We got our autograph books signed by all four Beatles. Someone went out to get Paul's signature for us. We also got autographs from Gerry and the Pacemakers and Billy J. Kramer and the Dakotas. After getting our autographs we went down to the theatre to watch our idols. We could hear the songs of the supporting acts but when the Beatles came on everyone was screaming and their songs could not really be heard. The excitement of meeting the Beatles that day and looking at the photos afterwards put everything else in the shade. ❞

CHRIS McGOWAN, TEACHING ASSISTANT, BENFLEET, ESSEX

MONDAY 17 JUNE

Sean O'Mahony received a letter from Brian Epstein agreeing to a monthly Beatles magazine. The contract was for three years and included a request from the group that they receive 33⅓ per cent of the profits, with which O'Mahony duly agreed. Teen mag *Marilyn* covered the Beatles for the first time under its regular column 'The Beatmakers'.

At 10.30am, the group began recording in Studio Five at the BBC's Maida Vale Studios in Delaware Road for the fourth *Pop Go The Beatles* programme, with guests, Irish trio the Bachelors. The Beatles performed 'I Saw Her Standing There', 'Anna (Go To Him)' (the first of two performances of Arthur Alexander's 1962 R&B classic), 'Boys', 'Chains', 'P.S. I Love You' (written by Paul in Hamburg), and 'Twist And Shout'. After they finished recording at 1pm, they had lunch in the BBC canteen, where Dezo Hoffmann was on hand to snap some photos. Brian Epstein joined the BBC crew at the nearby George pub for lunch. Afterwards the group went out onto Delaware Road, where John, George and Ringo were snapped bumping Paul, who was to celebrate his 21st birthday the following day. Afterwards, the group drove up to Liverpool to begin the celebrations. Jane Asher, who attended the recording session, joined them.

TUESDAY 18 JUNE

Paul turned 21, receiving thousands of birthday cards and presents – one an anonymous card twice his size saying 'Happy Birth Day Paul Love From'. Brian Epstein hosted drinks for Paul and Jane at the Epstein family home at 197 Queens Drive, Childwall, in the morning. Later, Paul joined the rest of the group and the NEMS stable for a photo shoot at the Childwall Fiveways Hotel in Queens Drive.

News spread that a birthday party was going to take place at Paul's aunt Gin's house at 147 Dinas Lane in Huyton. Traffic was held up and police with dogs were called out to keep order. Members of Gerry and the Pacemakers, the Fourmost, Billy J. Kramer, the Dakotas, the Remo Four, the Hurricanes and the Shadows (who had opened the 'Holiday Carnival' summer season at the newly reopened ABC in Church Street, Blackpool with Cliff Richard on 31 May) attended the party. The Shadows, sans bassist 'Liquorice' Locking, had driven down from Blackpool and met Paul and Jane outside the Empire Theatre before driving over to Dinas Lane. Pete Shotton, one of John's oldest friends, was also there – invited by Paul.

At 5pm, the third episode of *Pop Go The Beatles* aired, recorded on 1 June, with guests Carter-Lewis and the Southerners. During Paul's party, the Fourmost and the Scaffold – the trio which included Paul's brother Mike, now going by his professional name Mike McGear – performed live sets in a marquee in Jin's back garden. The Fourmost are still waiting for their 5/6 payment Paul promised them.

An inebriated John took umbrage when Bob Wooler approached him and said, 'Come on John. Tell me about you and Brian. We all know.' He laid into him, the resultant fracas requiring Epstein to take Wooler to a nearby hospital to treat his injuries, which over the years have been variously reported as broken ribs, bruised ribs, torn knuckles and a black eye. John suffered a bruised forefinger. 'He called me a queer,' John told Cynthia on their way home. 'So I battered his bloody ribs in.' Solicitor Rex Makin subsequently negotiated a settlement with Wooler, which was believed to be a payment of £200 in exchange for not taking civil action against John.

John did not stop there. After heckling the Scaffold while they performed, he was asked to leave the room and then had another altercation, this time with a young lady, who smacked him across the face after he tried to grope her. Kramer and the Fourmost's Billy Hatton interceded before John could do any more damage. 'I said "Lay off, John",' recalled Kramer. 'But he lashed into her. He'd had too much booze. I was semi-professional at the time, and he was winding me up as I left before him, shouting, "You're nothing, Kramer, and we're the top." Hatton was about to lay a fist on John when someone called out, 'Billy, if you hit him, the Fourmost are finished," he recalled. 'He was right, we hadn't even made a record then, and it would have been 'Bass Player In No-Mark Group Beats Up John Lennon".

Aunt Jin and her daughter Dianne Harris conveniently forgot to mention this aspect of the party to a reporter from the *Prescot & Huyton Reporter*. Jin said, 'We were worried at first but nobody tried to gatecrash and the whole evening was a wonderful success. Paul was full of praise for the way the youngsters outside behaved. They could easily have caused trouble if they had wanted to and everything would have been ruined. His one big regret was that the house wasn't big enough to invite everybody in.' Harris said, 'It was amazing how such a large number of people could stay so orderly. They were great. We had tried to keep the party a secret but with so many celebrities turning up it was just impossible. One or two were spotted and that started things off.'

> ❛ My family lived in Warrington and my parents sent my older sister to Huyton College in Liverpool as a day girl. When we moved less than 2 miles away over the Ship Canal to Grappenhall, we were then in Cheshire and she had to board. I followed her there five years later aged 11 or 12 as a boarder. That was the rule, you could be a day girl if you lived in Lancashire, but not if you lived in Cheshire! John Lennon's future wife Cynthia Powell taught art there. She came for one term, probably to do work experience. We called her 'Miss Powell'.
>
> It was my school friend Liz Simmons who introduced me to the Cavern. I remember queuing outside in the snow one Easter when the Beatles were due to play. In the holidays we went there frequently and it was easy then to get into the back room and have a chat with the groups. There was something about John Lennon that I just didn't take to. It was just chat but he was a bit sarcastic. Ringo was very quiet. He'd just listen and never really got involved. George was lovely but Paul was always my favourite. I used to buy everything connected with the Beatles and would send Paul letters to his home in Forthlin Road and he would write back. It

was all just chat, things like 'Shame on me, I was in Huyton and didn't call in on you', those sorts of things. Letter from Paul: 'PS I saw Liz in town today.' Little things like that he would write.

The first time I met Paul on my own was at the Grafton Ballroom in Liverpool in January 1963. I had all the letters from him with me, and I dropped them, in between the excitement of talking to him again and he picked them up. The letter on the top was one he'd sent me in an Air Mail envelope from Hamburg, and he said 'You're Fran Leiper from Huyton College, Huyton? Nice to put a face to the name!' I got him to sign my arm when he left. I covered the signature in sellotape and kept it dry for two weeks, hiding it from my house mistress who would not have approved. When I finally took the sellotape off the signature came with it and I gave it pride of place in my scrap book.

It was also there that I met Paul's cousin Diane, auntie Jin's daughter for the first time. I can't recall exactly how we became friends, but we did, and went on to go to several concerts together, screaming away with everyone else in the front row! They jokingly invited me to Paul's 21st birthday party. They said I could escape from the boarding house by climbing out of the dormitory window to get there. I thought about it, but no, I just couldn't have done. Even if I'd said it was a relative's birthday party, the school wouldn't have let me out. Afterwards they sent me a slice of birthday cake and some serviettes and straws. I kept the fruit cake and put some squashed bits in my scrapbook! I have a Christmas card Diane sent me in 1963, which says, 'Paul sends his Christmas wishes and says he's sorry he's not written for ages but 'you'll know how it is,' and says he hasn't forgotten you, honest.' I'd stopped getting letters from him by this time. The last letter I got was typed and had an obviously stamped signature. I never wrote again. When you get asked to send a stamped addressed envelope the next time you know it's not the money, it's the time. He'd have never said that. In 1992 I sold my well-thumbed scrap books, autographs and photos, even the signature and sellotape from my arm. I photocopied all the letters of course and still have some fabulous memories of those days. **❞**

FRAN BINNS, BUSINESS TRAVEL MANAGER, GRAPPENHALL, CHESHIRE

WEDNESDAY 19 JUNE

Brian Epstein told John to send the injured Wooler a telegram apologising for his behaviour. It read, 'Really sorry Bob. Terribly worried to realise what I had done. What more can I say?'

The group, minus John, took the train to London to record their second appearance on *Easy Beat* at the Playhouse Theatre. Epstein told a contrite John he had to go, packing him off on a later train. Afterwards, Epstein was interviewed by Derek Taylor at the NEMS offices. Taylor recalled the meeting: 'We got on awfully well, considering what a front he had. He was awfully remote. He did like the interview but also had this kind of sniffy front. I probably saw him two or three times in 1963 for dinner after the first interview. I'd recently met Ken Dodd, who was very hot, and he'd said [of the Beatles], "I like those lads, they're very cheeky. They should learn to dance." I said to Brian that's what Ken Dodd said. Brian said, "I've never heard such nonsense. How dare Ken Dodd offer such advice".'

Maureen O'Grady spoke with Paul, George, Ringo and Brian Epstein before the recording. John finally arrived with Cynthia, who was dressed in black from head to toe and wearing dark glasses. The session lasted from 8.45pm to 9.45pm and the group performed 'Some Other Guy', 'A Taste Of Honey', 'Thank You Girl' and 'From Me To You'. An attack of the giggles meant they had to record everything twice. The show aired the following Sunday.

❝ Back in the early '60s, I was a schoolboy living in Wembley. As soon as school was over I was straight on the Piccadilly line with my mate Richard Savage to go to recordings of live shows on BBC Radio. We were two of a kind. He was trying to learn how to play the guitar like Hank Marvin and I thought I was David Jacobs. In late 1962, we went to a recording of *The Talent Spot* at the BBC's Paris Studio in Regent Street. On that particular show, the Beatles were one of the guests and sang 'Love Me Do' and 'P.S. I Love You'. I thought they were great. The group used to go to the nearby Captain's Cabin pub. I wasn't allowed in because I wasn't old enough. So I waited for them outside and when they came out all four of them signed my autograph book. Lennon actually did a caricature of himself. I went out and bought 'Love Me Do' – that was my special record for that Saturday.

I was always listening to Radio Luxembourg. I had two transistor radios, one for each ear and I would listen every night for as long as I could stay awake. I was absolutely obsessed with the charts, and in the *NME* they would have an ad for the EMI releases to the left of the chart and one for Decca to the right, and on another page all the new Philips releases. They all had sponsored shows on Luxembourg and I would never go to sleep until I'd heard every one of those records. I remember seeing the ad for 'Please Please Me' and went out and bought the record that Saturday and continued buying their records from then on. The show I really liked going to was *Easy Beat*. It wasn't as easy to get tickets for this show but as time went by I got to know all the doormen and I would bribe them with cigarettes. 'In yer go mate,' they'd say and let me in. The show was recorded on Wednesday evenings. We'd turn up and most times we got in.

When I left school I wrote to all the record companies, the BBC, Radio Luxembourg and the ones that replied wrote, 'We'll put your name on file,' and of course I never heard from them. My parents were getting a little tired of the fact I couldn't get a job and had a friend who ran a couple of hairdressing salons and paid for me to have an apprenticeship with him. I absolutely loathed it. I was then offered a job by Vidal Sassoon and the upside of that was that I met quite a few show business people. They'd come in and have their hair done. I remember the Walker Brothers would come in after closing and go down to the basement and I'd stay behind and wash their hair. There was a journalist by the name of Penny Valentine who'd come in and always ask to have me wash her hair and we'd just chat. I told I couldn't stand the job and wanted to work in the music business and she got me an interview with Strike Records. She fixed up an appointment with them for me and that's how I got in, as a runner. That would have been 1966 around the time the label had its one and only hit, Neil Christian's 'That's Nice.'

In 1981, after twiddling my thumbs for about six months, I got a call from Johnny Beerling at Radio 1. He asked me to work on the 'Marathon Music Quiz' and that really was my intro into BBC radio. Initially I heard nothing from them, but I did work on a quiz show on Capital Radio which led to a few other things for them. Then when Richard Park came in to run the station, he asked me to help him set up Capital Gold. I was working with Roger Scott at Capital Gold when he went to Radio 1 to do a Sunday night show, and he asked me to produce it for him. I explained it wasn't as easy as that and then I heard from Johnny Beerling and told him I couldn't give up my Capital Gold job for one show a week on Radio 1. So he said, 'What else do you want to do then?' I told him I'd like to do *Pick of the Pops* with Alan Freeman and *Roundtable*, and he said, 'OK.' When Matthew Bannister came in as controller of Radio 1 and kicked everyone out, I thought I'd go and talk to Radio 2. I had a chat with Jim Moir about doing a show with Bob Harris and about a year later I got a phone call from him. 'Now listen here Swern. I've got eight programmes over Christmas and New Year. I'm going to let you do them with Bob Harris. If it goes well, we'll have a very nice lunch and a good conversation. If it doesn't, you'll never work in radio again.'

Fortunately we ended up having a very nice lunch and I've been at Radio 2 ever since. I've been producing *Pick Of The Pops* for more than twenty years and *Sounds Of The 60s* for ten years with Brian Matthew until his retirement. Anyone who recalls radio from the early '60s grew up with Brian, who was the host of *Easy Beat* and *Saturday Club*. He was instrumental in helping the Beatles reach a radio audience, interviewing them more than any other broadcaster. ❞

PHIL SWERN, RADIO PRODUCER AND CONSULTANT, CHISWICK, LONDON

THURSDAY 20 JUNE

'From Me To You' climbed back up one place to number 3 in the week's *Disc* chart. On the paper's letters page, Sandra Hayden won the Prize Letter, begging the Beatles not to go to the States. 'From Me To You' finally dropped from the top spot in the *NRM*, its place taken by Gerry and the Pacemakers' 'I Like It'. Taylor's interview with Epstein was printed in the *Daily Express*. He described the group as 'a gay quartet of ex-grammar schoolboys', while Epstein made the prescient comment, 'Whatever happens to popular music, whatever happens to beat groups, the Beatles are in the business for life'. Commenting on Tuesday night's fracas, he said, 'I did not see the incident. All I did was to drive [Bob Wooler] to the hospital. I can only hope he gets well soon'. John's telegram was sent from Covent Garden at 6.10pm to Wooler at his flat in Canning Street, Liverpool.

The production company the Beatles Limited was incorporated, with Epstein one of its directors. The group visited Dezo Hoffmann's studio in Wardour Street, who shot formal portraits of each member individually. Afterwards, he took them for lunch at the Budapest Restaurant in Greek Street.

FRIDAY 21 JUNE

The latest *NME* carried a thank you from Paul in the form of an ad, which cost him £15: 'TO MANY PEOPLE – Thank you very much for your Gifts and Greetings on my Birthday... Great! PAUL McCARTNEY'. 'From Me To You' dropped to number 5 in the Top 10. In the *Melody Maker* chart, it remained at number 3, while 'My Bonnie' dipped to number 46. In a front-page article headlined 'Beatles Blast Own Hit Disc', John told the paper, '['My Bonnie' is] just Tony Sheridan singing with

us banging in the background. They're flogging it but I wish they'd just shut up! It's terrible. It could be anybody. I wouldn't buy it!'

The *Daily Mirror* published an account of the scene at Paul's 21st birthday party on its back page ('Beatle In Brawl – "Sorry I Socked You"'), printing quotes – both subsequently believed to have been written by Tony Barrow – from Wooler ('I don't know why he did it. I was booted in the face. I begged him to stop. Finally, he was pulled off by other people at the party. I have been a friend of the Beatles for a long time. I have often compèred shows where they have appeared. I am terribly upset about this – physically as well as mentally.') and John ('Why did I have to go and punch my best friend? I was so high I didn't realise what I was doing. I had a great deal to drink at the party and very little to eat. By the time this happened I didn't know what I was doing. Bob is the last person in the world I would want to have a fight with. I can only hope he realises that I was too far gone to know what I was doing.')

In the evening, the group performed at the Art Deco Odeon on Epsom Road in Guildford. The queue stretched up Jenner Road and into Sydenham Road behind the cinema. Several female fans climbed over a wall, trying to get into the group's dressing room – one fell over and landed on a pile of coal, injuring her leg. Others tried to force their way through the stage door.

Vic Sutcliffe compèred the show which was billed as the Jimmy Crawford Package Show, with Jimmy Crawford, the Vampires, Rocking Henri and the Hayseeds, the Messengers, the Vikings with Michael London and Ricky Bowden taking the place of the advertised Lance Fortune. Bowden's manager Vic Keary had been contacted the previous month to ask whether the singer could fill in for Fortune. Bowden recalled, 'I jumped at the chance, arriving at the venue with the other artists about an hour before the Beatles. The crowds outside were huge. We had no idea

how they were going to get in, as access to the back was very difficult. In the end, they came in one by one, disguised as fans, with everyone else, through the front door! The plan worked, and they made their way through the cinema to the backstage area. We all had our own dressing rooms, but I was able to pop into theirs for a chat, and got their autographs, which I later gave to a close relative. I remember John Lennon tuning up his guitar behind me when I was about to go onstage – a bit distracting! It was a great show, and a great opportunity, but alas it didn't help my single to chart.'

> ❝ It was midsummer 1963. I was 13. My friend Pamela rang me and asked if I would go with her to see the Beatles. I was not aware that they were coming to Guildford but I knew straight away that I DID want to go with her. I remember that it was a fine summer evening and we met on the railway station platform. I don't remember what I was wearing but I do know that I would have been wearing a skirt – probably quite a full skirt or a dress. I had just started to wear stockings (no tights then) with a suspender belt from Woolworths. The height of sophistication! Before I was old enough for those 'American Tan' coloured nylon stockings I wore long white socks up to the knee. We caught the train to Guildford and made our way to the Odeon. There was a long queue to get in, and I was very surprised by it all because it was the first time I had been to a
>
>
>
> teenagers event like this. We used to go to the cinema on our own but this was different. There were few adults in the queue, it was a general impression of a huge crowd of excited teenagers, mainly girls. It was a new experience for me, and I think it was a new experience for society in general. I was in it and I was part of it.

ABOVE: Paul McCartney and Ringo Starr performing during an early television performance on *Thank Your Lucky Stars* on 17 February 1963. Photo: Hulton Archive / Stringer

RIGHT: Meal break in a canteen. Photo: Paul Popper/ Popperfoto

ABOVE: Pictured together rehearsing songs in their hotel room in Stockholm during their autumn tour of Sweden in October 1963. Photo: Popperfoto

LEFT: Posed together at Alpha TV Studios in Birmingham during filming of ABC TV's television show, *Lucky Stars* on 18 August 1963. Photo: Rolls Press/Popperfoto

ABOVE: The Beatles board the rear steps of an SAS airlines plane at Stockholm airport in Sweden for their return journey back to London on 31 October 1963. Photo: Getty

RIGHT: George and
Ringo Starr emerge
from a police van
at the Birmingham
Hippodrome Theatre
on 10 November 1963.
Photo: Getty

ABOVE: A group shot during a performance on Granada TV's *Late Scene Extra* television show filmed in
Manchester on 25 November 1963. Photo: Fox Photos / Stringer

ABOVE: In Huddersfield on 29 November. Photo: Mirrorpix

LEFT: The band in Plymouth,
13 November.
Photo: Mirrorpix

ABOVE: HRH Princess Margaret meets The Beatles at the Royal Variety Show, 4 November 1963.

<small>ABOVE:</small> The Beatles rehearse for an ATV Show with Morecambe and Wise, 2 December 1963. Photo: Mirrorpix

LEFT: The Beatles appear on *Juke Box Jury* with David Jacobs, 7 December 1963. Photo: Mirrorpix

RIGHT: The line-up for the Beatles Christmas Show at the Finsbury Park Astoria, 23 December 1963–11 January 1964. Photo: Mirrorpix

We had seats about halfway back on the ground floor. The seats were the usual red velvet and closed if you stood up. I thought lots of the girls were badly behaved. They were shouting out for the Beatles all the time. In between the other groups and solo singers a guy came onstage to introduce them. People were making it very hard for him because they were shouting, whistling, screaming, all the time. I remember thinking it was a bit awful for him, but thinking, 'Nobody wants to listen to all these other groups – we only came to hear the Beatles.' Girls really were hysterical. Everyone was shouting out and calling out at the tops of their voices.

At last the time came for the Beatles to come on the stage. They all wore suits and had the same kind of long haircut. It doesn't even look long nowadays, but at that time everyone else had short back and sides. The Beatles looked as if their hair had been cut round a pudding basin. The atmosphere was amazing. Totally mad. I remember thinking, 'I'm not going to scream' – I thought it was stupid. But the whole atmosphere was catching. I couldn't help myself and I screamed along with everyone else. I can't say now WHY all the girls screamed, because it meant we couldn't hear the songs at all, only the screams, and I don't think anyone really had experienced anything like it before, but Pamela and I became part of that seething hysterical mass. It was raw emotion. I don't remember any other details. I don't know how we got out of there, but I don't remember feeling unsafe at any time. I used to take a monthly magazine which came by post called *The Beatles*. I also had a big Beatles scrapbook with silly things like photos of dogs that looked as if they had Beatles haircuts, or interviews with greengrocers who had sold a Beatle a banana, or something. I wish I had that scrapbook now! I even remember a relative sending me four Beatle 'pins' in different colours, which were like a brooch to wear on a coat. These were like a ladybird shape and I thought them a bit pointless, but other people were impressed by them and I think I gave at least two of them away to school friends. There really was an air of mania about the early days of the Beatles. It was a new phenomenon. 𝕁

FAITH MOULIN, MAGAZINE EDITOR, YATTON, SOMERSET

SATURDAY 22 JUNE

George and Ringo travelled with Neil Aspinall to Abergavenny in Monmouthshire, Wales, for the evening's concert at the Town Hall Ballroom, arriving at around 5pm. Paul decided to take the train from Paddington, changing at Newport. Epstein had signed a contract with promoter Eddie Tattersall on 19 April for the group to appear for a fee of £250. Even though the group were now commanding more than twice that amount for live appearances, they honoured the commitment.

While waiting for the concert to begin, Paul, George and Ringo read fans' letters and signed autographs. Tattersall was a member of the local 1963 Freedom From Hunger committee and had urged fans to bring their autograph books for the group to sign to raise money for famine relief through the *Abergavenny Chronicle & Monmouthshire Advertiser*. Birthday boy Paul was presented with a huge birthday card by Tattersall's teenage daughter Lorraine, signed by hundreds of fans. Popular local singer Bryn Yemm also chatted with them in their dressing room.

John stayed behind to record an appearance on *Juke Box Jury* at Television Theatre in Shepherd's Bush, London. Fellow jury members included television personality Katie Boyle, Caroline Maudling (the 16-year-old daughter of the Chancellor of the Exchequer, who replaced the previously announced Zsa Zsa Gabor) and teen actor Bruce Prochnik. In October, Maudling told the *Daily Sketch* that the Beatles 'quite frankly' left her cold, and that she was certainly not one of their fans. She went on to say, 'The Beatles are quite efficient. They certainly have a good sense of rhythm, but I don't think that they offer enough... This is just a wild phase, and it will end as suddenly as it started. I'm convinced.'

Following the end of the recording at 9.15pm, John and Epstein were driven to Battersea's Westland Heliport, where a helicopter – chartered at a cost of more than £100 – whisked them off to Wales. They landed at football club Abergavenny Thursdays' Pen-y-Pound Stadium around 9.45pm, to a crowd larger than the club's average attendance. Extra police were called in to cope with the hundreds of fans who had shown up in anticipation of John's arrival. The club groundsman had painted a large white 'H' on the pitch to guide the helicopter down. Following a set by local favourites the Fabulous Fortunes, the Beatles finally went onstage at 10.30pm before a sold-out crowd of six hundred, who had paid 12/6 each for their tickets. Tom Davies, the Principal Officer of nearby Usk Borstal and father of the Fabulous Fortunes' lead singer Mike Davies, asked Tattersall whether three of his inmates, who all hailed from Liverpool, could be allowed to attend the show. In the company of a warden, they watched from the balcony.

After the performance, the Beatles attended a civic reception hosted by the Mayor and Mayoress, Councillor and Mrs Jack Thurston, where they drank tea and signed the visitors' book. Noting that last people to sign had been Queen Elizabeth II and Prince Philip – who had visited the town in May and signed as 'Elizabeth R' – John quipped, 'I wonder if that's her stage name?'

When the group returned to their dressing room, they discovered the door had been locked and the key could not be found. Overenthusiastic fans were held at bay. John said that it could have been worse. 'The fans are very good in some places or we would have been killed by now.' Tattersall recalled it was a pleasure to be associated with the career of the Beatles. 'They had a bit of a reputation for being rough diamonds but I found them polite and well mannered. John Lennon was the most outgoing, always cracking jokes, Paul McCartney was charming and both George Harrison and Ringo Starr were quiet. They really were nice lads.'

At about 1am, they walked the 100 yards down Cross Street to the Angel Hotel where they spent the night. At the hotel entrance they bid a fond farewell to Bryn Yemm, who walked home with a signed copy of *Please Please Me* under his arm. Yemm later said that he was bigger in Abergavenny than the Beatles were at the time.

❛ Three 16-year-old school friends Les, Graham and me boarded a train at Newport station. We were on our way to Abergavenny where the Beatles were performing at the Town Hall. Imagine our surprise, when walking along the corridor to find a seat, we spotted Paul McCartney sitting alone in the first-class compartment. Naturally, we stopped to say 'Hello,' and wished him a belated happy birthday! He invited us into his compartment, but we were apprehensive because we only had second class tickets. Paul said it would be OK, and if the ticket collector should question them, he would sort it out. The half-hour train journey went by so quickly with us asking all sorts of questions about the group. 'What are you doing next?' 'When is the next record coming out?' 'When are you on TV?' Les mentioned that he and I had recently started a group that had played at a few local youth clubs. 'What's the name of the group?' asked Paul. 'Well, we haven't thought of a good one yet.' Paul picked up his newspaper whose headline was something about a major court case that was going on at the time. He scanned the front page for a few moments, then said, 'What about the Witnesses? That sounds like a good name.'

When the train arrived at Abergavenny, Paul said, 'Seeing as you have bought tickets for the concert, you are welcome to share my taxi into town.' Paul sat next to the driver in the front seat with the three of us sat in the back. After a few glances at the young boys in the back seat, the driver asked Paul if they were the other Beatles. 'I don't know,' said Paul. He turned to us and asked, 'Are you the Beatles?' 'No,' we said, 'but we'd like to be!'

When the taxi arrived at Paul's hotel, we got out and crossed the road to join the rest of the fans in the hall. When the Fab Four took to the stage, the whole audience gathered at the front listening and watching in awe of their heroes. They played what everyone was there to hear, some great rock'n'roll and most of their *Please Please Me* album, finishing with John Lennon's fantastic version of 'Twist And Shout'. After the show, the group met their fans and signed autographs in the upstairs foyer area. We got a chance to speak to them and to especially thank Paul for the time he had spent with us on the train journey. He wished us good luck with our group and a safe journey home. More than fifty years later, whenever Les, Graham and I meet each other, the evening with the Beatles is relived as if we were 16 again. Well, why wouldn't we?

TEDDY FALLON, MUSICIAN, LLISWERRY, GWENT, WALES

SUNDAY 23 JUNE

The group checked out of the Angel and began the 90-mile trip to Aston to record *Lucky Stars - Summer Spin* at Alpha TV studios, filling up with petrol at the Esso garage in Hereford Road. While they were travelling, Wednesday's recording of *Easy Beat* aired at 10.31am. *Lucky Stars - Summer Spin*, also known as 'Thank Your Lucky Star-scouses', celebrated the Merseybeat boom, featuring Gerry and the Pacemakers, the Vernons Girls, Kenneth Cope with the Breakaways, Billy J. Kramer, the Big Three, Lee Curtis and the Searchers and was hosted by Pete Murray. 'Five Jealous Beatles Fans' from Brighouse had complained to *Pop Weekly* earlier in the month about a photo of the Vernons Girls sitting on the laps of the Beatles. 'We like both the Vernons Girls and the Beatles but PLEASE keep them separate.' The group mimed to 'From Me To You' and 'I Saw Her Standing There'. The show aired the following Saturday at the same time as John's appearance on *Juke Box Jury*. After making a beeline for the studio's cafeteria, the group enjoyed coffee, sausage rolls and salad.

I grew up in Liverpool, attending St Alexander's Primary School, then Major Street School, just off Scotland Road. There was a pawn shop just off Scotland Road called Young's, which sold secondhand stuff, and I bought a guitar called a Broadway. Then unfortunately I contracted TB and ended up in hospital for six months. It was actually quite good because they let me have the guitar in the hospital, and I could play it in one of the rooms late at night. I got out in 1956, and suddenly rock'n'roll was starting to happen. We were fortunate in Liverpool to have the sailors bringing the records and guitars back. They were even playing on the ships themselves. They were called 'the Cunard Yanks', and all playing guitars. I didn't take any lessons, I'd just pop a record on our Dansette 45 and play the records round and round and round to try and get them. You would think you were playing it right, but in fact you were playing it in your own style really.

After I'd left school, one of my mates was the last to be called up into the army, and unknown to me, he was stationed in Germany. When he came back, he said, 'Do you fancy starting a group?' and I said, 'Why not?' So we started this little skiffle group. His name was Tony West, and various people would go in and out, only the people who were really serious about it stayed. So it was myself and Tony, and we picked up a lad who played guitar from along the same road, Mike Prendergast. We'd

heard about a guy called Chris Curtis who was a drummer, so he was invited in, and we started to rehearse. We brought in a lead singer by the name of Ron Woodbridge, who lived in Anfield, right by the ground, but he wasn't suitable really. He was more Elvis Presley – he was doing all the moves but didn't have a great voice. We had a word and said it's not working, and he left. Then we heard of a lad who was playing at the Cross Keys by the Liverpool Stadium – the old boxing stadium. His name was Tony Jackson. He was a bass player and he was superb, so we asked him if he would join us.

We still needed a lead singer of sorts. We heard of someone through my mother, who was working at Blackledge's Bakery on Derby Road, and one of her workmates said, 'Oh, my son sings.' He was a fellow by the name of Billy Beck, who had changed his name to Johnny Sandon. The reason he was called Johnny Sandon was because he used to play in the Sandon pub, which is right next to Anfield. At that point, we became Johnny Sandon and the Searchers. We were doing really well and then Johnny got an invitation from the Remo Four, who were a great group and wanted a lead singer. Johnny said, 'It's good money. I'm off!' So in the end, we wanted to carry on, and decided we would all just start singing.

We became just the Searchers then, and the initial interest of all the good groups in Liverpool was suddenly beginning to happen. Brian Epstein wanted to sign us, so he came to see us at the Cavern, but unfortunately we were on last, and we'd been sipping the grapes all night, so when we went on, we were a bit 'pissycarto,' and didn't impress him. He said, 'I'll pass on you lads,' and that was that.

We decided to make a demo disc to send out to record companies. It was made at the Iron Door Club and cost us forty quid. We sent it out to all the record companies, and of course the interest in Liverpool was quite good at the time. Tony Hatch heard the demo and loved it, so the next thing we knew we had a message saying can you come down to Pye Studios in Marble Arch to record it properly. We were about to leave for the Star-Club in Hamburg, so we left a couple of days early and nipped down to London on the way. In the studios we recorded about five tracks just around one mic, and off to Germany we went. We all still had day jobs and had to get a month off work.

When they invited us back to the club later in the year, we thought we can't ask for another long holiday, so we met in the pub and said well, 'Shall we do it? Shall we turn pro?' The work was coming in and the money was getting good in Germany, things looked quite healthy, and in the end we said, 'OK, let's ask our parents.' I asked my dad, and he said, 'Well, you know, do whatever you want to do, but you'll never make a living playing that banjo!' While we were in Germany, a telegram came saying they're releasing 'Sweets For My Sweet', – 'Can you come back and promote it?' We thought, 'Oh God!' We'd been signed for a month, but in the end, Tito Burns, who'd by this time had become our manager, bought us out so we went back to England to promote the single.

It was initially what they called a sleeper. It was doing OK and selling well because there was such interest in Merseybeat at the time, but no one reckoned it was going to be a hit. Fortunately, a journalist then said to John Lennon, 'What's your favourite record at the moment?' and he said, 'Well, it's the Searchers' *Sweets For My Sweet.*' And that was it. It was number one within three weeks. So thanks to John Lennon he gave us a career really.

We were invited to an all-Liverpool special of *Thank Your Lucky Stars.* It was mostly Brian's groups. He came in to see us in the dressing room and said, 'Look, the lads have written a song for you.' It was 'Things We Said Today'. He asked if he could play it to us on his little portable 45 player, which he did, and we thought it was superb. We thought, 'This is great, the Beatles writing us a song!' We said, 'What's the catch?' He said, 'Well, I want you to sign for me,' which was great, and we thought 'Ah!' But the usual thing happened. We went to Tito Burns, and he wouldn't release us, so we lost the record. The work was constant. They worked us to a frazzle. They'd have us on the road, then Tito would nip us into the studio and say, 'Can you knock out an A- and B-side?' It was ridiculous, madness.

We've been touring for almost sixty years now, and I think it's really important that you look the part. You are playing with people's memories. We still wear our sharp suits, have good lighting, it's very important to put on a show. I still think of my dad saying. 'You'll never make a living out of playing that banjo!' and I think, 'Well, we've not done bad! 🎵

JOHN McNALLY, MUSICIAN, SINGER, CROSBY, LANCASHIRE

MONDAY **24 JUNE**

The group did some shopping, popping into A. Maknyick's Star Shirt Makers in Rupert Street, owned by Steve Stevens and his wife Katy. '[They] came up to us, on the top floor, but we didn't know who they were,' recalled Katy. 'They were just four scruffy boys who came up the staircase to see us. Ringo had a terrible figure, and I had to pin his shirt, because we did made-to-measure shirts.' George said the group needed some stock shirts to wear for the afternoon's recording at the BBC. She sold him one for £2 10s before showing the group a sample book, from which they ordered a further fifty shirts.

The group then headed over to the Playhouse Theatre for a 2.30pm rehearsal for *Saturday Club.* Their last *Side By Side* appearance (recorded on 4 April) with the Karl Denver Trio, aired at 5pm. Earlier in the day, Denver appeared in Manchester Magistrates' Court, charged – along with seventy-eight other people – for unlawful gaming at the city's Cromford Club.

At the hour-long recording of *Saturday Club* from 5.30pm to 6.30pm, the Beatles performed 'I Got To Find My Baby', 'Memphis, Tennessee', 'Money', 'Till There Was You', 'From Me To You' and 'Roll Over Beethoven'. The show aired the following Saturday.

Making good on his April promise to record the song, Del Shannon's version of 'From Me To You' became the first Lennon and McCartney composition to enter the US chart at number 96, set to peak at number 77 on 20 July.

TUESDAY 25 JUNE

The group drove north almost 250 miles to Middlesbrough for an appearance at the Astoria Ballroom on Wilson Street. Brian Naylor had booked them for £30 the previous October. It turned out to be an astute booking, with an overflowing ballroom of fans who paid 7/6 each to see the group. Like many other shows, there was a queue stretching around the corners of the Astoria. Soon after they arrived, the fourth episode of *Pop Go The Beatles*, recorded on 17 June, aired at 5pm (excluding 'A Taste Of Honey').

Vince King and the Stormers and the Johnny Taylor V supported the group at the evening's show. Laurence Atkinson was filling in for Johnny Taylor's Eric Shoosmith, who was taking an exam ('just my luck!' he said). Atkinson recalled, 'I was the lead guitarist with the Tempests and, although we played most nights of the week, I think that night was a Tuesday, a fairly quiet night for us, and I was available – so, happily agreed! The only practice we'd had together was a quick run through the set the week before the gig so it probably wasn't my finest performance on lead guitar. Good job there were thirty-five hundred screaming fans to drown us out! It was certainly the noisiest gig I ever played and the only time I ever played behind steel chain-link fencing. But that afforded me a great seat for the Beatles' performance. For their whole set, I sat on the front of the stage in front (and just to the side) of John Lennon.' DJ Rick Wilkinson shared a dressing room with them, but received a dressing down from George for turning his mic down during 'Roll Over Beethoven.'

The *Evening Gazette* commented on the evening: 'With swooning teen-age girls collapsing all round them, the latest craze in pop music, the Beatles, were all but pushed through the back of the stage when they visited the Astoria Ballroom. A cordon made up of the ballroom staff ringed the stage, trying to force back the hordes of fans as they pushed and screamed about forty deep. Chairs from the sides of the hall were piled in the middle by girls who then climbed upon them to gain a better view. Bouncers retrieved the chairs but no sooner had they been removed than they were dragged back to the middle. The heat and pressure of the crowd soon took its toll and over two dozen girls fainted. They were carried out and revived by ballroom staff. At the end of their performance the group ran across the stage clutching their guitars and protected by

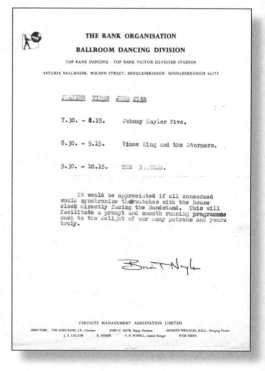

even more bouncers. George said, 'It was slightly wilder than usual, I'd say, but the strong-arm men did a magnificent job. Despite them, one girl kept knocking my guitar out of tune and one of us lost a string.'

❝ I started playing the guitar when I was 13. It cost 2/6 for an hour's lesson and that got me started into music. We had parties at home, and Dad would sing 'Teddy Bear', and I'd get up and play my guitar. That was where my interest came from. Soon after that, there was something going on at the Billingham Technical College. They were doing a Christmas show and wanted a few musicians, just to try to put a group together onstage and see what happened. I went along with my guitar and amplifier and spoke to the lad that was organising. I'd seen this drum kit onstage, and I walked over and had a bash. This chap came over and said, 'Hey! Get off those drums!' It was my first meeting with Brian Taylor! Since then we have been very good friends and still play together sixty years on.

That group was just a little quick group, but it was the start of what would become the Johnny Taylor V. We thought of all kind of names. In those days, everyone seemed to be called Johnny. Johnnie Ray, Johnny Kidd and the Pirates, so Brian Taylor became 'Johnny Taylor', and that's how it all started. 'Brian' didn't sound so good! There used to be a show called *The 625 Show* and you could write to the BBC for an audition to be on it. It was for up-and-coming acts, semi-professionals, and Jimmy Young was the compère. There was an orchestra there, and we got an audition. We drove down in our van to London and stayed in Sussex Gardens, paying £4 to stay in a B'n'B! We had a night out in London on the Saturday night in the West End, had a bit of fun, and the following morning, we made our way to this little church hall. We were in the foyer and looked through who was on the stage ahead of us for the same audition. It was the Beatles. As we were ready to go in, they were more or less ready to go out. John Lennon came out, and was looking to see who was on next, and Brian had the name 'Johnny Taylor V' on his bass drum. John said in his broad Liverpool accent 'Who the hell is Johnny Taylor anyway?'

The following year, we met them again when we played on the bill with them at the Astoria Ballroom in Middlesbrough. It was a typical old Victorian dance hall, which was eventually converted into a nightclub. The building is still there, but back then, it had an old-fashioned band, trumpets, trombones, a resident dance band with a singer. But as groups came in and became more popular, those old dance bands faded away. I said to our bassist Gordon, 'It's going to be chaotic there tonight because the Beatles are playing.' We went over early in the afternoon to set our gear up, and as we were setting up, they walked in. They were dressed in black. They'd got a bit of style about them by then, with high-heeled black boots, you know. They were different. They had moved ahead with their style, and they were going for it. The sky was their limit. They were wrapped up in themselves. These were just ordinary lads, who as time went on, got sophisticated. Good food, good wine, first class travel, they moved on. However, in those days, you could buy pies in dance halls. I can still see George Harrison walking over to the kiosk and buying one and eating it as if he'd never eaten one before. He must have been starving the way he ate it. I used to have a copy of the running list for the show, but somebody stole it. It said '7.30 The Johnny Taylor Five, 8.30 this group from Newcastle called Vince King and the Stormers, and 9.30 The Beatles' and at the bottom it said something along the lines of 'Would all participants please keep to the strict timing?' I can imagine what John Lennon said about that! The audience gave us a bit of respect – we were quite well known in the area – but they weren't really interested in us, they had come to see the Beatles. ❞

HENRY FAWCETT, MUSICIAN, HAULAGE CONTRACTOR, MIDDLESBOROUGH, CLEVELAND

WEDNESDAY 26 JUNE

The group made their fourth visit to Newcastle-upon-Tyne, an hour-long drive north on the A19, for a second visit to the city's Majestic Ballroom. After checking into the Royal Turks Head Hotel, where they had also stayed a couple of weeks earlier, John and Paul settled down in one of the rooms, sitting facing each other on twin beds and began to write 'She Loves You'.

Once the show started, ballroom staff managed to keep everything under control with the help of just two policemen. Outside it was more chaotic. Those unable to get into the ticket-only ballroom stood by the stage door in Westgate Road, chanting 'We Want The Beatles!' The group had to hide in Pilgrim Street police station, whiling away the time signing autographs for the local constabulary.

They played two twenty-minute spots and were greeted by screams and shouts as teens rushed forward to the stage. George later said, 'It was a fantastic reception.' Talking to the *Evening Chronicle*, he was asked how the group got its name. 'We were cleaning John Lennon's flat out when we saw a beetle crawl across the floor and Paul said, "That would be a great name for the group".'

Sharkeys, a local taxi firm, received a call to pick the group up from the Majestic. Nineteen-year-old Ron Thompson volunteered as he was a fan. As fares could not be picked up in the street, he had to drive to the stage door. He was taken up to the dressing room where the group were changing after their performance and told that only Paul wanted a taxi, to take him to Central Station. After being dropped off, Paul took the late train back to London to meet Billy J. Kramer at the latter's Abbey Road recording session the following day.

The Journal ran the headline 'Swoons And Screams Greet Beatles', reporting that 'ten teenage girls fainted' and 'hundreds of other screamed in adoration'. In his review, the reporter wrote that 'an occasional twang of guitars sneaked through the high-pitched screams which continued throughout their two appearances. The mainly female audience crowded against the steel safety barriers round the stage.' Still, he wrote, 'The Beatles performed splendidly; judiciously cast smiles and winks kept the screams at hysteria pitch.' Asked about the screams drowning out their music, George said, 'What can you do?'

❝ I was working in the offices of a high-end fashion store in Whitley Bay named Ryles in 1963. After work I'd sometimes hang out with a bunch of friends at the YMCA in Cullercoats. Girls weren't allowed in at that time, but we'd sneak in anyway; until we were chucked out. We'd all listen to the juke box and dance. Sometimes the manager would organize a Saturday night 'hop'. Then the girls could pay to get in and we'd all rock'n'roll with the boys. Most of the lads wouldn't (or couldn't) dance, so the ones that were good at it would hold onto two girls' hands, and the three of them would dance together.

One time at the end of the hop, another lad came rushing in and said he'd just seen an amazing group at the Majestic and we all had to go the next time they were there. We asked what the group's name was. He said, 'The Beatles'. We were all like, 'The Beatles, they'll never get anywhere with a name like that!' Anyway, a few of us purchased our five-bob tickets. The Majestic was a huge ballroom with a lovely shiny floor and a smallish stage at the far end. They had those metal barricades set up a few yards out in front of it. Big chandeliers hanging from the ceiling. Very fancy by our standards. We were all fascinated with the place. None of us had been anywhere like it. Everyone danced to piped-in rock and roll music, except it wasn't the kind of beboping we knew. Everyone (mostly girls) stood apart from each other (no hand holding) and just kind of shook their heads whilst maintaining very stiff bodies. We all copied what they were doing. The dancefloor was packed like sardines. Then party time!

The Beatles came out onstage and nobody danced from then on. Everyone rushed up to the barricades. I was right in the front row, off to the side of the stage. The Beatles were full of fun and laughing and talking to the crowd. Then they started performing and I have to say it was life-changing for me. Fabulous live guitar music and the sheer camaraderie of the group were intoxicating. Plus that amazing ungreased clean hair swishing all over the place. For me it was love at first sight. I fell for John's friendly antics right away. I shouted 'John! John!' And he looked right at me, laughed and shouted back, 'What! What!' He was so much fun. I was so caught up in the frenzy that I threw a brand-new bracelet my mam had bought me out onto the stage and John picked it up. Later on, every time they were on TV my mam would point at the screen and shout that he was wearing it (fat chance). All the girls were screaming and going nuts. I was so crammed up against the barricade that it was pushing right against my solar plexus. That, plus the heat from all the bodies, made me very dizzy. It is the only time in my life that I fainted. Luckily, it was

just for a few seconds, though. Someone told me to put my head down. I did, and then I was fine. I didn't want to miss a thing. The place went wild when they sang 'Twist And Shout'. I'd never heard it sung by anyone before. It was the epitome of happiness for a lot of people. A definite natural high. It seemed that everyone was an instant fan.

There was one gorgeous girl standing behind the barrier, front and centre of the stage – Meg. She was tanned, with long straight blonde hair. Beautiful. Apparently, she'd been with Paul the first time they were at the Majestic; and now everyone was watching the two of them flirting; all bedroom-eyes and smiles. I think she was with him again that night. Local girl. A looker.

During the intermission we asked a bodyguard if he could get us some autographs. We'd all bought postcards with a black-and-white glossy photo of them on the front. So he collected them from a bunch of us. He disappeared behind the stage for what seemed ages. We thought he wouldn't come back. But he did. The postcard I got back was missing Paul's signature. (Maybe he was being distracted by Meg!) But that was OK. I was in LOVE with John. The group became so famous so fast it was unbelievable. I was now a teen so lovesick that I didn't want to do anything except fantasise about being with John. My mam bought the *Please Please Me* album for me. That was the start of the 'lonesome blues' for me. I'd sit alone in the dark and play the album over and over till bedtime. I'd cry my eyes out when John would sing 'Anna' (How could anyone break John's heart like that?). I remember when my doctor came to the house and saw all the Beatles posters on my bedroom wall. He said, 'Good God, she's got Beatleitis!'

Back at the YMCA I was very happy that the juke box soon had 'She Loves You' and 'I Want To Hold Your Hand.' So life was bearable again. We never stopped playing those two records. All the girls stopped backcombing their hair, and I had a poor-man's version of the famous Beatle-cut. My uncle told me I looked like Hamlet. But that didn't stop me. The Beatles were instrumental in influencing soft, shiny hair coming back into fashion. It was fabulous. Especially after having to wear all the 'bouffant' and ghastly 'flips' – sprayed so much they were bulletproof. Gale force winds couldn't shift them. All the boys were jealous that the girls were falling all over the place for John, Paul, George or Ringo. Eventually, they too succumbed to the Beatle cuts, Nero jacket suits and Cuban-heeled boots. Fashion changed for the better because of the Fab Four. The day John was killed I was living on Long Island in New York. I cried all day. Even my small children understood why. I cried so much they thought I knew him. Then in 2000 my husband and I moved into the city. We'd often walk through Strawberry Fields in Central Park. There is a small crowd there on a daily basis; and always flowers, candles and peoples' personal mementos to our beloved John, laid across the famous 'Imagine' mosaic memoriam. Fans of every generation sit with guitars, playing Beatles music. It is always festive, rather than gloomy. Always a celebration of those four fab lads from Liverpool. **"**

FRANCES LIANE PRESTON, REGISTERED NURSE, FAIRFIELD, CONNECTICUT, USA

THURSDAY 27 JUNE

'From Me To You' dropped to number 6 in the *Disc* chart and number 4 in the *NRM* chart. The group's debut LP was reviewed in *Disc*. 'The Beatles are as rough as sandpaper in technical terms, but as entertainers they are top of the pile in Liverpool and many other places, too. They apply the same uninhibited enthusiasm to their work as do the Springfields, and the beat and atmosphere which they generate are compulsive and completely irresistible. That Liverpool sound? There's no such thing, of course. The Beatles are right slap bang on the rhythm and blues wavelength, and with other Liverpudlians, happen to be the best exponents on the pop side of R and B at present. There are eight Paul McCartney–John Lennon songs in the set and the two boys have an obvious goldmine knack of writing catchy melodies and easily dug lyrics which should stand them and their fellow Beatles in very good stead for a long time to come. Side one is as hot as a furnace, with the boys battering away in fine style and voice at a rocking collection of material. There's even a crazy snatch of classical piano making an unexpected contribution to 'Misery'. Side two is a little more relaxed and sedate, until 'There's A Place' restores the hectic punch of the flip. The lads do a nice waltzing treatment on 'Taste Of Honey' too. One of the most exciting and impressive British pop LPs for a long time.' The *Daily Express* reported the creation of Beatles Limited, with a starting share capital of £100. An accountant was quoted as saying, 'By doing this they can save paying considerable amounts of surtax.'

Paul spent the morning at Abbey Road while Billy J. Kramer and the Dakotas rehearsed 'Bad To Me' and 'I Call Your Name', which they recorded in the evening. He brought the lyrics to 'Bad To Me' written on a packet of Senior Service cigarettes. He returned to Liverpool in the afternoon and in the evening he and John finished 'She Loves You' in the dining room of his house in Forthlin Road, while his father Jim watched TV in the living room. Paul recalled, 'We sat in there, just beavering away while my dad was watching TV and smoking his Players cigarettes, and we wrote 'She Loves You'. We actually just finished it there because we'd started it in the hotel room. We went into the living room – "Dad, listen to this. What do you think?" So we played it to my dad and he said, "That's very nice, son, but there's enough of these Americanisms around. Couldn't you sing, "She loves you. Yes! Yes! Yes!" At which point we collapsed in a heap and said, "No, Dad, you don't quite get it!" That's my classic story about my dad. For a working-class guy that was rather a middle-class thing to say, really. But he was like that.'

FRIDAY 28 JUNE

The latest edition of the *NME* had 'From Me To You' and 'Do You Want To Know A Secret' both dropping one place to numbers 6 and 7 respectively in the Top 30. The Isley Brothers' version of 'Twist And Shout' charted at number 27, no doubt in part due to the Beatles performing the song live in concert. The paper's half-year Points Table revealed that the Beatles were in second place with 577 points, a distant second to Cliff Richard with 877 points. A letter from 'Devoted Beatle Fan' from Liverpool complained in the newspaper's 'From You To Us' column: 'I was annoyed to read in last week's *NME* that the Beatles are having a fan club Christmas party in London. Why can't it be here in Liverpool? I'm quite sure they have more fans up north than down south. Now I don't blame the girl who refused to buy their record because she didn't want them to become famous and go to London!'

In *Melody Maker*, 'From Me To You' was at number 5 and 'Do You Want To Know A Secret' at number 7. 'My Bonnie' dropped out of the Top 50. The group were guest reviewers in the paper's 'Blind Date' column ('The Beatles – what the Merseyside Wonders think of the latest batch of pop singles'), offering their comments on Elvis Presley's '(You Are The) Devil In Disguise', Rolf Harris' 'I Know A Man', Bo Diddley's 'Bo Diddley', the Chiffons' 'One Fine Day', the Dakotas' 'The Cruel Sea', Cleo Laine's 'Southend' (George said 'It could have been Margaret Rutherford for all I knew'), Helen Shapiro's 'Not Responsible' and the Tymes' 'So Much In Love'.

The group drove across the Pennines in heavy rain for a thirty-two-hundred-capacity sold-out concert at the Queen's Hall on Sovereign Street in Leeds. The show began at 8pm, billed by promoter Bernard Hinchcliffe as a 'Jazz-'n'-Pop Ball'. Tickets cost 10/6 (12/6 at the door). The group, who were paid £250, incongruously shared the bill with Mr Acker Bilk and His Paramount Jazz Band, the posters boasting 'Britain's Biggest Attractions Together For The First Time' – a claim that was not true – the Beatles had been on a bill with Bilk before at the 'Riverboat Shuffle' event on 25 August 1961, on board the MV Royal Iris, which sailed from Pier Head. During Bilk's performance, sandwiched between the Beatles' two sets, the clarinettist – sick of putting up with fans screaming for the group – told the crowd in his thick Somerset burr, 'Well, we're the bloody Earwigs!' Also on the bill were Sammy King and the Voltairs (returning by 'public request'), the Ryles Brothers with Gay Saxon and compère Garth Cawood (the 'North's Top DJ').

In the aftermath, the concert's organizer Mr Arthur Green reported that a steward 'was bitten during the performance on the top of his arm by a girl.' Despite some twenty stewards linking arms around the stage, which was built 5 feet high to prevent a stage invasion, fans managed to crawl under it. Green also reported that 'as the Beatles did their act there were screams and at times the dancers who had gathered tightly around the stage for the performances swayed in the fashion of a cup-tie crowd.' After the show, the Beatles headed back to Liverpool.

> ❝ My then boyfriend was lead guitarist in the Voltairs, who were one of the support acts that night. When the Beatles came onstage, I can only describe the sound from the audience as a volcanic eruption. The performance was very loud and totally magnetic! After the show I went backstage up some rickety steps and into a pokey dressing room. The entire time we were there with them, Paul and John were absolutely fired up (with adrenalin, I believe, but it may have been something else!). George and Ringo were rather quieter but still friendly. John spent the majority of the time sitting under the table
>
>
>
> clowning. The one exchange I can recall is Paul asking if anyone had a spare razor blade. When ask why he wanted one he said, 'To shave with.' Then he quipped, 'They're very hard to get hold of yer know!' The impression I'm left with was that they laughed and joked together a great deal. I just remember them being very down to earth; an energetic group of lads with a wicked Scouse sense of humour. I still have their autographs from that night signed, 'To Dinah'. ❞
>
> **DINAH BENTLEY, SPECIAL NEEDS TEACHER, HUDDERSFIELD, WEST YORKSHIRE**

SATURDAY 29 JUNE

The group had time in the morning to listen to Monday's recording of *Saturday Club*, which aired at 10am. But they were soon back on the road, heading to Handsworth and Old Hill for a double header on the Regan circuit - venues they had played in January and February.

At 6.05pm, Independent Television aired *Lucky Stars (Summer Spin)*, recorded the previous Sunday. The *Liverpool Echo* reviewer described the Beatles as the 'most potent' act on the programme, although was surprised that one or two of their numbers appeared to be mimed. Five minutes after the show finished, at 6.35pm, the episode of *Juke Box Jury* featuring John as a judge aired. John voted all eight records a miss. Cleo Laine's 'Southend', the Tymes' 'So Much In Love', Elvis Presley's '(You're The) Devil In Disguise' ('Well, you know, I used to go mad on Elvis, like all the groups, but not now. I don't like this. It's awful. Poor ol' Elvis... I don't like him anymore'), Miriam Makeba's 'The Clock Song', Tompall Glaser's 'On Top Of Spaghetti', Russ Conway's 'Flamenco', Paul and Paula's 'First Quarrel' and Julie Grant's '(Don't Ever Let Me Down)'. His predictions ended up being not too far off the mark, with only Presley's and the Tymes' records becoming hits.

Following the broadcast of the programme, John's critics attacked him as cynical, accusing him of not liking anything - but of course his fans defended his honesty and outspokenness. John defended his comments, saying he wasn't knocking Elvis. 'All I did was voice the opinion of many other Presley followers who think that his discs of late are ordinary! You can't dispute the fact that El is still the king'. The *Daily Herald* was less than impressed with the show. 'Apart from impish, intelligent Bruce Prochnik, last week's *Juke Box Jury* panel were the pinheadest I've seen. Have Caroline Maulding and the Beatles' John Lennon no sense of fun, no breadth of taste, no room for the ridiculous?'

The group arrived at the Plaza Ballroom in Handsworth for the first of two shows that night, on a bill with Mike Sheridan and the Nightriders and the Blue Stars. Local musician Brian Nicholls recalled the atmosphere being electric and full of anticipation. 'Ma Regan's husband Joe, resplendent in a smart black suit with black silk stripes down each side of his trousers and white shirt topped off with a dicky bow, announced to the audience in his inimitable style as emcee, 'We've got some great gear for you now!' 'One, two, three, four' BANG! – straight in. No soundcheck, no tuning up, no monitor/foldback speakers, no foot pedals, no personal introductions (they knew that we all knew who they were!). I remember, it was loud! All four were smiling and enjoying themselves – seemingly free from any of the tensions that were to beset them in later years. They sounded just like their recordings and, because of the then poor sound quality of live television broadcasts, much, much better in the flesh. That evening we all experienced first-hand why it was called Beatlemania!'

After finishing their set, they made the twenty-five-minute drive down the A457 to Old Hill, where they played a second show at the other Plaza Ballroom. Mike Sheridan and the Nightriders also played the double header, along with Dave Lacey and the Corvettes, the Cossacks and the Plazents. Jean Fawkes, who lived just a couple of minutes from the Plaza, remembered the evening well. 'I went the first time and couldn't get in. Everybody queued in String Meadow and after a bit everyone was told there was no room to get anybody else in. We went and queued again the following week and luckily got in. I decided I had waited that long, so I was staying there.'

Following the performance, the group drove to the Albany Hotel in the Birmingham district of Smallbrook, where they stayed the night. George took the opportunity to write a letter to his sister Louise, who lived in the US. 'We make our next record on Monday, called 'She Loves You'. By the way do you mind if Ringo and I pop over to see you all at the end of September?... I thought of flying over to see everybody, and maybe call in at Nashville for a few days too, to see Roy Orbison (whom we met on tour over here) and possibly Chet Atkins, a favourite of mine, if we have time. PS. I'm buying a new car soon, possibly a Jaguar'.

1963, what a year that turned out to be for me, the Beatles and the world! Although my life in show business had commenced several years earlier back in late 1960, at the tender age of 12, 1963 was to become the pinnacle of my career in the business. In April 1962 I was approached by the American producers of the planned Broadway version of *Oliver!* to play the title role. Two months later, accompanied by my mother as chaperone, I flew to New York to start rehearsals and then a pre-Broadway opening tour of the production. Whilst touring the US the English cast members were totally unaware of what was beginning to happen back home. The Beatles, in 1962, were busy building a fan base that was to explode by the time I travelled back to England in  the spring of 1963. On arriving home, now 14, I was soon totally embroiled in Beatlemania. I quickly acquired a Beatle haircut and Beatle suit that were by then all the rage. Like everyone else of my age I wanted to be a Beatle, or at least look like one!

That summer was to provide me with my one and only encounter directly with a Beatle. *Juke Box Jury* had been, and continued to be for many years, a very popular Saturday night, half-hour record review light entertainment programme on the BBC. The programme hosted a selection of four celebrities each week that would listen to and review half a dozen or so new single releases of the week and vote them either a 'Hit' or a 'Miss'. I was lucky enough to appear on the programme twice but the episode made in June of 1963 was to be my one and only meeting with John Lennon. We were both panellists on that week's show and we were introduced in the green room, the pre-recording meeting room for the guest celebrities. I don't think John thought too much about me or either of the other two guests to whom he was introduced and although polite, he was surrounded by his entourage and kept himself very much to himself. Of course, I was totally swept away by being on the same show as John Lennon but somewhat disappointed that he seemed a little aloof. I suppose he was the 'rebel' Beatle, the other two guests were of the elitist brigade and I was probably seen as the 14-year-old precocious little child star. Regardless, it was a wonderful, unforgettable experience and what a privilege it turned out to be! **"**

BRUCE PROCHNIK, IT ACCOUNT MANAGER, KINGS LANGLEY, HERTFORDSHIRE

SUNDAY 30 JUNE

The group left Birmingham and drove across country in drizzling rain to East Anglia for two concerts at the fifteen hundred-seater ABC on Regent Road in Great Yarmouth, the first in a ten-week series of seaside concerts. The two shows, at 6pm and 8.15pm, also featured the Brook Brothers, the Terry Young Combo, Erkey Grant, Tommy Wallis and Beryl and compère Ted Rogers.

Reporter Gianni Bisiach of Italian TV broadcaster RAI interviewed them in their dressing room, with the sound of screaming fans audible in the background. In a less-than-stimulating conversation lasting just under two minutes, they revealed their names and ages, talked briefly about fan letters and the suits they were wearing ('We got it from Paris – Pierre Cardin' – though in fact they were designed by Dougie Millings, based on a Cardin design). The interview aired on Italian TV, dubbed in Italian, in December 1963. Part of their second show was filmed from the cinema's balcony. The group spent the night at the nearby Carlton Hotel.

" I have great memories of the 30 June concert in Great Yarmouth – as it shaped the rest of my life. During May 1963, I had just started going out with Beryl. I first met her on 26 April and asked her out on a date, the same day the *Please Please Me* album came out in stereo. We still own the copy and argue over who actually bought it. However, sometime earlier, and before we had started to go out, I had planned a camping holiday with a few mates in Devon during early June. I became fond of Beryl but did not want to risk her drifting off whilst I was away so, to keep her interested, I asked her to come with me after my holiday to see this new exciting group, the Beatles. I had heard of them but knew little of them. She lived on the same road as me in Caister-on-Sea, a suburb of Great Yarmouth. She was a hairdresser and I was a full-time student at Norwich City College, doing HNC. We both had teas at our homes before the concert – in those days the

choice of places to eat out were very limited – no McDonalds, etc. – and it was an expense we could do without.

I picked Beryl up from her house in my father's lovely 1954 Consul – bench seats and three-speed column change – and drove to the cinema. The Beatles were very polished, if somewhat inaudible because of the noise. Sticking in my mind was 'A Taste Of Honey', 'Do You Want To Know A Secret' and, of course, 'Twist And Shout'. It was something we had never experienced before – the screaming, the music, the excitement. The audience seemed to be 90 per cent young girls. Afterwards, we met up with Beryl's bosses, Maurice and Doreen, who were also at the show, and went for a coffee. I jokingly mentioned that I fancied a Beatles haircut and before I knew it, I found myself back in her hairdressing salon where Beryl gave me an instant Beatles haircut! We stayed together and have now been married for over fifty years – had the Beatles not come, who knows what may have happened. **"**

JOHN GRIMMER, ELECTRICAL ENGINEER, GREAT YARMOUTH, NORFOLK

JULY

Oh, we do like to be beside the seaside

MONDAY 1 JULY

The second half of 1963 began with a sunny day at the English seaside for the Beatles - a far cry from the first day of the year. They had breakfast at the Carlton, before setting off on the three-hour trip back to London for a session at Abbey Road studios - the first time they had all been there since recording 'From Me To You' and 'Thank You Girl' on 5 March. Approximately an hour and a half into their journey, they stopped off for lunch in Dedham at Le Talbooth. After the meal they took photos outside with sous chef Derek Driver and chefs Kurt Friedl and Gerald Trueman.

Arriving at Abbey Road for an evening session, they had to force their way through a group of fans who had been waiting outside since nine o'clock in the morning. It didn't get any easier inside - a girl broke into Studio Two before the recording began. Several more fans made their way into the building, overpowering the five policemen on duty. Commissionaire John Skinner told second engineer Geoff Emerick to 'barricade the doors until we can round them all up.' Once order had been restored, recording began with George Martin, who had just returned from a two-week holiday, and engineers Norman Smith and Emerick. Emerick was working on his second session with the group. Earlier, he had walked into the studio to find Mal Evans setting up Ringo's drums and had also met Brian Epstein for the first time. Sean O'Mahony arrived with Philip Gotlop to take photos for his *The Beatles Book* venture, which hit the streets on 1 August. Terry O'Neill was also on hand to take photos, including a series of shots taken in the alleyway outside the studios.

The group cut 'She Loves You' - finished the previous Thursday, and 'Get You In The End' (subsequently known as 'I'll Get You'), penned a couple of weeks earlier at Menlove Avenue. During a break for supper, food was brought into the studio, for fear that even a visit to the canteen would cause mayhem. *Melody Maker* incorrectly reported that they recorded not only a new single but an entire second LP. After finishing the session, they made their way back to the Hotel President, where they spent the night.

❛ I was working as sous chef at Le Talbooth on the day the Beatles came. I was a fan, of course, and recognised them. Two weeks earlier, the Rolling Stones had turned up, and the governor, Gerald Milsom, turned them away. He didn't want anything to do with groups who had thousands of fans 'coming in and taking up the carpets as a souvenir.' It was frantic in those days. The manager at the time, my friend John, said, 'Derek, it's the Beatles, what do you think?' They turned up at 1.55, and we officially stopped serving at 2pm. I said, 'Let them come in.' Paul or John said, 'What have you got?' I said, 'I have a nice leg of lamb', so they all had that, with some mint sauce. It cost £10/6!

They were happy to sign the menu for me, and after the meal they agreed to have some pictures taken with us outside. They were messing around and wearing my chef's hat! Paul was in the lavatory when the group shot was taken, which was famous at the time for being across on the other side of the car park. Several pictures were taken, all of us taking it in turns, and then they thanked us, and set off on their way to London. It was a memorable day.

I kept the photographs and menu for years. Some years later, I decided to sell them, along with the signed menu, via Christie's. They went for about £9,000. In October 2014, whilst I was on holiday with my wife in Morocco, recovering from a triple heart-bypass, I was treading water in the pool of the

Sofitel Hotel in Marrakech. There was only one other couple there at the time, and we got chatting. I said 'What do you do for a living? and he said 'I'm an autograph authenticator.' I asked him if he meant as a hobby, and he said it used to be, but now he actually made a living out of it. I joked that I could have done with him a few years back, when I was selling my Beatles autographs. He asked me about the circumstances which they were taken in, and I told him about the group visiting Le Talbooth, and the pictures I had taken with them. He smiled at me and described the pictures. I had no idea how he knew them so well, and he just calmly said, 'I know, because I've got them. I bought them about eight or nine years ago.' The next morning at breakfast, he brought down his iPad, and proceeded to show me the photographs – there I was, with John Lennon wearing my chef's hat! We have kept in touch and met up with him and his wife at Le Talbooth, where it all took place, all these years ago. ❑

DEREK DRIVER, CHEF, CAPEL ST MARY, SUFFOLK

TUESDAY 2 JULY

John spoke by phone with *Disc*'s Jean Carol to clarify his comments about Elvis on *Juke Box Jury*. 'I wasn't knocking Presley. All I did was voice the opinions of so many other Presley followers who think that his discs of late are old hat,' he said. 'It's not the sound that myself and people of my age group want. That's why I criticised him. I didn't slam him, but I was just a big sick of hearing the same old stuff.' (The yet-to-be published edition of *Melody Maker* printed a letter from Helen Goddard, who revealed she was no longer a fan of John's. 'Elvis has sustained his place in the hit parade for nearly a decade. The Beatles are all the rage now, but what will they be doing in seven years' time?')

Dezo Hoffmann arrived at the Hotel President in the morning. He took a series of photos of the group, initially in Room 114, followed by the hotel's reception area and then, despite early morning rain, on the street outside and in the nearby Russell Square Gardens. Moving a mile away to the corner of Rupert Street and Brewer Street, he took more shots of the group buying bananas at a fruit stand, then to Dougie Millings' tailor shop at 63 Old Compton Street, followed by a visit to a nearby deli and onto Wardour Street – where they returned to Star Shirt Makers at number 31, collecting shirts they had ordered the previous Monday. Finally, they bought ice cream at the Kontakt Café at number 24, posed outside Garners restaurant at number 27 before going into Hoffmann's studio at number 29 to pose for further shots.

At 6.30pm the group recorded a session at the BBC's Maida Vale number 5 studio, their second visit, for the fifth episode of *Pop Go The Beatles*. They performed Arthur Crudup's 'That's Alright Mama' (recorded by Elvis Presley in 1954), 'There's A Place', 'Carol' (the only time they performed the Chuck Berry song, which the Rolling Stones subsequently recorded for their first LP), Arthur Alexander's 'Soldier Of Love (Lay Down Your Arms)' (dedicated on air to the girls at the St Therese Convent in Ryde on the Isle of Wight), Carl Perkins' 'Lend Me Your Comb' (the B-side of Perkins' last Sun single and a Hamburg favourite), 'Clarabella' (a cover of a Jodimars' B-side), the Coasters' 'Three Cool Cats', Chuck Berry's 'Sweet Little Sixteen' and 'Ask Me Why'.

The guests on the episode were Duffy Power with the Graham Bond Quartet, who released a cover of 'I Saw Her Standing There' in April – the *Liverpool Echo* panned the single, claiming it was 'disappointingly contrived, unimaginatively controlled'. Rodney Burke took over from Lee Peters as host of the programme. After the three-hour recording, they returned to the Hotel President. The show aired on 16 July, following a three-week break from the fourth episode to gauge audience reaction.

WEDNESDAY 3 JULY

The Beatles headed back north to Manchester, just over a month after their 30 May show at the Odeon. Some roads in the area had become impassable – a fierce thunderstorm had flooded houses and blocked roads, bringing rush-hour traffic to a standstill. In parts of the city almost three quarters of an inch of rain fell in less than three hours.

The group arrived in the city for a 4pm rehearsal at the Playhouse Theatre for the Light Programme's *The Beat Show*. After a short break, they performed 'From Me To You', 'A Taste Of Honey' and 'Twist And Shout' at the 8pm recording, which aired the next day.

THURSDAY 4 JULY

In the brand-new edition of *Disc*, 'From Me To You' remained at number 6. The Isley Brothers' 'Twist And Shout' bowed at number 23 on the chart. 'When it first came out nobody seemed very interested,' Paul recalled. 'We all thought it was fab. Everybody else – no go! I suppose people just weren't ready for that kind of music at that time. Still, it was such a great number we featured it from time to time.' The newspaper ran a feature with Cliff, Bruce Welch, Joe Brown, Billy Fury and Helen Shapiro. They were asked what they thought of the 'Liverpool boys'. Not surprisingly all were in favour. Cliff said, 'If any one group has a distinctive sound it is the Beatles.' *Disc* readers weren't in full agreement. Angela Eden and Tony Mutton both preferred Gerry and the Pacemakers, while Margaret O'Hara felt the Beatles would never beat Elvis, who would 'always be tops with 'the faithful.'

In the *NRM*, 'From Me To You' dropped to number 8. The paper featured its half-year chart survey, with 'Please Please Me' at number 7 with 603 points and 'From Me To You' at number 12 with 522 points, enough to put them in second place behind Cliff Richard with 1,282 points.

As the group drove back down south, George Martin mixed and edited the previous Monday's session. *The Beat Show* aired from 1pm to 1.30pm. In the evening, they went to see the Rolling Stones for the second time, performing at the Scene in Great Windmill Street.

❝ I don't really remember when I first met the Beatles. I guess it was Paul first but it was very shortly after my sister Jane met them. Anyway, I think I pretty much met the Beatles all at once but I don't remember where. I used to go and see the Stones as a fan at Ken Colyer's Jazz Club when it became Studio 51 on Monday nights. I remember on one of those Monday nights, them saying they had just recorded their first single 'Come On'. Later Paul and I went to see them at the Scene and I remember him on the way there saying that he was jealous of them because their manager let them wear whatever they wanted to onstage. I remember going to some of the Beatles' BBC sessions they did that year. They were amazing playing live together – incredibly good.

By this time Paul was living in the guest room of our house in Wimpole Street, having been offered the room by my parents. So we ended up sharing the top floor of the house. One night John came over and they were in the little music room in the basement where my mother used to give private oboe lessons when she wasn't giving them at the Academy. They just sat side by side at the piano writing this song. Paul stuck his head up the stairs and asked me to come down and listen to what they had just written. I sat down on the little sofa and they played 'I Want To Hold Your Hand' for the first time to anybody.

I had met Gordon Waller at Westminster School. He was more of a rock'n'roll fan and I was a bit more of a folk fan. The Everly Brothers were our idols as with any duo in rock'n'roll history. We started playing parties and the like while we were still at school. We got some professional gigs and there was a pub we played in at lunch sometimes. We'd play a half-hour set and then go back to school. We played at a wine bar called Tina's in Albemarle Street, a gig we got through Chad and Jeremy. They had been spotted there by John Barry who signed them to Ember Records. So they had to give up their gig there. Tina asked whether they knew anyone who could replace them. We knew them in passing and they suggested us.

I left Westminster a year before Gordon and went to King's College London where I read philosophy. There was a period when he'd have to climb over the fence at night and get out because he was a boarder and I would meet him outside and we'd go and play at the Pickwick Club. Norman Newell was there one night and invited us to his table to have a drink and asked us to come and audition for EMI. For the audition we were just singing the songs we were singing every night. After that he offered us a record deal.

Norman said to us, 'If you know any other songs that you want to cut for your first session, let me know.' Paul was working on several songs during the time he was living with us, including 'A World Without Love'. It wasn't finished and had no bridge. John didn't like it much and they weren't going to record it. I liked it though, so when we got our record deal I went back to Paul and asked him whether the song was still going a-begging. He said he hadn't finished it, but I asked him if we could have it. I had an idea of how we could do a duo version of it. He said, 'Fine. Take it.' The only mild nagging I had to do was to get him to write a bridge.

One of the things I'm asked all the time is, 'How did you get all those songs from the Beatles?' It wasn't like that at all. If you look at any of the interviews back then, the question that everybody asked them without fail was, 'What are you going to do when it's all over?' The assumption was that it was going to be all over in two years. In several of those interviews they said, 'We will be songwriters.' They took their songwriting responsibilities seriously. When we came back after doing 'A World Without Love' in America, we were touring, doing TV and all that, 'Nobody I Know' was finished and ready. 'Woman' he specifically played for us and said, 'I think this would be good for you.'

I had wanted to be a record producer from the moment I was first in the studio. The first record I ever produced was for Paul Jones. He had seen me in the studio working on some of our Peter and Gordon records and liked what I was doing and asked me if I would produce him recording a version of the Bee Gees' 'And The Sun Will Shine'. In fact, Paul McCartney played drums on the track along with Paul Samwell-Smith of the Yardbirds on bass, Nicky Hopkins on piano and Jeff Beck on guitar. I was spending a lot of time over at Paul's house talking about his ideas for Apple and he asked me to be an in-house producer for the label. He finally asked me to be Head of A&R. Danny Kortchmar had been a guitarist in the Kingbees who used to back Peter and Gordon on the road for several tours in America. He and I became very close friends. He was subsequently in a group called Flying Machine with his childhood friend James Taylor. When the group broke up, James ended up in New York. He had no money, but he did have a girlfriend in London he decided to go and stay with. Danny gave him my phone number and he called me up out of the blue one day, came over to my house and sang me some songs. I was completely knocked out. I told him I was starting a new job as head of A&R at a new record label and asked if he would be interested in a record deal. He said, 'Yes', and two days later I took him in to meet the Beatles and signed him to Apple. It was a multiple record deal, but I knew Allen Klein by reputation because of the Stones and I didn't like him and I suggested to James that when he came in, we leave. We thought we might get sued and there was talk of it, but Apple was in such a muddle that it never happened. That's when I became James' manager because we didn't know anybody else we could trust to do it. We moved to America and made a new record deal and I have been here ever since. ❚

**PETER ASHER, CBE, MUSICIAN, PRODUCER, MANAGER, CONSULTANT
AND LECTURER, SANTA MONICA, CALIFORNIA**

FRIDAY 5 JULY

The new *NME* revealed its full January–June chart points table. Cliff led the way with 877 points, followed by the Beatles with 577, Frank Ifield with 548 and the Shadows with 522. By year's end it was a much different story, with the group outscoring Cliff by more than four hundred points. In an article headed 'Worldwide Beatles', the paper reported that Del Shannon's version of 'From Me To You' had gone to number 87 in the *Billboard* chart – their own version bubbled under at number 116 the following month.

More noteworthy, in the week's 'Tail-Pieces', the Alley Cat (the pseudonym of the paper's publisher Maurice Kinn) revealed – against the wishes of Kinn's neighbour Brian Epstein – that Tony Barrow had admitted John was married. The week's *Melody Maker*, however, scooped the *NME* – John publicly admitted for the first time that he was in fact married, although he had never denied it. 'It is just that nobody ever asked me about it. But my wife, Cynthia, and I met during my days at art school and fell in love. It's as simple as that. The reason that I have never blazoned the fact all over the papers is that I regard my private life as being completely private.' In the following week's paper, Chris Roberts wrote an article asking the question 'Do wedding bells spell death for the big names?'

'From Me To You' dropped three places to number 8 and Roberts wrote an article titled 'How To Form A Beat Group'. 'It was ambition,' he said, 'that caused [them] to play themselves almost to exhaustion in German night clubs and Liverpool to weld their talent into a solid, saleable mass.'

Less than a week after a double header on the Regan circuit, the group returned to the West Midlands to do it again – this time at the Ritz in King's Heath, followed by another date at the Plaza Old Hill. At the Ritz, they shared the bill with Dane Tempest and the Atoms, the Redcaps and the Plazents. The Atoms' drummer Roger Stafford recalled the evening. 'We got a message to say they were short of groups at the Ritz and that we were to go over there. We thought we'd miss the Beatles, because they'd have to go on early there so they could get to Old Hill. So we made a mad dash, getting our equipment out of the Plaza, putting it in our van and going over to the Ritz. When we got there we didn't even unload our gear. We went in and went straight upstairs and the Beatles were already onstage. We saw part of their act and the only number I remember was 'I Saw Her Standing There'. Anyway, they finished their set and left in Ma and Pa Regan's Ford Consul driven by Bob Bailey, who worked for them as a jack-of-all trades. While the Redcaps were getting ready to perform, we helped the Beatles' roadie get their stuff out and into their van. I was a drummer, so obviously I went straight for the drum kit, took it down the fire escape and handed it to someone who put it in the van. While the Redcaps were performing we heard that they had to go over to the Plaza as well. When they finished their set, we went on and did ours. I picked up a broken drumstick off the floor, which I guess was Ringo's. I also found a postcard which had been thrown onstage by some fans, wishing Ringo a Happy Birthday. There's always been a mystery about that night that doesn't seem to have been answered. The following week all the groups and the regulars were talking about the Beatles' appearance. They left the Ritz by car to go to Old Hill, but their van, which left later, arrived at the Plaza before the car did and no one knows what happened to them in the meantime. People on that night wondered where they'd got to. The rumour was they'd popped off for some drinks in a pub somewhere.'

Arriving at the Plaza, Bob Bailey recalled a scene of 'utter madness. I had the shirt ripped off my back – I'd never seen scenes like it.' Support act Dave Lacey and the Corvettes had already finished their set while Denny and the Diplomats had to keep playing until the Beatles arrived. Lacey recalled, 'We couldn't hear a word that they sang. We had to get them out of the Plaza through the window of the toilet on to the roof outside because they would never have got out of the place alive. I clearly remember pushing them out through the window. The screaming from the girls was so loud they might as well have mouthed it.' Their late arrival meant the group performed a shortened set, comprising eleven songs.

On the way home to Liverpool, they noticed a strong smell of burning in their Ford Thames minibus. They piled out, while Neil Aspinall investigated the problem. A series of wires were crossed. Disconnecting them, they travelled back without the use of any lights. 'We used to keep a couple of torches in the back of the van,' Ringo recalled. 'John and Paul often got ideas for songs while travelling home. Me 'n' George used to hold the torches while they wrote down the songs. We tied those torches on to the front of the car and off we went – keeping one of the indicators winking as an extra warning that the Beatles were a-comin.'

❝ I left school at 16 and was going to go into the RAF. So I went down to Cardington in Bedfordshire, spent a week down there, did the whole rigamarole. At the end of the week they said, 'We want you,' and this was after National Service was finished. They asked how long would I sign up for. I said, 'Five years, maybe seven.' And they said, 'Ooh no, you have to sign for at least twelve.' I said, 'I'm 16 years old and you want me to sign up for twelve years of my life? I don't think so'. So I went back to Birmingham and got a summer job at Lewis's, which was the biggest department store in the city. Across the road was an amusement arcade and I used to go over there at lunchtime and play the pinball machines. I used to make more money there than at Lewis's. I truly was a pinball wizard. The guy on the next machine as it turned out was Euan Rose, who was also working at Lewis's. One day he leant over to me and says, 'I'm a drummer in a band. We've got a gig this weekend, do you want to come and see us?' I said, 'Well, I don't have a life, so why not?' I went to the gig and next week at work he said, 'What do you think?' I said, 'Well you're not bad but your singer's a bit rough in places.' A couple of weeks later he said, 'We're having rehearsals this weekend at my house. Do you want to come over and watch us?' So, I said, 'Sure why not?' I go over there and halfway through the rehearsal he says, 'Why don't you do one?' 'Well, I can't sing,' I said. 'Yes, you can,' he said, 'I've heard you in the stockroom at work.' So, we did some Buddy Holly stuff.

Euan said, 'We've got a gig on Monday at the George Hotel on Bristol Road.' You always remember the first place you ever played. Sometime in 1962 Denny Laine asked me to go and sing with him, so I sang with Denny and the Diplomats for a month or two. Later that year Dave Mountney was put in charge of putting together a house band for the Regan venues and that is how the Plazents came to be. We used to play at all four ballrooms. All these various artists came in, including all the American ones, so we came in in the afternoons and rehearsed with them and backed them on the night. We actually appeared at all four ballrooms on one night.

Every time the Beatles came to town, we went on before them so when we played the Ritz we went on first and while they were performing we headed over the Plaza in Old Hill and they came on later. We never got any credit for it and because we were the resident group we never got our names in any of the books. Whenever the Beatles played, I think the girls started screaming when they left school that afternoon and didn't stop until the next morning. On one occasion we were in the dressing room and the girls broke through the bar downstairs and came up the back stairs. We were at the top of the stairs pushing them all back down again. It was an absolute nut job. They were pretty friendly, ordinary guys. We didn't take much notice of them to be honest. We figured this was a flash in the pan like everything else was. If you had a hit record, you had a hit record and then you'd go back to your ordinary life again.

At the end of 1963 Decca came walking in one night and wanted to sign us. Obviously, we couldn't get the pens out quick enough. A couple of weeks later they came back to us and said they wanted us to do a one-off album of Beatles' songs. They said, 'You won't get any royalties, but we'll pay you well,' which they did – in fact they paid us very well. We went down to London and made the album on 4 December 1963. I know what day it was because it was my first wedding anniversary and my wife wasn't happy. We did nineteen songs. We went into the studio and six o'clock in the morning and finished at three o'clock the next morning and Decca said, 'We're going to call you the Merseyboys.' It was supposed to be for the American market to coincide with the Beatles' first visit to there. Around this time, we decided to call ourselves the Brumbeats, so for a while we were the Plazents, the Merseyboys and the Brumbeats. When we played on the Regan circuit we got to back all the American artists that played there. You name it, we backed them. I remember the time we backed the Four Seasons. Frankie Valli came running in the dressing room, swearing his head off, saying he was going to 'Shoot the bastard!' Apparently, some guy had told him to leave his girlfriend alone. Roy Orbison was cool. He sat in the dressing room and taught me how to do falsetto. I've always said this – I will quit singing when I can no longer sing 'Crying'. ⌡

**GRAHAM ASHFORD, ARTIST AND MUSICIAN, MARYVILLE,
WASHINGTON, US AND ONELOA, HAWAII, US**

SATURDAY 6 JULY

The Beatles travelled from Liverpool to Northwich in Cheshire, arriving at lunchtime to help crown the Northwich Carnival Queen in Verdin Park. They waited at the police station on Chester Way, where they were met by Memorial Hall manager Gwili Lewis. Lewis drove them around in a borrowed Parks' Steelworks van until it was time for their appearance – after two hours cooped up inside the vehicle and, with thousands of fans waiting for their arrival, they appeared at 3pm.

Pandemonium broke out as they made their way onstage. Part of the six thousand-strong crowd stampeded forward; girls passed out and were dragged clear to avoid being trampled on. Carnival committee chairman Councillor Don Nolan pleaded for the crowd to stay at the edge of the area, but to no avail. Councillor Tom Alcock asked the group to crown 16-year-old Cathryn Millington and leave the stage. Each Beatle kissed her on the cheek, Paul put her crown on upside down and the group hurried away, pursued by fans. Millington was celebrating her birthday; many of her gifts were trampled on and her white dress torn. She told the *Northwich Guardian*, 'I wasn't very nervous – just raging mad at all the stupid people who couldn't control themselves.' Eight people were treated by the St John Ambulance and a loudspeaker stand crashed to the ground slightly injuring 15-year-old Arlene Anderton of the Ormskirk dancing troupe.

Heavy thunderstorms broke at 5pm. Lewis drove the group to the Memorial Hall, known locally as 'The Morgue', for their evening performance, supported by the Cadillacs (who failed to show) and the Psychos. Ringo, whose birthday was the next day, was greeted by hundreds of presents, including the now perfunctory supply of Jelly Babies. He and Paul realised they had left their stage jackets back in Liverpool and made the hour-long trip home to get them. Bob Gannon, the Psychos' manager, was given a pile of autograph books and, in his own words, 'had the temerity to go in the Beatles dressing room and ask them to sign them. They all did except George who was in a corner strumming his guitar. Paul was very polite and gave me a cigarette and I remember Ringo's stool broke and he had to borrow our drummer's.' The Psychos' guitarist Chris Ackerley recalled the Beatles opening their set with 'There's A Place'. He said Ringo produced a wooden crate of beer – probably brown ale – and invited them to have a drink. He chatted with George for a while, asking what would happen if his guitar (it was a Gretsch White Falcon – even though it was black) was accidentally dropped and what it would cost to replace it. George replied, 'Don't worry about it. Gretsch will have one on my doorstep in the morning.'

At evening's end, Lewis, in his usual dinner jacket and black bow tie, came onstage – as he always did – to announce the numbers of the buses outside for the crowds to catch. A 'Policemen on Beatle duty were there,' recalled Lewis, 'and police cars on the ready were conveniently parked nearby. This gave weight to the idea that the Beatles would leave via the stage door. But the plan was to bring them out down the steps by the stage, into the auditorium and slip them out quickly through the emergency exit to a waiting car.' Nonetheless it was a relatively mild affair compared with the afternoon scenes in Verdin Park.

> ❮ I was a member of the Psychos who played as the support group that night. The group stemmed from our school days and consisted of myself on bass, Chris Ackerley on guitar, Barry Marshall on drums, who was a psychiatric nurse in Macclesfield, and Tony O'Hare on piano and saxophone. I don't remember too much about the actual evening, although I recall Chris went into the Beatles' dressing room because John Lennon had broken a string and didn't have a spare. Chris did and was asked to put it on for him.
>
> I do remember the noise of the screaming girls. It was absolutely deafening and all they had for a PA was a small Vox system, about three hundred watts max. It was the one where the column speakers were on a sloping stand on the stage. I think the system had 4' x 10' speakers, hardly adequate for the size of the room and drowned out by the noise.
>
> I was very impressed by their presentation, not only the suits they wore but the musical presentation was slick and very professional. Many groups today could learn a lot about the right way to put on a show. The whole set was well rehearsed and slick. No messing about between songs and McCartney was obviously the musical director. They all knew what the next song was and all Paul did was count in by tapping his boot heel on the stage. I was very impressed with this and even though I have played in, and seen, quite a few groups in my time, I have never seen anyone do that.
>
> I auditioned for the Fourmost and actually met Brian Epstein. I was offered the job but wimped out – I wasn't ready I suppose. Eventually I joined the Black Abbots comedy vocal group of Russ Abbot fame and eventually went back to my roots and developed a solo guitar vocal act which I still do today in Jersey where I live – some fifty years on. ❯
>
> **TONY HEART, CHARTER ANGLING BOAT SKIPPER, ST HELIER, JERSEY**

SUNDAY 7 JULY

Ringo celebrated his 23rd birthday at home in Liverpool. In the afternoon, the group drove to Blackpool for two shows at the ABC at 6pm and 8.15pm. The famed resort on the north-west coast of Lancashire was already in full swing: Morecambe and Wise, Matt Monro, Lena Martell and Paul Burnett were appearing at the North Pier Pavilion; the Big Star Show with the Karl Denver Trio, Eden Kane, Marty Wilde, Julie Grant, Daryl Quist, the Flee-Rekkers and Larry Burns at the South Pier; Albert Modley, Don Arrol, the Mudlarks and Barbara Law at the Central Pier; David Whitfield, Pinky and Perky, the Vernons Girls and the Dallas Boys at the Winter Gardens; the Billy Cotton Band Show with guest star Jimmy Edwards at the Opera House; Jimmy Clitheroe at the Grand Theatre; and, in his fourth decade,

Reginald Dixon playing the organ at the Tower Ballroom. For those who wanted even more entertainment, there was wrestling on Sunday nights at the Tower Circus.

With tickets priced between 6/6 and 9/6, the Beatles topped a bill with support from the Brook Brothers, George Meaton, Erkey Grant, the Terry Young Combo and the Fourmost (although incorrectly credited as the Four Mosts on the poster) and Jack Douglas, who had become a well-known figure as a regular on the BBC-TV children's show *Crackerjack*, compèring. Their Blackpool debut was announced in the local paper with a small piece about how blondes would stand a good chance with the group. Asked the type of girls they like, they commented – 'Blonde and intelligent' – John; 'Blonde, smallish' – George; 'Blonde, 5 ft 5 in, well built' – Ringo. Only Paul deviated, offering 'Any except soft ones.'

Fans Susan Whitehead and Sylvia Robinson brought a white squeaky dog for Ringo, while four pupils from Southport High School for Girls brought a card signed by sixty-five girls and a birthday cake. A fan also brought Julie Grant a fluffy yellow poodle won on a bingo stall that Grant named Ringo. 'Well, it rhymes with bingo doesn't it,' she commented.

The Beatles used Cliff Richard's dressing room. He was performing at the ABC throughout the summer with the Shadows. Sunday was their day off. The singer's promo cards were sitting on a dressing-room table, which the group showered on fans below, most of whom were chanting 'Happy Birthday'. No doubt confusion reigned. Ringo, at the suggestion of Brian Epstein, showed his face at the window, even though during the group's Sunday appearances in Blackpool, he enjoyed watching the western series *Laramie* on BBC-TV far more. The group were interviewed backstage by Kerstin McClure of the *Evening Gazette*. Ringo told her that he'd received 'several hundred birthday cards and I don't know how many presents'. George said that the group had not quite got used to their sky-rocketing success. 'We still haven't bought any new cars for example.' He had.

The Shadows watched the second show. Afterwards, the Beatles went to a party hosted by Hank Marvin and Brian Bennett at the house the two rented during their summer season. Marty Wilde, who had appeared at the South Pier, met the group for the first time at the party. 'They really are a modest group,' he said, 'very intelligent and they know exactly what they're doing over music.'

> ❝ I was appearing in the summer season show on the South Pier in Blackpool 1963 and was invited by Gerry Marsden on my day off to come and see the Beatles' show at the ABC Cinema. I had been born in Blackpool, but grew up in Leeds. I joined a dance group and took opera lessons with Madame Stiles Allen, who had taught Julie Andrews. I was asked to sing at the bar mitzvah of my dad's attorney, Julian Grant. Frankie Vaughan happened to be there and he heard me sing 'Moon River'. Afterwards he asked me to meet with his manager Eric Easton in London. Eric signed me on the spot to a five-year contract and immediately to took me to Pye Records, who appointed Tony Hatch to be my producer. They didn't like my real name – Vivien Foreman – so it was changed to Julie Grant, a play on my dad's attorney's name. I had had a hit with 'Up On The Roof' at the beginning of 1963 and was appearing on *Thank Your Lucky Stars* promoting the follow-up 'Count On Me' in April when I met Gerry.
>
>
>
> We got on really well and so when I was appearing on the South Pier in the summer he invited me to go and see the Beatles, and went to their first show there with my sister. Paul's dad was there and we stood in the back of the auditorium. You couldn't hear a thing. They could have been singing the phone book and you wouldn't have known. Paul's dad said, 'Can't hear a bloody thing. What a waste of time this is' in his thick Liverpool accent.
>
> After the show Gerry brought me backstage and that's when I first met the lads. It was Richie's

birthday so there was a cake, and that's the first time I met Brian – a real gentleman. Dapper with a beautiful leather briefcase. From it he handed out envelopes with their wages and George said, 'There's not very much here, Brian.' He said, 'You just bought a Jaguar.' Later I asked Brian if he could do me a favour and get me their autographs. He said, 'No problem,' and he opened his briefcase and out came four individual pictures done by Astrid [Kirchherr] and they all signed them to me. The biro was running out and so John, Paul and Richie signed using Brian's fountain pen. I treasure the photos to this day.

My birthday's on the 12th, so I invited them to my party, but they couldn't make it. But two weeks later, John and George came to the apartment, which my parents had rented for three months while I was doing the summer season. I had gone to see the show and afterwards we escaped over the roof with Neil Aspinall. They had to go back to Liverpool while I went back to the apartment. I told my mum and dad a couple of the lads were coming, but by the time eleven o'clock came around they hadn't arrived so my mum said, 'We might as well go to bed. They're not going to bloody show up. It's too late.' I said, 'No you've got to give them time, they had to go to Liverpool.' So, we're waiting – it was midnight. 'OK' she said, 'that's it – I'm off to bed.' So I took my wig off – I always wore wigs onstage in those days – and went into my bedroom. I then heard a car horn outside. I looked out of my window and saw a silvery grey-blue Jaguar, which George had just bought. I let them in and we ate a chocolate cake my mum had made earlier that day – John ate most of it, while George taught me how to play 'A Taste Of Honey' on this crappy little guitar I had. That's still the only thing I know how to play. I asked them if they would sign my autograph book and then pasted part of the doily the cake was on to the bottom of the page. Anyway, I consequently went a couple more times to see their show. We all got along like a house on fire. **J**

JULIE GRANT-CONNELLY, ENTERTAINMENT AGENT, GILFORD, NEW HAMPSHIRE, USA

MONDAY 8 JULY

The group set out on one of their longest drives of the year, a more than 300-mile journey to Margate on the north-east coast of Kent, where they began a week-long engagement, twice nightly at 6.30pm and 8.45pm at the Winter Gardens in Fort Crescent. The poster outside the venue read 'Britain's Fabulous Disc Stars – The Beatles – Billy J. Kramer with the Dakotas – Dean Rogers – Britain's Brightest Comedy Star Derek Roy – The Pan Yue Jen Troupe – The Lana Sisters – Reserved Seats 8/6 7/- 5/6 Guaranteed Unreserved 3/-'. Their set list for the week was 'Roll Over Beethoven', 'Thank You Girl', 'Chains', 'Please Please Me', 'A Taste Of Honey', 'I Saw Her Standing There', 'Baby It's You', 'From Me To You' and 'Twist And Shout'.

They had acquired new Vox amps following a visit to the company's headquarters at Jennings Musical Industries in nearby Dartford which they used for the first time during the week. 'We gave them whatever they wanted,' said Vox's Dick Denney, 'no questions asked.' They stayed at the Beresford Hotel in nearby Birchington-on-Sea. Sean O'Mahony and photographer Leslie Bryce spent the week collecting material for the first edition of *The Beatles Book*. Bryce took a photo of John placing the stylus on a copy of the *Twist And Shout* EP.

The *Isle of Thanet Gazette*'s reviewer saw the second performance and found them 'too loud' for his or her 'sensitive ears', noting that several older members of the audience made 'their exits discreetly before the performance was over'. 'The noise,' the reviewer commented, 'is indescribable, and throughout their playing and singing there is a continuous roar of squealing, howling, shouting and stamping of feet from the youngsters in the audience which drowns the so-called music from the stage, and believe me that is loud enough.'

❝ In the summer of 1963, my brother Vincent said he had a couple of tickets to see the Beatles at the Winter Gardens, and would I like to go? I'm not sure I even knew who they were, but I agreed to go with him. And my goodness, I never looked back! I knew Cliff and the Shadows were good, but I forgot about them after I'd seen the Beatles! We were absolutely knocked out by them. We couldn't wait for their new LPs to come out. We didn't have far to go to get to the Winter Gardens. We lived in Durban Road, by Drapers Mills School, in Cliftonville. I can't remember how we got there, but I think we probably walked. I don't think I had even bought any of their records before I saw them. Once I'd seen them, it was just 'Wow!' I bought them all. What annoyed me was the

noise. Oh the noise! [Fans] were banging their feet and screaming all the way through it. There was no need to. Why did they do that? I wanted to hear them. Why scream? I've read that in some places they couldn't even hear themselves play their own instruments.

The first time we didn't have tickets. Vincent and I just went up to the theatre and stood outside listening to the music. We were standing, probably near the end, and this couple came out and said there was no one on the door, so we could probably just go in. We just walked in and saw them for a few minutes for nothing! Vincent had paid 8/6 for the tickets for the night we went, then I went with Leonard Hayward, a friend of the family, later in the week for 3/6. I don't know how we got the tickets, probably he did. We were nearer the back then, more or less hanging on the windowsill. When I went with my brother, we went round the side afterwards, and he said, 'Well they won't come out here,' so we went round the back, and there was this blue car, and they had just got into it. I ran up to the car and said, 'Ringo, can I have your autograph?' and he signed it, but I really wanted John's. Having seen him onstage, he appealed to me, so he passed it over to John, and he signed his autograph, and he said, ''Ere you are luv,' just like that, and then went off with my pen! They were in the car about to leave, so I didn't manage to get Paul's or George's, and there were a few bouncers around. I still have the autographs. They're on my wall. John left the 'n' out in John, so it is unique! When he was sadly taken from us that was terrible. My son Lloyd was 3 months old and I was bringing him downstairs to feed him. I put the wireless on to hear John had been shot and was dead. I could not believe it. It seems like yesterday. I couldn't play his music at first. That was a very, very sad time. ❞

WENDY HOLLETT, HOUSEWIFE, MARGATE, KENT

TUESDAY 9 JULY

The Orchid Room in nearby Cliftonville opened its doors at 11am for a bingo session, while the Lido Theatre hosted the 'Miss Lovely Legs Competition' at the Bathing Pool in the afternoon. The Winter Gardens was back in action at 10.15 am with its 'Dancing Waters' in the New Sun Lounge – 'The greatest of all fountain spectacles! Forty-five hundred Jets! Twenty-five hundred Gallons of Water! Fantastic Designs and Gorgeous Colours, Played to the Music of the World's Most Famous Orchestras – Magic Waters That Actually Dance!'

Maureen O'Grady and Fiona Adams travelled down from London. Adams took a series of photos, while George gave O'Grady a toy dog called George. John asked her to dry his hair, but she said no. John offered half a crown in payment, which was enough to change her mind – and which she still has. O'Grady and Adams missed their last train home and were put up in a hotel for the night by the group. They hitched a ride back to London with George the following morning.

' I was born in Eastbourne and moved to Margate in 1960. My father, who was a lawyer, got the job as Deputy Town Clerk there. My older sister Hilary used to buy all the pop papers and I read them when she was finished with them. I, like every teenager at the time, listened to Radio Luxembourg under the pillow and I guess that's where I first heard the Beatles. My first job was washing cutlery and picking carcasses of chickens in a hotel in Cliftonville during the 1962 Christmas season. In June of 1963, I was coming home on the bus and had this ominous feeling you have sometimes. I got home and my mother was panicking because she thought my father was having a heart attack. I ran next door to our neighbour, who was a gynecologist, and she came over and then called an ambulance. He died soon after, aged 49.

My mother and father were friends of Jack Green, the general manager of the Winter Gardens, and his wife through social functions they loved to attend. The council were pretty awful after my father died. They didn't want to pay for his outstanding holiday time and I think Jack felt pretty lousy about the way we had been treated. Seeing the Beatles that summer was a last-minute thing. Jack got in touch with my mum and said he could get us tickets if we wanted them. It was myself and my younger sister Trish who was 9 at the time and we had another ticket. There was a girl who lived nearby who was very overweight and introverted and never had friends or anything. So I said, 'Why don't we take her?' Jack came round to our house on Westbrook Avenue and drove us over to the Winter Gardens.

We had front row seats and the concert itself was pretty overwhelming. I'd never heard so much screaming. At the end of the show, someone came and ushered Trish and I through a door to the backstage area. The Beatles' dressing room was down a long corridor on the right-hand side. We went inside and it was very quiet – just them and us. Paul was very welcoming, George was quiet and shy, Ringo didn't say anything and basically ignored us and John sat there with a blanket over his head and we never saw him. To be honest, I can't remember much else. It was all too much. We were only in there for about ten minutes or so. They gave us 10" by 8" photographs which they'd all signed and off we went out again and Jack drove us home. I was at Clarendon House Grammar School for Girls and although many of my school friends went to see them that week, I think we were the only ones to meet them that night. Margate in those days was a wonderful place to grow up in. I met my future husband Ian at a youth club when I was 12. We used to go to the Rendezvous Club at Dreamland on Sunday nights. All the girls danced and all the boys stood on the outside and watched – as you did at that age. They used to have all sorts of groups and singers there. The town really did become the armpit of the south for a while. It was like it was frozen in a time warp, but it's coming alive again, with the Turner Gallery and the Old Town Hall has been turned into a museum. Dreamland, which holds so many wonderful memories, has just reopened, trying to revive its glory days as a classic funfair. It has one of the five remaining wooden roller coasters in the world. I still go back regularly to visit family and friends, including several other people who went to see the Beatles that week in July. '

JENNY WILKIN, OFFICE MANAGER, COLE HARBOR, NOVA SCOTIA, CANADA

WEDNESDAY 10 JULY

The group rose early, travelling to London to record two more episodes of *Pop Go The Beatles* at the Aeolian Hall studio. At the three-hour morning session, beginning at 10.30am, they recorded 'Sweet Little Sixteen', 'A Taste Of Honey' (the sixth time they had recorded the song for the BBC), 'Nothin' Shakin' (But The Leaves On The Trees)' (originally recorded by Eddie Fontaine in 1958 and covered by Craig Douglas), 'Love Me Do', 'Lonesome Tears In My Eyes' (recorded by Johnny Burnette and His Rock and Roll Trio in 1957), and 'So How Come (No One Loves Me)' (a Felice and Boudleaux Bryant song written for the Everly Brothers). Their guests for the sixth episode – which was broadcast on 23 July – were Carter-Lewis and the Southerners. Their drummer Bobby Graham is reported to have been offered the role of the Beatles' drummer before Ringo. 'Why would I want to join a band in Liverpool that nobody's ever heard of?'

Following a break for lunch, they returned to record another episode at 1.30pm. For the seventh episode – broadcast on 30 July – their guests were the Searchers, and they performed 'Memphis, Tennessee' (which they had previously recorded on their first ever radio show), 'Do You Want To Know A Secret' (Billy J. Kramer's version of which had just dropped out of the Top 10), 'Till There Was You,' Carl Perkins' 'Matchbox,' the Marvelettes' 1961 US hit 'Please Mister Postman' (both of which Pete Best had taken lead vocals on when he was with the group) and 'The Hippy Hippy Shake' (which gave the Swinging Blue Jeans their biggest hit, peaking at number two in January 1964, held off the top by 'I Want To Hold Your Hand'). After finishing recording around 3.30pm, they made the two-hour return trip to Margate for the evening's two concerts.

❛ My family moved down to Margate from Birmingham when I was 3 years old, and as a lot of people did in those days, ran a guest house. It was just after the war and they'd read in the paper that this was the life – to live by the seaside. Ours was in the centre of the town by the clock tower. When we were full, the guest house held twenty-seven guests, so it was a lot of hard work. When I was 15 we gave it up, and moved to a house in the next road and my father started up a building business. I went to school locally at Clarendon House Grammar School in Ramsgate, followed by Thanet College, also in Ramsgate. To me it was all about the music in the early '60s. If I wasn't playing my 45s on my red-and-cream Dansette, I would be playing the juke boxes on the sea front. I would walk along there with friends, sometimes putting together our loose change to play another record. They always put the juke boxes near the doors so that the music would carry outside. When I was away on a course with the bank one week, my dad decorated my bedroom and bought me a radiogram. That was the living end! My mother would shout up, 'Turn that thing off, I can't stand another minute!'

In the summer of '63 the Beatles came for a whole week! I had left college that summer and joined Barclays Bank, enjoying having a bit of money to buy tickets with and Mary Quant dresses. My mother managed to get tickets for me and my best friend Gail to see them. We lived within walking distance of the Winter Gardens, so Gail took the bus into town and came to my house on Eaton Road. We were both wearing shift dresses, and set off to walk along to the harbour, then along the promenade to the back of the Gardens. The crowds outside were amazing. You could go in by the top entrance which was up on the main crescent, or you could go in through the back doors, which is the way we went. We had great seats, in the second or third row, but no one was sitting down! We had an aisle seat, and the one next to it, but when the Beatles came on I just remember getting up and stepping into the aisle dancing and screaming! There was a lot of screaming. When we came out, you couldn't move. It was phenomenal. Even now I think, 'Gosh, that was a little bit of history right there.' They were staying at the Beresford, about 5 miles out of Margate. When we could, we would go and sit outside and scream. They would open the windows and occasionally would send down one of their minions to pick out a few girls who would then be invited up to the room. My friends and I weren't brave enough to push ourselves to the front, so we were never chosen! The Winter Gardens is still going strong, and my local group, the Margate Operatic Society have appeared there many times over the last thirty years. Each time I walk up on to that stage, I stop in the middle and think, 'Yes, this is where John Lennon stood.' ❜

ANNIE YORATH, MARKETING COORDINATOR, WESTBROOK, MARGATE, KENT

THURSDAY 11 JULY

'From Me To You' dropped out of the *Disc* and *NRM* Top 10s to numbers 14 and 13 respectively. *Record Retailer* revealed that the group's new single, 'She Loves You', would be released on 23 August and that the EP *Twist And Shout* would be released on Friday. An EMI spokesman told the paper, 'Ever since we notified dealers orders have been flooding in. At the moment we have advance orders for over fifty thousand copies – one of the highest ever for an EP.' *The Stage* reported that fans were having a beetle tattooed on to their arms so they could join clubs named after the group. A couple of months later a teen was spotted in Upper Cwmbran with one tattooed on his forehead. A group of schoolboys were seen struggling near the post office in Victoria Street in Liverpool with a card measuring 3' by 2' made of hardboard. The pupils from the Liverpool Institute intended mailing the card to Brian Matthew requesting he play 'Thank You Girl' on *Saturday Club*. That evening, the group played their fourth night at the Winter Gardens while Brian Poole and the Tremeloes and Johnny Kidd and the Pirates were in town for a one-night stand at the Ballroom in Dreamland.

❛ Hard to imagine now but Margate was a lively seaside resort in those pre-cheap, foreign package holidays. Even in the winter there was a lively music scene thanks mostly to the Dreamland Ballroom which was 500 yards from where I lived. Every Saturday there was a guest star chart group and they all played there. Sunday was for up-and-coming groups and where Brian Poole and the Tremeloes were regarded as an up-and-coming group. Even before they had hits, the queue to see them stretched along the sea front. In the summer they put on extra nights but the Fabs never played there.

So imagine our surprise and delight when it was announced the Beatles would play there not just for one day but a week. I don't remember getting my ticket as a problem. In those days you just stood in an orderly line at the ticket office. Unlike today when ticket touts and block bookers appear to snap up tickets as soon as the box offices open. At work and in the pubs it was all people were talking about. I had a ticket for about three rows back. The screaming was so loud you couldn't hear much of what they sang, the only time the crowd was quiet was when John shouted, 'Shut up.' All too soon it was over but at least I can say I was there. The wooden podium that Ringo nailed his drums to (or his roadie) is still on the stage there. How I wish I had known how important the event would be, like most things we didn't realise we were part of history. If only we had digital cameras then. Didn't even make a note of the songs set. ❜

ROGER DAY, BROADCASTER, MAIDSTONE, KENT

FRIDAY 12 JULY

Beatles fans buying the latest issue of *Boyfriend* read about 'The Day We Took Off', in which Paul described their performance on Radio Luxembourg's *The Friday Spectacular* on 21 January. No doubt their eye caught the headline 'LUNCH WITH THE BEATLES! The opportunity of a lifetime! A chance to meet the most sought-after group anywhere! The prize of this fabulous competition is a lunch-date with the Beatles followed by a visit to a recording studio! Entries must be made by post card and include a song and no more than twenty-five words. (Closing date July 27th.)' The magazine also published some quotes from the group, 'The trouble is that our fans think we have a wonderfully easy life – just two shows a day, twenty minutes each show. They don't realise that our day begins at about ten in the morning with interviews, recordings and suit fittings. Ah, that reminds me – we must get a new suit. Fancy something different this time, don't you, Paul?' – Ringo. 'Well, I must admit that we couldn't keep going without all of the Jelly Babies that are thrust upon us by the girls. Although some of us,' (looking at the two main addicts John and George) 'are a little greedy at times, aren't they Ringo?' – Paul. 'Yeah! As I was saying, I think we're so busy we never get out of the theatres till after twelve usually. The girls are so persistent,' he said giving a ghoulish laugh. 'And that's another thing, you can't stand having your hair cut, can you, Ringo?' – George. 'You're only jealous 'cos my hair is longer than yours' – Ringo. 'Listen, what the eye doesn't see the harm doesn't grieve over. But I must say I can't see very far without them (his glasses). I can't even see the girls when they start running towards us – but I just follow George and he leads me to them!' – John.

The group's first EP, *Twist And Shout*, selling for 10/9, was released with advance orders of sixty thousand. An EMI spokesman said, 'Requests for the Beatles version of the song have been building for some time. They reached such a pitch that a special release was the only answer.' The *NME* wrote, 'Beatles go to town with the hit tune of the moment – 'Twist And Shout', plus the Kramer hit, 'Do You Want To Know A Secret'. And for very good measure, they add 'A Taste Of Honey' and 'There's A Place'!' Coincidentally – or not – a less desirable EP, released 'by popular demand' according to Polydor, with Tony Sheridan, featuring 'My Bonnie', 'Cry For A Shadow', 'The Saints' and 'Why' hit the shops. *Disc* wrote, 'Beatles Need Not Be Ashamed Of These Old Ones'. 'From Me To You' dropped out of the *NME* Top 10 after twelve weeks, falling to number 15.

Melody Maker reported that John was going through an 'Aussie kick' calling everybody 'cobber'. From 'From Me To You' dropped to number 12 in the paper's chart. The group visited a dentist in Margate. John had two teeth removed, George one, as well as two fillings, while Ringo proudly declared that all he had was a wash and brush-up. After returning to hotel, the *NME*'s Mike Butcher interviewed them in the lounge. After lunch they went swimming in the hotel pool, along with several other members of the week's Winter Gardens bill. Butcher was also invited, but unfortunately broke his toe. In between the two evening shows, George played some J. S. Bach on his guitar and listened to LPs by the Miracles and Mary Wells on the record player in their dressing room. A new concert promotion company, NEMS Presentations Limited, was incorporated.

❛ I remember those years like they were only last year. I was 14 years old, going to the Ursuline Convent in Westgate-on-Sea. It felt like one day I am quietly adoring Billy Fury, being a member of his Fan Club and collecting all his pictures to put in my many scrapbooks, and then POW ... THE BEATLES appeared on our telly and our lives changed forever. We all went mad for the Fab Four and I became a member of their Fan Club, collecting every single picture I could of them, my most prized possessions. When we heard that they were coming down to the Winter Gardens in Margate to do a show, we just went berserk. Luckily my father managed to get three tickets for me, my sister Trudi, and our friend Aileen. We were so excited, although Trudi, being nearly 17 years old, wasn't so 'madly in love' with them as I was, especially Paul.

In the afternoon I asked three of my friends from school, Melanie Roberts, Christine O'Callahan, and Olga Bedeski, if they wanted to see if we could get to meet the group at the Beresford Hotel, where I knew they were staying. Of course, the girls were up for it, as I was convinced that we would be able to. So, we all went down to Beresford Gap Beach, and had to climb round this large-spiked defence to stop people going round it, but we did manage it, with me going first and, being silly, I started to laugh as it was difficult and as the tide was in. It was either get round it or fall in the sea. Eventually we all did and climbed the steps that lead up through the cliff and up to the hotel grounds. But as we stealthily ran over the lawn, we were seen and got shouted at, so we just rushed back down the tunnel to the promenade, and of course back round the spiked thing. I felt so sorry for Melanie, Christine and Olga, as they couldn't afford to go to the show in the evening, and they had to get home to Whitstable. But I did promise that I would get them a signed picture of the group if I possibly could.

That evening our father dropped us off at the door of the Winter Gardens. Luckily, we didn't have to queue, like most of the kids at the door, we were so lucky and soon sat down in our fifth row back middle seats with great views. Then the lights changed and the Beatles walked onto the stage, and the whole theatre just erupted with this horrendous noise of manic screaming. It made me so frightened as I had never heard anything like it in my life. Everyone was stirred up into a frenzy and when they started to sing we never heard one note. I just sat there quietly at first not knowing what to do but as Trudi and Aileen had started to scream as well, I thought I might as well also. So we just sat and watched them. We certainly didn't hear one song, unfortunately, but it was a fantastic show and something that I will never forget. There certainly wasn't any chance of getting an autograph from them, as everyone wanted to see them, so we slowly made our way back up the stairs, to find our father waiting for us in his car.

The next day I asked Trudi, and her then boyfriend Roger, if they would come down to the Beresford with me just to see if I could get any of my many photos signed. I practically begged them, but they did agree to go with me. We went into the bar and sat over in the lounge part, and after only a few minutes, George and Ringo, walked in and stood at the bar, followed very quickly by Paul and John. I became so nervous – very unlike me at the time, but I had to practically force myself to move, and I was shaking from head to toe. I walked over to them and just said very squeakily, 'Please could you sign some of my photos for me and my friends please?' to which to my surprise they just said, 'Sure we can' and proceeded to sign lots of pics for me, and they were so nice and normal towards me, asking me if I'd seen their show, and I said, 'Yes. Last night. But, unfortunately, we didn't hear you sing a note because of the screaming,' to which they laughed and said, 'Yes. It was pretty noisy' but asked if I'd enjoyed it. 'Of course,' I said, laughing, and said my friends at school will be so jealous with meeting them and signing all my photos. I really wanted to ask Paul if I could give him a kiss – but I wasn't brave enough. I let Melanie, Christine and Olga have a picture each and put the rest in my scrapbooks, over the next two years I collected thousands of photos of the boys. And, of course, bought as many of their records that I possibly could. To say the Beatles changed my life is very true, just adoring those four fabulous Beatles. I seemed to grow up a lot that year, my silly childhood love of Billy Fury was something very different from how I felt for the Beatles and I never had a crush on any other group. ❜

NINA LE MAY, PHARMACEUTICAL ASSISTANT, MARGATE, KENT

SATURDAY 13 JULY

The week of performances in Margate, seen by a total of twenty thousand fans, came to an end at the Winter Gardens. All was not lost for those unable to get tickets. The glorious weather meant the Gardens' windows remained open during the shows. One fan recalled, 'The tide must have been out because there were people on the beach dancing. Every night after that we went down there to listen and dance on the promenade. It was a lovely summer. The noise coming out was incredible, and I remember

John Lennon belting out 'Twist And Shout', and the whole beach went wild! All we cared about was that they were there, and we were there.' In between performances, theatre staff managed to marshal thirty-four hundred fans in and out of the venue in twenty minutes, with the second show only beginning five minutes late.

❝ Margate was a marvellous place to spend your childhood. My mother ran a little guest house called Appledean. It had seven bedrooms and she used to let six of them out during the season. My sisters and I slept in the seventh, and Mum and Dad slept in the private sitting room. Of course, we all had to help on change over days and serving at the tables. The same people would come down every year – Margate was a popular seaside resort at the time. There was plenty to do in the town – Dreamland Funfair and Dance Hall, and the Winter Gardens, the bowling alley, and numerous coffee bars. The coffee bars would stay open late – there was Pelosi's and Ricco's, where you could drink frothy coffees and listen to the juke box. I was 13 in the summer of 1963, and a huge fan of the Beatles. My older sisters were into Elvis, but it wasn't until the groups came along in the early '60s that I really got into music. I'd go down to Thornton Bobby's, the music shop in Cliftonville, to listen to the records in the booths before buying them.

Our parents had taken us to shows at the Winter Gardens when we were young, but I had never been to a music concert there. We heard the Beatles were coming down for a week and were so excited. Mum knew someone who worked at the venue and managed to get tickets for me, my cousin Rita, and my school friend Jenny. The Winter Gardens are on the edge of Margate by Cliftonville where we lived, so it was only a ten-minute walk away. Our seats were in the second row! I don't know whether Mum got the tickets from the person she knew or if she had to queue, but we were thrilled to be there. George was my favourite! Everyone was screaming and jumping up and down. I'd never experienced anything like it. A security guard who also knew Mum came to find us after the show and took us backstage. The boys didn't really say much to us other than 'Hello' and they signed our autographs books and programmes. Dad came to pick us up as he didn't want us to walk home in the dark, and as you can imagine, we were full of it. We were buzzing. Such excitement! I knew the week was a sell-out, but I also knew that they didn't sell some of the seats on the balcony as you couldn't see the stage from them, so my sister and I went on the last night and sat in one of the seats on the balcony. I can't put into words how fantastic it was. After that it was all Beatlemania. I had pictures of them everywhere, and even had Beatles talcum powder! I followed them through all their musical changes and was heartbroken when they broke up. We went to New York a few years ago and went to Strawberry Fields to see John's memorial. It was so sad. ❞

BARBARA WATLER, MACHINIST, MARGATE, KENT

SUNDAY 14 JULY

The group left Margate for the six-hour drive north along the Thanet Way and through the Blackwall Tunnel for the evening's two performances at 6pm and 8.15pm at the ABC in Blackpool. Tickets sold for between 6/6 and 9/6. The group were supported by the Countrymen, Chas McDevitt and Shirley Douglas, Colin Day, the Red Price Combo and the shows were compèred by Jack Douglas. Afterwards, they stayed at the Imperial Hotel.

❝ Blackpool in the glorious summer of 1963. It was the swinging '60s. I was 17 and on holiday with my boyfriend, strolling down Blackpool's Golden Mile, holding hands and eating ice cream in Kiss-Me-Quick hats. We rode the yellow-and-red open-top electric trams down the promenade, screamed on the Big Dipper roller coaster at the Pleasure Beach fun fair and stole sun-warmed kisses on the Ghost Train. We spent sunny days on the beach (me in my first-ever bikini – navy with white polka dots). We danced the night away in the Winter Gardens Ballroom and climbed to the top of the famous Blackpool Tower. It seemed as though all the popular groups were appearing in Blackpool that week. I remember going to see the Karl Denver Trio and Marty Wilde and a matinee at the End Of The Pier Theatre with Des O'Connor and Peter Gordeno and his dancers.

But the highlight of the week for us was getting tickets to see the Beatles live onstage at the newly re-opened ABC. They were appearing on the Sunday night, so we had to stay on an extra day. Not a hardship. We would have happily slept on the beach rather than miss the chance to see them! Anticipation turned to frenzy once the Beatles came onstage. It was Beatlemania at its best. Girls stood on seats screaming and crying, pulling at their hair and shouting for their favourite. St John Ambulance volunteers rushed to help girls so overcome with emotion they were nearly fainting. I remember John Lennon yelling through his microphone for quiet before they gave up and belted out their songs at full volume, that had us dancing in the aisles and screaming for more. We would have kept them there forever if we could. It was a magical fantastic night I never wanted to end and one I have never forgotten. ❞

CHRISSY SENIOR, DRAMATHERAPIST, KINGSTON UPON HULL, YORKSHIRE

MONDAY 15 JULY

Tickets for the group's last-ever show at the Cavern, scheduled for 3 August, went on sale. It was sold out within half an hour.

Paul, pleading guilty by letter, was fined £15 for speeding and a further £2 for failing to produce his licence and insurance at Birkenhead Magistrates Court. In his letter of mitigation to the court, he wrote, 'There were people following us in a van so in an attempt to escape these people I drove faster and exceeded the speed limit. I thought I was still being followed when I was stopped by the constable. When I told him my excuse, he refused to believe me and told me that I had no excuse. He later asked what my 'excuse' was. Being unable to take my licence into the police station myself, I asked my father to do this for me but was later told that I had to do it in person. When I found this out, I was already involved in a tour of Britain which did not finish for three weeks.' Prosecutor Inspector J. H. McArdle revealed that Paul had had a previous speeding conviction earlier in the year. Following the fine, Brian Epstein said, 'When the group leave a theatre, a procession of fans often follows them. In future I will ask them to travel by coach when they are on tour.'

George popped round to Mendips, where he and John had fun recording on his recently acquired portable tape recorder. A few weeks later George told a reporter, 'Just lately we've all been having a bit of fun with a tape recorder. John writes down the words – you can't really call it poetry or verse – and then I read it out on the tape. It's weird stuff. I'm not sure that anybody else would know what it's all about.' Epstein took time to write to George's sister Louise in the US, telling her he would be sending three copies of *Please Please Me* and four of 'From Me To You'. The group met with Don Haworth from BBC-TV Manchester to discuss the possibility of a making a half-hour documentary on the group and the Merseybeat scene. Haworth had previously been an associate producer on BBC-TV's *Panorama*. In the evening, George and Ringo went to see Cliff Richard and the Shadows in Blackpool.

❛ I grew up in Anfield, near the football ground, and one day when we were about 15 or 16, a couple of boys who lived down the road said they were going to the Cavern to see this group. We hadn't heard of them but went along with them anyway and became addicted. By that time, I had left school and was working in a photographic studio called Jerome's, about ten minutes up the road from the Cavern. I worked there part-time whilst I studied at art school in Manchester. The studio closed for lunch from 12pm till 1.30, so we had an hour and a half for lunch. I would run all the way down the hill, not caring about eating, just wanting to hear the music. We went every other day during the week, and even took a week off in the summer so that we could go to the Cavern at lunch time, and in the evening. That was our holiday – a week in the Cavern! You couldn't hide where you had been – you would smell of the Cavern – not a very pleasant one. There was never any trouble there, no nastiness at all. I don't remember a single altercation. You could only get Coke and a hot dog though, no alcohol. But people in the main were very good-natured – they were more interested in the music. Most of the people who went there were teenagers.

We knew that it was only a matter of time before the Beatles would no longer be playing at the Cavern. So we were there in the queue when the tickets went on sale for a final show on August Bank Holiday. Just having a ticket wouldn't guarantee getting a good seat so on the day my friend Diane and I caught the first bus into town to get 'prime spec' in the queue. Our mothers thought we were mad. We'd dyed black in the old bath on the stove every item we were wearing. Our prowess with dye had not improved, as we judged by the expressions of the dockers who also awaited the first bus. The conductor, whose 'God, girls, who got you ready?' raised a guffaw from our fellow travellers as we boarded the bus, could not dampen our spirits. We thought we looked great and tonight we'd see the Beatles!

When we arrived, we were guaranteed a seat in the front row – there were only eight in front of us. They'd slept out all night and were hungry, so we gave them our sandwiches. They swore they'd be receiving their butties from a friend who couldn't sleep out, so were on 'rations' in exchange for a place saved in the queue. By noon we were about thirty back, the people who'd had spaces saved also did the same for other less hardy friends and we kept shuffling backwards. So much for the front row! By one o'clock we were starving. The promised rations hadn't arrived and we daren't leave the queue to buy more. But luck was with us – the four boys behind us had sandwiches, so we ingratiated ourselves and they grudgingly shared their curled-up egg sandwiches with us. It was a hot day – 'sarnies' rarely travel well stuffed in a duffle coat pocket, but we were in no position to complain. The queue had extended up Mathew Street into North John Street and continued into Victoria Street. People walked up and down to find friends in order to 'bunk in' further up. It was so hot we discarded our coats and sat on them in the dusty street.

It would be the last time I saw the group play live. I went to work for Peter Kaye in 1967. There were two branches of Peter Kaye Photography in Liverpool in the early '60s, one in the town centre, and one on the main road Brian Epstein travelled along to get to work. He spotted the studio and called in one day to ask the boss if he would photograph his group. At the time a chap called Les Chadwick worked there and was a good friend of Bill Harry [founder of *Mersey Beat*]. It was Les who took the first official photographs of them as a group. Les photographed all the local groups for *Mersey Beat*, and we had a vast collection of photographs. I'd always been interested in taking photographs and was employed originally to be the finishing re-toucher to do touch ups because I'd been to art school.

When I arrived, I happened upon a photograph of the Beatles in the waste bin. When I found out that Les had photographed the group I was very excited. I didn't know he had taken the original photographs of the group, and it was great because I was able to ask Peter and Les all about them. It was great working at the photographer's studio because we still did a lot of groups when I joined. We did a lot of work for *Mersey Beat*, and there was always something different happening. When Peter died, his widow decided to sell all the photos. They were sent to auction in around 1989 and were bought by Apple for £160,000. However, although we sold the negatives, we didn't sell the copyright. I live near Penny Lane, and hardly ever walk down there without seeing a bus full of tourists. They all take pictures of themselves at the sign that says Penny Lane. It still goes on. It's incredible, the impact the Beatles had on everyone. **"**

MARGARET ROBERTS, PHOTOGRAPHER, LIVERPOOL, MERSEYSIDE

TUESDAY 16 JULY

An EMI spokesman reported that sales of *Please Please Me* had passed one hundred thousand and the *Twist And Shout* EP had sold more than one hundred and fifty thousand copies since it went on sale the previous Friday. John talked to *Disc*, 'We're completely knocked out by it all, and never realised our combined sales were anything like this.'

The group headed back down to London to record the eighth, ninth and tenth episodes of *Pop Go The Beatles* at the Paris Studios. The first recording had been planned for 10.30am but was rescheduled to begin at 3pm. Rather than record the third show the following day, they opted to do all three in one day. At the first session they recorded 'I'm Gonna Sit Right Down And Cry (Over You)' (which they had heard listening to Elvis Presley's 1956 debut), 'Crying, Waiting, Hoping' (a Buddy Holly song the group had performed at their Decca audition and the only time they performed it on radio), 'Kansas City/Hey-Hey-Hey-Hey!' (a medley combining songs by Jerry Leiber and Mike Stoller and Little Richard), the Teddy Bears' 'To Know Him Is To Love Him' (requiring a change of gender from 'Him' to 'Her'), 'The Honeymoon Song' (a Mikis Theodorakis song written as the theme to the 1959 film *Honeymoon*) and 'Twist And Shout'. Except for 'Kansas City/Hey-Hey-Hey-Hey!' and 'Twist And Shout', this was the only time they performed these songs at the BBC. *Melody Maker*'s Chris Roberts, who was present at the recording, was asked to join in on the former. While the group were taking an hour-long break, the fifth episode of *Pop Go The Beatles*, recorded on 2 July, aired at 5pm, leaving out 'Three Cool Cats', 'Sweet Little Sixteen' and 'Ask Me Why'.

At 6pm, they began recording the second episode. They performed 'Long Tall Sally', 'Please Please Me', 'She Loves You' (the first opportunity for fans to hear the song on radio), 'You Really Got A Hold On Me', 'I'll Get You' and Ray Charles' 'I Got A Woman'. With only a fifteen-minute break, they continued their marathon at 8.45pm, performing Buddy Holly's 'Words Of Love' (which they subsequently recorded in September 1964 for the *Beatles For Sale* LP, 'Glad All Over' (a Carl Perkins' cover which had been in their live set since 1960), 'I Just Don't Understand' (a US Top 20 hit for Ann-Margret), '(There's A) Devil In Her Heart' (the B-side of a 1962 single by Detroit girl group the Donays, which they recorded at Abbey Road two days later) and Larry Williams' 'Slow Down'. By the time they finished recording at 10.30pm, they had recorded eighteen songs during the day. The three shows aired on 6, 13 and 20 August.

At one point during the sessions, Ringo took advantage of some down time and sat at the piano, playing a song he was working on called 'Don't Pass Me By'. It was finally committed to vinyl on the group's double LP *The Beatles* in 1968.

WEDNESDAY 17 JULY

The group recorded a session for an episode of *Easy Beat* at the Playhouse Theatre between 8.45pm and 9.45pm. Performing before a live studio audience, they played 'I Saw Her Standing There', a cover of Arthur Alexander's 'A Shot Of Rhythm And Blues' (the only live recording of the song they ever made), 'There's A Place' and 'Twist And Shout'. The show aired the following Sunday.

By now, fans had become aware of where recordings were taking place and started to show up in droves. One BBC doorman, a veteran of the El Alamein campaign, complained they got the brunt of the excited fans' behaviour. 'The lads show themselves and we get the knocks,' he said.

During their two-day stay in London, they were interviewed by *Disc*'s June Harris and *NRM*'s Peter Jones. They told Harris they were dumbfounded by the success of their first EP. 'I know people won't believe us when I say this is beyond anything we expected,' said John, while Paul commented, 'It's the royalty cheques that get me. We received one not so long for what seemed a huge lump and were told it was only part of our royalties. If that wasn't the total sum, I think I'll retire at the end of the year and go and live in the Mersey tunnel.'

THURSDAY 18 JULY

'Fantastic chart success – Beatles EP Hits 17!' exclaimed the headline of *Disc*. It reported that the *Twist And Shout* EP had sold more than one hundred and fifty thousand copies in less than a week and *Please Please Me* had passed the one hundred thousand marks in six weeks – second only to Elvis Presley's *Blue Hawaii*, which reached the target in little over a month. 'From Me To You' dropped to number 16 in the new Top 30. John's comments on *Juke Box Jury* a month earlier still rankled with some. The *Disc* post bag printed a letter from J. Hilton and J. Holden in Blackpool. 'How dare John Lennon criticise Elvis's latest record. He talked about originality but you can't really say that the Beatles are original. We are disgusted.'

A photo of the group was featured on the front page of the *NRM*, taken by Dezo Hoffmann. It appeared to show John sticking a biro into George's right ear. The paper reported that the *Twist And Shout* EP entered its EP chart at number 7, while 'From Me To You' dropped three places to number 16. Reader Ken Ward was particularly scathing about the group's version of 'Memphis Tennessee' on *Saturday Club*, 'Perhaps the biggest joke of all was when [they] started singing Peggy Lee. Sorry, did I say singing?'

Paul and George went to see Tony Barrow at his NEMS' office, bringing a copy of 'She Loves You' with them. At 7pm, in a session lasting three and three-quarter hours, the group began work on their second LP in Studio Two at Abbey Road. They recorded eleven takes of 'You Really Got A Hold On Me', seven takes of 'Money' (already familiar with fans after performances on *Saturday Club* and *Pop Go The Beatles*), six of '(There's A) Devil In Her Heart' and three of 'Till There Was You'. John upset Brian Epstein, who commented on Paul's vocal on 'Till There Was You'. John shot back, 'We'll make the records. You just go on counting your percentages.'

FRIDAY 19 JULY

The latest *NME* revealed that the *Twist And Shout* EP had entered the singles chart at number 13 – the first EP to have ever sold enough copies to do so – while 'From Me To You' held steady at number 15. The front page of the *Melody Maker* featured the headline, 'Beatles blast-off!' reporting that EMI had had orders of forty thousand within half an hour first thing Monday morning. 'From Me To You' dropped four places to number 16. Interviewed in the paper, Ringo said, 'Well I'm not very good as some of these top boys because I should really practice more than I do. I never tune my drums to anything in particular – just to what sounds right.'

Billy J. Kramer's new single was released, 'Bad To Me' with B-side 'I Call Your Name' – both tracks penned by Lennon and McCartney. Keith Fordyce's review in the *NME* revealed that the 'tune and tempo are both very catchy and the arrangement for the backing is first class.' He went on to write, 'I love the way that the words "there" and "fair" are rhymed with "fur"!' The *NRM* felt it would be 'a roaring great hit for sure. For absolute sure,' while *Disc* described it as 'very easy on the ear.'

After a night spent at the Hotel President in Russell Square, the group set off for North Wales – a four-plus-hour journey, taking them to the coastal town of Rhyl, Flintshire – for two shows at the Ritz Ballroom. Situated on the Promenade in part of the Alhambra Restaurant, it was the most popular dance hall on the North Wales coast at the time. It was somewhat short lived however, opening in 1955 and burning down in 1968. Their appearance followed almost a year to the day after their first show in the town – an inauspicious affair at the Regent Dansette located in the High Street above Burton's Tailor. A cocktail waitress brought drinks for the group into the green room. She tripped and spilled them on Paul.

SATURDAY 20 JULY

Diego Breuer, a waiter at the Westminster Hotel, recalled the Beatles 'were supposed to stay at the hotel but the management were worried about the fans so they did not. John, Paul and Ringo came in during the afternoon to pass the time before going to perform. I served them refreshments in the upstairs lounge and John asked me to sort the television for them which I did in exchange for their signatures for my wife.' During the day, George went to see his aunt Janey and uncle Jimmy in Broughton.

In the evening, the group played a second night at the Ritz Ballroom. David Roberts travelled by coach from Aberystwyth to see them. He recalled them coming through the front door and across the dance floor to get to the stage. 'They kicked off with 'I Saw Her Standing There' and the place erupted. The last number, 'Twist And Shout', was fantastic – everybody was singing and screaming. They had to cross the dance floor to leave.

This time everyone was ready and tried to make a grab for their favourite Beatle. They made it out minus a few buttons off their jackets.' Ringo had his hair pulled by an overzealous fan who refused to let go. 'She was gripping it real hard, trying to tear it out by the roots and I can feel it right now.' Afterwards, they drove back to Liverpool. Ringo went to the Blue Angel and stayed until the small hours.

> **'** My dad was from Llandecwyn in Wales where he grew up on a farm. He met my mum and they got married. My sister was born eleven years before me and my mum got poorly giving birth to me so I went to live in Llandecwyn with my grandparents for six or seven weeks. While I was there they noticed I wasn't moving my left arm. So when I went home, my mum took me to the doctor's where it was discovered I didn't have a left shoulder blade, but because my bones were still growing, they couldn't operate. When I was 8, they decided I was old enough to have an operation. So in the summer of 1963 I was taken into Gobowen Orthopediatric Hospital near Oswestry. We lived about four houses down from George Harrison's Uncle Jimmy and Auntie Janey who were brother and sister of George's father Harold. They were ever such little people. I remember when they walked past our house you could only just see them above the hedge. Janey had been talking to my mum and said she would get our George to sign his autograph and when he came down to see them, maybe he would come and see me in hospital. And my mum said, 'Oh she'd love that.' While I was in hospital he did go and see them and was planning to come to the hospital but ran out of time. So instead he gave them an autographed photograph of the Beatles to give to me, signed 'To Janet, Love' and then their names. When my mum came to see me, she said, 'George Harrison of the Beatles has been to see Janey and Jimmy and brought this for you.'
>
> After I was discharged and went home my dad and mum asked me what I wanted as a present for being a good girl and I said, 'A record player.' So they bought me a Dansette and my sister got me the Beatles' EP. That was the first record I had and she also bought me a Rolling Stones EP. When I left Broughton in 1980 to get married, Janey and Jimmy were still living there. I used to see them passing up and down going to the shops. Being in my teens and twenties, you didn't really talk to older people, but my mum and my dad used to chat with them quite often. I remember soon after moving, my mum telling me that a big posh car came to their house. Some years later my dad said, 'Do you want your stuff out of the attic?' I said, 'It's all right. Leave it there for now.' So then my mum died and years went on and my dad got another lady friend and then my dad died and, of course, I kept asking this lady friend, 'Could I have my things out of the attic?' She said, 'There's nothing up there,' and she was very awkward with me. I thought there's no way my dad would have thrown my things out. He was a hoarder if anything, but she told me there was nothing there. Anyway, last year she died and someone bought the house and they obviously went up into the attic. She contacted me and said, 'Are you Janet Evans that was?' I said, 'Yes.' She said, 'I'm living in 25 Mold Road and we've been up in the attic and we've found some things and they belong to you.' I knew there were things up there, but there was no Beatles picture. **'**
>
> JANET WADESON, HAIRDRESSER, BUCKLEY, FLINTSHIRE

SUNDAY 21 JULY

A s the group enjoyed a lie-in at their respective homes, Wednesday's recording of *Easy Beat* aired from 10.31am to 11.30am. A short article in the *Radio Times* commented that, 'The last time the Beatles appeared in *Easy Beat*, their fans filled the street outside the studio.' They might have been surprised to read in the *Sunday Mirror* that, according to Jack Bentley, Mitch Murray had helped them and many others to the top.

After Sunday lunch, they had a second meeting with BBC-TV Manchester's Don Haworth, before setting off for Blackpool at about 3.15pm for two performances at the Queen's Theatre. The venue was

263

hosting 'Putting on the Donegan' starring Lonnie Donegan, Miki and Griff, Des O'Connor, Jill Westlake, Peter Goodwright, the Clark Brothers, the Kestrels, the Tiller Girls and Ken Moule and the Orchestra for the summer. An estimated four thousand fans blocked the streets around the theatre on Bank Hey Street as the Beatles arrived at 4.45pm for the evening's two shows at 6pm and 8.10pm. Theatre manager Archie Stewart took the group up some ladders and scaffolding in a nearby builder's yard, across the roofs of adjoining buildings, to enter the theatre through a skylight. He later commented, 'This is the first time we have ever brought our stars in that way. I don't think I am very popular with the fans, but if the Beatles had gone in through the front they would have been mobbed.' John recalled, 'We might have got through the massed ranks of fans if we had been inside a tank or if we had been mounted on elephants, but any other way was impossible.' After the show, police using loudspeakers failed to disperse the crowd outside the stage door. The group stayed backstage eating fish and chips and drinking Coke, finally getting away at 1am, even though Stewart proclaimed that they had left 'long ago without any trouble at all'. He added, 'How I got them out is my little secret because I have other Sunday "pop" concerts coming up.'

❛ We were in a state of abject panic because it was already late on a Sunday night and we [the Fourmost] had to be down at Abbey Road to do our first recording on the following Wednesday afternoon, but we still did not have an A-side. Thankfully the Beatles came to our rescue and our immediate problem was solved by the timely assistance of John and George. The plan was that, after the show had finished, Brian O'Hara and I would meet up with them at Mendips. A red-eyed Brian and I arrived at the house and were shown into the front room. Then, in the cold early morning, with George on guitar and sporting exhausted and croaky voices, two sleepy Beatles sang a song into an old tape recorder. The song was 'Hello Little Girl' and it was a John Lennon composition that they had placed into our grateful hands. After thanking our friends, an extremely relieved pair of putative popsters crept wearily away into the gathering daylight. We realised that our group had to travel down to London the next day to record a song that we had never heard before. So I went home and worked out the chords etc. from the precious tape and then tried to get a little sleep. Our group had to do all the rehearsing whilst on the way down to London and to add just a little more unwanted tension to the affair, all of this work had to be completed for the recording session on the following afternoon. The actual session was in Studio Two and it lasted from 2.30pm until 6.45pm and the songs that we recorded were 'Hello Little Girl', 'Just In Case' and 'Little Egypt'. It was a tall order, but it produced our first hit record. ❜

BILLY HATTON, BASS GUITARIST, LIVERPOOL, MERSEYSIDE

MONDAY 22 JULY

The group drove to Weston-super-Mare in Somerset – a 200-mile trip to the south-west of England – to begin another Arthur Howes-presented six-night engagement at the town's eighteen hundred-seater Odeon on Walliscote Road. They were scheduled to play two shows nightly at 6.15pm and 8.30pm with Gerry and the Pacemakers, the Lana Sisters, the Sons of the Piltdown Men, Billy Baxter, Tommy Wallis and Beryl and Tommy Quickly. The latter was another Brian Epstein protégé who made his professional stage debut that evening.

While the Beatles were making their way to the town, so too were teenagers Barbara Herron and Joan McNulty, hitch-hiking their way from Liverpool to visit friends in Cheddar and see the group. At around 9.30pm, they were picked up by three men near Gloucester. Heading down the A370 to Weston, driver

Douglas Blunt turned left at the West Wick Roundabout towards Banwell. Two-and-a-half miles down the road on Wolvershill Road, the men forced the girls out of the car. Blunt produced a u410 shotgun from under his seat and attacked McNulty, while Edward Webb did the same to Herron. Herron bit him, and he then picked up an axe from the back of the car and attacked her, battering her skull. Webb then attacked McNulty. Colin White, the third man in the car, tried to stop them. They drove off leaving both girls for dead. Just after midnight, Captain John Gwyn of Pool Farm was awakened by knocking on his door. He found a bleeding McNulty. She was rushed to the Queen Alexandra Memorial Hospital in Weston-super-Mare, where she received twenty-eight stitches for her wounds. Gwyn went looking for Herron and found her lifeless body on a grass verge in Cannaway Lane.

❝ Back in July 1963 I was in a group called the Iveys. We had been playing a gig a few miles out of town at Rossholm School for Girls at Brent Knoll. After the gig, we made our way back to Weston. I was on my Triumph Tiger Cub motorbike with our drummer Bob Davies on the back, while rhythm guitarist Remo Ferrari was on his Vespa scooter with his brother Mario. As we reached town, we were astonished to see thousands of highly excited people surrounding the Odeon. Then it clicked. The Beatles were in town and had just performed their first night of a week-long series of concerts there.

It was obvious from the crowds that they hadn't yet left the cinema, so we got off our bikes to savour the moment. After about five minutes, the hubbub from the crowd turned into a roar as a white fifteen hundredweight Thames van backed up to the exit opposite the Bristol and Exeter pub. The Beatles were about to leave the building! Neil Aspinall was at the wheel and was gingerly reversing the vehicle through the crowd trying to position it so the Beatles could jump straight into the back from the stage door. Not an easy manoeuvre given the frantic crowd. Then the Fab Four burst through the exit and dived into the van, still finding time for a smile and a wave to their fans. The back door slammed shut, and they were away.

We jumped on our bikes, following in hot pursuit, and soon realised they were hopelessly lost, going around in circles and getting nowhere. On their second excursion to Wadham Street, the van stopped. They must have seen us following them, as one of the back doors opened. George Harrison's head appeared, and asked me in his unmistakable Liverpool accent, 'Can you tell us the way to the Royal Pier Hotel, please?' Trying not to show my excitement at this unexpected encounter, I said, 'Sure, follow us.' So, we headed off with the Beatles in tow, reached the hotel on Birnbeck Road, and still grasping the moment followed them inside. However, we felt a little awkward standing in the reception with them, not knowing what to do, we turned and said goodnight. John Lennon looked at us. 'Thanks very much lads – goodnight!' Still excited, I thought that was the end of our Beatles experience – but it was only the beginning!

We had booked our tickets for the second night's concert months before and enjoyed every second of it – they were a great, great group. I knew one of the Odeon's managers, and that night he asked me 'was that you on the motor bike last night?' I said 'Yes.' He said, 'We just can't get the Beatles away after the show, the crowds are far too big, so we've made a plan. We are going to use decoy vans at one of the other exits, if you can be backstage each night, we will decide which one we intend to use at the last minute, you can be there waiting with your bikes to guide them to their hotel.' We jumped at the offer and for the rest of the week became the Beatles official 'outriders'!

One night when they spilled out of the designated exit, we were waiting for them, but the van didn't appear. There we were on the pavement with the Fab Four, with thousands of screaming fans just around the corner looking for them! Any second we expected someone to shout, 'There they are!' and to be engulfed. George said what I thought was 'let's get the car.' It so happened that week George had put his Mark 10 Jag in for a service at Victoria Garage, which at that time, had an entrance directly opposite the exit being used that evening. One of my team, Mike Millington held the keys to the garage. He was a mechanic there. We all ran across the raised grass plantation to get to the garage's entrance on Alexandra Parade. On the way John Lennon fell over with a curse. I helped him up and we carried on running, genuinely frightened we would be spotted by the mob at any moment. We entered the garage, where Mike took the group to George's car. They all looked bemused. George said, 'What the hell are we doing here?' I replied, 'You said let's get the car.' 'I said cab, not car!' replied George. OOPS! There we were with the four Beatles, stood in a dimly lit garage at 10.30pm – it was surreal! They all jumped in George's car, and we escorted them home safe and sound.

Being backstage with them for the next four nights, we had many conversations and were on first name terms. When some of my friends realised we were in such a privileged position, they naturally tried to take advantage of this and get closer themselves. We delivered many love letters, along with fluffy toys and other presents. On one occasion as I handed Paul a love letter with hearts all over it, the sender had asked me to tell him exactly which seat she would be sat in that night. 'Paul, this is from a girl with blonde hair who will be blowing you kisses from the third row.' John, coming down the stairs from the dressing room, overheard me and said, 'Girls? Where are the girls?' 'I thought you were married?' I said. Being just 16, I was taken aback by his response. 'So what!' until he followed up his comment with a broad grin.

Every night we spent at least fifteen or twenty minutes alone with the group waiting for our exit instructions. There was many a conversation and many memories – John composing on a piano backstage – composing what I wonder? ...being told off by all four of them because the brake light on my motorbike wasn't working, and having to promise to get it fixed... a long animated conversation with George about his love of cars... the time their van stopped at traffic lights, girls recognizing them and screaming, only for Ringo to grin at me pointing vigorously to his chest assuring me that the girls were screaming for him not me (Ringo did have a great sense of humour) ... and lastly, backstage at the Odeon I watched every performance from the wings, and was never more chuffed than when Paul glanced at me and gave a wink of recognition.

Eighteen years later I had the chance to return the gesture. Paul invited my group Fumble to appear with him and others at the Hammersmith Odeon in London. As we were playing our set, I saw him stood in the wings watching, just as I had done eighteen years earlier in Weston-super-Mare. I nodded at him and winked – Paul raised his thumb and nodded back, but he could never have known that this exchange had taken me back to Weston when, aged 16, I had been so proud to be a Beatles outrider! ◗

DES HENLY, MUSICIAN AND TEACHER, WESTON-SUPER-MARE, SOMERSET

TUESDAY 23 JULY

The group woke at the Royal Pier Hotel, their base for the week, and drove around town with Gerry Marsden. Marsden was wearing a big hat and dark glasses, recording exchanges he had with locals, asking where the town's golf course was. 'We got some dead funny replies,' George recalled, 'just like *Candid Camera* it was, only in sound!'

The town was abuzz with the first commercial crossing of the hovercraft service between Weston and Penarth. Thousands queued for the £1 tickets for the 11-mile crossing which took just under twelve minutes. Two days later the hovercraft returned to port after one of its engines overheated. The sixth episode of *Pop Go The Beatles*, with guests Carter-Lewis and the Southerners, aired at 5pm. The group played their second night at the Odeon.

❛ The summer of 1963 when the Beatles visited Weston-super-Mare is a time I shall remember forever. How could I ever forget those few days when the Fab Four visited my hometown. I was 13 years old and my best friend Judy and I were mad about pop music. We danced around my red Dansette record player for hours to Cliff and the Shadows, Elvis, the Tornados, Frank Ifield and Susan Maughan. Nothing, however, prepared us for the sounds of those four young guys – John, George, Paul and Ringo. Although we didn't realise it this was to be pre-Beatlemania time. Imagine our excitement when we read in the *Weston Mercury* that the Beatles were billed to appear at the Odeon. We couldn't believe it – no one famous ever came to Weston! Judy and I rushed down to town to buy our tickets.

Finally, the day came and we caught the bus down to the Odeon. Considering what was to happen during the next few weeks and months, I recall that the queue was not that long, but the buzz of excitement was unmistakable. The odd screams started to be heard from the crowd – mostly girls of around our age – to the sound of Gerry Marsden singing 'How Do You Do It?' and 'I Like It' but the screams were beginning to get deafening as the moment came for the Beatles to be announced. They ran onstage and the audience erupted. It was wonderful. We couldn't just sit there, we had to join in with the screaming and singing. I'd been a rather reserved young lady until that point, but I couldn't contain myself any longer and had to join in with the screaming and shouting. It was not something really expected of a privately educated young lady.

After the performance with our ears still ringing, we waited at the stage door in hope of getting some autographs, but after an hour or so we were told they had left by another exit, and had gone off to their hotel. Luckily for us this was not the end of the story. Well, how could we possibly leave things like that when we knew they were staying in Weston for a week? We found out that they were staying at the Royal Pier Hotel at Anchor Head, so the next day armed with our autograph books and cameras Judy and I caught the bus up to the hotel. A few other fans were hanging around with us in the hope of seeing John, Paul, George and Ringo, but nothing much seemed to be happening. Judy and I decided to wander around the back of the hotel and see if anything was happening there. How lucky could we be! We actually heard the voices of the Beatles and a transistor radio playing up on the balcony. The balcony, however, was only about 10 feet tall. So near and yet so far but nothing was going to deter me now. How I climbed the wall I cannot for the life of me remember. I think Judy must have given me a leg up and somehow my head just about reached the balcony and I was able to see the boys with their wives and girlfriends. There they were, it was a dream come true. They were so friendly even though I had invaded their privacy. With just a head showing through the railings, and hanging on for dear life, our autograph books and magazines were passed round and autographed. They autographed everything for us. We were over the moon. John even asked my name. That afternoon I was supposed to be going to tea with Judy. We rushed to catch the bus just leaving from outside the hotel. Judy leapt aboard – I just didn't make it in time and missed it. I also missed my tea but I didn't care one bit. I walked all the way home clutching the autographs. I treasure the one that says, 'To Ann, Love John Lennon'. ❜

ANN BAXTER, VETERINARY NURSING ASSISTANT, WESTON-SUPER-MARE, SOMERSET

WEDNESDAY 24 JULY

F ans Sandra Blaken and her friend Joyce visited Weston and, by offering two ghost train operators on the Grand Pier ten Woodbine cigarettes each, found out the Beatles were staying at the Royal Pier. They got Paul's autographs as well as those of Pacemakers' Gerry and Fred Marsden and Les Chadwick. John, George and Gerry whiled away the afternoon recording themselves on a portable tape recorder in one of the hotel rooms. For reasons only known to themselves, they recited psalms from the Bible, and sang 'The Lord Is My Shepherd' and 'There Is A Green Hill Far Away'. After they drove off, the girls went into the hotel with a few more fans and wandered into Room 49, where the Beatles were staying –

information gleaned from Fred Marsden. They found a letter for George and an LP sleeve with John's name on it. They then left, heading to the group's second show.

Transglobal, a music licensing firm in New York and an affiliate of EMI's, wrote to Vee-Jay Records requesting a royalty statement and immediate payment on sales of 'Love Me Do' and 'P.S. I Love You'. The record label failed to respond to the request, even though all they owed was $859. The group heard the news that Brian Epstein had signed a contract for the group to perform for three weeks at the Olympia Theatre in Paris, France, the following January. They played their third night at the Odeon.

❛ As soon as I first heard the Beatles I was hooked and I quickly became one of the thousands of screaming teenage fans. Not only did I scream when they were onstage and on television, but I screamed when their records were played on the radio and I remember my dad commenting, 'It's those Beatles again.' He would go off down the garden to get away from my screams! I went to see them perform live as many times as possible. I saw them in Bristol, Bath and Torquay. My friend and I went to stay with an aunt of mine in Plymouth so we could easily get to Torquay to see them and I remember we spent the afternoon screaming outside the stage door where we could hear them performing their matinee show and then we went to the evening performance before getting the train back to Plymouth. I was also lucky enough to be picked to go to the fan club's show in London where, after their performance, we shook hands with the Fab Four as we filed past them. The screaming at that show was immense and girls were carried away as they fainted!

My most exciting Beatles' experience was when they were in Weston-super-Mare. Here is my diary exactly as I wrote it at the time: 'Went down Weston on the Wednesday morning (24 July 1963) with Joyce. Found out what hotel Beatles staying in by buying 2 chaps ten fags each. Went to hotel (Royal Pier) in afternoon. Got Paul's, Fred's & Les Chadwick's autographs. Gerry, John & George came out but were in a hurry but managed to get Gerry's autograph. Chap on duty at door left in car so as Fred had told us Beatles' bedroom number was 49 about six of us went up. Door open, went in, no one there, ward-robe open. Bible open on one of the two beds. Letter for George on dressing table & record cover with John's name on in ward-robe so must have been John & George's bedroom. I took big card label from one of a pile of Wolsey Cotton rib X briefs!! Nearly got police on us because we went up to bedroom. Went to show (2nd performance) – fab!!! They recognised us especially Paul & Fred. Went down Weston on the Friday morning (26 July 1963) with Stephanie & Ros. Went straight to hotel. Got rest of Beatles' & Pacemakers' autographs and also Tommy Quickly's. Got label from pants signed by Beatles. Paul knew I'd been up in bedroom!! Took photos. Stayed outside hotel all day (7½ hours). THEY'RE FAB!!! ❜

SANDRA WOODRUFF, MINISTRY OF DEFENCE, BRISTOL, AVON

THURSDAY **25 JULY**

❛Twist And Shout' climbed to number 9 in the *Disc* chart as 'From Me To You' dropped to number 18. In an interview with the group conducted by June Harris, Paul mentioned that Claude François was selling four thousand copies a day in France with his version of 'From Me To You'.

In the *NRM* chart 'From Me To You' climbed back up one place to number 15, while *Twist And Shout* jumped seven places to the top of the EP chart. The Isley Brothers' version also made a one-week appearance in the chart at number 42. The paper published its EP and LP six-month survey. Even though *Please Please Me* was still sitting at the top of the LP chart, it had only accumulated 247 points, putting it at number 8. As a group, they settled one place outside the Top 10.

While fans continued to search Weston for the Beatles, four thousand people attended the Modern Venus Bathing Beauty Competition held at the Pool. Twenty-four-year-old Reading secretary Margaret Bristow was crowned the winner, giving judges Hugh Lloyd and Terry Scott a big hug and receiving the £50 prize. The group visited Joan McNulty at the Queen Alexandra Memorial Hospital on the Boulevard, who was recovering after being attacked three days earlier. Paul bought her a box of chocolates from a nearby newsagents. In the evening, they played two more shows at the Odeon.

❝ I was born in a house on Upper Church Road in Weston, not far from the sea front and the Royal Pier Hotel. It was a lovely family home, lots of kids running around, and our playground was the beach and under the pier. I left school at 15 and went straight to work at Lloyd and Osborn, a hairdressing salon with a wig room at the top of the building. I wanted to do something unusual, something other than office or shop work, and heard about wig making, and thought I'd like to give it a try.

I worked in the wig room with lots of other young women and learnt the trade. I made lots of friends there, and we had a wonderful time. Mr Lloyd ran the office downstairs, Mr Osborn ran the hair salon, and we had a fantastic boss in Mr Lloyd's son-in-law, Mr Chichester, who ran the wig room upstairs. The premises were at 26 the Boulevard. It wasn't just a ladies' hairdressers. On the ground floor was the shop, where they sold creams, perfumes and hair products, and at the back was the gents' salon, where the Beatles had their hair cut. I can't remember the names of the hairdressers who did their hair, but I know one of them was Stanley, who was a lovely man. I'm not sure if they made an appointment but I'm guessing they just walked in. The news came upstairs to the wig room that they were there and – oh wow! Had I known then they were to become so famous I would have swept the floor and kept their hair. Needless to say our boss wouldn't let us go down to see them. There would have been chaos.

I went to see them twice, although I can't remember an awful lot apart from screaming! There was a photo taken by the local paper with everyone standing outside the theatre and I'm there near the front. When I tell people now about the Beatles coming into the hair salon. They say, 'Really? I can't believe that!' People just can't believe it. And here we are over fifty years later, and people are still asking me about it! Their music will live on for generations to come. ❞

SYLVIA BROOMHALL, WIG MAKER, WESTON-SUPER-MARE, SOMERSET

FRIDAY **26 JULY**

'Twist And Shout' climbed to number 8 in the *NME* singles chart and entered the *Melody Maker* chart, including EP sales, for the first time, at number 14. 'From Me To You' dropped down to number 18 in the former and held steady at number 16 in the latter. *Melody Maker* interviewed several musicians for an article titled 'Beat Crazy – That's Britain'. Vera Lynn said she liked 'a lot of the current hit parade music', but less enthusiasm was shown by Ted Heath ('It is strictly adolescent music'), Tubby Hayes ('I try not to listen to it. I think it's a row. I think it's bad for youngsters to be brought up on this kind of music.') and Steve Race ('It passes the time, but what's new in it?'). Their views were echoed by Mr R. G. Harrison in the letters page. 'The beat boys have arrived, with their supposed new sounds, banal melodies and lyrics which clearly illustrate the nadir of one's imagination where songwriting is concerned. Some claim this new trend is healthy in pop music. But ten years from now will a disc-jockey say, 'And now, here is that much-loved standard of a decade ago, I Like It'?'

Brian Epstein signed a contract with the Rabin Agency for the group to perform at the Wimbledon Palais on 14 December for 50 per cent of the takings. By the time the date rolled around, the gig had become exclusively for fan club members.

As the group played their fifth night in Weston-super-Mare, the weekly *Weston Mercury & Somersetshire Herald* reviewed the opening night. 'THEY HAD THEM TWISTING IN THE AISLES! Wildly Enthusiastic Reception for the Beatles at Odeon Stage Show. Hundreds of frenzied teenagers cheered, screamed, twisted in the aisles... finally surged to the front of the auditorium at the climax of a wonderful opening night at the Odeon... Well before the end of this number ['Twist And Shout'], hundreds of twisting teenagers had progressed from the edge of their seats to within feet of where the Beatles where performing. Two wildly excited youths scaled the barrier on the stage to shake hands with each member of the quartet. Joan McNulty was visited in hospital by her mother.

❝ I was born in Weston during the War. My father was in the army and stayed in it and eventually became Brigadier Councillor Austin, CBE. But I didn't take after him. I wasn't particularly interested in anything when I was young because I was very reclusive and peculiarly underweight. I was ill for a while and ended up being 6 feet tall and under 10 stone. I could sing very well and play the piano, but nobody was particularly interested in that. Suddenly I realised I could do Jerry Lee Lewis, Little Richard and Ray Charles very well because I was daft enough and not inhibited and that went down awfully well with the ladies. We had a massive Teddy Boy thing around Weston and there was a gang in the late '50s who were particularly notorious.

I didn't do very much of anything else until 1962 when a lady from the College Players Dramatic Society came to see me. She was a very nice ex-professional lady called Aileen Lundman and she said, 'Would you like to come and be in a play?' I said, 'I don't know. It sounds a bit sissy to me.' She stood on my front door and said, 'But we've got some very nice girls.' I remember saying, 'I'll give it a shot then.' So I went and did this play *Dear Charles* and was a big success. Somebody said, 'You're good at that. Why don't you try and audition for the Rapier Players Theatre in Bristol?' I had nothing else to do, so I did. I went up there and auditioned without a care in the world. I was interviewed by a lovely man called John Dufty and two of us got in from 400 applicants. I became an apprentice in rep for one year. Receiving £1 a week minus tax, which was a take home pay of 12/10½.

Everything changed around this time because of the Cuban Missile Crisis and we had audiences coming to see us in comedies and shows like *The Boyfriend* and we all thought we were going to die. We just got over that when we ran straight into the most horrendous winter. I was staying in the YMCA and the heating failed and I had to go to bed in all my clothes and my duffle coat with all the blankets over me. But the two things put together changed everything. There was this cafe just across the balcony from the Little Theatre inside the Colston Hall. It was very much a place for people in the hall and wasn't really open for the public. We used to have a coffee at 11am, one at lunchtime and one in the afternoon. One afternoon in March 1963, the Beatles came in with a couple of other people and some management bods. They sat down and were joshing and joking about and we didn't take much notice of them but they weren't really known at that point. Actors didn't think much of 'pop' people. We were 'serious' actors.

A couple of years later I was in *Great Expectations* at the Little Theatre with Jane Asher, and Paul McCartney turned up to see her and came backstage. By that time the tables had turned and he was super famous and we weren't the kind of people he talked to. Then suddenly the Bristol Old Vic took over the Rapier Players and we all lost our jobs. So in July 1963 and I returned home and found myself at a bit of a loose end. When the theatre shut, I was fairly depressed and didn't know what I was going to do next. I wandered around town and was amazed by the vast crowds outside the Odeon hoping to catch a glimpse of the Beatles. A guy I went to school with by the name of Dave Brown had tickets to see the show with his girlfriend, but they had an argument beforehand and he asked me to go in her place. Like most people, all I can remember is a lot of screaming and not being able to hear anything. It was the first show and I think if he'd offered me a ticket to go and see the second show I wouldn't have gone because there was something good on television.

I did several shows that following year, including *Under The Sycamore Tree*. My father never said anything when I did stuff, but I was told that he turned to someone and said, 'Thank God we've found something he can do properly.' Someone saw the play and said, 'Why don't you audition for the Bristol Old Vic Theatre School?' So I went up there and did their weekend –and did a little bit of everything with different teachers. I particularly enjoyed that – especially a teacher called Rudi Shelley who had his own way of doing things but I can look back now and know I owe him a tremendous debt. He helped me stop being so insular. He taught me physical exercises that were totally simple and I've done virtually every day since. I'm now in my late seventies and most of my school friends are dead. I went through the Vic school experience and at the end of that my father was working in London as a high ranking National Service staffer and he had contacts. So he got me my agent and I went to live in London and started picking up odd bits on television, changing my name to Simon Cord. At the start it was hard work, getting an interview and things. I thought I must go back to basics here and one of the keys to my career in theatre was early on I realised that most male actors wanted to play the leads and be loved. I didn't want any of that and wanted to play the bad guys. I knew how to do that because of my youth in Weston. Then I made a wanted poster for the murder of everybody I had killed onstage up to that point and sent it off to all the BBC-TV producers and later I would go to Shepherd's Bush for interviews and it was on the wall. I managed to pick up roles in Z Cars, Softly Softly, Steptoe And Son, Dick Emery, Armchair Theatre and a whole load of other bits and pieces. I was working at the Royal Court in Edward Bond's *The Sea* and there was a scene when Coral Browne threw ashes out of a vase into my face. These were tiny pieces of plastic and one of them went into my throat. It was sharp and cut me and after a couple of days I lost my voice and after that I found I couldn't act for more than about four or five days without my voice being affected. That really put an end to my acting career. As for the Beatles, I went off them a bit after *Sgt. Pepper*. I always identified with Lennon, was a great admirer of McCartney, George kept himself to himself and Ringo's very clever because he never allowed it to overwhelm him as far as I can see. They certainly changed the face of popular music. **"**

BRIAN AUSTIN, SENIOR RESEARCH HISTORIAN AND ACTOR, WESTON-SUPER-MARE, SOMERSET

SATURDAY **27 JULY**

I n the morning's *Liverpool Echo*, Peter Layton wrote an article about jazz, reporting that John and Paul wanted no part of the genre. 'They look on it as something of a triumph that jazz has been driven out of so many Liverpool spots by their inexorable advance.' During the day, the group enjoyed a day out, having their photos taken by Dezo Hoffmann. They were first snapped riding donkeys on the sea front. Pete Swaysland was working as a donkey boy when they went for a ride. 'They were larking about and I thought 'What a strange bunch of lads with long hair and strange accents." The donkey rides were

owned by a local character by the name of Don Trapnell. He reputedly had gone eight rounds with British heavyweight Don Cockell and, in 1964, appeared with his donkeys in the opening scene of the film *The Beauty Jungle* starring Ian Hendry and Janette Scott. Hoffmann and the group then drove to Brean Down where they donned Victorian bathing outfits, which had been hired by Hoffmann from the costumiers Berman's. After stopping off for petrol in Warren Road, they went to the Sunny Holt Caravan Park on South Road, where they were captured riding go karts. Hoffmann also recorded with an 8mm movie camera. Footage of the day was included in the 'Real Love' promo video in 1995. When they returned to their hotel, still photos were snapped, which were later used for a Typhoo tea advert. They played their final night at the Odeon. After the second house, George, trying to avoid fans, crashed his Jaguar into a wall at the hotel garage.

> ❝ My grandfather was from Shirley in the West Midlands and owned John Neilson Engineering, a company bearing his name, which made hand operated presses and undertook general engineering work. He'd been to the West Country many times and saw an advert in the 1950s for a caravan site for sale in Brean. So he decided to sell the engineering company and move there with my grandmother, uncle, my parents and me. My brother Ron was born four years later. Originally my parents moved to a shop in Burnham-on-Sea selling fruit and vegetables, later moving to the caravan site, which was called Sunnyholt Caravan Park. After seeing photos of go-karts in a magazine, Grandfather had

the idea of building a go-kart track at the caravan site, as there weren't many amusements in the nearby area. He made the go-karts himself and they were operated by my father and were opened to the public as well as holiday makers, on the site. We had an amusement arcade as well and installed a juke box there in the early '6os. As I was in my teens by then, Grandfather allowed me to choose the 45s for the juke box. I'd go down to the local record store in Jotcham's Sport Shop in Burnham-on-Sea. I would buy them, and then press the middles out so we could load them into the juke box. It was on that juke box that I can still remember hearing 'Love Me Do'. That was the beginning of my love affair with the Beatles.

All of my friends at school and I loved the Beatles, and when we heard they were coming to play at the Odeon, my friend Margaret and I decided to go over early one day on the bus and see if we could get tickets. We caught the bus from outside the caravan park and joined the queue for tickets. Everyone was very excited. We spent the day wandering around the town, excited about the evening's show. We must have gone to the early performance, as I know we didn't get back too late. You could hardly hear anything. I think they started with 'I Saw Her Standing There' and finished with 'Twist And Shout'. I can remember after the show, they appeared on the roof of the Odeon waving. We were all just standing there, it was mesmerising!

We travelled back home on the bus, and when we got there, we could hardly believe it when Dad said, 'Oh you'll never guess who's been here on the go-karts! The Beatles!' My brother says that when they did show up, Dad said, 'Who are those long-haired lads over there, have they paid?' When he asked who they were, one of the boys said, 'We're The Beatles' and Dad said, 'My daughter's gone to Weston to see you.' I was absolutely devastated. Can you imagine? I had been in Weston for the day, and they had been here on our caravan park, on our go-karts! I just couldn't believe it and was mortified. You know what parents are like though, they thought it was quite amusing. After word got out they had come to the park, people would come in and ask, 'Which seat did Paul sit on? Which one did Ringo sit on?' Some of them even kissed the go-kart seats. 〕

SUSAN BULLOCK, TOURIST ATTRACTION MANAGER, WESTON-SUPER-MARE, SOMERSET

SUNDAY 28 JULY

After breakfast at the Royal Pier Hotel, the group set off on a cross-country drive – a six-hour journey to Great Yarmouth. They played two shows at 6pm and 8.15pm at the ABC, with tickets priced between 4/6 and 9/6, promoted as the 'Big Sunday Night Stage Show'. The Kestrels, the Trebletones, Freddie Starr and the Midnighters (whose debut single 'Who Told You?' had been released on Decca a couple of months earlier), Barry Barnett, Alan Field and Glenda Collins were also on the bill. Not much more than a stone's throw from the cinema in Regent Road, Adam Faith, with whom they spent some time before the shows, and Joe Brown were performing at the Wellington and Britannia theatres, respectively. Ken Dodd, who was appearing at the ABC all summer, visited the group backstage and trod on John's toe. As on their previous visit, they stayed at the Carlton Hotel.

> ❝ I was 12 years old and my older sister took me to the concert as an early birthday present. I especially remember John Lennon introducing what in his words 'would probably be our new single 'She Loves You'.' They finished off the gig with 'Twist And Shout'. There was much screaming, the girl next to me was crying for half the concert. The group in those days were using little Vox AC30 amps for their guitars and a small PA system so at times it was impossible to hear what they were singing. An urban myth came into being after the concert as a story went round that the following morning the group were in a large Jaguar car and stopped a local person by the side of the road in the town to ask for directions out of the town, having allegedly stayed overnight in a local hotel. Don't know how true it is, but it's a good tale anyway. ❞

DENNIS BEAN, CHARTERED ENGINEER, BECCLES, NORFOLK

MONDAY 29 JULY

The group checked out of the Carlton and headed to London for a photo session with Don Smith, which was to be featured as part of the *Radio Times*' 'Portrait Gallery' series. The session took place at 4pm in a room at the Washington Hotel in Curzon Street. Afterwards, they were snapped on the hotel's roof by Marc Sharratt, while Paul was interviewed by the *NME*'s Alan Smith for a forthcoming feature, 'Close-Up On A Beatle'. A session at Abbey Road was postponed as fans had caused problems outside the last time they were there.

The Sunderland Empire Theatre Junior Society stand at the Seaburn Ideal Homes and Holidays Exhibition was inundated with teenagers wanting to sign up. Within the first two days of the exhibition more than one hundred and fifty had become members. It was not the free drama coaching that interested them – but the chance of being first in line to get tickets for the Beatles' shows at the Sunderland Empire in November. 'As soon as the young people heard that the Beatles [were] coming in November they rushed to our stand to join,' said Mr J. D. Harrison, the society's secretary. 'They were obviously frightened of not being able to get in, so are taking no chances.' Membership cost 2/6 per year and started on 2 September. The two shows were almost sold out within forty-eight hours of tickets going on sale.

TUESDAY 30 JULY

The Beatles arrived at EMI studios for a 10am session in Studio Two lasting three and half hours. They recorded nine takes of 'Please Mister Postman' and ten of 'It Won't Be Long', the first Lennon/McCartney song to be recorded for their second album. Just after 1.30pm the group drove to the Playhouse Theatre to make an appearance on the BBC radio programme *Non Stop Pop*. They were interviewed by bandleader Phil Tate for the programme's 'Pop Chat' segment. Asked about songwriting, John said, 'All the better songs that we have written – the ones that anybody wants to hear – those were co-written... Sometimes half the words are written by me and [Paul will] finish them off. We go along a word each, practically.' Paul was asked how he avoided being recognised if he took a girl out, 'Uhh, I don't know... just sort of run.'

Immediately afterwards they recorded 'Long Tall Sally,' 'She Loves You,' 'Glad All Over,' 'Twist And Shout,' 'You Really Got A Hold On Me' and 'I'll Get You' for an episode of *Saturday Club*, which aired on 30 August. They returned to Abbey Road in time for a 5pm session, coinciding with the broadcast of the seventh episode of *Pop Go The Beatles*, recorded on July 10 and featuring the Searchers as guests. The evening session lasted six hours (though was scheduled for only five). They recorded seven more takes of 'Money,' five of 'Till There Was You' with George playing an acoustic Jose Ramirez Guitarra Estudio, eight of 'Roll Over Beethoven,' thirteen of 'It Won't Be Long' and fourteen of 'All My Loving,' a song Paul had written during the Roy Orbison tour.

WEDNESDAY 31 JULY

The group headed back north-west to make a return visit to the Imperial Ballroom in Nelson, performing to a sold-out crowd of eighteen hundred. It was less chaotic than their previous visit in May. Teenagers Christine Brown and Lynn Peake were allowed backstage to meet their idols after being chosen as 'Nelson's biggest Beatles fans' by Imp manager Bob Caine. Mrs Margaret Curran and her two children flew over from Belfast to see the concert. Girls were crushed in the crowd and taken outside to recover. The *Nelson Leader*'s sub-editor, 26-year-old Roger Siddall,

asked for his opinion, said, 'Horrible discord... about as musical as a regiment of cavalry charging over a tin bridge! If this is being with it, then I'm obviously being a so-called square.'

The *Leader*'s review of the performance reported that 'the ingredients which went in to making it a night to remember for most young folk were similar to those when the Beatles last visited Nelson – a capacity audience, hysterical girls, overcome by either the almost unbearable heat or excitement, fainting like ninepins, photographer's flashbulbs and, of course, a royal helping of 'Scousound.'

During the month, more British records were played on the BBC than ever before. Out of twenty-seven hundred items broadcast, 55.15 per cent were British and 36.78 per cent were American. Only five years previously, the figures had been flipped, with US records garnering more than 63 per cent and British records a mere 36 per cent.

❛ In 1963 I was 14 years old when I saw the Beatles. I was lucky enough to see them on both occasions that they appeared in Nelson, not because I was a particularly big Beatles fan but because it was Saturday night – so where else would I be! Going down Th'Imp was a rite of passage for most teenagers in the East Lancs' towns of Burnley, Nelson and Colne in the '60s. The Imperial Ballroom, its 'proper' title, looked little more than an extremely large Nissen hut, built on the canal banks but OOOH once you got inside it was a naive teenager's dream of modern, 'with it' sophistication. It had a large sprung dance floor with a small stage at the front, around which were a couple of rows of seats, plus two bars (one cocktail) and a cafe. It was one of the few places where Mods and Rockers could mix with little more trouble than a few thrown fists and handbags. How much of this was down to the bouncers and how much to the sheer enthusiasm of being able to see top performers live I'm not sure. Romances blossomed and failed in this heady environment. The doors opened at 7.30pm and closed at 11.30pm, the building had to be empty by midnight due to the Sunday laws of the time. Almost every week one of the top stars of the day would be appearing, and at a price that even a schoolgirl with a Saturday job could afford to buy a ticket and still have a bit of money left for the rest of the week. We didn't realise just how special those times were until much later, going to see a top group or singer now is such an expensive, special occasion!

The Beatles' debut performance in May was the first time I'd ever seen girls get so hysterical over a group onstage, several of them fainted from hysteria or heat. I'm not sure which – after all there were nearly two thousand of us in a ballroom full of people smoking (it was the '60s) and there was no such thing as air conditioning. Hell, there weren't even any windows! Health and Safety would have had a field day. As far as I was concerned the group were good but nothing memorable. Their second appearance in July was different. There were the Beatles on the stage, but no one heard them singing – a corny joke but true. The screaming began before they came onstage and didn't stop until long after they had gone. People came to see them, not hear them. They could buy their records to do that! Happy memories of past times and friendships. ❙

JOYCE LATHAM, LIBRARY ASSISTANT (BRITISH LIBRARY), BURNT OAK, LONDON

AUGUST

Goodbye to the Cavern

THURSDAY 1 AUGUST

Shortly after 6.30am, Joan McNulty was discharged from hospital. As she left, she said, 'I can't help thinking about her [Herron]. She was such a wonderful friend. I am just beginning to be able to relax again. I couldn't sleep for nearly a week.' Ambulance driver Daniel Brewer was waiting outside the Alfred Street entrance of the hospital to drive her to Bristol Temple Meads station where, accompanied by a nurse, she took a train back to her home in Sefton Park, Liverpool. She carried with her the box of chocolates given to her by the Beatles. Arriving at Lime Street station, she was met by her uncle and driven home by taxi where was greeted by her mother Beatrice, the assistant matron at the Parkfield House old people's home where they lived. 'It's good to be home,' Joan said.

The front page of *Disc* featured a photo of the Beatles sitting on donkeys on the beach, taken the previous Saturday, headlined 'Ridin' High!' In the Top 30, 'Twist And Shout' climbed to number 5 as 'From Me To You' dropped to number 23. The paper announced the group had been booked by the Variety Club of Great Britain for the 'Beatles' New Year Ball' at the Royal Albert Hall. In October, however, at a Hall council meeting, it was proposed that the Beatles should be banned from appearing at the venue. Minutes taken at the meeting recorded, 'The President said he felt that this particular group represented first-class entertainment and had in fact been chosen to appear in this year's Royal Command Performance. Undoubtedly unfavourable comment would arise if the Council refused to allow them to appear.' Despite this, they did not perform at the Ball, following suspicions that council members had put pressure on the Variety Club to take them off the bill.

In the *NRM*, 'From Me To You' dropped to number 17. The first issue of *The Beatles Book*, edited by Sean O'Mahony under the name Johnny Dean, hit the newsstands. The winners of a competition in the magazine were Lyn Russell, Christine Canning, Anne Stevens and Dorothy Franklin – their prize was a transistor radio and a letter from the Beatles. Run from a one-room office on the Edgware Road, the first edition sold eighty thousand copies and by December it had reached monthly sales of three hundred and thirty thousand. O'Mahony later commented, 'That lift-off period was fast and dramatic. In publishing it's very rare for that to happen. Then it went into a very extended decline.' The magazine continued until December 1969.

Following a rehearsal at noon, the group recorded the eleventh and twelfth episodes of *Pop Go The Beatles* at the Playhouse Theatre in Manchester. At the first recording at 1.30pm they performed 'Ooh! My Soul', 'Don't Ever Change' (their sole radio performance of the Goffin/King song originally recorded by the Crickets), 'Twist And Shout', 'She Loves You', 'Anna (Go To Him)' and 'A Shot Of Rhythm And Blues'. At 4pm after a short break, they recorded another episode, playing 'Lucille', 'From Me To You', 'I'll Get You', 'Money', 'Baby It's You', 'There's A Place', 'Honey Don't' (the flipside of Carl Perkins' 'Blue Suede Shoes' recorded in December 1955) and 'Roll Over Beethoven'. The two shows aired on 27 August and 3 September. While in Manchester, George took his Gretsch Country Gentleman into Barratt's to be repaired. The shop lent him an Australian guitar, the Maton Mastersound MS-500, as a temporary replacement. After the recording the group drove back home to Liverpool.

> ❝ The first time my sister Linda and I heard the Beatles was on Radio Luxembourg, singing 'Love Me Do'. She was two years older and probably the biggest fan, and I was always trying to keep up. The signal was terrible, coming and going, but through the crackles, it was enough to get us hooked. By the time 'Please Please Me' was in the charts, we were obsessed, listening to them on *Saturday Club* and Alan Freeman's *Pick Of The Pops*. The first concert we went to was at the Southampton Gaumont

in May, when they were on the bill with Roy Orbison. For some reason we decided against throwing Jelly Babies, too run-of-the-mill for us, and settled on, for reasons none of us can remember, a bottle of Cedarwood aftershave. It was something we bought for our dad, and so assumed they would like some too! Someone took it from us when we got near to the stage and promised it would be passed on.

I recall us having a huge mural of the Beatles on our bedroom wall, with them wearing old-fashioned, striped bathing costumes. They had been an insert in a magazine, and it took up almost all of one wall in our small bedroom. It was huge! We found out that there was going to be a Beatles monthly magazine. Most people would be able to pick it up from their local newsagents, but we lived out in the sticks. However, as luck would have it, a newsagent lived opposite us. He would make up his orders and go and pick them up, bringing them back in his car. Anyway, we would go over to his house when the Beatles magazine was due. We would wait for ages – his wife was very kind and understanding! Of course, we had to have one each, it would have been impossible to share. 】

NORMA SCOTT, HOUSEWIFE, TROWBRIDGE, WILTSHIRE

FRIDAY 2 AUGUST

"The Year's Greatest Solo Singer From Liverpool – Tommy Quickly Sings Tip Of My Tongue – Another Smash Hit From The Sensational Writing Team John Lennon And Paul McCartney' boasted the front cover of the week's edition of the *NME*. Unfortunately, the single, released on the Piccadilly label, failed to make inroads in any published charts. The Beatles had played their own version of the song to George Martin at a session on 26 November 1962. John subsequently described it as 'another piece of Paul's garbage, not my garbage.' Maybe Martin thought the same thing – they never recorded it. 'Twist And Shout' climbed to number 6, while Billy J. Kramer's 'Bad To Me' was the highest new entry at number 19. 'From Me To You' dropped to number 27. Derek Johnson wrote a detailed survey on the Beatles' chart achievements in the first seven months of the year under the heading 'Beatles Join Select Few To Get EPs (and LPs) In The Best Sellers', making the point that Cliff Richard's recent EP *Holiday Carnival* had not made the *NME* singles chart and yet at 10/9, costing 4/1 more than singles, the *Twist And Shout* EP had become the first EP to do so. He went on to write that despite Frank Sinatra making number 12 in the singles chart with an album, he considered it 'highly unlikely that any more LPs will appear in the Top 30 in future'.

Melody Maker ran the front page headline, 'Boiling Beatles Blast Copy Cats – Even Our Hair Styles Are Aped'. John told the paper, 'Certain groups are doing exactly the same thing as us. I wouldn't have brought the matter up, but some guys are having digs at us. Look – we copied nobody. I'm not a Negro so I can't copy a Negro singer, can I? We've got our own style, our group.' In a centre spread article, 'What Makes The Beatles B-E-A-T', John also said, 'I'm sure in four years' time we won't be so popular,' with Ringo adding, 'It can't last forever, I know that. I'm saving like mad. Never want to work for anybody else. When things get rough, I want enough money to buy my own business. Definitely.' The paper reported that the Beatles, Gerry and the Pacemakers, and Billy J. Kramer with the Dakotas had sold over two and a half million records in the UK in the previous six months. In its chart, 'Twist And Shout' climbed eight places to number 6 and 'From Me To You' dropped to number 19.

In the evening, the Beatles returned to the Grafton Rooms in Liverpool, topping a bill with Chick Graham and the Coasters, the Dennisons, Sonny Webb and the Cascades and the Undertakers. They earned £100 for two half-hour sets at 9.30pm and 11pm - considerably less than they were now usually earning. It was their fourth and final appearance at the venue. The first time they had played there was on 3 August the previous year, when they had been paid £10 each.

❛ I was a pupil at Roscommon Street Secondary Modern in 1962 and remember a lot of people had suddenly become aware of the Beatles. My elder brother John was very much into music, as was I. He came in one day and said to me, 'Have you ever heard of a group called the Beatles?' I wasn't old enough then to go into the clubs in town, so I would never have heard of them. He said, 'They're playing at the Cavern, and I'm going down to see them.' So off he went, and came back and said, 'They're amazing!' Then just a couple of weeks later, he came running in up the hallway shouting, 'Put the radio on!' We quickly put the radio on, and the Beatles were on singing 'Love Me Do'. That was it really, and since then they have always been the backdrop soundtrack to my life.

I'd seen them several times before getting the tickets to see them play at the Grafton. I'd had to queue for the tickets when they went on sale at the box office a few weeks earlier. The Grafton was a dance hall – there was the stage, then the floor area, and round the floor were small tables and chairs. I was wearing white bell-bottom trousers, short black boots and a mustard-coloured, polo neck sweater, hand-knitted by my auntie Annie! It was probably too hot in August to be wearing a knitted sweater, but they were fashionable at the time, and nobody took any notice! I was 14 years old and had blonde hair down to my waist. There wasn't a lot of screaming. That didn't happen in Liverpool! Screaming was a rest of the UK thing. But this evening, there was a lot of noise – people singing along with the songs and cheering and clapping loudly at the end.

I kept my ticket stubs from various shows but when I went to live abroad, one of my brothers ransacked my bedroom when he moved in. He saw all these things under my bed and threw them away because he didn't think they were important! He's kicking himself now! I had a piece of the original Cavern stage that I took myself, and it was in the suitcase with all my other bits and pieces. It had a note on top saying, 'Jean's things, do not touch.' All my treasures were gone. My two younger brothers were in bands at that point and I discovered when I came home that all the stuff that had been in the suitcase has been thrown away, and it was full of band leads and pedals!

I moved to Norway in 1972. My friend Sandra had come home to see me – she had married a man who was half Norwegian and was living in Norway, but had come home to Liverpool to visit friends and family. She said, 'Well, if I get you a job, will you come to Norway?' So I said, 'Yes,' as I'd already resigned from my job of nine years. She rang the place where she worked, and they told her to tell me to go to the Norwegian Consul in Liverpool and get a work permit. In the meantime, they would write to the Consul with an offer of employment for me. Two weeks later I was living in Norway! It was a different experience, but I had a wonderful time. I spoke the language fluently and still do today. I met my husband in Norway, even though he comes from Huddersfield! When I came back from Norway, I worked for a Norwegian company in Liverpool. I worked for them for five years and left to go to Royal Insurance, where I worked for twenty years. After that I went to work at the Liverpool Institute for Performing Arts, which was Paul McCartney's old school in Liverpool. I was PA to the Chief Executive there and managed to mingle and mix with Paul quite a lot. I worked there for five years before retiring from there. I had been retired for four years when the man who owns the company where I work now, Cavern City Tours – they own the Cavern Club, the Cavern Pub and the Magical Mystery Tour – I had known him for over thirty years and had often asked me to come and work for him, made me this offer, while I was sitting in the middle of a show at the Royal Court Theatre in 2015. The following week when the office reopened, he called me and said, 'I meant what I said. I know you're not looking for a job, but you'd be perfect for what I've got in mind.' He made an offer I couldn't refuse, so I was dragged out of retirement! 〞

JEAN CATHARELL, EXECUTIVE PERSONAL ASSISTANT, LIVERPOOL, MERSEYSIDE

SATURDAY **3 AUGUST**

The group played their 274th and final show at the Cavern club. They were paid £5 for their first gig on 9 February 1961, for this evening, the pay cheque was £300. Epstein had demanded a limit of five hundred tickets - at 10/- a ticket, the club lost money on the door. The booking had come about because of Albert Kinder and Les Ackerley's insistence they honour the Grafton Ballroom performance the previous night. Epstein could not book them into the Liverpool area prior to that show, so, in a fit of pique, made this booking to get back at them. The Mersey Beats, the Escorts, the Roadrunners, Faron's Flamingos and Johnny Ringo and the Colts rounded out the bill.

Fans began standing outside at 6am. Commenting on the occasion, Cavern Club bouncer Paddy Delaney said, 'The crowds outside the club were going mad! By the time that John had got through the cordon of girls, his Mohair jacket had lost a sleeve. I grabbed it to stop the girls getting away with a souvenir. John immediately stitched the sleeve back on' The Merseybeats' Billy Kinsley remembered the show. 'The Beatles were really cheesed off that night. They'd already had two number ones, playing theatres, roadies getting their gear in. You couldn't do that in the Cavern. Plus, it was August Bank holiday so it was absolutely chocka, never mind the Beatles being there. It was back to the nitty-gritty for them, where you got electric shocks off the microphones because condensation was streaming down the wall. Then the fuses blew. John was in a bad mood. John and Paul went into this old-time music-hall song, with Paul on the piano. We didn't realise until *Sgt. Pepper* came out... 'When I'm 64'! (Paul had written the song when he was 16 on the piano his father had bought from Harry Epstein at the NEMS store.) But, for the most part, the humour and the ad-libbing had gone. Backstage, Paul actually said to us, 'I told you we shouldn't have come back.'

After the show, George and Ringo adjourned to the Blue Angel where they met up with Tony Sheridan. George was also interviewed by the *NME*'s Alan Smith for its forthcoming 'Close-Up On A Beatle' feature. Sipping on a Pepsi with an always lit cigarette held between his fingers, he told Smith about how he met Paul and the early days of the group. Taking a break from the interview, he welcomed Bob Wooler, who had just walked into the club. Talking about the group and the future, George said, 'We've known each other for six or seven years. If we couldn't get along, we'd know it by now all right. I know I'm very happy. Ringo says I'm an irritable so-and-so, but I think he's just having me on. I think the future holds a lot. I'd like to invest money and perhaps branch out in different show business ventures.'

THE BEATLES AT THE CAVERN
10 MATHEW STREET (OFF NORTH JOHN STREET) LIVERPOOL (Telephone: CENtral 1591)
SATURDAY 3rd AUGUST
ALSO ON THE SAME TERRIFIC PROGRAMME:
THE MERSEY BEATS
THE ESCORTS
THE ROAD RUNNERS
THE SAPPHIRES
JOHNNY RINGO & THE COLTS
SHOW STARTS AT 6 p.m. & FINISHES AT 11-30 p.m.
TICKET PRICE 9/6
The sale of which is strictly limited to Cavern Club Members only, who must produce their Membership Card when purchasing the ticket and both ticket and Membership Card must be presented at the Club on the night. This rule will be strictly enforced.

> ❛ By the time I first met the Beatles I was working for *Mirabelle*. They were performing at the ABC in Croydon, which was quite close to where I lived. I had an instant rapport with them; we were like mates immediately. They had this awful dressing room at the top of the building. They opened their dressing-room window and said, 'Listen, listen,' and they put their heads out of the window and the girls screamed. And they went, 'We're famous, we're famous.' I said, 'I don't think you are. I think I could put my head out of the window and they'd scream.' They said, 'Go on then.' I put my head out and they screamed. They said, 'Oh no, we're not as famous as we thought.'
>
> I knew them really well by the time they played their last show at the Cavern. I went up [to Liverpool] the night before with *Mirabelle*'s photographer Trevor – I can't remember his last name – and stayed at the Adelphi. I met up with them the following day when I went to the Cavern. I had never been there before. I thought it was awful – the most hideous place on earth. It was empty, but I thought it was dreadful. I'm claustrophobic and it was a Health and Safety nightmare. They were down at the other end in these arches where they changed. There were no dressing rooms. It was all fun and they were jamming and then the audience started coming in. They kept playing and it seemed most of the people knew them.
>
> But before the show started it got really frightening. You couldn't move and I'm there with them. I looked at the door and realised I couldn't get out. Ringo looked at me and said, 'You're going to faint, aren't you?' I said, 'Yes.' So Eppy said, 'I'm going to get you out' and he picked me up and staggered through that seething crowd to get me to the door. And that's my memory of that day – I was listening to them play sitting on the steps outside the Cavern having made a complete fool of myself. I've never forgotten it because it had a vibe that I've never experienced before or since. It was a hideous place but they were amazing. Trevor couldn't get any pictures because of the heat and the humidity. So Ringo said, 'You'll never get a picture. You'll have to warm your camera up.' He went back to the Adelphi in a taxi, had it wait there while he wrapped his camera in tin foil and put it in an oven until it was hot enough and then came back to the Cavern. Technically I might be talking rubbish, but that's what he did and it worked. After the show I went to the Blue Angel. Anyway, Trevor and I left the club and drove through the night straight back to London. It was an awfully long drive. We didn't get home until about five in the morning.
>
> I saw them many more times after that. I remember Paul loved my mum. When I went and did interviews, my mum would often drive me and whenever I interviewed Paul in a hotel or somewhere, my mum would just sit in a corner and have a coffee. So Paul got to know her and he really liked her – she was very glamorous and very warm. When they came back from America, there was that famous scene at the airport. All the press were there and it was live on TV. I brought my mum into the press conference. The Beatles arrived and Paul saw Mum in the corner and came straight over to her and told her everything about what happened in America. I think he still needed a mother figure. They were chatting away and everyone was wondering where Paul was and I remember John saying, 'He's with Dawn's mum.' So they dragged him back to the press conference. Looking back, the Beatles really were in a class of their own. ❜
>
> **DAWN SLOUGH, JOURNALIST, COBHAM, SURREY**

SUNDAY 4 AUGUST

The group drove to ABC-TV's studios in Didsbury to tape a segment for *Lucky Stars - Summer Spin*, which aired on 24 August. They arrived a couple of hours early and had to wait for technicians to set up their equipment. After miming to 'She Loves You' and 'I'll Get You', they spoke with *Disc*'s Barry Cockcroft in their dressing room. George told him about their recent

experience at the dentist's and that all was still not right. He informed Cockcroft that despite having had two fillings and a tooth removed, he had toothache. Ringo chimed in that all he had 'was a wash and brush-up – my teeth are beautiful'. When it was time to leave, some two hundred fans were waiting out front, so they left through a side entrance. They departed before Cliff Richard and the Shadows showed up to record their appearance for the following Saturday's one hundredth anniversary programme of *Thank Your Lucky Stars*.

The Beatles then drove to Blackpool for two concerts at 6pm and 8.10pm at the Queen's Theatre. The town was experiencing a heatwave over the Bank Holiday weekend. Sixty-eight special trains had been laid on with 1,300 buses and coaches arriving at the bus station. It was also the first weekend that the new Preston-Warrington motorway link had come into effect and all police leave was cancelled. At the end of the three-day weekend, an estimated 61,000 people had visited the town. The Beatles used the same escape route as on their previous visit.

❛ Being a kid of 14 in 1963 was a perfect age to be when I first heard the opening of 'Please Please Me', because it was like nothing I had ever heard before and I became a Beatles fan for life and I had to see them when they came to play Blackpool, which they did eleven times. I remember seeing them at the long-gone Queen's Theatre, seeing being the operative word because all we heard was demented screaming from the girls, but the atmosphere was incredible. It was my first-ever live concert and I was really looking forward to seeing the group that everyone at school could not stop talking about. After the show we ran around like headless chickens with our jacket collars turned up trying to fool the girls into thinking we were the Beatles escaping from the theatre.

'Please Please Me' is in a direct line of musical signposts that changed my perception of rock music, it followed 'Jailhouse Rock' and afterwards came 'Hey Joe' from the inimitable Jimi Hendrix. These three records were like thunderbolts from another planet and still sound vital today, but to be 14 and in Blackpool at the start of the '60s, we were blessed and we took the Beatles as ours, being from the North, fresh and brash. This was a time when there were no drugs or unemployment and we still had a motorcycle industry. We spent many happy hours playing on the flipper tables (usually Gottlieb) and teenagers had their own identity for the first time with their music and clothes, we were FREE, and to paraphrase Spike Milligan, 'Queen Victoria finally died in 1960.' The Beatles were the '60s, all the other groups paid homage and copied and followed respectfully. I have never felt as alive as I did in those early '60s halcyon days. Harold Macmillan was right, 'We never had it so good'. ❜

STEVE GOMERSALL, OWNER OF STEVE'S PRO SHOP AT
LAKESIDE SUPERBOWL, PRESTON, LANCASHIRE

MONDAY 5 AUGUST

Undeterred by persistent rain and high winds, Pat Brackett, Marjorie Jones and Dorothy Willson began queuing at 5am at Abbotsfield Park, Chassen Road, Urmston – fourteen-and-a-half hours before 'A Twist And Shout Dance' concert was due to begin as part of the annual Urmston Show. Rain continued to fall at the show's 11.30am opening, but stopped during the afternoon. A queue for the concert began taking shape at around 4.30pm, ultimately stretching more than 200 yards from the entrance. The now familiar heavy police presence featured, along with a mounted force, members of the St John Ambulance service and the Red Cross on standby in Flixton Road. By 7.30pm, when the concert began, more than a thousand people were crammed inside the marquee, paying 2/6 in addition to the 10/- ticket for the main show.

Following an opening set by Johnny Martin and the Tremors – most of which was drowned by chants of 'We Want The Beatles!' – Brian Poole and the Tremeloes took to the stage performing their debut hit 'Twist And Shout' – then at number 4 in the *NME* chart, two places higher than the Beatles' EP version. Compère David Hamilton, embracing his future 'Diddy' David persona, then whipped the already excited teenage fans into a frenzy by calling out 'Give me a B! Give me an E! Give me an A...', as he introduced the Beatles, who had been smuggled into the marquee in a council dust cart driven by Ronnie Powell. Girls climbed up ropes to get a better view and an assortment of coins, hair slides and other items were thrown on to the stage.

The group, paid £26 18s for their performance plus £2 18s for train tickets, left the way they came – in the dust cart. The Dennisons had the less than enviable task of following them, seeing the audience disperse as they performed. Councillor A. E. Williams, Chairman of the Show Committee, paid tribute to those who turned up – 'they enjoyed themselves and behaved themselves as I thought they would.'

> ❝ My sister Susan and I had been to the Urmston Show earlier in the day enjoying toffee apples and riding the merry-go-round with its fabulous artwork, colours, mirrors and music. My pet rabbit was entered in the show and was in the marquee adjacent to the one erected for the concert. She won first prize ... not bad for a rabbit that started out life as Ringo, surprising us all by giving birth and later becoming Priscilla. Her marquee would later serve as a recovery tent for the St John Ambulance as they treated streams of hysterical girls carried off in quick succession from the Beatles' performance. Our  mother took us back to the show to see the Beatles that evening. We stayed at the back of the crowd which was not a bad position considering you could see over the heads to the stage. It was impossible to hear the music clearly with the continued screaming. With the weather closing in Mum decided we should leave and not living far away we reluctantly went home. We were delighted however to find that because of where we lived in Weston Avenue, close to the railway line, which was between us and the marquee, we could actually see straight down and across onto the stage and hear the sound really well from my first-floor bedroom window. We had the best seat in the house. ❞

LYNDA SMITH, ORGANIC FARMER, NORTHERN NEW SOUTH WALES, AUSTRALIA

TUESDAY 6 AUGUST

The group flew to the Channel Islands aboard a British United flight for a week of concerts in St Helier and St Peter Port. Arriving in St Peter airport in Jersey, they took the ten-minute journey to their hotel, the Revere, in Kensington Place. Even though it was the height of the summer, 1.3 inches of rain had fallen on the island two days before. With the afternoon to kill before the evening's show, the group sunbathed by the hotel pool and went go-karting.

NEMS Enterprises, comprising Brian Epstein and a staff of three, moved to new premises in Liverpool, 24 Moorfields, above the Wizard's Den magic shop. One of Epstein's first pieces of business in his new surroundings was to sign a contract for the group to appear on the BBC's *The Mersey Sound* documentary later in the year.

The eighth episode of *Pop Go The Beatles*, recorded on 16 July, was broadcast on the Light Programme at 5pm. Their guests were the Swinging Blue Jeans. In the evening the group played their first concert promoted by John Smith, at the Springfield Ballroom on Janvrin Road. Frankie Howerd was performing at the nearby Plaza throughout the week.

> ❝ My brother Geoff and I were both captivated by the dynamic and innovative sound of the Beatles and were looking forward to their visit to Jersey. But my brother was only 10 at the time and, unfortunately, our parents wouldn't allow him to go to the concert! So, our father drove my 16-year-old sister Jenny and me, aged 14, in the family's maroon-and-cream-coloured Morris Oxford to the Springfield Ballroom to watch their first concert. I remember the ballroom being rather dark and cavernous and lacking any atmosphere, but as soon as the boys appeared onstage the audience went crazy with excitement – it was an electrifying experience!
>
>
>
> Our father knew Marshall Doran, the owner of the Revere Hotel, very well. It was then, and still is, a small boutique hotel located in a side street near the centre of town. Four days later, during the late afternoon our father drove my brother, who was now extremely happy, and me to the hotel. We spent about half an hour with the group who asked us to join them over tea and sandwiches in the hotel's lounge. They were very welcoming and funny, always cracking jokes and generally messing around! I recall John being the funniest of all the Beatles. And to top it all, we also managed to get their autographs! Meeting the Beatles was a very special occasion which we both will never forget. ❞
>
> **MALCOLM CORRIGAN, MARKETING CONSULTANT, ST OUEN, JERSEY**

WEDNESDAY 7 AUGUST

Sisters Carol and June Browne and their cousin Elaine Lamb, of Prittlewell, Essex, were on holiday on Jersey when they saw George walking down Kensington Place. 'We first knew they were there when I saw George walking down the street,' recalled Carol. 'We went round the back of their hotel and asked the manager if we could see them. He was very nice about it and let us in. When we got there, George was standing beside the pool and Paul, John and Ringo were swimming. When they came out of the pool we went over and sat with them and had our photographs taken with them.' June, a 14-year-old pupil at Westcliff High School, got George's autograph and was one of those who queued all night to buy a ticket to see them in Southend-on-Sea in December. Later in the day, the group went go-karting again, and Ringo met up with Valerie Callam at the Runnymede Court Hotel in Roseville Street, where she was working – Callam was a Redcoat Ringo had worked with at Butlins. In the evening, the group played their second date at the Springfield Ballroom.

> ❛ On Friday 3 August, I saw the Beatles at the Grafton Ballroom in West Derby Road, Liverpool, which was less than a mile from where I was living at the time. I was 16 and had just left the Liverpool Institute High School. I had seen them at the Cavern in 1962 at a lunchtime session along with several lads from school. The Grafton was the first big venue I had seen the Beatles play in and the contrast with the Cavern was fascinating. Apart from the difference in size this was an opulent arena and everyone seemed to be in their best bib and tucker. In between numbers Paul mentioned that the following week they were off to the Channel Islands. By amazing coincidence, I was going to Jersey that Sunday for a week's holiday with three mates – my first holiday without my parents.
>
> We set off early on Sunday in a Fiat 500 car to catch the ferry. An extremely small car owned by the oldest member of our group, Ian Stewart, who was 19 and seemed very old to us 16-year-olds – a man in fact. On arriving in Jersey after a rather uncomfortable journey including a choppy crossing, we booked into our digs and ascertained that the Beatles were appearing at the Springfield Ballroom on the Tuesday and Wednesday. Tickets had been sold out for the Tuesday but we managed to get two for the Wednesday. Four into two is difficult, so we drew lots and Ian and I were the successful recipients of the prized tickets. The Beatles performed a similar set to that at the Grafton but the most significant difference was the number of girls in the audience – probably three quarters of the crowd, whereas at the Grafton it was equally divided with males and females. Consequently, the screaming at Jersey was quite intense. The first time I had experienced it and it was much more difficult to hear the numbers. Having first seen the Beatles in 1961, when in my opinion they were at their rawest and best, I was a little disappointed with the Jersey performance and remember commentating to my friends afterwards that they had lost a bit of their early dynamic stage act. Happy days though. ❜
>
> **RAY O'BRIEN, BEATLES AUTHOR, BIRKENHEAD, MERSEYSIDE**

THURSDAY 8 AUGUST

I n the latest edition of *Disc*, 'Twist And Shout' reached number 3 and 'From Me To You' dropped to number 28. On its front page, the paper featured one of Dezo Hoffmann's pictures of the group wearing Victorian swimsuits taken at Brean Down two weeks earlier. 'From Me To You' dropped to number 20 in the chart. The *Daily Mirror* also printed one of Hoffmann's Brean Down photos on page 11, headlined 'The Roaring Sixties Beatles'. 'Back to the Roaring Twenties' the paper reported, the 'days of the Blackbottom and Charleston. The sun is shining. On the beach, four young men in striped bathing suits and straw boaters go into a song and dance routine. But the song's not 'Silvery Moon' or 'Bye Bye Blackbird'.

As the annual St Brelade's Summer Fête and Winter Carnival began on Jersey, the group flew to neighbouring Guernsey on board a BEA plane. They were met on the tarmac by Les de la Mare, assistant to the shows' promoter Baron Pontin, to avoid them having to going through the public terminal. Afterwards, they were driven to the Duke of Richmond Hotel in Cambridge Park, St Peter Port, where they stayed for the following two nights. On their arrival they enjoyed lunch, which included Fresh Guernsey Salads and New Jersey Potatoes.

A lucky fan got their autographs in the hotel's foyer as they headed to the Auditorium at Candie Gardens for two performances at 7pm and 9.15pm, where twelve hundred fans at each performance paid between 10/- and 17/6 - expensive by UK prices. Billed as the Fabulous Beatles, the show was compèred by Vic Sutcliffe with support from Les Dell, the Rob Charles Combo, the Robert Brothers and Mike Kelly. In their dressing room, John broke a guitar string and asked Ivan Robert of the Robert Brothers whether he had a spare. When Robert obliged, John said, 'What do I owe you?' Robert asked for his guitar strap. His brother Bonny felt they held their own, but when the Beatles left the Candie 'we got flattened, it was unbelievable'.

Guernsey Evening Press reporter Sam Brown interviewed the group backstage between shows. Fans who were unable to get in stood outside and listened to the show through the canvas side of the auditorium. Pontin's then 15-year-old daughter Gill recalled, 'We sat in the front row right in the middle and the low stage was only a few feet away, however, although we screamed most of the way through, we all stayed in our seats as did the rest of the audience.'

Returning to their hotel, John had dinner with Royston Ellis and his girlfriend Stephanie. Ellis, a Liverpool beat poet who claimed to have suggested the group's name change from Beetles to Beatles, was working as a ferryboat engineer on the island. After consuming a lot of alcohol, Ellis, Stephanie, John and Suzanne Sellers, who was working at the hotel that summer, adjourned to Ellis' flat where he apparently suggested the four of them had sex dressed in oilskins and polythene bags. Sellers made a hasty departure.

Vee-Jay Records received a telegram from Transglobal demanding that the label immediately cease manufacture and distribution of any and all records containing performances of Frank Ifield and the Beatles (once again spelt Beattles). Despite Transglobal regarding this as a demand for termination, Vee-Jay subsequently went ahead and released *Introducing The Beatles* and four other albums' worth of material from the previously acquired master tapes.

❛ It was quite an exciting time being around in the '60s. I moved to Guernsey from Manchester when I was about 15 to work for my brother who had bought a hotel in St Peter Port. I found it rather insular, you always knew who you were going to meet at parties. My friend Maureen, who I met there, was working at a hotel in town called the Richmond, and the Beatles were staying there. We'd all gone over to the hotel after they had done the show at the Candie. I'd been working that evening, so would have gone there after work. At the end of the evening, we were all invited back to this party at Royston's. He lived in a very strange flat. I didn't know him at all and didn't even know he was a writer. I don't know how I ended up there, as I'd never met Royston and I've never seen him since, but John and I had been chatting, and sort of paired up as it were. We got to the party, and nobody else had arrived. It was just John and myself, and Royston and his girlfriend. It was quite strange, because when we got there, Royston and his girlfriend went off and made fried egg sandwiches. I'd never had a fried egg sandwich before, so that's why that sticks in my mind. After we ate the fried egg sandwiches, Royston and his girlfriend went off again, and then came back wearing these black plastic bags. John and myself kind of looked at one another, and they said, 'Do you want to join in?' and we said, 'Join in with what?', and they said, 'Well we kind of play games with these plastic bags then end up having sex.' They offered John and I a plastic bag each, I said, 'No, thank you very much.' I didn't want anything to do with that sort of thing, and as far as I can remember, neither did John. I recall afterwards that I decided to go, and John came down the stairs with me and gave me money for a cab to get home. What happened after that, I have no idea, but according to folklore, he went back, and did play the game! As a result of that, he wrote the song called 'Polythene Pam'. I certainly wasn't involved and 'Polythene Pam' certainly wasn't me! It was all very innocent between John and I. He was charming, just a real ordinary guy. We got on very well. He was very factual and not at all arrogant. Nice guy, very chatty. We mostly talked about music, and what was happening at the time – it was an exciting time in music. ❜

SUZANNE ROTHWELL, INSURANCE BROKER, HONITON, DEVON

FRIDAY 9 AUGUST

The front page of the *NME* ran with 'Close-up on Beatle, Paul McCartney'. 'Twist And Shout' climbed to number 4 in the chart, knocking Brian Poole and the Tremeloes' version down a place to number 5. This instalment of the weekly 'Close-Up On A Beatle' series took much of its material from Alan Smith's interview with Paul, conducted on the roof of the Washington Hotel on 30 July. The paper's Alley Cat announced that Wayne Fontana's next single was likely to be a Lennon/McCartney song.

'Twist And Shout' was also at number 4 in *Melody Maker*, up two places, while 'From Me To You' dropped five places to number 24. The paper's Mailbag section printed letters in response to the previous week's comments from John about being copied by other groups. Peter Vining from London N22 wrote, 'My image of the Beatles has been slightly crushed by their little tantrums on the front page of last week's *MM*. If they are the top beat group and expect not to be copied, it's about time they grew up in pop ideas. They should be proud to know that groups think their style good enough to copy. Or do they think they'll be ousted from the top by copycats? Aren't they good enough to hold their own yet? You won't last for ever, Beatles, but don't dig your own grave by annoying the groups that idolise you.' D. Hyams of London

EC1 wrote, 'I am surprised that any group should want to copy the Beatles. They are much worse on radio than on record. As for other groups climbing on the bandwagon, John Lennon must surely have made this claim with tongue in cheek. The bandwagon belongs to the entire gravy train called pop music.' C. Bean of Lincoln was even more critical, writing, 'So the Beatles complain that other groups copy them. What are they afraid of? That some of the copyists are better than the originators? The Beatles have been outclassed in at least two songs – 'Twist And Shout' by Brian Poole and 'There's A Place' by the Kestrels.'

The *Daily Mail*, Adrian Mitchell calculated the most successful chart acts of the first half of the year on a points basis. Naturally the Beatles were on top with 165 points, followed by Gerry and the Pacemakers with 139. The highest American act, Ned Miller, came in at number seven with 57 points.

Fog caused delays of up to an hour from Guernsey airport in the morning, as the group returned to Jersey for their last two shows at the Springfield Ballroom. While they were waiting to leave, John was asked whether he would like a holiday. His reply? 'Mate, it's all a holiday.'

SATURDAY 10 AUGUST

The group played their final date at the Springfield Ballroom in St Helier. The five nights netted them £1,000. Following the show, the group had dinner at the Hotel de la Plage.

> ❛ My boyfriend Eric was a Beatle fanatic with the polo-necked jumper and cardigan and Beatle haircut with full fringe. As a 16th birthday present for me, he bought two tickets to see them. He picked me up in his car and we drove to the Springfield. I didn't realise until I was inside that that was the surprise birthday present. I was absolutely amazed. We sat upstairs in the balcony, so we got a good view of them. It was so exciting. Everyone was out of their seats dancing and singing to their music. It was a packed house, upstairs and downstairs. Anywhere they could fit people in. To round off the evening, Eric took me to the Battle of Flowers Carnival and asked me to marry him. I turned him down because I was only 16. My parents were very happy when I told them I had done so. Anyway, we got married four years later when I was 20 and we had two sons together. It didn't work out and I got married a second time and have been for more than forty years. But I've never forgotten that very special night all those years ago. ❜
>
> **MARLENE JONES, ACCOUNTS OFFICE SECRETARY, ST SAVIOUR, JERSEY**

SUNDAY 11 AUGUST

The group flew back to England. Mal Evans, who began his first day as a full-time Beatles employee, met them at the airport. From this point on, he drove the Ford Thames van packed with the group's equipment, while Neil Aspinall acted as their chauffeur, driving them from place to place in an Austin Princess.

After a four-week break from the ABC in Blackpool, which had seen Frank Ifield and Gerry and the Pacemakers head the bill the previous three weeks, the Beatles returned for two shows at 6pm and 8.15pm. They topped a bill which was compèred by Jack Douglas and also featured Freddie Starr and the

Midnighters, Patti Brooks, Terry Young, Sons of the Piltdown Men, Gary and Lee. After the second show, they drove back to Liverpool.

American singer Pat Boone, in the UK filming scenes for the film *Never Put It In Writing*, played his first-ever game of cricket, appearing for the Stars XI against the Sussex county team in Hove. He said that during his stay he hadn't been able to turn on the radio without hearing the Beatles. 'I really love their 'Twist And Shout' – those screams get me – but I like 'From Me To You' best. I'd like to record it myself.'

❝ I went to see the Beatles at the ABC in 1963. Although they played a major role in challenging the deferential, class-ridden culture that hung over after the war in Britain, those pressures to conform to social norms were still very strong at that time. The fact that I bought a ticket for a seat in the posher circle, not the stalls, is evidence of this. Revolution might have been in the air that night but the influence of our parents' generation on entertainment was still strong. The variety theatre theme still dominated. The radio's *Billy Cotton Band Show* played after roast lunch on Sundays and ITV still spent *Sunday Night at the London Palladium*. As a result the Beatles were not the only 'act' to appear on the stage. The show started with a set from Freddie Starr. He would have been more at home with our parents' generation in the audience. However, bowing to the norms, we listened to Starr politely (well, mostly) and clapped as required. But the Beatles topped the bill and they were the ones the all-teenage audience wanted to see. Bowing to that theme of post-war respectability, Brian Epstein had the boys wear suits – albeit with unconventional collars; a minor detail today but a significant spark to the revolutionary kindling in those days. As the Beatles played, the stalls filled with the sound of screaming, but not the circle. Professional and slick, the boys went into one famous number after another. It came to 'Twist and Shout' and as we were encouraged to 'shake it up, baby', some girls in the circle stood and screamed too. It's difficult to believe now but the single, uniformed usherette on duty in the huge expanse of the circle merely motioned towards them with her hand to sit down and shushed them – and they stopped. Can you imagine that today? The girls merely stopped and sat down. Another social revolution crushed for a moment – but not for long. No smashed guitars or Jim Morrison nakedness that night as the lads finished with the conventional, variety hall, four-man, choreographed bow before the curtains closed on a different world. ❞

GEOFF SHOESMITH, COLLEGE LECTURER AND WRITER, LYTHAM, LANCASHIRE

MONDAY 12 AUGUST

At 3am, four girls from Epsom in Surrey – Megan Molyneux, Diane Weir, Kathryn Bowry and Rona Graham – all wearing sunglasses despite the darkness, began queuing outside the Princess Theatre in Torquay to buy tickets for the following Sunday's concerts. The Beatles, billed as 'Britain's Fabulous Disc Stars', began another week of concerts at a seaside resort, this time at the 1,883-seater Odeon on Gloddaeth Avenue in Llandudno, Caernarvonshire, on the North Wales coast – the town had enjoyed a visit from her H. R. H. Queen Elizabeth and Prince Philip the previous weekend, when they attended the National Eisteddfod at Craig-y-Don. Also featured on the Beatles' bill were Billy J. Kramer with the Dakotas, the glamorous Lana Sisters, the Sons of the Piltdown Men, Tommy Wallis and Beryl, Gary and Lee, Tommy Quickly and compère Billy Baxter.

Not for the first time, the Beatles' vehicle broke down on the way. They arrived at about 5.30pm, an hour before the first of the twice-nightly shows. *North Wales Weekly* cub reporter Judy Phillips had already been waiting more than two hours for them. She recalled 'getting a coveted interview with them was more difficult than I'd envisaged. My first approach to their management was turned down, but with the tenacity of youth I refused to give up, and finally through a contact made with Brian Epstein through a family friend, an interview was agreed. Eventually a somewhat breathless John, Paul, George and Ringo turned up, but with only an hour or so to go before the show started, I was told there was no time for an interview. My face must have dropped in disappointment.' Neil Aspinall suggested that Phillips watch the first show and then interview them before their second performance. At the end she was shepherded backstage and taken to their dressing room. 'I would say they weren't best pleased to be faced with the prospect of an interview after just coming off stage, but the initial chilly atmosphere soon dispelled, and we were quickly chatting away like old friends. John and Paul did most of the talking, with the odd interjection from George, but I recall Ringo staying silent on the periphery of the conversation.' Even faced with the sight of Paul standing in front of her with nothing more than a towel around his waist the young reporter wasn't fazed. After the second show, they made the two-minute drive down North Parade to the Grand Hotel on Happy Valley Road, where they stayed the week.

❛ 1963 stands out in my memory as a very special year. I was 16 that May and felt very grown up as a prefect at school. I had a boyfriend who lived opposite me – we used to spy on each other from our bedroom windows which was considerably easier in the winter months with no foliage to hinder our views. It was also the year of the dreaded O levels and exams loomed large in the summer months. Did anyone ever make sense of *Paradise Lost*? How to combine studying when all around me Beatlemania was exploding like a volcano? I had three school friends who all agreed with me that the Beatles were something entirely different from any sound we'd heard before. Seeing them live became something of an odyssey in 1963, and we managed to get tickets to see them four times, twice in Croydon, once in Guildford, where my father worked (he went to the Odeon and bought the tickets for us!), and once in Torquay. Although living in Surrey, my family had a guest house in Paignton so I was allowed to have friends to stay in the summer in return for helping out with the chores.

The Beatles were booked to appear in Torquay on Sunday 18 August, with the box office opening the previous Monday. So Kate, Diane, Rona and I left my parents' house at 3am and walked in the dark to the Princess Theatre on the Torquay seafront. My journal, as opposed to my tiny diary, tells me that we stopped at the telescope on the seafront to study the moon as it was a clear cloudless night. We really thought the queue would snake around the building, even at that early hour – but, joy of joys, we were first! We each wore three jumpers, jeans and had brought with us blankets (no sleeping bags then) and a flask of hot coffee. We sat down on the steps of the Princess and settled down, too excited to sleep. Unbeknown to us my mother had telephoned the local newspaper to tell them about our early-morning stroll. She loved all the excitement around music and theatre, as both she and my father were keen theatregoers in the 1930s and 1940s. A photographer arrived at about 10am, by which time the end of the queue had reached way past Torquay Harbour, about a mile away. He posed us at the box office, then took another photo of our rear as we had designed four placards, pinning one each on our backs. They read BE, AT, LE, S! and we walked four abreast so that the letters made sense! I was the 'S!' During the coming week we caused quite a stir wherever we went into Torquay that summer, as with our jeans, straw hats, sunglasses and placards, we stood out from the crowd. We had decorated the hats with Beatles' names and even drawn beetles! We threw them onstage during the show on the following Sunday, and each of the four Beatles picked up a hat and wore it at the end of their set. We really were in Beatle heaven. I maintain that being 16 in 1963 was the optimum age to enjoy the British music scene – freedom to enjoy following groups around but with few responsibilities. A very special year. My son and daughter studied Beatles' music and lyrics at their senior school in the 1980s, how cool was that? **,**

MEGAN MOLYNEUX, ACCOMMODATION MANAGER FOR
FOREIGN STUDENTS, TEIGNMOUTH, DEVON

TUESDAY 13 AUGUST

EMI Records announced that sales of the *Twist And Shout* EP had passed two hundred and fifty thousand, becoming the company's first EP to qualify for a silver disc award as well as being its fastest-selling EP. (The previous highest-selling EP had been Elvis Presley's *Jailhouse Rock*, which sold two hundred and thirty thousand.) In addition, *Please Please Me* passed one hundred and seventy-five thousand sales. The news reached the Beatles during an interview with *Disc*'s Alan Walsh in their hotel suite. George said, 'You know this fab news calls for celebration. Let's go mad and have something really strong,' at which point he phoned room service and ordered iced Cokes. Meanwhile, constant chanting of 'We Want The Beatles!' filtered in from outside.

Valerie Puckering, who worked as a chambermaid at a bed and breakfast on Claremont Road, called Dalston, recalled the evening.
'I served the guests afternoon tea every day and then had the evening off before returning to give them cocoa and biscuits. After we served tea, a fellow chambermaid, who was from Sweden, the landlady's daughter Ruth and I walked down Claremont on to St Mary's Road and Deganwy Avenue and onto Gloddaeth Street, where the Odeon was. When we got there, I discovered I'd left our tickets behind, but the people in the box office found us three which we were in the 6/6 section. I'd bought 4/6 tickets. We saw the first show and then afterwards went round the back of the building where there were some stone steps. The Beatles came out and signed autographs, but there were so many people in front of us and we had to get back to serve cocoa and biscuits, that I never got their autographs.'

294

> ❝ I was born in Huyton, Liverpool, in 1954, and was only 9 when my family went to Llandudno on holiday in the summer of 1963. We went there every year on holiday and stayed in a flat in the town centre. It was a major trip in those days. We went on the bus. It would have been about two or three hours but seemed like a week. We used to stay on the seafront, but the people who owned the property moved, and so we moved to a place in Caroline Road. My dad wasn't a particular Beatles fan and my sister was not so keen as she was a Cliff Richard fan, but my brother was. We just happened to walk past the Odeon and the ticket office was open, and Dad just walked in and got five tickets, all in a row, which would be unheard of these days. I don't remember a huge amount about it, other than they came on last, and did about half an hour. It was the era of Jelly Babies, and I have this vision stuck in my head of them flying through the air. There was some screaming, but it's all a bit vague. I recall sitting to the left of the stage at the back of the auditorium. It was the last holiday that we had together as a family, as my brother was 16 or 17, and after that year, he went on holiday on his own or with friends. My brother and I both got married eventually, and although we kept in touch, we were miles apart, and didn't get back in touch until our parents died. I said, 'Do you remember when we went to see the Beatles?' I can remember the group used to appear on local news programmes in the evening, and it must have been the end of 1962/beginning of '63, and my brother shouted, 'Oh! The Beatles are on!' and I went to have a look on the black-and-white television. At the end of the year, he bought me *With The Beatles* for Christmas. There may be more anorak-ish Beatles fans than me, but I loved them with a passion. I loved the music, I loved the era, the whole association with that era right up until the end – well it was just magic. ❞
>
> **BRIAN SMITH, SALES MANAGER, HASTINGS, EAST SUSSEX**

WEDNESDAY 14 AUGUST

Teenage girls began queuing outside Granada TV Centre in Manchester at 3.30am. Advance orders of 'She Loves You' passed two hundred and thirty-five thousand copies. EMI Managing Director Len Wood had been presented with a manufacturing order of three hundred and fifty thousand. Thinking it was far too high he agreed to two hundred and fifty thousand, despite the company's marketing manager insisting it wasn't enough. He was right – 'within weeks we had sold over a million'. John and Paul signed an agreement 'to assign to Northern Songs the full copyright in all their compositions published during a three-year period commencing February 28th, 1963'. Fifty-six copyrights were published during that time; John and Paul received 40 per cent each and Brian Epstein the remainder.

The group drove to Manchester to record two episodes of *Scene At 6.30* at Granada's Studio Four. They mimed to 'Twist And Shout' for that night's show and 'She Loves You' for the following Monday's. When they tried to leave through the studio's main entrance, they were besieged by hundreds of fans. They did a quick about-face – two of them fled back into the studio and the other two through a set of disused offices. 'I held his hand for just a minute,' one fan cried, 'I think he's gorgeous.' Even Bill Roache, *Coronation Street*'s Ken Barlow, was mobbed when he arrived at the studio. Afterwards, the group drove back to Llandudno. Mal Evans, following them in the Ford, failed to make it in time for the first show. The group used the Dakotas' equipment, which meant Paul had to play a right-handed Gibson bass upside down.

❛ My grandfather was the drummer for the Llandudno Town Band for forty-two years. They were a brass band who played on the promenade and he was the one who got me into music and taught me how to play the drums. I left the local secondary modern at 15 and got a job as an apprentice watch and clock repairer at H. Mansell's. I earned £12 10 shillings a week at the shop, and in the evenings would play as a drummer in local groups. The night the Beatles played at the Odeon was life-changing for me. I was a big fan and the place was absolutely packed. The girls were going crazy and I thought, 'I wouldn't mind a bit of that!' That evening the Beatles stayed at the Grand Hotel, and a friend of mine, who was actually a hairdresser, posed as a journalist and asked if he could have an interview with them and they let him in! There is a photograph of him with Paul and John in the Grand taken that evening having a pint.

The pivotal moment for me came when I got a call from the Kids in Geneva. They were a group from nearby Conwy Bay and had been touring with the Moody Blues. They were playing at a wedding in Switzerland, and Si Stewart was there, and fell in love with the group. He owned two clubs, one in New York and one in London. He asked them if they would be his resident group in the club in Leicester Square, so they rang me and said they were getting rid of their drummer, and would I like to join them? I jumped at the chance, and the day I joined them was the day England won the World Cup. I turned professional that day, and the next few years were the best years of my life. After our stint there, we moved to Liverpool and when we first started playing at the Cavern Club, Bob Wooler was the manager and used to guarantee us at least another gig on the same day. So, on Friday and Saturday, more often than not, we'd have three gigs on the same day. There were six of us, and it was quite hard going. The money wasn't very good, and we'd have to book into a hotel, but the experience was just outstanding. We were very impressed by Bob because he had a Mercedes convertible and lots of connections in the music industry. It was Bob who arranged for us to play on the same bill as Chuck Berry. By the end of the '60s I'd had enough and gave up drumming. The group split up, and we went our own ways. The Kids have a brick on Mathew Street, opposite the Cavern, so that is great reminder of the good old days.

A few months ago, I was in a pub in Llandudno and there was a waitress walking around with a T-shirt on that said I LOVE THE BEATLES. I got talking to her, and I said I liked the Beatles and had seen them in Llandudno in 1963. She said, 'Oh yes, I heard they came here and played at the Palladium. I read in John Lennon's biography that it was their favourite venue.' I told her it was actually the Odeon they played at, and that I couldn't imagine Llandudno Palladium being their favourite venue anyway. It wasn't until I was walking home that night that I realised it would have been the London Palladium John actually meant, but she had obviously never heard of it, and assumed the only Palladium was the one in Llandudno! It is now a Wetherspoons. ❜

PHILIP GRIFFITH, BARTENDER, LLANDUDNO, WALES

THURSDAY 15 AUGUST

The week's issue of *Disc* revealed the Beatles were going to be the subject of a BBC-TV documentary to be produced by Don Haworth. A large part was filmed in Liverpool, featuring interviews with the group and scenes shot in several local clubs. The paper also announced the release of two new EPs, the first in September, including the group's first three singles alongside 'Thank You Girl', and the second in October with 'I Saw Her Standing There', 'Misery', 'Anna' and 'Chains'. Their current EP *Twist And Shout* stayed at number 3 in the chart, while 'From Me To You' dropped out of the Top 30. In the *NRM* chart, 'From Me To You' dropped to number 27.

Tony Barrow travelled to Llandudno for the day to interview the group, in the guise of his 'Disker' persona. 'It used to be very simple to chat with folk like the Beatles and Billy J. Kramer,' he wrote. 'A trip to

Liverpool's renowned Cavern basement almost any lunchtime would take care of the whole thing. Now the barriers of stardom have closed around the great names.' John told him that, 'At theatre shows we can't even hear ourselves singing when half the audience screams through every number. It ruins the enjoyment of the other half. We've pleaded with the screamers but it hasn't made a scrap of difference.' While Ringo said, 'We feel sorry for our road manager, Neil Aspinall. Even if he parks the van miles from any theatre or studio, some fool covers it with lipstick. There are also the more harmful idiots who take parts of the vehicle as souvenirs and let down the tyres. Long after we've left by car Neil has to pump up his tyres and clean his windscreen before he can get home.'

The group played their fourth night at the Odeon.

❛ In 1963 I was 15 and attending boarding school in Cheltenham. I spent the summer holidays at home in Chester during which we had a visit from my aunt, uncle and three cousins from Kent. We managed to get tickets for a pop concert in Llandudno. On the day of the concert we headed out early and spent the day on the beach and at the funfair in Rhyl and then continued to Llandudno where we all changed in the back of the car before going to the theatre. We had balcony seats and the show featured several other acts, none of whom I can now remember. Finally the Beatles appeared and my main memory is of lots of very loud screaming. On my return to school the following month I told my school friends about the concert and four of us (can't remember who) decided to write to the Beatles in the hope of receiving a response. I decided to write to George Harrison and was the only one to include a stamp addressed envelope. That November I received a letter from George together with a copy of all four Beatles autographs. This caused much excitement in the school. The letter was read out in assembly (I can't remember by whom – certainly not me as I was too shy). When I returned home at the end of term my dad framed the letter along with the autographs, the ticket and a picture of George from a chewing gum package!

Rolling forward fifty years to September 2013, I noticed BBC-TV's *Antiques Roadshow* was visiting Exeter which happened to be the city in which the Beatles had performed the very day on which my letter from George was posted. George made reference to having had a great time in the US, but as I knew the Beatles did not visit there until 1964, I had always wondered whether the letter and the autographs were genuine so decided to take it along to the roadshow in the hope of getting them authenticated. Hilary Kay, one of the BBC researchers and presenters, took a great interest in the letter and as a result I was very lucky to be amongst a small number of people selected to be included in the actual programme. When Hilary interviewed me she explained that George and his brother had visited their sister in America in 1963 and that the letter had been written by George on their return and indeed was genuine. That was the good news. The not so good news was that George had forged all the signatures and that this was a party trick of his which he apparently continued until the day he died. The programme was screened nationally and several old school friends who saw it contacted me after a gap of fifty years but sadly their memories are not a lot better than mine! ❜

SANDRA SMITHEMAN, HOUSEWIFE, WEST HILL, DEVON

FRIDAY 16 AUGUST

The *Daily Mail*'s Adrian Mitchell wrote about them again in an article headed 'Amazing How The Off-Beat Beatles Wow All The Family.' He had been in Llandudno to interview them and see them onstage. 'The show began and the Beatles came on to a solid wall of screams,' he wrote. 'But not everyone screamed. Some fans in the 3- to 6-year-old age group preferred beating their seats with their fists. Mothers leaned forward and gazed at the Beatles as if they watched their own sons. Fathers, full of lunch, listened happily enough. Everyone smiled. That's probably the Beatles' most extraordinary achievement. Without trying at all, simply by being themselves, they have captured that famous and elusive animal, the family audience.'

In the *NME*, 'Twist And Shout' remained at number 4. EMI took out an ad in the paper – 'Still going like a bomb! The first ever EP to get in the *NME* Top 10.' The second instalment in the 'Close-Up On A Beatle' series featured George. The paper also reviewed Tommy Quickly's debut single, described by Keith Fordyce as a 'medium-paced beat number with what might be termed 'tune appeal" by 'a newcomer with a cheeky grin and a likeable personality.'

In *Melody Maker*'s chart, 'Twist And Shout' climbed to number 2, held off the top by the Searchers' 'Sweet For My Sweet', while 'From Me To You' dropped to number 28. The paper announced the Beatles would appear on the fifth birthday edition of *Saturday Club* the day after making their debut on Associated-Rediffusion's *Ready, Steady, Go!* The group played their fifth night at the Odeon in Llandudno.

❛ It was 1962 and I was an 11-plus year-old music mad schoolboy. Younger sibling of Kathryn Margaret, our parents Tom and Jean Mackey were proprietors of the Shelbourne – a central promenade hotel on the magnificent north shore of the classic Victorian holiday resort of Llandudno. I was a tall lad for my age, and probably a little ahead of others in my age group in all matters music and motors, having already learnt to drive the family car (a Triumph 2000) on the relatively deserted black rock sands at nearby Porthmadog. My somewhat rebellious mother was my chief instructor in all things gears, brakes and wheels (unbeknown to my father who would have killed us both!) and she was probably also the main influence of my youthful taste in music. With that familiar childhood memory trait of seemingly (incorrect) endless hot summers drifts back a time when pop groups would be at number one in the charts for months on end. However, just like the title of an earlier late '50s hit by the Platters, to me – these guys were all just 'Great Pretenders' to what was to become known later as the Fab Four. Imagine our reaction then when my sister and I heard that they were coming to town. The venue was to be one of the town's two (or was it three?) cinemas – the biggest and best of them all – the Odeon. Originally built in the 1930s as the Winter Gardens, this impressive two thousand-seater music hall, theatre and ballroom soon changed hands – and names, eventually becoming the Astra. Now a block of retirement apartments, this place was well known to '60s teenagers in and around the area, hosting amongst other things the weekly Friday night Teen-Beat Dance and 'Adolescent Development' night. So on a Saturday morning, sis and I made the five-minute walk from home to the Odeon, and simply lined up in the box office queue. As I recall my birthday was on the first opening night – Monday the 12th, however we could only get tickets for a later performance that week. Around a month's pocket money was duly handed over for two mid row seats at just over 6 shillings each (around 30p in today's money). Crikey!

The big night came, and we joined the full house audience for the early show. I honestly can't remember the batting order as all we were really interested in was the main event. I think the main thing that sticks in my mind, as they were announced as the final act, was the noise. My goodness there was noise! Floors were thumped with two thousand pairs of shoes and boots, seats were clapped open and shut, and young girls screamed their lungs out as baby faced Paul and bad boy John appeared stage left. This applause quickly built into a crescendo of whistles and screams the likes of which I had never heard in all my young life. Sadly, this completely drowned out the music but strangely took nothing away from the night. What an experience – the guys just battled on against all the odds – well used to this reception by now I'm sure. They could have literally simply stood there or even hidden behind the curtains all night and the reaction would have been the same. Adulation. The show was over all too soon, but the night was by no means over.

We, along with several hundred others, gathered around the rear stage door area, in the hope of seeing them leave. After what seemed like ages, they emerged to a waiting van, and it drove off slowly and carefully as the whole road was just full of fans. We ran up to the Grand Hotel on the pier and gathered at the main door, having been tipped off that this was where they were staying. Sure enough, in a few minutes they arrived and climbed out to get inside the lobby. There seemed to be no security at all, so the fans just crowded around them, myself included. Clutching my alternating blue/pink pages' autograph book – I squeezed my way in closer and closer to the lads until I was standing, jostled up next to Paul McCartney. I thrust the book into his hand shouting, 'Please sign it!' He took the book from me, scribbled in it and passed it to George, who in turn passed it to Ringo. From there I lost sight of it in the crowd. A few seconds later a hand thrust the book out towards us, but, as I tried to reach it, someone jumped up on my shoulders and grabbed it. Turning around quickly I saw the culprit running off back down towards the town, with my big sister in hot pursuit. She caught him up and wrenched the book from his thieving mitts. I caught up with her and we made our way along the short stretch of promenade. Upon arriving back home we checked the pages and I was very happy to see all four signatures intact on one page.

So after the drama of nearly losing the book, you'd think I would have guarded it with my life, eh? Sadly, it was later lost again – I know not where or how. Along with various vinyl LPs, photographs, loudspeakers, turntables, guitars, crushed velvet trousers, shoulder length hair and flowery shirts... simply gone. As I've come to realise over many years of attending music gigs, it's not just about the music, or the lyrics, or the lights, it's about 'being there.' I'm glad I was there, and that my big sister was too. 〕

TIM MACKEY, RETAIL FOOD DIVISIONAL STORES DIRECTOR, LLANDUDNO, NORTH WALES

SATURDAY **17 AUGUST**

Details of Tony Barrow's travels to Llandudno two days earlier appeared in his weekly 'Disker' column for the *Liverpool Echo*. He revealed he used the Beatles' record player to review the week's singles while there.

The Beatles' six-day stint at the Odeon came to a close. During the week's chaos, cinema manager Roy Bentley had to lower the safety curtain when the audience wouldn't leave at the end of show; St John Ambulance were called in to deal with fainting girls; fans waited round the back of the Odeon to get the group's autographs; and cinema staff exited through the stage door in overcoats and Beatle wigs, to allow the Beatles to leave through the front into an awaiting car. Before the final show, Alan Smith interviewed Ringo in his hotel room while he packed. He told Smith that he could see himself owning

a hair salon at some point in the future. 'I figure it would be a good business move. Girls will always want their hair doing, and if the Beatles ever fell through I'd have a good side-line. I could go round from time to time saying, "Is everything all right, madam? A cup of coffee, perhaps? Or would you like a tot of whisky?"' When the article appeared, Paul mentioned that the group were thinking of having Ringo out front dancing for a few numbers, while one of the other Beatles (presumably Paul) took over on the drum kit. After the second show, Neil Aspinall drove Ringo, Paul and George back to Liverpool.

The *North Wales Weekly News* reported that the Beatles 'had a devastating effect on some teenagers during their visit. One girl who paid 8s 6d for a seat near the front of the theatre is reported to have fainted as soon as the group stepped onstage and to have missed the whole of their act. Perhaps she thought the glory of being carried out of the theatre in full view was worth the sacrifice.' Not everyone felt the same way. A. T. wrote, 'I was appalled and disgusted at the unbelievable display of mass hysteria which took place at the theatre,' while 'Square' Visitor said he 'wouldn't have missed the experience,' but would never go again when staying in Llandudno.

❛ My mother Georgina emigrated to the United States in 1956 and I was born three years later in Sacramento, California. In 1963 we returned to the UK to visit relatives. My uncle Jon met us off the ship when we arrived in Liverpool. He had been a young art student at Liverpool Art College where he made friends with another student there, John Lennon. The family myth goes that John even asked Jon to play drums in the group. When he declined because he didn't know how to play, John said, 'That's all right, none of us know how to play.' He told us that John was a tough guy and would protect him from the bullies. He was a good friend to have.

Later that summer we went to stay with my grandmother Doris at 33, Bryniau Road in Llandudno. Being only 3 at the time I can only remember parts of what happened, but fortunately my mother wrote down her memories of what happened. Uncle Jon came to stay as well. While we were there the Beatles were performing at the Odeon. They were already so famous that he was hesitant about contacting them. He felt that because of their notoriety they would not remember who he was. Eventually he plucked up courage and decided to go to the stage door and ask for John Lennon. A few minutes later John came running down the stairs, so pleased to see him. Apparently, they were tired of being mobbed by strangers that seeing someone they knew was a great pleasure. The following day was my 4th birthday. Jon took me to the Grand where they were staying. I remember climbing this gorgeous circular staircase. When we arrived they were all still asleep. As we walked through the door, Paul jumped out of his bed in his undershorts. They called room service and ordered breakfast. After eating his corn flakes, John decided it was time to shave. His face was covered in lather when he heard a small group of girls screaming outside the window. He leaned out and to all the girls' delight, he flicked the lather off his face and it fell down on them. Then he turned to me and teasingly said he would throw me to the fans below. I hung onto my uncle's leg – I was too young to realise he was joking.

In the afternoon, Jon took John and Paul to Conwy where they rented a rowing boat and went out on the river. Then he brought them back to Bryniau Road for tea. My grandmother had made salmon sandwiches, jelly and, of course, birthday cake. John and Paul duly sang 'Happy Birthday' to me. Paul gave my mother a box of chocolates. My grandmother was running a bed and breakfast at the house at the time and employed a young girl to come in each day to wash the dishes. She took that Saturday off to go and see the group. She never got over the fact that they came to the house when she wasn't there. Apparently after the show she caught a close-up glimpse of them. When they left the theatre and got into their car, she was almost run over as she clung to their car door. A mother and daughter were staying in the house and as John and Paul were leaving the daughter bumped into them. She immediately ran upstairs and told her mother that the Beatles were downstairs. Her mother said, 'You must be crazy. The Beatles wouldn't be in a bed and breakfast house in Wales.' Four years later, John and Paul sponsored an art exhibition for my uncle. Three thousand people attended the opening. By the time the show was over, every one of his paintings had sold. Sometime later, Jon found a house in Leamington Spa that he wanted to buy, but none of the banks would lend him any money. He had a job teaching art at University two days a week. One evening he was out with John and told him about the house. John asked, 'Where is it and how much does it cost?' The next day John phoned him and asked him to come over to his house. When my uncle got there, John showed him the deed on his desk – bought and paid for with everything in Jon's name. They made an agreement that Jon would take out a life insurance policy with John as his beneficiary. He thought that when the policy matured he might be penniless. Jon continued to pay the policy and after John died he went to a solicitor and asked him what to do about it. 'Are you mad?' he said, 'if you died, Yoko Ono would get the money. She's one of the richest women in the world. You have fulfilled your obligation. Cash it in.' Jon never did like Yoko, so he took the money and ran. That February after meeting them in Llandudno, I saw them on *The Ed Sullivan Show*. I couldn't understand how they'd got inside the television set. ∎

CATHY MILLS, TEACHER, RENO, NEVADA, USA

SUNDAY 18 AUGUST

Mal Evans, Tony Bramwell and John left Llandudno in the bus late in the morning and headed to Torquay. They travelled on the A5, with John at the wheel – yet to take his driving test. He almost drove the bus off the road at Horseshoe Pass, a notoriously dangerous stretch outside Llandegla. Paul, George and Ringo drove in their cars from Liverpool. They all arrived in time for the first of two shows at the Princess Theatre on Torbay Road, where Bruce Forsyth was starring in the resident summer show, *Show Time*.

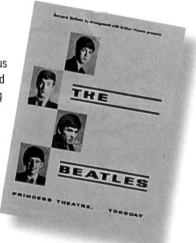

Crowds had begun gathering in the early afternoon, and hundreds of fans without tickets were turned away. A 6/- ticket was selling for £1. Extra police were called in to protect the group once they arrived at the theatre, which was surrounded by a solid mass of screaming teenagers. The show also featured the Fourmost, Rod and Carolyn, Lynne Perri, Bob Bain, Barry Barnett, Harold Collins and the Princess Theatre Orchestra. A second show followed at 8.30pm. For one autograph hunter, John signed 'Benny Higgins (Juggler)'. Following the show, the group adjourned to the Imperial Hotel, where John, Paul and Ringo, celebrating his first anniversary with the group, played snooker with a fellow guest. A tired George went to bed.

The *Paignton News* commented, 'I was certainly looking forward to seeing the Beatles at the Princess Theatre on Sunday evening. But I wondered after the show, whether it had been worth it. For me, their act was spoilt by the continuous screaming of hundreds of girls who made up two-thirds of the audience ... the Beatles pounded their way through their act, apparently unperturbed by the mass hysteria which they had generated in the audience.' The *Herald Express* remarked, 'The screaming was continuous during the show, but there was no trouble. It was fantastic that so many youngsters could get so excited and yet behave themselves.'

> **❝** My friend Diane and I went regularly to the Princess Theatre in Torquay on Sunday evenings, so we were particularly excited when we found out that the Beatles were coming. Diane worked in Torquay and got up early on the day the box office opened and joined the long queue at the theatre to get tickets. Even being there by about 6am, she still only managed to get us seats in the back row. On the day of the concert I can remember we were very excited but didn't want to forgo our afternoon on the beach. Her family had a beach hut so we planned to go to the beach after lunch, spend the afternoon there, then get changed in the hut and go off to Torquay on her Lambretta. I can remember we thought we were very daring, haring about on a scooter, I even had a long black scarf tied around my crash helmet; the idea had been that it would flow out dramatically behind us but it didn't work like that; it spent lots of time wound around my face – fortunately not Diane's! Diane picked me up and we set off for the beach but the dear old Lambretta broke down. We, of course, knew nothing about what to do but stand by the roadside looking helpless and two guys stopped and helped us to get it going, so we invited them down to the beach for the afternoon. All very innocent, even gave them a cup of tea. They then left us and we changed to go to the theatre. I remember Diane wore grey hipster trousers and looked great. I could have scratched her eyes out! However, the guys hadn't earned their cups of tea because the Lambretta wouldn't start. We gave no thought to the security of the scooter, we had to get to the concert, so we toiled in the sun up a very long steep hill and caught the bus into Torquay and got there in time for the concert. The theatre was packed and the atmosphere was amazing. I'm not sure we heard a word of what they sang. It was enough just to be there and see them and we came out reeling with excitement. We had seen the Beatles! We had to ring Diane's mum to come over to Torquay and fetch us. She was very, very angry. She could just not understand how much more important it was to see the Beatles than to worry about the Lambretta. But the scooter was OK when Diane collected it the following day and it was repaired. **❞**
>
> **JAN NICHOLLS, SECRETARY, THAME, OXFORDSHIRE**

MONDAY 19 AUGUST

The group made their way east along the south coast to Bournemouth for a week-long stint at the 1,755-seater Gaumont on Westover Road, with Billy J. Kramer with the Dakotas, Tommy Quickly, the Glamorous Lanas, Sons of the Piltdown Men, Garry and Lee, Tommy Wallis and Beryl in support and compèred by Billy Baxter. Cynthia accompanied John for the week's visit and Paul's father also stayed the week. Under cloudy and thundery skies, Ringo arrived in his new car at the Palace Court Hotel next to the Gaumont. His previous car, a Ford Zephyr Zodiac Mk II, had so many messages from fans scratched on its paintwork that he decided to sell it. (Unfortunately for the buyer, drummer Brian Redman, fans weren't aware it was no longer Ringo's and continued to vandalise the vehicle.)

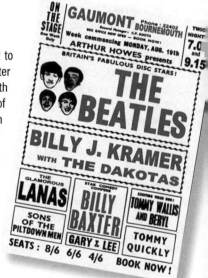

AUGUST

The box office opened at 10am for nightly 7pm and 9.15pm shows, with tickets selling between 4/6 and 8/6. A queue formed, blocking the entrances to the ABC and the Bournemouth Ice Rink further down Westover Road. In between shows, a party was held backstage in their dressing room for birthday boy Billy J. Kramer, now 20 years old. The Beatles, who sent a telegram with the message 'Happy Birthday, from your proud parents – the Beatles', and the Dakotas toasted him with iced Cokes. Kramer said, 'This is just about the most fabulous birthday anyone could ever have. A record at the top of the hit parade for the second time and a birthday party with the Beatles and the Dakotas – what more could anyone want?' The previous Wednesday's recording of *Scene At 6.30* aired on Granada TV.

❝ My dad had a small shop in a suburb of Bournemouth selling second-hand guitars, and I began to learn the electric guitar. A fellow teenager by the name of Al Stewart spotted the shop on his way into Bournemouth from Wimborne, hopped off the bus and came in. We got chatting and became immediate friends from that moment on. By 1963, there was so much happening. That August, Al and I talked our way into meeting the Beatles. I was then 16, but looked slightly older, Al was 17. We were both involved in the local music scene. As the audience at the first performance began to leave, I suggested to Al an idea that might get us backstage. With some trepidation he agreed. Instead of leaving the theatre we went to the manager's office, where I told him we had come down from London and had Rickenbacker-related business to discuss with the Beatles' management and couldn't get through the huge stage door crowds – could he help? Slight pause – he reached for a phone to the stage door. 'A Mr Kremer and a Mr Stewart are coming round – let them in.' This duly transpired.

I found myself knocking on their dressing-room door with Al just behind me. It was opened by Neil Aspinall. He took one look and obviously thought, 'How on earth did they get here?', but as we'd managed to actually get backstage, he assumed that we must have some connection. Rickenbacker were relatively obscure guitars at the time – Al and I must have been two of only a handful of people who had ever heard of them in Bournemouth – so he must have thought, 'Oh what the hell,' and went to get John. Door closed. Minutes passed. The door opened again – this time by Lennon, wearing black horn-rimmed glasses, and had changed from his stage suit into a blue denim shirt. He said it was too busy in the dressing room so we started chatting in the hallway. He seemed to enjoy chatting with us and went back into the dressing room and reappeared with his Rickenbacker and handed it to me. I very nervously strummed a few chords and passed it to Al – even then a vastly superior guitarist. While we were strumming his guitar, he was just looking on laconically. While talking about their first house performance we mentioned the relatively low volume from his Vox amp. He said he'd turn it up for the next house. Next day the *Bournemouth Echo* review raved about them, of course, but complained about the overwhelmingly loud guitar of John Lennon.

The Beatles and the supporting groups stayed at the Palace Court Hotel. Hotel staff kept the main entrance doors closed, restricting to guests only. The first time Al and I passed this 'guard' was the following day with Ray Jones of the Dakotas. After this we just came and went as we pleased, as it was erroneously assumed we were connected with the Dakotas. The lounge was on the first floor with balconies overlooking Westover Road. The girls across the road kept their gaze on the balconies, and of course the hotel entrance. Part of the lounge had been temporarily partitioned off for the Beatles and the other acts. We would sit around there with the Dakotas. Eventually, well into the afternoon, the Beatles would appear – well three of them. Paul McCartney wasn't about when we were there. They sat around a low, lounge table near to us. Al and I didn't exchange many words with them, striving to seem cool and be part of things – aware that we might be asked to leave at any moment.

303

That afternoon I sat at the next table as John, George and Ringo were interviewed by *The Beatles* monthly. During this, from time to time, someone, not a Beatle, would go out onto the balcony, causing the girls waiting across the way to break into screams. To my amazement when this happened, John, in the middle of the interview, would shout, 'SHUT UP!' at the top of his voice. After a while he got up, went out onto the balcony for a moment, causing a predictable cascade of screaming. At one point, casting 'cool' aside, I thought I'd better get their autographs. The problem was I only had a pencil. George, who seemed quiet during the interview, got as far as 'George' and broke the pencil. He said, 'Sorry, I broke your pencil. John give me your pen.' So for all these years I've had George's signature in part pencil and part ink, followed by John and Ringo in ink. On the Thursday afternoon the Beatles went to Southampton to film a TV slot and the Dakotas decided to meet up with Billy J. Kramer at the Gaumont. We left with them. As soon as we reached the street, the crowd of girls, recognising a group connected to the Beatles, broke into a screaming run and to my delight chased us into the theatre, where someone slammed the doors shut after us. Our very own *A Hard Day's Night* moment. Later that evening I briefly stood in the wings while the Beatles performed till spotted in the gloom and told to leave by a stage hand. **⌡**

JON KREMER, AUTHOR, BOURNEMOUTH, DORSET

TUESDAY 20 AUGUST

Sean O'Mahony, Leslie Bryce and Peter Jones arrived in Bournemouth to photograph and interview the group for *The Beatles Book*. When the contents of the interview appeared in future issues, Jones used the pseudonym Billy Shepherd. The group spent time sitting in the lounge of the hotel. John had some fun with his new tape recorder, recording the phrase, 'A pot of tea and some cucumber sandwiches please,' playing it when an elderly waiter came to take an order. Unable to work out who was placing the order, the waiter wandered off. O'Mahony and Jones chatted with John, George and Ringo, while Paul went off on his own. O'Mahony later wrote, 'Standing at the side of the stage in Bournemouth was a bit like watching four people playing to a volcano. Everything they did brought great roars of approval and any extra movement or sound produced an immediate reaction which at times threatened to overwhelm them.' During the week John was also interviewed by Alan Smith for the last 'Close-Up On A Beatle' article.

Photographer Robert Freeman drove down from London and was greeted in reception by Brian Epstein, who took him into the lounge, informing him that they would be down about midday. 'They're late risers.' Freeman had sent a portfolio of his work to the group while they were performing in Llandudno, featuring large black-and-white prints of jazz musicians including Cannonball Adderley, Dizzy Gillespie, Coleman Hawkins, Elvin Jones and John Coltrane. His shots of Coltrane particularly appealed to the group. Freeman's first recollection of meeting them were of 'old ladies surrounding them and asking questions. The Beatles all assumed Oxford accents and every time they were asked questions like, "How old are you?" they would give their age and ask, "And how old are you?"'

The 'Rickenbacker representatives', Jon Kremer and Al Stewart, now passing themselves off as reporters with the *Echo*, managed to gain access to the hotel's lounge, with the help of Dakota Ray Jones. For the rest of the week, hotel staff thought they were members of the Dakotas. They invited the group to a party at Le Disque a Go! Go! where Stewart's group the Trappers were playing that night. They declined.

The tenth episode of *Pop Go The Beatles*, recorded on 16 July and featuring guests Russ Sainty and the Nu-Notes, aired at 5pm. The recording of 'She Loves You' from the ninth episode, recorded on the same day, opened the show. The group played their second night at the Gaumont, where Freeman saw them perform for the first time.

Following a three-week run at the Manchester Opera House, the revue *Six Of One* opened at Liverpool's Royal Court Theatre. One of the show's sketches featured Dora Bryan, Amanda Barrie, Pamela Hart and Sheila O'Neill donning black wigs and Cardin cardigans as the Cockroaches in a sketch called 'The Liver Poules'. The *Liverpool Daily Post*'s review said it 'brought the house down'.

❛ My twin sister Dilys and I were born and bred in Bournemouth, attending the local primary and secondary schools. There was quite a lot to do in the town in the early '60s. It was still a popular holiday resort, and there was an international foreign language school which brought lots of young people to the area. In those days you left school early to work, which I did when I was 15. I had a godfather who worked at the *Bournemouth Evening Echo*, and he managed to get me a job there. I wasn't particularly interested in photography at all, but I went, was trained, attended college, and stayed there for twelve years.

In August 1963, a press release arrived at the newspaper's office announcing that the Beatles were coming to the Gaumont for a week. I can't say I really knew of them that well, but being a young member of staff I went along with a camera and press pass to take some photographs. It was around the time of our 20th birthday and Dilys persuaded me to take her along. Brian Epstein was standing outside the dressing room. I had my pass, so was allowed in, but it took a bit of persuading to get Dilys in. I said to Brian, 'This is my twin sister, and it's her birthday today,' which wasn't strictly true, it was a week later! He said, 'They all say that,' but let her in anyway. The group were absolutely charming. We were in there for a little while. Dilys sat on a stool and they all gathered round, and I took some photographs. The next day at the morning conference in the office, I submitted the pictures, and the editor, Douglas Simms, said, 'Who the devil are these? The Beatles? Never heard of them!' So he never used the pictures.

I suppose we weren't really a progressive newspaper at the time, certainly not as far as music was concerned, but when they returned later that year to the Winter Gardens, it was a completely different story. They were really big by then, and I would never have got Dilys in to see them then. A group of local journalists were ushered in for seven minutes while the group were playing Scalextric. It was all stage managed. I remember loads of cuddly toys the girls had sent them, and John Lennon said that he was saving them all for Julian. This time we used the pictures I took! **"**

DAVID EVANS, PHOTOGRAPHER AND JOURNALIST, SWINDON, WILTSHIRE

WEDNESDAY 21 AUGUST

The group spent most of the day relaxing at the hotel when they could. By now, teenage girls were sleeping outside the back of the hotel, some finding their way inside through back doors and roaming the floors in search of their idols. Others patrolled out front with binoculars. One morning, an enterprising group got into the Gaumont through the stage door and tore the buttons off the Beatles' stage suits. The less enterprising just sat there and kissed their Cuban boots. One less fortunate girl from London, spending the week on holiday at the seaside resort, discovered on her return that all her Beatles records had been stolen from her home.

The Beatles performed their third night at the Gaumont. Columnist Nancy Spain, who thought 'Twist And Shout' was the most diabolical noise ever recorded by anyone, drove to Bournemouth to write an article for *She* magazine. She spent the evening in the Beatles' dressing room and had dinner with the group after the show. She lent her pink Jacqmar scarf to Paul, who needed a tie to enter the hotel's dining room. 'He turned it into a tie with Windsor knot [and] carried it off with an air'. George ordered a whisky and Coca-Cola but sent the whisky back because it was bourbon, while John enjoyed a whisky and lime.

At Abbey Road, George Martin and his engineers Norman Smith and Geoff Emerick edited and mixed tracks for the group's new LP.

" As I look back now I realise that my journey as one of the first teenagers, started on a day in the autumn of 1962 when four young men appeared on the television singing their new song. Their sound and appearance was different. My boyfriend, now my husband of more than fifty years started laughing, he was a rock and roller through and through. My dad [Tom Mellor, Chief Technician/ Engineer at the Gaumont] declared, 'We've got them coming to us next year in August... What ****** idiot booked them during our peak season?' Dad didn't know who they were, but I did. It was THE BEATLES. It was Monday 19 August and I took the yellow trolley bus as usual into work at Bobby's Department Store in Bournemouth Square. During that morning my dad came across to the store to give me the very sad news that my grandfather had died and that he had put my mum and my brother on the plane to Manchester. This news had not been received earlier because the telegram boy had called on the Sunday and posted the telegram through the letter box of the shop below. Dad said to me, 'You had better come across to the theatre after work; you can have your dinner in the restaurant and then come and join me on the sound desk.' My dad had overall responsibility for everything that happened onstage, front and rear and in the theatre. So began my amazing week into seeing and hearing the Beatles live, twice nightly. As I made my way across Bournemouth Square I became aware of the crowds gathering in front of and either side of the theatre. I walked past them and into the theatre foyer and asked for my dad. The fans were piling into the auditorium. There was a great atmosphere of excitement and anticipation as the show began. As the second half of the show began some of the girls began screaming and calling out 'John! ...Paul! ...George! ...Ringo!' Yes, the girls screamed and called out, but when Paul did the introductions most of the fans listened and when they began to scream again Paul shushed them and they became quiet. John was so funny, clowning around and making us all laugh, he would echo Paul's 'Clap your hands... stamp your feet.'

The audience was very well behaved as they performed their songs. Each day the fans thronged the main road and pavements around the theatre, the shopkeepers complaining because their customers couldn't get in. The crowds brought the traffic to a standstill. Whenever an upstairs window in the Gaumont opened the fans would scream and shout. Every day I would walk past the queues and make my way into the theatre, much to the puzzlement of the fans outside. Once inside I would make my way up to the circle and join my dad on the sound desk. On the Wednesday, something special happened. During their performance, Paul announced they had a new song which was to be released on Friday. John shouted, 'Buy your copy please.' They then sang 'She Loves You' to us all, days before its release. None of us knew then the impact this new song was going to have.

It was part of my dad's professional practice to record every artist and group for sound purposes only. He would use his reel-to-reel tape recorder, capturing the ambient sound in the theatre. Dad was an expert in acoustics. He did this for all shows. I knew that Dad did this and had even heard the LIVE recording from that Wednesday. I never ever screamed during performances because I didn't want to miss anything and if I had, Dad would not have let me stand alongside him. I will never ever forget hearing Paul singing 'A Taste Of Honey'. It was so beautiful. Then when John sang 'Baby It's You', everyone went silent. You could hear a pin drop. These two songs were stunning and very moving. The audience joined hands and swayed when they sang 'Chains', it was wonderful. My journey up to and experiencing Beatlemania was only the beginning of yet another story. ❞

**IRENE DRAPER, SOCIAL WORKER AND MANAGER OF DAY
CARE CENTRE, BOURNEMOUTH, DORSET**

THURSDAY 22 AUGUST

The front page of the week's *Disc* wished Billy J. Kramer a 'Happy Birthday!', reporting that the Lennon/McCartney-written 'Bad To Me' had topped the chart. A photo of Kramer cutting his birthday cake, surrounded by Beatles and Dakotas, graced the cover. 'Twist And Shout' dropped a place to number 4, alongside news that 'She Loves You' had reached advanced orders of two hundred and fifty thousand, Don Nicholl reviewed the single. 'The Beatles, of course, will zip straight into the parade with their latest release. Their sound is extremely exciting on this 'She Loves You' half... instruments pounding and the boys chanting powerfully. Admittedly that's all that will be needed, just now, to give the group another hit seller. But – forgive me if I carp – what a pity to waste such energy and rhythmic enthusiasm on such an ordinary song. The lyric is feeble and unimaginative. I would have thought that a team of such youthful vigour, riding high on such a wave of approbation, could afford to set its sights a little higher than this. This song's about as ambitious as sitting in an armchair waiting for your pension to be delivered!'

In the *NRM* chart, 'Bad To Me' also made it to the top while 'From Me To You' dropped to number 37. The paper's 'She Loves You' review raved, 'That noise you hear is the Beatles' newie rushing straight into the charts – an advance order of quarter of a million, for a start. Two Lennon-McCartney numbers. Top side is strictly fab, pushed along at precisely the right pace, with a stack of vocal attack. Solid instrumental fair pounding along behind the vocal work. We just can't think of anything to have a go about. Flip is slightly slower and features another swingingly commercial slice of Merseybeat. A value-for-money coupling but the top side will attract most of the attention. Just clear that number one spot, that's all.' They gave it a four-star rating.

The group met Robert Freeman around noon. Using a Pentax SLR with 180mm telephoto lens – with its aperture set at F22 – he took a series of shots for use on their forthcoming LP. He recalled that 'they had to fit in the square format of the cover, so rather than have them all in a line, I put Ringo in the bottom right corner, since he was the last to join the group. He was also the shortest, although he still had to kneel on a stool to get in the right position.' The session took no more than an hour. Freeman subsequently photographed sleeves for *A Hard Day's Night*, *Beatles For Sale*, *Help!* and *Rubber Soul*. For this first sleeve, Epstein persuaded EMI to pay Freeman £75 rather than the originally proposed £25.

After eating lunch in the hotel dining room, the group drove – with Freeman – to Southern ITV Centre in the Southampton suburb of Northam to appear on *Day By Day*, miming to 'She Loves You'. It aired later in the day between 5.55pm and 6.40pm as the group prepared for their fourth night at the Gaumont. After the session, John, George and Ringo returned to their hotel, where they were interviewed by Chris Roberts. Paul and his father drove to Pontins in Bracklesham Bay to see Mike and Bett Robbins. Paul patiently signed autographs for thrilled teenagers who were on holiday. They got back to Bournemouth just as the group were getting ready to go to the Gaumont. Roberts described the scene: 'From the hotel balcony, you can see them outside. A knot of girls patiently waiting outside the swing doors, a long line of girls sitting on the wall opposite the hotel, scanning the balcony, the windows for the breath of a Beatle. Time to leave the theatre. Female faces squashed against the glass. The screams and thumping, muffled by the doors and a phalanx of policemen and hotel porters, rises to explosion point as the rest of the Beatles saunter downstairs.' During one of the shows, a 5" metal blanket pin was thrown onstage. Paul told Roberts to tell fans not to throw things at them. 'It's the girls, you see. They can't throw properly, they just aim for the stage and hurl away. It's bloody dangerous. This could have taken someone's eyes out.'

❝ Summer, Bournemouth and the Beatles were going to be there for a week. Three of us, my sister and I and a school friend were ardent fans from first hearing 'Love Me Do'. We'd seen the group in Southampton where they were on the bill with Roy Orbison, and also at Salisbury City Hall, just a dance hall where we were sandwiched close to the stage, but this was going to be special. We planned our week with care. We lived 20 miles away but could buy a cheap train ticket to travel every day. Our plan was to wander the streets and beaches and come across the group relaxing on the beach where we would be able to talk to them. We knew we needed to be eye-catching, so during that sunny August week we wore hot, hairy jumpers, because they had to be black and polo necked, just like the Beatles own gear. As we were penniless schoolgirls this required some ingenuity, I think they call it upcycling now. We borrowed my dad's work jumpers, one had to be dyed black, a very messy process carried out in our kitchen sink, and on the front embroidered huge beetle emblems, with the slogan, 'Wanted Beatles'. It was based loosely on the Western movie posters of the time and we like to think they were forerunners of slogan T-shirts that came later. At the end of the week they had to be unpicked and handed back!

We soon discovered the group were staying at the hotel right next to the theatre where they were to perform each night, so we spent much of each day at the little park across the road with forays to the back of the hotel and theatre. I can't remember seeing that many other fans, but during our wonderful week we managed to startle George by squealing when he appeared and rapidly disappeared from his balcony, and we chatted to Paul and his dad (who was charming) and managed to get autographs when they all set out for the TV studios in Southampton. We could only afford to go to the show just once, but of course it was fabulous. During the week this photographer came over to us and told us that Paul had noticed us and asked to take our photograph. At the time we thought little of it but much later learned it was Robert Freeman. Looking back, that year of our lives seemed a bit of a dream, a very intense period. The week before we had been sulky teenagers on a family holiday on the Isle of Wight, hearing about the Great Train Robbery. A week later it was GCE results. My friend started work and my sister and I went back to school. In the autumn during my French A Level class I was stunned to find our photo in a French magazine.

We saw the Beatles one last time in November again in Bournemouth but by this time Beatlemania had taken off. Perversely this was the point our ardour cooled as fans, we still loved the music but the attraction had been to be an early fan. My sister and I pestered our local newsagent each month to make sure we had an early delivery of the Beatles magazine, and of course we each had our own copy. We couldn't bear to wait and share. We collected all our memorabilia and stuck it onto a roll of wallpaper, left it in our parents' loft, and later our mum threw it away. My husband Chris, who I met up in Birmingham while I was studying at Library School just three years later in 1966, contacted Robert Freeman in the 1980s to ask for a good copy of the photograph of the three of us. We'd seen the picture again in his book *Yesterday*. I wrote to him and to my surprise saw the letter reprinted in his next book, *The Beatles – A Private View* and because it included my address in full, had loads of fan letters from all round the world. Recently I was rummaging through some of my memories and came across a play I wrote at the time called *Beatles In Our Belfries*. 〕

LINDA BURROWES, LIBRARIAN,
BASINGSTOKE, HAMPSHIRE

FRIDAY 23 AUGUST

The group's fourth single, 'She Loves You', backed with 'I'll Get You', was released. Keith Fordyce reviewed the single in the *NME*, headlined 'Another Beatles' Winner'. 'It wouldn't need a remarkable prophet to predict that the new release from the Beatles is going to be another No. 1. Gigantic advance orders ensure success for 'She Loves You', a bright entertaining and catchy sample of the Mersey sound.' Alan Smith's interview with Ringo the previous Saturday was published – the third of four 'Close-Up On A Beatle' articles.

The front page of the week's *Melody Maker* read, 'Beatles – The D-J Verdict'. David Jacobs described the single as 'rather disappointing', while Brian Matthew said, 'It is the first Beatles record that hasn't knocked me out.' On the other hand, Alan Freeman thought it was a 'great record' and Jimmy Savile offered the opinion, 'Great, man, great. Great beat, great atmosphere all the way through. What? Have I heard it? No.' Guest reviewers the Temperance Seven were somewhat less complimentary. 'The lyrics are fatuous and erotic. If this is the Beatles, they're heading downwards, although there was something about their other records that was good. They have descended to the general mire. Once they were distinctive. No longer. Poor beat stuff, this.' 'Bad To Me' went to number one in both the *NME* and *Melody Maker* charts, while 'Twist And Shout' dropped one place to number 3 in *Melody Maker* and to number 5 in the *NME*. 'From Me To You' dropped to number 35 in *Melody Maker*.

A doctor was called to George's room and prescribed tonic and bed rest. Taking his advice, George spent the day in bed, writing the song 'Don't Bother Me'. George later recalled, 'I don't think it's a particularly good song, it mightn't even be a song at all but at least it showed me that all I needed to do was keep on writing and then maybe eventually I would write something good. I still feel now "I wish I could write something good". It's relativity. It did, however, provide me with an occupation.' He also found time to write to Astrid Kirchherr. After the fifth night at the Gaumont, the group were interviewed in their dressing room by Klas Burling for Sveriges Radio. When asked whether they would like to visit to Sweden, Paul said, 'We want to come because we've heard about the girls in Sweden. All gorgeous blondes, you know.' They explained that 'I'll Get You' was intended to be their new single until they penned 'She Loves You'. Burling, accompanied by English singer Michael Cox, had driven to Bournemouth in his Fiat Juventus by way of the Gothenburg ferry.

Later the group – minus George, who was still not feeling well – attended the Variety Artists' 10th Anniversary Ball at the Exeter Hotel. John and Cynthia, celebrating their first wedding anniversary, took to the dance floor for a leisurely waltz or two, while Ringo settled for the hully gully. Ringo and Paul drank rum and Cokes at the bar while chatting to the *Bournemouth Times*' Tony Crawley. They told him they'd bought all two hundred and thirty-five thousand advance order copies of their new single. 'Well, we've bought them. That's why we've come out tonight. Can't move in our hotel suite for discs!' Cynthia was having her first true experience of the mayhem. 'It's fantastic. I just popped out to do some shopping and lots of them asked me for my autograph.'

GAUMONT THEATRE
BOURNEMOUTH
The Beatles & Billy J. Kramer
with The Dakotas
1st Performance 7-0
FRIDAY
AUGUST 23
CIRCLE
O53 4/6
No Tickets exchanged nor money refunded
TO BE GIVEN UP

❝ My parents had a business in a village called Kinson. Until reaching my teens, my mother insisted – quite rightly – that I be attired in short trousers, tweed jacket and a school cap. I was quite an accomplished musician – I played the guitar and trumpet – and in the late '50s joined the Jan Ralfini Orchestra. Later I served as a rifleman and section NCO in the Royal Green Jackets. I played trumpet with the Bournemouth Silver Band whilst at school, playing at half-time on the pitch at Dean Court football ground, and in the bandstand in Fisherman's Walk and Bournemouth Gardens. Around this time, I formed the Sandstorms, and we were soon playing every Tuesday and Saturday for the Beat Nights held at the Pavilion, opposite John Stewart Ladies Hair Fashions, where I was serving as an apprentice ladies' hair stylist. (I had the good fortune to style Millicent Martin's hair when she was performing at the Pavilion the week the Beatles played at the Gaumont.) Long before [the Beatles] got to Bournemouth, I'd gone into Bright's record shop in Gervis Place to order their first album, *Please Please Me*. They didn't

even know who the Beatles were and subsequently ordered the wrong record! Once I got the right copy, I bought it, took it home and sat down to listen and learn as many tracks as possible. Once I had them under my belt, with the words on paper and the chords in the correct pattern, I immediately convened a Sandstorms' emergency rehearsal. Unbelievably, through diligence, blistered fingers, sweat and frayed tempers, we managed to learn the complete album and performed it to great effect and audience adulation at the Pavilion Beat Night the very next evening.

The hair salon was my day job, and while the Beatles were performing for a week at the Gaumont, I had the privilege (I felt quite blasé then) while at the salon, to see John, Paul, George and Ringo on more than one occasion – the first time I went with my parents, the second on my own. One thing that stayed in my mind was their Cuban-heeled boots. Up until seeing the Beatles, the Sandstorms used Fender Stratocaster guitars, but subsequent to seeing them, we changed our instrument line-up to match that of the Fab Four. From then on, I played a Gretsch Chet Atkins Country Gent, Harrison-type which I'd ordered from the US. Our rhythm guitarist bought an Epiphone Dreadnought acoustic guitar like Lennon's, and our bass player sported the proverbial McCartney Hofner Beatle violin bass guitar.

During the Beatles' week-long performance at the Gaumont, it was arranged that several groups, including the Sandstorms, would perform in a marquee erected near the beach at the Pier Approach. All the groups were gathered and played to the excited throng of fans who awaited the arrival of their heroes. The Beatles had been scheduled to sign autographs in the group marquee, on a six-foot trestle table, complete with four gold chairs, paper and pens. The time came and went, and everybody's disappointment was confirmed when a hot, embarrassed representative came down after speaking to the Beatles to announce that they'd had to leave in order to get to their next gig. ❞

ROGER DOWNTON, MUSICIAN, BOURNEMOUTH, DORSET

SATURDAY **24 AUGUST**

Saturday Club, recorded on 30 July, aired on the Light Programme while the 4 August recording of ABC-TV's *Lucky Stars – Summer Spin* aired at 6.05pm. 'She Loves You' was, not surprisingly, voted a hit on *Juke Box Jury*. It was opening day of the 1963–1964 Football League season. The group's new-found wealth made doing the pools an unnecessary pursuit. The previous season they had each given 5/- to Ringo's stepfather who filled in the coupon for them.

They played their sixth and final night in Bournemouth. It was a week that had seen the group cooped up in their hotel for most of the week. Even after they had left Bournemouth following their final show, fans were still milling around the hotel and some returned at daybreak the next day. Langley Johnson wrote in the *NRM* that they were 'four young men who rarely see the light of day except through a hotel room window.' Ringo decided to drive back to London afterwards. His arm was badly scalded on the journey, when he took the cap off his overheated radiator.

❝ My mother died when I was very young, and I was brought up by an elder sister and her husband. There were three sisters, more or less the same age, then I appeared a long time afterwards, almost twenty years later. When my elder sister Doreen got married, her husband was in the merchant navy. He was a radio operator, and when he came out of the navy in the late 1950s, he worked in Liverpool at Speke, as a radio operator. I came down from Birkenhead to live with them at Burnham-on-Sea, but every summer I would go back up to stay with my auntie Rosie. My cousin Jean, who was a few years older and studying to be a hairdresser, started telling me about this wonderful club in Liverpool called the Cavern. She was doing an apprenticeship, and had a half day on a Thursday, so this is when she would take me. I could have only been about 12 or 13. At lunch time, we would go over on the ferry and it was amazing. The Beatles weren't that well known out of the area. I'd come back down to Burnham and rave about them, and nobody knew what I was talking about! They all thought I was mad. They'd say, 'Every time you go up there you come back and go on and on about them.' I must have seen them a dozen times, at these lunchtime sessions.

If you'd ever been to the Cavern, you would know how cramped it was in there, so this was quite something. There was a door on the street, and then you went down steep steps, right into this cavern. You couldn't move in there. When I first went there I was frightened, I thought I was going to suffocate. It was jam-packed – and that was lunch time. I wasn't allowed to go in the evening. I was too young, and my aunt would never have allowed me. I was under age for the lunch time sessions as well, but Jean always managed to get me in. If they'd known my age, I would have been thrown out! You came out of there, and you just smelt of it. They were all dancing and jumping about and singing, and it was quite a sort of sweaty atmosphere. The walls were damp with condensation.

When I was back in Somerset a friend and I went to see the group when they spent a week at the Odeon in nearby Weston-super-Mare. The following month, I went down to stay with my friend Margaret's aunt in Southbourne. She was old-fashioned and very strict and would only let us go to one of the early shows to see the Beatles at Bournemouth. Before the show, we went down the side entrance of the cinema. It was right down in the middle of town, where the gardens go through. I was determined to make myself known as it were, so I dragged Margaret round to the back door. We just wanted to get their autographs, but we got such a mouthful. At that age, they were words I had not even heard of. I remember at around that time a magazine came out, every month, and I had every single one of them! Over the period of time, with moving house and so on, they have been lost somewhere along the way. I'm in my seventies now, and think, 'If only I'd kept them!' We bought them at the local newsagent, G. W. Hurley's, in Burnham. We'd buy the records in a sports shop in Victoria Street – the guy who was running the sports shop twigged on that all these kids were mad on pop music, so he started selling records as well. Over the years I've never lost my love for the Beatles. At the very beginning of their career at the Cavern, I covered my bedroom walls with pictures of them, and collected all of their records. I still have them in a box under the stairs! ❞

MARGARET OWEN, BANK CLERK, BURNHAM-ON-SEA, SOMERSET

SUNDAY 25 AUGUST

The group, minus Ringo, checked out of the Palace Court Hotel, and headed north on a 300-mile trip to Blackpool to perform two shows at 6pm and 8.15pm at the ABC, with the Sons of the Piltdown Men, Gary and Lee, Terry Young, Patti Brooks, Jack Douglas, Chas McDevitt and Shirley Douglas, and Colin Day in support. McDevitt filmed part of their performance from the wings. Present for the shows was Bill Harry, whom George thanked for pestering him to write his own material after a meeting earlier in the year outside the Cabin Club in Wood Street. Harry had taken him to *Mersey Beat*'s office and played him Kingsize Taylor's new record from Germany and asked him whether he'd written anything since 'Cry For A Shadow'.

> ❛ In 1963 I was an 18-year-old apprentice motor mechanic working for my father at his Rootes car dealership in St Annes on Sea. Being the son of a garage owner had its advantages, which meant I always had use of a car! We regularly went into Blackpool on a Saturday night to dance at the Winter Gardens. Part of my apprenticeship was day release to the Blackpool Technical College, which I normally travelled to by train with another guy on the same course as me. I remember sometimes sharing the same train compartment with collegiate schoolgirls! I suppose living next door to Blackpool made one blasé about what it had to offer. It was nothing to pop to the shops there, and in my work at the garage, having to drive in to collect customers cars or spare parts. Driving down the prom, past the Pleasure Beach, the Tower etc. I took it for granted. In those days we had no commercial radio, so if you wanted to listen to the latest hits you had to frequent a coffee bar, go to a record store, or listen to Radio Luxembourg on 208 metres on the medium wave. My local coffee bar was the Tender Trap in St Annes, and it was there where I first heard 'Please Please Me'. At the time I was asking, 'Who are these Beatles?' For me, a major event that year was the launch of the Hillman Imp, a new generation rear-engined car. I was lucky to be sent to the regional distributors in Southport to collect our first one for the showroom. It was a red one, and I remember feeling quite chuffed driving it back to the garage on trade plates, as the first person at the garage to drive one. I can't remember which Beatles show in Blackpool I went to first. I know I went with my then girlfriend, and sat near the front, surrounded by screaming girls. It was probably one of the shows at the Queen's Theatre, because afterwards I certainly went to another show at the ABC. It was quite good being at the garage, because most of the Summer Season stars playing at Blackpool would stay in St Annes for the duration. They would rent local houses, and many of them visited our garage for petrol and service etc. I remember that Cliff Richard came for petrol in his Ford Thunderbird, sometime that summer. Also, one of our other apprentices was a guitarist in a local group, and he got quite excited when Bert Weedon came in with his car. I remember that we both got invited backstage on one of the Blackpool piers where he was playing. They were innocent happy days! ❜
>
> **TONY ELLISON, MOTOR MECHANIC, COFFS HARBOUR, NEW SOUTH WALES, AUSTRALIA**

MONDAY 26 AUGUST

Paul received his third speeding conviction of the year at Wallasey Magistrates Court, receiving a £25 fine, plus a further £6 on two summonses for failing to produce his driving licence and insurance certificate – as well as a twelve-month disqualification from driving. He admitted driving his car at 50 to 55 miles per hour in Seabank Road on 14 June. Magistrates' chairman Alderman William Hannaford said, 'it is time you were taught a lesson.'

In a day that brought scattered showers, the group drove north to Southport to begin a week-long stint at the Odeon, with Gerry and the Pacemakers, the Fourmost, Tommy Wallis and Beryl, the Sons of the Piltdown Men, Gary and Lee, Tommy Quickly and compère Bob Bain. Shows were twice nightly, at 6.25pm and 8.40pm. The Beatles arrived half an hour after the show started. Southport was in the midst of its annual Flower Show. Hundreds of fans travelled by coach from Cheshire, the Wirral and other parts of Lancashire. Queues six deep stretched into Lord Street and Post Office Avenue. Extra police were on duty for the week and several different routes in and out of the theatre had been planned to protect the group from being mobbed.

The *Southport Visiter* reported that, 'There were screams, shrieks and cheers when the Beatles made the spotlights and captivated everyone. Each number was greeted with a roar, which swelled until it exploded like a rocket... This is definitely a 'show stopper' show and to anyone who goes, if they don't get with it before the night is out then they have definitely something lacking. There is just one drawback. When the Beatles give out that Mersey music something seems to grip. You just feel like getting out of your seat and twisting it up in the aisles. That's the one thing that is out, and you have to be content with gripping your knees and yelling and wriggling in your seat – hardly the easiest thing to do with an atmosphere like this!'

Ringo, playing with a bandaged arm after his accident returning from Bournemouth, had to modify some of his drum breaks.

 I was 18 at the time and I was trying to impress a girl called Ginny, who worked as a nanny at a vicarage in Crosby. I asked her if she would like to see the Beatles, who were appearing for a week in Southport and, with a chat-up line like that, she naturally said 'Yes'. She was a popular girl, as the previous year six boys had given her 'Ginny Come Lately' for her birthday or for Christmas. I was the first person to give her 'Ginny In The Mirror' by Del Shannon.

We went from Crosby to Southport on the train. We sat about five rows from the back of the stalls and they were good seats. The compère was Bob Bain, who was born in Scotland but put on an American accent and sounded impressive (the handbill says Billy Baxter but my notes say Bob Bain). The opening act was Gary and Lee and I see they performed Johnny Kidd's 'I'll Never Get Over You' and 'Twistin' To The Locomotion', which when you think about it was an odd concept. So little is known about them that I can't even find them on Google. Brian Epstein nursed high hopes for Tommy Quickly and he sang 'Heaven Only Knows', Buddy Holly's 'Everyday' and 'Tip Of My Tongue'. The girls screamed for him. I'm not sure what Tommy Wallis and Beryl performed but Tommy played a xylophone on wheels while wearing roller skates. Beryl wore a swimsuit and also glided around on roller skates. No one paid any attention to them and the girls were calling out for the Beatles. They were from the dying days of variety – however, if they'd swapped their roller skates for the new American craze, skateboards, they could have cleaned up. Gerry and the Pacemakers closed the first half. They opened with a Beatles' favourite, 'Some Other Guy' and then their first B-side, 'Away From You', which Gerry had written in Hamburg. This was followed by Chuck Berry's 'Sweet Little Sixteen' and a very good version of 'How Do You Do It', which got the crowd going. Next came Arthur Alexander's 'A Shot Of Rhythm And Blues' and then Nat 'King' Cole's 'Pretend', although they followed Carl Mann's arrangement. This was greeted as warmly as any hit single. Then Gerry performed 'You'll Never Walk Alone', which was going to be the next single and was very well received. They ended with another number one, 'I Like It'. According to my notes, I preferred Gerry and the Pacemakers to the Beatles. I know I thought I would have been pompous declaring that the American originals were always better than the Liverpool covers. I still largely think that now but I also appreciate that the Liverpool cover versions have charms of their own.

The second half opened with the Fourmost who started with a B-side 'Just In Case' and moved onto Doris Day's 'Everybody Loves A Lover' with an arrangement borrowed from the Shirelles. Their hit,

'Hello Little Girl' was next and then Brian O'Hara did excellent impressions for 'September In The Rain'. I recall that Donald Duck and Frankie Valli were in there somewhere. Effectively, they were a cabaret act masquerading as a beat group. The screaming was at fever pitch when the Beatles came on and I remember Ginny pounding my arms as George opened their set with 'Roll Over Beethoven'. The pounding continued for 'Thank You Girl', 'Chains', 'A Taste Of Honey' and 'She Loves You'. Girls all around me were screaming and it was like being in the monkey house at the zoo. John took the lead vocal for 'Baby It's You' and then it was 'From Me To You', Ringo's offering 'Boys', 'I Saw Her Standing There' and the closer, a great, raucous 'Twist And Shout'. Naturally, I would have preferred to have heard the Beatles without all the screaming but, on the other hand, I was with a girl who was enjoying it immensely and so I have mixed feelings about it. I enjoyed my train journey home but I remember her saying, 'My previous boyfriend was David Noble and he turned out to be David Ignoble.' When I took her back to the vicarage, the vicar was asking questions about the Beatles and trying to fathom what this phenomenon was all about. It must have worked out well with Ginny as I see that I saw her on Thursday, Friday, Saturday and Sunday too. A few weeks later she changed jobs and I never saw her again.

As fate would have it, I was inside that very Odeon recently. It is now Sainsbury's and some of the customers may have wondered who was that crazy loon smiling in the aisles. They didn't realise I was thinking back to 1963. In some form or other, I think of the Beatles every day – but Ginny, well, I hadn't thought of her in years. **♪**

SPENCER LEIGH, AUTHOR AND BROADCASTER, LIVERPOOL

TUESDAY 27 AUGUST

A forty-five knot gale passed through Southport in the middle of the night. At 9.30am filming began on Don Haworth's documentary at the Little Theatre in Hoghton Street. The theatre was the home of the Southport Dramatic Club. Scenic artist Arthur Nugent, assisted by Charles Preston, set the stage with a rostrum upstage left for Ringo's drum kit and a grey velour curtain backdrop. The Beatles arrived at 10am and immediately changed into their familiar grey collarless suits and were filmed miming to 'Twist And Shout' and 'She Loves You'. During a break the TV crew changed the backdrop to create the impression the group were being filmed at more than one venue. They changed into black suits and mimed to 'Love Me Do'. Footage from the previous night's shows was interspersed with the songs. Preston recalled the filming taking all day and finishing about 5.30pm. John asked him to go to Boots to buy him some throat pastilles. 'During a break I recall sitting in

the stalls with Ringo Starr who admired the theatre and asked how one went about joining the Club! Sadly he never did!'

The eleventh episode of *Pop Go The Beatles*, recorded on 1 August, aired at 5pm with guests the Cyril Davies Rhythm and Blues All Stars featuring Long John Baldry. The group played their second night at the Odeon in Southport.

WEDNESDAY 28 AUGUST

The group drove to BBC-TV's studio at Dickenson Road in Manchester for another 9.30am start. They were interviewed in a dressing room for *The Mersey Sound* programme. Asked about their origins, George said: 'Actually, we'd been at it a long time before that. We'd been to Hamburg. I think that's where we found our style... we developed our style because of this fella. He used to say, 'You've got to make a show for the people,' and he used to come up every night, shouting 'Mach schau! Mach schau!' So we used to 'Mach schau', and John used to dance around like a gorilla, and we'd all, you know, knock our heads together and things like that. Anyway, we got back to Liverpool and all the groups there were doing Shadows' type of stuff, and we came back with leather jackets and jeans and funny hair – maching schau – which went down quite well.' In response to how much longer they thought the group would keep going, John said, 'Well, you can't say, you know. You can be big-headed and say, "Yeah, we're gonna last ten years." But as soon as you've said that you think, "We're lucky if we last three months," you know.' Paul added, 'Well, obviously we can't keep playing the same sort of music until we're about forty – sort of, old men playing 'From Me To You' – nobody is going to want to know at all about that sort of thing.' George reckoned that the group would keep going 'for at least another four years.' Once again, Ringo mentioned his desire to open a ladies hairdressing salon.

After filming they drove down the A34 to the Parrswood Hotel for a pint. In the evening, they played their third night at the Odeon in Southport. The *Manchester Evening News* printed letters from irate Beatles fans in response to an earlier letter from 'Adenuff'. Tina North, a self-described 'Fed-Up Teenager from Southport', complained, 'If Adenuff isn't half-way to Cubesville, I don't know who is,' while an unnamed 'Record Fan' from Manchester vented, 'Adenuff claims to be "with it." Someone had better tell him the Charleston went out years ago, along with the Penny-farthing bicycle.'

Brian Epstein's new signing Cilla Black recorded 'Love Of The Loved' at Abbey Road, produced by George Martin and with an arrangement by Les Reed. The song was mainly written by Paul on one of his walks home to Allerton after taking a girl to the cinema and recorded at the Beatles' 1962 Decca audition. The song had been slated for fellow Liverpudlian Beryl Marsden, as John was a particular fan. On hearing the song, however, Epstein said, 'I want that for Cilla'. Black, even though she had heard the song many times in the Cavern, claimed John and Paul had written the song with her in mind. '[It] didn't exactly commend itself to me when I first heard it. When I heard their demo I nearly died. I mean, demos are bad at the best of times, but this one!'

THURSDAY 29 AUGUST

'She Loves You' Chart Sensation – Beatles beat Cliff in race for top' trumpeted the front page of *Disc*. The paper revealed that 'She Loves You' had stormed into the chart at number 3, two places above Cliff Richard's 'It's All In The Game', which had climbed six places, while 'Twist And Shout' dropped to number 7. 'Hello Little Girl', the Fourmost's Lennon/McCartney-penned debut received a four-star review from Don Nicholl, who felt that the single would bring the group 'quick success'. In the *NRM* chart, 'She Loves You' entered at number 12, while 'From Me To You' dropped to number 41 after a twenty-week stay. 'Hello Little Girl', the third song John had ever written and given a three-star rating, 'should do pretty well' according to the paper's singles reviews.

The group continued filming Don Haworth's documentary, taking the Liverpool Pier Head to Wallasey ferry, signing autographs and meeting fans, as well as acting out an arrival at Speke Airport. They signed a photograph for Haworth, who gave it to his daughter Elaine. The crew also filmed background shots around the Odeon, including exterior and interior shots of the building, crowd scenes in the foyer and queues outside. A spokesman said, 'If it got out where we were we would be inundated with fans and our job is to make sure the boys get onstage during the evening.'

In the evening, they played their fourth night at the Odeon in Southport. Ken Lloyd reported that thousands had been turning up nightly and hundreds phoning ('I am the aunt of one of the Beatles. Get him to the phone for an urgent message.') He told the *Southport Visiter*, 'So far the Beatles have had dozens of pretended aunts, uncles, grandfathers, grandmothers and hundreds of very personal friends ringing. It is a bit of a headache for us because early in the week both of our top groups here did have actual relatives who came and sat in the audience to cheer them on. However, we are getting to understand the genuine voice, for usually the fan who rings up finds herself tongue-tied with excitement by the time she has got the first few words out.'

Cilla Black made her live debut, filling in for the Fourmost, who had driven down to London to appear on *Ready, Steady, Go!* the following day. Backed by the Sons of the Piltdown Men, she sang 'Summertime', 'A Shot Of Rhythm and Blues' and 'Fever'. Epstein's father, Harry, standing in the wings, remarked, 'She'll be the next Gracie Fields.'

❛ My dad was mad on tape recorders and had several. The best one he got was a Stella four track, with overdub and everything. I used to record the programmes on the radio on a Sunday. I'd record *Two Way Family Favourites*, *The Billy Cotton Band Show*, and *Pick of the Pops*. I came across the old reel to reel tapes a few years ago, and was able to transfer some to a cassette, and then onto my computer, so it's great to be able to listen to them all again. The very first time I saw the Beatles was on the TV show *People and Places*. I was sitting in the parlour and my dad shouted, 'Come and see this group on the telly!' and I went in, and there they were doing 'Love Me Do'. I grabbed my guitar and played along with them. When they'd finished, I said, 'They're rubbish them!' Mum and Dad didn't pass comment. My mate Gerald Keegan, better known as Geggsie, was well into the Beatles from the word go, and  it was really because of him that I became interested in them. We used to go and see each other's groups. His was called the Dresdens and they were very, very good. I remember seeing them one night at the Sea Cadets' hut, and they opened up with 'Please Please Me'. I said afterwards, 'Wow, I liked that song, who did that?' and he said, 'the Beatles of course!' So that got me into looking at their other stuff. I've always been a bit slow on the uptake!

I left school in July 1963, but didn't get a job immediately, because I was going to be a pop star! I was on the dole for a bit, until my dad, along with the DHSS, decided that getting a job was the best thing for me. I was sent from home in Wallasey to Liverpool with Geggsie for a job interview at a carpet shop. So we were both being sent for this interview, and got the boat over from Wallasey to the Old Pier Head. I was looking for a bus, when Geggsie said, 'Hey, look! There's the Beatles by the meat pie stall!' I hot-footed it to the pie stand and I got all their autographs. Next thing we were running, all feet and flapping coats, across the gang plank, because they were filming on the ferry. We decided we wanted to be in the film as well, so we hid behind a funnel, and jumped out at the last minute! I got their autographs on the back page of a 1962 Liverpool Streets Directory – this was before A-Zs came out. If you looked up a particular street, it would give you an address of where that particular street or junction started. I have no idea what happened to it. I can still see it in my mind, and Ringo's greasy thumb print where he'd stuck the pie in his mouth! We never did make it to the interview. **"**

IAN HEATH, MUSICIAN AND TELEVISION ENGINEER, LIVERPOOL, MERSEYSIDE

FRIDAY 30 AUGUST

The week's filming came to an end with a scene of Ringo pushing his way through extras, pretending to be fans, outside his home in Dingle and getting into George's open-top Jaguar. Ringo was also filmed walking past several ladies under hooded hairdryers in the salon inside Horne Brothers in Lord Street. 'I've always fancied having a ladies hairdressing salon, you know, a string of 'em in fact… trotting around in my stripes and tails and everything… 'Like a cup of tea, madam?" Paul told *Mirabelle* that he had fallen over a cameraman on the floor of his bedroom. 'The place is swarming with them and technicians. See, they're living with us for a week.' Three of the group went to a camera shop on Lord Street to buy a cine camera. When word spread that they were in the shop, fans assembled outside chanting 'We Want The Beatles!' The manager phoned the police but in the meantime the group were smuggled out through a rear exit. 'It was hectic while it lasted,' said shop assistant Dennis Smith. 'It took some time to convince the teenagers that the Beatles really had left. We were astonished when scores of young people suddenly invaded the shop demanding autographs.'

'She Loves You' entered the *NME* chart at number 2, behind 'Bad To Me'. 'Twist And Shout' dropped down to number 10. In the *Melody Maker* chart, 'She Loves You' entered at number 12, 'Twist And Shout' slipped down one place to number 4 and 'From Me To You' placed at number 43. The final 'Close-Up On A Beatle' article, featuring John, appeared in the *NME*. John said, 'When I think about it, I suppose I'm a bit of an exhibitionist. I've always been performing in one way or another, making jokes or wanting to get up on to a stage and sing. Still, I suppose you have to be like that in show business. I know that success has changed me for the good. I'm probably better at being nice to people, now the Beatles are doing so well and we're all so happy.' Keith Fordyce reviewed the Fourmost's 'Hello Little Girl' with the bold statement: 'I wouldn't mind betting that it goes right to the top.' In the 'From You To Us' letters page, J. Evans from

Liverpool wrote, 'Can't the public of today see that the Beatles are just four ordinary young men who need a haircut.'

The 30 July recording of the 'Pop Chat' segment of *Non Stop Pop* aired on the Light Programme at 5pm. The group played their fifth night at the Odeon in Southport.

SATURDAY 31 AUGUST

The group played their sixth and final night at the Odeon in Southport. Thirty thousand fans saw them during the week, some of whom bought tickets for every night. During the week postmen delivered a bag of fan mail a day to the theatre. Coach firms had organised day trips to Southport for fans to see the group. One firm had booked ninety-five tickets. Many people made the hour-long journey from Blackpool. The second edition of *The Beatles Book*, with a photo of the group playing table tennis on the cover, was published.

SEPTEMBER

A number one single, a number one EP and a number one LP

SUNDAY 1 SEPTEMBER

I n an article titled 'Pop Goes The Whimper' in the day's *Sunday Telegraph*, Ian Christie described the Liverpool music scene 'as the breeding ground of guitar-bashing, hoarse-voiced, money-spinning talent.'

The Beatles travelled to Didsbury to ABC-TV's Studio Centre to tape an appearance on *Big Night Out*. They arrived about an hour late for rehearsal, Jane Asher carrying Paul's guitar as they walked through the door. When hosts Mike and Bernie Winters arrived at the studio earlier in the day, there was already a massive crowd waiting outside. The group rehearsed during the day and recorded at night, miming to 'From Me To You', 'She Loves You' and 'Twist And Shout' and part of 'I Saw Her Standing There' as the credits rolled in front of the six hundred-strong studio audience. The show also featured Billy Dainty, Sally Barnes with Bobby Beaumont, Patsy Ann Noble, Lionel Blair and His Dancers and the ABC Television Showband. A few days later, the group watched a playback of the show at ATV House.

> **'** I started out as an actor, appearing in a touring production of *Watch On The Rhine* when I was a teenager and then attended the Royal Shakespeare Theatre during the Second World War. In 1947, I realised that I wanted to dance more than I wanted to act. I was in the touring productions of *Annie Get Your Gun* and *Kiss Me Kate* in the late '40s/ early '50s and then went on to do a lot of TV in the 1950s. By 1963 I had already appeared on *Play It Cool, Thank Your Lucky Stars, The Benny Hill Show, Sunday Night At The London Palladium* and the *Royal Variety Performance*.
>
>
>
> My first experience of the Beatles was meeting Paul McCartney in Sportique, the tailor's in Old Compton Street, next door to The 2i's coffee bar. He must have recognised me and said, 'Hello Lionel!' We chatted for a while – he was buying some new clothes for a trip to Hamburg they were about to go on. I asked him the name of his group, and he said the Beatles. I hadn't heard of them!
>
> The next time I bumped into them it was 1963 and they were huge. I was appearing with my dancers on the same television show called *Big Night Out*. We recorded our slots at different times, although I do recall there was a piano on the set, and Paul was tinkering around on it. It was a busy year for me and my girls – the Lionel Blair Dancers. At the beginning of the year *The Cool Mikado*, the first of two films I did with Michael Winner, was released, with a cast that included Frankie Howerd, Tommy Cooper, Stubby Kaye, Dennis Price and Mike and Bernie Winters. The following year Richard Lester, the director of *A Hard Day's Night*, approached me and asked if I would appear with the girls in the film. The Palladium always had dancers on, and they wanted the Lionel Blair Dancers. It wasn't actually filmed at the Palladium, but in a theatre in Charlotte Street called the Scala, sadly long gone now. One night I went gambling with Brian Epstein and he won almost £100,000! I went on to do many more television shows with the Beatles and have been so lucky to have had such a long career. **'**
>
> **LIONEL BLAIR, ACTOR, SINGER AND DANCER, BANSTEAD, SURREY**

MONDAY 2 SEPTEMBER

The Official
Beatles FAN CLUB
First Floor, Service House,
13 Monmouth Street, London, W.C.2

The group had a scare when they flew to London for the following day's BBC radio sessions. Take-off was aborted and, following a delay, as the plane was about to take off again, an emergency exit flew open. George, sitting the nearest, recalled the experience: 'We were taking off when the plane suddenly came to a halt just as it was about to leave the ground. They gave me the jitters but what was to follow will make me sympathise with Elvis Presley's fear of flying for the rest of my days! As we made the proper take-off the emergency exit by which I was sitting suddenly flew open! I had heard bloodcurdling stories about people being sucked out of aircraft, and I don't mind admitting I was pretty terrified. Brian Epstein, who was sitting next to me, grabbed my arm and I yelled out for the air hostess – but she thought I was fooling as we often do since we fly in this plane so frequently'.

In the day's *Guardian*, Charlotte Loewenthal wrote on the subject of mothers trying to communicate with their offspring. She suggested that distinguishing 'intelligently between the Beatles and the Shadows' would be useful.

‘ I was 16 and working as an office boy at the *NME*, when one of the writers there – a guy by the name of Mike Butcher – stopped me as I was passing by and said, 'Hey Tony, I wanted to have a word with you – I've got a friend who works round the corner, and he's looking for an office boy.' He said, 'He's the Beatles' Press Officer.' I said, 'Oh yeah,' sounding interested. He sent me round to Tony Barrow and I was offered the job. I went back to the office and said I would be starting a new job on Monday. The guys there said, 'Oh yeah, where are you going?' and when I said, 'I'm going to be working for the Beatles' Press Officer,' they were absolutely gutted! I'd only been at the *NME* for a few months, but this was too good an opportunity to miss.

Thirteen Monmouth Street was above a seedy bookshop, next door to a French Polishers. It was a narrow Soho-type building – you went up rickety stairs to the first floor, and up again to the second floor where the fan club was based. Basically, it was one room, with a back room off it, which was used for storage. It was a nice little area, tucked off the main road between Seven Dials and Shaftesbury Avenue. Tony Barrow had the first-floor front office, which always had the shades down, with just a lamp on. Val Sumpter was his secretary and Jo Bergman his PA, who was an absolute whizz. They had two phones in there, and she'd be talking on both at the same time. She kept the whole thing together, and never mixed with anyone in particular. She was always professional and too busy. I was up and down between the two, always running errands for Tony, so I had a lot to do with both floors. Upstairs, Mary Cockram, who was 'Anne Collingham' to the fans, worked with Bettina Rose, who had joined from ATV. She had run a fan club for the group in her spare time and joined NEMS full-time when things began to take off.

The day I got there, there were two half full Royal Mail sacks. Within three months, the whole room was absolutely full! Full of mail bags, with a new bag being delivered every day. You'd spend all day opening envelopes, taking out postal orders, and sending off fan club stuff. Mary and Bettina would type up templates of letters, and we'd print them off on a mimeo machine. We'd do the same with press releases for Tony. A lot of time was spent signing autographs – yes, we learnt how to fake them! Over the course of the next six months Tony brought in a load of extra people. Because we only had this one room, we brought in some trestle tables which we put in a square, and we would get a sack of mail and tip it out on the tables. There would be gifts, letters, Jelly Babies, money, all sorts of things. It was fairly manageable at first, then it got a bit mad!

By the following year, Brian Epstein had decided to move NEMS down from Liverpool and I went with Tony when they opened the office in Argyll Street. By then we were handling all his other artistes as well. Tony surrounded himself with professionals, the accountant Mr Montgomery and Alistair Taylor, who was a bit frightening. You never went into Brian's office unless he asked you. He had an intercom system installed, long before things like that were commonplace. It had a buzzer and a big red flashing light, and you would have to answer politely, 'Yes, Mr Epstein?' At the fan club it was really just youngsters there messing around, but Argyll Street was a different kettle of fish. The receptionists were great, two girls from Liverpool, who seemed to spend a lot of time finding out which parties were going on! You could always rely on them to let you know what was happening and where. They went on to work for Apple after NEMS. The reason I left NEMS was really just that I lost interest. It sounds mad now, but being a musician is what I really wanted to do. Tony tried to persuade me to stay, saying, 'Stick with me, I'll teach you all the tricks of the trade,' and I didn't do it! I wanted to be a musician. It sounds stupid looking back, but I've managed to make a living as a professional musician all my life, so I suppose I haven't done too badly! **J**

TONY CATCHPOLE, MUSICIAN AND PROPERTY CONSULTANT, SHEFFIELD, SOUTH YORKSHIRE

TUESDAY 3 SEPTEMBER

MI Records announced that 'She Loves You' had reached UK sales of five hundred thousand copies. (It went on to sell 1.6 million units in the UK alone and remain Britain's best-selling single until 1977.) The group began recording the first of the last three *Pop Go The Beatles* shows at the Aeolian Hall studio at 2pm. At the first two-and-a-half-hour session, they recorded 'Too Much Monkey Business', 'Till There Was You', 'Love Me Do', 'She Loves You', 'I'll Get You' and 'The Hippy Hippy Shake'.

After a half-hour break, as the twelfth episode of *Pop Go The Beatles* aired on the Light Programme with guests Brian Poole and the Tremeloes ('Lucille', 'Baby It's You' and 'She Loves You' were not broadcast), the group recorded a second session, with guests the Marauders, performing 'Chains' for the fourth and last time on radio, 'You Really Got A Hold On Me', 'Misery', 'A Taste Of Honey' (transferred to an earlier show), 'Lucille', 'From Me To You' and 'Boys', for all the girls in the Lower Fourth at Blackburne House, Liverpool and Jill, Janet, Mary, Brenda and Lynn from Wakefield. The third session, beginning at 8pm following another half-hour break, saw the group record 'Ask Me Why' (the fourth and last time they performed the song on BBC Radio), '(There's A) Devil In Her Heart' (the second and last time they performed it), 'I Saw Her Standing There', 'Sure To Fall (In Love With You)' and 'Twist And Shout', with Tony Rivers and the Castaways as guests. 'She Loves You', recorded at the first session, was included in the programme when it aired. The three recordings aired on 10, 17 and 24 September.

❝ As with most of our contemporaries, we began by forming a skiffle group in the late '50s. I started the group and persuaded my schoolmate Ken Sherratt to join me playing the tea-chest bass. We eventually morphed into a beat group. Originally, myself, Ken, and drummer Barry Sergeant worked as a trio, doing clubs and dance halls throughout the north-west and gaining a large following. In late '62, our management suggested that we upgrade to a four-piece which seemed to be the flavour of the day, so we were joined by rhythm guitarist Danny Davis, a Pye recording artist, who we had previously backed on a few occasions. 1963 was a cathartic year for us, we had featured on quite a few radio shows and made a couple of local TV appearances when we learned that Decca Records were scouting for talent in the north-west and our manager secured an audition with Peter Attwood. He liked what he saw and sometime in the early summer we found ourselves in the Maida Vale studios where we began our recording career.

The year had begun with our usual round of dance hall and club dates including an appearance at the Cavern Club in Liverpool on 27 January. We shared the bill with the Swinging Blue Jeans and the Merseybeats. By September our recording of 'That's What I Want' was getting lots of airplay and eventually made it into the charts. This gave us the opportunity to be featured as guest group on what was probably the most iconic pop music radio show of the day, *Pop Go The Beatles*. Imagine how we felt about appearing on a show with the Beatles. We drove down to London the night before and stayed at the Aaland Hotel in Bloomsbury, which is where we always stayed when we were in the city. Our call was around teatime. We met producer Ian Grant and performed the A- and B-side of our single. We recorded our set in this big empty studio, so imagine our disappointment when we found out we weren't going to be meeting the Beatles. We had watched them perform live a couple of times, but it would've been good to have met them face to face. ❞

LES BRYAN, COMEDIAN, KIDSGROVE, STOKE-ON-TRENT, STAFFORDSHIRE

WEDNESDAY 4 SEPTEMBER

Brian Epstein told the *NME* that the Beatles and Billy J. Kramer would be starring in a two-and-a-half-week Christmas show at a major London theatre, compèred by Rolf Harris. 'We aim to make it a slickly produced show with much more entertainment value than anything the Beatles and Billy J. have had the opportunity of doing before.'

A year on from the group's first recording session proper for EMI, they travelled to Worcester to play two shows – the first of four dates promoted by John Smith for which the group were paid £250 a night – at 6.30pm and 8.45pm at the Gaumont. The show was compèred by Ted King with supporting acts the Fourmost, Rockin' Henri and the Hayseeds, Mike Berry and the Innocents, Ian Crawford and the Boomerangs.

Between shows, the group were once again interviewed by Antony Willard from the *Worcester Evening News*. John complained about things being thrown at them onstage. 'I always thought they threw at performers they didn't like. We don't mind them screaming together but not one after the other. That puts us off.' In his review, headlined 'They Screamed Their Heads Off At The Beatles,' Willard mentioned that his ear drums nearly crumbled. 'The screaming was the loudest and most intense I have ever heard, rising to a crescendo for 'She Loves You', at number one in the Top 10 to-day and 'Twist And Shout.'

❝ I went to Worcester Grammar School for Girls from 1954 to 1959 travelling each day by train from Malvern Link. The building is now retirement apartments so I could end up going back to school! During 1959/60 I went to Malvern Technical College to do a secretarial course. The Careers Officer

then found me a job at Whatley and Mellor, a solicitor's office – now a restaurant. I went to evening classes at the Technical College for several years in order to get further qualifications in shorthand and typing and worked as a legal secretary until I retired in 2010. In our spare time we went to the local cinema and theatre in Malvern and I also went to dances at the Winter Gardens with my school friend, Gillian. I remember buying *Melody Maker* from the local W. H. Smith and would go home from work at lunch time to play my Beatles' records. I was 20 years old in 1963, and Whatley and Mellor's office was opposite the theatre, and my friend from there, Jean, another legal secretary, and I were both fans of the Beatles. We had become aware of them around the time of 'Please Please Me'. I would queue up outside Ralph Hales music shop in Malvern Link whenever a new Beatles' record would come out. You could listen to the new releases on headphones in the booths, and I would take my treasured 45s home and listen to them on the red-and-cream Dansette my brother had handed down to me when he got himself a new one.

I can't remember how Jean and I managed to get tickets to see the group when they came to Worcester Gaumont for the second time that year. I certainly don't remember queuing up for tickets. We went to the early evening show, travelling the seven miles from Malvern to Worcester on the bus. It was a really enjoyable evening, but you couldn't hear the music because of the screaming. I still love the Beatles' music and every year my husband and I, together with our son, go to Malvern Theatre to see the Bootleg Beatles. My husband was a printer in Abergavenny in 1963 and his claim to fame is that he printed the tickets for the Beatles' dance there and also went along to it. **J**

RUTH REECE, LEGAL SECRETARY, DROITWICH, WORCESTERSHIRE

THURSDAY 5 SEPTEMBER

In the new edition of *Disc*, 'She Loves You' went to number one, knocking 'Bad To Me' off the top, as 'Twist And Shout' dropped to number 11. In the *NRM* chart, 'She Loves You' climbed nine places to number 3, while 'From Me To You' dropped to number 44.

The group set off for a return visit to Taunton, where they played two performances at 6.30pm and 8.45pm at the Gaumont Palace. In a piece headlined 'Screaming Girls Marred Beatles Show', the *Somerset County Gazette* commented, 'Finally, the moment everyone had been waiting for came – "The Beatles" were onstage. They gave their usual excellent performance, which, however, was somewhat marred by screaming and whistling from the audience. Indeed, one girl was so moved that she dashed up on the stage and began dancing with the group, until she was forcibly removed. This was not part of the act as many people suspected.' The *Somerset County Herald* thought the evening might have been 'a fairly disastrous experience' if the Beatles hadn't been on the bill. With them, it 'turned into full-blooded teenage entertainment.' The reviewer went on to say none of their songs would stand a chance in the Eurovision Song Contest and didn't 'bleat about lost loves, unfaithful girl friends, carrying school books or being too young.' A subsequent leader article said that 'Hysterical scenes must have made school teachers wonder what they had done to deserve such results of their efforts. Exuberance and high spirits are right and natural in young people, but the "Beatlemania" and irrationality that so many are exhibiting show that our education and training are leaving a mental and spiritual vacuum'.

❛ I came from a farming family on my father's side, and a butchering family on my mother's. Most of my teenage years were missed to a certain extent because I was at public school. I could never listen to *Saturday Club* or *Teen and Twenty Disc Club* because of lessons. We were very restricted. They say your school days are the best days of your life but as a friend of mine said, 'Well, what the hell have we to look forward to?' When you were at public school, you were at school every day of the week, lessons on a Saturday morning, and games on a Saturday afternoon. Probably about 85 per cent of the pupils were boarders, but the day boys had to adopt the same regime as the boarders. If they were doing prep, so were we, and we weren't allowed out without written permission and wearing school uniform.

When we did get out into Taunton, there was a coffee bar run by a chap called Paul Shepherd and his wife. It was one of those places where you'd go in with a group and sit there for hours for the price of a cup of tea which cost sixpence. At the top of the High Street was the Merlin – now that was a real coffee bar, along the lines of the 2i's in Soho. It was the thing in those days for young people to go to a coffee bar, and there was a pub across the road called the Full Moon. I first had a record player when I was about 14 or 15. There was an electrical shop called Taylor's which had a very, very small record department and they had listening booths in there. There was also a record shop in town called Wyman's. It was a stationery shop if I recall, with a record department upstairs. The first record I ever bought was one by Lonnie Donegan, and I was a fan of Elvis. A friend of mine, Andrew Rugg, was a regular reader of the *New Musical Express* and very keen on '60s music. He was the one who organised tickets to see the Beatles when they came to the Gaumont when we were in the Lower Sixth at school. To be honest what I remember most about the concert was screaming girls drowning out any chance of hearing the group. The old Gaumont building where we saw the Beatles is still there. It had been a cinema come theatre, then closed before reopening as a Mecca bingo hall. The Gaiety Cinema became a pool hall but has just been pulled down and turned into flats. It's amazing how I remember the words of the songs of the '60s but can't remember what I did yesterday! It was a good time, a good time. ❜

CHRISTOPHER BEVAN, CHARTERED SURVEYOR, TAUNTON, SOMERSET

FRIDAY **6 SEPTEMBER**

The front page of the week's *NME* announced 'The Fabulous Beatles! – 'The Famous Foursome from Liverpool reach new heights this week. Their new single, 'She Loves You' is No 2 in the *NME* Top 30 this week. Their 'Twist And Shout' is Britain's Top Selling EP. And their LP, *Please Please Me*, sits firmly at No. 1 in the LP chart. Congratulations to the Fabulous Beatles!' The announcement was already out of date as 'She Loves You' had moved up to number one, knocking 'Bad To Me' off the top. 'Twist And Shout' slipped out of the Top 10 to number 13.

In the *Melody Maker* chart, 'She Loves You' climbed twelve places to number one, also knocking 'Bad To Me' down to number 2, as 'Twist And Shout' fell to number 9 and 'From Me To You' dropped out of the Top 50 after twenty weeks. Chris Roberts' article, 'Tilting For The Top – Cliff versus the Beatles', questioned whether the Beatles now had the upper hand. 'They are still going to be the showbusiness toast of 1963.' The group's second EP, *The Beatles' Hits* was released, featuring 'From Me To You', 'Thank You Girl', 'Please Please Me' and 'Love Me Do'. Brian Epstein wrote to Alun Owen, asking him whether he would consider writing a screenplay for a planned Beatles film. Owen had written several episodes of *Armchair Theatre* for ABC Weekend Television.

The Beatles travelled to Luton to play two shows at 6.30pm and 8.45pm, the third date on the mini-tour, at the Odeon on Dunstable Road. Chris Hutchins chatted with them backstage about their forthcoming holidays. Even though the group were now becoming a household name, the *Luton Saturday Telegraph* failed to review the shows, instead reporting that a portable radio had been stolen from the home of Mrs Ivy Abbott. *The Luton News* commented that fans 'raved over the 'Bs' visit,' but the paper's reviewer, the singularly named Alvin, thought there was 'one blot on the show however. The persistent screaming of schoolgirls frequently drowned the singing. The screamers kept up a constant barrage of squeals throughout the opening acts and really let loose when the Beatles arrived. At times I was actually forced to hold my hands over my ears to keep my eardrums from bursting. I'm sure there is no need for this selfish display of appreciation.'

After the show the group drove back to London, returning to their rooms at the Hotel President. Artist Peter Blake, his wife Jann Haworth and Robert Freeman – who had all seen one of the Luton shows – arrived at the hotel and had coffee and sandwiches, before heading to the Crazy Elephant club with John and Ringo. 'John had never really spent time in London and wanted to go to the clubs,' Blake remembered. 'George was tired and went to bed, so John, Ringo, a friend named Joe Chelson and I went on the town. We drove around in Joe's old jeep. We went to a club called the Crazy Elephant and asked, 'Can we come in?' The man at the door said, 'Are you members?' We said no, but they were actually playing a Beatles song. So John said, 'You're playing our song. You must let us in.' The doorman said, 'I don't know what that is. I don't know who you are. You can't come in.' Then a voice came from inside the club and said, 'It's all right. They're friends of mine. They can come in.' We went in and it was Paul, who was already there at the smartest club in town.'

Later, they went to the Flamingo Club at 33–37 Wardour Street. By the time they arrived, the Ronnie Ross Quartet had finished playing, so they went upstairs to the All-Nighter Club to hear Georgie Fame and the Blue Flames play well into the night.

‘ I first heard the Beatles in late 1962 when Radio Luxembourg played 'Love Me Do'. I wasn't absolutely knocked out with the song, although I found it intriguing. I remember thinking it sounded a bit Eastern. It was something to do with the inflections in Paul's voice. And then 'Please Please Me' came out and completely blew me away. From that time onwards, they were just magic. Everything just got better and better all the time. Absolutely wonderful, and we just couldn't get enough. It was a great time to be in love with music. When I heard they were coming to Luton – just up the road from me, I just had to go and see them. I've got very vivid memories of going with Col [Blunstone]. We were completely blown away. Obviously at the time, there was so much screaming going on that you couldn't really hear them, but it was really, really magical. A huge amount of energy. There aren't any bigger fans of the Beatles than our group [the Zombies]. We thought they were a wonderful breath of fresh air. Their craft is still fantastic when you listen back to all the songs they put together, a wonderful coming together of them and George Martin. George produced them absolutely wonderfully and it's just great music, and truly timeless.

At the end of 1964, the Zombies went to the US for the first time to perform on one of Murray the K's package shows. We opened at eight o'clock in the morning, six shows a day, doing just a couple of songs, playing with the likes of Patti LaBelle, Dionne Warwick, Ben E. King, the Drifters, Chuck Jackson and the Shangri-Las. They really dug what we were doing, we were so knocked out.

A couple of years passed by and we were getting very frustrated by our producer Ken Jones, who I thought had done a terrific job at the beginning of the Zombies' career, but he was very autocratic. We said to him, 'Look, we want to produce an album ourselves,' and he was great. He said, 'OK, if you want to do it yourselves, I'll help you.' He used his contacts to get us into Abbey Road. We wanted to make a clean start, and because we were so in love with the Beatles, Abbey Road was the obvious choice, and Ken booked us in, and literally about a week before we walked in, the Beatles had just walked out, having finished *Sgt. Pepper*. They had left stuff around in the studio. John had left his mellotron there, and that's why you can hear mellotron all over our album [*Odessey And Oracle*]. It was just there, so I used it. It wasn't ours to use, but we used it. A lot of technical innovations that the Beatles had introduced, we were lucky enough to be able to take advantage of. We had engineers like Geoff Emerick and Peter Vince. The album didn't sell at first, but after a decade or so, it started to sell and people started talking about it and have never stopped really. From that time onwards, people started to quote *Odessey And Oracle* in the same breath as *Sgt. Pepper* and *Revolver*, and things like *Pet Sounds*, which is a huge compliment. Then eighteen months after the album came out, 'Time Of The Season' became a number one in almost every country in the world apart from the UK, but even then the album wasn't particularly selling well. I often say onstage that it sells more now than when it was first out. As far as I know we were the first group who were allowed to record at Abbey Road who weren't an EMI signing. The group split up before the single came out, because the guys who weren't writers in the group, in other words everybody except Chris [White] and myself, were making no money. When the single was a hit, we were offered large sums to reform, but we turned them all down. We didn't want to just look back and restart everything up. The Beatles were a huge influence on our music, but I think that's true of every single other group who was around at the time, and none more so than the Rolling Stones. I think the Rolling Stones took so much from the Beatles, and the press put forward this big competition between them both. The Beatles would come out with something like 'I Feel Fine', a guitar picking thing, and the next record from the Stones you knew would be something similar. Everybody at the time, you could not be hugely influenced by the Beatles. Hugely ahead of their time. They were very honest, and the production was very earthy, meaty, and it wasn't full of gimmicks, it was very honest and the records had great grooves, and a chunky feel to them. Lennon was a wonderful rhythm guitarist. I've always loved Ringo's drumming. I was on the Ringo Starr All Starr tour in 2006 and playing with him was great. ❚

ROD ARGENT, MUSICIAN, PETERSFIELD, HAMPSHIRE

SATURDAY 7 SEPTEMBER

The group recorded a three-hour session beginning at 1pm at the Playhouse Theatre in London for the fifth birthday edition of *Saturday Club* - its 262nd broadcast. They performed 'I Saw Her Standing There,' 'Memphis, Tennessee,' 'Happy Birthday Saturday Club' (an adaptation of the song in the style of Heinz's 'Just Like Eddie'), 'I'll Get You,' 'She Loves You' and 'Lucille'. The show aired on 5 October. During a break, Paul was interviewed by Rosemary Hart for the BBC Home Service series *A World Of Sound*, subtitled 'Liverpool: A Swinging City,' which aired on 21 November.

At around four o'clock, the group drove to Croydon for two concerts at the Fairfield Hall at 6.15pm and 8.45pm, with local group the Quiet Five added to the bill. After the show, about five hundred screaming teenagers, mostly girls, mobbed the group as they tried to leave. St John Ambulance Brigade volunteer Alan Dives was knocked to the ground and trampled on by the surging crowd. He was taken to hospital but not detained. One policeman said, 'I've never seen anything like it. It's a miracle no one was killed.'

The *Croydon Advertiser* reviewed the shows: 'They demonstrated why they have shot to the top at such a rapid pace. They were self-assured, smart in appearance and gave the customers what they wanted - although what this precisely is poses rather a doubtful question. It has been said somewhere that "The quality of Mersey is not strained" ...It was very severely strained – the Noise Abatement Society would have had a hey-day! Continuous high-pitched screaming throughout the group's entire act from a capacity audience, composed mainly of teenage girls, prevented any attempt at a critical assessment of the Beatles' performance. During their fifteen-minute appearance onstage, the numbers they played included, I believe, 'Please Please Me', 'From Me To You', a frenetic 'Twist And Shout' and their current success 'She Loves You'.'

Richard Green in the *Times-Herald* was equally euphoric. 'It hardly seems possible, but I believe the foursome have improved since I saw them last in June. Their whole presentation seems to have become much more polished and the way Paul chatted with the audience was far removed from his earlier on-stage aloofness.' However, he did comment that he would take a tin hat with him the next time he saw them so Jelly Babies hitting him on the head would have less impact. Sunday's recording of *Big Night Out* aired at 7.40pm, except in the London region.

> ❝ The Quiet Five was formed by Pat Dane (real name Patrick Adamson) around 1962, with Richard Barnes, Nick Ryan, Paul Hoffman and myself on keyboards and vocals. We started off playing around the Croydon and South London areas and were popular and successful as a live group, performing covers of current material as well as our own stuff. We had a couple of attempts at recording and produced some good demos, particularly when the well-known DJ Shaw Taylor took an interest in looking after us. But we never flew as a recording outfit. Although we had ambition, it was really only Barnes who wanted to make a career of it, the rest of us had other jobs which, of course, curtailed our progress professionally. That's not to say that we wouldn't have grabbed the chance for the big time if it had come our way!
>
> Anyway, I remember that night with the Beatles very well. We did most of the first act to a wild, tumultuous reception from the audience, clearly practising in anticipation of what was to come! The screaming was so loud we could hardly hear what we were doing. Then, as we made our exit stage right, we passed the Fab Four in the wings waiting to go on. We didn't have any other interaction with them – I wish we had, but we all had our own dressing rooms, we were on at different times, and it was quite literally, passing in the dark. At the time they had newly embarked upon what was to become the biggest roller-coaster since Elvis, complete with sharp suits and muppet haircuts so none of us really knew what to expect. And small – that's what I remember most; to a man they were at least 4 inches shorter than us, their southern counterparts (or so we liked to think).
>
> We'd had a good set and got a huge ovation and I remember wondering what they could do that we couldn't. Well, we didn't have long to wait to find out! They started to play and there it was, the unmistakable originality, the unique sound, the wit, the sense of mischief – so different and so much better than us. Quite simply, there had never been anything like the Beatles before. Of course, performing with them was a great experience for us but it also brought it home that, even

though we were still in our early twenties, something had changed, things had moved on and the music scene would never be the same again. Just as we had got started, it felt as if we were being left behind. Of course, we weren't the only ones. The Beatles were unique and different and represented the beginning of an entirely new era and one that was to last for the next twenty-five years; some would argue longer. And that new era started for me in September 1963. The world of music, film, television and art was changing. It was undergoing a huge revolution, particularly in this country, so it was a very exciting time to be going into what previously was considered a hopelessly insecure line of work. Anything artistic was flamboyant and exotic and to be discouraged by parents but, of course, it wasn't the case and I did perfectly well having changed direction. I worked in publishing and advertising in the '70s and '80s and later became a TV producer, devising and producing *A Touch Of Frost*, *The Darling Buds Of May*, *My Uncle Silas*, and *Pride Of Africa*. The musical theme I wrote for *The Darling Buds Of May* won me an Ivor Novello Award – an honour I share with John, Paul and George. **⁊**

PIP BURLEY, TELEVISION PRODUCER, ADVERTISING EXECUTIVE, MUSICIAN AND COMPOSER, HEADLEY, SURREY

SUNDAY **8 SEPTEMBER**

The Beatles drove north to Blackpool for two more concerts at 6pm and 8.15pm at the ABC, performing with Chas McDevitt and Shirley Douglas, the Countrymen, Lee Leslie, the Sons of the Piltdown Men, Terry Young and host Jack Douglas. Marty Wilde and the Wildcats, Bruce Welch and Eden Kane all sat at the back watching the Beatles show. Wilde was writing a weekly column for the *NRM* during his summer season at Blackpool's Rainbow Theatre and observed girls leaving the theatre during 'Twist And Shout' so they could get to the stage door before the Beatles left. He also commented, 'They've got one really great advantage over many recording artists. They manage to make their numbers on the stage have exactly the same sound as their records. They went down a storm.'

The Beatles did not return to Blackpool until the following summer when they made a further three appearances – although in December, Brian Barker, the licensee of the Eagle and Child in nearby Weeton, told the press that the group had arrived at his pub, sat in a corner and ordered turkey sandwiches and fruit juices. 'I'm certain it was the Beatles,' said Barker. 'They obviously wanted to be left alone so I saw that they weren't bothered by anyone. In fact, the only other persons to recognise them were two girls whose boyfriends wouldn't let them ask for autographs.' However, Barker was mistaken – the group were on the other side of the country, performing in Leicester.

❛ I was doing the summer season in Blackpool in 1963 at the Rainbow on the South Pier. At that particular point, I was writing record reviews for the *Record Mirror*. I can't remember how I got the job, but I do remember I got into quite a lot of trouble! If you speak your mind and you're known, it's a bit like Twitter or Facebook these days, potentially you're going to get yourself in one big pile of trouble – I used to say what I thought.

I was asked to review the Beatles when they did a one-off show at the ABC. I thought the lead guitar played by George Harrison was too loud and I mentioned this in my review – it kind of took some

of the edge off for me. Other than that, the set was brilliant – just a bit too loud. I don't think that went down too well with George! They were a big name by then, even though it was at the very beginning of their career. I'd known them before, as I used to work around the country, including the Liverpool Empire. There were always people talking about the Beatles, giving me Beatles magazines, stories about them, etc. I didn't know much about them until 'Love Me Do' came out but I thought it would be a big hit. I remember saying in my article that anyone who could get shares in them should do so because they were going to be enormous! I did have an advantage over lots of people because one of the places I worked was in a ballroom in Chester, and they'd been there and had torn the place apart. Wherever I went kids were talking about them. They'd say, 'Have you seen the Beatles?' Loads of people were asking me. They were creating this following before they even made it as recording stars.

I wrote for *Record Mirror* for about a year and a half, but I used to write what I thought. The mail that was coming in was phenomenal. In a way I was relieved when I did stop writing the reviews because I think somebody would have shot me or hung me otherwise! I didn't hold back. I didn't tell lies, I just told what I thought was the truth. They were paying me to write though, and I thought well if you're going to be a journalist, be an honest one. In the case of the Beatles, I would never have done anything to have harmed them because I respected them tremendously. I met them during that summer season at a party there. They were there, as were Cliff and the Shadows, who were also doing a summer season in Blackpool that year. It was a good time for pop records, a very interesting time. There's no question that there was a lot going on. **〕**

MARTY WILDE, SINGER/SONGWRITER AND MUSICIAN, WELWYN, HERTFORDSHIRE

MONDAY **9 SEPTEMBER**

The group travelled first-class by train from Blackpool to London. They hadn't had breakfast and when the ticket collector came to clip their tickets he was asked what time they started serving lunch. 'No restaurant car,' was the reply. Several fellow passengers were spotted eating lemon cake – apparently all that was available in the buffet car. 'We found the only thing between us and the cake was a long queue,' George recalled. 'We stood in it and shuffled slowly forward with the rest of the queue. But when we got near the cake, we could see supplies were running low. We got nearer and nearer. Then what happens? Only one bloke ahead of us – and he buys the last bit of cake! He paid nine pence for it.' Despite George offering 3/- for the slice, the man proceeded to eat it in front of them.

At Crewe Station, the train stopped for a few minutes. Ringo was delegated to find food, returning with hot dogs and Cokes with moments to spare. On their arrival in the capital, they met with *Daily Mirror* photographer Bela Zola, who shot them in various locations, including St James's Church Hall and Garson

House in Gloucester Terrace. Afterwards, they were interviewed by the paper's columnist Donald Zec in his nearby flat at 28 Maitland Court in Lancaster Terrace, where he served them tea. Zec had seen one of their shows in Luton the previous Friday. It was later reported that the group were none too happy with the subsequent feature. Taking advantage of a rare night off, the Beatles moved into their new base at 57 Green Street in Mayfair. After Paul and John moved out later in the year, their neighbours Harry and Carol Finegold on the floor below sometimes cooked for George and Ringo.

Marilyn magazine featured the first of four articles titled 'Beatle Box'. In the first article, Paul answered a series of not particularly interesting questions from readers.

TUESDAY 10 SEPTEMBER

The *Daily Mirror* published Zec's interview under the heading 'Four Frenzied Little Lord Fauntleroys Who Are Making £50,000 Every Week'. The group spent part of the morning at the NEMS office, before travelling to the Savoy Hotel for the Variety Club of Great Britain Luncheon. They were awarded *Melody Maker* Pop Poll's Top Vocal Group of the Year. Other attendees included Millicent Martin, Norman Vaughan and world heavyweight boxing champion Sonny Liston, 'giving punch to the lunch'. After the celebrity-packed proceedings, the group joined Billy J. Kramer and Susan Maughan to pose for photographers in Victoria Embankment Gardens. John and Paul left by taxi to head back to Green Street. As the cab drove down Jermyn

Street, they saw Andrew Oldham, who invited them to see the Rolling Stones in rehearsal at the Studio 51 Club at 10–11 Great Newport Street.

With the Stones unable to decide on a second single, John and Paul played an unfinished song they were working on, 'I Wanna Be Your Man'. Keith Richard commented later, 'John and Paul came down to rehearsal and laid the song on us. We hadn't heard their version. We just heard John and Paul on a piano banging it out. We picked it up, and it was just one of those jams. They got enthusiastic, we got enthusiastic and said, "Right. We'll cut it tomorrow," and that was it.' John commented, 'We weren't going to give them anything great, right?' The Beatles recorded their own version the following day, with Ringo on lead vocals. The thirteenth episode of *Pop Go The Beatles*, recorded on the 3rd with guests Johnny Kidd and the Pirates, aired at 5pm.

❝ I started working for NEMS on 10 June 1963. I went for the interview in my lunch hour, and when I arrived at 13 Monmouth Street, the book shop owner downstairs said that a company had taken a couple of rooms upstairs, and that my interview must be up there. (It was a 'dirty' book shop.) I went up, and knocked on the door. An American girl opened it. Her name was Jo Bergman. She was Tony Barrow's assistant and introduced me to him. Much of what he was saying didn't sink in because he spoke so fast. He asked me if I'd heard of a group called the Beatles, and I said I hadn't. He explained that they were a northern pop group and had been touring and had had a number one! I said, 'I'm sorry, but I haven't heard of them.' I think that was what clinched it. I was the only person to be interviewed. We got on very well, and at the end he said, 'Well, I'll let you know.' By the end of my lunch break, Tony had rung and offered me the job.

Back in my office, I wasn't sure whether or not I wanted it. I had felt comforted when I arrived back in my familiar surroundings. Did I want to work for a fan club? In the end, I decided to go for it. What followed was three years of mayhem! I was initially taken on to be the face of 'Anne Collingham'. Tony had come up with the name as he felt they needed someone for the fans to write to. What was happening was that fans would come to the office asking to meet 'Anne Collingham', and she didn't exist! Jo's American accent didn't really cut the mustard, so I was to be the face of 'Anne Collingham'. I was paid £10 a week, and initially we just had the two rooms – Tony's office, Jo's and mine, and a reception area. By the end of August, beginning of September, things were getting a bit crazy. We were having to get through about sixty sacks of mail a week, and you couldn't get any admin done during the day, because the phone rang non-stop. We had to do lots of overtime. Fans would ring up or turn up expecting the group to be there. We had to be polite, but all we had time to do was ask for their details, and say we'd send them a membership pack!

Bettina Rose had been running the Beatles fan club from home, as well as doing a day job as a secretary at ATV and it became obvious that it wasn't going to be possible to continue doing the two jobs, so she was brought in at this time to work full-time as Joint National Secretary. We took over two more rooms upstairs, and employed some eight new members of staff.

It wasn't until September that I actually met the Beatles. I didn't know I was going to meet them that day, but Tony said that he had some guests coming, and would I make some teas and coffee? It was such a nuisance because it was an old building, with a rickety staircase, so I ended up staggering into his room, and the Beatles were in there. They were lovely, and he introduced me to each one, like a who's who. I was so embarrassed because they were all giggling and the atmosphere in the room was really smokey and quite dark. It was very clubby. I put the tray of cups and saucers down and tried to serve, and they said, 'We'll do it. It's OK', which was something else and really quite special. Up until then, I didn't really know them, but through my work I knew what they were up to, but not really being a fan as such, but as soon as I met them it was all a bit different after then.

The following month, I remember Paul coming to the office to take us girls out for lunch. We went to a steak house near the office. It wasn't anything palatial, just a normal restaurant. Paul played footsie with me under the table. He probably did that to all the girls, but it was fun anyway. Unfortunately, it wasn't fun for everyone though. Tony sent Tony Catchpole on an errand to buy toilet rolls! He was so upset he couldn't come. It was really funny because he had to get a dozen toilet rolls, and normally we had Andrex or other soft tissue, but Tony being Tony, he had such a good sense of humour, and he was so annoyed about having to get these toilet rolls and not going to lunch, that he went out and bought twelve Bronco rolls – the cheapest paper you could get – it was like Izal – see through! We thought it was hilarious. But Tony B and Brian didn't think it was at all funny.

Towards the end of September, I posed in the official Beatles sweater for a print ad. I remember Tony called me into his office, and said, 'I've got something for you to do' and showed me the sweater. I thought, 'What's this for?' He said, 'You'll be modelling it for the flyers that are going out.' Dezo Hoffmann took the photo in his Soho studio and it was actually taken at Cilla Black's first photo session. I really didn't want to do it to be honest. I didn't like having my picture taken but he said I had to, so we headed for the studio with Cilla and Bobby Willis. It was quite a session, because I wasn't a model and wasn't animated at all. I was so hot in the jumper, which was itchy and very uncomfortable. Dezo said, 'This is not right, this is not right, what we need to do is ...' and he decided to pull it in and peg it, to give it a bit more shape for the photographs, adding to my embarrassment. He told me to, 'Make like you're twisting,' but there was no music, and it was all very awkward. Bobby was standing off-camera, and he said, 'It's OK, we can do this,' and he was twisting off-camera just to help, so I did it.

Another memorable highlight was when Tony took Bettina and I up to Liverpool for the Northern Area Fan Club Convention in December and we met Freda Kelly for the first time. The Beatles were the panellists on *Juke Box Jury*. We – the three girls – Freda, Bettina and I were on the second jury. The rehearsals were brilliant. The Beatles disagreed on every single record that was played, and we were thinking this was great, our families were going to see it because we were there. We were seen at the beginning and introduced by David Jacobs, but that was the last that was seen of us! When it came to the show itself, they agreed on everything!

I left NEMS on 22 May 1966, after three hectic years. My friend Pat and I had spent some time in Jersey, and loved it so much we decided to work there for a few summers and would come back to London to temp. I was never a career girl as such, a job was a job, and as long as it paid for what I wanted to do, I was happy. I spent many happy years in Greece, which was quite an adventure, but returned home to England and settled. Looking back at those early days, it's hard to believe how lucky I was to be in the right place at the right time and have such unique memories. Over the years, it has become apparent that people seem to have forgotten the early days of the Beatles Fan Club in Monmouth Street, focusing mainly on Argyll Street. However, it should be worth remembering that this was NEMS first office in London and was visited by many hundreds of loyal Beatle fans from 1963 to 1966. I know – I was there! **"**

MARY COCKRAM, SECRETARY, ISLINGTON, LONDON

WEDNESDAY 11 SEPTEMBER

One year to the day since the Beatles went into Abbey Road to record 'Love Me Do', the group returned to continue recording tracks for their new LP. The two sessions took place between 2.30pm and 10.15pm and included the first take of 'I Wanna Be Your Man' – Ringo's first lead vocal, two takes of 'Little Child', fifteen of 'All I've Got To Do', nine of 'Not A Second Time' and seven of George's recently written 'Don't Bother Me'. *Melody Maker's* Chris Roberts was present at the recording and reported that a mouse sitting on a ledge looking through the control room window caused much jocularity. Roberts, himself a guitar player, was asked by John whether he knew anyone who could fix the electrics on his Rickenbacker 325. 'Yes I do,' replied Roberts and took the instrument to guitar maker Jim Burns at his factory in Buckhurst Hill, Essex. When repaired, Burns handed it over to Leslie Andrews who re-fretted the instrument. Roberts returned the instrument to NEMS after John returned from his holiday in Paris. The *Daily Mail* suggested that the group's 'beat music' was earning them £5,000 a week.

" My granny gave me the *Twist And Shout* EP for my 8th birthday on 11 September 1963. She was a tremendous pianist and had led Mrs Hutson's Boys with my dad on drums and my uncle Pete on piano accordion. Anyway that birthday present, much to my mother's horror, kicked off this obsession with the Beatles. I'm not sure why my granny bought it for me other than it was current, she thought it was good stuff and that I'd like it and she wasn't wrong. My mother never really forgave her for it. I wasn't really that conscious of who the Beatles were. They had played in Margate that summer and had stayed at the Beresford Hotel, about half a mile from where

we lived. Some years later when they tore the hotel down, I prised a bucket load of blue tiles from the swimming pool they swam in.

That Christmas I put an ad in the local newsagent to sell some of my Corgi and Dinky toys. They were still in their boxes and I flogged them off and made enough money to go and buy my first Beatles' LP. I went into Skinner's Records in Westgate. I said, 'I want a Beatles LP,' and they said, 'Which one do you want? We've got the first one *Please Please Me*, *With The Beatles* and this new one *A Hard Day's Night*, which had just come out. So I had to have the new one and I think I paid 32/6 for it with the money I got for my Corgis and Dinkys. And now winding the clock on more than fifty years, I'm thinking of selling my Beatles vinyl and going out and buying some of those originals Corgis and Dinkys.

We had a mono record player back at home at the time; my local record shop in Birchington didn't have a mono copy of *Sgt. Pepper* so I cycled 4 or 5 miles into Margate to Henry's Records and forked out my 37/11 to buy the mono version of the LP. Since then I've just gone on collecting Beatles stuff, finding out as much as I could about them. I've managed to do a bit of writing about them, some radio shows for the BBC, and then you get hauled in as a so-called expert, which I'm not at all, just to talk about the Beatles. I hope to be discovered, but it hasn't happened yet. I can well remember being in Skinner's, waiting for the first releases on the Apple label. I wanted *Hey Jude* and they said it hadn't come in. So I said, 'Can I wait?' We waited until the postman arrived. This package was there and they opened it and there, for the first time, was this Apple record in a black sleeve. There was also Mary Hopkin's *Those Were The Days*. My poor mum and dad had to drive me to the record store on the day each of their records came out.

I later went back to a second-hand shop in Herne Bay, a rather grubby place that sold magazines that my mum and dad wouldn't have wanted me to have, but under the counter he had the Beatles' and the Rolling Stones' magazines. I then found that the *Beatles Monthly* had been printed by a firm in Margate. So my mum and I went along because I thought they must have copies. So I dragged my mum along to see the manager. He saw this little boy come along asking if he had any copies of the magazine. He said he hadn't and then I discovered someone at school had the complete set because his father had worked for the printer's. He had some in his loft so I bought all of them off him. I've continued to pursue music as my hobby ever since. I still have all my Beatles vinyl, but of course like everyone else I've also got their music on eight-track, cassette, I've even got some on reel to reel, CD, the remastered CDs, the mono boxed set and the stereo boxed set. Some of my best friendships are from music. I've met an awful lot of nice people through my love of music. A lot of kindred spirits, but we're a little bit different. There are those who have to have every sleeve and that sort of thing, and that's an illness, whereas with me it's just a brief hobby. **J**

**JOHN HUTSON, MEDIA RELATIONS, CORPORATE COMMUNICATIONS,
PUBLIC AFFAIRS AND BROADCASTER, BANWELL, SOMERSET**

THURSDAY 12 SEPTEMBER

In the week's *Disc* Top 30, 'She Loves You' stayed at number one, while 'Twist And Shout' dropped two places to number 13. The group told Dick Tatham about their forthcoming holiday plans. John was going to Paris, explaining his reasoning. 'I did the trip two years ago when I was near enough broke. I hitched most of the way and stayed in some pretty low dumps. Now I want to see what it's like being there with money in your pocket.' Paul and Ringo were going to Greece; Paul 'to have all my teeth out', while Ringo claimed 'to get my toenails tattooed'. George said he was looking forward to seeing his sister Louise in the US, a place he had never been to before. The front page of *NRM* read 'No. 1 Again' as 'She Loves You' went to the top, while 'From Me To You' dropped out of the Top 50 after twenty-one weeks. With 'She Loves You', *Twist And Shout* and *Please Please Me* topping the Singles, EP and LP charts, the Beatles became the second act to achieve the feat – the other being Elvis Presley in June 1962.

In the new edition of the *Radio Times*, the magazine's weekly 'Portrait Gallery' offered portraits of the group. It described the group as a 'very much a do-it-yourself outfit,' who played their own compositions (over 100 to date), wrote their own lyrics and scored their own arrangements. 'Equipped with brooding good looks, they inspire devotion of traffic-jam proportions among their fans wherever they appear. If imitation be indeed the sincerest form of flattery, the number of eyebrow-level Beatle haircuts to be seen around the coffee bars is flattery indeed.' More than two hundred and fifty thousand applications came in for the 10 x 8" photos at 2/-.

Photographer Norman Parkinson captured the group at the Hotel President, including a shot of them holding the *Financial Times* with the headline 'Steel Production In August Best Since Early 1961.' Parkinson later commented that they were 'collectively and separately the most talented and primitive young men' he had ever met. He went on to say, 'If they started a political party 90 per cent of the country's teenagers would vote for them. They are the voice of youth. Perhaps we should lower the voting age.'

At 2.30pm, another recording session began at EMI Studios. In four hours, they recorded radio clips for Australian DJ Bob Rogers on Sydney station 2SM and an open message for general use and ten new takes of 'Hold Me Tight.' After a half-hour break, they did ten new takes of 'Don't Bother Me,' sixteen more of 'Little Child' and six more of 'I Wanna Be Your Man,' finishing at 11.30pm. Parkinson snapped them recording in the studios and having cups of tea in the canteen.

FRIDAY 13 SEPTEMBER

In the latest editions of the *NME* and *Melody Maker*, 'She Loves You' stayed at number one in both, while *Twist And Shout* dropped to numbers 15 and 12, respectively. Cliff Richard's 'My Top 10' in the *NME* included the Kestrels' version of 'There's A Place' ('They sound like a good US Negro quartet, praise indeed!') but nothing by the Beatles themselves. Only two days after its previous mention of the group, the *Daily Mail* warned Cliff that there was 'a Beatle on [his] back'. However, the writer also felt that 'by the time the Beatles have vanished back to Merseyside, Cliff could still be enjoying himself on *Housewives' Choice*, in film, and on the West End stage and round the world'. The paper's show business correspondent Barry Norman also wrote a piece titled 'Top Of The Long-Hair Pops', comparing the meteoric rise of three young actors – Ian Holm, Ian Richardson and David Warner, who were all playing leading roles at the Royal Shakespeare Company - to the Beatles.

The group drove back up north to perform at the Public Hall in Preston's Market Square, where they had appeared on 26 October the previous year. The concerts were promoted by Epstein and Vin Sumner, who had booked them in August 1962 at the Preston Grasshoppers Rugby Club Dance, paying £18. This time the Beatles were paid £538. They changed into their stage clothes in their Ford Thames minibus as it was being driven around the town centre. When they finally arrived at the hall, they almost immediately walked onstage to perform to an audience of two thousand. Outwitting fans after the second show, they crawled through the hall's cellar and out through a side door.

Paul, because of his driving conviction, was driven by Epstein's assistant Barry Leonard to nearby Nelson, to sit on the panel of judges for 'Miss Imperial 1963'. Part of an annual 'Young Ones Ball' promotion by the *Nelson Leader*. Singers Eden Kane and Julie Grant were also on the panel. Paul arrived just after midnight and helped vote Virginia Lonsdale, an 18-year-old dairy maid from Simonstone, the first ever winner. Fans were invited onstage to get autographs. Grant remembered the ensuing chaos. 'It went to hell in a handbasket. Hundreds of kids running up and jumping on Paul. They scuffed up against my dress and my brooch fell off. Paul said, "Here I'll keep it safe for you." I never saw the bloody thing again.'

The newspaper's Leigh Morrissey, among the seventeen hundred attendees, wrote, 'It was gay. It was heavy with the twanging guitar beat of rock group music. It was spectacular. It was star-studded. And, let's face it: it was noisy, too.' The Mayor of Nelson, Councillor O.S. Cox commented, 'An unusual evening but an enjoyable evening. It was good to see the youngsters having a gay fling and at the same time helping the old folk.' Fellow Councillor Taylor Smith, Burnley Rural District Council, added, 'A very enjoyable evening and I will not forget it in a hurry. Two o'clock is a little past my normal bedtime, though.' The rest of the group returned home to Liverpool after the show.

❝ I had no idea that Cliff included our [the Kestrels'] version of 'There's A Place' in his favourite Top 10 at the time. He's certainly never told me about it. We made the record in between the two tours we did with the Beatles in 1963. It was their idea. They said, 'Do you want to record this song?' So, we did. EMI, in their wisdom, released an extended play with the Beatles' version on it a few weeks after ours came out. Very annoying! It was recorded at Pye Studios with a Johnny Keating arrangement and Ray Horricks producing. I remember Reg Guest was the keyboard player on it.

My singing career had begun back in the mid '50s. I had met Roger Greenaway, who is my oldest friend, when I was 16. We used to play football together and do all sorts of things. We weren't at school together – I, for my sins, went to a minor public school called Colston's, and Roger went to a grammar school. Around this time, when I was working for E. S. & A. Robinson's in Bristol, we formed a skiffle group and we used to rehearse in the company's basement. We soon became a vocal group and played at the Colston Hall. We then entered a Carroll Levis' Discoveries contest at the Hippodrome. We were all old enough in 1958 to do National Service and managed to get into the same unit – the Royal Army Pay Corps at Devizes, so we were able to continue with our music. We were called all sorts of names back then – the Belltones, the Belltonaries, but ended up as the Kestrels. We'd been trying to think of a name to settle on and were writing down names. Kestrel happened to be the name of the pencil I was writing with. So I said, 'What about this? Look,' and held up the pencil.

Just before we were demobbed, we went to see Eddie Cochran at the Hippodrome in Bristol. We drove back to Devizes and passed where the car he was travelling in crashed. We didn't know it was him who had been killed until the following morning when we read about it in the newspaper. We kicked off 1963 with the Helen Shapiro tour with the Beatles and Kenny Lynch, etc. She started off heading the tour, but halfway through it was getting ridiculous, so Helen closed the first half and the Beatles closed the second half. We were actually paid extra money to go on immediately before them, because no one else wanted to. Nobody could hear anything and it was just one big scream. We all travelled on the coach together. It was brilliant fun, just wonderful. It was a popular tour, but by the end, the audience weren't really interested in anyone else other than the Beatles.

We also did the autumn tour with them as well. I remember Stockton-on-Tees clearly. That's when we heard that President Kennedy had been shot. John Lennon came off stage and said, 'This is unbelievable.' Our biggest claim to fame, is that we actually taught the Beatles how to bow! Everything was very regimented in the army, and so we learned to all bow together and come up again together, two, three, four, up! Before they appeared on the Royal Command Performance, we rehearsed with them, and that's what they did on that show. We watched it on TV, and counted 'two, three, four... up' and they got it right!

I was a studio musician for thirty years and had a wonderful time. Elton, Cliff, Tom Jones, other classic singles – can't think of any though! I did Edison Lighthouse's 'Love Grows' and the Pipkins' 'Gimme Dat Ding,' which was banned in Italy – they thought it was something rude. I was also a member of the original Brotherhood of Man and White Plains and sang the lead on 'Beach Baby' by First Class. It was played to Brian Wilson when he was in Australia, and he said, 'Well, it's definitely West Coast American.' I've since met Brian on several occasions and he confirms that they always play the song before their concerts. It's been an enjoyable career, I've had a lovely time. I still go to America a couple of times a year, and still sing the same old, same old. ❞

TONY BURROWS, SINGER, WOKINGHAM, BERKSHIRE

SATURDAY 14 SEPTEMBER

The *Daily Mirror* printed eight letters in its 'Viewpoint' column, following Zec's article the previous Tuesday. All the writers, bar one, were critical of Zec's article. The one who agreed, a Mr J. Yaman of Oxhey, Hertfordshire wrote, 'Have we all gone mad allowing the Beatles to earn £5,000 a week for making a noise they have the cheek to call singing.'

The *Preston Evening Post* reported on the previous night's visit, its front-page headline reading, 'Beatles Invade Preston – And, Boy, What A Scream.' However, nothing was written about the concert given by 'the world's best in beat music' – instead the writer commented on observant fans who spotted the group arriving in their car, 'a blue Vauxhall Victor, GSS 421.' As the car drove away at the end of the show, 'showers of autograph books, programmes, pictures and Jelly Babies – Beatle fodder – were thrown after the car.' The paper also claimed that screams and shouting was heard as far away as Friargate.

In the afternoon, the group gave press interviews at NEMS' Liverpool offices. On his way, George visited a record shop and bought two Shirelles' LPs (*Baby It's You* and *The Shirelles Sing To Trumpets And Strings*) as well as Mary Wells' *The Golden Girl Of American Hits* and Ketty Lester's *Love Letters* along with several singles. Once at NEMS, he slipped one of the Shirelles' LP onto the record player, turned up the volume and sank into a luxurious leather armchair.

Two girls arrived outside the Memorial Hall in Northwich at 7.15am for the evening's concert by the group, who didn't arrive until twelve hours later. They made their third appearance of the year at the venue, supported by the Landsliders and Gerry De Ville and the City Kings.

❝ As we lived in the sticks, life was a bit limited to access to dances or music. We didn't have phones or cars in those days, so had to make our way by bus, or didn't go. When I left school I worked in our local Co-op No. 10 Branch in Middlewich's Bull Ring. I then went to work at Powell's Tailors, making men's coats as a seamstress on piece-work. My friend Mary Lamb worked there too. Saturday was when we donned our glad rags, mainly a pencil skirt and jumper and winkle-picker shoes, same every week, dressed alike, everyone thinking we were twins, to go off flirting and learning to jive. The local cobbler Jack Steele warned us that it would be bad for our backs and our feet would go

out of shape as we got older, wearing 'rubbish stuff' like this. How right he was. The dancing school was run by Bernard and Kay Dodd. It was the best thing Mr Dodd ever did when he taught us to jive to 'Please Please Me'.

Saturday night was of course our regular visit to the Memorial Hall, if we managed to catch the 6.10 bus that is. Dressed to kill, off we went with our net petticoats having been dipped in starch all week, thrust and crushed into our clutch bags. I had seen the Beatles on their earlier visit and Mary and I were desperate to see them again. When we arrived, Mary ran to the local chippy as we had had no tea, leaving me there by myself. No sooner had she gone, when the Beatles rolled up in their limousine, jumped out, bounded up the steps to see me waiting alone at the top. They all signed my autograph book which I pushed at them. When I gathered the courage to speak I touched Paul's hair. He said, 'Why did you do that?' I said, 'Because I can tell everybody that I have touched your hair.' He then lifted mine, which then was down to my waist and said, 'Is it all right if I tell everybody I have touched yours?' They then shot into the dressing room and were gone. Mary had missed them so I showed her my autograph book. In those days we put all our handbags on either side of the stage for the whole evening while we danced. Nobody ever touched anyone else's or stole anything, but to my great horror and disbelief my bag was gone by the end of the evening. 🔗

ELLEN MATTHEWS, PROFESSIONAL CARER, MIDDLEWICH, CHESHIRE

SUNDAY 15 SEPTEMBER

The *BEATLES* are heading a fabulous line-up at
THE GREAT POP PROM
ROYAL ALBERT HALL, LONDON
SUNDAY 15th SEPT.
AT 2.15 p.m.
Sponsored by Valentine, Marilyn and Roxy in aid of the Printers' Pension Corporation
PRICES OF ADMISSION : 3/6, 7/6, 10/6, 15/- and 17/6
TICKETS NOW ON SALE at the Pop Prom Box Office, Royal Albert Hall, Kensington, London, S.W.7 and usual Ticket Agencies
IT'S THE SWINGIEST SHOW OF THE YEAR—BOOK NOW !

The *Sunday Times* printed its first article on the group, headlined 'The Beatles Beat The Lot'. The paper's music critic Derek Jewell described their sound as 'vigorous, aggressive, uncompromising and boringly stereotyped. It is exaggeratedly rhythmic, high-pitched, thunderously-amplified, full of wild, insidious harmonies'. Paul told Jewell, 'Once you could get on being a fake; sequin shirts, dyed hair, false eyelashes, no talent. Not now. All that phoney image-building. When I used to read about those pop singers who didn't smoke or drink and went for a run in the mornings I thought, what's wrong with them. Most teenagers do smoke and drink and miss their morning exercise. It's the healthy thing to do.'

The Beatles and the Rolling Stones played on the same bill together for the first time, at the 'Great Pop Prom' at London's Royal Albert Hall. The group arrived in time for a 12.30pm rehearsal. The Stones opened the 2.15pm concert, attended by six thousand fans, and which also featured Shane Fenton and the Fentones, the Brook Brothers, the Lorne Gibson Trio, Arthur Greenslade and the Gee Men, the Viscounts, Kenny Lynch, Clinton Ford, Susan Maughan, the Vernons Girls and compère Alan Freeman. Cathy Donaldson, a Beatles' fan from Kingston-upon-Thames, screamed so loudly that a loose tooth fell out – which she swallowed. She had to be carried outside, missing their final number, 'Twist And Shout'.

The *Daily Mirror* reported that, 'It was the siege of the Beatle-crushers... Never has the Royal Albert Hall seen scenes quite like it. Even for Britain's newly elected top vocal group, the Beatles, it was bewildering... They were the target for anything the teenagers could lay their hands on. Girls swept out of their seats and tried to rush the stage. They were repelled by a solid block of forty commissionaires. After their final hit number, 'Twist And Shout', the four Beatles fled from the stage and out of the Hall into a waiting cab'. Even the staid *Daily Express* saw fit to make comment on its front page, headed 'Beatle Fans Riot'. 'Hundreds of screaming girls broke a police cordon when the Beatles, pop stars, arrived at the Albert Hall for a concert.'

❛ I was born in Canada and at the age of 4 moved over to England to live in Aldershot. My dad had met my mum there during the Second World War, because all the Canadian troops passed through the barracks there on their way to fight in Europe. When I was about 12 years old my aunt came from Canada to visit and she bought me a plastic ukulele. A year or so later I got my first guitar. When I was about 16, I saw an ad in *Melody Maker* – 'Lorne Gibson looking for a guitar and bass player.' I applied for that job and got it. We [the Lorne Gibson Trio] recorded 'Some Do, Some Don't', probably our biggest claim to fame, which happened to be released on the same day as 'Love Me Do'. That winter, in addition to playing pop concerts, we played the northern working men's club circuit, spending a considerable period of time driving at 2 miles an hour in the fog on the M1 going up and down there.

Brian Epstein took a liking to the Trio and wanted to sign us up to NEMS. Although nothing came of that, in 1964 we did a series of concerts at the Prince of Wales Theatre in London as part of his *Pops Alive!* season. We had always been lucky enough to do a fair amount of radio work for the BBC and were booked for the first programme of a series called *Pop Go The Beatles*. The next time we saw them was at the Pop Prom. We were already inside and I remember them coming crashing through a side door. That always seemed to be the way they made an entrance. John had an acoustic Gibson guitar he played on one of the songs. I was standing and watching them from one of the tunnels that leads off from the stage and the audience was all around us. John put the guitar down at the back of the stage area as they finished their set and then they made their mad dash to get out. I looked up the tunnel and there was John's guitar disappearing in the hands of a fan. So at that point I ran up the tunnel and said, 'Come on, love. You can't have that. That belongs to John.' I ended up having a tug of war with her. She was on one end, I was on the other. I won and I took it backstage for them. It was all so hectic on the one hand, but me being 17 years old at the time, it went right over my head. It didn't occur to me that much that I was playing with the Beatles.

When we did one of the Prince of Wales' concerts in 1964 I got to chat with George and he showed me a twelve-string guitar the Rickenbacker people had just given him. Anyway, I stayed with the trio for a few more years, we released an album and several singles as well as doing a lot of radio work for the BBC. We even had our own show called *Three's Company* on which the Beatles made a guest appearance! In 1969, I was – as we like to call it – 'in between gigs' and was working in a lumber yard. I had an accident and lost the top of my left index finger. So that put a stop to my guitar playing for a while but I ended up working as a tape op at Olympic Sound. One of the things I worked on was *Jesus Christ Superstar*. I ended up playing a short piece of guitar for it, which was pretty cool. A few years ago we did three reunion concerts down in Devon and in 2004, the year after Lorne died, they did a memorial for him at the same venue and Vic [Arnold] and I went down and played as a duo. Since retiring I've been entertaining in retirement homes, including twenty minutes or so of Beatles' material. I talk about the times I met the Beatles, something I had never done in the past. It wasn't that I was embarrassed by my musical journey. Just that I didn't want to deal with the 'wing nuts' who would have said, 'Yeah, right mate, and I was the first astronaut on the sun!' 𝗝

STEVE VAUGHAN, MUSICIAN, BRAMPTON, ONTARIO, CANADA

MONDAY 16 SEPTEMBER–WEDNESDAY 2 OCTOBER

'She Loves You' and 'I'll Get You' were released on the Swan label in the US (Swan 4152). Swan's Bernie Binnick had acquired the rights from EMI in August while on holiday in the UK, after Capitol once again turned down the opportunity to release a Beatles' single – as had A&M, Columbia, Decca and RCA Victor. *Cash Box* reviewed the single, 'The big English hit, by the Beatles, could do big things in this country via the artists' release on Swan. Tune, tagged 'She Love You' [sic], is a robust, romantic rocker that the crew works over with solid sales authority. Backing's a catchy cha cha-twist handclapper.' The magazine chose it as their 'Newcomer of the Week.' The record was played on the

'Rate-A-Record' segment of TV's *American Bandstand*. It scored a modest 73 out of 98, with DJ Dick Clark subsequently recalling that he figured 'these guys were going nowhere'. WINS DJ Murray the K spun it on his record review contest, where it came third out of five, behind the Excellents' 'Coney Island Baby' and the Four Seasons' 'New Mexican Rose'. An exasperated George Martin would contact Capitol, saying 'For God's sake, do something about this. These boys are breaking it, and they're going to be fantastic throughout the world.'

The group flew out from London Airport for a well-deserved holiday. John and Cynthia travelled to Paris, later joined by Brian Epstein. While there Epstein told Barry Norman he would never sell his interest in the group. George and his brother Peter flew to New York, making their first ever trip to the US, to visit their sister Louise Caldwell. Paul, Jane Asher, Ringo and Maureen Cox flew to Athens where they stayed for a couple of days before travelling to Corfu.

A few days into their trip, John and Cynthia returned to their room at the George V Hotel in Paris to find a note from Astrid Kirchherr. They met up with Kirchherr and a girlfriend in the evening and hopped from one wine bar to another. As dawn broke the quartet was so paralytic that they could only stagger back to where Astrid was staying. More wine was consumed before they all collapsed on Astrid's single bed. They fell asleep, woke up with hangovers and John and Cynthia made their way back to their hotel. During the holiday, John bought Cynthia a grey coat, white beret and a bottle of Chanel No. 5 and filmed much of their trip with his cine camera. They returned home to Liverpool after eight days, ostensibly because John missed his guitar. 'I went potty without it,' he told Maureen Cleave. On their return to England, Epstein organised family snaps taken by Robert Freeman. During the session, Freeman mentioned to the couple that there was an empty top floor flat where he lived in Emperor's Gate off the Cromwell Road. They took it sight unseen in November.

Paul and Ringo spent their first week in Corfu living in chalets before spending a few days at the Miramare Beach Hotel on the island of Rhodes. For the remainder of their holidays they stayed in Athens, where they booked into the Acropole Palace Hotel; Paul used the name McCarthy and Ringo was misspelled as 'Starky'. On their last night at the hotel, they played with the resident group Trio Athenia. Ringo told the *NME*'s Alan Smith that they 'were living in chalets and we used to get up about ten in the morning and go sunbathing. The trouble was, it was so hot we used to have to give up after an hour or so.' Paul had difficulty adapting to the local cuisine. 'The only part we didn't like was having to take the garlic from all the food, and there were times when I longed for a good old steak and chips, or a few cheese slices.'

After an overnight stay at the Pickwick Hotel in New York, George and Peter took the two-and-a-half-hour flight to Lambert Field Airport in St Louis, Missouri, where they met Louise and her husband Gordon. They drove the 120 miles down Route 3 to 113 McCann Street in Benton, Illinois in the family's 1961 white Dodge Dart. It was the first time George had seen his sister since she left Liverpool for Canada in 1956. 'It had been a long time since I had seen my two brothers, and they had never met their niece and nephew,' Louise later recalled. On his first full day in Benton, George met Gabe McCarty, dry-cleaner by day, musician by night, and leader of local group the Four Vests. Over the next ten days, they spent a fair amount of time together, with McCarty driving George around in his light green 1961 Chevrolet station wagon. McCarty and fellow Four Vest Vernon Mandrell drove George to Mt Vernon, half an hour north on Route 37. They went to the Fenton Music Store at 601 South 10th Street – the only music store in the area which stocked Rickenbacker guitars. After trying several out, George picked a Rickenbacker 425 Fireglo solid body. Wanting one in black and not the fire-glow red he had chosen, George took up owner 'Red' Fenton's offer to refinish it for him in black. George paid around $400 for the guitar, accessories and the refinishing. With only the four of them in the store, George, with McCarty and Fenton on bass and piano respectively, jammed for a while – there was no instrument for the left-handed Mandrell to use. Afterwards they went to the Taco Villa drive-in restaurant, where George got into conversation with one of the roller-skating waitresses at the nearby A&W. McCarty also took George to Barton and Collins Furniture Store on the north-west side of Benton's town square. They were greeted by manager Bob Bonenberger. Among the twenty or so LPs George bought was a copy of James Ray's *If You Gotta Make A Fool Of Somebody*, which included the track 'Got My Mind Set On You.' (George's cover version of the record gave him one of his biggest hits in 1988.) On 20 September, George, Peter and the Caldwells had dinner with Judge Everett Lewis and his wife Lilian, who lived opposite.

The following day, George, Peter and Louise were driven to the Freeman Coal Company in West Frankfort, where Gordon worked. They walked two miles south on Route 37 to the studio of radio station WFRX, to visit Marcia Schafer, the 17-year-old daughter of one of its owners who had her own weekly *Saturday Session* show. When they arrived at the station, they discovered Schafer had already gone home. She was called back and conducted a fifteen-minute interview, which Peter filmed on George's 8mm camera. Before leaving, George gave her a copy of 'She Loves You' and an autographed photo of the group. Later in the year, Schafer penned a piece about the Beatles in *Redbird Notes*, the West Frankfort high school newspaper. 'Their music is wild and uninhibited and outsells the world's greatest recording artists, although not one of the Beatles can read music,' she wrote.

On the following Saturday, George, Peter and the Caldwells travelled to Eldorado, 30 miles south-east of Benton on Route 34, to see the Four Vests at the VFW Post 3479 hall. After their first set, McCarty asked George whether he would like to sit in with them. George took over from lead guitarist Kenny Welch using his hollow-bodied Rickenbacker. The group played a selection of country and western and rock'n'roll classics. Jim Chady, a friend of McCarty's, recalled that when George started playing, 'it was like someone threw a switch in that room. The difference was that dramatic.' One audience member told McCarty, 'That new kid that's trying out for your band – you'd be crazy if you didn't take him on.' Louise remembered people banging their fists on the tables and stomping their feet. 'The whole place was electrified.' After taking a break, the group played a further set, with George joining them on another few numbers. Fewer than a hundred people witnessed the first time a Beatle performed in the US. The next day George attended a birthday party at the Boneyard Boccie Ball Club at 500 South Wilson Street in Benton. He played with the Four Vests again, filling in for Welch, who was unable to make it.

During his ten days with the Caldwells, George spent two days camping in Shawnee National Forest, saw a handful of movies at the Marion Drive-In just north of the town of Benton on Route 37, including Cliff Richard and the Shadows' *Summer Holiday*, (titled *Wonderful To Be Young* in the US) and *The Nutty Professor* with Jerry Lewis. While watching the Cliff Richard film, George leant over to Louise and said, 'I know him.' One night he hung out at Teen Town on West Main Street in West Frankfort to hear a group.

On the 30th, George and Peter bade their sister farewell, and travelled to New York to spend the remaining days of their holiday there. He went to see Anthony Newley in *Stop The World I Want To Get Off* at the Ambassador Theatre on West 49th Street, visiting the actor backstage after the show. Peter took photos of him at the top of the Empire State Building. George went on to say that his time spent in New York was a disappointment – 'It's a lonely sort of place.'

In the 19 September edition of *Disc*, 'She Loves You' continued at number one for a third week, while *Twist And Shout* dropped two places to number 15. The single spent a second week at the top in the *NRM* chart, while *The Beatles' Hits* bowed at number 6 in the EP chart. In the same week's editions of the *NME* and *Melody Maker*, 'She Loves You' enjoyed its third week at number one in both charts, while *Twist And Shout* dropped four places to number 19 in the *NME* chart and climbed one place to number 11 in *Melody Maker* chart. *Melody Maker* listed the results of its Pop Poll. The Beatles ran off with the British

Vocal Group honour, taking 54.75 per cent of the vote – streets ahead of the second place Springfields. 'From Me To You', with 20.79 per cent and 'Please Please Me', with 12.13 per cent took the first two places in the British Vocal Disc category. *Pop Go The Beatles* took fourth place in the Radio Show category and the Beatles inexplicably were runners-up in the Brightest Hope section behind Billy J. Kramer. The group did less well in the World Section, coming second to the Four Seasons in the Vocal Group category, while 'From Me To You' was a distant fourth in the Vocal Disc section behind Andy Williams' 'Can't Get Used To Losing You', Roy Orbison's 'In Dreams' and Ray Charles' 'Take These Chains From My Heart'. The fourteenth edition of *Pop Go The Beatles*, with the Marauders, had aired on 17 September on the Light Programme at 5pm, and on the 24th, the fifteenth and final episode aired, recorded on 3 September with guests Tony Rivers and the Castaways.

The following week's edition of *Disc* had 'She Loves You' enjoying a fourth week at number one, while *Twist And Shout* dropped nine places to number 24 and *The Beatles' Hits* EP entered at number 29. 'She Loves You' began a third week at number one in the *NRM*, with 'From Me To You' dropping to number 39. In the *NME* and *Melody Maker*, 'She Loves You' continued its run at number one. The Fourmost's 'Hello Little Girl' entered the *NME* chart at number 22 and the *Melody Maker* chart at number 26, which also listed the group's two EPs in its singles chart – *Twist And Shout* dropped nine places to number 20 and *The Beatles' Hits* new at number 44.

Asked his feelings about the likelihood he would be the runner-up in the *NME*'s year end points table, Cliff Richard said, 'Make no mistake – I'd love to win the points table. But if the Beatles do overtake me, I shall have nothing but praise for them, because they're a great group!' On *Ready, Steady, Go!* host Keith Fordyce asked viewers to send three questions to pop to the group on their appearance the following week, with a prize of an autographed copy of their LP for the most original questions. The most often asked questions from the two thousand replies they got were: 'How did the Beatles get their name?' and 'What size pudding basins do they use for their fringe haircuts?' On 30 September, at the opening of the twenty-first season of the Halle Orchestra in Manchester, conductor Sir John Barbarolli had been presented with a gold medal for twenty years' service as its conductor. Interviewed by the press, Barbarolli said, 'Beat music isn't music at all. Terrible. Good jazz – yes, I admire. Duke Ellington enormously. But the Beatles? No!'

Two days before the group returned to the UK, George Martin and engineers Norman Smith and Geoff Emerick edited and mixed tracks at Abbey Road from 10am to 1.15pm, with Martin adding piano on 'Money' and Hammond organ on 'I Wanna Be Your Man'.

On Tuesday 1 October, Beatles fans rushed out to buy the new edition of *Reveille*, which was offering a 70 x 40 inch free poster of the group – featuring a photograph taken by Dezo Hoffmann on Brean Down at the end of July. Inside the magazine, Bunny Lewis wrote: 'Meet The Beatles, the hottest product to hit show business since Cliff Richard. It is always hard to analyse the exact reasons for enormous success in show business, but I believe that in the case of these Liverpool lads it is because they have an extremely virile and beaty sound. They arrived on the scene at a time when everyone was tired of what had gone before. This sound of theirs is their own, and is not, as many people suggest, rhythm and blues, although this type of jazz has a strong influence on them. They did not consciously invent it. It just grew on them ... Another reason for their success is, of course, that they write their own material... The Beatle haircut, like the Beatle sound, came rather by chance. After they had washed their hair, they could not make it lie down in the more orthodox position.'

George and his brother Peter returned from New York, arriving at London Airport, paying £22 customs' duty on his new guitar. They then flew back to Liverpool. Paul, Ringo, Jane and Maureen arrived late at London Airport, returning via Zurich and Frankfurt due to an Olympic Airways strike. Asher's mother Margaret suggested Paul stay the night.

❛ In the summer of 1963, I was 17 years old and preoccupied with starting my senior year of high school, getting together with my girlfriends, making Chef Boyardee pizzas and watching *American Bandstand*. I was also fortunate enough to be the host of my own teenage show on a local radio station. That summer, a vivacious blonde with a delightful British accent started dropping by the station with records of her brother's group from England that had been sent to her by her mother. My father, who was part-owner and manager, introduced us. Since I was the teenage DJ, and the only one playing rock'n'roll music on WFRX, he suggested that I might play them on my show. I started playing 'From Me To You'. Later, she said her brother would be visiting her and would like to meet the DJ who had been playing the Beatles regularly on her show.

I had already gone home for the day when I received the call that George, Louise and their brother Peter were at the station. I jumped in my father's 1958 black Oldsmobile Delta 88 with tail fins and drove back to the station. Two of my most vivid memories of that meeting were George's fascination with my dad's car and seeing George standing in the main lobby of the station when I arrived. He was wearing jeans, a white shirt and sandals. Of course, the haircut really caught my eye. I thought he was kind of cute, but in a different way than the boys I was used to. As we talked that day, he told of two of the boys, John and Paul, writing their tunes and having enough numbers to keep them in original songs until 1975. I wish I had thought to ask him where he thought the Beatles would be in ten years and what would be their place in history.

He said he liked the States, but not the hot weather. He liked the variety of music found in the local music stores and was fascinated by the car hops on skates at a Mt Vernon drive-in restaurant. He enjoyed drive-in theatres since they did not have them in England. My senior year I was Editor-in-Chief of my high school paper and if I had not written about my interview with George in the November 1963 issue of the *Red Bird Notes*, most of it would be forgotten. My classmates were a little intrigued with the story, but even after the Beatles appeared on *The Ed Sullivan Show*, the significance of George's visit to Southern Illinois did not sink in. For all we knew, the Beatles were just a passing phase and might be forgotten in a few years. When they continued to gain worldwide stardom, many of us were too busy going to college or to war, getting married, and starting families to pay a lot of attention. I remember my daughter Beth being so fascinated with the Beatles that she asked me if she could take 'She Loves You' to Show and Tell at her grade school. Not really grasping the significance of the record even then, I let her do this. It's something we can laugh about now, especially since the record has remained intact.

It was not until the mid '90s, that I began getting requests to tell my story of meeting George from local newspapers. Then after Bob Bartel stepped in to save George's sister's house on McCann from demolition and filmed his documentary *A Beatle in Benton* and Jim Kirkpatrick wrote his book *Before He Was Fab*, did people start realising how important George's visit to Benton in 1963 was. When the Beatles said they played beat music, I wrote in my *Red Bird Notes* article in 1963, that whatever beat music was, it was catching. If my family had not been involved in radio, if we had not moved to West Frankfort in 1956, if my father had not been at WFRX, if I had not been a teenage DJ in 1963, if Louise and her family had not moved to Benton none of this would have happened. All I can say is what I have been saying for years – 'I was in the right place at the right time and very fortunate to have played a small part in the history of the Beatles'. ❜

MARCIA RAUBACH, MARKETING CONSULTANT, WEST FRANKFORT, ILLINOIS, USA

OCTOBER
The weekend starts here

THURSDAY 3 OCTOBER

George flew back to London after spending the night at home. On board with him was *Disc*'s Alan Walsh. He recounted his holiday in the US, 'The whole trip was really tremendous from beginning to end. I just can't tell you how much I enjoyed America. Their standard of living is so much higher than ours in every way – they all have central heating and air conditioning and every house has a big television.' He was probably less happy with the news that 'She Loves You' had been knocked off the top of the new *Disc* Top 30 by Brian Poole and the Tremeloes' 'Do You Love Me'. *Twist And Shout* dropped two places to number 26 while *The Beatles' Hits* climbed two places to number 27. The *NRM* still had 'She Loves You' at number one. After nine weeks at the top, the *Twist And Shout* EP was replaced by the Searchers' *Ain't Gonna Kiss Ya*.

At 10am, Ringo overdubbed his vocal on 'I Wanna Be Your Man' with takes 14 and 15, and John and Paul overdubbed theirs on 'Little Child', takes 19, 20 and 21, at Abbey Road. The session ended at 1pm. Mid-afternoon, Michael Colley interviewed the group at NEMS' office for the Light Programme's *The Public Ear*. In covering a variety of topics, Paul said, 'It wasn't so much that we foresaw a big success. We just never thought that anything particularly bad would happen to us... We never sat down at one particular point at all and, sort of, worried about anything. We've always thought that something would turn up sometime.' George commented, 'But we've also got an accountant and a company, Beatles Limited. They see the money... We aren't doing it for the money, really, because don't forget we played for about three or four years or maybe longer just earning hardly anything... But the money does help, let's face it.' John talked about his musicianship. 'I haven't got the patience to practise to become a "perfect" guitarist, you know. I'm more interested in the combination of my voice and the guitar I know, and to write songs, than I am in the instrument. So, I never go through a day hardly without playing it whether I'm performing or not, you know.' Pete Best told the story of being fired from the group, and Bill Harry, Millie Sutcliffe and Royston Ellis were also featured on the programme, which aired on 3 November. In the evening, Ringo travelled to Southend-on-Sea to see the Everly Brothers, Bo Diddley and the Rolling Stones perform at the Odeon.

FRIDAY 4 OCTOBER

In the week's *Melody Maker* 'She Loves You' began a fifth week at number one in the Top 50, while *The Beatles' Hits* climbed seven places to number 37 with *Twist And Shout* dropping to number 29. Naysayers continued to write into the paper's Mailbag. 'I don't think we need worry who is top between Cliff Richard and the Beatles,' wrote Ann Davies of Bellshill, Scotland. 'In my estimation the Beatles will not be heard of in about six months' time.' Like *Disc*, the *NME* chart had 'Do You Love Me' at number one and 'She Loves You' at number 2.

When the Beatles arrived at Kingsway's Studio Nine to begin rehearsing for the evening's live performance of *Ready, Steady, Go!*, there was already a huge queue outside hoping to get in. Fellow guest Jet Harris walked out during rehearsals, saying, 'I've finished with show business,' leaving his partner Tony Meehan to perform solo. Harris was found two days later in a seafront flat in Brighton, under sedation. The show aired live at 6.15pm, with the Beatles miming to 'Twist And Shout', 'I'll Get You' and 'She Loves You'. Dusty Springfield, whose solo career was about to begin in earnest, asked the group several playful questions. When host Keith Fordyce posed the question, 'Would you rather spend a night with Brigitte Bardot or have £1,000?', John chose the money while Paul and Ringo picked Bardot. George replied, 'both please'. The group also appeared with Helen Shapiro as she mimed to her latest single 'Look Who It Is'. Paul

chose 13-year-old Melanie Coe as the winner of the show's miming contest, who lip-synched to Brenda Lee's 'Let's Jump The Broomstick'. After the recording of the show, the four had a meal at the nearby Star Steak House in Shaftesbury Avenue.

❛ A friend and I were huge fans of *Ready, Steady, Go!* and were determined to be in the audience the first time the Beatles appeared. To get on the show as a dancer, you had to attend auditions at the studios in Holborn. When we arrived on that Friday morning, there was a queue of young people from all over the country that stretched around the block. I thought we'd never get in! We were ushered in en masse. You had to dance to the music, and they would come round and tap people on the shoulder. That was the sign you weren't going to be one of the dancers. They narrowed us down to about thirty or so. It wasn't just how you danced, it was also your clothes, and how you looked. It was the time when looking 'fabulous' was just beginning. We took great care over our appearance, and these two gay guys who worked with my mother were the inspiration for what I wore and they did my hair specially, a Vidal Sassoon bob. I was very into fashion and wanted to look the part! Paul and John were very serious and aloof all day and kept themselves to themselves. But George and Ringo were very friendly, Ringo in particular, just chatting away, showing us his rings. I was madly in love with George and kept looking at him, going weak at the knees. He was very friendly too, and an absolute gentleman. I was selected to take part in the lip-synching contest. We had been at the studios since eight in the morning, and had done the mime about eight times, and when it came to the final cut, I felt I really didn't want to have to do it again! I had the feeling that I might win, as I had heard the producers talking in the morning to Paul and heard my name being mentioned. The winners of the contest were allowed to dance on the show every week, and so I ended up going there every Friday afternoon. I had to make endless excuses to get out of school. I think the teachers knew, as everyone had seen the show and were talking about the girl from school who had been on it, so I seemed to get away with it! Two things happened after I'd been on the show. Suddenly girls who hadn't talked to me wanted to be my friend, and other girls that had been sort of friendly, didn't want to know me. It was jealousy I suppose. So it was quite interesting what happened.

By the time I was 17, I was hanging out in various London clubs. My favourite was the Bag O' Nails. All the pop stars and actors of the day used to go there and getting in depended on your appearance. You had to be dressed in the latest fashions. I made friends with a girl called Margrit, who was married to Ritchie Blackmore. She was German and came from Hamburg. She told me she had met the Beatles there and knew them quite well, but I didn't believe her until one night when we arrived, John Lennon was there and motioned us over. I sat at his table all evening but didn't speak to him!

In early 1967 I ran away from home. The *Daily Mail* ran a story headlined 'A-level Girl Dumps Car

> And Vanishes', saying that my dad had spent the day searching for me. Paul McCartney apparently read the story and it inspired him to write 'She's Leaving Home'. I got married the following year and went to live in the Bahamas, then Miami, Los Angeles, Spain and now I'm back home in Suffolk. I still don't know if Paul knows that he met the girl he wrote about all these years ago three years earlier on *Ready, Steady, Go!* It was nice to be immortalized in a song, but it would have been nicer if it had been for doing something other than running away from home. **J**
>
> **MELANIE COE, ANTIQUE DEALER, ALDEBURGH, SUFFOLK**

SATURDAY 5 OCTOBER

Eleven million listeners tuned in to listen to the fifth birthday recording of *Saturday Club* with its all-star line-up headed by the Beatles. It was also the first anniversary of the release of 'Love Me Do'. The group travelled north to Scotland for the first of three shows, again promoted by Albert Bonici.

ALBERT A. BONICI
PRESENTS

THE BEATLES
Supported by
HUSTON WELLS & THE MARKSMEN
THE OVERLANDERS ● MALCOLM CLARK
THE CRESTERS

In the GLASGOW CONCERT HALL
On SATURDAY, 5th OCTOBER, 1963
TWO HOUSES: 6.15 and 8.30 (Doors open 5.45)
SEATS: 7/6 to 17/6, bookable from
J. D. Cuthbertson, 226 Sauchiehall Street, DOUglas 5182

By the time they arrived at the Concert Hall in Argyle Street, Glasgow, there had been a bomb scare after thirty-five hundred fans had already packed the hall to see them. While the group, supported by Mike Berry and Freddie Starr and the Midnighters, performed 'Twist And Shout', sections of plaster fell from the balcony. Close to a hundred seats in the hall were reportedly damaged after fans stood on them screaming and cheering. George's Rickenbacker 425 guitar, valued at £150, was stolen from the group's car parked on St Vincent Street outside the venue. After the show, the group were smuggled out through a side door and taken on the five-minute drive to the Central Hotel on Hope Street, where three suites had been booked for them. Hundreds of fans found out where they were staying and milled around the main entrance.

The Evening Times published an article headlined 'Beatles Fans Tore Up The Hall', reporting that, 'so much damage was done by spectators at the Beatles jazz group concert in Glasgow Concert Hall on Saturday that it was unlikely the corporation would again let the hall to similar groups. The screaming of spectators, some of whom danced on the seats, caused plaster work at the side of the balcony to come loose.' City Treasurer, Councillor Richard Buchanan, talked of 'semi-savage conduct' amidst fears that the balcony would collapse under the strain of stamping feet. 'This kind of behaviour will not be tolerated. There was so much shouting and screaming that the group could not be heard. The balcony was actually felt to be shaking with all the pandemonium that was going on.'

> **❝** 1963 was a busy year. At the time I was a member of Joe Brown and the Bruvvers. We toured with Dion and Del Shannon, did a summer season at the Windmill Theatre in Great Yarmouth on the same bill as the Tornados and Mark Wynter and made many radio and TV appearances, several of them with the Beatles. We did a couple of *Saturday Clubs* with them, including the fifth birthday show, and were on the *NME* Poll-Winners' Concert in April. I had first met the group the previous year when we played several venues in the Liverpool area, and were supported by this up and coming local group. John used to tape a set list to the top of his guitar, and on a few occasions, they played 'Picture Of You', our biggest hit, which I had written with Johnny Beveridge.

I was dating Beryl Braithwaite, who was a friend of fellow Bruvver Brian Dunn. When we used to have a bit of time off, I'd stay with Brian and his mum and dad in Ripon and meet up with Beryl. Because I knew the Beatles, we went along to the theatre when they were playing in Leeds, and just went round to the back door, like you could in those days. We were still riding high, and there was never a problem getting in to see a show. We went backstage after the show, and afterwards, down to the hotel where they were staying and had some sandwiches and a beer.

During the summer season in Great Yarmouth, my brother Tony and I rented a house in Jellicoe Road, near the racecourse in Caister, which was a scene of socialising after various shows. The Beatles came back there for a few drinks after playing one of their Sunday night gigs at the ABC in the town.

At the end of 1963 I moved on to join Lonnie Donegan. I'd had a bit of a disagreement with Joe about something in the studio, as did our drummer Ron Parry. It was reported in the papers the following day under the headline 'Bruvvers walk out on Joe.' I decided to get away for a few days, and popped up to see some friends in Lichfield, and to pay a visit to Ann, who was still my girlfriend at the time, and lived in Birmingham. When I got back to Lichfield, one of my friends said, 'Lonnie Donegan's been on the phone, he wants you to ring him!' He'd seen the stories in the press, and got in touch with my mother, asking for my number. He was a fan of the Bruvvers and asked me if I'd like to join his group! There was no time to go back home, so my mum packed a bag, and Lonnie picked it up – he was in South Woodford, and I was in Wanstead, so only a couple of miles away. We met up at Coventry railway station, and I jumped into his Alfa Romeo, and headed up to the Globe Theatre in Stockton, and there I was, back again, with Lonnie Donegan! It was to be the beginning of a working relationship that lasted years until his death in 2002. In the late '60s I was in a group with Albert Lee called Country Fever, rejoined Joe and his wife Vikki in his group Home Brew, had a hit in 1972 with 'New Orleans' as part of Harley Quinne and now more than half a century on, I'm on the road as a member of the Swinging Blue Jeans. My story with the Beatles didn't finish in 1963 though. In 1989, I had a call from Paul McCartney to ask whether the Bruvvers could play at his daughter Stella's 18th birthday party. I still have his telemessage which reads, 'Thanks lads for providing a grand evening of rock'n'roll music ... We all had a ball.' **⟩**

PETER OAKMAN, ARTISTE, MUSICIAN AND SONGWRITER, ROMFORD, ESSEX

SUNDAY 6 OCTOBER

The group had a lie-in before setting off from Queen Street railway station for the hour and a half train journey to Kirkcaldy, a town of fifty thousand people – many of whom worked in the linoleum manufacturing industry based there. The group went directly to the fifteen hundred-seater Carlton Theatre in Park Road. Promoter Kingsway Entertainment had given away priority tickets to the Carlton bingo club members. Billed as 'The Beatles In Scotland', the two concerts took place at 6.30pm and 9pm with support from Andy Ross and His Orchestra featuring Sue Taylor and Bryce Wilson, Houston Wells and the Marksmen and the Clifton Hall Stars featuring the Fortunes.

During the first house, some members of the audience, which included Glasgow Rangers' international Jim Baxter and his girlfriend Jean Ferguson, left early, complaining that they could not hear the music because of screaming fans. The half dozen *Daily Record* winners were ushered into the group's dressing room, two at a time. Fifteen-year-old Valerie Hunter recalled her experience, taking the bus home after the gig: 'It felt like I was walking on air all the way to the bus stop. It was just brilliant.'

The second house spilled out on to Park Road and down to St Clair Street. Four bingo stewards left the building through a fire exit as decoys with coats over their heads, allowing the group to run to their car and make their escape. John didn't quite make it and had to run after the vehicle. The group drove north on the A92 and A91 to Perth, where they stayed overnight at the Salutation Hotel, which had been 'welcoming guests since 1699'.

At 9pm, 16-year-old Belfast Royal Academy school girls Diane Halley and Rosemary Stuart arrived at the ABC in Belfast to be first in line to buy tickets when the box office opened at 10am the following morning. As the evening wore on, the pair had been joined by a hundred or so more fans. By dawn the crowd had grown to a thousand and when the box office opened there were thirteen hundred waiting to buy tickets.

> ❛ I was 17 years old and working in the Lockhart linen factory office. I loved dancing and took all day on a Saturday to get my hair done and choose the perfect outfit. All of the '60s groups started coming to Kirkcaldy, it was a popular venue. My mum wrote poetry. She had already won a competition for my friend Thelma Duncan to win tickets for Cliff Richard and was fascinated by the Beatles. She wrote a poem for a *Daily Record* competition to meet the Beatles, and I entered it and was one of the winners! The prize was high tea (a Scottish description of fish and chips, scones, cakes and tea!)
>
>
>
> at the Station Hotel, and tickets for the show afterwards at the Carlton Theatre. Sunday came, and I was really excited, although if truth be told, more excited to be going to the dancing from midnight to 4am at the Raith Ballroom in Links Street – Mum and Dad had let me go! I had bought myself a new suit. My friend Val had a similar dress, with a long black collar. So off I went from Dunsire Street on the number 3 bus to the rail station stop, which was next to the hotel.
>
> On arrival, we were told that Brian Epstein had called the tea off, so the six of us had to have it on our own. The tea was lovely even though the Beatles weren't there! At the interval we went to the dressing room, two girls at a time. It was absolutely tiny, hardly bigger than a toilet and the Beatles were sitting just with T-shirts on and towels wrapped round them, I suppose maybe they were very hot, just having a laugh really. John said, 'Hello girls, come in, sit down.' He never stopped talking. He was very chatty. 'Do you live in the area?' 'Do you work?' He asked plenty questions. George was very quiet, but very nice. I found Paul very standoffish, not in the least bit interested as how I would have described him. Although he spoke when we spoke to him. When you lived in Kirkcaldy you really didn't hear anything other than Scottish accents, so I was quite fascinated with Ringo's accent because it was very Liverpudlian. He said he loved the atmosphere in the Carlton. Brian Epstein was keen to keep these visits short, so soon after, we were all done. The group of us chatted afterwards and discussed who we liked best and what they said, and then we all left and went home with our ears still ringing due to the noise of the screaming. I often think perhaps at 17 I was not quite ready for this experience and didn't appreciate it more at the time. However, I was lucky enough to see them when they were just starting out, in fact meet them, how lucky was I? ❜
>
> **RITA PAGE, FIFE COUNCIL WORKER, KIRKCALDY, FIFE, SCOTLAND**

MONDAY 7 OCTOBER

The group had breakfast in the hotel dining room. Two men on a business trip to Glasgow at the adjoining table approached them and were provided with autographs, apparently as a peace offering for the incessant noise from fans through the night. The *Daily Express* began a week-long series of articles written by Merrick Winn under the byline 'An Express Inquiry' into the Liverpool Sound. In typical Fleet Street style, it was a condescending look at what had happened in Liverpool over the past year. The teaser for the following day's article read, 'It's better than knocking down old ladies with bicycle chains.' The new edition of *Mirabelle* began the first of a four-part series on the group titled 'This Is Our Life'. First up was John, who described 'a happy, contended childhood' being shattered when his mother died before his 14th birthday. 'Only those who have experienced such a tragedy can imagine how awful it is. I don't like talking about it because it's too great a sorrow to be publicised, but I hope all of you who have two parents living, will appreciate them... After Mum died I went to live with my aunt Mimi. She's the greatest, bless her heart. We have a little house, with frilly curtains as the windows, and an old apple tree in the front garden.'

The Beatles drove north on the A92, a thirty-mile journey to Dundee, for the last of three one-nighters in Scotland, for which they were paid £500 per show. The first fans started queuing outside the Caird Hall in City Square in the middle of the afternoon. The group arrived at around 5.30pm and found a transistor radio, a record player and records, a selection of magazines, a television set (which didn't work) and food laid on for them in their dressing room, where they spent a few moments with two Dundee football club players, winger Hugh Robertson and centre half George Ryden. They also invited two fans from Bridge of Allan backstage, Janis Watson and Maureen Smith, who had seen them in Glasgow and Kirkcaldy. Janis had the group autograph her arm.

After a supporting bill of the Caravelles, the Overlanders, and local groups Malcolm Clarke and the Cresters and Johnny Hudson and the Teenbeats, the Beatles appeared onstage at 7.40pm. They performed nine songs. John spent his time unravelling his amp cable during the opening number, 'I'll Get You'. The set closed with 'Twist And Shout'. Half a dozen teenage were girls treated for hysteria at the ambulance post, set up in the smaller Marryat Hall. After the performance, the group were ushered by police through the hall's switch-room, then downstairs, through the boiler-house and out into Castle Street, where a getaway car was waiting to take them back to Perth. In the equipment van, right behind the car, sat two enterprising teenage girls who had lain in wait for the group. Four paratroopers of the 15th Battalion Perth Parachute Division had started a diversionary action and were pursued by teens chanting, 'We Want The Beatles!' Spreading the rumour that they were to act as bodyguards, the paratroopers drew attention to themselves before diving into a parked car at the hall's main door. Police blocked off that exit leading to Castle Street. Long after the Beatles had left, about two thousand fans stood outside the stage door. At midnight, fans could still be seen waiting outside the Salutation Hotel in the pouring rain.

The *Dundee Courier* reported, 'Never have I witnessed such mass-hypnotism or had my ears bludgeoned by such a noise... Until last night the nearest parallel I had come across was 'The Courier' machine-room in full cry, with papers pouring from the presses... When it was all over the silence hurt my ears. People spoke, but I heard nothing except a popping sound – the kind passengers in an airliner hear as it climbs from the runway.'

❛ I fell in love with music at an early age. My dad played banjo and four-string guitar in his uncle's band as a lad, then in RAF concert parties. He taught me some chords when I was about 11 and I'd play his guitar in the lunchbreak at the convent school I went to in Barnet. I finished my education at Clark's College doing a secretarial course and left school at 16. I started work in a local estate agents as a secretary and in the evening played rhythm guitar at a club in Soho London called The Tatty Bogle. Meanwhile, I left my job and joined Lawson Piggott Motors to become secretary to the general manager.

Just after I arrived so did a shy young girl called Andrea Simpson. I found out she could sing, so I asked if she wanted to be part of a duo. We started rehearsing – folk songs, pop songs and classic standards from song books borrowed from her sister Carole, a very accomplished jazz singer who was then working at Peter Cook's Establishment Club. One evening, a musician by the name of Tony Pitt came to Barnet Jazz Club. Afterwards he came back to my mum and dad's flat and I told him about my newly formed duo. 'I know a great song I think would suit you, called 'You Don't Have To Be A Baby To Cry'.' The next day I taught it to Andrea and got to work to find an interesting harmony. It took a while but it was well worth it. The name the Caravelles was chosen by Bunny Lewis. He released the single on his Ritz label through Decca Records. I was just 19, Andrea nearing 18.

I can remember everything about that evening at the Caird Hall. We decided after our set that we would go out to the front and watch the Beatles' performance and see what was happening. We were ushered up into the circle and were standing there with all these screaming girls! It was quite exciting in some ways, but almost impossible to hear them because the sound systems then were only column speakers, and two or three microphones. It was all a bit Heath Robinson really compared to nowadays, but we certainly got the feel and the atmosphere of it all.

'You Don't Have To Be A Baby To Cry' reached number three in the US that Christmas. Negotiations went ahead for a six-week tour with TV, radio and live dates. Then most spectacular of all was being asked to appear with the Beatles at the Washington Arena in their very first US concert. Andrea and I briefly shared the dressing room with Paul and Ringo. We were just put on the stage, with minimal backup, and had to sing to promote our records, not something that we enjoyed. We thought it was going to be glamorous and lovely, but of course it wasn't at all! We knew that we had preceded the Beatles, so to speak, with our single in the Billboard Top 100, and when they talked about 'The British Invasion', they completely forgot about the fact that we, the 'Whispering Twosome', had got there first! Nobody took much notice, but why would they? We never repeated it, but they did!

It was February 1964 with snow on the ground and that was our last appearance before flying down to Miami for a short holiday in the Bahamas. The Beatles went to Miami too, on the train, but that was just the beginning for them. We returned home to do the northern club circuit, the Star-Club in Hamburg, recording for Polydor and sadly no more hits – but a fantastic life experience and enormous fun! In 1966 we split up. I went solo and Andrea worked with several other partners for a number of years with a few more single releases. When you're that young you think that it's going to go on forever, but your experience of life is so limited, and I thought we would sing together for years. But so many things happen to you at that time in your life, and I was always the enthusiast, I was the one who wanted to do it. Andrea was more reluctant, but happy to go along with it. The good thing was that we had a great laugh together. She had a great sense of humour, and we shared that. ❜

LOIS PUSEY, SINGER/SONGWRITER AND VOICE-OVER ARTIST, SUNBURY-ON-THAMES, MIDDLESEX

TUESDAY 8 OCTOBER

*T*he *Guardian* published a piece by Stanley Reynolds, 'Raver's Requiem'. He interviewed Bob Wooler who told him of an afternoon he was sitting in the Jacaranda Club in Slater Street. 'Two long-haired, leather-jacketed boys came in. They said they had just come back from Hamburg. They were the advance party of the Beatles.' He went on to describe their Litherland gig on 27 December 1960. 'When they came out they sang 'Long Tall Sally', the place went mad. I've never experienced anything like it.' Reynolds warned that 'The problem with the Liverpool Scene is striking a balance between the publicity and overexposure that seems to plague any likely newcomer in sports, letters or show business, nipping him neatly in the bud.'

The *Glasgow Herald* reported on the damage at Saturday's concert in an article headlined '100 Seats Damaged At Concert'. It read, 'So much damage was done by spectators at a concert given by the Beatles' singing group on Saturday at the Glasgow Concert Hall that the hall is unlikely to be let again to similar groups. Treasurer Richard Buchanan said yesterday, "The hundreds of screaming teenagers who packed the hall damaged a hundred seats, and it was necessary to have forty policemen and fifty attendants on duty. We are not going to tolerate wild behaviour in that hall."' The *Dundee Telegraph* viewed the group's visit differently. 'The kids were marvellous and exploded the myth that they are vandals at such shows. They've also proved they are much better behaved than their Glasgow counterparts.'

The group left the Salutation Hotel and drove back south to London, arriving in the evening. Just after midnight they went to Ronnie Scott's club at 39 Gerrard Street in Soho to see jazz saxophonist Roland Kirk, leaving in the early hours.

WEDNESDAY 9 OCTOBER

*J*ohn celebrated his 23rd birthday. The group ate breakfast together at their flat, having the day free until an evening rehearsal at 6.30pm at the Paris Studio for *The Ken Dodd Show*. They had met the Liverpool comic two years earlier when they appeared on the same bill of a charity concert at the Albany Cinema in Maghull, Liverpool. The recording took place in front of a studio audience between 10pm and 11pm; the group performed 'She Loves You'. The show aired on 3 November on the Light Programme.

Two 15-year-old girls smuggled rum and wine into Grove Park Grammar School in Wrexham, North Wales, to celebrate John's birthday. After the teacher found the girls 'tiddly', they were banned from school for a month. One of the girl's less-than-sympathetic father, a metal worker, said the girls deserved the suspension. 'I feel particularly sore because it was my rum.'

BBC Television aired *The Mersey Sound*, Don Haworth's half-hour documentary, at 10.10pm in the north of England and London. The *Radio Times* described the show: 'The Mersey Sound... nobody knows quite what this is, but it is very loud indeed, and profitable. The story of this frantic boom is lightly told by those who make the noise. Music by the Beatles, Group One, the Undertakers, narration, Michael Barton.' Maurice Richardson, in his review for *The Observer* the following Sunday, described it as an 'excellent little documentary', using the first documented instance of 'Beatlemania' in print: 'Light and fast yet packed with significance, it gave you a strong contemporary feeling. The degree of Beatlemania, with fans sleeping under Beatles' windows and sending them Jelly Babies by the ton, seemed to be fairly acute. One of the odder features was the extreme youth of many of the fans. Some of them were barely out of the toddlers' group.' He noted that 'The Beatles themselves made a distinctly agreeable impression.

They weren't exactly modest but were quite free from megalomania and perfectly prepared to fade the possibility of a short reign before oblivion set in.' An unnamed *Sunday Telegraph* reviewer wrote, 'I'd been as ready as the next man to join in a Help Stamp Out Beatles campaign, but they emerged as a very endearing group.' Hundreds of fans protested to the BBC because they were not allowed to stay up to watch the show.

❛ I'd always fancied having a go at playing the guitar and got my first one on my 16th birthday in February 1957. I formed a group at Birkenhead School with some friends, and we called ourselves the Firecrests. The next group I was in was a mixture of the ones before, this time we called ourselves the Jaywalkers. By this time we started going over to Liverpool and doing all the gigs – there were so many clubs around, and we must have played them all. We played at the Cavern quite a lot from 1960 onwards. We went on the *Carroll Levis Show*, although we didn't win our heat. Rory Storm and the Hurricanes were on the same show, and he'd seen us a couple of times before.

A few days later the telephone rang in our house – we were one of the few with a telephone on our street – and Rory, who had a bit of a stutter, said, 'We saw you playing at the Empire on the *Carroll Levis Show*, and we'd like to know if you'd want to join our group?' I knew of them, but I didn't know him very well, and I actually said, 'Well no, not really, I'm quite happy with the group I'm in.'

Brian Epstein also approached us at one point. He wanted us to be available to do gigs on his package tours all over the country at short notice if there was some problem, and one of his groups couldn't make it. We turned him down, only because we were all working day-time jobs as well as gigging in the evening. He wasn't very happy about it, but we couldn't really give that all up on the off chance of some gigs with him. By the beginning of '62, groups were starting to go abroad, to Hamburg and to the American Air Force bases in France.

After a little while, Harry Prytherch [drummer of the Remo Four], who I knew well, rang up and said, 'How do you fancy forming a group?' It was to be with what remained of the Jaywalkers and the Remo Four, and so I did, and we called ourselves Group One. The Remo Four were a bit like us, a bit more mature, smartly dressed, and quite up on the music scene. We played well without being too raucous and were together for a couple of years.

We played at the Cavern in March 1962, the first time the Beatles played an evening gig. I remember one evening in Chester we were playing on the bill with them, and it turned out that John had got married earlier that day. We didn't know for months later. He kept it quiet. I recall him being in a bad mood. He wasn't very happy at all. He'd got married earlier in the day and was out gigging in the evening! We were playing some of the Beatles repertoire, in our own style of course, and John came flying onto the stage from the dressing room and said, 'Hey, stop that, you're playing our fucking numbers!' Harry told him to fuck off. They didn't hate each other, but there was always that tension with John. He could be difficult. I remember when we had played a gig with them at the Aintree Institute, and they came off stage and John had this very unusual guitar. I hadn't seen one like it before. It was a Rickenbacker, which he had brought back from Germany. I said, 'Excuse me John, what's that?' pointing to his guitar. He said, 'It's a guitar' sarcastically. That was the sign to clear off. He wasn't interested in talking about it!

On Good Friday in 1963 we appeared at the Rhythm and Blues Marathon at the Cavern. In general, you got away from the Cavern fairly early, well before midnight on an ordinary night. The marathon started in the afternoon, with a long list of local groups, but we didn't really know everybody. You would fly in and out and didn't have time to stop and chat. The getting in and getting out was the same set of steps, so if you had a double, where you played two gigs in one evening, you had to get your gear up through the crowd and up those steps. You'd have sweat absolutely pouring off you, because of the number of people in there. They certainly didn't need heating! There was a sort of dressing room – one of the archways to the left of the stage as you look at it, had a small room, a bit like a cave, and you had to get ready in there. It was chaotic, with one group coming off, and the next going on. There wasn't enough room for everyone's gear in there, so if you were on later in the evening, you'd just have to leave it in the car or somewhere.

We did a BBC documentary that year called *The Mersey Sound*, which was about the Beatles and the music scene in the Liverpool area at the time. Although it was edited to look like we were all together filming, we didn't actually see them at all that day, we just turned up and did our thing. It was a very interesting film. It gave you an idea, so soon after the war really, of how things were. About three years ago I did a little spell with Mike Byrne. As part of the act, Mike tells little stories about the members of the group and their past. He always says of us, 'They used to play with the Beatles at the Cavern, and Dave, John Lennon spoke to you once didn't he?' and I say, 'Yes. He said, "Get out of the way"!' **"**

DAVID WILLIAMS, INSURANCE SALES EXECUTIVE, ELLESMERE PORT, CHESHIRE

THURSDAY 10 OCTOBER

The new edition of *Disc* included a four-page Beatles supplement and offered seats for the forthcoming Beatles' package tour on its front page. 'Anne Collingham' announced that all fan club members were going to receive a very special Christmas gift from the boys. Paul revealed he had changed his diet, which now included bananas, meringues, pancakes and crêpe suzettes, while John said that he had an LP of Stravinsky along with albums by the Shirelles and Chuck Berry. Paul also talked about his Greece trip and commented on the group's success: 'It's fab – the success and all that – but I wish people wouldn't think that because we're successful, we're unapproachable. It's not true. We're just the same now as we always were, and I hate it when maybe someone who lives in the same street now ignores me because they're frightened I'm going to turn my head away.' George chimed in on the subject as well: 'The most obvious change is financial. That's very nice, but I don't think it's the most important thing. It's nice to be able to buy a new car and new clothes when you want them, but I was happy when I couldn't afford these things.' John said, 'I can't stand it if someone plays one of our records in public knowing we're there.' Ringo talked again about owning hair salons. 'Eventually I think I'll open up a chain of hairdressing shops in and around Liverpool. I'd like my main shop to be in the centre of the city and be THE place. I have enough hairdressing friends to keep the shops well staffed but feel with a haircut like mine it would be best for me to stay away from them!' 'She Loves You' remained at number 2 in the chart, while *The Beatles' Hits* went down one place to number 28 and *Twist And Shout* dropped out of the Top 30. 'She Loves You' dropped to number 3 in the *NRM* chart.

The *Liverpool Weekly News* ran the front-page headline 'Please, Please Us, Wail The Beatles' Fans'. Fan Club secretary Freda Kelly explained that when mail they received reached over one thousand letters a day, she decided to move to London. 'We do our best but we can't comply with all their requests or else Paul and the others would have been bald long ago.' She cited Ringo's model of Fred Flintstone playing drums from two girls in Cardiff as one of their favourites. In the evening the group went to the Strand Theatre in London to see the hit musical *A Funny Thing Happened On The Way To The Forum*, starring Frankie Howerd. John enjoyed it so much he saw the show a second time in November, taking Cynthia along.

Mr James Draper, the spokesman for the Export Council for Europe, claimed there was a possibility the Beatles might lend musical backing to a forthcoming British Shop Window Week in Dusseldorf, West Germany. They didn't.

FRIDAY 11 OCTOBER

The *NME* reported that the Beatles were about to receive their first gold disc for 'She Loves You', which had just passed sales of seven hundred and fifty thousand and that *Please Please Me*, still at number one, had now reached two hundred and fifty thousand sales. 'She Loves You' dropped to number 3 in the *NME* and the *Melody Maker* charts, as *The Beatles' Hits* climbed eight places to number 29 and *Twist And Shout* dropped to number 31 in *Melody Maker*. The paper also featured a Ray Coleman interview with Brian Epstein. Epstein was asked what would happen if one of the members of his stable of groups went solo, such as John Lennon. After spending a while to frame his answer, he replied, 'Why does everybody pick on John Lennon? Don't you know there are four Beatles?' Asked how much the Beatles earned, he said, 'Between £1,000 and £1,500 between them each week, exclusive of record royalties.'

First thing, Sean O'Mahony and Leslie Bryce visited the group at their flat, bringing a sack of birthday cards and gifts for John. Bryce took a series of photos of the group having breakfast, looking through the bag of mail and wearing fake beards and moustaches.

The group performed a half-hour set in front of a three thousand-capacity crowd at the Ballroom on Stone Road, Trentham, near Stoke-on-Trent. A solid mass of fans stood at the end of the Ballroom, stamping their feet and shouting, 'We Want The Beatles!' – at times drowning out the resident Ken Jones Band. Even an announcement that the group would not be appearing until 10.30pm failed to move them. The group were escorted into the Ballroom by police, minutes before they were due onstage. Police dogs kept guard outside the padlocked stage door.

During the show, the crowd tried to storm the stage from the dance floor. Three teenage girls were taken to hospital, while dozens were given first aid by Red Cross attendants. Mr L. W. Johnson, the venue's Entertainments Manager, said, 'I have never seen anything like [it] in twenty-three years. If I had had enough tickets, I could have filled Stoke City football ground.' Police, dealing with the largest-ever crowd seen at the Ballroom, described the scene as 'phenomenal.' Nearly an hour after the show, dozens of fans waited around to see their idols, who had already left the area for the North Stafford Hotel, carrying a sack filled with letters from fans. The group were captured backstage with Miss Harp and several local dignitaries.

> ❛ As a 20-year-old, I was very excited to represent my hair salon and get to meet the Beatles. After a long day at work and then getting ready for the evening, I arrived at the Ballroom with my fiancé, Don, my family and Ken, my boss. I had never seen so many people. Boys with Beatle jackets and haircuts, girls with beehives. The Ballroom was a mass of people. Never mind dancing around your handbags, you couldn't get a pin in between you. The atmosphere was electric. Then Ken and I had to go backstage to meet the judges. They asked me a few questions about myself – where I worked, what I did? We were then asked to go back into the Ballroom and enjoy the Beatles and to return after the show was over. Then the moment came – girls began screaming and shouting 'We Want The Beatles!' The four of them came onstage and went straight into 'From Me To You'. When they finished with 'Twist And Shout', you could feel the floorboards rocking under your feet. Girls were fainting

and it was all over. I went backstage with the other contestants. We could hear the Beatles in the next room but didn't have the privilege of meeting them. As we came out of the room, the Beatles walked by and John said they'd never had a night like it. All I saw of the other three were the backs of their heads as they left the Ballroom. We were called onstage and I was declared 'Miss Harp Lager Trentham Gardens 1963'. I won £30 – which was a lot of money in those days – and a charm bracelet. The perfect end to a perfect night. **"**

PAULINE BASKEYFIELD, FREEHAND PAINTRESS, STOKE-ON-TRENT, STAFFORDSHIRE

SATURDAY 12 OCTOBER

The Beatles woke to the sound of about forty fans who had been waiting outside the North Stafford Hotel since 6.30am. They drove from Stoke and arrived an hour late at the Donmar Rehearsal Theatre at 41 Earlham Street. They had a clothes fitting, before being interviewed by the *Daily Sketch* columnist Godfrey Winn, alongside Brian Epstein, who was about to move into a flat in Whaddon House. The group then rehearsed through the evening for the following night's *Val Parnell's Sunday Night At The London Palladium*.

The box office for the two concerts on 8 November opened in Belfast. Fans had started queuing outside the Ritz cinema the night before. Sixty-two-year-old grandmother Mrs W. Simpson took her place in line among thousands of teenagers to buy tickets for her 9-year-old grandson Michael, as well as her neighbour Mrs P. Briggs and her 13-year-old son, Andrew. Raymond Liggett recalled, 'Heading for night class, I met a girl and her brother on the bus. They were going down to queue overnight for tickets. I only had a ten-shilling note in my pocket, so I handed it over. We met the next day and I found out that she had obtained the three middle seats in the balcony, looking straight down on to the stage. Best seats in the house and I had done nothing!' When the Beatles returned the following year to the King's Hall, Liggett was there too. 'A young lady behind me spent the entire time they were on reciting their names "John, Paul, George and Ringo" over and over.'

" At this distance in time it's hard to appreciate the scale of the excitement generated by the news that the Beatles were coming to town. Although Northern Ireland was still something of a social and cultural backwater – bars and restaurants had to close at ten o'clock and, like theatres, cinemas and dance halls, weren't allowed to open at all on Sundays – the local papers were full of titillating stories about the group's tour and the only dissenting voices were those of the Reverend Ian Paisley and some of his followers who disapproved of the 'worldliness' of it all. I was a 16-year-old schoolboy and a member of a youthful pop group that was having some modest success sharing the stage with the likes of Jerry Lee Lewis and a virtually unknown Van Morrison.

I was also determined to be amongst the first in line for tickets when they went on sale at the Ritz Cinema, situated just yards from the front gates of my school, the Royal Belfast Academical Institution. The box office was due to open at nine on Saturday morning and the day before, as soon as school was out, I went there with a couple of classmates to review the situation. There weren't many people about so we decided to return in shifts during the night with my friend Chris Hill going first. Arriving at the cinema on my Honda 50 motorbike to join Chris shortly after 6am, my disappointment at finding a dozen or so other fans had beaten us to it was soon dispelled by the camaraderie that developed amongst us, and the realisation that we were in a much better place than the hundreds of hopefuls who joined the queue in dribs and drabs behind us. When the box office opened our vigil was rewarded with seats in the second row. On the appointed day I was in my seat and the performance began. The relative calm was short lived and when the main attraction appeared the audience went wild.

Exactly ten years later, at the beginning of a career that would put me close to the heart of the Irish peace process for more than three decades, I was Private Secretary to the Chief Minister of Northern Ireland, Brian Faulkner, and shared an office with one of our press officers, none other than Jimmy Robinson, the journalist who'd been the first to meet the Beatles on their journey north and who'd swapped the glamour of a life in television for an altogether more staid one as a public servant. At a stroke, that placed me at only two degrees of separation from the lads themselves. Wow! As my career progressed as a senior British government official on the political side of the Northern Ireland Office I travelled afar and had the privilege of working with a many remarkable people including prime ministers, presidents and princes, and witnessing some extraordinary and wonderful things. But that evening in November 1963, so long ago, will forever remain one of my most cherished memories. **"**

**CHRIS MACCABE, COMPANION OF THE ORDER OF THE BATH, INDEPENDENT
CONFLICT RESOLUTION CONSULTANT, BELFAST, NORTHERN IRELAND**

SUNDAY 13 OCTOBER

The group arrived at the London Palladium in Argyll Street at 11am to begin rehearsing for the evening's live broadcast at 8.25pm. During the afternoon, close to a hundred girls smashed a pane of glass, broke through a back door and stampeded through the back stalls of the theatre. Ringo was onstage and retreated to the group's dressing room – where the other Beatles were enjoying a lunch of roast lamb, potatoes and sprouts, before the girls could overwhelm him. The Palladium's manager David Wilmot dialled 999 as staff tried to hold the pack at bay – commissionaires threatened to turn fire hoses on them. As more than thirty police ran into the theatre the girls rushed outside, joining a further five hundred screaming fans. Five managed to get on to the theatre's roof but staff found them. Parnell told the group, 'I am not risking letting you out. It could be dangerous.' Mal Evans and Neil Aspinall, who was celebrating his 22nd birthday, were sent out to a nearby cafe in Carnaby Street to buy hot dogs and Coke.

A reported fifteen million viewers watched the show as it aired live to their homes, seeing the group perform 'From Me To You', 'I'll Get You', 'She Loves You' and 'Twist And Shout', attired in brand new suits. At the show's conclusion, the group joined the other acts on the night's bill, waving goodbye from the revolving stage. Host Bruce Forsyth later said, 'We could have gone round fifty times and those young fans would have kept screaming.'

As the group left, police sealed off the front of the theatre and held back more than a thousand screaming fans. A police motorcycle escort stood by as the group dashed to their car. Unfortunately, it was parked 50 yards up the street and they had to outrun the fans. The group drove to the Grosvenor House Hotel, where they celebrated the evening's success at a party hosted by Brian Epstein in Room 704. With the party still going strong at about 4am, someone suggested buying the morning papers to read the press coverage. As George headed off to bed, he said, 'Well, that's that. We've just about done it all now. Don't want to sound pessimistic, but honestly everything that happens from now on must be just anti-climax.'

Clifford Davis wrote in the *Daily Mirror*: 'The Beatles – whose mere names had the girls squirming and squeaking in the Palladium audience last night – seemed a very cute bunch. And with a sense of fun, too. They did nothing especially to excite their fans. Their singing and instrumental work wasn't particularly inspiring or provocative. And their movements, lacking all cohesion,

production and polish, were remarkably restrained. Nothing calculated here, just four kids, with grins, having a ball. All the same, one shake of those monk-like hair-dos had the girls screaming with the same fervour as Palladium audiences showered squeaks and yells a few years back, on Johnnie Ray and Frankie Laine.' Val Parnell said, 'It is fairly obvious that we shall ask them back again soon.'

❛ In October 1963 I was an 8-year-old schoolboy growing up in Blackburn, Lancashire. I lived near the football ground, Ewood Park, and Blackburn Rovers were the only 'stars' many of us were aware of. My dad had played football and my mum had been friends with Bryan Douglas, a famous local player who played for England. My dad was a joiner and part time drummer playing jazz and swing music with piano, bass and drum combos in the pubs around Lancashire on weekend nights. He told us he'd visited the Cavern Club in Liverpool with a friend to see the Beatles one night in 1962, like many he was caught up in the feeling which was sweeping the north of England that the group were really going to 'make it big'. Maybe even as big as George Formby!

His sense that something was happening meant that my brother and I were allowed to stay up late on this particular Sunday night (even though it was a before-school night). It was a big enough deal for my dad to break out his new 'toy', a reel-to-reel tape recorder with a little plastic microphone, an Elizabethan Popular 400. This was a basic domestic tape recorder which in later years became a great source of entertainment and experimentation for my brother and me. That night my dad set up and held the little square microphone to the TV to record the entire Beatles performance. I became an instant fan and I even remember getting a pair of Beatle boots and wearing them to school with the uniform short trousers (now there's a look!). Who knew that in 1967 the whole world would hear of Blackburn, Lancashire, when the Beatles released *Sgt. Pepper's Lonely Hearts Club Band*.

I left Blackburn at 18 and then emigrated to the United States in 1975. The Beatles were always a part me and in 1983 and 1984 I organized the very first package tours to Liverpool and London for American Beatle fans under the name Rock Apple Tours. These were ten-day package holidays built around the annual Beatle Conventions held in Liverpool back then. The tours introduced me to MTV and I even had a working relationship with Abbey Road Studios which presented me with an entree into the real music business. I'm pretty sure I'd be in a different business if my dad hadn't been so interested in them on that memorable Sunday night. I still have the tape! ❜

TONY RAINE, CONCERT PRODUCER AND ARTIST MANAGER, CHATHAM, MASSACHUSETTS, USA

MONDAY 14 OCTOBER

The group and their parents took the train back to Liverpool. John remained behind to go to a Billy J. Kramer session. When John made fun of Kramer's performance, George Martin said to the latter, 'I give you full permission to come to the Beatles session on Thursday and shout at John whenever you like.' The Fourmost cut 'I'm In Love' a few days later and it became their second single. *Mirabelle* featured George in its four-part series 'This Is Our Life.'

Four girls had started queuing in Portsmouth on Thursday, taking turns to keep their place at the head of the queue for ninety hours. The Guildhall box office opened an hour early, a spokesman saying, 'These girls have waited long enough. They have got to get to school.' The queue stretched along one side of the Guildhall, with blankets, sleeping beds and transistor radios littering the pavement. One girl asked that her name not be published because she got 'a rocket when I was late for school after queuing for tickets for Cliff Richard.' Councillor Leonard Evans complained about 'girls lying down on the pavement surrounded by vacuum flasks' in the queue for tickets at a meeting of the Portsmouth Entertainments Subcommittee. 'It was a terrible sight. We ought not to allow it outside our Guildhall. It is not dignified.' Councillor F. A. Currey disagreed, saying, 'Nonsense. It's all good publicity. I don't care if we have dead bodies lying round the Guildhall, if it provides such publicity.'

At 8.45am, when Charles Lockier arrived at his Queen's Road office in Clifton, Bristol, the line for tickets for the Colston Hall shows stretched into Berkeley Square. Marion Hayes, Nora Lacey, Andrea Chappell, Bridget Swanson and Angela Hickey, who began queueing at 10pm the previous night, were the first to get tickets. Lacey told the *Bristol Evening Post* as she set off for school that 'it was cold, hard and miserable, but I wouldn't miss the Beatles for anything.' Seventy-two-year-old Marie Stock, who got up at 5am and then decided to go back to bed because it was too early, stood in line with her two grandsons. Within three hours, all five thousand tickets had sold.

In Coventry, two middle-aged mothers, Mrs E. Blewitt and Mrs B. S. Bishop, were at the head of the queue, hoping to buy thirty tickets for a coach party of the Birmingham Beatles fan club. Mrs Blewitt had taken her daughter Jane's place in line at 7am. Before long, more than a thousand people were queuing outside the theatre and up Cook Street Gate, with many camping out all night. The Burns sisters told a reporter from the *Coventry Evening Telegraph* that 'none of us who waited all night got a lot of sleep. We listened to the radio and had a dance now and then, but Radio Luxembourg finished at three o'clock. We took it in turns to wander about then to help pass the time and we snatched a bit of sleep, but I don't think anybody really got much sleep.' All 4,020 tickets sold in four hours, with around two hundred and fifty in the queue missing out.

❛ I've lived in Portsmouth all my life, so you could say I'm a real local lad. Every couple of months they would have concerts at the Guildhall in town, and there was a group of six or seven of us who used to go along, a mixture of school friends and friends from the local football and cricket clubs. Every Saturday we would meet up at the coffee bar above the Fine Fare Supermarket in Cosham High Street. There was another coffee bar called Mary's Milk Bar on the High Street, although that one was a bit dodgy as the rival Mods and Rockers would meet there. There were several music shops in Portsmouth, Weston Hart being the famous one. I lived on the outskirts of Portsmouth so there was a Weston Hart in our local high street, and several more in the town.

I turned 18 in 1963 and had bought tickets to see Chris Montez and Tommy

Roe at the Guildhall in March. Also on the bill, the Beatles. We'd heard of the Beatles, because we'd all bought 'Love Me Do', but certainly hadn't bought the tickets because of them. They ended the first half, and everyone was shouting, 'Bring back the Beatles! Bring back the Beatles!' – particularly when Chris Montez was on. They were, in fact, absolutely brilliant, and it was my first experience of them live.

Later that year we queued up all night one night in October hoping to get front row seats for their headlining show in November. We were about second or third in the queue, and I remember it just getting longer and longer. It was pretty cold. I'd like to say we were there with a couple of coffees, but it was probably more like a couple of beers! We knew from our position in the queue we were guaranteed to get front row, which thankfully we did. The concert was due on 12 November, but Paul McCartney had gastric flu, and the show was postponed to 3 December. After about the third number, Paul said, 'Girls, can you please stop screaming because people want to listen to us?' It was chaos. I'm still a Beatles fan, and it amazes me the number of younger people that we know who are real Beatlemaniacs. Sadly, over the years the tickets and programmes I collected from the shows have gone, along with the tickets and programmes from every game I went to of the World Cup in 1966, victims of several house moves. **❜**

RICHARD TOVERY, HIGHER EXECUTIVE OFFICER, CROWN PROSECUTION SERVICE, COSHAM, PORTSMOUTH, HAMPSHIRE

TUESDAY 15 OCTOBER

I n the evening, the group gave their fourth and final performance at the Floral Hall in Southport, where they had first performed on 20 February 1962. In the wake of the scenes outside the London Palladium two nights before, reporters from the capital travelled north to the seaside resort, no doubt in the hope of more mayhem. One hundred or so fans without tickets waited patiently outside and were allowed in. A police sergeant said, 'It's the way you handle them more than anything that counts and the crowd has behaved excellently, giving us no trouble at all.' The *Daily Express'* Derek Taylor went backstage to interview the group and found them chatting to film actor John Gregson, his uncle Paddy and nephew Arthur Johnson, a local newspaperman. The group, supported by Bruce Harris and the Cavaliers and Vic and the Spidermen, played two twenty-minute sets. Reporters headed back to London disappointed – in the evening's worst incident a girl received a cut on her face, after being pushed off the stage area into the audience six feet below. The *Southport Journal* commented, 'The expected "riot" never happened. The foresight and good humour of the police prevented a repetition of the scene outside the London Palladium. Half a dozen burly policemen controlled the influx.'

❛ I grew up in Northwich and played a bit of guitar at school. Around 1959, I formed a group with school friend Brian [Booth]. Our first booking was at the Royalty Theatre in Chester supporting Wee Willie Harris, and that was followed by lots of other local gigs, including the Cavern in 1960, and a spot on a pilot show for ABC Television which was recorded at the Didsbury Studios in 1962. In November that year at Earlestown Town Hall we played our first gig with the Beatles. We'd known Ringo for some time from his days with Rory Storm and the Hurricanes, and that evening we were sharing a dressing room with them. We all got on well and I was chatting to John in the corner. He

had two mouth organs and was alternating between the two. He said, 'One of these isn't working very well – it doesn't sound right.' I suggested he play me something on both to see, and he said, 'I'll play the intro to our next record, it's called 'Please Please Me' and it's going straight to number one!' Everyone in the room cheered. I said that one sounds just fine, and he said, 'Do you want it?' I told him I didn't, as I didn't play the mouth organ. How many times since then I wish I had accepted it!

We didn't play with them when they played at the Mersey View in April 1963, but Percy Lawless was the manager there, and I used to sit in his office chatting to him after shows. One night he said, 'I've got a letter here from Brian Epstein to have the Beatles, and they want £100!' I said, 'Listen, book them! You'll never regret it.' He still wasn't sure, but eventually I persuaded him to book them, and it ended up being the busiest night they had ever had. After that night, Percy would always say to me, 'Thank you for persuading me to book the Beatles!' We would have gone along, but being a Saturday night, we had gigs of our own, so missed a great evening.

How things had changed the next time we played with them. The group had appeared on *Sunday Night At The London Palladium*. Two days later, we were appearing with them at the Floral Hall in Southport. That evening as I drove up to the theatre, it was a lovely sunny evening for October and all these girls started rushing up. I wondered if they were going to get out of the way, but no, they mobbed the car – I drove a Vauxhall Estate, and they thought I was Ringo! I was pulled out of the car, and my shirt was ripped, before someone shouted, 'It's not him!' It all happened in seconds. I managed to get myself together and make my way to the stage door. A man's voice yelled, 'Go away! You can't come in!' Luckily Brian had heard my voice, and shouted to him, 'He's one of us', and I was let in. We all had to lean on the stage door to shut it! I told the others I had been mobbed, causing much amusement. My son lives in California now and happened to say to one of the local radio stations in Lakeport, 'Oh my dad's coming over and he used to play with the Beatles' and they said, 'The Beatles?' They are all Beatles mad over there, and I ended up on a talk show recounting the days of the Cavaliers and when we shared a dressing room with them. **J**

RALPH HORNBY, MUSICIAN AND ELECTRICAL ENGINEER, TARPORLEY, CHESHIRE

WEDNESDAY 16 OCTOBER

A press reception was held in the stalls bar of the Prince of Wales Theatre in London. Impresario Bernard Delfont announced that the Beatles would perform at the year's Royal Command Performance in November. He explained that his 16-year-old daughter Susan was responsible for the group being invited, saying, 'I didn't know who the Beatles were until five months ago. Susan asked me for an extra ten bob pocket money to buy one of their records. I had to ask her, "Who are the Beatles?" I told her not to worry about the cash as I could get the record 'Please Please Me' at wholesale price. But she was so insistent about it that when I got to work, I sent my secretary out to buy it.'

363

At 4.30pm, the group did a photo session with Leslie Bryce at their flat. Afterwards, they rehearsed for their fourth and last session for *Easy Beat* at the Playhouse Theatre. Epstein informed the BBC that, concerned with their safety, the group would no longer perform in front of a studio audience, cancelling a planned fifth appearance on the show. George spoke to *Disc*'s June Harris during a break in rehearsal, commenting on their Royal Variety appearance. 'I don't want to sound ungrateful or anything like that, but why are the Beatles on the same stage as a mass of show business greats? It's not like we've acted in *Hamlet* or written an Academy Award winning song.' They also conducted a short interview for the Light Programme's *Radio Newsreel*. Interviewer Peter Woods asked a series of condescending questions, such as, 'How much of this is getting popularity by acting the fool a bit and playing around?' and 'But your funny haircuts aren't natural?' Answering the question, 'How do you find all this business of having screaming girls following you all over the place?' George said, 'Well, we feel flattered.' John added 'and flattened,' the comment passing over Woods' head. Woods asked, 'Now, are you going to try and lose some of your Liverpool dialect for the Royal Show?' Paul replied, 'We don't all speak like them BBC posh fellas, you know.' The interview was broadcast later that evening. The group also met film director Richard Lester for the first time. The hour-long *Easy Beat* recording, which aired the following Sunday, began at 9pm, with the group performing 'I Saw Her Standing There', 'Love Me Do', 'Please Please Me', both of which were their last performances on the BBC, 'From Me To You' and 'She Loves You.'

THURSDAY 17 OCTOBER

The front page of the *NRM* was dominated by a recent Dezo Hoffmann picture of the Beatles. Neil Aspinall wrote an article, 'Look What Happened In Just A Year...' John commented 'It's been fab. There's no other word for it. What can you say about the things that have happened to us?' He praised the fans, 'We believe in our fans. We appreciate the way they've stuck loyally to us and the help they've always given us. Sometimes we have to turn and run – but that's because we don't want to cause riots. But the fans have been so generous with their presents and their letters. Honestly, we love 'em all.' 'She Loves You' stayed at number 3 in the chart and moved down a place to number 3 in the *Disc* chart, *The Beatles' Hits* dropped out of the Top 30, while Cilla Black's debut 'Love Of The Loved' entered the Top 30 at number 25.

Four teenage girls, known only as Karen, Anne, Vicky and Susan – no doubt to protect their identity from jealous fans – arrived at the offices of *Boyfriend* at 11.45am, the winners of the magazine's 13 July 'Why I Like The Beatles' competition. They were driven to the Old Vienna restaurant at 94 New Bond Street, a favourite of *Boyfriend*'s publisher Reg Taylor, to have lunch with the group. Meanwhile, Maureen O'Grady went to the NEMS office to pick up the Beatles. Only Paul was there. The others were running late. As Paul and O'Grady approached the restaurant, the sight of the large crowd caused Paul to lean over and say, 'Must be someone like Princess Margaret coming along.' Paul opened the door for O'Grady, who promptly stumbled on the pavement. As they waited for the remaining Beatles to show up, Paul commented, 'I hope they're all right. They're probably being torn apart by the crowds outside – and loving every minute of it!' George and Ringo arrived shortly thereafter, followed by John, who had obviously just washed his hair – it was still wet. The girls had shrimp cocktail, followed by steak for all – except John who had jelly and Coke – and Jozsi's Malakoff Torte for dessert. The group signed autographs and photos for the girls, and the restaurant manager asked the group to write their names on one of the restaurant's walls. A police officer came in to say that the chauffeur had been driving round in the car for the past half hour.

The group left the lunch early to get to Abbey Road for a session at 2.30pm, where they were booked in as the Dakotas to throw off eager fans. The girls were meant to join the band at the session as part of the contest, but George Martin vetoed the idea and were taken back to *Boyfriend*'s offices instead. The studios had begun using a Studer J-37 four-track machine earlier in the month. Up to this point, George Martin had recorded everything in twin-track mono.

Once the three-hour session started, the group recorded their first Christmas record, described later by Tony Barrow as a 'damage limitation operation' in response to unopened sacks of mail throughout the NEMS office. Barrow wrote 'a few, so-called funny lines... they came out with a very funny first Christmas record.' Afterwards, they tried a twelfth take of 'You Really Got A Hold On Me,' before beginning work on 'I Want To Hold Your Hand' and 'This Boy.'

A second three-hour session started at 7pm; the group completed seventeen takes of both 'I Want To Hold Your Hand' and 'This Boy.' Dick James showed up for the evening session, prompting George to say, 'Is Mr James here to count his money?' As John, Paul and George worked on their harmonies for 'This Boy,' Ringo enjoyed a cigarette while reading a comic book.

The *Evening Standard* began a three-part series written by Maureen Cleave. She started the first article by writing, 'The Beatles are the first people to make rock'n'roll respectable. They have won over the class snob, the intellectual snob, the music snob, the grown-ups and the husbands.' Commenting on Edward Heath's comment that the group didn't speak the Queen's English, John told Cleave, 'He is a politician and he oughtn't to go round saying how people speak. Probably the people that voted him into his comfy little seat didn't speak the Queen's English either.'

> ❝ When I drafted a script for the group to follow I was relying on them to mess around with my words and make them funnier. They didn't let me, or themselves, down. Although part of their Christmas message was a genuine 'thank you' to fans, the rest of the material I gave them provided ample scope for plenty of clowning around. I took the finished recording to Paul Lynton's place just around the corner from my Monmouth Street office and we edited it to fit on one single side of a 7' flexi-disc. When I say edited I mean we actually cut the tape recording with scissors, patched the pieces together and let the discarded bits drop to the floor. Lyntone's staff pulled out all the stops to produce some thirty-one thousand copies of the edited disc and we got the eagerly awaited Christmas present in the post just in time to beat the seasonal rush. Epstein's grudgingly given budget for the venture left us with little cash to spend on a conventional EP-style cover or sleeve to house the disc. We had to make do with a cheap, vomit-yellow-coloured container, overprinted in black and made of an inexpensive cross between paper and board. It was put together with staples that came open too easily. This was the one part of the product of which I felt ashamed. Otherwise, the record did the damage limitation job for which it was intended, and much more. ❞
>
> **TONY BARROW, PRESS OFFICER TO THE FAB FOUR 1963-1968, MORECAMBE, LANCASHIRE**

FRIDAY 18 OCTOBER

'She Loves You' dropped a place to number 4 in both the *NME* and *Melody Maker* charts. In the latter paper's chart, *The Beatles' Hits* and *Twist And Shout* both dropped two places to numbers 31 and 33, respectively. In reviewing the Palladium show, *Melody Maker*'s Chris Roberts wrote, 'Not since the heyday of crooner Johnnie Ray in 1955, has the world-famous theatre been spotlit by near-riots, scenes of mass hysteria, and frantic fan behaviour. To say that the Beatles' appearance was eagerly awaited would be the understatement of 1963. It was the Last Night of the Proms, and New Year's Eve in Trafalgar Square a minute before midnight all rolled into one, for the predominantly teenage audience.'

John told the paper, 'It was the greatest experience we have had so far. As soon as we were clear of the theatre, we all agreed on that. It was nerve-racking, waiting for everything to start, but once we were onstage, everything was great. There's a marvellous atmosphere there, about the whole place, and as soon as we were on we lost our nervous feeling. We arrived at the theatre in the morning, with eight hours to go, feeling sick with nerves. We went in the front door – most of the girls were round the back. The worst part was coming out. The police had the front entrance street – Argyll Street – cordoned off. We rushed down to a taxi and found there wasn't one there. We rushed over to a car we thought was a taxi, and it turned out to be a police car, and they wouldn't let us in. Eventually we got to a car and got out, with police motorbikes on each side. It was like royalty. Some cars tried to follow us, but the police must have forced them into side streets or something.'

The group filmed a spot for the evening's *Scene At 6.30* in Studio Four at the Granada Television Centre in Manchester, miming to 'She Loves You'. They were a last-minute replacement for Brian Poole and the Tremeloes. Seventeen-year-old Michael Belger was arrested after being spotted breaking into a shop in Blackstock Street, Liverpool. At his court hearing, Mr E. Rex Makin, his solicitor, told the judge Belger wasn't a criminal, but 'like so many youngsters today thinking more of clothes and hair styles than hard work. He wanted this black mac for Christmas, being one of many with Beatlemania, and now found himself in court because of this stupid act.' Magistrate G. N. England conditionally discharged him.

SATURDAY 19 OCTOBER

By 10am, fans were already queuing for the Beatles' evening's show at Buxton's Pavilion. Local group Derrick and the Falcons opened the show, including 'Please Please Me' and 'Chains' in their set. Also on the bill were Manchester group the Deltones. The crowd officially totalled twenty-five hundred but increased in size when the main exit doors were opened to allow people to breathe. Terry O'Malley of Derrick and the Falcons said, 'It was the only time I have played there and not seen one inch of the floor. There was more room on the stage even with three sets of gear!'

The Beatles played two twenty-minute sets, one at 9pm and the other just after 10.30pm – at the first, eighteen girls fainted, at the second, forty-four. Police Sergeant Jim Earl, standing on the floor-level stage, had to ask for order, as fainting girls were taken outside across the road and lain down in the yard of St John the Baptist Church. A force of twelve policemen tried to keep the surging crowd back. Burly men were positioned on the steps at the side of the stage, but girls still rushed towards the group, determined to break through the human barrier. Policeman John Swain found himself on the stage and developed a strategy of grabbing each girl by the arm as she rushed towards the group, and then spinning her round through 360 degrees, causing her to be flung back where someone else grabbed her and propelled her down the steps and back into the hall. Fellow policeman Grahame Hibbert was also on duty. He was standing on the steps leading backstage to stop the crowd entering the area. The Gardens' foreman Jack Redfern asked him to go backstage with

366

the group so they could sign a few autographs books. As he was going down the narrow passage with a bundle in his arms, George took advantage of his situation and pinched his truncheon. 'I hadn't a clue who he was, and I dumped the autograph books on a chair, grabbed his arm and took the truncheon from him and was about to eject him from behind with my truncheon between his legs when there was a camera flash and a rowdy cheer from the open dressing room – it was then apparent he was one of the group! The incident was the subject of much humour to the group and onlookers. I was somewhat embarrassed and returned to my post on the stairs.'

After the show, the Beatles made a quick getaway from the Pavilion's St John's Road exit, whisked away before any fans got a chance to see them. The week's *Buxton Advertiser* report of the concert, headlined 'Dance-Extraordinary Puts Up Pavilion Temperature', singled out Henry Sherwood, a sergeant in the Buxton Division of the St John Ambulance Brigade, as the hero of the hour. According to the story, he was 'kept busy throughout the night attending to young girls who had seen fit to pass out rather than endure the excitement any further.' Maureen Cleave's three-part series in the *Evening Standard* came to an end, the final instalment headlined 'It's Like Living It Up With Four Marx Brothers'.

> ❛ I went, with my friend Jenny, to see the Beatles just before my 14th birthday. A neighbour had purchased a couple of tickets but could not go so decided to give them to me. Buxton is a small town and nothing much seemed to happen there. I used to go to the local youth clubs with my friends, where we'd play badminton and sit around chatting. One of the youth clubs used to have groups on and they played a lot of American R&B tunes. I also used to meet up with my friends in the holidays in a local cafe, where we used to sit in a back room chatting and listening to the juke box. I was so excited at the thought of going to the Beatles concert, as I had never been to anything like it before. Jenny and I took hours to get ready and I remember the crowds of people as we walked into the Pavilion Gardens. We managed to get into the crowd and when the Beatles came on everyone started to push forwards. I am only small and I found being in such a crowd overwhelming. You couldn't hear what the Beatles were playing for all the girls screaming. I passed out and was carried over everyone, as did many others, towards the stage. I remember coming round just as they carried me past John and George and then they threw me out of the back door. I stood there for a couple of minutes before the door opened again and Jenny appeared. Just then they began playing 'Twist and Shout' and we ran back in by a side door. I feel privileged to have seen the Beatles so early on in their career and followed them until they split up. ❜
>
> **LESLEY MARCHANT, MARKETING OFFICER, OLD WHITTINGTON, DERBYSHIRE**

SUNDAY **20 OCTOBER**

Wednesday's recording of *Easy Beat* aired at 10.31am. It turned out to be the group's last appearance on the show. Fans listened in while camping outside the municipal booking offices in Charles Street, Leicester, to buy tickets for the 1 December concerts – causing two roads to close to the public. Seventy police struggled to control three thousand fans who had been queuing to buy tickets for up to sixteen hours. A plate-glass window of a nearby shop on the corner of Charles and Halford Streets caved in from the mass of bodies pressing against it. 'In the midst of the melée,' a policeman on duty recalled, 'a young man's hand shot up and held the massive plate glass aloft. He held it for long enough to enable us to get everyone out from underneath and to get hold of the glass and lower it to the ground. In my opinion, his action saved lives and certainly serious injuries that morning.'

The group were still in Liverpool, meeting with Peter Yolland, who had been hired to produce their Christmas show. Yolland had produced several regional pantomimes over the previous decade and had just completed a series of Intermediate French for Schools TV programmes. He had been recommended by agent Joe Collins, who was promoting the shows. Yolland

realised this was going to be something different altogether, telling the press, 'I've been in show business since 1948, but this will be the first time I will have worked in a theatre with policemen trying to keep people out of it.'

A crowd had assembled outside the Alpha TV Studios in Aston Road, Birmingham, in the hope of seeing the group arrive for a recording of *Thank Your Lucky Stars*. Some had arrived as early as 6am – one told the *Birmingham Evening Mail & Despatch*, 'We were told the Beatles would arrive at 8am disguised as electricians.' Girls went round to the back of the studios and scaled a 10-foot wall. As they dropped down behind it, police lying in wait grabbed them and lead them back outside. Plate-glass windows out front were boarded up. Fans hopes were dashed – the group switched cars and entered the studio through the back entrance. Margaret Beresford said, 'Why don't the Beatles show themselves? Some of us have waited since six o'clock this morning.' Another fan complained, 'We've helped the Beatles get where they are. We can pull them down again.'

The press was allowed five minutes with the group; Brian Epstein explained that they hadn't eaten all day. *TV Times*' writer Brian Finch interviewed them for the forthcoming four-part series, 'Read A Beatle A Week', as did Tony Barrow for a six-part series in the *Liverpool Echo*, which ran from Monday through Saturday. After a few minutes, the group went to the studio canteen, where they ate lamb, cabbage and potatoes, followed by fruit pie and tea.

At the show, the group performed 'She Loves You', 'All My Loving' and 'Money', the first time the latter two had been played on television. They played in front of a studio audience of 380, unaware that the crowd outside totalled more than two thousand. About twenty girls burst through the police cordon and stormed the main entrance. A taxi, called to pick up a technician, was surrounded and its windscreen was damaged, its mirrors broken and bodywork dented. Fans stopped chanting 'We Want The Beatles!' after thirteen hours as police finally gained control. A plainclothes policeman tapped three times on the studio's steel roller door to signal the start of a thirty-second master plan to get the Beatles away. As he rapped on the door, other police jumped out of a van outside a side entrance and formed a human chain to keep the crowds back. The group jumped into their car and headed back home to Liverpool with Finch on board. He described his experience thus: 'Getting the Beatles to talk is like trying to get one of those foreign radio stations. You tune in and hope that they stay on the wave-length long enough to give you something.' The show aired the following Saturday.

❝ In 1963, my best friend Mavis and I were 15 and totally besotted by the Beatles. She loved John and I was mad about Paul, so when we heard they were coming to Leicester we just had to get tickets to go and see them. My dad was very strict, but Mum (bless her!) eventually persuaded him to give me permission to queue all night. Mavis's parents only agreed when Dad assured them he would make regular visits to check on us throughout our vigil. That momentous Saturday evening he duly took two very excited girls into town in his old Ford Escort and settled us in the queue, promising to come back a few hours later to make sure we were OK. It was thrilling to be sitting on the pavement outside the back entrance of Lewis's with all the other fans. Everyone was so friendly and the atmosphere was buzzing with excitement. Two lads our age were next to us in the queue and when Dad paid us his first visit with a flask of coffee and sandwiches he commented how daft one of them looked, sitting in a deckchair wearing a ladies' headscarf on his head! Dad was as good as his word and came two or three times throughout the night, even sitting in our places in the queue so we would warm up in his van. The night was quite cold and, too excited to sleep, Mavis and I went for a walk along the queue at around four in the morning, leaving the lads to save our places.

Suddenly someone shouted they were opening the doors of the municipal offices and the crowd surged forward. It was a false alarm, but it gave us the opportunity to nip into the queue virtually outside, making us so much closer to the front. When the doors did open, Halfords' shop window smashed with the weight of the crowd and we were counted into the building one at a time by policemen – I was twelfth and Mavis was thirteenth in line to get our precious concert tickets. We came out totally euphoric. We had seats on the second row of the left-hand curve of the balcony overlooking the stage and screamed and sobbed the whole way through the Beatles' performance. It was absolutely magical!

Four years later while reminiscing the night of 'The Queue' with my new boyfriend and my parents, we were all astounded to realise that Will (the new boyfriend) had been located in the same spot as Mavis and I had been originally. It was even more astounding that he remembered Dad bringing us refreshments throughout the night and when Dad commented on the lad in the deckchair with the headscarf... yes, it turned out to be Will! The 'Deckchair' lad and I have been married for more than fifty years, and we STILL love listening to the Beatles. ❞

LYNDA BARTHOLOMEW, SECRETARY, WIGSTON, LEICESTERSHIRE

MONDAY 21 OCTOBER

The *Daily Sketch* began a four-day special featuring each Beatle in turn, starting with Ringo. He told interviewer Kenneth Passingham, 'None of us have quite grasped what it's all about yet. It's washing over our heads like some huge tidal wave. But we're young. Youth is on our side. And it's youth that matters right now. I don't care about politics. Just people.' Under the heading 'Beatle Battle Rages', the paper also described scenes in Leicester. The *Daily Mail* ran a piece by Vincent Mulchrone, 'This Beatlemania – What, I wondered, was it all about?' Mulchrone described a scene on board the Liverpool-London express where the Beatles shared a compartment with an older gentleman who complained about their presence. The exact scene appeared in *A Hard Day's Night* the following year. Mulchrone described the group as 'shatteringly honest, incredibly modest and immediately friendly'. He went on to write, 'Above all, they are refreshing; they are fun; they are kind. I feel better about life for having been in their company.' The new edition of *Mirabelle* featured Ringo in the third of its four-part series 'This Is Our Life'.

Well over a thousand teens, along with several adults queuing for their children, lined up to buy tickets for the Christmas Show at the Astoria in Finsbury Park. At the head of the queue were three 15-year-old girls who had arrived at 8am the day before and patiently camped on the pavement, enduring torrential rain, until they got their tickets at 10.30am. They bought twenty-seven tickets for themselves and school friends. George Martin spent the morning mixing and editing 'This Boy' and 'I Want To Hold Your Hand.'

A top-level police conference finalised safety precautions for the two Winter Garden concerts in Bournemouth. Manager Samuel Bell declared, 'The demand for tickets for the shows, by post alone already, is nothing short of Beatlistic.' He added, 'We can't let them freeze to death. So supplies of Beatle soup, sausage rolls, tea and coffee will be available at about 9pm, 1am and 6am, served on trolleys. We're not doing this for profit. Just as a service. These kids – we expect over a thousand – aim to queue up all night until the box-offices open tomorrow morning. Needless to say, none of the crowd would dare leave the queue to eat or drink in our cafe.' He remarked that the only time anything came close to this was in April 1956, when fifty fans queued all night long to buy tickets for a Stan Kenton concert.

❛ I first became aware of the Beatles when their first single came out. When we heard they were doing a week at the Astoria, we made a decision to buy tickets for virtually all our close friends at the time, I think it worked out at about fifty. There was a group of us who agreed to get down there really early to start queueing, taking it in shifts. We all had pushbikes and worked out a relay system. It started about nine or ten o'clock the night before. I got the short straw and had to be there in the early hours. There were about eight of us involved, and we were to do a couple of hours each in pairs. When we arrived, there were already some girls in front of us, and so we were second in the queue. The girls had come a long way and were camping overnight. We ended up with the middle of the front two rows, quite unbelievable now if you think about it. The show was great. I don't know if anybody actually heard them though! We were lucky to be that close.

I went to another two shows – one with a friend, and one on my own. When I went the second and third time, I just bought an odd ticket and I can remember being halfway the back, and Billy J. Kramer stood up and sang 'Scarlet Ribbons' without any accompaniment, and someone shouted out 'Sexy!' and it really affected him. I'd turned 15 in the August of that year, and left school to take up a job. One of the things that was really important in that era was how you dressed. If you didn't have a Beatles jacket, well you weren't anybody. If your hair was longer than your ears, you were a bit of a scallywag. Carnaby Street was the 'in' place. I can remember spending a month's wages on a pair of hand-sewn shoes – a fortune! We actually knew somebody who made up Cuban-heeled boots. There was a record shop in Crouch End where we'd buy all the records, on the right-hand side up by the Clock Tower. You'd order the next Beatles single before it was released in order not to be disappointed and find it sold out. Scooters were everywhere – I had a Lambretta – and slept under Brighton Pier a few times! It was great growing up back then, playing football in the street etc. We were out all day playing with our mates and bicycled everywhere. It always amazes people when I tell them that I saw them three times. It does make you laugh when you see the photographs of Beatlemania though! ❜

STEVE 'STEP' HARBUD, HEALTH AND SAFETY OFFICER, RICHMOND-UPON-THAMES, SURREY

TUESDAY 22 OCTOBER

George was the focus of the day's *Daily Sketch* feature. He revealed he had received a fan letter from a 6-year-old girl telling him to 'hang on for me for a few years – and please don't tell my big sister.' Alfred Stevenson, headmaster of Adelaide Private College in Ilfracombe, Devon, blamed slumping homework standards on the Beatles. He said that too many of his pupils listened to the radio in the evening when they should be doing their homework. 'They tell their parents the Beatles help them concentrate when they do their homework. Even if they succeed in completing their prep their results are often bad because of lack of concentration and poor reading.' He appealed to parents to switch the radio off so their children could do their homework in silence. Stevenson had already written to Radio Luxembourg to ask whether they wouldn't mind not playing the Beatles until after 9.30pm. A Luxembourg spokesman commented, 'We wouldn't dare! I'm afraid we have to consider a large public, and you can imagine what their reactions would be!'

The second day of Edward Webb and Douglas Blunt's trial came to a quick end at Somerset Assizes in Taunton, after Webb changed his plea to guilty. Mr Justice Streatfeild in passing a life sentence said, 'You have pleaded guilty to this awful murder. It is a most lamentable and disgraceful case.' After the verdict, Joan McNulty, her mother Beatrice and sister Betty Milne had lunch and went window shopping before catching the 4.18pm train back to Liverpool. On leaving, McNulty said, 'Barbara [Herron] and I were going to see Cheddar, and then go to Weston, where I have friends. We were also going to see the Beatles, who were playing there at the time. I never did get to see Cheddar. I might do one day.'

By noon, 32,000 tickets had been sold for the 'Beatles Christmas Show' at the Astoria in Finsbury Park. Manager Cyril Higham said that the remaining 50,000 tickets would likely be sold 'within a week or so' and that meant that the previous record of 40,000 for a single show, set by three and four week runs of *The Longest Day* and *The Guns Of Navarone* would easily be broken. Postal bookings had been so heavy that the cinema was rejecting them. There had been 10,000 applications for block bookings on a special form printed in the *NME* the previous week.

WEDNESDAY 23 OCTOBER

John was featured in the day's *Daily Sketch*, saying 'I don't want to be singing at 80. Who wants a croaking Beatle at 80?... But we've got lots of things to do, yet. Exciting things, I believe. In fact, there's only one thing I don't want to do. Grow old.'

The group began a session at 10am at Abbey Road, recording a sixteenth take of 'I Wanna Be Your Man.' Fans began queuing at 10.45 in the pouring rain outside the ABC in Hull to buy tickets for their two concerts on 24 November. Police announced that they had to move along and could not wait outside the venue until Friday night. When asked by a *Hull & Yorkshire Times* reporter why the fans were not at work, one teen said, 'We haven't got jobs. There aren't any.' Tickets for the 22 November shows in Stockton-on-Tees also went on sale.

After the recording session, the group, Aspinall and Evans left London Airport, flying aboard a BEA flight to Arlanda Airport, 25 miles north of Stockholm. Upon their arrival, they were presented with bouquets of flowers and met by some thirty to forty female fans. John said, 'Where's all the snow, folks?' They were then driven to the Hotel Continental in Vasagatan in the Swedish capital, where they booked into rooms 205 to 210. Epstein arrived in Sweden later, after being interviewed on Southern TV's *For Art's Sake*. The group held a press conference in the hotel, before visiting Nalen, a music venue on Regeringsgatan, a short walk from the hotel – described by Ringo as 'a bit more elegant than the Cavern.'

Charles Groves, the musical director of the Royal Liverpool Philharmonic Society, spoke to the Crosby Recorded Music Circle. 'I personally cannot stand the noise [the Beatles] make, but I would fight to the death to allow those who do like that noise to enjoy it.'

THURSDAY 24 OCTOBER

In the final segment of the Beatle series, Paul – describing himself as 'the Beatle with the choirboy face' – was featured in the *Daily Sketch*. He remarked that the group's impact was akin to 'what my old aunt enjoyed when she heard Bing Crosby for the first time.'

Gripped by Beatlemania, the national and regional morning papers reported on the phenomena's many effects. The *Daily Herald* revealed that Derek and Hilary Gray of Kelsey Way in Beckenham had asked the Post Office for a new telephone number, after being inundated for five months with phone calls from Beatles fans dialling BEA TLES (BEC 8537). 'Some fans seem to think the Beatles live at my home,' Mrs Gray commented, 'I don't even like the Beatles.' In a letter to the *Daily Express*, 13-year-old Janet Cooper from West Heath in Birmingham suggested that the Duke of Edinburgh Award for 'Initiative and Fortitude' be given to the Beatles, citing that 'to attain their present popularity [they] must show initiative, and to face such crowds of fans as they do surely shows fortitude.'

While the older generation gleaned the latest news on the Fab Four over a nice cup of tea, groups of teenagers began queuing outside the Winter Gardens in Bournemouth at 8.30am, anticipating the ticket office's opening at 10am two days later. Not wanting to be recognised, they hid their faces from the camera behind copies of the new edition of *Disc*, which featured a photo of the Beatles drinking Cokes with straws from bottles. They probably were not too happy to read that 'She Loves You' had slipped down a place to number 4, although it did stay at number 3 in the *NRM* chart. Some six hundred fans stayed overnight, causing the queue to stretch from the steps of the venue – described by the *Bournemouth Evening Echo* as 'a vast open-air dormitory' – down the paths to the edge of Cranborne Road, then up the path and around to the back of the theatre.

At 6pm a more tranquil scene was taking place in the Manchester district of Ardwick with 15-year-olds Betty Francis and Andrea Clay queuing outside the ABC, a full two days before the box office opened for the group's 20 November concert. Francis told a *Manchester Evening News* reporter that, 'It's not just a question of getting in, you've got to get on the front seats. That is, of course, if you want to see them near to.' The pair had come prepared for their forty-hour wait, bringing along three copies of *The Beatles Book* monthly, several Beatles souvenirs, various photos of the group and a quick pencil sketch or two by Francis. By the time the box office opened at 10am on Saturday, there were more than five thousand fans standing in line – half of whom went home empty-handed.

In the late afternoon in Stockholm, the group caused chaos at a press conference. The group repeatedly interrupted to chant 'aex-bel-abit' in unison after hearing someone say 'aktiebolaget', the Swedish term for package show. At 5pm, they recorded a seven-song set for the Swedish radio programme *Drop In*, hosted by Klas Burling, at the Karlaplansstudion in the Karlaplan plaza. Some of their equipment hadn't shown up, so they had to borrow support group Hasse Rosen and the Norsemen's Fender amps. Sound engineer Hans Westman recalled the recording as 'the worst I've ever made, totally chaotic.' It was broadcast on 11 November. After the recording, attended by an audience of more than two hundred and fifty – though only a hundred had been expected – they left the studio through the main entrance, making their getaway in Burling's blue Fiat 1500, which received a dent or two in the melée. Burling commented, in English, 'That's show business.' Fan club secretary Freda Kelly, accompanying the group on the trip, had her toes trodden on and then run over by the car.

❝ My friend Betty and I both attended Cromwell Secondary Modern School in Salford and were both mad keen Beatles fans. When we heard they were going to be doing a concert in Manchester, we decided, instead of going to school, we would go and queue up for tickets! We were 15 at the time. I'd seen them once before at a lunch gig at the Cavern. I went there on the train to Liverpool. I didn't dare tell my dad, but when he found out, I got into trouble! I must have only been about 14, and Pete Best was still the drummer then. I'd never been to a proper pop concert before.

I had told my mum about skipping school to queue for tickets for the Beatles, and she said, 'Well, if you really want to, I'll let you do it.' My dad didn't know (again!), so off we went on the bus into town. We arrived around teatime, two days early. I can remember it was still light when we arrived, and people were on their way home from work, obviously thinking, 'What's happening here?' We were all set up, with our blankets and flasks, and would take it in turns to go and get something to eat. By the time it reached midnight, there were so many people behind us. We took it in turns with the two girls behind us in the queue to go to the loo. We got six tickets each.

When my dad found out, he went mad! Unfortunately, one of the staff at our school had seen the *Daily Mirror* the next morning, and there we were, on the front page! Betty and I were suspended from school for three days. In these days, you just didn't do things like that. We were sent to the Education Officers on Chapel Street in Salford. It was quite serious, but we were very famous! It was definitely worth it, and when the day dawned, we were right there in the front row for the show. I took my friends Josie Brown, Anne Barratt and Anita Rowley. I don't remember who else came with us. Betty took her own friends. The night of the concert was just wild. It was absolutely fantastic! I remember what I was wearing. It was a Beatles coat a friend's mum had made it for me. It was a collarless jacket made out of plastic, which I wore with a checked skirt, and knee-length boots.

I never saw them again live, but almost fifty years later, I went with my husband Les and son Michael to see the Beatles Experience in Liverpool. To enter the exhibition, you have to walk down a flight of stairs, and there, in full view in front of us, was a huge photograph of me from 1963, screaming! Michael said he wasn't going to walk in with me, he was so embarrassed! The same picture was used on the front of a record cover by someone not particularly famous, and also for a birthday card. Just one day in life, and it is still with me to this day. ❞

ANDREA SHEFFIELD, SECRETARY, SALFORD, LANCASHIRE

FRIDAY 25 OCTOBER

The group jockeyed for position as 'She Loves You' climbed back up a place to number 3 in both the *NME* and *Melody Maker* charts. *The Beatles' Hits* and *Twist And Shout* dropped to numbers 35 and 38 in *Melody Maker*. The paper reported that, 'Beatle Fever Hits Britain – All concerts sold out – and now a Royal Show spot'. Paul told the paper that, 'the Royal Variety Show is a challenge to us in that it will be the type of audience that we haven't played to very much. We'll probably be the biggest flop on earth – but we are not particularly worried about flopping there. If we flop, we'll try and think of what made us flop. I think what we ought to do is just to play in front of that sort of audience and try to do our best and see what happens. If we don't quite make it, then we should try and analyse what happens and why we weren't particularly successful.'

Meanwhile, on their second full day in Sweden, the group posed for the cover of what was the *Long Tall Sally* EP. Photographers Bo Trenter and Robert Freeman held the session at the Stadshus before moving on to Hötorget Square in the centre of the city and in front of the Sergel Teatern. After some sightseeing, the group met with fans, then left for Karlstad, driving the snowy 300 kilometres to the Stadshotellet in a convoy of six cars and one trailer. They drove to Nya Aulan, a secondary school hall in Sundsta Läroverk, Sundstavägen, for two concerts at 7pm and 9pm. The support acts were Jack Dailey, Mona Skarström, the Telstars, Svend Millers Popstars and Cambridge group the Phantoms, who had moved to Sweden in 1961. They made their first appearance on a foreign stage with John, Paul and George running on with Ringo bringing up the rear with a drum under his arm. The hall was only three-quarters full, with an estimated seven hundred and fifty ticket holders; however, twenty-eight policemen were on hand. The group performed 'Long Tall Sally', 'Please Please Me', 'I Saw Her Standing There', 'From Me To You', 'A Taste Of Honey', 'Chains', 'Boys', 'She Loves You' and 'Twist And Shout', during which John's mic broke. After the concert they went back to their hotel and had a late dinner.

The group failed to impress *Nya Wermlands-Tidningen*'s reviewer Johnny Olsson, who thought they had a 'monotonous style' and sounded rather 'corny'. Another newspaper commented, 'My god, I knew they were longhaired, but not that longhaired!'

> ❛ I was doing an apprenticeship at Marshall's Aerospace in Cambridge when I formed my first group, the Scramblers and, in time, we became the Phantoms. One evening we had a gig at the Guildhall in Cambridge, and a couple of Cambridge students came to talk to us. They'd been writing some songs, and wondered if we could learn to play them, and do a demo disc for them. We agreed, and they hawked it around London, got a bite from a little record company called Palette Records and cut a couple of songs with them. They had a Norwegian singer on the label by the name of Per Elvis Granberg. He was looking for a group to accompany him  around Norway for a summer tour, and somehow we got the job. We headed out to Norway and did six months from June to December. I remember at the beginning of December, we had to go from Oslo to Bergen, which was on the west coast of Norway. You could either go round the bottom or straight over, and we decided with a bit of bravado, that we would go straight across. Ken Leverington our guitarist had his car there, with a trailer on the back with all our little bits and pieces in. We got about halfway, and it began to snow heavily. Needless to say we got stuck, and had to wait for the snow plough to come, which luckily didn't take too long. Back in Oslo, we heard that we had got a few gigs at a club called Nalen in Stockholm in Sweden. So we did two or three gigs there, returning to England shortly

before Christmas. The following spring, we had an enquiry from someone in Stockholm. Would we care to go over for a couple of weeks to join a tour that was going to be called 'Tourney Twist'? This was at the height of the Twist phenomenon. Being as poor as church mice, we said 'Yes, please, we'll come.' We toured with several Swedish artists and a Danish girl singer called Diami, who ended up marrying our rhythm guitarist Cliff Gentle. Ken was by now going by the name of Ken Levy, because it was easier for the Swedes to pronounce. After two weeks on the road, the tour was extended for another two weeks, but it was getting very cold. We travelled around on a coach, and I remember when we arrived at a bridge over a river, we went down to the river, and drove across the ice! They tended to work on the bridges over there in the winter, because the ice was hard enough to drive over.

Spring became summer, and summer became autumn, and we just carried on. We were on the road mostly and would stay in hotels and what they called 'pensionnatts' – boarding houses. The following February we went to Finland for six weeks. After one gig, I remember walking outside, and it was so cold – I found out the next day it had been minus 46! It was something we got used to and the snow was very crisp under your feet.

Back in Stockholm in the autumn, we were gigging again locally, and I don't really recall how it came about, but we ended up doing a few shows with the Beatles. We knew of them of course, but we had spent all of the year in Scandinavia, so weren't totally up with what was happening back home. To us they were just four lads from Liverpool. Their success hadn't gone to their heads at all. The Swedish fans were a bit more restrained, still enthusiastic, although I'd say the screaming wasn't that loud. They would play a song, and chat afterwards. It wouldn't have been possible to do that in England at that stage. It was all great fun. The amps that the Beatles had were Vox – they were slightly doctored so they were a bit louder and better than when you just bought them in the shop. Somehow we ended up with two of them after they had gone. John and George had been using them and left them behind. I didn't get Paul's bass amp unfortunately! The Phantoms eventually disbanded in 1967, having spent most of the '60s living in Scandinavia, only coming home to England for holidays. Summertime was a big time for groups travelling around in Sweden, playing in what they call out there 'Folketspark' meaning 'Folks Park – People's Park,' and in the winter, we played in the 'People's House' – the inside venue. Altogether, I was in Scandinavia for eighteen years, managing to earn a living as a musician. I returned to Cambridge in 1980, and was working in the motor business, and bumped into an old friend who played guitar with a group called the World's End. I ended up joining them, playing songs written by a local student called John Cook, who was a prolific song writer. I am now the last surviving Phantom, and although now retired, played until recently around Cambridge. We were like kids in a sweet shop, being in Scandinavia, with all these lovely girls! **"**

DAVID COOKE, MUSICIAN, SAWSTON, CAMBRIDGESHIRE

SATURDAY **26 OCTOBER**

Long queues for Beatles' tickets were by now the norm, and police forces were struggling to improve strategies for Beatle crowd control. In Cambridge, six policemen had formed a cordon to hold back a crowd of fans – numbering one thousand from all over the country, including Bristol, London, Norwich, Southend and Leicester and a fifty-strong contingent from Liverpool – when the ticket office doors opened at 7am, three-and-a-half hours earlier than advertised. Although each person was limited to six tickets maximum, by 10am all thirty-eight hundred tickets had been sold. Afterwards, City Council workmen were left to clear away the debris from the overnight queue. Fans smashed the windows at nearby St Andrew's Street Baptist Church by throwing empty beer bottles being thrown over the church wall. One youth was taken to the police station but later released. Church caretaker Percy Pauley said, 'This morning I found greasy fish and chip papers all over the lawns and plastic lemonade cups. Even a City Police "No Parking" sign with a heavy concrete base was lying on top of one of the graves.' The queue had stretched 200 yards along Downing Place. Transistor radios, blankets, sleeping bags, thermos flasks and even primus stoves were used during the wait.

At 5pm, the group played the first of two concerts at the thirty-five hundred-seater Kungliga Tennishallen, Lidingövägen, in Stockholm, playing second on the bill to 'Peppermint Twist' US hitmakers Joey Dee and the Starliters. Also on the bill were Jerry Williams and the Violents and Suzie. Williams was responsible for the short tour: he had worked with the Beatles at the Star-Club in Hamburg the previous year and recommended them to promoter Bengt-Åke Bengtsson. During the performance, John and Paul both got electric shocks. As they performed in Sweden, the previous Sunday's recording of ABC-TV's *Thank Your Lucky Stars*, aired at 5.50pm in the UK.

At the group's 8pm performance, fans invaded the stage and one girl threw herself at George. He commented later, 'It wasn't very funny at the time, but so long as you can keep on playing it's not too bad.' Ringo added, 'You play better when you're scared.' Hundreds of youngsters stormed the stage to touch their idols. Some fifty police were forced to form a chain to stop them; the concert was interrupted for twenty minutes before it could continue. The police could not stop the girls from rushing to the stage, despite their commands as the concert continued. The audience whistled and screamed out its applause – the riot completely drowning out the artists. After the show, John and Ringo went to a party hosted by Dee at the Foresta Hotel that lasted until 5am. Paul and George returned to the Continental.

One local paper wrote: 'When it was time for the black-dressed Beatles to sing, there was a wild rush of fans toward the stage, but this time the guards were able to control the young folks in time. Still, everyone refused to return to their places. The Beatles went through their whole repertoire successfully, and during the last song, 'Twist and Shout', hundreds of young fans could no longer control themselves and stormed the stage. To summarize my impressions of this craziness, I would have to say that only the Beatles had any redeeming value. They are a gang of well-brought-up and talented rock artists who present their songs with style and at the same time do so in a pleasant way. One would certainly want to see them return to Sweden, while we can do without such jumping jacks as Joey Dee.'

❝ I became obsessed with the Beatles in my mid-teens. Their appearance on the music scene was a very exciting time for me. In 1963, when I was 15 years old, it was announced that they would be appearing in Manchester at the ABC Ardwick, and the concert was expected to be a sellout on the first day. Some friends and I decided that we would queue overnight for tickets. Knowing that our parents would forbid it, we told them that we would be staying overnight at a friend's house and going to school from there the following day. We set off on the train the evening before the sale of tickets, very excited, and set up camp on the pavement outside. However, we were filmed dancing, wearing Beatles tights, by the Northern News Channel *Scene at 6.30*, unaware that they were TV cameramen! Some of our parents and teachers saw us on TV. We were mortified, as you can imagine! We were suspended from school for a week. My dad was fuming that I had lied to him and confiscated my very precious ticket. I was heartbroken, especially as my friends were told off but allowed to keep theirs. The day before the concert he gave my ticket back to me. The concert was amazing. The following year we queued overnight for tickets again, but this time at the ABC in Wigan, our hometown, with our parents' consent. My boyfriend at the time also went to the concert, he annoyed me after it ended by mimicking me trying to climb on the stage, and also screaming for Paul, who was my favourite. We had a row and didn't speak for a couple of days. However, we later married, and have been together over fifty years. ❞

CHRISTINE KENYON, HOUSEWIFE, WIGAN, LANCASHIRE

SUNDAY 27 OCTOBER

At 8.30am, in Newcastle-upon-Tyne, someone yelled 'The box office is open,' two hours before scheduled. More than four thousand fans – some who had been queuing for forty-eight hours – stampeded the box office. Many in the front of the queue were trampled on and more than a hundred and twenty were given first aid. Several were taken to hospital with shock. Forty policemen battled for three quarters of an hour to hold the mob at bay and restore order. Superintendent John Martin told the crowd through his patrol car loudspeaker, 'Unless you calm down I will cancel all bookings and the show.' Ambulance men provided liquids and used two gallons of sal volatile to revive those suffering from exposure. People living in neighbouring flats, fed up with the noise from the transistor radios, threw water over the youngsters, drenching them. One girl, who lost her jeans in a stampede, had to wrap herself in a blanket to buy her tickets. Thirteen-year-old Marjorie Harrison commented, 'It was terrifying. Hundreds of stupid screaming people suddenly descended on us and grabbed our places. I had been sitting near the front of the queue since Friday morning, too. Now I can only hope one of my friends will give me a ticket,' while Carol Paine, aged 9, said, 'My mummy is in the queue somewhere. We have been here since Saturday night.'

At 10am, the Beatles set off to drive 300 miles to Gothenburg, checking into the Park Avenue Hotel at Kungsportsavenyn 36–38 on arrival. They were scheduled to play three shows at the Lorensbergs Cirkus in Lorensbergsparken, at 3pm, 5pm and 8pm – the third added after the first two had sold out. There were different support acts for the shows, including Jerry Williams and the Violents, Trio Me' Bumba, currently enjoying a Top 10 hit with 'Spel-Olles Gånglåt', the Telstars, Jack Dailey, Mona Skarström, the Prickles and Ken Levy and the Phantoms. A local newspaper commented, 'Never ever had so many shoes stamped the floor at Cirkus in Lorensbergsparken as this particular day.'

❛ I grew up in Whitley Bay and went to the local co-ed grammar school. There were four of us who were really good friends at school. I was probably very unusual in that I didn't have a record player back then. It's just not something we had in the house at the time. I had one of these old reel-to-reel tape recorders that looked like a suitcase, and I used to record the Top 20 on a Sunday afternoon. I had a little radio which I bought myself. I paid so much a week from my pocket money to this little independent electrical shop. I had a crush on the boy who worked there! I first heard the Beatles singing 'Love Me Do' on Radio Luxembourg. I think it's fair to say that initially I was carried along by peer pressure in terms of my adulation of the Beatles. It was a case of 'We all love the Beatles.' We all had to have a favourite, and mine was Paul. He was very pretty! I should of course have liked John, I realised that in later life. He was the one that had the intellect and was much more interesting, but obviously I went for looks at the time! I have a memory of being in a room in school and singing along to 'She Loves You', all of us singing the 'Ooooooh!' bits together, shaking our heads like mad! I went to see [the Beatles] in June with my friend Lesley, but this time, we had to queue overnight. It was bitterly cold, and we had no sleeping bags, but there was a good atmosphere there. Everyone was well mannered, with no pushing. That was of course until the box office opened, and then there was a stampede! The four of us – myself, Lesley, Brenda and Lyn were pretty inseparable at the time. We all told our parents that the other parents had said it was OK! My parents went along with it. Lesley's were a lot less liberal, but they ended up bringing us flasks of soup and blankets in the middle of the night! I recall not being embarrassed about them coming, as we were so grateful for the warmth and food. Lesley remembers going to a public loo in the middle of the night, and everyone looking ghastly! I can't remember what I did on that front, but remember I wore a pair of blue pearlised shoes, that I wouldn't take off my feet, and wore them until they fell apart.

Everything was very orderly until the Chinese whispers went around that the box office was opening, and everyone started running. We took flight, and ran with them, because we thought instinctively that all the people in the queue behind us were also running. There was a plenty of squashing and people fighting their way forwards, and I remember getting to the box office, and having the tickets in my hands. It must have been around ten in the morning.

My abiding memory of the concert is being miffed because I couldn't hear anything. It was a complete disappointment, which is why I value that first experience, because that was my real experience of hearing the Beatles live. That second time, it was just screaming, and everybody standing on their seats. You couldn't hear anything at all, and at that point I was in R39, so a little bit further forward! The tickets this time were 10/6, so they had gone up two shillings in a matter of months! It would have taken about half an hour to get back to Whitley Bay on the bus. My parents were quite concerned with their own lives and not too worried about the time I got home, but Lesley's were. As for the Beatles, well I think I was just carried along on the wave in my teenage years, and never saw them again, but am still in touch with my friend Lesley who I went to the concerts with, and we still reminisce about those fun times. 〕

JOANNA CLOSE, ART AND DESIGN LECTURER, TYNEMOUTH, TYNE AND WEAR

MONDAY 28 OCTOBER

Sixteen-year-olds John Logan and Bob Parker began queuing outside the ABC in Lincoln a week before tickets went on sale, trying to set a one hundred and seventy-hour queuing record in a nationwide Beatles-drive. After twenty-seven hours police moved them on and banned them from queuing again until midnight Saturday. Logan got his ticket on the following week, dashed back to the garage where he worked as a panel beater and managed to clock in on time. Still, his manager Mr Clifford Broadley called him in to his office and promptly fired him. 'I asked earlier if I could have the morning off to get my ticket but was turned down. He said if I was more interested in the Beatles than in my job I was no good to him.' Mr Robert Barnard, manager of the garage, said, 'No, I'm not a Beatles fan. Personally I wouldn't walk across the street to see them.'

In Newcastle, an anonymous clerk in the city's new Civic Centre gave his ticket to Rosalie Moffatt, an 11-year-old from Ashington. She had written to the Corporation to ask whether her ticket could be mailed to her because she couldn't afford the bus fare. Her father, a 37-year-old miner, had not worked regularly for a decade due to ill health. The clerk said he was going to send her the money for the bus fare as well.

After a well-deserved morning off while travelling 40 miles to Borås and 'resting, sightseeing, getting voices back,' the group signed records at the Waidele Musik record shop in the afternoon. Paul told the press, 'We are having a wonderful time, but we can't wait to get home.' At 7.30pm they played a concert at the Boråshallen on Bockasjögatan in front of twenty-five hundred fans, once again supported by Jack Dailey, Mona Skarström, the Telstars, the Sven Millers, Ken Levy and the Phantoms, Trio Me' Bumba, the Prickles and Terry Wayne. At one point during the show the power went out – 14-year-old Krister Karlsson saw a power outlet and decided to pull the plug out for fun. Amongst the noise, much of the audience was probably unaware of a few minutes of unplugged Beatles. Future music critic Kjell-Åke Dahlin said,

'We stood on the chairs and screamed.' A reviewer for the *Vastgota Demokraten* commented, 'When the Beatles entered, the audience went totally wild. People in the back seats tried to move forward towards the stage, and the police had difficulty keeping the stage free from screaming kids. It reminded more of a religious meeting than a music event. On the last song no one could hear anything of the music, although the very best speakers in the market were used.' For some reason the reviewer translated the group's name to 'De Brutala', meaning The Brutal. They spent the night at the Grand Hotel.

❛ In the small village of Gållstad, outside Borås, we were four guys and a girl who started a guitar group in the beginning of 1963. We took the initials of our last names TAGG, which means thorn in English. We checked the English dictionary which translated the word Tagg to Prickle. So we named ourselves the Prickles. We were playing guitar hits of the Shadows and a quite famous Swedish group called the Spotnicks. There was a Swedish musician by the name of Lennart Wahlström, who also owned a music store, and he took care of us, taught us to play, and to sing in harmony. He also became our manager and was the one who booked us for the Beatles concerts in Gothenburg and Borås.

The first of the two concerts, which were called 'Popfestival', took place in Gothenburg. The Beatles were top of the bill and closed the show. At the time not many knew of them in Sweden. They'd had a hit with 'Twist And Shout', and that was all. For some reason the Sven-Ingvars couldn't make it, and we were asked to play in their place. Of course, this was a big adventure for us, to play for so many people, in the big city of Gothenburg. The Beatles played three concerts that Sunday, but there were different opening acts for all three concerts. We got to the concert hall in the afternoon, the same time as the Beatles made their first appearance. All of the few dressing rooms were occupied, so we just walked in and sat down in one of them. After a while these four English guys came in, probably wondering why we were in their dressing room. But they didn't say anything about it. John laid down on a wooden bench with a coat over him to rest. We talked to the other three a little. When we said our name was the Prickles, John chuckled. 'Ho, ho, ho' from the bench, and Paul said, 'Don't mind him, he's just a bit tired.' (Some months later, when a record company was going to sign us, they explained, we need to change our name, otherwise we'd be known as 'prick less'. It wasn't until then that we realised why John had laughed. To solve the problem, we added an 'r' and called ourselves the Pricklers.)

Paul stood beside the stage listening to us when were playing. When we met after our set, he asked how long we had been playing. 'Half a year,' I said, and he said, 'Oh good,' or something like that. Later we stood beside the stage and watched the Beatles playing. They played very loud, we thought, and with an energy totally new to us. I remember, when they came off stage and singing 'Twist and Shout', they were breathless, and Paul said to John, 'Well done John.' We watched their last show at the Cirkus out in the stairs just behind the audience. This was the first time we saw a wild audience, and this was only a breeze of what was coming the next day in Borås. We were again booked as an opening act. The Beatles came and said hello to us. We asked for their autographs, and they signed the cards they had brought with them. It was hard to get John to sign, so Paul copied John's handwriting and signed them all in John's place. I remember our manager Lennart wouldn't give up and finally got John to sign. On the fiftieth anniversary of the Beatles concert in Boras, I was invited to talk about it on local radio. I told about my memories of our two meetings, and for some reason they talked a lot about Ringo's qualities as a drummer compared to Pete Best. They played three different version of 'Love Me Do.' With Ringo, Pete Best and Andy White. In a vote for the best Beatles song, George Harrison's 'While My Guitar Gently Weeps' won. Quite surprising to me. ❜

ULF GÖTHAGER, PRODUCTION MANAGER, BORÅS, SWEDEN

TUESDAY 29 OCTOBER

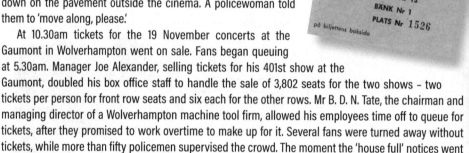

ESKILSTUNA SPORTHALL
Sittplats HÖGER
SEKTION **G**
NEDGÅNG Nr 13
BÄNK Nr 1
PLATS Nr 1526
på biljettens baksida

Some pupils from Mirfield Grammar School showed up to buy tickets for two shows in Huddersfield five days before the box office was due to open. Wrapped in scarves, woollen jumpers and blankets with hot coffee to keep themselves warm, they settled down on the pavement outside the cinema. A policewoman told them to 'move along, please.'

At 10.30am tickets for the 19 November concerts at the Gaumont in Wolverhampton went on sale. Fans began queuing at 5.30am. Manager Joe Alexander, selling tickets for his 401st show at the Gaumont, doubled his box office staff to handle the sale of 3,802 seats for the two shows – two tickets per person for front row seats and six each for the other rows. Mr B. D. N. Tate, the chairman and managing director of a Wolverhampton machine tool firm, allowed his employees time off to queue for tickets, after they promised to work overtime to make up for it. Several fans were turned away without tickets, while more than fifty policemen supervised the crowd. The moment the 'house full' notices went up, tickets started being sold on the black market for £3 each. Despite fears of riots, clashes with police and screaming from uncontrollable teenagers, the one thousand-strong crowd caused no trouble.

The *Washington Post* became the first major American newspaper to comment on the Beatle phenomenon, publishing an article 'Thousands of Britons "Riot" Over the Beatles.' Flora Lewis wrote about riot squads being called out in four British towns. Describing the Beatles as looking like 'limp, upside-down dust-mops,' Lewis wrote, 'When they sound off, everything begins to fly and it seems that everyone in the country not yet anchored down by age and dignity begins to shiver, shake and scream... They have put guitars, electrified and ordinary, so much into vogue that one hundred and ninety thousand have been sold since the Beatles burst on the scene a year ago and sales continue at fifteen hundred a week.'

Meanwhile, the Beatles made the four-and-a-half-hour journey north-east to Eskilstuna, for a 7pm performance in front of two thousand fans at the Sporthallen on Hamngatan. Supporting them were Jerry Williams and the Violents, Trio Me' Bumba, the Telstars, Jack Dailey and Mona Skarström. Swedish newspapers commented, 'The Beatles made a K.O. on the audience' ... 'Young and wild ecstasy' ... 'A hand full of girls heating each other up and to help them there is this noise from the guitars of the twist idols.' While the group were performing, Brian Epstein met with movie producer Walter Shenson and United Artists' European head of production, Bud Ornstein, at the latter's apartment to discuss the making of a film starring the Beatles. Neil Aspinall married Ornstein's daughter Suzy in 1968. After the show, the group drove back to Stockholm, where they spent the night.

> ❝ On the Tuesday before the tickets were going on sale at the Ritz in Huddersfield, a group of us, who all went to the Starlight Dance Studio, had agreed to do a rota queuing for tickets. My pals, sisters Sue and Anne, and I went during the day. We bunked off school, but unfortunately we were on the TV programme *Look North* that night. Their dad was furious, mine didn't know. On the Friday we did it again and arrived in the morning and took our places at the left of the building not far from the front of the queue. Part way through the night the police decided to move us to the other side of the building. In the rush, our place in the queue was moved further back. We were visited by Sue and Anne's dad (mine still didn't know) who bought us some 'Beatle Soup' (Bovril) which was on sale. During the night it poured with rain. We were sodden. In the early hours Sue and Anne's dad came again with bacon sandwiches – a life saver! The tickets were supposed to go on sale at 9am, but

at 6am something happened and everyone rushed to the front of the building. The police couldn't cope and they formed a line, linking hands. People were coming into the town, pushing through and getting tickets. The glass doors at the front of the cinema were broken. Sue's boyfriend pushed her to the front and she got six tickets in the fifth row, which we shared. Another friend grabbed hold of the back of a policeman's uniform, pushed him to the front, then pretended to faint. He took her in and she got tickets. When the night of the performance came we screamed all the way through, and we just about heard what they were singing. ❜

BEVERLEY MEECH, HOUSEWIFE, HUDDERSFIELD, WEST YORKSHIRE

WEDNESDAY 30 OCTOBER

The *Daily Express* and the *Daily Telegraph* revealed that the Beatles had signed up to make their movie debut – reporting that Alun Owen was to write an original screenplay for the group, produced by Walter Shenson and distributed by United Artists. Owen had first met George at the Blue Angel and then the remaining three Beatles earlier in the month. The production, filmed totally in black and white, had a budget of £200,000; shooting began in February 1964, following a series of concerts at the Olympia in Paris. Owen told the *NME* that, 'I aim to create the story around ninety minutes of their own fantastic lives at the top of the pop music profession. But it will be fictional, despite the fact that the things which happen to them in the film are probably the sort of things that happen to them in reality. I aim to utilise their fantastic personalities and sense of humour.' Shenson said, 'I don't want to make a conventional film because the Beatles are not conventional. In an exciting musical I want to capture them

on the screen as they really are.' The group told reporters they wouldn't do 'a rags-to-riches story, or the one about the record being smuggled into the studio and put on by mistake. We've *seen* that one.'

John was sharing a room with Robert Freeman on the Swedish trip. At 10am, he wandered into Room 206, where Neil Aspinall was polishing his boots. Wearing his vest and trousers, he munched on Neil's toast. Ringo came in wearing his pyjama top with trousers, soon followed by George. In Room 209, Paul waited for his breakfast to be delivered. After waiting three quarters of an hour for an egg, he decided to go out. The group were driven to the Arenateatern, a small theatre in Stockholm's Gröna Lund amusement park, for camera rehearsals for the Sveriges Television music show *Drop In*. Lunch followed at a restaurant in nearby Solliden, where they were joined by Mal Evans, Neil Aspinall, producer Klas Burling, presenter Kersti Adams-Ray and several photographers. John and Paul both sat down and played a piano. After lunch, Bo Trenter took a number of widely used shots of the group.

After *Drop In* rehearsals came to an end, Paul and Ringo went shopping. They dropped into the city's largest department store, NK, where Paul bought some perfume for Jane Asher. Back at the hotel, they rehearsed for the forthcoming UK tour. They worked on 'I Wanna Be Your Man' for Ringo and performed an acoustic version of 'I Want To Hold Your Hand' for Burling, who later said he immediately knew it would be a hit. They met members of their Swedish fan club and signed autographs. At 7pm, the recording began in front of a studio audience. Gals and Pals, Lill-Babs, Doris Olsson and Boris were also on the bill. During the show, Aspinall and Evans went out for food, returning with sausages and pommes frites. The Beatles performed 'She Loves You' and 'Twist And Shout', and then launched into 'I Saw Her Standing There' at Burling's request. As presenter Adams-Ray attempted to start up the show's theme tune, the group played 'Long Tall Sally'. Finally, as the credits rolled, they joined in with handclaps. After the show, the group was driven back to the Continental in a green police car. The recording aired on 3 November.

THURSDAY 31 OCTOBER

'S he Loves You' continued its climb back up the charts, moving up to number 3 in *Disc* and to number 2 in *NRM*, which also featured *The Beatles' Hits* EP knocking the Searchers' *Ain't Gonna Kiss Ya* off the top of the EP chart.

Before the group headed to the airport to return home, Klas Burling chatted one last time with Paul and Ringo. Teen Bengt Eriksson (later a journalist at the Swedish pop magazine *Schlager*) took John and Neil Aspinall on a shopping trip. John bought a dark grey coat at Stroms on the corner of Sveavagen and Kungsgatan. Several fans made the 25-mile journey to Arlanda Airport and mobbed the group when they arrived. The group flew back to London aboard an SAS Caravelle jet, as second-class passengers. During the flight, those in first-class came into the second-class compartment asking for autographs.

When the group landed, they were greeted at London Airport by a huge crowd, estimated variously at anything between fifteen hundred and twenty thousand, on the roof gardens of the Queen's Building, adjacent to Terminal 2. The fans, some of whom had slept overnight, undeterred by pouring rain, had been directed to the gardens by airport officials. Thirty extra police were called in and crush barriers erected to contain the crowd. Anne Butler in the *Daily Herald* described the scene. 'I touched a Beatle last night. Two fans, little more than 12 years old, grabbed me later and kissed my gloved hand. The fever is now an epidemic. I trod on a Beatle too. Couldn't help it. There was a scrum at London Airport when the group returned from their week in Sweden. The Beatle fans were at the airport to give a squealing welcome. Hundreds and hundreds of bedraggled girls and boys waited hours in the rain to see them. Officials specially arranged for the Beatles' Caravelle from Stockholm to touch down near the Queen's Building.

Everyone who looked like a Beatle fan was directed to the rooftop gardens. For just 6d each they could watch their idols – but from a distance.' One man surveying the scene said, 'The country's gone mad. Bloody kids. Makes you sick.'

The Ministry of Aviation considered the Beatles so important that it issued a directive giving the group's arrival priority over Prime Minister Sir Alec Douglas-Home's departure to Edinburgh. In the midst of the commotion, even contestants for the Miss World competition passed through the terminal unnoticed. Ed Sullivan and his wife Sylvia, on their annual visit to London, took notice of the hubbub. He later said, 'For years we've visited London, and it was during one of our arrivals at London Airport that Mrs Sullivan and I saw hundreds and hundreds of these youngsters and I asked what celebrity was arriving.

They told us that the youngsters were waiting to greet the Beatles on their return from Sweden. Always on the lookout for talent, I decided that the Beatles would be a great attraction for our TV show.' He described seeing them as being like the time he travelled the American south and heard 'the name of Presley at fairs. But these boys had people even wilder than Presley, and they didn't have the wriggling and sex. I caught their act in England, and the reaction, and I said to my wife, 'These boys have something, I want them.''

Police escorted the group through customs. The press snatched a few words with the group about their forthcoming appearance on the Royal Variety Show. Paul replied to a question about whether they would be changing any of their act, 'We'll have to change it I'm sure. We can't do the same thing all the time. We haven't thought about what we're gonna do yet.' Asked about his accent and comments made by Edward Heath, John responded, 'I'm not going to vote for Ted.'

To evade the swarm of fans, the group left the airport via a side staircase, getting into their Austin Princess for their journey through London. The tyres on their bus had been let down and required repairs costing £11 13s 6d, including parking charges. In the evening, George went to see Little Richard, the Everly Brothers, Bo Diddley and the Rolling Stones in concert at the Odeon in Lewisham. Wearing a suede cap, with a wig underneath, fake beard, leather coat and a pair of glasses, he managed to go unnoticed. He stood in the wings watching the show, only to hear Little Richard proclaim, 'I taught the Beatles how to rock!'

❝ An only child, I grew up with my parents in Queensland in a tiny place called Tungamull, between Rockhampton and the coast. My mother had tried to teach me violin, but I was more interested in playing with the other school kids. It wasn't till my late teens, when I heard Roy Orbison's 'Only The Lonely' on the radio, that I decided I wanted to be a singer/songwriter, so I bought an old guitar. I was by then working a nine to five job in the Main Roads Department in Rockhampton. After a short stint in a local group called the Rockets, I started singing solo in pubs and beer gardens on the weekends. In October 1963 a friend and work colleague, Peter Egan, asked me if I had heard the Beatles. I was a little sceptical. Having heard many predictions about 'the next big thing' at that time, who were never heard of again, I showed a rather cynical lack of interest. But he insisted that I listen to them, and loaned me their album *Please Please Me*. He brought it to work, I played it that night and returned it the next day. Someone else had lent me an LP sometime earlier, which I kept for weeks, accidentally leaving it in the sun and had

to buy him a replacement. Word had spread around the office of my negligence. I learned a valuable lesson, so I returned Peter's copy promptly the next day. When I heard it, I was absolutely stunned. I instantly became one of the Beatles' greatest fans, and I have remained that way to this very day.

Not long after that introduction to the Beatles, in the same year, my friend Barry had started a group called the Candy Men and asked me to join. There were other groups playing in Rockhampton in the rather healthy dance scene at that time, but we played far more Beatles than the others, and that certainly worked in our favour. So that year or so amounted to a nine-to-five job in the Public Service, playing and singing Beatles and other songs at night, and at lunchtime a friend, Robert Caswell, and I would go to the local record shop, Munros, and listen to all the latest releases, while discussing how we would one day leave that area and take over the world. He wanted to be a screenwriter, I wanted to be a singer/songwriter. Big dreams, in a small place.

About the same time, I too left Rockhampton with my wife Jill, heading for Sydney, and after signing with an independent record label, Sweet Peach, I broke through with a number one record in Australia, 'Bonnie Please Don't Go (She's Leavin')'. I followed that with an album, on the Good Thyme label, the title track of which was *Rock And Roll (I Gave You The Best Years Of My Life)*, the sad tale of an unrequited love affair with rock'n'roll, the eventual acceptance of failure, but also a gratitude for the great times that journey had brought. I drew on many of my own times, when writing that song, especially the line, 'Bought all the Beatle records, sounded just like Paul.' I probably never really sounded like Paul, nor John for that matter, but in my own mind at the time I guess I wanted to think I did and experiencing the crowd's reactions to our humble renditions of the Beatles' hits, it wasn't hard to imagine anything. That song became a world hit for me, and also for the many other artists around the world, who covered it. I have, perhaps subconsciously, followed the Beatles' example, whereby there is a variety of styles, and influences of rock, ballads, country, period pieces, children songs, blues, folk etc. in all my albums. And in one of those albums, I once again touched on my early experiences with the Beatles, in a song called 'Friends Of Mine'. A tribute to my early heroes, James Dean, Roy Orbison, and of course the Beatles, summing up the positive effects they had on me, in those very early formative days. I never met any of the Beatles, although I did have a long meeting in London with their producer George Martin, who had expressed an interest in producing one of my albums. From that first introduction in 1963, to now, the Beatles have had a profound and lasting effect on me. As I sung in 'Friends of Mine', I may not have been a friend of theirs, but they sure were friends of mine. ❞

KEVIN JOHNSON, SINGER/SONGWRITER, SYDNEY, AUSTRALIA

NOVEMBER

'And the rest of you, if you'll just
rattle your jewellery'

FRIDAY 1 NOVEMBER

At 10.30am, the first fans began gathering outside the Odeon in Cheltenham, as a prelude to the evening's two shows; the start of the group's thirty-three-date nationwide tour, for which they were now earning £300 a night. Already a hundred and twenty thousand tickets had been sold; promoter Arthur Howes commented, 'Such scenes as this have only been equalled by Cliff Richard. The tour is a sell-out all the way – and I could sell it over and over again right now.'

Queuing fans read copies of the latest editions of the *NME* and *Melody Maker* in line; the latter ran the headline 'Beatles Beware!' on its front cover. 'She Loves You' remained at number 3, with *The Beatles' Hits* at number 31 in the singles chart, 'Twist And Shout' at number 38 and 'Bad To Me' at number 44. The *NME* reported that the group had overtaken Cliff Richard in the 1963 points table, with 1,151 points to Cliff's 1,129. 'She Loves You' moved up one place to number 2. *The Beatles (No. 1)* EP went on sale, featuring 'I Saw Her Standing There', 'Misery', 'Anna (Go To Him)' and 'Chains'.

The group set off for the Regency spa town. An hour and a half west of London, they stopped for lunch, ordering mixed grills and steaks at the Windrush Inn on the A40 Burford Road in Witney, Oxfordshire. Landlord Ted Thompson was asked if lunch could be served, being told that the Beatles were 'feeling tired and could their presence be kept quiet?' Waitress Margaret Hill later commented, 'I didn't know whether I was coming or going'. When pupils from Wood Green School heard of the visit, they arrived in droves, picking up bits of gravel from the car park.

Madge Barter and Sandra Warner, friends of Louise Harrison's from when they worked together at the Rotol Airscrews factory in Staverton, were invited backstage to meet the group. The group finally got a chance to snack on hot dogs. 'Operation Escape' swung into action as the group ran out of the cinema and into a waiting minibus. Twenty or thirty teenagers standing in the rain hammered on the side of

the vehicle as it drove away, followed by a posse of motorcycles and cars with flashing headlights. A startled *Gloucestershire Echo* reporter and photographer Mike Charity were on board. The driver took a circuitous route through side streets and alleyways, swerving to avoid a parked car. They got to the Savoy Hotel car park in Bayshill Road only split seconds before pursuers. The group rushed through the back door while police blocked the way. Sensing the potential chaos, two other Cheltenham hotels had turned them down.

> ❝ My best friend Patsy and I had joined the fan club and when the tour was announced we watched the news to find out when each town's tickets went on sale. Even with the new-found freedom the '60s had given us, there was just no way that our parents would allow 16-year-olds to sleep on a pavement all night to get tickets. So, we hatched a plan. I told my parents I was sleeping at Patsy's and she did the same with hers. Safe enough as no one had home phones, so they couldn't check up on us. We travelled to Huddersfield from our homes in Halifax and arrived early in the evening to find hundreds of girls already encamped on the pavements. There were friendly policemen there as well to take care and watch over us during the night. We weren't well prepared though. I had snuck a little blanket out, but the evening was cold and the pavement uncomfortable. Vendors were selling 'Beatle Soup', which was just Oxo – but it was warm and wet so we drank it. We couldn't sleep and were exhausted. We'd never done anything like this before and we were beginning to regret it. The police decided to avoid a dangerous situation forming, as by now there were more girls than there were tickets for and dawn hadn't even arrived yet, when numbers would swell even more. So, they had staff open up at six o'clock and tried to manage us by letting us in in blocks of about twenty at a time. At one point I was so tired I dropped to the floor on some steps and was trampled on. The Red Cross arrived and was helping girls in distress. I shouted to Patsy to stay where she was as I didn't want to leave my place in the queue. I was half helped through the door by the Red Cross, but, as soon as I caught sight of the box office, I just went for it and bought four tickets. We caught the bus back to Halifax and must have looked a right sight. I fell asleep and had to be woken for my stop. My dad was up when I got home and he took one look at me and knew what I had done. He told me to go to bed and I slept all day. After we had seen the show, we both lost our voices from screaming and on the Monday after, Patsy had a job interview with the Post Office as a telephonist. She got the job but she still doesn't know how. ❞
>
> LINDA KITSON, JEWELLER, NORLAND, WEST YORKSHIRE

SATURDAY 2 NOVEMBER

Jo Davis, Marylyn Clarke and Di Franklin, fans who had seen both of the previous night's shows, discovered the group were staying at the Savoy. At 10am, they wandered in through the front door and casually asked to speak to George. Much to their amazement, he came down shortly afterwards and chatted with them. The girls were so excited that they didn't even realise until later that they hadn't touched the cups of coffee brought to them. As George and John walked to the car, Paul arrived in the lobby and offered the girls cigarettes before heading outside to meet with forty or so waiting fans.

The group headed north for two shows at the City Hall in Sheffield, travelling with *Melody Maker* editor Ray Coleman. They passed the latest copy of the paper around as they drove, stopping off for lunch at the Bull's Head pub on the A38 in the village of Shenstone, signing autographs for the staff. Once the word was out, local licensees had to cope with phone calls, answering queries from fans. The rest of the package tour ate at a transport cafe 15 miles north near Burton-on-Trent. Driver Ron King commented, 'If it's good enough for Cliff Richard here, it's good enough for you.'

By 4pm, the City Hall was surrounded by thousands of fans, some who had arrived at dawn with sandwiches. All police leave was cancelled. The group went straight to police HQ, traveling to the venue in a Black Maria. They rushed in through the front door surrounded by police. John arrived separately a short time later, sneaking in through a lift shaft at the side of the hall, wearing a trilby. There had been fears that he

had been kidnapped as part of Sheffield University's Rag Week. Aspinall brewed some tea for John. 'He's tea-mad. My duty in life is to make sure he gets tea.' George asked Coleman to 'write down that we've had enough Jelly Babies now. We used to like them but even we can get spoiled. Thank the fans very much, but we'd like them to stop throwing them.' John was sprawled on a sofa reading *Twikker*, the Rag Week's comic, Ringo listened to a Chuck Jackson record and George wandered around doing nothing, leaving Paul to talk to the *Sheffield Telegraph*'s Frazier Wright. 'Let's face it, we love it most of the time. Who wouldn't? All those girls going crazy for you. But now and then you just feel fed up with it... We're on five weeks of these one-night stands. Play, pack-up, move on. Sleep when you are travelling, sleep in the dressing rooms sometimes.'

At soundcheck, with Paul on drums, George on tambourine and Jaywalker Lloyd Baker on piano, they jammed on 'Moanin''. Aspinall brought a record player and some food. Before the first show at 6.10pm, two girls were found hiding in a cloakroom and a 12-year-old boy was found under the stage. Geoff Moss of the Jaywalkers was sent out to get some sandwiches, but when he returned, pushing through the throng outside, they resembled an 'unappetising sort of bread sauce'.

By the end of the 8.40pm show, the stage was ankle deep in Jelly Babies, love letters, programmes and sundry gifts. Girls ripped off bracelets and necklaces and flung them on to the stage, and some wept hysterically. Joyce Elgie, a secretary from Worksop, was carried from the hall in tears and treated for hysteria by members of the St John Ambulance Brigade; she was allowed to return to the hall to watch the remainder of the show.

The group, still wearing their stage suits, were escorted out of the building by police into their waiting car and driven at high speed to Doncaster, where they stayed the night. The *Sheffield Telegraph* music critic G. F. Linstead waxed lyrical. 'The quality of Mersey is not restrained', Portia might have said had she been called upon to judge the Beatles' Show at the City Hall on Saturday. Far from their sound dropping 'as the gentle rain from heaven' it poured out in a mighty flood during an electric storm set up by an army of microphones, amplifiers and the agonised cries of damp teenagers. It is difficult to believe that four homely lads, for all the world looking like trim young bisons, could have produced so many decibels of sound.'

> ❝ My friends and I were just 17, we had our tickets for the first AND second shows and were very excited indeed. By sheer luck, we got chatting to Bill Ellman from the *Daily Mirror*, a lovely man who smuggled us backstage to have our ecstatic photo taken with Paul McCartney. It is on my wall to this day. But the best thing about our contact with the press was that we had found out where the Beatles were staying. It was the Savoy Hotel in Cheltenia – very grand and very staid. So the next morning, we turned up there and trembling enthusiastically, asked at reception if we could see the Beatles, please? Be still my beating heart, I can still remember the joy when George and Paul appeared before us. Paul even gave us a cigarette, which covered me with confusion as I didn't smoke, and so managed to blow his lighter flame out. The shame. John and Ringo appeared too, muttering niceties (not terribly nice, on John's part) and we were all regarded with great suspicion by the Cheltenham dowagers enjoying their morning coffee. Then the group all disappeared into their stately black car. And we felt Beatified. ❞
>
> **JO REES, LEGAL SECRETARY, WINCHCOMBE, GLOUCESTERSHIRE**

SUNDAY 3 NOVEMBER

The group slept in until midday and had a large lunch before making the hour-long trip on the A1 north-west to Leeds and the Odeon, where they had previously performed on 5 June. At 2.30pm, *The Ken Dodd Show,* recorded on 9 October and also featuring John Laurie, Judith Chalmers, Wallas Eaton, Percy Edwards, Peter Hudson and the BBC Variety Orchestra conducted by Paul Fenoulhet, aired on the Light Programme, followed by *The Public Ear*, which featured an interview with the group recorded on 3 October. Introduced by Allan Scott, the show also featured Pauline Boty, Tony Hall and the Max Harris Group. The 30 October recording of *Drop In* aired on Swedish TV.

Just over 6 miles east of Leeds on the A63 Selby Road, as tour manager Johnny Clapson phoned to check whether the Odeon was ready for 'Operation Beatles', the group met with local police, who escorted

them into the city. Crush barriers had been set up at the Vicar Lane end of Harrison Street behind the Odeon to keep an estimated eight thousand fans back. The road at the back of the cinema was blocked off, with police dogs, police cars, police on foot and police on horses. Naturally, all police leave was cancelled, with one hundred and twenty officers on duty. Shops in the vicinity boarded up their display windows. Eight ambulances were on standby.

At 3.15pm, as the group's car approached the venue, George filmed the crowd with his cine camera. Once inside, Ringo jammed on Peter Jay's drum kit and 14-year-olds Sharon Sanderson and Geraldine Milles, who had baked a giant cake with drawings of the group in icing, got the chance to meet the group. Their reward for their endeavours was a kiss from each Beatle. The cake was donated to a local children's hospital. A waiter from a nearby Chinese restaurant arrived with a menu, announcing, 'Hiya fellas, I'm from Liverpool as well.' They chose English dishes. The group were also photographed reading the *Sunday Mirror*, featuring the headline, 'The Dynamic Sunday Newspaper'. The 5.15pm show went off with the usual frantic scenes – but five minutes from the end of the 7.45pm performance a bomb hoax was phoned in. Three fire engines raced to the cinema while more than 2,500 fans were leaving. Ten or so female fans needed to be treated for exhaustion. A segment of one of the two shows was recorded for a forthcoming court case involving the Performing Right Society.

MONDAY **4 NOVEMBER**

An EMI spokesman told *Record Retailer*, 'This is completely unprecedented. Normally we are extremely busy at this time of year, just before Christmas. But this year we have this phenomenal demand as well... *Twist And Shout* has sold three hundred thousand, *Please Please Me* LP two hundred and fifty thousand'. The group appeared on the front cover of the new issue of *Mirabelle* and featured Paul in the last of its four-part series, 'This Is Our Life'.

At 8am, the group flew from Leeds' Yeadon Airport on board a BKS Air Transport flight (BK401) to London. Fans began assembling outside the stage-door entrance of the Prince of Wales Theatre in London's Whitcomb Street in anticipation, where the group were performing at the evening's 33rd annual Royal Command Performance. When the group arrived around 10am, some forty fans spotted them and ran down Coventry Street after them. The group took their turn to rehearse and then adjourned to the Mapleton Hotel next door for some lunch. Sue Delfont, who was with her younger sister Jenny, recalled, 'We were lucky enough to watch them rehearse. I remember sitting in the stalls with only a few technicians and the producer there as we sat and listened... After they finished we were taken to the hotel next door through a specially constructed covered way behind the theatre where we met the four of them

as they sat eating.' During their rehearsal, fellow performer Marlene Dietrich was seen twisting in the aisles. She later told a journalist, 'It was a joy to be with those youngsters. I adore the Beatles.' Bob Adams, manager of Sound City music shop, rushed to the theatre to bring George a replacement Gretsch Country Gentleman guitar after his own began playing up.

Her Majesty Queen Elizabeth, the Queen Mother, Princess Margaret and Lord Snowdon arrived for the performance; as they stepped out of their royal limousines they were greeted by shouts of 'We Want The Beatles!' Undoubtedly the stars of the night, the Beatles appeared seventh on an eclectic entertainment bill of nineteen acts. The group performed 'From Me To You', 'She Loves You', 'Till There Was You' and 'Twist And Shout'. Before performing 'Twist And Shout', John made a request to the audience – creating a stir in the next day's morning papers. 'For our last number I'd like to ask your help. The people in the cheaper seats clap your hands, and the rest of you, if you'd just rattle your jewellery. We'd like to sing a song called 'Twist And Shout'.' The Queen Mother reportedly tapped her feet during the song, leading to the royal comment, 'It is one of the best shows I've seen. The Beatles are most intriguing!' Ringo later told *Mirabelle*'s Dawn James that after asking John where their next date was, in reply to 'Slough', she said, 'That's near us'. Princess Margaret followed with 'Slough Slough quick quick Slough'.

Outside fans gathered by the stage door. The group moved to the Mapleton's. Afterwards, they returned to the theatre, where they were smuggled out by a side door into a taxi at 1.20am and driven to the Hotel President to spend the night. Aspinall described the evening as 'more of a theatrical family affair. There was not such a tense atmosphere and the rest of the cast were very helpful. The reception last night was better than expected'.

The Times headed its article on the show 'The Beatles On Parade'. Referring to the performances by Charlie Drake, Harry Secombe and Tommy Steele, the writer asked what 'connexion any of these pleasures has with the youthfully private world in which the Beatles exercise the combination of musical naivety with electronic sophistication which suits their engaging, irreverent cheerfulness and the loudest common chords since the end of *Ein Heldenleben*'. The Old Stager in *The Sphere* felt the group stole the show, commenting incomprehensibly that they 'wheeled their droning flight, only the moping owl (or square) complained that they molested the ancient solitary reign of yesterday's stars'.

❝ I joined the Talk of the Town in Leicester Square in February 1963 as a dancer at the age of 16. We were known as the Billy Petch Dancers. It was during that year that I, along with several other of the dancers, was asked to perform at the London Palladium for the Royal Variety Performance. During rehearsals all the artists sat in the auditorium awaiting their turn, so if we were sitting close to someone we'd chat with them, but we were all there to work. We met most of the other artists, including the Beatles, who I was already a fan of, but we were in a professional work situation so I wasn't there as a fan.

It was a wonderful time to be working and living in the heart of London. Everything seemed so alive. Vegetarians were making the headlines with the launching of a specialist restaurant named Cranks, there were many more to follow. Fashion was at a very 'expressive' time, Carnaby Street, along with Mary Quant and Biba, with all the striking makeup (false eyelashes were a big thing), all that went to make the image with the clothes. And not forgetting the inspirational hairdresser Vidal Sassoon, with his trendsetting salon in Bond Street. I was one of his clients for several years. So, if you wanted 'The Look', that was where you acquired it. And Bond Street had the most wonderful shops, my favourite for shoes. Working in the theatre demands that you always look your best, so clothes, hair and makeup were very important.

Dancers are not very well paid and often have more than one job. So, after I had finished the show at the Talk of the Town at about 10.45pm in the evening, I and four or five of the other girls would make our way across town to the Savoy Hotel to dance in the midnight cabaret. There, we were the Irving Davies Dancers. I remember one evening in particular while on my way up to the dressing room when Danny Kaye stepped into the lift. He was visiting London and staying at the Savoy at that time. As time passed on I expanded my career into fashion modelling on the catwalk, also working with cosmetic companies at Bourne and Hollingsworth and then Harvey Nichols. ❞

GWEN NICHOL, PROFESSIONAL DANCER, NORTHAMPTON, NORTHAMPTONSHIRE

TUESDAY 5 NOVEMBER

For Beatles fans in Slough the day began at 9.15am. Pat Turner and Brenda Koning began sitting on the cold ground with flasks of tea and sandwiches outside the Adelphi; they were wearing men's socks and mackintoshes to keep warm, but later in the day got soaked by the rain. Turner, who worked at ICI Paints and Horlicks employee Koning were both interviewed by an ITN film crew. Jennifer Gilder, Monica Mollinger, Pauline Burnett and Patricia Druce, who had taken they day off from their jobs at a Maidenhead radio firm, were also interviewed. Their foreman told them, 'It's your jobs or the Beatles.' They chose the Beatles.

Following breakfast, the group met with their accountants. They spent the rest of the morning in the back of a car driving around London with an Associated-Rediffusion TV crew filming them for a segment included in the following Thursday's *This Week* broadcast. Ringo and George were interviewed first, followed by John and Paul, because they couldn't all fit in the back of the car. George was seen reading the *Daily Sketch* with the front-page headline 'Beatles Siege'. The usually staid *Daily Telegraph* headlined its coverage with 'Beatle Mania At Royal Variety Show'.

'Operation Beatle' swung into effect several hours before the concerts. Half of the eighty officers on duty were Special Constabulary, with some drafted in from High Wycombe. At 2.30pm, fans mobbed a Black Maria outside the Adelphi, thinking the Beatles were inside. A band of girls from Warren Field and Slough High School marched down the High Street with a 15-foot Beatle banner. Madelynne Harridge made the banner from an old sheet pinched from her home in Iver Heath, saying, 'Mother won't mind. She's a Beatles fan too!' As they marched, they sang, 'Unward loyal Beatle fans, marching to the show, with the Beatles banner going on before. George and Paul and Ringo, John the leader too, Twisting, shouting, screaming, marching to the show' to the tune of 'Onward Christian Soldiers'.

Brian Epstein flew Pan Am from London Airport to New York with Billy J. Kramer to meet with executives from Capitol Records as well as Ed Sullivan. In his possession was a stack of newspaper cuttings, including the *Daily Mirror* front page headline 'Beatlemania As Princess Arrives', which described the previous night's Royal Variety Performance. Epstein and Kramer stayed at the Regency Hotel on Park Avenue, where laundry staff lost a pair of gold cufflinks Clive Epstein had recently given his brother.

The Beatles set off for the evening's shows, arriving at 4.25pm. Some one hundred and fifty girls, lined up along the A4 Bath Road, rushed the car. They were stopped by the police who blocked the way as the group ran in through the front entrance. Attendant police watched George and Ringo jam with a couple of the Jaywalkers. During the first show, which began at 6.30pm, all kinds of items rained down on the stage – balls of paper, posies and even a toilet roll, which got caught in Paul's bass guitar. At about 8.20pm, as the first house left, leather jacketed youths who were unable to get in began throwing fireworks – bangers landed in the midst of the crowd. Police stamped them out as fast as they could; many guarded the garage next door, which had eighteen thousand gallons of petrol stored underground. Several girls lost their shoes as the bangers exploded amongst them. In between shows, three large boxes of autograph books awaited the group, which they signed to raise money for the 'Slough Freedom From Hunger' campaign, launched that day by Eton and Slough Labour Member of Parliament, Fenner Brockway. They formed a chain to sign the books and managed to get through two of the three boxes – no doubt with the help of the by-now-proficient forgers Neil Aspinall and Mal Evans. During the second show, which began at 8.45pm, two girls sprinted down the aisle and tried to climb onstage but were dragged back by attendants.

Less than thirty seconds after the final curtain fell, the group's Austin Princess raced down the Bath Road through the four hundred-strong crowd. Jaguar police cars acted as a convoy, headlights blazing and sirens wailing. Chief Superintendent Laurence Harman later described the evening, 'It was nice to see the young people enjoying themselves. I saw some of the girls fainting in the audience now and then. I'm not sure whether that was caused by mass hysteria or just by Beatlemania.'

❝ My first date with my boyfriend, who later became my husband, was in June 1963. We went to see *Peyton Place* at the Adelphi in our hometown of Slough. I left school a month later and started work as a junior shorthand typist at Giddy and Giddy, a local estate agents in the centre of town. I'd done typing and shorthand at school, and also a secretarial course at college. I was a Beatles fan, and my boyfriend was a Rolling Stones fan. We managed to get tickets for the Beatles show in November, I don't think we queued – we both lived near the box office, so would have been able to get there quickly as soon as we heard they were coming. They were good seats, in the fifth row, but the screaming was unbelievable. You couldn't hear a word they were singing or a note they were playing, it was that bad. My boyfriend said, 'Well, you can come with me next week to see the Rolling Stones!' perhaps suggesting we would be able to hear them better. That was at the Carlton on the High Street. We later saw them regularly at the Ricky Tick club in Windsor. The Carlton would have these events on during the week, but on Sunday afternoons, they would have live groups on and dancing. That was our regular thing, and when it finished around six o'clock, we would then head down to the Adelphi. There was no alcohol at either venue, just Coke and Fanta, but it didn't stop us having a great time. [It] was a beautiful building in its heyday. It was really an old-fashioned picture house which doubled as a concert hall. The dancing took place in another part of the building. I haven't been back for a long time, but I know it was flattened inside to make a bingo hall, and is still standing. ❞

NORMA ZACHARCZUK, DAIRY CO-ORDINATOR, SLOUGH, BERKSHIRE

WEDNESDAY 6 NOVEMBER

The *Daily Mirror* headlined an editorial 'Yeah! Yeah! Yeah!' The article read: 'You have to be a real sour square not to love the nutty, noisy, happy, handsome Beatles. If they don't sweep your blues away – brother, you're a lost cause. If they don't put a beat in your feet – sister, you're not living. How refreshing to see these rumbustious young Beatles take a middle-aged Royal Variety Performance audience by the scruff of their necks and have them beatling like teenagers. Fact is that Beatle People are everywhere: From Wapping to Windsor. Aged 7 to 70. And it's plain to see why these four energetic, cheeky lads from Liverpool go down so big. They're young, new. They're high-spirited, cheerful. What a change from the self-pitying moaners crooning their love-lorn tunes from the tortured shallows of lukewarm hearts. The Beatles are whacky. They wear their hair like a mop – but it's WASHED, it's super-clean. So is their fresh young act. Good luck, Beatles!'

Less enthusiastic was Robert Pitman, writing in his *Daily Express* 'In My Opinion' column, 'The middle-aged people who are trying so hard to appreciate the Beatles are making idiots of themselves. For the truth (if we face it honestly) is that these four ordinary young men produce an extraordinarily unpleasant noise... In my opinion the Beatle influence on schoolboys is also sad. No longer does their hope of a fortune lie in finding a rare issue in a packet of assorted foreign stamps. Even in prep schools they are busily buying electric guitars and drums instead. With thousands of rival groups strumming madly, their chance of success is no higher than with the stamps. And guitars cost so much more.' No doubt the news that advance orders of 'I Want To Hold Your Hand' had reached seven hundred thousand and *With The Beatles* two hundred and sixty-five thousand sent him into an apoplectic fit.

The group headed north for two performances at the ABC Northampton at 6.30pm and 8.45pm. They drove straight to the Campbell Square Police Station on Upper Mounts. With heavy rain falling, they reluctantly got out of their car. PC Norman Edmunds asked for John's autograph, who started by writing down prisoner number 0943417. They were driven to the cinema in the back of a Black Maria, escorted by PC Ted Dawkins. Dawkins had banned his 14-year-old daughter Mary from going to the show and tried to placate her by getting the group's autographs. The heavy rain kept fans without tickets away when the group arrived.

Just before the second show started, the previous Sunday's *Ken Dodd Show* was repeated on the Light Programme. During their performances, screaming drowned the group out as per usual. The noise was too much for five children who had to be treated by nurses for shock. After the second concert, as the National Anthem was still being played, a decoy vehicle drove away from the venue's Lower Mounts exit, while the group escaped in a car waiting in St Michael's Road, driving back to Campbell Square. Fans, hoping to catch a glimpse of their idols, waited in Abington Square and at two exits from the ABC car park. Teens headed to the Hind Hotel, in the mistaken belief that the group were staying there overnight, even though it was north-east of Northampton – and the group were already on the M1 heading back to London.

❛ My love of the Beatles started in 1962 when classmate Michael Johnson brought in a portable record player to school and played 'Love Me Do'. Immediately it struck me as something quite different and exciting, so much so that Michael joined the fan club and became one of the first members! (Amongst our friends also amazed that day was a certain Reg Dwight – better known now as Elton John!) Unfortunately, due to my parents moving house, I had to change schools to Welwyn Garden City, but I took my love of the Beatles with me. I can remember my room with pictures over every surface and a life-size picture of John Lennon above my bed! He was always my favourite as he seemed more adult than the others. I was too young to really understand the power of raw sex appeal.

I heard they were playing in Northampton, so I organised a coach trip to see them there and sold the tickets to my new school friends – I think it enhanced my popularity briefly. I can remember chiefly the horrendous noise, such screaming. I'm sure by today's standards it would be very tame but at the time it was tremendously exciting to see John do 'Twist and Shout' and 'Money' – and I use the words 'see' as no one could hear a thing! I can remember the terrific noise and being there to see them. I worked out that by putting my fingers half into my ears, I could cut out the worst of the screams and still hear them singing. I'm so glad I went to see them and managed a Christmas Special at the Finsbury Park Astoria, too. They were very special. Luckily, I am still friends with my friends from the first school. And I am still a Beatles fan. ❜

JANET EDROFF, SPECIAL NEEDS TEACHER, STEVENAGE, HERTFORDSHIRE

THURSDAY 7 NOVEMBER

At 8.30am, retailers were informed that the group's new single, 'I Want To Hold Your Hand', would go on sale on 29 November. By 3.30pm, over half a million copies had been ordered. Photos of the group at the Royal Variety Show, including one with Her Royal Highness Princess Margaret, graced the front cover of the week's *Disc*. The paper announced that *Thank Your Lucky Stars* would feature a special Merseybeat edition on 21 December. 'She Loves You' stayed at number 3, while *The Beatles (No. 1)* EP debuted at number 24. In the *NRM* chart, 'She Loves You' stayed at number 2 while *The Beatles (No. 1)* debuted at number 10 in the EP chart. The paper reported that *With The Beatles* had the biggest advance order for an LP in history. Peter Jones wrote a track-by-track review of the record.

Just after midday, the group arrived at Dublin Airport on a specially chartered Aer Lingus Viscount (flight EI 155) from London Airport. They were scheduled to play two concerts at 6.30pm and 9pm at the Adelphi, followed by a further two shows in Belfast, a trip sponsored by the Guinness brewery. There had been twenty thousand requests for the 2,304 tickets on sale.

As they arrived at the airport, they were welcomed by some four hundred fans, despite cold and damp weather. Paul Russell of Starlite Artistes greeted them on the tarmac. Airport and regular police smuggled them through a back door and into the VIP lounge. They met Frank Hall, who interviewed them for Radio Telefis Éireann's *In Town* TV show. After the interview, they were driven by Russell in his white Chrysler Saratoga to the Gresham Hotel for lunch with the Adelphi's manager, Harry Lush. They were interviewed a second time, this time by Russell, for RTÉ's TV show *The Showband Show*. Ringo and John found time to sneak out to a nearby pub with Kestrels Roger Greenaway and Geoff Williams for a Guinness.

At around 4pm, the group were driven to the Adelphi on Middle Abbey Street, where they were escorted into its Princes Street entrance. Ushered upstairs to the cinema's boardroom, they immediately met press and photographers. Paul told one reporter that he no longer owned a car because, 'Thanks to Mr Marples' he'd been 'had-up three times for speeding.' Another reporter asked how long their success would last. Paul replied, 'It could end tomorrow, but I hope it won't.' Crowds began gathering outside at around 5.30pm with the Gardai keeping a vigilant watch on both sides of the street. A lone figure, with a red nose and glasses standing on a little wooden box outside the *Evening Press* office talking about Salvation, went largely ignored.

Crowds emerging from the first show clashed with thousands waiting for the second. The Gardai formed cordons to clear the street. Girls began screaming and shouting to be pulled to safety. Ambulances rushed nearly a dozen people to Jervis Street Hospital and many more were treated on the spot. Two plate-glass windows gave way under the pressure of fans. At 9.10pm, the group's Tuesday interview aired on ITV – an eleven-minute segment for *This Week*.

At the end of the second show, 'Rescue Beatles Operation' swung into action. The group jumped into an *Evening Herald* van with Mr Jack Flanagan behind the wheel – Flanagan had been parked outside for half an hour. Ron King signalled for him to start the engine and he drove down Princes Street to the back entrance of the Gresham. Reporter Liam Kelly and photographer Jack Murphy drove along with them. The group ran inside, through the kitchen into the Aberdeen Hall, and took the lifts up to their rooms.

The rioting continued after the second show. Fifty Gardai tried to move the crowd out of Middle Abbey Street and into O'Connell Street. An unruly section resisted and tried to overturn parked cars. Batons were drawn and more than a dozen young men were hauled off in squad cars and a Black Maria. A number of girls were injured in the crush and one man fractured a leg as the St John Ambulance Brigade ran a shuttle service to the hospital. The police chief commented, 'It was all right until the mania degenerated into barbarism.'

Once things quietened down, the group walked down Cavendish Row to Groome's Hotel for a pint or two. Several members of the cast of the musical *Carrie*, in the middle of its run at the Gate Theatre opposite the Groome's, were enjoying a post-show drink. George asked cast member Rebecca Wilkinson whether she would like to dance. *Carrie*'s author Wesley Burrowes recalled her telling George 'to shag off. Afterwards, when she realised who it was and what she had just turned down, she was very mortified.'

❛ By the time the autumn tour started, 'Beatlemania' was in full swing. Big crowds would be waiting at the theatre in each town as our tour coach arrived and each day, we would see the bizarre sights of maybe a hundred police officers sitting in the empty theatre before going out to control the show crowd, with us and 'the boys' hanging around on the stage, jamming a little. It was at these sessions I realised how good a drummer Paul was. He was playing many of the cross rhythms that were unheard of then. I got on well with Ringo – being a fellow drummer. George seemed very much the youngster of the group and John already started to seem more arty and withdrawn, but we all got on well together and would often go back after the show to their hotel and play cards and talk until late into the night. During our act they would always stand in the wings and take the mickey out of our bows at the end of our act which I always counted in. One, two, three, BOW! I particularly remember the trip to Ireland. In Dublin, O'Connell Street turned into a riot zone with cars being overturned and burned – we loved that!

On returning to London, we experienced first-hand the amazing reception the 'boys' received. Brian Epstein stage managed these events so well, letting the fans know exactly when the 'boys' would be flying in – the result was thousands of fans screaming from the observation roofs of London Airport as we stepped from the aircraft onto the steps and, bearing in mind at this stage all the Jaywalkers had the Beatle look – the hair, the leather coats and boots, the hysteria that welled up was incredible, reaching a crescendo as the 'Fab Four' themselves appeared – a moment never to be forgotten! The group were particularly impressed with our Cuban-heeled boots and vowed that when they made some money they would go down to London and buy some. We had purchased the boots from Anello and Davide's on the Charing Cross Road, a stone's throw from London's 'Tin Pan Alley' in Denmark Street.

We were with them at Stockton when it was announced that President Kennedy had been shot. It was such a shock. I remember everybody running around saying, 'Are we going to have to cancel the show?' In the end they decided to do the show, because if they didn't, there would have been a riot. It was only when we got to Bournemouth and a CBS film crew from America turned up that we started to suspect we were witnessing a bigger thing than had ever happened before and might reach further than the British Isles. America in those days had its own completely separate and distinct 'pop' scene.

It all kind of runs into one. I can't believe we did that tour with them, and I didn't keep a programme or get their autographs. I have nothing. We scored a big success on the autumn tour, closing the first half. We were a good contrast to the Beatles in the second half with our different sax lead line-up, light up drums and even the comedy routines – we'd got on well with the 'boys' and so we were gutted when our archrivals Sounds Incorporated were booked for the Beatles London Christmas show, which followed the tour. Although they were much better musicians than us, we had a vastly better show and big fan following. We were even more upset when they got the Beatles first American tour including the classic Shea Stadium gig. It was years later that I found out that our then agent Ossie Newman had asked for an extra £200 a week for us and lost the Christmas show and probably the American tour because of this – something I've never forgiven him for. We were completely unaware of the increase in our price. We'd have done it for nothing to be part of what now is pop history. **⁊**

PETER JAY, SHOWMAN, GREAT YARMOUTH, NORFOLK

FRIDAY **8 NOVEMBER**

As dawn broke, the damage caused around the Adelphi became painfully apparent. Cars near the cinema had dented roofs and bodywork and windshields smashed. A traffic bollard at the corner of O'Connell Street and Lower Abbey Street had been uprooted. A Garda sergeant, who lost his cap to a flying object, said, 'I have seen everything now. This is really mad. What can have got into them?'

At 6.30am, teens Valerie Harvey (who was wearing a special Beatle sweater), Agnes Maguire, Maria McCann and Eileen Hawkins arrived at the stage door of the Ritz in Belfast. McCann told the *Belfast Telegraph*, 'We can't wait to start screaming.' Hawkins complained, 'Everyone has been telling us lies. We've been sent from hotels to railway stations and all round the place by the police.' They were soon joined by John Logue, who said he'd been 'dashing around all the hotels.' Fans standing in line with the latest editions of the *NME* and *Melody Maker* saw *The Beatles' Hits* EP enter the *NME* chart at number 30 and 'She Loves You' staying at number 2 for a second week. In *Melody Maker*, 'She Loves You' climbed one place to number 2. *The Beatles (No. 1)* EP entered at number 40, *The Beatles' Hits* and *Twist And Shout* both climbed to numbers 23 and 32, respectively. The *NME* revealed that the group had made history with advance orders of over a quarter of a million for their new album, seven hundred thousand for their new single and sales of *Please Please Me* had passed two hundred and sixty-five thousand.

The group left the Gresham at 11.45am in atypical November weather – sunny intervals and 48 degrees. They drove the 103 miles from Dublin to Belfast on the Dundalk to Newry road, stopping at the border town of Killeen. Customs officers asked whether they had anything to declare – one asked Paul for his autograph, saying, 'Your fame spreads, you know.' Meeting at a pre-arranged location just inside the border, they filmed an interview with Ulster TV's Jimmy Robinson for the evening's *Ulster News*. At the beginning of the one-minute interview, George tried to push John into the road as a white van passed by. They signed some autographs before they continued on their way, escorted by members of the RUC. They arrived in Belfast at 2pm and headed to Broadcasting House on Ormeau Avenue. An hour later, they recorded an interview in Studio 8 with Sally Ogle for the evening's *Six Ten* programme. Afterwards, they made their way to the Ritz in a police motorcade, arriving just before 4pm; they entered through the front entrance with a major police presence forcing a passageway through the crowd.

Once inside, they met their 17-year-old local fan-club secretary Audrey Gowar, who presented them with shillelaghs and then posed for pictures at a press call in the auditorium before heading to their dressing room. She managed to plant a kiss on Paul's left cheek. Three enterprising male fans asked whether they could bake a cake and bring it down to the cinema, just in case the group got hungry

- which they obviously had, because the four starving Beatles were given Kit-Kats by *News Letter* reporter Kay Kennedy. Their chauffeur, Dubliner John Brennan, a taxi driver by day, went to the pictures. 'I didn't expect to be called back because we thought after the Dublin riot in which cars were overturned, that the car would be wrecked.' Minutes before the 6.30pm show, the group's performance of 'She Loves You' on 4 October's *Ready, Steady, Go!* was repeated and the *Ulster News* interview aired.

During the first show, several teenagers stripped off before policewomen intervened, and one girl in knee-high boots climbed onstage and threw her arms around Paul. Seventeen-year-old Joan Strain was the first casualty carried into the foyer. 'I was swept away,' she explained. Others were treated in the foyer and more than a dozen were taken to hospital by ambulance. Outside, a section of the crowd broke through a barrier, injuring several people. Four were taken into the cinema for treatment by the St John Ambulance Brigade.

Between the end of the first show and the start of the 8.45pm performance, the group ate chicken and salad, blissfully unaware of the mayhem outside. The crowd numbered around six thousand in total, as fans from the first show left and those coming to see the second show arrived, along with those without tickets hanging around. Downtown traffic was disrupted for hours. After the second show, the group were escorted through the front door flanked by two groups of policemen. Girls lying on stretchers outside the cinema sat up and shouted, 'I love you,' while the group got into their limo. They were taken on the five-minute drive to the Grand Central. In an exercise in futility, several fans ran after the car only to see it disappear into the night. At the hotel, traffic was brought to a standstill. Crowds were still there well after midnight. Mrs W. Simpson, the 62-year-old grandmother who stood in line to buy tickets on 12 October, said, 'I've always thought they were great, just fine.'

❛ I was a student at Royal Belfast Academical Institution, where I was a member of the school camera club. It was a remarkable year. From the American dominated charts came this wave of British groups. The Beatles lead from the front and to my 16-year-old self, there was only one group. Brought up with a diet of Elvis, Brenda Lee, the Everly Brothers, Roy Orbison, Bobby Vee and the Drifters, their fresh raw sound was what all '60s teenagers wanted to hear. I had been given a 35mm camera for my birthday and by the time the Beatles came to Belfast I had my own darkroom in the attic of my house and I was ready to go. I had one roll of film – thirty-six shots – which looking back was rather naive.

I kept a diary in those days and two entries from that time read – 'Sat 12 October 1963. Got up at 3am and cycled down to the Ritz arriving at 3.45am. Waited there with about twenty others while the queue got bigger and bigger. Chris came at 6.30 and I told him and the others I had been there since 2am! A long and tiring wait before the box office opened at 10am. Got autographs of two of the Bachelors who had been playing the night before. Also Cilla Black walked past. Got second row seats and was quite pleased with this.'

Diary entry – 'Friday 8 November 1963. Very excited about the Beatles show. High fever in school. In evening took photos of them on TV. Went down early and took photos of the mass of people outside from the first show and those going to the second! Bunked queue and met Chris and the rest inside. Took a few photos of the early groups and kept twenty shots for the Beatles. When they came on there was a near riot inside. Stood on the arms of the chair while Chris held on to my legs. Beatles were absolutely fabulous and I think I got some great photos. Can't wait to get them developed and printed and bring them to the Inst. Dance tomorrow.'

By the time the Beatles came onstage this had been cut in half to around eighteen shots left. Still I knew I had got something. I remember the excitement of processing the film and doing the contact sheet – and then the first prints. The next night I went to my school dance with a pouch of prints from the night before. The talk all night was about the Beatles show and to be there with these original prints was a great buzz. All night I took orders from friends and a couple of girls wanted sets so they could sell them for me at their schools. Over the next four weeks I printed some one thousand prints and did almost no school work. I always wanted to become a professional photographer but when I left school I went to college in Manchester and then into the family clothing business. That lasted nine years before I walked out and started my own photography business. I have been a professional photographer for the past forty years and I always think back to my first commercial venture in November 1963. Needless to say, I failed my mock O-levels but managed to get my act together for the real thing the following June. ❞

CHRISTOPHER HILL, PHOTOGRAPHER, BELFAST, NORTHERN IRELAND

SATURDAY 9 NOVEMBER

The clean-up of central Belfast and the Ritz began in earnest first thing. Cinema projectionist Danny Devlin recalled the stage being awash in Jelly Babies. 'If they hadn't been dirty, I would have eaten them myself.'

'Nearly all the teenage girls suffer from it... Beatlemania, a sickness which quickens the pulse, tests the larynx, and makes the heart pound whenever the Beatles play their rhythm-and-blues music,' wrote David Reece in the *Belfast Telegraph*. 'The mob symptoms: girls queue all day (and night) for tickets to see them – some faint by the kerbside – and when they get inside the hall they do what apparently comes naturally – squeal, shout and stamp their feet. Should the girls reach the advanced stage, they find themselves trying to rush the stage to hug their pin-up guitar player. But why don't the boy pop fans act similarly and scream over girl singers? I have been moving in pop music circles in search of an explanation.'

At 6am, fans began waiting outside the Granada in East Ham for the evening's two shows at 6.45pm and 9pm. The group slept late and had to make a mad dash for Aldergrove Airport to catch their plane back to London. Detectives calling at the hotel found them fast asleep. After a quick breakfast, they slipped out of the back door, where some thirty fans were waiting. They made the 12-mile journey to the airport driving along back roads and ran to the plane, which was waiting for them on the runway. The flight back to London was a bumpy one. Rain and clouds greeting them on their return – along with screaming fans, again waiting on the airport's roof gardens. Other travellers were held back by a cordon of policemen as the group made their way through the main concourse, down an escalator and into their waiting Austin Princess. Paul commented, 'All we want to do now is put our feet up and have a sleep.' There was not much chance of that.

The group arrived at the Granada at 3.50pm; a police motorbike came out of Campbell Avenue, followed by their limousine. Leave for about a hundred men of K Division Metropolitan Police had been cancelled. An estimated six thousand fans waited outside the cinema. The crowd surged forward and girls screamed as the group jumped out of the car and rushed through the stage door. At 5.15pm John Perdoni, whose cafe was across the road from the Granada, took the group three cheese sandwiches and three cups of tea – one without sugar. He also took his two children to meet them. Some fans brought a cake with 'Congratulations, Ringo, Paul, John, George' on it. The cake cost them £2.

At 9pm, as the second show was starting, Perdoni took them a supper of steak, chips, tomatoes and mushrooms for George and Ringo and egg salad for John and Paul, as well as more cups of tea. He slipped in through the front door, unnoticed by all – but when he returned later to collect the dirty dishes and cutlery he was mobbed and had to be rescued by police. In the following days, he was asked by fans whether he would sell them a knife or fork used by the group. He said, 'I'm going to hold a raffle, charging 6d a ticket, with the proceeds going to the spastics and the Toy for a Child Christmas fund.' The telephone backstage rang. It was *Daily Mirror* photographer Monte Fresco, inviting the group to washing-machine tycoon John Bloom's 32nd birthday party later that night.

A crowd of more than five thousand were waiting outside as the first house left. By 10pm, more than seven hundred fans had gathered in St John's Road to see the group leave. Police cordoned off the area and closed Campbell Avenue completely to pedestrians and traffic. At 11.08pm the crowd surged forward as the group got into their car. With its engine running, they made a break for it, but Ringo tripped and fell flat on his face. The others got out of the car, picked him up and threw him in as it sped off to London and to the party in Aldford House, Park Lane. Twenty minutes later, a thousand girls still waited in Barking Road outside the cinema.

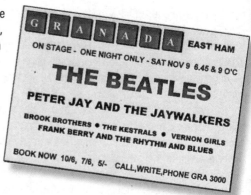

When the Beatles arrived at Bloom's flat, the 68-year-old porter Arthur Dyer refused to let them in, unaware of who they were. 'I don't care a bugger who you are, you're not coming in dressed like that.' Fresco, leaving the party, encountered the scene and persuaded him to change his mind. Once inside, they mingled with around a hundred and fifty guests, including singers Adam Faith and Shirley Bassey and comedian Max Bygraves. Mrs Lou Levey took the opportunity to dance with Ringo. (The group's tax adviser Walter Strach suggested that investing in Bloom's company wasn't a good idea. The following year Bloom filed for bankruptcy.)

> ❛ The ninth of November 1963 was a big day for Beatles fans in East Ham as they were coming to play at the Granada. Tickets went in a flash when they'd gone on sale weeks before. They had played there earlier in March of that year, but then they had been down the bill. At that time, they'd only released a couple of singles, but by November 'Beatlemania' was well and truly with us. Everyone was talking about it. Even mums and dads and grandparents! Close to the Granada was a Church Army hall where a jumble sale was being held. A huge banner outside proclaimed, 'There is no truth that the Beatles are appearing here today but everyone else is!' Not everyone in East Ham was as delighted, however. The Beatles weren't at all popular with a group of local rockers who were threatening to disrupt the show with a bomb scare and a call to the Fire Brigade, but thankfully that didn't happen and the show went on. There would have been a riot if it hadn't. I don't remember much about the rest of performers on the bill but they must have been very disillusioned as right
>
>
>
> from the start of the evening the audience was shouting for the Beatles. Then at last the curtain went up again and there they were. The four young mopheads from Liverpool that everyone had come to see. The noise was deafening. Not from the group, but from the girls screaming! I could just about hear their opening number – 'I Saw Her Standing There'. And that was the way it continued, but it didn't matter. It was just so great to be there and be a part of it. All too soon it came to an end and 'Twist And Shout' signalled the finish of their performance. It had been wonderful. An exciting evening that I'm sure most of us there have never forgotten. ❜
>
> **BARRIE POWELL, FINANCE DEPARTMENT OF THE COUNTY BOROUGH OF WEST HAM, ROMFORD, ESSEX**

SUNDAY 10 NOVEMBER

Fans were gathering at the Birmingham Hippodrome. The Beatles' car broke down on its way north on the M1; the RAC were called in and towed the vehicle to a nearby garage. The group had to wait awhile and decided to eat at the Newport Pagnell service area while the car was being repaired. Afterwards, they were driven to Birmingham Police headquarters in Steelhouse Lane, arriving an hour late. They had a nice cup of tea with the police officers and signed autographs, then borrowed police helmets and uniform raincoats and drove to the theatre in a Black Maria, with four constables as company and accompanied by decoy police cars. George said later, 'They put us in the Black Maria and told us to put helmets on. We didn't really need them, but it was great fun. The police seemed to enjoy it as much as we did.' John chatted briefly with PC Gordon Russell, whose helmet he had purloined.

John was not aware that his son was being christened that day at Hoylake Parish Church in Trinity Road, Hoylake, Cheshire. Unlike John, twenty or so fans heard about it and sat in the back of the church during the ceremony. They were said to be 'very quiet'. Cynthia's brother and his wife, her mother and her mother's best friend Frances Reeves witnessed the Reverend Ifor Davies conduct the ceremony. Anticipating a large crowd, Hoylake police had sent two police constables and a duty sergeant to Trinity Road at 4pm.

Between the 5.30pm and 8pm shows, *The Royal Variety Performance* was broadcast on ATV and the Light Programme, at 7.35pm. The man delivering the group's dinner had to be escorted into the building by twenty policemen. During the second show, both Paul and Ringo were hit by missiles thrown from the audience. Theatre orchestra musicians, electricians and members of a local Territorial Army unit helped stewards keep order. At the end of the second show, the group left during the National Anthem, by which time only about two hundred fans remained at the stage door. A number of girls were treated for hysteria and one youth put his foot through the roof of a nearby building.

❝ I kept a diary in 1963 which I still have, and there were many entries which mentioned the Beatles. I saw them three times that year. Firstly at the Town Hall with Roy Orbison, secondly at the Ritz in King's Heath, and lastly at the Hippodrome.

Tuesday 4 June – 'Saw the Beatles at the Town Hall, absolutely great, and all the rest, love them all.' It was the Roy Orbison show. I don't know where I got the tickets from. Probably my sister got them.

Friday 5 July – 'Went to Ritz saw Beatles, lovely. Met a boy from the platters also Redcaps (Smashing)'; the platters was some sort of industrial thing where he used to deliver stuff, and I used to see him when I was walking past the delivery area. He was at the show as well. We danced before the Redcaps and the Beatles came on. That was the evening I met Dave, from the Redcaps, who I went out with for a while. He broke my heart that evening because he told me that John Lennon was married! I did love John for his nonconformist attitude, but Paul was so gorgeous looking, so I was torn between the two. My friend Sue and I met in Birmingham and when we were waiting for a bus to go to the show, this girl was there. We said we were going to see the Beatles at the Ritz, and she said, 'Oh, are you a member?' and we said, 'No?' She said we wouldn't get in unless we were members or with someone who could sign us in. So, she suggested as she and her friend were members, that if we waited in the queue, she'd go home and get her card, and get ready, and she would sign us in, so that is what we did. We got in because of the girl we met at the bus stop! This was the evening that I held onto Paul's shoe. We went in, and it was a dance, but most people there were intent on seeing the Beatles, that's why we were all there. I sat on the stage on the left-hand side, it was just a put-up job, just a foot or so higher than the dance floor. When the Beatles came on, Paul was standing right in front of me. I couldn't believe my luck! It was a lovely show and I reached out to touch Paul's foot, which he was tapping away as he did, and I just held it, and he looked at me, and he was smiling at me, and John was looking at him and smiling. I just kept holding his foot, I just loved it, it was lovely, such a thrill.

Sunday 10 November – I just put 'The Beatles!' It was the show at the Hippodrome in Birmingham. It is a theatre in the middle of town, which also shows pantomimes and ballet. It's a big theatre. I can't remember how we got the tickets. I know we didn't camp out. I went with my friend Susan who lived next door to me. We used to go everywhere together and were Beatle fanatics. We just loved them. I was Susan Spears at that time, and she was Susan Spooner, and my mum used to call us 'Sis and Sas' because our initials were the same. Everyone called us that. That night we were in the balcony, and they seemed so far away. When we saw them at the Ritz, they were mine, it was like they belonged to me. I could sit on the stage, but when they were at the Hippodrome, they were big stars by then, and it wasn't as intimate. Sue and I just wanted to listen to them, we were looking at each other and saying 'Why don't they be quiet?' and 'I can't hear them!' We didn't scream, we were just disappointed that we couldn't hear anything. It was so different to the other shows we'd been to. All these years later, I still get excited talking about seeing the Beatles! They were magical times. **"**

SUE FLANAGAN, WAITRESS, HALESOWEN, WEST MIDLANDS

MONDAY 11 NOVEMBER

The group took advantage of a day off. Paul and Ringo went shopping in Soho. Paul later said, they were 'in the pouring rain, carrying parcels and only two or three people recognised us.' George took an unnamed blonde girl out on a date, later saying 'It's probably the last time I shall see her.' John and Cynthia went to see *A Funny Thing Happened On The Way To The Forum*. They also moved into Flat 3, 13 Emperor's Gate, for which they paid £15 a week. The name Hadley appeared on the intercom.

Brian Epstein was still in New York. He met with Ed Sullivan and his producer Bob Precht at the Delmonico Hotel to negotiate appearances on *The Ed Sullivan Show* for the Beatles and Gerry and the Pacemakers. Precht recalled, 'I found him a most genial fellow. After a lot of discussion, we arranged bookings for three *Ed Sullivan* shows for the Beatles and two *Ed Sullivan* shows for Gerry and the Pacemakers. A fine working and personal relationship was set up between the two of us.' The arrangement saw the Beatles make three appearances (two of them live) for $10,000, with round-trip air fares and hotel accommodation in New York and Miami in February 1964. Epstein also gave CBS-TV exclusive rights to the Beatles on US television for one year. Epstein visited Capitol Records' offices on Sixth Avenue to meet with director of East Coast operations Brown Meggs. The label had previously turned down an option to release the group's records in the US, but after playing 'I Want To Hold Your Hand' to Meggs, an agreement was reached to release the record in January 1964. Epstein also met with Vee-Jay Records; General Artists Corp. agent Sid Bernstein, who booked them for a show at Carnegie Hall and the Coliseum in Washington, DC; attorney Walter Hofer, who hosted a cocktail party for him two days earlier; and *16* magazine's editor-in-chief Gloria Stavers. He was also interviewed for *The New Yorker* during his stay. The entire trip cost him £2,000, partly because he booked into an 'extremely good hotel,' the Regency. At 10.05pm 24 October's recording of *Drop In* aired on Sveriges Radio.

TUESDAY 12 NOVEMBER

Before setting off for Portsmouth for two shows at the Guildhall, a sickly Paul saw a doctor in London. A spokesman said, 'Paul has a temperature. He is under strict doctor's orders, but is being allowed to carry on with the two shows in Portsmouth tonight, provided that he rests for the rest of the day.'

The group headed south, arriving at the Royal Beach Hotel in Southsea, where they were to spend the night. John Johnston interviewed them for BBC-TV's *South Today*, which aired at 6.10pm. A planned interview on Southern Television's *Day By Day* show at the broadcaster's studios in Northam, half an hour away, was cancelled. This despite more than forty policemen drafted in to guard the studios, a quartet of announcers dressed in Beatles wigs and suits to act as decoys and the Television Centre's glass doors and windows boarded up.

At 3.35pm, the group arrived in a yellow Corporation van at the Guildhall's front entrance. They made their way to their dressing room by way of the stage. Looking tired, drawn and unshaven, they posed for photos. After the photographers left, they asked for cups of tea. John told the press, 'We've all got flu, and Paul has got gastric flu.' A brief interview with Jeremy James for *Day By Day* was hastily re-arranged. His first question was, 'Are you beginning to find the strain of this going around the country at this tremendous speed getting you down a bit?' During the two-and-a-half-minute interview, Paul looked increasingly uncomfortable.

Local doctor John Langmaid was called to the theatre and shortly thereafter press officer Charles Gillet announced the shows had been cancelled. Langmaid billed NEMS £4 4s for his house call. Reading from a prepared statement, Gillet said, 'Dr J. R. Langmaid has examined Paul. He has a temperature of 101 degrees, which is much higher than when he left London this morning. It is not safe for him to go on. People can write for their money back or keep their tickets for a new Beatles show.' The press went outside to tell the fans. Brian Epstein, still in New York, was kept abreast of the situation, spending more than £100 on transatlantic phone calls. At 4.55pm, they were driven back to their hotel. When Paul went to bed at 7pm, he had a temperature of 102 degrees. Spinner from the *Evening News* and fellow journalist Kay Stanhope were there. 'We sat downstairs with the hotel manager, talking about VIPs upstairs,' reported Spinner. 'No-one else in the hotel knew that the Beatles were guests. They rushed to their bedrooms after the show was cancelled. Supper was sent to their rooms; to have ventured downstairs, would have been courting trouble. That is life for the Beatles these days, they are prisoners of their own success. They live on the run from their devotees. The only relaxation they can find is in one another's company. They receive more publicity than many a star. Now they face the rumours: "Are the Beatles cracking up?"

At 5pm in New York, Epstein had dinner at the Delmonico with Precht to finalise the deal to appear on *The Ed Sullivan Show*. The deal was sealed with handshake. Sullivan later told *The New York Times*, 'I made up my mind that this was the same sort of mass hit hysteria that had characterised the Elvis Presley days.'

405

❛ I was a family doctor in Southsea having joined my father's previously single-handed practice in 1962. On the morning of 12 November I had been called to visit a young girl patient of mine who had had a bad attack of asthma – I think she was 12 years old, or thereabouts. She had a ticket for the Beatles concert that evening and there were floods of tears when I said that she wasn't well enough to go. Later in the day I was told by my secretary that there had been a phone call from the Guildhall requesting me to go there as soon as possible to see one of the Beatles. When I arrived, I was taken in via a back entrance and thence upstairs to a room where Paul McCartney was lying down on what I think was a settee. The other members of the group were in the same room and I remember John Lennon pacing up and down looking rather anxious. I examined Paul and prescribed some medicine. It was quite clear to me that there was no way that the poor chap would be able to perform that evening, so the show was cancelled – much, as I imagine, to the relief of all of them! The following morning, I visited him again at the Royal Beach Hotel and found him looking and feeling much better. I remember saying that it would be OK for them to travel onward that day. I was thanked politely and then fought my way out through a barrage of press reporters in the hotel lobby. I then visited the girl I had seen the previous morning. I was greeted by a beaming child who thanked me for cancelling the Beatles' concert and wanted to know whether the stethoscope I used to examine her was the one I had used for Paul! ❜

JOHN LANGMAID, DOCTOR, SOUTHSEA, HAMPSHIRE

WEDNESDAY 13 NOVEMBER

Dr Langmaid visited Paul at the hotel at 9am. Lily Morin, who took the group warm milk the previous night, brought them boiled eggs, toast and tea. 'I think they are lovely,' she said. 'They are good boys. They were very considerate to me and I would like to wish them luck!' The *Daily Mirror* featured a front-page picture of Paul, with the headline 'A 'Very Sick Boy'. At 10.45am, as the group set out on the 170-mile trek to the ABC in Plymouth, Paul appeared first from the back entrance, revealing to the waiting press and photographers that he was 'much better'. George, who also had a temperature, said, 'I wasn't as bad as Paul. I think nearly everyone in the show caught it. Of course, the show takes it out of you a little bit, but it is just the same as everything else. If you have a regular sleep every night, it is OK.' He also announced that they would be returning to Portsmouth. 'The promoter is already fixing up the date. It depends on what everyone is doing.' Tony Barrow said, 'Paul's pulse and temperature are back to normal, although he is still feeling somewhat groggy. He is taking drugs three times during the journey, primarily to keep down his temperature. It won't be very comfortable for him, but all being well they will appear tonight.' The group set off for Plymouth.

Dempster Paul, the assistant manager at the 1,958-seater ABC in Plymouth, said that he arrived two hours early and that 'the phone has not stopped ringing.' The ABC manager Tom Purdie reported that the group's two concerts were 'the biggest demand for tickets that I have ever known here for anything. It is a great pity that we have them for only one night. I could have filled the place every night for a week.' Halfway through their journey, the group stopped for lunch at the Asker's Road House Hotel on the main Dorchester to Bridport road, near Askerswell in Dorset. After eating, they continued on their way, driving through Charmouth and Lyme Regis, before meeting up with a Westward Television crew in the car park of the Lyneham Inn in Plympton off the A38. They filmed a sequence getting out of their car and putting on winter coats for the show *Move Over Dad* ('a gay new show with the accent on the beat of the young').

As the group drove down Plymouth's Royal Parade, a sole teen, standing at the crossing opposite Dingles department store, spotted them and began screaming, much to the amazement of fellow pedestrians. Their car drove into Westward's studios; the group were whisked inside and interviewed, then taken to the Athenaeum Theatre by way of an underground passage, where they encountered a prop skeleton hanging from the ceiling. They crossed Athenaeum Place and walked through the cinema's stage door. At a brief press conference, Paul met a girl who claimed to be his second cousin, telling him that her mother Elizabeth was his aunt. He told her he didn't have an aunt Elizabeth. The girl did get his autograph before being ushered out.

Two hours before the doors opened for the first show, teens Joan Dunlop and Margaret Hosking made sure they were first in line. They were buoyed by a notice on the front door, which read 'The Show Is On With Beatles'. The cinema's sound engineer Ted Sparrow fetched an electric fire from his home to provide some heat in the group's dressing room (and brought his copy of the *Please Please Me* LP for the group to sign). In between the 6.15pm and 8.30pm shows, the group were brought dinner – Paul, now obviously feeling a little bit better, had two fried eggs and a glass of milk; John, egg salad, jelly and a glass of milk; Ringo, fillet steak, chips, peas and cream caramel; and George, fillet steak, chips, peas and a glass of milk. During the evening, BBC-TV broadcast *The Mersey Sound* to a nationwide audience for the first time. Initially aired in the north of England and the London area only, it was now broadcast across the country because the demand was so great.

Following the second show, they left the cinema the way they came, through the underground tunnel. Few saw them as they came out of the back of Westward's studios and sped away under a police escort. The group set off east on the A38, driving one hour to Torquay. They spent the night at the Imperial Hotel, occupying three rooms in the recently built west wing. More than a thousand fans waited outside the cinema in Plymouth for over three hours, hoping for a glimpse of the group. The proprietor of a hotel a few miles outside of the city was woken up at 1.30am by two teenage girls who said that they understood that Paul was staying at the hotel and wanted to see him.

> ❝ I met the Beatles at the 4pm press call that day. This was after their previous concerts at Portsmouth the day before had to be cancelled with Paul suffering from flu. But they were all under the weather. Anyway, it was the start of a very busy day and night. I was a staff photographer for the *Western Morning News* and the *Western Evening Herald* and after taking the press call pix, I then had to dash a couple hundred yards to the office for the first lot of them to be processed. Then back to the ABC to photograph the massive queues of girls. With the best view in the house along with BBC cameraman Colin Rowe, we took pictures of the Beatles in their first set. Then another dash to the office before returning for the second show. Being a Beatles fan I think I was running on adrenaline that night but they just took everything in their stride. They were just so relaxed and laid back. At the press call we just sat on chairs drinking tea and talking to them as though they were our mates. It seemed that there was no security and once inside the cinema away from the screaming hordes they could just relax and be themselves. I remember getting their autographs but the funny thing was I was talking to George the most but I ended up with programme signed by the other three and John had signed twice for some reason. Onstage they were fantastic; light years ahead of everybody else. Next day normality returned. ❞
>
> **MIKE COX, PHOTOGRAPHER, PLYMOUTH, DEVON**

THURSDAY 14 NOVEMBER

I n the new edition of *Disc*, 'She Loves You' spent a third week at number 3, as *The Beatles (No. 1)* EP climbed three places to number 21. The paper reviewed *With The Beatles*. 'Well, folks, this is it. Certainly, the LP of the year where phenomenally high sales are concerned and also, I suspect, in terms of punch, spirit and general liveliness. Reviewing Beatle discs and predicting their success now is like saying with confidence that strawberries and cream will be a popular sell-out next summer. With an advance order shooting up to the half-million mark, nobody anywhere needs any encouragement from me to get this LP. All you have to do now is place your order and wait patiently for fourteen tracks of great and boisterous Beatledom.' Valerie Lloyd from Criggion in Shropshire, reading the paper during her afternoon tea, screamed through a mouthful of cream cake, 'Mum! I've won!' when she saw she had won tickets to see the group in Wolverhampton. Her mother picked herself up off the floor and phoned her husband at work, Valerie's brother who lived near Wolverhampton and 'just about anyone else she could think of'.

'She Loves You' dropped a place to number 3 in the *NRM* chart. As *The Beatles (No. 1)* EP climbed seven places to number 3 in the EP chart, behind *The Beatles Hits* and *Twist And Shout*. The paper, which claimed it was the first national record paper to give the group a write-up, published its first-ever colour front page – naturally they chose a photo of the Beatles.

The group left Torquay and headed north on the A380, a short forty-five-minute drive to the ABC in Exeter, where they had previously appeared on 28 March. Now they were ushered through a side door unnoticed, while Peter Jay and the Jaywalkers signed autographs out front as decoys. The curtains were drawn and hundreds of fans already outside chanting 'We Want The Beatles!' with three hours before the first show at 6.15pm. Over a pot of tea, the group offered their thoughts to *Bristol Evening Post* reporter Roger Bennett. Ringo, playing cards with Ron King ('Double solitaire. Ronnie taught me. I could only play patience before. Now we have a match every night.') told him, 'Boredom, that's what we're really up against. Travelling is really the biggest drag. A hundred miles a day. Bit wearing. Then there's all this hanging around locked up in hotels and dressing rooms when we daren't go out. So we get sort of crazes on things. Like movie cameras. That's the latest. We poke them through the car windows when we're travelling at anything that looks interesting. We haven't quite got the hang of it yet.'

As if on cue, Neil Aspinall arrived with a large brown paper parcel with an £8 Scalextric set inside. The group eagerly pulled the parcel apart and plugged the set in. Half a mile away, fans began congregating outside the Rougemont Hotel in Queen Street, when news spread that the group were staying there.

The second show began at 8.30pm. Afterwards, with an ambulance parked in New North Road as a decoy, the group escaped by way of a side door, into a private car driven by Ann Madison, the daughter of a friend of Robert Parker, who took them to the Rougemont. A hotel waiter took up a turkey and ham supper with Horlicks to one of the rooms and found the group sitting on the floor playing with a train set John had just bought for Julian. They got to bed at 2am.

❛ It was a typical winter's day, rather chilly, the clouds hung like pudding bags in the sky and a slight mist pervaded the air of our seaside town, but it was most definitely not a typical day for my two friends and I as it was to involve a certain amount of derring-do and breaking the rules. As I left home that morning dressed in my school uniform, to my parents everything looked outwardly normal. However, a plot was being hatched that involved keeping fingers crossed and a huge dollop of hope in pulling this adventure off and not being found out. The Beatles had played Plymouth the night before and I twigged that they would stay at the Imperial Hotel in Torquay before travelling to Exeter for their next concert. The hunch was confirmed by the fact that the manager of this prestigious hotel had a daughter in a younger class at our school and he had told her that THEY had been booked to stay there. So this spurred on our hi-jinx and naughtiness. Absolutely no way were we going to sit in a classroom whilst our boys were back in town.

We were so desperate to see them again that we plotted to go to school, be present for registration, so it looked like we were at school for the day and then mischievously disappear. This we managed to do and the escapade began. In our convent school uniforms (we could not have smuggled other clothes to change into), the three of us looked indubitably obvious and this drew attention on our arrival at the hotel. We were joined by various photographers and reporters who had wind of their stay plus some hotel staff and also the sister of one of my friends and her pal who were in on the secret, also escaping school. The reporters started talking to us and we begged them not to print anything about us being there as this would spell big trouble with a capital T. We even pretended to be from another school so adding to the subterfuge. I don't think the reporters were wised-up to the fact our uniforms didn't match that school.

I can't quite recall the exact time John, George, Paul and Ringo emerged from the hotel but can remember the sudden flurry of activity and we found ourselves in the midst of it all, face to face. We could have touched them and even breathed the same air. What exquisite moments! They merrily greeted us, chatting and signing autographs, remarking about our school uniforms. So, we told them what we were up to. I remember we thanked them for their music and how much they meant to us, with a quick peck on the cheek. They all looked very smart. John, George and Ringo were wearing dark overcoats and Paul in a shirt tie and suit. John had an eye-catching black-and-white dotty shirt which was quite adventurous for the time. We wanted time to stand still but all too soon they were whisked away and we were left, as if in a dream, with all that had just happened and a great feeling of mission accomplished. We were the luckiest girls in the whole world. We were invincible but very soon we would be wishing we could be invisible.

The three of us planned to return to school for the evening homework class. We walked up through the town chatting excitedly but our exuberance was soon turned into that of sheer horror. What a juxtaposition. Outside a newsagent's we saw a placard for the late edition of our local newspaper proclaiming 'Torquay Schoolgirls Cut School To See The Beatles'. We bought a copy and were filled with terror. We had not expected to find ourselves in print on the front page. Thankfully no photos of us or names mentioned as we had told them we could be expelled (which was true), but we had not reckoned on a reporter making a story of us being there. On arriving back at school we could have done with Harry Potter's 'invisibility cloak' as we tried to sneak back in but we were seen by the Mother Superior looking extremely cross. It was obvious she had been waiting for us to return and catch us. Needless to say we were trembling and quaking. This was not looking good. It felt as though the whole world had come tumbling down around us. Fleetingly I had thought of us making up a story but we should not have left school anyway without permission for whatever reason even if it was to buy something in town we needed for school.

I noticed the Mother Superior had one hand behind her back which we were soon to realise, and half guessed, was that evening's paper. 'It's about you girls, isn't it?' she enquired, looking even sterner. Of course, you cannot lie to a nun (well, let's just say you dare not) and so the game was up. So we feared the worst as we stood before her awaiting our fate. Then something strange happened – and I saw a twinkle in her eye. This was totally opposite to the normally extremely strict Mother

Superior. Yes, we received a huge telling off but to our utmost surprise we were told that this time our parents would not be informed, there would be no further inquisition and unbelievably – no punishment. We just could not believe it, what on earth had come over her? It was indeed a miracle. As she turned to go back into her office she winked at us and I truly believe that although she was at least middle-aged at the time, she had put herself in our shoes and seen her young self in us and possibly wished she too had been at the Imperial and been part of that excitement. Maybe she was a secret Beatles fan. **🗩**

ROWENA HOUGHTON, OFFICIAL BEATLES FAN CLUB AREA SECRETARY FOR DEVON, CORNWALL, SOMERSET, DORSET AND WILTSHIRE, TORQUAY, SOUTH DEVON

FRIDAY 15 NOVEMBER

Readers of the *NME* were greeted with the front-page headline 'Beatles Album Secrets'. *The Beatles' Hits* EP dropped out of the Top 30, *The Beatles (No. 1)* EP entered at number 27 and 'She Loves You' stayed at number 2 for a third week. 'She Loves You' also stayed at number 2 in the *Melody Maker* singles chart, with *The Beatles' Hits* at number 24, *Twist And Shout* at number 25 and *The Beatles (No. 1)* at number 27. Ray Coleman interviewed the group in an article titled, 'We Have Our Rows – Nothing Serious.' Paul said, 'All jobs are hard if you do them well. I don't know – what does an artist have to do. I know travelling is tiring, but it's part of the job. When you get to a place, you set yourself up, go onstage for say half an hour, and that's that. Everything should be worked out beforehand. People who grumble about the tough part of this life should go over to Germany, and work there, then they'd know how well off they are working in Britain.' While John commented, 'I know we've got some knockers. People say it isn't real rhythm-and-blues. Who ever said it was? Certainly not us. We have never claimed to be R&B – it's a tag that some people put on us presumably because they had to label us somehow. That put us in for it among the diehards and I'd like to put the record straight. Our music is just – well, our music. Call it a variation of rock'n'roll if you like. It just happens to come out with that sort of sound.' Ringo said, 'I let the others do all the worrying – I'm happy to go on up there and play drums, and that's all. Well, I know I'm earning more money, like, but that doesn't make a lot of difference – just more and better suits, that's all I spend the extra on. And food.' George, again referencing their fans, said, 'The crowds have a right to scream the place down it they want to. If that's their way of enjoying themselves, good luck to them.' Alan Smith previewing *With The Beatles* in the *NME* wrote, 'If it doesn't stay at the top of the *NME*

LP chart for at least eight weeks, I'll walk up and down Liverpool's Lime Street carrying an "I Hate The Beatles" sandwich-board!'

At 9.30am, the group woke and had fruit juice, corn flakes, toast, marmalade and tea sent to their rooms. Half an hour later, they were back in bed – fast asleep. At 12.30pm, they left the Rougemont in the Austin Princess, accompanied by a police escort. Reaching Checkpoint Ringo at the city boundary, a Devon county police car took over, escorting them on the A38 to Checkpoint McCartney just past the village of Holcombe Rogus, the boundary line of Devon and Somerset, where Somerset police picked up the baton. When they reached Bedminster Down, 3 miles from Colston Hall, Bristol police took over. 'Operation Get The Beatles Into Colston Hall Safely' kicked into gear and the group were escorted into the city by a *Bristol Evening Post* van.

The afternoon edition of the *Evening Post* revealed the extent of the preparations of the operation: 'Look out Bristol – the Beatles are coming. And with them, a fantastic hush-hush security system like something out of James Bond. The city was gripped with Merseymania this afternoon as Operation Beatle went into action. The object of the operation: To smuggle the four most valuable pudding-basin hair-cuts in Britain into and out of Bristol for their Colston Hall show... Hundreds of girls in tight jeans laden with sandwiches and flasks of coffee besieged all the entrances to the hall for eight hours before the Beatles were due to appear... Scores of girls never turned up at work today. They said they would rather lose their jobs than miss the Beatles'. By lunchtime, the hall's red doors were covered in graffiti. Seventeen girls were found hiding in the toilets hoping for a glimpse of the group.

At the second performance, an estimated five thousand fans blocked the road outside the theatre, despite rain. Thirty people fainted or became hysterical and several stood on car roofs, rocking the vehicles. One man was restrained by four policemen, while one girl was carried away unconscious. Nearly a hundred police forced the crowd back. Inside the hall, 17-year-old Margaret Heath from Cardiff leapt onstage and threw her arms around John and tried to kiss him. She was dragged off stage and escorted from the hall, screaming all the while. Taken to a rest room by ambulancemen, she lay on a bed her red skirt rumpled, her face flushed and her long hair dishevelled. She said, 'I feel lovely. I know John is married and I can never have him, but it doesn't matter. I felt there was such a short distance between us. I don't know how I got to him. I just grabbed him and flung my arms round his neck. John looked terrified. I would do it again if I got the chance.' After the show, she was taken to Bristol Temple Meads station in an ambulance so she could take a train home. Girls ran down the gangways but were stopped by security men. One policeman asked his inspector, 'Can I go outside? I can't stand any more.'

At the end of the show, the group escaped out of the back exit, piling into a taxi. They switched to their car and were driven to the Francis Hotel in Queen Square, Bath. The state of siege lasted for another two hours, as teens prowled the streets of Bristol trying to find out where the group were staying.

> One winter's afternoon during the 1962 Christmas holiday period, Ian Dibble called on Tim Vickery and, dumping a large stack of Roneoed pages on the table, announced, 'We're going to do a pantomime!' Ian had decided that the performing group would consist of contemporaries and be called the Yatton Youth Club, whose management committee would fund us in return for the profits from out little endeavours. A few months after that first notoriously eventful and l-o-n-g pantomime, Ian had the bright idea that we should hold a fund-raising raffle. The prizes were to be an inexpensive Civic record player, which I was able to buy with staff discount from the store where I worked, and – here's the brilliant bit – a Beatles LP and a Beatles EP, autographed by the Beatles themselves! Somewhat easier said than done. We knew that the Beatles would be appearing at the Colston Hall in

November. That gave us several weeks. Ian was sure that, as it was for a good cause, we would have no trouble at all in arranging to call at the theatre, meet the group and get the record sleeves autographed.

The weeks leading up to mid-November saw us spending all our spare change telephoning all around the country to wherever the Beatles were performing in the vain hope of speaking to someone who could give us the authority to meet them at the Colston Hall – but all to no avail. D-Day grew nearer. Tim and I were getting desperate; Ian, as usual, was naive, over-confident and dismissive.

'Oh, it'll be all right.' On Wednesday the 13th, we failed to reach anyone in authority at the ABC Plymouth, ditto the next day at Exeter. Finally, there was only one thing left to do; go to the Colston Hall and try to talk our way in.

We jumped into a taxi and Ian instructed the driver: 'Colston Hall please!' then added 'Stage door.' As we approached the hall we could see the place surrounded by female fans. Our taxi turned into Pipe Lane and slowly inched its way along until it got to Trenchard Street. It started to turn, heading towards the stage door, when the driver said; 'That's it; I can't go no further.' The taxi stopped, and we suddenly found ourselves to be the centre of attention of thousands of screaming girls (remember, it was dark). We struggled to get out of the taxi, Tim losing a button from his overcoat in the process – luckily for him that that was all he lost. Famous for fifteen minutes? We were famous for fifteen seconds.

We asked to see the theatre manager and when he arrived we told him of our mission. Eventually, out came Neil Aspinall. He then took the sleeves from whoever was carrying them. A few minutes later he returned with them autographed. We never actually got to meet the Beatles, and could not, in fact, authenticate the signatures, but I think that they were genuine. One of the *Clevedon Mercury*'s reporters lived in Yatton and as the drama group's so-called 'Press Officer', I used to give him our news, written up as an article, for him to re-write or edit as he wished. Usually my efforts were published, uncredited and with minimum changes. On this occasion he clearly thought that my report had been too modest and added that we had actually met the Beatles, reporting that we intrepid three had 'walked into the Colston Hall, chatted with the Beatles and walked out again.' The story was later picked up and repeated by the *Weston Mercury*. Made a good story, I suppose – and probably infuriated any of those screaming girls who happened to read it. I think that the record player and autographed LP went together as first prize and were won by one Barry Kellow from Wakedean Gardens. Twelve years later Ian was working as temporary doorman at the Bristol Hippodrome. One of his tasks was forging autographs. **⟫**

TERRY WEIDS, RETAIL MANAGER, BRISTOL, AVON

SATURDAY 16 NOVEMBER

B y morning, three hundred fans were chanting outside the Francis Hotel, while thirty police stood by. One 15-year-old girl in school uniform broke through the cordon, calmly entered the hotel through the kitchen entrance and reached the lift before the head porter spotted her. She was taken away in tears. Two other girls attempted to apply for jobs as waitresses in order to get in. The group breakfasted in bed on cornflakes, boiled eggs, toast and coffee. They left by a side entrance to a waiting police van, but not before some fans tried to reach them. The Chief Constable of Bath, Mr George Nichols, helped hold them back. Most fans were attempting to make their way through the hotel's revolving doors – some were crushed and trampled on in the surge. Police cordoned off the building, leaving guests waiting nearly three hours to get out.

The van sped off through morning traffic, ignoring a one-way sign, taking them to Sydney Gardens, where they got into the Austin Princess to take them on the two-hour drive on the A36 to Bournemouth for two shows at 6pm and 8.30pm at the Winter Gardens on Exeter Road. On their way, as they drove through scattered, thundery rain, the group stopped at the Old Thatch Restaurant in Ferndown, run by Mr and Mrs G. Carpenter. They all had orange juice, except Ringo who had chicken soup. John, Paul and George had lamb chops for their main course, Ringo chose rainbow trout, followed by banana fritters. Pints of milk were ordered all round. Shortly after leaving the restaurant, they met with local police and were driven to Bournemouth in a Black Maria.

At 4.30pm, the windowless police van drove up to the front of the building and reversed against the steps. A small army of policemen formed a corridor linking arms to let the group run the gauntlet. At the venue, the group immediately met with the press. Afterwards, they were ushered into manager Samuel Bell's office, who introduced them to the Mayor and Mayoress, Alderman and Mrs Harry Mears. Bournemouth councillor's wife Mrs Phillip Whitelegg and her daughter Sandra sold black velvet beetles to fans. Proceeds went to the Mayor of Bournemouth's Christmas Appeal Fund for the Old Folk of Bournemouth. At 5.15pm, *Move Over Dad*, featuring the group's interview in Plymouth, aired on Southern TV.

The group were interviewed in their dressing room by CBS-TV reporter Josh Darsa. During a rather awkward couple of minutes, Darsa asked them a series of frequently asked questions. The highlight was when George pointed at a mute Ringo and said, 'This is Ringo'. Darsa remarked, 'It's the sort of story we could hold on to for a week of more, but now the other networks are here, we'll have to rush it home pronto.' Fellow US networks, ABC and NBC also had camera crews on hand. William Sheehan interviewed them for ABC-TV, while NBC's Edwin Newman filmed a dismissive report that aired two days later in the US.

Between shows they watched *Thank Your Lucky Stars* and *Juke Box Jury* on a portable television lent by Corbin Lockyer Ltd, played Scalextric, signed autographs and were interviewed by press and television. Sid Green and Dick Hills, writers for Morecambe And Wise, whose show the group were going to be on, came to see their performance. Three young girls behind journalist Tony Crawley told him, 'We didn't pay to hear the Beatles. We can hear them at home any time on discs. We paid to see them – to scream for them. We practiced screaming last night without records.' Concert-goers at Billy J. Kramer's show at the Streatham Odeon obviously wished they were elsewhere, shouting 'We Want The Beatles!'

During the second show both George and Ringo were hit in the eye by Jelly Babies. After the performance, the group went for a late-night meal at a nearby restaurant. They were initially turned away by the doorman as the restaurant was closed for a private party. Newlyweds Javier Revuelta Pineiro and his bride Joan were celebrating with friends and family who had been unable to attend their wedding the previous month. Pineiro later recalled that, 'Ringo came over and said, "We've eaten here before after the show. Can we join the party?" Pineiro remembered them being 'smashing lads and one of them asked how they could repay me. I said I didn't want anything. So, they offered to go and get their stuff and play for my guests. They played and mucked about for an hour. Twenty or thirty girls also turned up and the party went on till two o'clock in the morning. John Lennon gave me his personal number and the Cavern Club number and said they would repay me. I told them I was a classical music fan but I liked their music.' Fans waited outside the Carlton Hotel and even the Crown Hotel in Blandford, unaware that the group were staying at the Branksome Towers in Poole.

‘ My father was a pentecostal minister, and my parents moved down to Bournemouth to retire. They were quite old really compared to other people's parents. I grew up [in Bournemouth], and when I left school, I went into journalism because I didn't know what else to do. In those days we didn't tend to go to university but I had been told I was good at writing essays. There were no journalist training programmes, but there was a position with a local press agency in Christchurch. I joined them as an apprentice, and would go out on my bike to the local police and ambulance stations and the courts to get stories for the BBC and such like. I was really thrown in at the deep end. I remember the time I got my first story on the local BBC news – somebody had stolen the RSPCA charity collection dog from Christchurch quay – that was my first big story!

I had a good relationship with Sam Bell, the manager of the Winter Gardens. He was pretty useful to me as we got on well, and he would arrange tickets and such like. That was really how I got in to see the Beatles when they came back to Bournemouth that November. It was a nightmare getting in there, getting through half a dozen doors. It was like getting into a prison because they had closed all the doors and had these hefty guys on each one. Eventually I got in to see them in the dressing room. People were making cracks, but I had no idea what they were! I introduced myself and asked what they were doing. They were playing Scalextric, so I asked if I could have a go. I picked up the little trigger thing and I remember I lost my car straight away! I can't remember who was actually playing – one or two of them. I'm now retired and spend too much time on the internet studying UFOs and parapsychology! I would never have guessed that the evening I spent playing Scalextric with The Beatles would still be talked about nearly sixty years on. ’

DAVE HAITH, JOURNALIST, BOURNEMOUTH, DORSET

SUNDAY 17 NOVEMBER

At 11.15am two policemen arrived at Branksome Towers. About half an hour later, the Beatles left through the hotel kitchen and stepped into their waiting car. Paul was photographed by Terry Spencer holding his ever-present transistor radio to his ear and listening to *Easy Beat*. Spencer travelled with the group to their next show in Coventry. George told a waiting journalist, 'Doubt if we've ever slept so well. Usually the fans find out where we are and stay outside until late at night and they come back very early in the morning chanting our names.' Shortly afterwards, the two policemen came out of the hotel to inform the teenagers that the group had never been there. They left disappointed.

The Austin Princess headed north-east on the A34, stopping off in the rain for lunch at the Oriel Hotel and Restaurant in Ock Street, Abingdon, Berkshire at about 1.45pm. The group arrived half an hour late at the Little Park Street police station in Coventry at 4pm. Local police escorted them up the High Street, lined with hundreds of fans immune to the pouring rain, then to Broadgate, the Burges and finally to the back entrance of the Coventry Theatre. They were greeted by stage-door lady, Nan Egginton – who later had her photo snapped having a nice cup of tea with John.

Before the 6pm show, actress Julie Christie, then a company member at Birmingham Rep, spent time with the group. She recalled, 'I really wanted to meet them to satisfy my curiosity. I liked their sound and I just asked if I could meet them.' She was captured on film trying to play a guitar, surrounded by the group, who appeared before press and photographers. Paul was asked how he was feeling, saying, 'I'm perfectly all right now. All the stories about me cracking up are quite groundless. Honest, I've never had a serious illness in my life.' John interjected, 'Now everyone is waiting for us to crack up under the strain. I'll tell you this: when we are breaking down, we'll make a public announcement so everyone can come and take pictures.' Paul also told a reporter, 'We're tickled pink over all this American interest, of course.' On not being able to leave the theatre and go for a walk, George said, 'It's a bit like being in prison, but we are not fresh-air types.' John said he didn't mind the continual screaming, adding, 'If I go to a football match and someone tells me to shut up, I'd soon have something to say.' In an interview printed in the day's *News Of The World*, Alun Owen was quoted, 'They live in a series of boxes all the time. A hotel room box, a car box and a dressing room box. They can't move away from these boxes in case they are recognised and mobbed.'

The St John Ambulance brigade had fifteen members on duty rather than the usual six. As the show got underway, they were kept busy treating a number of girls close to unconsciousness with hysterics. Divisional Superintendent Mr W. Heath said, 'One was so hysterical and frightened by all the screaming that she just stood sobbing uncontrollably for several minutes. It was really quite dangerous.' During the second show at 8.30pm, table tennis balls rained down on the group. John was hit in the chest by a doll and Ringo received a blow on the head from a woman's errant shoe.

They left the venue in their car accompanied by a policewoman seated in the front passenger seat. The car sped back to the Little Park Street police station, before driving the 2-mile trip along the A4114 to the Brooklands Grange Hotel in Holyhead Road, Allesley, where they spent the night.

❛ I was working at the Oriel Hotel and Restaurant where we had a sign outside saying, 'Famous for Food'. It was lunchtime and we had quite a few rally drivers in the restaurant already, who were on their way home after an event. Then the door opened and somebody walked in who I recognised immediately as Brian Epstein. He said that he would like to bring the Beatles in to have lunch but that they would not sign autographs until after they had eaten. I was very excited and ran to the kitchen to tell the proprietors Kathleen Clements and Averil Hobbs, 'The Beatles are coming in for lunch!' Mr and Mrs Kemp, who

owned the building and leased it to Kathleen and Averil, also happened to be having lunch in the restaurant at the time. Mrs Kemp rushed to the telephone in reception to tell her friends, so it was ages before I could telephone my husband, hoping that he might be able to bring our two young children down to the hotel. Unfortunately, he said that he was too busy stirring custard, as he had been left to prepare lunch for the children.

The Beatles were so friendly. John and Paul were joking the whole time and it was difficult to get them to concentrate on choosing from the menu. They kept following me round the room and I found it quite difficult to persuade them to sit down! John, Paul and George ordered a large jug of milk to share between them, while Ringo chose something different. After their roast meals, when it was time to choose desserts, the menu offered peaches and ice cream. George, who was a lovely quiet boy being the youngest member of the group, asked whether he could have custard with his peaches. Averil was very pleased to make custard specially for him. They were lovely boys, very friendly and all very smartly dressed. John tended to act as spokesperson for the others, while Ringo was probably the quietest. After everybody had finished eating, Brian allowed them to sign autographs. I brought several sheets of the hotel's headed notepaper to the table, which all four of the group autographed, so that the hotel staff could all have copies. Brian also gave me some fan club photographs of the group. One of the rally drivers came to their table with a banknote and asked them to autograph it. They refused, saying that they would not deface one of the Queen's banknotes. It was a wonderful experience, serving the Beatles just at the point when their fame was spreading around the world. ❜

BERYL RIDGE, WAITRESS AND HOTEL RECEPTIONIST, ABINGDON, OXFORDSHIRE

MONDAY 18 NOVEMBER

In the early hours of the morning, Mal Evans was rushed to Staffordshire General Infirmary suffering from head injuries, after he hit a lamp standard driving the Ford Thames minibus. The van overturned at Longford Island on the A5 at Watling Street in Bridgtown near Cannock, about 9 miles from Wolverhampton where the group were playing the following day. Fan mail was scattered everywhere and firemen were called to

wash petrol off the road. Nine guitars and some amplifying equipment remained virtually undamaged. The left front side of the van and left passenger door not so. Tony Bramwell took over until Evans was fit again. With news of this reaching the group, they had to continue with their back-breaking schedule, checking out of the Brooklands Grange Hotel and driving back to London – a two-hour drive down the M1.

Police and security men – more than enough to cope with the handful of fans – secured EMI House in preparation for the group's visit at lunchtime. On arrival, they attended a cocktail party. In the ground floor studio, they were presented with eight silver discs for 'She Loves You', the *Twist And Shout* EP, *Please Please Me* and the yet-to-be released *With The Beatles* by EMI head Sir Joseph Lockwood, *Disc*'s managing editor Gerald Marks and George Martin, who gave them a miniature 2-inch framed EP. Afterwards, they had a formal lunch in the sixth-floor boardroom with Epstein, Martin and EMI executives. Lockwood said, 'They have created a disc success without parallel in these twelve months.' He tripped up during his speech and Lennon quipped, 'You're fired!' Photographer Terry Spencer took his daughter Cara along to the group's photocall. After the lunch, Paul went to see the recently opened *The Trial* at the Cameo Poly and went with John to see Dora Bryan in *Six Of One* at the Adelphi Theatre in the evening.

American TV audiences got their first look at the Beatles when NBC's *The Huntley Brinkley Report* aired Edwin Newman's dismissive and condescending report. 'The hottest musical group in Great Britain today is the Beatles. It's not a collection of insects, but a quartet of young men with pudding-bowl haircuts and who spell Beatles B-E-A-T-L-E-S... they've sold two and a half million records and they earn $5,000 a week... Those who study such things say that at last the British juvenile has someone immediate to identify with, not some distant American rock'n'roll hero... One reason for the Beatles' popularity may be that it's almost impossible to hear them... the London *Times* has carried the sobering report the Beatles may bring their Mersey sound to the United States... one Robert Percival, an artist, proposes to capture

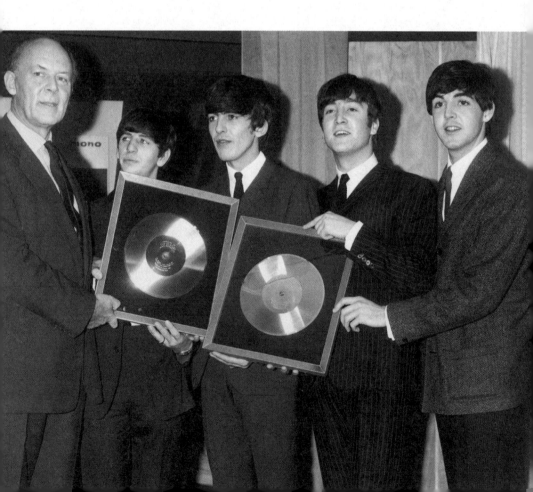

the Mersey Sound on canvas. Percival, mercifully, is deaf.' He also said, 'the quality of Mersey is somewhat strained' and 'show us no Mersey,' as if no one had done so before. Chet Huntley, before signing off with the show's nightly quote, added, 'So anyone looking for some mute inglorious Milton will just have to keep on looking.'

It was early in 1963 when my mother and I went to London Airport to collect Dad [Terence Spencer] from a story he had been covering in Africa for *Life* magazine. I was then 13 years old and very caught up in the music of the day. I was also always on the look-out to make a little extra pocket money and Dad had promised me and my mother that, if we suggested a story that was taken up by *Life*, he would give us £5. That was a lot of money in those days! I could sense there was something pretty special about a new group that was taking the UK by storm. After greeting Dad at the airport, I said to him, 'Dad, I think I have got a good story for you. It's about the Beatles.' Well, he asked around a bit and realised they were becoming a sensation in England and, still rather reluctantly, sent a telex to New York with the story suggestion. At about the same time, the managing editor of *Life* was driving around the city with his 13-year-old daughter. One of the Beatles' songs came on the radio and she got very excited and told her father this new British group were really amazing. He remembered seeing my father's telex – and made the decision to send Dad off on the trail of the Beatles!

For the next few months, off and on, Dad followed them around England. He hung around with them in their dressing rooms, at their hotels, etc., until he became almost invisible to them. This gave him the chance to take thousands of unposed photographs of them fooling around, playing with a train set, helping Ringo to learn about photography, etc. They were often bored as they had to be taken to the theatres very early in order to avoid the screaming fans who would turn up outside. In those days, they were totally natural and unspoiled and just let Dad take any photos he wanted. One day, Dad asked the Beatles if they wouldn't mind recording a short message on his dictaphone for me – one of their biggest fans (or at least that's what he told them!). They readily agreed and each one proceeded to say something into the machine. Some of it included rather bad language, along the lines of 'Hello Cara. John here. Your ***** father is here with us ***** around.' The message went on for about ten minutes. When he got the message home, he played it to my mother and asked if he should let me hear it as there was all that bad language in it. She pointed out that there wasn't a word in it that I hadn't already heard my father use! (Typical journalist.) I was therefore allowed to listen to it and was, of course, thrilled beyond measure. I played it to all my friends and once, on the bus home from school. Even the bus conductor came to listen to it, as did everyone on the bus!

Sometime later, my father had the dictaphone in his office when he called the Paris bureau of *Time-Life* about a new story. He often recorded those conversations. This particular day, he managed to record over the precious Beatles message. It took all his courage to admit this to me – and we cried together! He told me how awful he felt about it, which of course he did. Poor Dad. And poor me! Many years later still, Dad sold ten thousand of his black-and-white Beatles negatives at an auction at Sotheby's. To our huge surprise and delight, they achieved a sale price of £74,000.00! As Dad realised that my original idea had made him a lot of money over the years, he paid off my first mortgage – of £18,000.00. The negatives were bought by Bloomsbury Publishing. They used them – with the text written by my father – to produce a coffee table book, entitled *It Was Thirty Years Ago*. I now have in my ownership ten colour images of the Beatles, the best of which were shown at the 'Living Dangerously' exhibition a couple of years ago.

CARA SPENCER, PHOTO ARCHIVIST AND TRAVEL ADVISOR, SHREWSBURY, SHROPSHIRE

TUESDAY 19 NOVEMBER

Before the group drove north for two shows at the Gaumont in Wolverhampton, they popped into the recording of the week's *Saturday Club*. On their arrival at the Gaumont, the group dashed inside. Ringo, complete with rolled umbrella, passed by Peter Jay, saying 'Hello, Charles. Going to the club tonight?' Paul sat down at the piano and played some jazz. Half an hour later John arrived. Fans hearing that the group couldn't get food into the theatre, sent in packets of sandwiches – although soon after a local cafe sent three steak and chips and one steak and salad. Valerie Lloyd, one of three *Disc* winners, took the day off school ('I would never have been able to concentrate on lessons, anyway', she said). Her parents drove her from her home in Criggion to Wolverhampton, where she met up with her brother Christopher, the other two winners and their companions. They had to go into the dressing room in threes because it was so small. Afterwards, they had their photos taken on steps outside the dressing room.

At the 6.30pm show they were visited by *The Beatles Book*'s Sean O'Mahony and Leslie Bryce, who brought a selection of hats for them to wear. Paul sat down at a piano while George and Ringo posed for photos. Ringo soon called for a doctor because of an earache in his left ear. John arrived late, and then jammed with Peter Jay and a couple of other musicians for a quarter of an hour. Before the 8.40pm show, the group ate the meals from the local cafe, and then posed for more photos with their guitars, which had been repaired at a local music shop following Monday's accident. During the performance, bottles, Jelly Babies and a stuffed white rabbit rained down on the group and two screaming girls rushed onstage. Hundreds of teenage girls wept uncontrollably as they left the cinema, having shouted themselves hoarse. After the show, a police car drew up in front of the group's vehicle – both drove off in one direction, while the group escaped in a van going the opposite way.

They drove home to Liverpool in heavy rain. Fans assembled outside the Stafford General Infirmary, where Mal Evans was still hospitalised, in the hope that the group would visit him. They didn't. The *Express & Star*, in the article '100 Aspirins, Twist, and Shout!', described the evening as, 'Mass hysteria. That is the only adequate way to describe last night's visit to Wolverhampton of the Beatles.'

> **❝** The Beatles were on a British tour and in March 1963 they came to Wolverhampton and played at the Gaumont. I couldn't get a ticket but my older cousin Jackie went and she was bitterly disappointed because John Lennon didn't play. They returned again in the November and this time I was determined to get a ticket. Along with a couple of mates, we skived school and pitched up very early on the day the tickets were being sold. It was bitterly cold and we had no blankets or sleeping bags but we stuck it out. We were about one hundred or so places back and by early afternoon the queue stretched all the way round the block up Temple Street. I had done some portrait drawings in pencil of each one of the group about A3 size. I had done them as preliminary sketches for a large mural painting that I did at the local youth centre in Ashmore Park, the area of Wolverhampton where I lived at the time. The painting had been photographed by one of the local newspapers and a reporter saw the drawings. He suggested that I should try and present them to the Beatles at the concert and said he would try to help arrange it. Anyway, I thought great and took the drawings with me on the evening on the concert. I didn't really think anything would come of it but to my surprise the reporter

found me and took them to the Beatles' road manager and came back with a backstage pass for me to meet the group after the concert.

I never did get backstage to actually meet the Beatles. It was mayhem. Hundreds of screaming girls and older boys all pushing through the narrow corridor leading to their dressing room. Not all was lost though. The group received my drawings and there were photographs of them looking at the portraits of them in the local newspapers. The euphoria didn't last too long. Three days later I was playing five aside football at the youth club and there was a public address announcement that JFK had been shot. By the late '60s I was at art college where I took my first degree in fashion and textiles moving to painting for my postgraduate study. In the summer of 1972 I had finished at art college and was trying to begin life as a freelance artist. By 1972 the local band Slade were regular visitors to my dad's pub. They began to throw parties at the pub when they had a hit record. Their manager Chas Chandler had taken the group down the path of a 'skinhead' look but by 1973 glam rock had begun to make its mark with Bowie and Marc Bolan. One evening during a conversation with Chas and Noddy Holder it was suggested a shift in identity was necessary. Between late 1972 and the summer of 1975 I made all of Dave Hill's stage costumes and many for the others in the group culminating in the costumes for the onstage sequences in their feature film, *Slade in Flame*. This was a really enjoyable time. I was designing and making crazy costumes and getting paid for it. I travelled around places in Europe and, for a change, stayed in posh hotels. It was a blast! After working as a teacher for over forty years in the UK, Europe, the Middle East and Asia I retired at the young age of seventy-one and began a new career as a painter. I love teaching art but have always painted and always loved music. It is surprising that the kids today in Hong Kong know all the words to the Beatles songs. **7**

STEVE MEGSON, ARTIST AND ART TEACHER, HONG KONG, CHINA

WEDNESDAY 20 NOVEMBER

t was raining in Manchester at lunchtime when fans began lining up outside the twenty-six hundred-seater ABC in Ardwick for the two evening shows at 6.30pm and 8.45pm. By the time the group arrived mid-afternoon, the area was covered in a blanket of fog. They were met with the usual platoon of press and photographers, but this time there were movie crews from Granada Television and British Pathé News. They posed for photographers with the day's unofficial fifth Beatle – an oversized toy panda, which John later took home for Julian. Asked whether the police should protect the Beatles, George replied, 'Mr Macmillan gets protection. Why shouldn't we and the fans? If they stopped the police doing it, the hospital bills would be three times as big.' A mobile police station was set up in the cinema car park and a hundred additional officers were called in to support the local C Division. A bus stop in Stockport Road outside the ABC was moved and the cinema's rear entrance was locked and barred. 'We do not anticipate any real trouble. Manchester fans are usually quite good-tempered about it all,' said a police spokesman. In their dressing room, Ringo emptied a mailbag full of fan mail before playing solitaire, John feigned a nap and Paul put on a black astrakhan hat that had been sent to him.

Granada interviewed the group about their forthcoming visit to the United States, while Michael Barton, who had narrated *The Mersey Story*, conducted a two-minute interview for the evening's BBC North Home Service programme, *Voice Of The North*, which aired that evening before the first show at 6.10pm. Barton also interviewed George about the Liverpool and Hamburg rock scenes for the show *Wacker, Mach Schau*, which aired the following Wednesday. During the evening's first concert, British Pathé filmed 'She Loves You' and 'Twist And Shout', for an eight-minute movie called *The Beatles Come To Town*, shown on cinema screens across the country for a week from 22 December.

At the invitation of the *Manchester Evening News*, Professor John Cohen, head of the Psychology Department at Manchester University, watched the effect the Beatles' performance had on an audience. 'There is a touch of hysteria. It's just healthy exuberance, a thousand times healthier than the reaction to the American crooners. Remember, this is the only world they have that's completely theirs... This is not really hysteria. Hysteria is pathological. It is a disease. This is emotional release. It is a healthy thing that these girls can release themselves in this way. They will be better for it. This is something new in this country. It is a very fine thing that they can reach this pitch. African tribes are known for it. And it is something like voodoo. But the nearest thing I know to it is the Hitler Jugend before the war. It is a similar sort of enthusiasm, but that enthusiasm was wrongly directed. This is harmless. And it will occur so infrequently in their lives that there is little damage. There is no single ingredient. There are many. Sex is only one of them and of that they are completely unaware... They don't even want to hear the music. It doesn't matter to them. They have a complete adoration for the image onstage... These were all unawakened girls, 13, 14, 15. No awakened girl could react like that. They would associate sex too much with what they were feeling and be restrained. Just remember, this is their world. The only world in which they can be completely unrestrained.' He also said he couldn't hear a thing.

❝ The day that was going to become the most memorable in my teenage years was put into motion some two weeks before. My friend Lorraine Greenhalgh and I were bemoaning the fact that the Beatles were coming to Manchester and we didn't have tickets for their concert and there wasn't a dog in hell's chance of ever getting to meet them. I remembered Lorraine telling me she had heard that the boys loved Jelly Babies and thousands of girls had been throwing them on the stage at their concerts. We then had a brainwave. Why not write to Bassett's Licorice Allsorts, the makers of Jelly Babies, and ask for their help. So, tongue in cheek, we wrote to them addressing the letter, Dear George (the founder of the company), explaining our dilemma and how we needed their expertise to help us meet our heart-throbs. Never in our wildest dreams did we really expect a reply. We were amazed to receive a marvellous letter from the Managing Director explaining that although George had been dead for over a hundred years, he hoped that we would be pleased with the efforts of the present-day management. Pleased? We were ecstatic. A giant Jelly Baby had been made especially for us to present to the Beatles. Tickets materialised from somewhere and the press and television were involved. It was a whirlwind of fun and excitement. We were eventually taken to meet the Fab Four and they were fabulous in every possible way. We were made to feel very special chatting away and having photographs with the boys. It was just an amazing time. The Beatles were everything a young teenage fan could have ever hoped for and Bassett's Licorice Allsorts were wonderful. They made our dreams come true. What happened to the giant Jelly Baby? Well, that was sent to the children at Booth's Hall children's hospital. So we were all winners. ❞

JOYCE AINSBURY, ANTIQUE DEALER, DISLEY, CHESHIRE

THURSDAY 21 NOVEMBER

The latest edition of *Disc* published the first review of the group's new single 'I Want To Hold Your Hand'. Don Nicholl in his 'Disc Date' column, headlined 'Look Out Top Spot... The Beatles' smash-hit new single is here!' wrote: 'Here it is, the disc which is very nearly a million seller before it even reaches the counters! I wonder what all those record dealers – and Parlophone – would do if the Beatles suddenly went out of fashion? Imagine it... shelves stacked-high with this disc and the customers saying: "We've changed our minds." Not likely to happen though! No, this Lennon-McCartney composed coupling is going to delight the group's fans. 'I Want To Hold Your Hand' has a crisp hand-clapping gimmick and there's an identifying falsetto tremble on the end of the title phrase. Not as wild as their previous release, but a steady compulsive beater. A gentle ballad on the other side for interesting contrast. 'This Boy', in fact strikes me as one of their most thoughtful offerings.'

In the paper's latest singles chart, 'She Loves You' climbed one place to number 2, as *The Beatles (No. 1)* EP moved up three places to number 18, the *Twist And Shout* EP re-entered the chart at number 21 and *The Beatles' Hits* EP entered at number 23.

'She Loves You' climbed one place to number 2 in the *NRM* chart as well. 'Another from the prolific McCartney-Lennon pen is slightly-slower-than-usual number that's already sold to the tune of three-quarters of a million,' wrote Peter Jones in his review of the group's new single. 'There's a bluesy guitar-and-drums backing with a plaintive tune running through the whole thing. It tends to build and grows on you with each play. Falsetto breaks intrude on this one, which is probably one of their best singles to date.' The record has 'a heavy, pounding sound which gets the teen tootsies tapping inside a fifth of a second.' Paul's interview with Rosemary Hart on *A World Of Sound*, recorded on 7 September, aired on the Home Service between 4.30pm and 5pm.

The group set off from Liverpool, heading north on the A6 for Carlisle, a 120 mile-plus trip, for the two shows at 6.15pm and 8.30pm at the ABC. In the build-up to the concerts, Chief Superintendent Donald Roy said, 'I do hope Carlisle teenagers will behave more sensibly than teenagers in other towns.'

On arrival, the group liaised with local police at the Cavaghan and Gray factory on the London Road. They transferred to a police vehicle and were driven down Greystone Road, to the cinema's side door on Warwick Road, and entered the projection room. Forty police constables were guarding the entrance. Ringo carried an umbrella and donned a black cossack hat, presumably the same one as Paul had worn the previous day. There were fewer fans than expected because of heavy rain; the following day's headline in the *Carlisle Journal* read, 'Beatles Get A Cool Carlisle Reception'. Before the show, the Mayor of Carlisle, Councillor David Hamilton, hosted a reception for the group. His wife, his daughter Olwyn, the Town Clerk's daughter Caroline Robertson and Judith Pope, the daughter of the Mayor's secretary, were also present. *Disc* winners also met the Beatles backstage, who had just been handed a telegram by Brian Epstein which read, 'You have just sold one million copies of 'She Loves You'.'

Police dogs Paddy and Ursula and their handlers ensured the crowd of close to two thousand was kept moving as one group of fans left the venue after the first show and another waited to go in for the second. Thirty security guards were on hand inside the venue. In a television interview for *North East Reports*, the group were asked about the telegram they had received. John pulled it out of his pocket and read it. 'Just got great news about 'She Loves You' swelling a million', he said.

The concerts were largely uneventful. George was hit by an apple core thrown from the audience, which gave him a slight black eye. Police and cinema officials remained near the stage throughout the two performances. A single seat was broken. After the second show, the group left the theatre in a Royal Mail van. PC John Walker drove them to the Stanwix suburb, where they met the Crown and Mitre Hotel's

manager and transferred to other cars. They were driven the 2 miles back into the city to the hotel - where they had been ignominiously ejected from the hotel ballroom the previous February - entering through the garage and into the linen room. John and George shared one room, Paul and Ringo another. They ate a cold snack before going to bed. A rumoured stay at a local country club, and a 2.30am private cabaret for members never transpired.

> ❛ I can't remember how, but my best friend Janice and I had got tickets for the show at the Lonsdale Cinema, which had just been renamed the ABC. It was a school day, so I went off as usual, in my uniform, to the Carlisle and County High School for Girls. I was 14 years old and the Beatles were my absolute idols at the time. Paul McCartney was my favourite. My father, David Hamilton, was Mayor of Carlisle. During the morning at school, I was taken from my lessons as the mayor's chauffeur had arrived at the school to collect me to take me home.
> Unbeknown to me there was to be a 'civic reception' held for the group in the upstairs foyer of the Lonsdale. When I arrived home and was told why I had been brought out of school, I was totally

stunned. I had to get myself out of my uniform and into something suitable to 'meet' my all-time favourite pop group. As was the fashion in those days, I backcombed my hair to within an inch of its life, put on my black 'Beatles' sweater (a black polo neck) and a pair of trousers. You can imagine, there was no way I was wearing my school uniform for such an exciting venture. We were then driven off in the mayor's limousine to the Lonsdale.

When we arrived in the foyer the mayor's secretary and his daughter, and the Town Clerk and his daughter were also there. I can remember I couldn't really believe that I was sitting there waiting for the Beatles to join us. I'd been looking forward to the show that night, but this was something I honestly never expected. The lift could be heard heading up to the foyer and in a few seconds John, George, Paul and Ringo appeared from inside. It was unbelievable, here I was in the foyer of our local cinema with my idols – I reckon I was speechless (for a change!). They mingled with everyone and then photos were taken. I had some taken sitting between all four of them and then some others taken with just Paul and my father. I did ask Paul if I could have his tie as a memento but he offered me a sixpence (old money) instead, so I had a photo taken with him handing me the sixpence. I still have it mounted with the photo of him giving it to me. It really was a dream come true, and it certainly felt more like a dream than real life. I can't remember what I said to them or they said to me although we were all together in the foyer for quite some time, you have to remember I was only 14 and this was my favourite group. It all seemed to be over in a flash, then I wondered if it really had just been a dream.

Janice and I went off to the show that night and we didn't hear a word they sang or a note they played because everyone, including us, was screaming so hard. I did feel sorry that I hadn't been able to take her with me earlier in the day, but we still stayed best friends and, in fact, we still are to this day. Janice and her family were very unfortunate to be badly flooded during the awful floods in Carlisle of 2005 and everything downstairs was totally ruined, including lots of their photographs and, unfortunately, her copy of the Beatles autographs. However her husband had the presence of mind to lay them carefully on a radiator and managed to dry them out until they were almost as good as new. When I left school and went on to take a Commercial Course at our local college, part of the course was Shorthand. My record collection, as you can imagine, was pretty much all Beatles – singles and albums. To practice my shorthand I used to put the singles on 'repeat' and take down the words in shorthand. My mum was just about driven to distraction through having to listen to the same song multiple times. She was regularly heard to say, 'Pleeeeeeease change the record!' It obviously worked for me though, I went on to be a shorthand typist when I left college. I have many photographs and cuttings from the newspapers back then and whenever I look at them they bring many, many happy memories of that very special day in my life. **❞**

OLWYN GIBSON, CUMBRIA LIBRARY SERVICE PERSONAL ASSISTANT, CARLISLE, CUMBRIA

FRIDAY 22 NOVEMBER

With advance orders of three hundred thousand, *With The Beatles* was released. *Melody Maker* commented, 'A great album, with variety of tempo and a raw style that puts the Beatles unmistakably at the top of the beat tree'. Demand was such that EMI had forty presses on the go at its Hayes record factory. Production manager George Manning said that the factory had taken on an extra 100 workers since the start of Beatlemania. 'We are working just about as many hours as we can, twenty-four hours a day seven days a week,' he said. 'Production resources are stretched to the limit'. Overrun by customers, NEMS record store in Liverpool had to call in the police. In all five hundred and thirty thousand copies were sold nationwide by the end of the day.

The front page of the week's *NME* featured an ad for Dora Bryan's 'All I Want For Christmas Is A Beatle', voted a hit on the previous Saturday's *Juke Box Jury*. Bryan later said, 'I didn't even know what a Beatle was until we started rehearsing this show last summer... I think they're marvellous. So with it, but I don't even know which Beatle is which... When I tried to talk to them at a ball where they were in the cabaret, a security man pulled me away. I felt such a fool. At that stage in their careers I found them very bright, unspoilt, and friendly boys. I don't think any Christmas goes by without the record being played on the radio.' A telegram from the group was delivered to her dressing room shortly thereafter. It read, 'We think the record is fab. All We Want For Beatmas Is A Crystal. But seriously – we hope it is a big hit. Signed John, Paul, George, Ringo.'

In the paper's Top 30, 'She Loves You' returned to the top of the chart after seven weeks, where it had dropped to number 4 and climbed back up again. *The Beatles' Hits* EP re-entered the chart at number 30 as *The Beatles (No. 1)* climbed three places to number 24. The *Twist And Shout* EP also re-entered at number 29. Derek Johnson reviewed 'I Want To Hold Your Hand', writing, 'Worth every single one of its fantastic advance orders – that's my judgement on the Beatles' new single. It's repetitious almost to the point of hypnosis, has an easily memorised melody, and some built-in hand clapping to help along the infectious broken beat. And there's a plaintive and much quieter middle eight, which proves a mighty effective buffer to the remainder of this power-packed disc.' 'Beatles TV Sensation' read the headline of an article that featured news that 'She Loves You' had passed sales of nine hundred and seventy-five thousand two days earlier, and an upcoming appearance on *Juke Box Jury*, a Boxing Day radio show called *Beatle Time*, a series on Radio Luxembourg starting on 22 December and the rescheduling of the group's Portsmouth shows.

In *Melody Maker*, 'She Loves You' also returned to the top, after a six-week break. *Twist And Shout* and *The Beatles' Hits* climbed back into the Top 20 to numbers 15 and 18 respectively, while *The Beatles (No. 1)* climbed to number 22. Bob Dawbarn, the paper's modern jazz expert, wrote, 'I like the Beatles! There will now be a short pause while jazz club proprietors tear up my membership forms, my landlord prepares notice to quit and Dave Brubeck fans cry "I thought as much."... On reflection I think my main reason for liking the Beatles is that they [are] genuine.'

The group woke up late, had a quick snack around midday and left the Crown and Mitre the way they came. Just three fans were on hand to see them go. They drove south on the A6 to Penrith before turning west on the A66 for the two-hour journey to Stockton-on-Tees, where they played two shows at the Globe Theatre at 6.15pm and 8.30pm. As fans were waiting for them at the stage door, the group arrived at the front and walked unencumbered through the foyer. They had cheese sandwiches backstage, posed for photographers and talked with reporters. During the first show, theatre worker Alan Day broke the news to the group that President Kennedy had been assassinated. Vernons Girl Jean Owen remembered, 'We were just about to go onstage, and John came down and was standing at the side. He said, "Eh, did yer know, Kennedy's just been shot?" We looked at him in disbelief. Mo said, "Oh don't be so bloody sick!", and he said, "I'm telling yer, he's just been shot!" Just as he said that, we were announced and had to go on. It wasn't until we came off stage that we heard it was true.'

A few hours earlier, the *CBS Morning News With Mike Wallace* segment recorded in Bournemouth aired in the US. It had been scheduled to be repeated in the evening on the *CBS Evening News With Walter Cronkite*, but was pre-empted by news of the assassination. The report by Alexander Kendrick, who had covered the Russian front in the Second World War and preceded Dan Rather as the network's London bureau chief, was only slightly less condescending than Edwin Newman's earlier in the week. 'Yeah yeah yeah, those are the Beatles those are and this is Beatleland, formerly known as Britain, where an epidemic called Beatlemania has seized the teenage population, especially female. Some of the girls can write and they belong to the Beatle fan club. The Beatles sound like insect life but it's spelled B-E-A-T Beat and these four boys from Liverpool with their dish-mopped hairstyles are Britain's latest musical and in fact sociological phenomenon. They have introduced what their press agents call "the Mersey Sound" after the River Mersey on which Liverpool stands and though musicologists say it is no different than any other rock'n'roll except maybe louder, it has carried the Beatles to the top of the heap. In fact, they have met royalty, and royalty is appreciative and impressed. Wherever the Beatles go they are pursued by hordes of screaming swinging juveniles. They and their press agents have to think up all sorts of ways to evade their adoring fans. Thousands of teenagers in every city and town stand in line all night to get tickets for their touring show. Girls faint when the tickets run out. The other night the Beatles played Bournemouth, the south coast family resort, and Bournemouth will never be the same.'

During 'Twist And Shout' in their second set, two girls managed to get onstage and make a beeline for George, hugging him before making their way over to John. As stewards grabbed hold of the girls, the curtain came down and the group made a quick exit through a back door and into a waiting police car. They were driven half an hour north to the Eden Arms Hotel in nearby Rushyford. Six girls were treated at Stockton and Thornaby Hospital for fainting and hysteria.

❝ I was 9 years old living with my mum and dad and my brother Laurence in a flat in Nunhead, south London. My dad was the manager of G & S Roseman's, a tailor's shop in the Old Kent Road, and on the day *With The Beatles* was released he went to Jones and Higgins, a department store in Rye Lane, Peckham, and bought me a copy. The family used to shop there all the time and there was a mynah bird in there that used to say 'Look out boys. Here come the cops.' It had the premier record department in the area and you had to go past the mynah bird to get to it.

I used to listen to the Light Programme, the forerunner of the very station I work at now, and remember hearing the Beatles for the first time on *Saturday Club*. My mum used to tune into the Light Programme so we could listen to *Listen With Mother* and so at the weekend it was still tuned into the same station. I also remember watching *Juke Box Jury* once when David Jacobs said, 'Young people love the Beatles. They are revolting,' and Pete Murray, who was one of the panellists that week said, 'Yes, young people are revolting.' But when I heard them the excitement quotient was off the scale. I hadn't heard anything so exciting. So my dad knew I was crazy about them.

That evening, I was watching television. In those days, ITV would switch at 7pm from Associated-Rediffusion to ATV, and I remember an announcer by the name of Redvers Kyle doing the hand over into *Take Your Pick* and during the show news came through of Kennedy's assassination. Shortly afterwards my dad walked through the door and said, 'Here's something that might cheer us all up', holding a copy of *With The Beatles*. The first track I listened to was 'Don't Bother Me'. I was never very good at getting the needle to land in the right place on the record. I was allowed to stay up late that night to listen to the album. I played the whole album over and over again until it was worn out. This is a terrible admission, but I've never been much of a carer of records. I respect the music but not the system. I remember scratching 'All My Loving' until it jumped. So Paul goes 'I'll pretend... missing.' That was the only record my dad ever bought me – afterwards I bought everything by the Beatles with my 2/6 weekly pocket money. Every Saturday my uncle Jack would come round and he had a Norton motorbike with a sidecar and on that particular Saturday I wanted to stay indoors and listen to the album, so my mum, Laurence and Auntie Maureen all went out, got in the sidecar and went for a drive. They were driving down Pepys Road in New Cross and the sidecar came loose as they were going down the hill. The sidecar slid into the bus depot across the other side of the road. However, if it had kept going to the intersection of the New Cross Road, they certainly would have been killed. My uncle Jack never drove it again. Years later, the bosses at BBC Radio 2, wanted to do a photo for the front cover of the *Radio Times* with Terry Wogan, Jonathan Ross, who had just joined Radio 2, Mark Lamarr and me. They asked me whether I was up for it and I said 'Yes, absolutely.' 'What do you want to do?' they asked me. 'Well I'd like to do the cover of *With The Beatles* and recreate it. So on the front of the *Radio Times* it said, 'Radio 2 and the new Beatles'.

STEVE WRIGHT, BBC BROADCASTER, LONDON

SATURDAY 23 NOVEMBER

The Beatles left the Eden Arms and headed up the A1 to the City Hall in Newcastle-upon-Tyne for the evening's two shows at 6.30pm and 8.40pm. Just before the first show, *Juke Box Jury* aired. 'I Want To Hold Your Hand' was one of eight records voted a hit by the panel – the only one that turned out to be a hit. Fifteen-year-old Elizabeth Robson was invited backstage to meet the group after her black-and-red shoulder school bag decorated with six photos of the group had been spotted by officials at the stage door. 'I was thrilled to find them so natural and friendly. John Lennon, particularly, has a wonderful sense of humour.' During the second show, while George was playing a guitar solo, two girls made it past the twenty bouncers, leapt up onstage and grabbed hold of a microphone. It took stewards nearly a minute to get them back into their seats.

After the show, with a hundred police on duty outside the hall, the group ran down a short flight of stairs, through a doorway and headed back to the Eden Arms. They had planned to stay at Shotley Bridge's Crown and Crossed Swords Hotel, but police had them drive down the Great North Road where they were delayed with engine trouble in Rushyford, so they stayed a second night at the Eden Arms. Ted Blench, the host of the Crown, denied they were at his hotel. 'Nonsense. The black-haired little so-and-sos were nowhere near.' The Eden Arms manager didn't seem too keen on them either, saying, 'This Beatlemania makes me sick.'

In a review titled 'These Screaming Fans Beat The Beatles' Beat', the *Evening Chronicle* commented on fans' reactions. 'If you have ever wondered how Baron Frankenstein might have felt when he realised what a monster he had created, put yourself in the shoes of the small group of journalists (myself among them) who first recognised and publicised a quaintly-named recording group now universally acclaimed as the Beatles. Until Saturday night my acquaintance with the Liverpool lads had been that ideal combination of pleasure and power which control of a volume knob or a television switch gives one. Then I was pitched headlong into a vortex of mass hysteria the like of which I have not seen since I witnessed the almost unbelievable vilification of Mussolini's corpse in Milan at the end of the war. Newcastle's City Hall reverberated to the rhythmic stamp of more than two thousand pairs of feet and the decibels rose well beyond tolerance level as two thousand teenagers screamed themselves hoarse, and effectively destroyed any chance of hearing the very sounds they had queued for hours and paid good money to listen to. Solid phalanxes of gyrating bodies and imploring, outstretched arms blotted out the view of the stage and the sweating, shouting performers. Fever-pitch was reached and passed. The fans had whipped themselves into a near-delirium in which nothing mattered but that they were involved in the mass adulation of the Beatles. To them it was "fab" – though if they heard one word or caught one strangled guitar chord of that futile projection from the stage, they achieved more than I did.' The review ended, 'Oh for a "quiet" concert – the '1812 Overture' or the soothing normality of The Planets for example!'

Only after a few hours after two glossy pictures of the Beatles were displayed in the offices of the Leigh Chronicle, the window was smashed and the photographs taken. A few days before another window in the office was smashed. Mr. H. Whittaker, the paper's branch manager said, 'two down, four to go.'

❝ In 1963 I was 14 and living in Newcastle-upon-Tyne. My friends Mary, Caroline and myself were enjoying our youth and the changes that the '60s brought. The Beatles were the most exciting thing to happen in our lives. When we heard that they would be playing at the City Hall in November 1963, we resolved to queue all night for tickets. My sister Denise, who was 17, decided to come along with us, although she was slightly less interested in the Beatles as she was somewhat more sophisticated, having just finished secretarial college! The tickets went on sale at the City Hall which was only about a mile from my home. By the time we arrived at the queue we were only about 500 yards away from my house. I can't remember much about the night spent queuing except that lots of parents were checking on their children, after all we were mostly young teenagers. Hot flasks of coffee and food were supplied by my parents and my friend's mother. There were police patrolling all through the night, so we never slept, just talked and laughed.

At around seven o'clock in the morning the word went out that the box office was open (not true) and there was a grand scramble and stampede! I was separated from my sister and friends. I tried to stay in the queue although I was being squashed, the thought of the opportunity to see my idols kept me going for a while. The night without sleep and lack of air got the better of me, I fainted! I was quickly lifted over the heads of the crowd into a policeman's arms. He wanted me to go to hospital for a check-up but I just wanted to go home and sleep!

At home I went straight to bed devastated that I had lost my chance of seeing the Beatles. My friends had left the queue when the stampede started. My sister had not returned home. Later in the day I awoke to find that she had actually been able to buy a ticket (only one per person). When she heard what had happened and how distraught I was, she gave me her ticket! To thank her for her grand gesture I gave her my most precious possession, my wicker school cookery basket!

I went to the Beatles concert and it was FAB, even though I was on my own. My seat was in the balcony with plenty of other young teenagers, mainly girls. When the Beatles came onstage the place erupted, with lots of screaming girls. The concert continued in the same way. I always say I saw the Beatles live in 1963 as I certainly didn't hear them! I moved to Italy in 1970 where I have lived ever since. My sister moved to Melbourne in 1973 and is still there. The Italian state television has in their library images of the piece of black-and-white film which shows my exit from the queue. I have seen myself on their news programme when they reported the deaths of both John Lennon and George Harrison. **,**

SUSAN MANFRONI, ANTIQUES DEALER, RIMINI, ITALY

SUNDAY 24 NOVEMBER

nterviewed by John Deane Potter in the *News Of The World*, Brian Epstein said, 'I had no idea of managing them at first. I chatted with them and found they were rather browned off. They were well known on Merseyside, but never seemed to get anywhere near the big time. We liked each other and gradually the idea grew between us that I might manage them. It revived all my show business instincts and I felt I could help them with my knowledge of the theatre.' Across the ocean, *The New York Times* wrote about the Beatles for the first time. Stephen Watts described them as 'wearing floor-mop haircuts which remind one of nothing so much as an adolescent version of the Three Stooges.'

As the group prepared to leave the Eden Arms for two shows at 5.15pm and 7.45pm at the 2,360-seater ABC in Hull, it was discovered their car could not start. An AA patrolman arrived but was unable to repair the fault. A Humber was hired from Minories Garage in Newcastle and the group were on their way after an hour's delay. Afterwards, the patrolman found himself trapped in the hotel car park by fans. The group arrived in Hull mid-afternoon, late for their rendezvous with police at the city's boundary, who took them Gordon Street Police station. As they discussed arrangements for their journey to the cinema in the charge room, Sergeant Ted Holt told John, 'If you don't stop swearing in my charge room, the only place you're going is them cells.'

The group were taken to the venue in a van, with PCs Andy Lowthorpe and Don Sylvester on board. They met with the press in the cinema's Regal Room. George turned off his transistor radio, Ringo lit a cigarette and John and Paul sat down. Cokes were brought in. John, asked what it was like to have adoring fans, replied, 'It changes other people around us... We get very little peace and quiet, but we find it no more tiring than we find anything else.' Joe King of the *Hull & Kingston Times* asked Paul whether he would be prepared to meet 17-year-old Lynda Hill, who had queued all night to buy a ticket, but at 8.45am was still 10 yards from the booking office and had to go to work. The group came downstairs and went outside to meet her. Her employer Mrs Canty had given her a ticket to see the first show with her 13-year-old daughter Heather.

The first show ended at 7.15pm. Mounted police cleared a way through thousands of fans to allow buses in and out of Ferensway station between the two houses. At the second show, a teddy bear landed at Paul's feet. Twelve fans fainted at the first show, eleven at the second. Girls had to be restrained by police, who numbered forty inside the building, alongside twenty-two stewards and four international rugby league players. Eighteen-year-old Pat Hall lost her ticket at a wrestling show the previous Tuesday, throwing it away with some green raffle tickets. 'I nearly fainted on Friday when I realised what I had done. We had lived on fish and chips and queued all night for those tickets.' She got in touch with police and an official at the ABC. After a friend in the audience vouched for her and her two friends, Janice Irwin and Irene Ahmed, they were let in.

With a decoy car out front after the second show, the group escaped in a police van at the rear of the cinema and were whisked back to the police station.

> ❟ At the time I was a constable in the Hull City Police Force and was assigned one evening to go with a driver and another PC to pick up the Beatles at the City boundary on Boothferry Road, Hull, which we did. We took them to the Gordon Street Police Station where they showered and changed into their stage gear. We then got into the police van again and took them to the ABC. We had an interesting chat with them about their career so far and a comical point in the journey was when John Lennon insisted on wearing my helmet which was much too small for him. It looked like 'a pea on a drum.' I managed to obtain all their autographs for my daughter and her friend which as far as I'm aware she still possesses. On arrival at the cinema, we smuggled them into the building through a side door but the horde of screaming girls spotted us at the last minute, but we got them inside without any trouble and I escorted them right on to the stage. By the time their gig finished I had gone off duty, but it was a very interesting episode in a thirty-year police career. ❟
>
> **DON SYLVESTER, POLICE CONSTABLE, KINGSTON UPON HULL, EAST YORKSHIRE**

MONDAY 25 NOVEMBER

The *Bradford Telegraph & Argus* reported that police leave had been cancelled in anticipation of the Gaumont box office opening: 'Two thirds of Bradford City Police force have had their leave cancelled for next Sunday so that adequate supervision can be given to the thousands-strong queue expected at the Gaumont Theatre when the booking office for the Beatles show on 21 December will be open at 10pm.' At the suggestion of the Chief Constable, the box office opened at 8.30am at the Doncaster Gaumont. Ann Rowlands and Rita Sutcliffe were particularly concerned: 'We factory girls have to start work at 7.30am. We don't mind queuing for tickets, but we do mind losing our jobs.' The plan had been to open the box office on 22 November, but the date clashed with the Doncaster races. However, tickets had been offered that day as spot prizes at the Doncaster Press Ball at the Earl of Doncaster Arms. Cinema manager Colin Meggison said that desperate fans had offered to wash his personal laundry and to scrub the floors of the cinema in exchange for tickets. He provided hot dogs for those who queued through the night. Police Superintendent Robert Coggan of the Doncaster Borough Police said, 'They are a credit to Doncaster. They behaved themselves when they queued for tickets.' By dawn, it was raining and the queue stretched down East Laith Gate. Wet and cold, twenty at a time were admitted into the box office.

The group, taking a day off from their tour, recorded spots for *Late Night Extra* and *Scene At 6.30* at Granada TV Centre in Manchester. They mimed to 'I Want To Hold Your Hand' and 'This Boy', and were interviewed by Gay Byrne for the two shows. Byrne asked the group and fellow guest, comedian Ken Dodd, 'We have always thought that it might be a good question to put to Mr Kenneth Dodd and the members of the Beatles, er, to what extent do they attribute their success to their hairstyles?' George said that it might have been better for Dodd if he had been bald. Commenting on the similarities between him and the group, the comedian said, 'We talk the same language – it's the draught from the Mersey Tunnel which causes the Liverpool accent.' It was one of the last times John used his Gibson J-160E guitar (which was stolen while they were performing their Christmas show at Finsbury Park). The two shows aired on 27 November and 20 December respectively.

TUESDAY **26 NOVEMBER**

The group set out for Cambridge, where the tour continued with two concerts at the Regal Cinema. At 2.15pm, they met with police several miles outside the city and transferred into a Black Maria, driving the remaining few miles to the cinema. Manager D.J. Archer said, 'The cinema is like a fortress with the drawbridge off. Every entry and exit point is being guarded by extra men.' On hand was a twelve-man Vespa motor scooter team, which included former Cambridge United goalkeeper Roy Coxon, and members of the Shelford Football Club helped keep order inside – they had also helped out at the earlier concert in March. The Red Cross had a dozen men in pairs, with the foyer resembling a miniature battle station, with stretchers, blankets, pillows and large bottles of smelling salts.

Arriving in the city, the group drove along Lensfield Road and Tennis Court Road into the grounds of the University Laboratories on to Downing Place, and to the back of the cinema on St Andrew's Street. Inside, they met press in the circle lobby, drinking Scotch and Coke. John was asked how his wife reacted to seeing so little of him. 'It gets a bit tough at times,' he responded. 'If I get really lonely, though, I send for her, although we move round the country with such speed that I have little time to take account of my personal life.' He also commented on his impressions of the city, 'I wish I had more time to spend in Cambridge. It looks like such a lovely place. I think we shall have to come back again to see it – only in disguise. The town seems very dignified.' When asked what their film was going to be about, Paul replied, 'Sort of a fantasy-type thing.' The group were also interviewed by Jean Goodman in their dressing room for BBC's live *East At Six Ten* television show at 6.38pm. She found them at their most mischievous. Asked 'How long do you think the group will last?' John replied, 'About five years.' One of the few sensible answers given.

Promoter Arthur Howes arrived in his Jaguar with passengers Maureen O'Grady and Fiona Adams. After the 6.15pm show, following the National Anthem, the audience left to the strains of *The Bridge On The River Kwai* theme. Someone was overheard saying, 'I guess I like them, but really Cliff's better.' The group met with Peter Yolland again. He took twenty minutes to record the group's lines for the Christmas show in a nearby dressing room, half an hour before they went back onstage.

Less than a minute after their last curtain call, the group were out of the building. They ran down a flight of stairs backstage and scrambled into a waiting van, driven by Police Sergeant Arthur Quinney. As Quinney pulled away from the kerb, a decoy Black Maria, with headlamps blazing, drove towards the crowds standing at the end of Downing Place, while police cars pulled up outside the front entrance in St Andrew's Street. The group were driven through the grounds of the University Laboratories to Tennis Court Road, left on to Lensfield Road, to Gonville Place and left on to Parkside for the roundabout journey to the University Arms. As soon as they passed through, Chief Inspector Ronald Barlow, head of the City Police Traffic Department, ordered the gates to be closed. Crowds outside the cinema completely blocked the road while hundreds more waited patiently outside the hotel.

Within ten minutes of arriving at the hotel, the group were sitting down to dinner. American journalist Michael Braun interviewed them over their meal. He had joined them on the road for an in-depth view of the Beatle phenomenon for a book he was writing. After dinner the group stayed up late listening to records, watching films and chatting to hotel staff.

Traffic blocks built up through the town centre and well into Hills Road. When rain began to fall, the crowd began to disperse. A senior police officer commented, 'Things went very well indeed, although I am sorry so many people were disappointed about not seeing the Beatles.' Following the two concerts, a Red Cross spokesman said, 'We dealt with three hysteria cases and one girl who went temporarily deaf and asked us for earplugs.'

Varsity reviewed the concert, 'They played their numbers against a solid wall of shriek. Girls waving programmes like maddened metronomes pleaded for recognition. Only the National Anthem could end it all. The police and the fire hoses were waiting in the street. But drizzle dampened the hysteria.' The paper also printed a segment from the diary of an unnamed undergraduate: 'Was sick in the afternoon. Query – over-excited anticipation or dyspepsia? Surely not... Find myself panting so loudly I can hardly hear them. Emotive music and other phrases flash through my mind in a last minute bid for proper intellectual non-participation. Hear scream – it's me I think. The Girtonian in the row in front looks round in scornful superiority... Later in the quietness of Newnham, I struggled with the disgrace of succumbing to the mass influence. Prostituted sensibility, feels exhausted. Why did I let it happen? Why did it get me like that? Then the idea hits me – of course, the birth trauma again.' At the London Rotarians lunch in London, Sir Henry Jones, the chairman of the Gas Council, said, 'I prefer the Beatles to old-time dance music, and gas heating to log fires.'

❝ I was at Drama School in Bristol, having commenced my 'formal' training as a singer, dancer, actor and stage manager that September. It was the first time that I had lived away from my home and family in Lincoln, which was where I had started my career in entertainment in 1958 at the Theatre Royal. I was intending to spend my first Christmas away from home working on a production of *Around The World in Eighty Days* at the historic Theatre Royal in King Street. Life was good at this time for an 18-year-old, with the youth culture at last finding its feet and more importantly, its voice. Paramount to this in the 'Kennedy Years', was the development of music, on both sides of the Atlantic and the emergence of the Mersey Sound. I had listened to the early releases of the Beatles earlier in the year and was blown away by their unique sound and the pure energy that they produced. So much so, that on all my letters back home to Lincoln, I put the letters J-P-G-R on the back of every envelope. As a student living on a grant at that time, I couldn't afford to buy a ticket for their concert at the Colston Hall on the 15th of November, but joined the crowds outside that virtually closed off the city centre. Knowing that their second LP was due for release the following week, I was determined to buy my own copy at the earliest opportunity, and began to save the funds required. The tragic event in Dallas, when JFK was assassinated, was on everyone's mind that weekend and on the day after his funeral, I went down to my local record shop and bought my copy of 'With The Beatles' for 32 shillings and 6 pence. My first impression was of the striking cover photo by Robert Freeman, and the image that the four portrayed. I listened to all 14 of the tracks with my girlfriend Maggie in her flat in Clifton, whilst eating jars of Shipton's Salmon Spread, the height of student indulgence! Our personal favourite was 'All My Loving' and it became an anthem of ours. It was also nice to hear George get a solo on 'Don't Bother Me' and 'Roll Over Beethoven.' As a student, I tried to emulate their style of dress, and to this day still have in my wardrobe the Wolsey-made collar and lapel less jacket that I would wear with my Levis 501s and roll neck jumper back in 1963. My association with the Beatles grew stronger when I left Bristol in 1966 to work in Liverpool at the Playhouse, Royal Court and Empire Theatres. I became the unofficial First Night Party Social Secretary and would take many eminent visiting artists to the Cavern Club, the Shakey or, more often, to the Blue Angel Club. This was owned by Allan Williams who was the first Beatles Manger and who personally drove the van over to Hamburg in 1960 for their season at the Indra Club. Allan was a larger than life character and we soon got to know each other very well. On one occasion I recall, he decided to hold a Spanish bullfight in the Basement Bar. He somehow 'obtained' a young bull locally, and kept it locked up all day in the beer store, until the advertised time. Then he let the animal loose and everyone scattered, as the frightened animal showed how he felt by relieving himself all over the dance floor. We became close friends and I went on holiday with him and his delightful wife Beryl Chang to Palma where he was opening an 'automated' alley. His idea was to employ two local pensioners to stand at the far end of the alley with old mattresses round the shins, and roll the balls back again. He later fell on hard times and sold coffee mugs in Camden Market with the inscription 'I'm The Mug Who Sold The Beatles' embossed on them. Great times and a privilege to remember what I was up to over fifty years ago. **"**

JOHN TOOGOOD, WEST END THEATRE GENERAL MANAGER, LINCOLN, LINCOLNSHIRE

WEDNESDAY 27 NOVEMBER

MI announced that sales of 'She Loves You' had surpassed a million, *With The Beatles* had sold five hundred and thirty thousand copies since the previous Friday and that advance sales of 'I Want To Hold Your Hand' had reached nine hundred and forty thousand. Gerald Depinns, sales manager of George Bassett's, the largest Jelly Baby manufacturers in Sheffield, told the *Daily Mirror* that, 'They've been going at least sixty years. And there is a ritual about the way to eat them. Some eat the limbs off first, while others prefer to decapitate them. Few people suck them.'

A doorman at the University Arms told girls waiting outside that the two men standing at the hotel entrance were international rugby players.

After having a lie-in, the group left in the Austin Princess at midday, heading to the Rialto in York for two shows at 6.40pm and 8.45pm. The main gates leading into the hotel were closed five minutes before they left. After waiting four hours to get the group's autographs, 17-year-old Edwin Jones came away empty handed.

The group arrived half an hour earlier than expected to their pre-arranged rendezvous with police on the Tadcaster Road, so they dropped into the York Motel for a meal. George phoned the police to say they had arrived. A Z-Car with Derek Lacey on board headed to meet them.

Arriving at the cinema, they jumped out of the still-moving car and ran through the front doors. Some four hundred fans, jammed behind crush barriers, were there to greet them, keeping up an almost unending chant of 'We Want Paul! ...George! ...Ringo! ...John!' John felt ill, apparently because he'd eaten his meal at the York Motel too quickly, and spent the following three hours in their dressing room. Paul said, 'He'll be all right after he's had a kip.' Inside, more than two dozen journalists and photographers were waiting. Paul held 7-month-old Jane Vize from Hull in his arms so that her mother Margaret could photograph them. Christine Glensor and Bronwen Pickering interviewed the group for their Queen Anne

Grammar School newspaper, chatting with Ringo, George and Paul. John thought the teens' presence was 'probably just an excuse to get into our dressing room. Anyway, women should be obscene and not heard.' When the group were finished, they downed Cokes and headed off to their dressing rooms.

During the first show, the lights in the theatre fused and the curtains failed to close after the draw cable jammed on its drum. For the rest of the show, the curtains had to be wound by hand. Following the second show, the group were whisked out of the building into their waiting car and driven to the Royal Station York Hotel. George went to bed soon after they arrived, while John joined Paul and Ringo in their room. George wrote to a young fan who had asked to marry him. 'If you really want to marry me then send a photograph, as I can't very well say yes without even seeing you can I? I will see what can be arranged, but I think you had better ask your parents first!'

Joan Home reviewed the shows in the *Northern Echo*. 'Have you ever tried listening to a thirty-minute long scream from 1,626 pairs of lungs, with a Merseyside beat for backing?' she wrote. 'It is fabulous, or I suppose it is if you like that kind of thing. Like the rest of the kids in this country the York ones love it.'

During the evening, several Beatles-related programmes appeared on television and radio. At 6.15pm, ATV's *Fair Play* aired on London ITV. Its host Edgar Lustgarten interviewed Epstein, saying, 'The more popular the Beatles get the more the kids rave and the more the fans need police control. For all this the rate-payers pay.' At 8pm, *Wacker, Mach Schau*, aired on the BBC North Home Service, an extended version of the *Voice Of The North* programme that had gone out the previous week. *Late Night Extra*, featuring the group miming to 'I Want To Hold Your Hand', was broadcast on Northern TV at 11.45pm. Talking with Michael Braun, John said they'd always hated Cliff Richard, while Paul talked about the film *The Trial*, which he had seen the previous week, and the plays *Next Time I'll Sing To You* and *A Severed Head*, both of which he was unimpressed with. One being 'a dead bore' the other 'the crappiest thing I'd seen for years.'

❛ I was a 17-year-old sixth-former at Queen Anne's Grammar School in York in the autumn of 1963, and we were all crazy about the Beatles. I had seen them a couple of times that year, once with Chris Montez, and once supporting Roy Orbison. By November, they had become so popular, we had taken it in turns to queue for tickets with my friend Bronwen Pickering, whose parents ran Pickering's Bookshop in the Shambles, and another friend drawing the short straw, and having to miss school to take their turn. Unfortunately, they were found out and hauled up in front of our teacher, Miss Whittaker. She asked them who they had bought tickets for, but they refused to say, and were consequently banned from the sixth-form common room for a week! They had to move their desks out into the hall, but to us they were heroines – firstly because they got tickets for the front row, and secondly because they didn't tell on us!

About this time, the sixth forms of the four grammar schools in York, including ours, got together and decided to produce a magazine, to be sold in aid of Oxfam. Our sixth form was asked if it would write some articles, so Bronwen and I came up with the idea of interviewing the Beatles when they came to town for the show. So, one Saturday at my house, we got ourselves psyched up, and decided to ring Stacey Brewer from *The Yorkshire Evening Press*. We told him of our plan and asked for some advice of how to go about it. He suggested ringing the manager of the Rialto to explain what we'd like to do, which we did, and I nearly fell off my chair when he said yes! He suggested coming to the cinema around 4.30, straight after school, on the day of the concert. We were very excited, but also mortified that we would have to go in our school uniforms! In those days we had berets, with a badge on the front. You were not allowed to take your beret off whilst in uniform, but as soon as we got off the bus outside the Rialto on the big day, we put our berets in our bags!

We couldn't believe the crowds when we got there. There was a police cordon around the cinema, keeping the fans on the other side of the street. We went up to one of the policemen and told him we were interviewing the Beatles for our school magazine, and that the manager had asked us to come along. He took us inside, and sure enough, the manager remembered us, and we were ushered through to the inside of the theatre. There were various other press reporters, although no one else of our age, all waiting for the group. Paul, Ringo and George duly appeared, but not John – we were told he wasn't feeling well. We were all allowed a short time with each Beatle, before moving on to the next. We had a list of questions we wanted to ask, including their views on politics, although they wouldn't answer questions of that nature. My strongest memory is of Ringo sitting on the edge of the stage, as things calmed down, just talking to Bronwen and I. He told us about a book he was reading called *Mila 18* by Leon Uris, which was set in Warsaw during and after the Second World War.

When we got home, we quickly changed out of our uniforms, and into our mini-skirts, and back on the bus to take up our seats in the front row for the concert. It all seemed like a bit of a dream that we had been there earlier, interviewing them! Fortunately, John was feeling better, and was onstage for the show. Even down at the front, it was almost impossible to hear them sing for the screaming! The next day when I got up, my father was listening to the radio in the kitchen, and they mentioned that there was a story in the *Northern Echo* about two schoolgirls who had interviewed the Beatles. Our English teacher at school got hold of a copy and read it out in class. I was quoted as saying, 'We were curious to discover how the Beatles induced hysteria.' She thought it was absolutely hilarious that I had said this! Over the next couple of days, Bronwen and I put our heads together, and wrote the story of our wonderful encounter, calling it 'With The Beatles'. I later looked up the book Ringo had told us about and took it out of the local library to read. I still look back with fondness to my encounter with the Beatles, it was just one of those days that you never forget. ❜

CHRISTINE DOWIE, MAYOR, KIRKBYMOORSIDE, NORTH YORKSHIRE

THURSDAY 28 NOVEMBER

The front page of *Disc* read 'Boots For The Beatles' and featured a photo of the group trying on various types of footwear in a shoe shop. In the paper's new Top 30, the Beatles and the songwriting team of Lennon and McCartney dominated the chart, with 'She Loves You' returning to number one, *With The Beatles* at number 14 (already with sales of more than five hundred and twenty thousand), the EPs *Twist And Shout*, *The Beatles' Hits*, *The Beatles (No. 1)*, at numbers 17, 20 and 21, respectively, and the Rolling Stones' 'I Wanna Be Your Man' at number 30. Inside the paper was an article written by Mike Scott titled 'The Beatles Talking On America, Money, Girls And Marriage'. George felt that going to America was 'going to be hard', while John commented on how successful their Swedish trip had been – even though the group were not very well known there when they had arrived – before adding, 'On the other hand, we are being paid a fortune to go to America and probably nothing will happen.' The paper announced that a two-hour all-star radio show, *From Us To You*, headlined by the Beatles, was scheduled to air on the Light Programme on Boxing Day. For those considering what to ask Santa for, the paper suggested Beatle jackets, a Beatle dress, Beatles sweaters, Beatle badges and Beatle boots.

'She Loves You' also returned to number one in the *NRM* chart, while *With The Beatles* entered the LP chart at number 2. Langley Johnson posed the question, 'Are the Beatles bad for pop business?' After making mention of the current tour, the three-week Christmas show, their trip to America and their appearances on *Juke Box Jury*, he reached the conclusion that 'Beatlemania is on the way to 'infecting' the whole world. Which is GOOD for business, whatever the sufferers have to say about it.' The *Daily Express* reported that Mitre United, who played in Birmingham's Coronation League, had only won two games since changing their name to the Beatles. Secretary John Weaver theorised about centre forward Bernard Kemp, who had a Beatle haircut and hadn't scored for a while; 'I think his hair is getting in his eyes.'

As the group were about to leave York, fans from York Technical College found them in their car at the tea square behind the hotel and got their autographs. As the car moved off, Paul wound his window down to sign a piece of A4 ruled notepaper. The group drove south on the A19 for two shows at the ABC in Saltergate, Lincoln. During the journey, George took the wheel of the Austin Princess to embark on a race with Arthur Howes in his Jaguar. They arrived shortly after 3.30pm.

Vendors in the city's High Street were selling souvenir newspapers, crying, 'Get your Beatles paper here!' Richard Cooper, who had travelled down from Scunthorpe to see one of the two shows, vaulted a fence which he believed led to a towpath – but ended up in the river Witham. He was rescued by his friends Stephen Drury and John Gilgallon, then taken to dry out at the City Police Station. Before the 6.15pm show, a doctor was called to the cinema to treat Ringo, who was suffering from an earache. It took her twenty minutes to convince those guarding the group that she was a doctor. On her advice, he was taken to Lincoln County Hospital to have his ear syringed. He left wearing a trilby, dark glasses and a heavy overcoat, a disguise that 'made him look like Brecht being smuggled out of Germany,' according to one eyewitness. An ABC spokesman reported that, 'He has been suffering from a painful earache all week,' while a nurse at the hospital proffered the view that 'It's a Beatles' occupational disease, all that hair getting in their ears.'

During the second house, twenty or so teenagers made a mad dash for the stage. The group performed 'I Want To Hold Your Hand' live for the first time. Following the 8.30pm show, they left the cinema in stage make-up. As they were about to make their getaway, the police chief came over and asked for their autographs for his daughters. The group hurtled down West Parade and into a cul-de-sac, followed by two housewives – June Clarke and Anne Blair – who pointed them in the right direction in exchange for autographs. They drove to Punch's Hotel in Doncaster. On their way, they ran out of petrol and had to flag down a passing lorry at 1.30am. By 10am the next day, they had a new driver.

6 It seemed like summer to me because we were SO HAPPY. The group had never been to Lincoln before (nor since, I guess), and it was our chance to show them how we felt. I would have just turned 16 at the time – and I was a young, naive 16 – green, wet behind the ears, all that. I barely knew what sex was although I certainly did like boys by then, especially George Harrison (my allegiance later switched to John). We must have queued for hours somewhere and been ecstatic when we held those tickets in our hands. I went with my friend Mary Hopkinson, who was a Paul fan, and we clung to each other screaming. Mary tells me that I would occasionally tell her to 'shut up' because I couldn't hear the music! And believe me, even in November 1963 (just shortly into their careers), I knew every word of every Beatles song, and I could sing all of the parts. I would go to our front room and play my Beatles records over and over and over, with my ear right next to the speaker because I couldn't play it too loud. My parents despaired but I was no different than most other 15/16-year-olds at the time. In fact, I think the Beatles were saviours – our lives were rather dull, expectations were shallow (more dullness), and they brought us such joy and something like madness or gleefulness that carried us through. (My own daughter

had the same experience at 14 with Depeche Mode, and the generation before me it was Elvis, and before that probably Frank Sinatra). Isn't it wonderful that we were 'normal' teenagers – doing what teenagers for generations had been doing?! I'm so glad I'm a baby boomer and lived through that period! **"**

KATHERINE COOPER, FINANCE MANAGER, WELLS FARGO BANK, KENT, WASHINGTON, USA

FRIDAY 29 NOVEMBER

In the *NME* chart, 'She Loves You' remained at number one, while *With The Beatles* placed at number 15, and the EPs *Twist And Shout* and *The Beatles (No. 1)* at numbers 16 and 26. The paper also reported that sales of 'I Want To Hold Your Hand', released on this day, had passed nine hundred and forty thousand two days earlier, 'She Loves You' had passed the million mark, reaching 1,050,000, and *With The Beatles* had passed the half-million mark with sales of five hundred and thirty thousand, becoming the first million-selling LP in the UK. In 'From You To Us', Linda and Jane Coombes complained that in the previous week's issue the Beatles had been mentioned seventy-nine times.

'She Loves You' also remained at number one in the *Melody Maker* singles chart, with the three EPs all climbing – *Twist And Shout* (14), *The Beatles' Hits* (15) and *The Beatles (No. 1)* (21). *With The Beatles* knocked *Please Please Me* off the top of the LP chart, where it had been for 29 weeks (*NME*) and 30 weeks (*Melody Maker*), respectively. Combined, the two LPs held the top spot on the chart continuously for fifty-one weeks, from May 1963 to May 1964.

The group were playing at the ABC in Huddersfield in the evening and met up with their police escort 6 miles away near Thunder Bridge on the A629. They arrived in the town at 4pm, accompanied by PC George Banks in a white police car. Their Austin Princess car was driven to the front entrance and they entered through the front door of the 2,036-seater cinema. They immediately held a press conference, indulging in cocktail sausages while answering questions. They were asked about their fans and Paul responded, 'I admit that the majority of our audiences are girls, but they only scream where a man at a football match would cheer.' Ian O'Brien and Michael Hartley, two pupils from St Gregory's Roman Catholic Grammar School, attended the conference, writing for their school magazine *Crank*. The group were also interviewed backstage by Gorden Kaye for *Music Box*, a record request show for local hospitals, as part of the Huddersfield Tape Recording Society. Kaye asked George what he thought of fans screaming throughout their performances. George answered, 'Well, they've paid the money so they can scream, can't they? I mean, if they haven't paid and they were screaming, it'd be a liberty, wouldn't it?' Asked what his ambitions were, he said, 'to join the Navy and be a lieutenant commander on HMS Queen Victoria.' (Kaye went on to be an actor, notably playing the role of René in the BBC1 Television sitcom *Allo 'Allo!*) The *Huddersfield Daily Examiner* had four reporters and two photographers covering the event.

Several hundred fans began gathering outside the White Swan Hotel in nearby Halifax chanting for their heroes. Traffic was held up and as the evening wore on and more fans arrived with sandwiches and flasks of tea, telling police they were prepared to stay – some of whom did so until after midnight. Back in Huddersfield, a crowd began to gather at 5pm. Those without tickets assembled in the car park adjoining the YEB Showroom. A group of nurses from Huddersfield Royal Infirmary saw the concerts for free, in exchange for selling ice cream during the intermission. Half an hour before the group were due to onstage for the first house, as fans milled around four-deep on either side of Market Street, three fire engines from the Huddersfield Fire Brigade arrived at the cinema. A phone call had been placed claiming there had been an explosion at the cinema. Its manager Roy Hartle was in the foyer when the firemen arrived, assuring them that it was a false alarm. Before the start of the 6.15 show, the St John Ambulance treated a girl for a sprained ankle and another suffering from a bad case of hysteria.

After the first show, a black kitten with a pink bow was found on a stalls seat inside a tartan shopping bag, accompanied by a note saying it was a present for John. At 10.30pm, within ninety seconds of the curtain coming down at the end of the second show, the group had left the building. A Black Maria, usually used to take prisoners to Leeds Prison, backed up to an emergency door on Fox Street and drove the group away. Crush barriers at the junction of Market Street were moved aside, allowing the van to drive through and ignore a red light. The group was driven to Peel Street headquarters, where they changed into street clothes, got into their own car and made way to their hotel outside Huddersfield. Meanwhile, a police car and Black Maria waited outside the main entrance, as the group's instruments were loaded into their van. A St John Ambulance Brigade member said, 'Even Wembley has nothing on this,' noting a fellow member spent both shows with cotton wool stuffed in her ears.

❛ I was just 16 (not 17!) as my birthday was 9 November and I had queued overnight to secure tickets in the front row. I was with my school friends and there was a great sense of excitement with parents coming along with hot drinks to keep us warm as we lay under blankets on the pavement. I nearly didn't go to the concert as my grandad had collapsed and died in Nottingham on 22 November (yes – the same day as JFK) and I went to Derby with my mother for her to sort out the funeral arrangements. If I had stayed for the funeral, I would have missed the concert but everyone agreed that I shouldn't do that. So I travelled back to Huddersfield on the trains by myself. Very adventurous for me. The train journey from Derby to Huddersfield seemed quite tortuous in those days as it went via Chesterfield, Sheffield and Penistone. I had to change stations in Sheffield which were about one mile apart. At Penistone (which always felt like the coldest station on earth) passengers had to be led across the train track to get to the opposite platform. At least by 1963 there was a train to Huddersfield.

I still have the letter that I sent to my mother the day after the concert, telling her all about it. After she died, I found it amongst her collection of papers which she had kept. I wrote, 'Had a fabulous time at the Beatles last night. They sang about eight songs and all of them fabulous. The noise was terrific. We couldn't really hear them. I've got a sore throat after all the screaming. The police (about one hundred) had barricades up all round the cinema and the queue went into the car park. We weren't allowed to throw any Jelly Babies as they threatened to stop the show. All along the edge of the stage there was about forty men crouched down in case anybody ran up and St John Ambulance men all along the side coping with the fainting girls. There was a girl behind me who cried all the time. Every time Paul or John (they were nearest to us) looked we screamed, shouted their names and waved our hands. Paul looked at me and Anne twice and smiled and raised his eyebrows. For their last song 'Twist And Shout' quite a few stood up and went absolutely mad (including us) and all the men stood up ready to stop them so we all sat down again. We heard Miss Hamer (she was the headmistress of my school – Huddersfield High School, a girls' grammar school) went to see them to study their psycho-something or other. I didn't mention in my letter that George was my favourite. ❜

CHRISTINE SKINNER, CHEMICAL RESEARCH ANALYST, KNUTSFORD, CHESHIRE

SATURDAY **30 NOVEMBER**

By 10.30am, there was already a gathering of teenage girls waiting outside the stage door of the Empire Theatre in Sunderland, shouting 'They're here!' at each passing car. A nearby furniture store boarded up its plate-glass windows. One of its directors, Mr M. Gillis, said, 'We are taking no chances with our windows.' By the middle of the afternoon, the crowd had grown to more than a hundred and twenty, and by 5.30pm close to two thousand were waiting. Many girls in the crowd refused to give reporters their names for fear of parental wrath. A rumour spread that the group had been involved in a car accident and would not be appearing. Like many towns hosting shows during this tour, shops had various Beatle-related items for sale – Joplings was selling Beatles suits for £8, Caslaw Bros had velvet jackets for £5, and Walkers jewellers had fan badges for 6/-. In perhaps a first, a dog parlour was offering a Beatle cut for poodles.

Before the 6pm show, *Sunderland Echo* reporter Barry St John Neville interviewed the group backstage and twenty teenage winners of the Freedom From Hunger competition got the opportunity to meet their idols. The Empire's Roman Catholic padre, Father Leo Coughlin, also talked with the group backstage, all partaking in a brandy and soda. Paul asked the priest, 'Why are there so many big churches in countries where people are starving?' The seemingly innocent encounter became controversial after Coughlin told members of St Benet's Youth Club the following day. He said, 'Some loaded wisecracking went on and there was a pushing incident. That is all I can say.' Twenty-two-year-old schoolteacher Pat Cummings told her pupils at St Hilda's Secondary Modern school in Sunderland that the group had been rude to the padre. The following weekend, a Beatles spokesman responded, 'The boys were having an innocent joke on the priest. As far as I know there was no pushing incident when Father Coughlin left after an hour. He was very happy. For he left with a 10s note autographed by Paul McCartney.' George added, 'It was just a leg-pull, Father Coughlin knew we were joking. When he had his drink, I just chipped in to say, "I thought that you weren't supposed to drink," or something like that. It wasn't meant to be serious. We like the padre and were surprised that he's taken it this way. We would like to tell our fans we were not being rude.'

After the second show, the group walked through a backstage corridor, ran down Dun Cow Street and into the nearby Central Fire Station. They amused themselves by sliding down the fireman's pole, making their getaway from Sunderland in a police car, while decoy fire engine number one, clanging its bell, drove off. The group were driven a ten-minute drive across the River Wear to the corner of Seaburn Terrace and Whitburn Road, where they spent the night at the Seaburn Hotel, overlooking the North Sea. They conducted a phone interview with a DJ in Melbourne, Australia. In the aftermath of the shows, police called it a 'quiet affair,' revealing that a sole middle-aged woman had fainted.

> ❛ It was a Saturday and I was 9½. But it was no ordinary Saturday as this was the day I'd looked forward to for weeks. I was going to see the Beatles. The sound of the Beatles had first reached me via the faltering waves of Radio Luxembourg in late 1962. My big brother Graham had already mentioned them to me and I remember that my first mental image of them was as a group of eight or so men wearing checky jackets and playing instruments like the double bass and the clarinet. Graham would feed me the odd morsel of information he'd managed to find about the Beatles and he was already a big fan of theirs. 'I think one of them's called John McCarthy', he told me one day. Gradually one wall of our bedroom was submerged beneath a collage of photos and clippings of the group, though in those pre-Blu Tac days Graham just glued them onto the wallpaper. There was great excitement about the two shows and tickets were hard to find but through my mam, who was secretary to the director at the theatre, we got tickets in the upper circle for the 6.30 show for me,

Graham, my sister Linda and her best friend Liz, and for Mam herself. The day before the concert I was in the playground at school waiting in line for my turn at rounders when one of my mates behind me said, 'Let's get Moley! He's got a ticket for the Beatles.' He was only joking but it was indicative of how keen all of us were to see them.

Finally the big night came and even the very stodgy *Sunderland Echo* got into the spirit, devoting a couple of pages to the group under the headline 'The Beatles Come To Town!' That afternoon hadn't started well as Sunderland A.F.C., who were pushing for promotion to the First Division, after missing out narrowly the season before, lost at home to Southampton 2-1, but nothing could quench my high spirits. *Doctor Who* had started on the BBC the week before and we watched the beginning of an episode about cavemen, but we had to be off to get to the show. I was still in short trousers in those days and I was wearing a thick overcoat as we made the fifteen-minute walk in the dark to the town centre. When we arrived at the theatre the lights above the foyer beamed out the Beatles. The upper circle was accessed by a side door and the stairs seemed endless to my 9-year-old legs as we spiralled our way up. There was an electric buzz in the air as we took our seats while MAM took up a position at the back somewhere. A few rows away Graham spotted a schoolmate of his who was brandishing a packet of Jelly Babies. The lights went down and the slick young American compère at once launched into his basic tactic of the evening, which was to tease the audience as much as possible about the impending arrival of the stars of the show. Every time he did this a torrent of screams would pour from the audience. I'd never heard anyone scream like this before, except when someone had thumped them. After the interval the curtains parted and there they were – in their Beatle suits and standing in their classic stage positions. John stood with his legs slightly apart on the right with George and Paul sharing a mic on the left as Ringo thrashed away and smiled on the drum podium centre stage behind them. The noise from the moment those curtains parted was like nothing I'd heard before. The music itself was loud but it was almost drowned out by the constant screaming and shouting, while Jelly Babies, identity bracelets, sealed notes and God knows what was hurled towards the stage, which incidentally was well cordoned off.

The climax of the show was undoubtedly 'Twist and Shout' with John and the audience screaming their guts out as the song built up and up till it seemed that something had to give. 'She Loves You' is probably the definitive anthem of Beatlemania with its 'yeah, yeah, yeahs' and Paul and George combining to hit those 'Whooooos!' as they shook their mopheads. Paul regularly waved up to the fans like us in the cheaper seats and no doubt we weren't the only ones to insist afterwards that 'he was definitely waving at us.' He was! All too soon our thirty minutes was up and the grinning foursome had disappeared behind the lowering curtains with many a bow. Even after all the noise had stopped I still couldn't hear what the others were saying to me as we surged down the stairs and my ears didn't return to normal till the next day. We floated home on a wave of excitement but the Beatles still had their 8.30 show to do. I couldn't wait to tell them about it at school on Monday morning. ❜

IAN MOLE, ENGLISH TEACHER/TOUR GUIDE, LONDON

DECEMBER

'Ladies and gentlemen,
for the first time on air in the
United States, here are
The Beatles singing "I Want To
Hold Your Hand".'

SUNDAY 1 DECEMBER

At 3am, brothers Kenneth and David Heath, Paul Kettlewell and Terence Bostock began queueing outside the Gaumont in Bradford for the 21 December concert. Despite the bitter cold, they were sheltered by the theatre canopy and a cinema ventilator blew warm air on them. The first girls in the queue were Maureen Wilkinson and Colleen Stockdale, who walked from her home in Shipley. By mid-morning, the queue, which started at Quebec Street and was fenced off by linked crush barriers, was about five hundred-strong. Girls sat on the pavement and huddled in blankets. Just after 1pm freezing rain began to pour. 'Operation Beatlecrush' swung into gear. The upstairs lounge at the theatre was turned into an emergency ward, where girls suffering from exhaustion caused by hours of waiting were treated. At dusk, the queue was one thousand-strong. The casualty list climbed above fifty. Standing by were four ambulances and an ambulance trailer, manned by nearly one hundred Red Cross, St John Ambulance Brigade, Civil Defence and regular ambulance staff. Bradford's champion police horse Angus stood proud at the head of the queue.

Mounted police sorted the crowd into sections, and then into three ticket queues. Most members of A Division of Bradford police were on eight-hour shifts, while ambulance men were on three-hour shifts. At 5.30pm it began raining again. Maureen Wilkinson was squeezed out of the queue. 'This is the last time I'll queue for the Beatles,' she said. Sixty police held back the two thousand-strong crowd as the ticket office opened at 9.35pm, half an hour earlier than planned. By the end of the day, five thousand of the 6,660 tickets had sold and piles of belongings ended up in the lost property office.

The group left Sunderland and headed south on the A1 - over 180 miles - to De Montfort Hall in Granfield Street, Leicester. 50 miles north of their destination, they stopped for lunch at the Normanton Inn in Worksop, before continuing on their journey. Footpaths from the gates to the hall itself were fenced off to prevent people from straying into the gardens, which were patrolled by police officers with dogs. The group arrived at the front entrance on Regent Road - where only about fifty teenagers were waiting - escorted by a Jeep and motorcyclists. More than two hundred police cordoned the grounds and patrolled the hall in relays. Thirty officers and stewards blocking anyone's way to the stage; some front seats were removed to create a no man's land. Student Union members from Leicester University met the group and persuaded them to launch Leicester students' 1964 Charity Appeal by buying the first tickets in their Rag Car Contest. Rag organiser Colin Eden said, 'We are sure that their patronage will give a tremendous fillip to this year's competition, which is intended to be one of the principal fund-raising activities of the 1964 appeal.' The group's only backstage request was a TV set. Promoter Arthur Kimbrell asked the owner of Slaney's if he could borrow one. He also asked whether the owner's teenage daughter Jenny would like to see the show. She jumped at the chance - and was also taken to the group's dressing room, where she had her photo taken with them and her programme signed.

A refreshment room attendant was overheard saying, 'Why on earth these girls stood so long in queues for tickets and spent so much money just to scream and drown every note beats me, but perhaps I'm a square.' Autograph books, a doll, an umbrella and a toy panda were thrown onto the stage. Steward Mr Ray Millward was scratched and punched by a girl as he tried to take her back to her seat: 'We are

443

used to it, but I have never seen anything like this. We used to get a lot of hysteria with Cliff Richard, but this beats everything. I had a shoe and umbrella thrown at me. One girl fought with me like a wildcat. I had to force her arm behind her back to get her to sit down.' At the end of the second performance, one youth leapt from a balcony onto the stage. He flung his arms around a startled George and tried to follow them off stage, until the police intervened. Afterwards, the group drove to Nottingham where they spent the night – a new ploy to avoid fans who waited outside hotels in the towns where they were playing.

ABC Weekend TV announced that to combat the Beatles' appearance on *Juke Box Jury* the following Saturday Patrick Macnee and Honor Blackman, stars of *The Avengers*, would appear on *Thank Your Lucky Stars*. In a *New York Times* editorial headlined 'Britons Succumb to "Beatlemania"', Frederick Lewis wrote: 'They are fighting all over Britain. Rarely a night passes without an outbreak in some town or other. Sometimes it is a mere skirmish involving a few hundred police, but more often there is a pitched battle, with broken legs, cracked ribs and bloody noses. The police do their best, but it is well known that they are secretly in sympathy with the battlers. The cause of this shattering of the English peace is a phenomenon called the Beatles. To see a Beatle is a joy, to touch one paradise on earth... They are working class and their roots and attitudes are firmly of the north of England. Because of their success, they can act as spokesmen for the new, noisy, anti-establishment generation which is becoming a force in British life... The Beatles are part of a strong-flowing reaction against the soft, middle-class south of England, which has controlled popular culture for so long.' Lewis went on to say that 'by comparison, Elvis Presley is an Edwardian tenor of considerable diffidence.'

❛ I was 15 years old and had just started in the sixth form at school and had just discovered boys. I had become a Beatles fan after hearing them on the radio and seen them on TV. My friend Sue and her boyfriend Paul queued to get tickets for the early concert. They bought four, two for themselves and two for Paul's friend, also called Paul. I somehow managed to get him to invite me to go with him. By coincidence Paul McCartney was my favourite member of the group. The two boys lived some distance away from Sue and I, so we met them on the bus into Leicester. It was run by Gibson's Comfort, the same company that provided our school bus. We walked from the stop to De Montfort Hall which took us a good thirty minutes. We had seats downstairs in the middle to the left. They didn't have tiered seating then so the seats were all on one level which made it more difficult to see especially as I was five feet two inches tall. I can't remember much  about the performance other than they looked just as they did on TV, moptop haircuts, collarless suits and very clean cut. I do remember the screaming, my own included, which completely drowned the music, and standing on the seats to try to see the stage. I was wearing thin heels and it was difficult not to punch a hole in the canvas seat. I don't know how Paul felt as all my attention was focussed on THE Paul and the other three Beatles onstage. Sadly, we only went out together until Christmas – barely a month. Sue eventually married her Paul. After the concert we walked back into Leicester and caught the bus home. I think we were all in a daze. When Mum asked me how it had been when I got home, I told her 'I didn't hear anything and I didn't see anything. But it was fab.' She worked next door to the offices of the *Leicester Mercury* and told a reporter what I had said. The next morning my quote appeared in the paper and I got some comments at school because of it. **❜**

BARBARA HODSON, CIVIL SERVANT, LEICESTER, LEICESTERSHIRE

MONDAY 2 DECEMBER

Tickets for two shows at the Southampton Gaumont on 13 December went on sale. Scheduled for 10am, the box office opening was brought forward because of the size of the crowd. Clerk-typist Julie Barlow was first in line, buying a box ticket 'nearest to my favourite John Lennon', after an all-night vigil. Thirteen-year-old Pat Stewart, who had been queuing since Friday, was taken to Royal Hants Hospital, suffering from exhaustion, minutes before tickets went on sale. Cinema manager Ken Watts made sure she got one: 'I thought it was only fair after she had been there so long.' Fifteen-year-old Pauline Kelleher was expelled from a Southampton commercial college after playing truant so she could buy tickets. Her headmaster, Mr W. A. Nicholls said, 'I am not against the Beatles, but this was the last straw.'

More than two hundred fans welcomed the Beatles as they arrived at ATV's studios in Eldon Avenue, Borehamwood, Hertfordshire, to record an episode of Associated-Rediffusion's Morecambe and Wise show *Two Of A Kind*. The group were accompanied by Brian Epstein, new PR man Brian Sommerville and Dezo Hoffmann. They performed 'This Boy', 'All My Loving' and 'I Want To Hold Your Hand' and finished with a version of 'Moonlight Bay', joined by their hosts, wearing boaters and striped jackets while Eric Morecambe donned a Beatle wig. They also took part in a sketch during which Morecambe repeatedly said 'Hello Bongo' to Ringo. The show aired on 18 April 1964.

In the evening, the group performed in the Grand Ballroom of the Grosvenor House Hotel in London, a charity event for the Stars Organization for Spastics. A drunk in a dinner jacket heckled them and was told to shut up. After a second encore, there was an onstage rush, so Cyril Stapleton led his orchestra into 'Twist And Shout'. The group met with Dora Bryan and the Countess of Westmorland, who had organised the event. John Deane Potter in the *News Of The World* described 'lace-and-pearl debutantes clutching their aristocratic bosoms with the same eye-rolling expression of ecstasy as the girls in Portsmouth.' Apparently some of those in attendance preferred Joan Turner's act to the Beatles'. John, no doubt in agreement, said, 'If anybody tells us we were good tonight I'll spit in their faces; we were awful.'

❝ I was a 13/14-year-old schoolgirl in Southampton at the time. My friends and I queued out for two days to get tickets for their show. It was cold whilst queuing. My parents wouldn't let me queue at night, so I did the days and my friend Pat Marsh took over at night. The tickets went on sale on Monday morning and we got second row tickets. We went back to school in the afternoon. My mum wrote a note saying why I wasn't at school in the morning. The teacher didn't tell me off. I think it was an unknown thing, so they let it go! We all really, really enjoyed the show, we screamed and screamed. My favourite was John. It was packed in the theatre and I don't think we heard too much of the music because of the screaming. We were just pleased to see them and to be breathing the same air as them! I always loved the boys and have all their records on vinyl and CDs as well. I have the Beatles fan club magazines in pristine condition from number one. Admittedly I didn't collect all but I have other stuff as well. My one regret is that I didn't keep the theatre tickets, lost in the mists of time I expect. ❞

JENNY GALE, NURSE, FREEMANTLE, HAMPSHIRE

TUESDAY 3 DECEMBER

*T*oday began a weekly *Meet The Beatles* series, featuring Ringo in the first instalment. He yet again said that he would open a ladies' hairdressing salon if it all ended tomorrow. He also made the point that if public money was not used for police protection at their concerts, it would cost a fortune in hospital bills. He described his ideal girlfriend as 'smaller than me, she'll be slim and feminine, she'll be intelligent but not too smart, she'll be a marvellous cook and she'll be able to talk. I can't.'

An unnamed London store received an inquiry about its Mersey Beat Wig from Buckingham Palace. The identity of the interested party was not revealed. The *Hampshire Telegraph* reviewed Portsmouth Players' *Gilbert & Sullivan For All*, headlined 'You Can Keep The Beatles' – so the news that the group were delayed again, when the water pipe in their car broke on the A3 on the way to the Guildhall to play postponed concerts, was probably received with glee.

Local College of Art students Vicki Mitchell and Bernice Goodall spent some time with the Beatles before the first show, having won a contest to design clothes for them. Paul smuggled the girls and a *Portsmouth Evening News* reporter through security. Mitchell told the *News*, 'We all sat round a table. Paul looked through the sketches. He and John liked them very much. Ringo hardly said anything. They thought one suit looked like something they were already having made. They liked the capes, too. Tea was brought in. Paul, Ringo and George had fish and chips, but John joked, "Due to an accident I can't eat fish and chips." He wanted salad, but ended up with tomato soup.'

The Lord Mayor and Lady Mayoress of Portsmouth, Councillor and Mrs Harry Sotnick, stood at the back of the stalls during the Beatles' first spot. Their daughter Caroline wrote a plea for her father to use his civic influence to get the group's autographs, on behalf of eight fellow schoolgirls at Roedean. Several coins were thrown onstage as they sang 'Money (That's What I Want)'. 'If you try to get on the stage you will be burnt by the footlights, or electrocuted. I have a lot of policemen and strong-arm men who will take you out if you do not behave – and you will not come back,' came the stern warning from David Evans. Jacqueline Capstick from EMI France stood in the wings, alongside two French reporters who interviewed the group in anticipation of their scheduled February visit to Paris. The group were now using 60-watt Vox amplifiers. Reg Clark, the Sales Manager of Jennings Musical Industries in Dartford, said, 'Formerly they were using 30-watt amplifiers which is the average amplifier for any professional group, but they told us the screaming and shouting of the fans made it impossible for anybody to hear.' At the beginning of the year, Clark had agreed with Brian Epstein to provide the group with two free Vox amps after Epstein had told him that as long as he was the group's manager, they would use no other amps.

❝ I was 16 in late 1962, living in the south of England and spending my evenings at the local clubs and dance halls jiving to the then current sounds. At a club this particular evening I noticed a group of youngsters gathered round the record player nodding their head and tapping their feet to the sound of a record I had never heard before. Being curious I went over and asked who the group were with this great bassy sound and wailing harmonica. 'The Beatles' they said, so I thought this must be a new folk group, but stood listening and thought they sounded interesting! Then I happened to see a photo of them in *Punch* magazine. Wow! I thought they are really good-looking and even better they were from my hometown up north in Liverpool. Well, I was born across the Mersey in Wallasey. This is when I began collecting any pics I could find in the paper or magazines in bookshops, I was raving over them. Everything seemed different, I just wanted to stay in and listen to my LP instead of roaming the streets with my friend. I had Beatles on my cupboard door, Beatles on the record player, Beatles in our conversations, Beatles on my mind, they were four dream boys! I joined their fan club and still have all my letters and things I received from them. I also have the complete set of Beatles monthly books. Then I heard the Beatles were coming to Portsmouth. Twelve of us in our typing class in the fifth year in my high school decided we would queue from the Saturday morning, through the afternoon, Saturday night, Sunday morning, afternoon and night in shifts, the final Sunday night being myself and two friends Jill and Coral. We had everything planned and the first girls bagged the space outside the Guildhall where we would be queuing for the next three days. I had to go to work as a Saturday girl so had no idea whereabouts we were in the queue. On the Sunday evening Jill's dad took us over in his car and we took our places for the night. It was a night never to be forgotten, no chance of sleeping with fifty Beatles fans singing, playing guitars and transistor radios blaring Radio Luxembourg. We were looked after by some strict policemen who kept checking to see everything was OK – we had to keep the noise down or we would be taken to the nick and fined £10 for vagrancy! We made so many friends and had a good laugh sharing soup and tea, and being very silly. Suddenly the Guildhall clock struck midnight and we all said 'Good morning' to each other. We were visited by worried parents, giggling drunken boys and boozy groups of men going home in the early hours but the police kept their eyes on us. Eventually daylight appeared and more and more people joined the queue shivering on the steps. The time dragged by until 9.45am when people began gathering up their blankets and bags of food and guitars, then suddenly the doors opened and a surge towards the door lost us our place. It was chaos as we pushed our way towards the front to try and get in next. They only allowed a certain number in at a time and we were only allowed six tickets each, which was fine as we wanted twelve. Triumphantly we emerged from the booking office with our twelve tickets – four rows from the front in the centre – how exciting! We went and had some coffee, then wearily travelled back on the ferry to Gosport singing, 'We've got our tickets – four rows back.' We caught the number 6 bus back home much to the amusement of the bus conductor Mr Wyatt with the pink cheeks. He knew us from travelling to school every day. Annoyingly we had to go back to school on the Monday afternoon and had to tell our tale to our excited friends. Our plan had worked, we were going to see the Beatles in real life. Two days later we were up in front of the headmaster and got a good telling off for taking the morning off to get our tickets, we were nearly suspended! We hung our heads in shame (with fingers crossed behind our backs) as our typing teacher told us how disappointed he was that pupils of his would waste valuable working time queuing for tickets to see four stupid men shaking their stupid heads off.

We couldn't wait for 12 November. The day was approaching, we were so excited, on the 11th we were jumping about, hardly able to work. We were so excited and the day just dragged slowly. At last the day arrived we had been waiting for, I had terrible stomach ache and couldn't eat any tea. Oh no! It was announced on the teatime news the show was cancelled – what??? Three days later we learnt they were coming back on 3 December. At last, the day was approaching when we would see our lovely Beatles in real life. I was so excited I didn't know what to do, so I just got ready. I pressed my red tartan pinafore dress and my black polo-neck jumper, did my hair and had a bath, then made my way over to Portsmouth on the ferry with my friends. We arrived at the Guildhall and it was full of screaming girls chasing any car that appeared, thinking the Beatles were arriving in a decoy vehicle. Every delivery van was climbed on and peered into. Was it them? We ran from the front to the back trying to get just a glimpse of them in the windows at the back. Every time someone passed a window, screaming rang out around the building. We sat in our seats and were warned if we left them we would be removed from the theatre. We sat through the show watching the other acts impatiently waiting for the second half. The compère kept teasing us and making us scream even louder. 'Yes, We Want The Beatles!!'

The curtains opened and there they were picking up their guitars and excitedly singing 'She Loves You'. We couldn't believe how gorgeous they looked in real life – like our pictures moving. We were right in front of Paul, and George sometimes joined him at the mic. Oh, what could we do – just stand and stare, cry, clap, scream, there wasn't time to think, just take in the moment. I wasn't bothered about hearing the music I could hear that on my records. So, I took in every minute watching them and smiling and laughing along with them. I swear George smiled back at me – oh he was so lovely and they all looked so good-looking in their suits with the dark collars. John spoke and the place erupted. 'Shurrup,' he shouted and everyone laughed. Paul said, 'Now we want you to clap your hands and stamp your feet,' and John did his usual silly handclapping and made us all laugh. How we loved them. I couldn't believe I had seen, looked at and breathed the same air as my lovely Beatles. They were just fabulous. The curtains closed and they were gone. We ran to the side entrances but they were twelve deep in girls and police, so we ran to the back, but everyone was saying, 'They've gone, they've gone.' We were disappointed but not surprised they had got away before everyone had come out of the theatre. We met up with some of the queue people, got our programmes and went to the car where my dad was waiting to bring us home. I can never forget that night, the most exciting time of my teenage years. **"**

SHEILA ROGERS, LEGAL SECRETARY, FAREHAM, HAMPSHIRE

WEDNESDAY 4 DECEMBER

Ringo travelled back to Liverpool on a Starways Viscount flight. Fellow passenger Margaret Fletcher, who was visiting her parents in Litherland with her 3-year-old son Jeffrey, recognised him – despite living 13,000-miles away in Darwin, Australia, and never having heard his records. 'I recognised him by his haircut,' she said after landing at Speke Airport, 'We have seen pictures of them in Australia, but I have never heard them sing. We don't have television in our part of the world and I've never even heard them on the radio. But I am dying to hear one of their records while I'm here.' Meanwhile, George slept in, getting up at noon for a suit fitting with Dougie Millings. He ate lunch with Michael Braun. Afterwards, he visited Dick James to see how much the group were owed in royalties, while Braun headed to John's flat in Emperor's Gate. Braun drank tea, John Scotch. They discussed several subjects including Elvis, the Beatles' forthcoming film and John's still-untitled book – which would become *John Lennon In His Own Write*.

Henry Price, the Conservative Member of Parliament for West Lewisham, told a women's lunch at Cobb's department store in Sydenham, 'We have got to beat the beat of the Beatles... The beat of the Beatles has captured the imagination of a proportion of our young people. This is only a small proportion, but some of them have been carried too far by it... It is quite useless decrying it, being rude about it and about those who like it – unless we can offer them something they like better.' He talked about twisting: 'This has a strange hypnotic effect on them. Their eyes become glazed, their mouths gape, their hands wobble loosely at the ends of their wrists, and their legs wobble just as loosely at the knees. This is known as being "sent." It doesn't send me, but this is not because there is anything wrong with the teenagers. It's because I'm not "with it." I'm a square... I belong to a different generation.'

In the US, Capitol Records issued a press release, 'New English Madness To Spread To US; Beatlemania Will Be Imported Here' – announcing it had acquired US rights to the Beatles catalogue and would be releasing 'I Want To Hold Your Hand' on 13 January 1964.

THURSDAY **5 DECEMBER**

On its front page, *Disc* reported 'Beatles Make Disc History – Again', revealing that 'I Want To Hold Your Hand' had crashed into the singles chart at number one, knocking 'She Loves You' off the top – the first time an act had had the number one and two spots on the singles chart. As both records passed the million sales mark, the group picked up their first two gold discs. *With The Beatles* climbed three places to number 11, while the EPs *Twist And Shout*, *The Beatles' Hits* and *The Beatles (No. 1)* stood at numbers 16, 17 and 26. Alan Walsh revealed that the group's first visit to America would only feature TV appearances. Brian Epstein, who Walsh interviewed earlier in the week, said, 'I don't believe in pushing artists in where they are not wanted. I'll wait until there is a definite demand for the Beatles before I allow them to do personal appearances. The only exception will be those connected with their film.'

'I Want To Hold Your Hand' entered the *NRM* chart at number 10, while 'She Loves You' stayed at number one. *With The Beatles* knocked *Please Please Me* off the top of the album chart, where it had been for thirty weeks, and the group continued to dominate the EP charts, still holding down the top three spots.

In the latest edition of *Reveille*, Bunny Lewis wrote: 'The Beatles' activities are fast becoming a bore. Their slightest deviation from plan or minutest deterioration in health is presented as a matter of paramount importance. I hasten to add that this is not their fault nor, indeed, that of their publicist. The bandwagon is rolling, and momentum does the rest... I, like most other inhabitants of this island, admire the Beatles, but I am not entertained by a daily blow-by-blow account of their progress from one one-night stand to another... Teenagers are highly protective and possessive. In the case of the Beatles there is no longer anything to be protective about. Their parents are often even barmier about the boys than they are... The boys themselves are endearing, lively characters. I wish them well, and a long and successful future. We shall see.' John and Paul flew back home to Liverpool while George travelled more sedately by train.

FRIDAY **6 DECEMBER**

The *NME*'s front-page banner read 'Beatles' Amazing Xmas Disc.' Inside, Alan Smith wrote a detailed review of 'The Craziest Xmas greeting of all!' Cliff Richard told Derek Johnson that he didn't in any way begrudge the Beatles' success. 'What the Beatles have accomplished is good for everybody in show business. It gives the whole profession a boost – just as it did when Bill Haley or Elvis first came on the scene.' In the paper's chart 'I Want To Hold Your Hand' debuted at number one, knocking 'She Loves You' down to number 2. *With The Beatles* hit number 11, breaking Frank Sinatra's record of reaching number 12 with *Songs For Swinging Lovers* as the highest charted LP in the history of the singles chart. *Twist And Shout* reached number 15 and *The Beatles' Hits* number 19. *With The Beatles* entered the *NME* LP chart at number one, knocking *Please Please Me* down to number 2. Dora Bryan's 'All I Want For Christmas Is A Beatle' debuted at number 28. An EMI spokesman said, '*Twist And Shout* has sold more than half a million.'

In the first of a four-part series titled 'That Was The Year That Was', Derek Johnson wrote in the *NME*, 'In the far distant future, when our descendants study their history books, they will see one word imprinted against the year 1963 in the chronological table of events – Beatles! For just as convincingly as 1066 marked the Battle of Hastings, or 1215 the Magna Carta, so will this present year be remembered by posterity for the achievements of four lads from Liverpool.'

'BEATLES Hits Charts For SEVEN!' ran the headline on *Melody Maker*'s front page. 'I Want To Hold Your Hand' entered the singles chart at number one, knocking 'She Loves You' off the top. *Twist And Shout* climbed to number 11, *The Beatles (No. 1)* to number 19, while *The Beatles' Hits* dropped two places to number 17. In the paper's Mailbag, Miss A. Phillips of Hackney wasn't too enamoured with the group's new LP. 'I entirely disagree with the *Melody Maker* review of the Beatles new LP. I don't know what happens to stars when they reach the top, but the quality of their records has certainly dropped. It seems they have just gone into a recording studio and said "Come on, fellas, we've got to make another LP and it might as well be now." I am sorry to have to say this, as I am an ardent Beatles fan. But I think somebody should have the courage to protest.'

Police investigated reports that fans buying tickets for the group's Wimbledon Palais appearance had fallen foul of forgers. Palais boss Bernard Rabin said, 'I have told police that some youngsters say they have been offered tickets for 25s each. We made certain that all tickets were sold in ones and twos, so we think the tickets being offered must be forgeries.' Without any advance publicity, tickets sold out in a matter of hours. Local police were told that all leave had been cancelled for the group's forthcoming visit and would be on 'Beatle Duty.'

SATURDAY 7 DECEMBER

Just before 11am, the Beatles arrived at the Empire Theatre in Liverpool in preparation for a long day where they appeared on *Juke Box Jury* as well as perform two concerts – one at the Empire and the other at the nearby Odeon. There were thirty police on duty outside and just three fans – rain kept many away, as well as Christmas shopping no doubt. Eight mounted police showed up at one point, but left when it was obvious their services were not required.

The group set up their equipment during a camera rehearsal, then had a coffee break. Afterwards, they rehearsed the opening and closing of *Juke Box Jury*. Paul's former English Literature teacher Alan Durband was present. At 1pm, they had lunch – a 9/6 three-course meal with Scotch salmon, honeydew melon, roast lamb, minced chicken duchesse and gooseberry pie. After lunch, there was a photo call where John said, 'I can't stop imitating an American reporter who is on tour with us,' referring to Michael Braun.

A portion of the expected twenty-five hundred members of the north-west section of the Beatles Fan Club began pouring in when the doors opened at 1.30pm. At 2.10pm a short rehearsal for *Juke Box Jury* began, followed immediately by the recording. Host David Jacobs described the scene later on, 'The audience was so excited that when, eventually, I introduced the Beatles and they walked onstage, the roar from the crowd sounded like the whole of the BEA and BOAC jet fleet were taking off at one time. The noise was probably the loudest and most deafening I've ever had to sit through.'

On the programme, the group voted the Chants' 'I Could Write A Book', Elvis Presley's 'Kiss Me Quick', described as 'like Blackpool on a Sunday afternoon,' the Swinging Blue Jeans' 'Hippy Hippy Shake', Steve and Eydie's 'I Can't Stop Talking About You', Billy Fury's 'Do You Really Love Me Too?' and the Merseybeats' 'I Think Of You' hits, while Paul Anka's 'Did You Have A Happy Birthday?', Shirley Ellis' 'The Nitty Gritty Song', Bobby Vinton's 'There, I've Said It Again' (the record they knocked off the top of the US charts the following February) and the Orchids' 'Love Hit Me' misses – the latter group were in the audience. After the Billy Fury record was played, Ringo commented that he went to school with the singer, but couldn't remember which day. Fan club secretaries Freda Kelly, Bettina Rose and Mary Cockram were

the alternative panellists. After an hour-plus break, the group recorded a performance at 3.45pm, which aired in the evening on the programme *It's The Beatles!* They played 'From Me To You', 'I Saw Her Standing There', 'All My Loving', 'Roll Over Beethoven', 'Boys', 'Till There Was You', 'She Loves You', 'This Boy', 'I Want To Hold Your Hand', 'Money' and 'Twist And Shout'. They finished with an instrumental reprise of 'From Me To You' and a snippet of the 'Third Man Theme'. They then recorded a two-minute interview to be broadcast on the Christmas Day *Top Pops Of 1963* special.

At 5.30pm, they left the Empire and ran a short distance down Pudsey Street, which separated the Empire and the Odeon. With fans leaving the Empire and more arriving at the Odeon, around seven thousand congregated outside. One hundred extra police were drafted in – some on horseback. First-aid was given to some thirty teenage girl casualties, most of whom had fainted.

Settling down in their dressing room, the group switched on the TV set, provided by the furniture and TV department of NEMS. It had no aerial, so they used a piece of metal screwed to a coat rack. They watched the *Telegoons* and then *Juke Box Jury* at 6.05pm. During the broadcast, the signal was lost, and a TV engineer was called to fix it. In the interval between shows, they posed in their dressing room with Oxford University undergraduates Jeffrey Archer and Nicholas Lloyd, who were trying to raise £1 million for Oxfam. Brian Epstein was not happy about this. He had been approached by Archer and was not keen for the group to get involved with any charities. Four days earlier, however, Archer had already announced to the press, 'The Beatles have told us they want to join in this message to the youth of Britain: "Swing along with us and give all you got to famine relief." Archer and Lloyd, who had earlier described Archer as 'a nut' who'd 'believe in fairies,' arrived in Liverpool armed with Oxfam posters and collecting tins and inveigled their way into the group's dressing room.

For those at home unable to be present at the concert, the BBC offered up *Dixon Of Dock Green* and *Wells Fargo* before *It's The Beatles!* aired at 8.10pm. The group watched the programme between the first and second shows; Ringo ate sausage and chips while watching himself sing 'Boys'. Twenty-two million people watched *Juke Box Jury* and 21.5 million viewed *It's The Beatles!*. *Juke Box Jury* had its highest ever rating, coming in seventh place in the Television Audience Measurement (TAM) weekly survey, while *It's The Beatles!* was ranked tenth. Despite these viewing figures, *Melody Maker*'s Bob Dawbarn was very critical of the shows. 'Production was unbelievably bad, with poor sound, cameras on the wrong person, terrible balance and no attempt at presentation. The Beatles themselves were way below form on their own show – out-of-tune singing and general lack of punch. They had little of interest to say on *Jury* and John Lennon was too intent on playing for laughs that didn't come.'

Following the show at the Odeon, John and Pete Shotton went to the latter's sister Harriet's to collect some drawings and writings he wanted to take to London with him. They took them back to Mendips in a large canvas bag and sat up into the small hours. John asked Shotton how his Old Dutch Cafe enterprise was going and gave him his pay packet. When Shotton opened it later in the day, he found ten £5 notes inside.

❛ I began my career in television in the early days of commercial television, working as a cartoonist and presenter on *The Weekend Show*. This led to me drawing in vision on *World Of Sport* and *Cool For Cats*. I was also a strip cartoonist for *Eagle*, *Robin* and *Girl*. I was determined to be a producer for the BBC and was eventually accepted along with Bill Cotton Jr. We became the youngest directors/ producers on BBC-TV and I was asked to take over *Juke Box Jury* in August 1962. It had all been a rather staid affair, so my aim was to open it up a bit and invite all sorts of people from every walk of life, and that was a departure really, certainly from the first intention. I had scouts on the streets at that time, looking for unusual people. People who were interested in music, but who also looked different. It was such an easy format. It was the first time the public were actually seen on screen in that kind way, big close ups, reaction shots as the music was being played. That was the kind of thing we really went for. We had long-focus lenses that we got big close ups on. We had to find inventive ways to hide artists behind the screen whilst their record was being reviewed, as it was rather obvious when the camera panned round. We would record two each day, one which would go out live, and one which would go out the following week. The BBC was keen to do that, so that is how we operated. Most of the shows were done from the theatre, but some were done from the Centre.

John Lennon's first appearance on the show was in June 1963. A music publisher had said to me, 'You've got to come and meet this guy, he's one of this group, and is really worth seeing.' So, he came, and I had this unique experience of having lunch with John when no one really recognised him in the BBC canteen at the Television Centre. He was just one of the lads really. I was intrigued with him. He turned up wearing this leather jacket. We spoke about where music was going, or where he thought it was going, and he was just very funny, and very outspoken, and I thought he would be ideal for the show. We needed people like that. What took us by surprise were the Replace with: hordes of people who had come down from Liverpool to see him, or to try and get into the television theatre as it was then. I thought, 'My God, this must be something!' because of all these kids. I don't know how they expected to get in, because all the seats went so quickly in advance, and really, they were just queuing outside hoping to catch a glimpse of him. On the day that all four Beatles appeared on the show, Everton were playing Chelsea at home, and we were doing the show live from the Empire. The venue changed and we had an outside broadcast crew, who were not really light entertainment people at all, most used to sports, and we had a really small budget. It was decided that the Empire was too small to record in, so we moved to the Odeon. The following month, along with fellow producer Johnnie Stewart, I began producing *Top Of The Pops*, recorded in a church hall in Manchester, which had been converted into a studio by the BBC. 🥟

NEVILLE WORTMAN, CEO OF THE CONFIDENT VOICE, EXECUTIVE PRODUCER OF POLESTAR PICTURES AND DIRECTOR OF SPEAK GOOD ENGLISH WELL, LONDON

SUNDAY 8 DECEMBER

The queue for the two evening concerts at the Odeon in Lewisham started at 9am, even though both houses were sold out. One hundred police and special reserves, eight horses, twelve motorcycle patrolmen and four Black Marias were on hand. The Beatles caught the train to Euston Station. On arrival, they were picked up and driven to Ladywell Police Station, where they met local police and a photographer from the *Lewisham Journal & Borough News*. Paul got out of the car and signed autographs, while the others stayed inside. They were escorted for one mile to the venue, with patrol cars both preceding and following their car. They arrived at 4.30pm, just as a bingo session was finishing. As the crowd outside worked itself into a frenzy, a glass panel collapsed in a doorway because of pressure put on it by fans. A girl was already halfway through it before she was removed by police. Another girl was badly kicked; Sandra Simms and Avril Lewis fainted and were taken to Lewisham Hospital. Two policemen were thrown to the ground.

Paula Gracey, who had interviewed the group on their previous visit in March, talked with them; they offered her some of their Butter Krisps. *Disc* ticket winners were taken backstage to meet the group before the 6.30pm show. One St John Ambulance man dealt with 'three faints and one nose bleed' in the first half. The group were pelted with Jelly Babies and teddy bears and, as the show came a close, scuffles broke out between girls who were trying to gain access to the venue via a side door and uniformed attendants. Four schoolgirls made a cardboard heart, suitably decorated with their names and notes of their undying love for the group. They all put their autograph books into the heart and one of them, Jennifer Coglan, was delegated to run to the front of the venue, throw the heart onto the stage and hope the Beatles would see their books, sign them and throw them back. Needless to say, it all went wrong. She threw the heart, but it missed and fell into the orchestra pit – the girls lost their autograph books and any hope of autographs. In addition to losing her book, Linda Eldridge screamed so much she lost her voice, and despite having to take a maths test the following day, skipped school as she could not speak. One fan described his experience as the group left the cinema, 'Boy, I thought I had them until one huge policeman carried me back several paces as though I was a feather.'

As fans poured out of the cinema, they were greeted by thick fog. Some were disoriented, having waited in the rain during the day, going without food and screaming themselves silly. One got on the wrong bus and ended up stranded miles from home. Kindly staff laid on a special bus to get her home. The *Kentish Times* reported that, 'The mighty shout of adulation that lasted throughout the Beatles' entire act seemed more cruel than kind. Anybody who witnesses the sort of reception the four boys from Liverpool are being given to-day cannot fail to feel some sympathy for them for the moment the cheers die away and stop, as they will have to eventually. Paul struggled to announce each number and ineffectively shouted "Shaddup" at the tearful ecstatic girls. But in the face of such violent approbation there was nothing much to do but play the numbers.' The *Lewisham Journal & Borough News* wrote, 'I tried to listen but like a beetle, I could only crawl away through the fog exhausted by my efforts at the finish.'

The Beatles drove into the West End to attend the 21st birthday party of Peter Jay and the Jaywalkers' saxophonist and pianist Lloyd Baker. Tommy Steele, the Vernons Girls, the Brook Brothers and TV host Hughie Green were also present at Baker's flat.

> ❝ When I got *Disc* ('The Top Music and Record Industry Weekly') – a now defunct UK pop music newspaper – and found a competition to meet the Beatles, I had to enter. The competition was to suggest a name for a new Beatles EP for America. My entry was alarmingly original – 'Meet The Beatles' (In January 1964, the first US Beatles album was called *Meet The Beatles*. I like to think that they got the idea from me). I popped my entry into an envelope and posted it without much hope of winning. A couple of weeks later, I bunked off school and went to the Lewisham Odeon and started queuing up the side of the cinema for tickets. Armed with a ground sheet, sleeping bag, umbrella, sandwiches and thermos flask of coffee, I settled down at number five in the queue. Next

in the queue were two girls, one of whom, as it grew dark, I was soon snuggled up to. Before we parted we'd arranged to meet the next Friday on the Barclay's Bank corner in Lee Green. The smog arrived on Thursday and by Friday evening you could hardly see a hand in front of your face. Unsurprisingly, I suppose, she failed to turn up. She had no phone (phones were quite a luxury in those days) and, although I knew she lived in Eltham Road, being a mile long and full of houses and flats, I had no hope of ever finding her again. I got home to be greeted with the news that JFK had been assassinated... But I digress.

The next morning, my father arrived at about six o'clock to check if I was OK and with my school uniform, which I struggled into under the umbrella. By seven o'clock the queue had grown to several hundred and soon dozens of police turned up to hold back the crowd. The ticket office was due to open at 10.30 but the police made them open an hour early and I was soon the proud owner of four tickets for the second row for the second performance at a cost of 12/6d each. I was over the moon. I got a raft of detentions and other punishments for my pains, the headmaster not thinking that queuing for Beatles tickets was a good enough excuse for taking a day off and arriving very late, dirty and tired for school, but it was worth it.

When I got home from school there was a letter waiting for me from *Disc*, signed by all four Beatles, saying I'd won two front-row tickets for the Beatles – and I'd get to meet them backstage. So now I had six tickets for the show! The next three weeks seemed more like three years as I counted down to the concert. I whiled away the days constantly playing the new LP *With The Beatles*, writing out the lyrics in my Beatles music notebook and working out the chords. Then a week later my world was really rocked when I heard 'I Want To Hold Your Hand' for the first time on the radio.

8 December eventually arrived. I arrived at the Odeon at midday and found myself hanging around with about thirty or forty others who were there to just soak up the atmosphere. Just after I arrived there was some excitement when a big van showed up and started unloading instruments and amplifiers in through the stage door. At four o'clock there was a flurry of activity and screaming and we all rushed up the side of the cinema to find a Black Maria parked across the pavement surrounded by police. It backed right up to the stage door and we could see the Beatles' legs and feet under the van door as they ran into the cinema. The first show kicked off at 6.30 and dozens of us jostled along the side of the Odeon, sticking our ears to the emergency exit doors trying to hear what was going on – but all we could hear was screaming. As the police cleared us away from one door, we'd rush to another. At about seven o'clock my father turned up with Diane, my 'date'. Diane lived in my road and I'd fancied her since we were at primary school together. Somehow we met up in the midst of the heaving crowds of (mostly) teenage girls. I had already sold two of the tickets to two girls from Prendergast School I was hoping to impress, so I gave my dad the other two tickets and asked him to sell them for me outside the cinema. When I got home after the show he said he'd been very fortunate to sell them for 'almost what I'd paid!' Clearly, he was not a natural ticket tout!

As the audience for the first show was leaving, Diane and I fought our way into the cinema where we were met by someone from *Disc* and we were escorted through a maze of green-and-mustard painted brick tunnels to a tiny dressing room. As we entered John was sitting at a tiny table, tucking into a mountain of beans on toast. He looked up at us and said, 'Excuse me stuffing my face, will ya?' Paul, George and Ringo were all drinking tea out of cups and saucers that looked like my granny's best china. 'Want a cup of tea?' asked Paul. I don't know what I was expecting, but I certainly wasn't expecting such a bizarrely ordinary scene. And, as much as I had thought about meeting the Beatles, I hadn't thought about what I'd say to them. In any event, I was too gobsmacked to say anything coherent apart from, 'I'm in a group.' Paul seemed interested and amused when I told him that that my group played Beatles songs to kids at 8.30 in the morning before Saturday morning pictures. 'We've done worse gigs than that,' he said. George didn't say much and Diane cornered Ringo and I heard him laughing a lot – but I don't know what they were talking about. They all seemed genuinely humble and interested in us. John asked me what sort of guitar I played. I told him I had a Hofner Sunburst Senator – he thought that was cool. Then the photographer came in and took some photographs. After a final rush of autograph signing – I got my programme autographed (I've still got it) – we were ushered out. Paul shouted after us, 'Enjoy the show' and it was over.

As we entered the cinema from a door by the stage everyone started screaming – maybe they thought we were the Beatles – and we were escorted to our seats in the centre of the front row. The curtains went up at 8.45 and the chants went up – 'We Want The Beatles!' Frank Berry, the compère did his best – he must have been used to trying to combat the screaming hordes. He cracked a joke or two and hurriedly introduced, in turn, the Vernons Girls, the Brook Brothers, the Kestrels and Peter Jay and the Jaywalkers – all of whom were greeted with polite attention during their numbers and a smattering of applause before the chanting started up again. 'We Want The Beatles.' Berry was losing the battle by the end and joined in the chanting and then screamed, 'The Beatles!' The first chords of 'I Saw Her Standing There' rang out before the curtain was pulled back. and as the curtains slid apart the screaming hit peak decibels – and I was screaming, too. As the cinema filled with a mild aroma of urine, the boys were barely audible over the screaming as they went through their set, bowing after each song. I nearly wet myself as well! The Beatles left the stage smiling and waving and when they had gone a ghostly hush descended for a few moments as the realisation sank in that the show was over. Then a rush for the doors. I met John and Paul again on 9 May 1965... but that is another story... 🟦

DAVID ROSE, SCRIPTWRITER, STOCKWELL, LONDON

MONDAY 9 DECEMBER

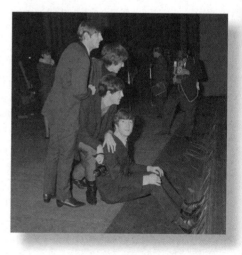

The Beatles received an early morning call at their flat, when a reporter from *Fabulous* arrived to go on the road with them for the week. Ringo let him in. John was still asleep and George had just woken. Paul soon returned from visiting a friend, followed by Tony Barrow. A busy morning was in order. The group had a couple of photo sessions and interviews, visited Monmouth Street, and ended the morning at Abbey Road to meet with George Martin. They had a snack in the canteen, signing autographs for the waitresses. Afterwards, the Austin Princess arrived to take them to the Odeon in Southend-on-Sea for two shows at 6.35pm and 8.50pm.

The group's Christmas single for fan club members was mailed out with the message, 'Sincere good wishes for Christmas and the New Year from John, Paul, George and Ringo'. To receive the Christmas record, fans had to have enrolled and paid their dues by 30 November. Pressing plant Lyntone Records pressed thirty-one thousand copies.

The group arrived in Southend at 2.30pm. They met with police at the borough boundary and climbed into a police van. The van turned right onto Ashburnham Road, and then left onto Gordon Place and into Middleton garage at the back of cinema in Luker Road. The group's own car arrived at the stage door, accompanied by a police motorcycle escort, carrying driver Bill Corbett and four local men disguised as the Beatles. They were paid £1 each for their deception. As the group arrived at the cinema, they ran from the garage across an open space and into the venue. John was the first to enter, wearing dark glasses and a suede cap, recently bought at a Chelsea boutique, followed by Paul and George in identical black polo neck sweaters and leather jackets, with Ringo not far behind.

Local and national press were waiting, alongside Chief Constable McConnach, two Rank theatre regional controllers and half a dozen policemen. Henry Cloke, headmaster of Westcliff High School, let 14-year-old pupils Stuart Connall and Dennis Sherwood out of school early to interview the group for school magazine *Tempo*. Sally Ross, a pupil at Crowstone Prep School, had spent two nights making a model of the Beatles from dolly pegs, cigarette tops and chocolate boxes and left it at the Odeon hoping it would be autographed. Arthur Levenson phoned her to say if she came to the theatre she might be able to meet the group. She ended up posing with them onstage. Linda Daniels and Susan Pledge, who usually provided backstage needs for artists visiting the Odeon, were on hand to give the group food and drinks.

Backstage, the group spoke with *Disc*'s June Harris. They talked about what it was like to tour, their upcoming visits to America and Australia, and the making of their first feature film. John commented on the sound of screams coming from outside. 'A year ago, before all this happened, we could enter and leave any theatre, stay in an hotel, have a night out and go shopping without being mobbed.' Asked what his plans where for Christmas, Paul said, 'I intend to eat and sleep,' as he chewed on a chicken wing. John and George concurred, and all agreed that their New Year's resolution was to never wear their collarless Beatle jackets again.

During the shows, eight members of security company Securicor, as well as members of the Southend Judo Club, stood between the fans and the stage, while a fifty-strong contingent of St John Ambulance Brigade and Red Cross waited in the gangways. Pat Grimes, aged 16, almost fell into the orchestra pit as the group played 'Twist And Shout'. As she rushed forward, a cinema attendant grabbed her, stopping her from falling down eight feet. She broke away but was stopped again. A near riot erupted – the fire curtain was brought down and the performance stopped for five minutes. Police moved in from the sides of theatre. Earlier in the show, Grimes had thrown a toy miniature dog on the stage. In return John threw her a Beatle brooch. Later her mother told a reporter, 'Pat had always been a bit headstrong and a tomboy.' She went to work at a local cafe the following day proudly wearing the brooch.

Following the 6.35pm show, the group were interviewed in their dressing room by a BBC-TV news crew. At the end of the show while the National Anthem was being played, the group left the way they came and headed back to London, getting to bed at 3am.

Across the Atlantic, the week's edition of *Billboard* reported that 'Capitol Has New Beatles Bashes', revealing that Capitol Records had completed negotiations with EMI for the exclusive distribution of the group, while *Cash Box*'s headline read, 'Capitol Gets The Beatles For US', reporting that the Queen Mother had found them 'young, fresh and vital.'

❛ In 1963 I was living in Eastwood, then a village, about 3 miles from Southend-on Sea. I attended Eastwood High School for girls, which although a secondary modern was very progressive for its time. I had a friend who unlike me was very cool and gradually got me interested in the group, especially after showing me magazines which pictured them. For that time they were quite unlike any group before with their strange hairstyle and suits without collars! My first crush was on Paul, as I thought he had such an angelic face, but later switched to George as with my impending puberty he seemed slightly more edgy and dangerous looking! I seem to remember just about every girl in my school was mad about them, much to the despair of our teachers. My parents at first were rather disapproving but mellowed with time. I think even my father, a rabid classical music lover, had to admit they wrote some good melodies. In fact I remember I told him their music would still be played in fifty years' time – which indeed it has been.

When I knew they were coming to play in Southend, I queued up like everybody else. People had started queuing three days before the box office opened, but I showed up quite early on the Sunday – maybe around 8am. I must have travelled by bus, as my dad didn't get a car until his job supplied him with one a year or two later. When I rejoined the queue after having some lunch it was much shorter, but I still didn't think I'd get a ticket. Members of the Odeon staff were going up and down the line telling us we may as well go home! When I reached the ticket office, I heard someone say, 'That's it.' Suddenly I saw flash bulbs going off and lots of reporters asking me my name, how old I was, which school I went to, etc. I felt very confused and slightly intimidated by it. It felt rather like a dream. I do recall some of my teachers who'd seen the article in the local newspaper speaking to me about it at school.

As for the concert, well I don't think anyone could hear the Beatles sing, speak or play due to the huge noise level. Everyone was on their feet screaming, shouting and whistling. I think my devotion began to waver when they started to become a bit weird and grew their hair and beards. Although I had a secret longing to be old enough to be a hippy, I had a strange feeling I'd been let down by them in some way. Round about this time I discovered boys and various other styles of music so I left the Beatles behind, but will always be glad that I was a part of that amazing era. **,**

LINDSAY SPRING, DISPENSER, IPSWICH, SUFFOLK

TUESDAY 10 DECEMBER

nterviewed in the *Daily Express*, Cliff Richard said, 'I think the Beatles will ride high for maybe a year – then they will have to look to their laurels.' John Whyte-Melville-Skeffington, the 13th Viscount Massereene and 6th Viscount Ferrard, wrote a letter from the House of Lords in Westminster: 'I cannot understand this Beatle mania. I appreciate they have attractive personalities but when it comes to a question of rhythm, Elvis Presley has it all the way. Yours faithfully.' In the second of *Today*'s features on the group, John admitted they weren't great musicians. 'I'd be the first to admit that our success is out of all proportion to our musical talent.'

GAUMONT ∷ DONCASTER

ARTHUR HOWES presents

THE BEATLES SHOW

2nd Performance 8-30 p.m.
TUESDAY
DECEMBER **10**

CIRCLE 7/6

BLOCK
6 O35

No ticket exchanged nor money refunded
THIS PORTION TO BE RETAINED

Just after midday, the group set off on the long journey to Doncaster for two evening concerts at 6.15pm and 8.30pm at the Gaumont. They stopped off for lunch at the George Hotel in the High Street in Stamford and signed autographs for staff and fellow diners. They arrived at the pre-determined rendezvous of Doncaster Rovers' football ground on Bawtry Road at 4.40pm, about an hour late. Policeman Cyril Vickers described the group as 'a bunch of long-haired idiots,' but still got his son Martyn their autographs. They climbed into the back of a yellow *Yorkshire Evening Post* newspaper delivery van, using copies of the day's paper as seats, and were driven to the cinema five minutes away. The van pulled up outside and drove down an alley to a side entrance. Once inside, the group sat down for a ten-minute interview with Australian journalist Dibbs Mather for the BBC Transcription Service.

During the National Anthem at the end of the second show, the group quickly left the cinema through the emergency exit on Thorne Road and jumped into Inspector J. Oldfield's car. Oldfield drove them to the Regent Hotel, where they stayed the night. The *Doncaster Gazette & Chronicle* commented that the evening was 'marked by a singular lack of the riotous behaviour which, reports would indicate, has occurred where the group have appeared.' The paper was under the impression that two of the group were named David McCartney and Richard Starr.

In the US, the *CBS Evening News* re-aired the four-minute segment which had gone out on the morning of 22 November. Anchor Walter Cronkite later said, 'It was not a musical phenomenon to me. The phenomenon was a social one.' Cronkite arranged for his teenage daughters Kathy and Nancy to attend the dress rehearsal of the group's Ed Sullivan show appearance in February 1964. 'I don't think up till that time they really cared very much what their father did, but I suddenly was a hero in their eyes,' he commented. Silver Springs, Maryland, teenager Marsha Albert, a ninth-grader at Sligo High School, watched the item and put pen to paper. She wrote to local DJ Carroll James Jr. at Washington's WWDC radio station, asking, 'Why can't we have music like that here in America?' Intrigued, James contacted the British Embassy, which was unable to oblige so instead spoke with BOAC airlines. They arranged for a copy of 'I Want To Hold Your Hand' to be brought over by a stewardess the next time she flew to Washington. He aired the record for the first time on the 17th, inviting Albert into the studio to introduce it.

❝ I remember going down to the Co-op on a lovely summer's evening in August 1962. The first thing I noticed was the board outside, which spelt the name the B-E-A-T-L-E-S. When I went into the dance hall, there they were – the four of them with Pete Best as the drummer. Their haircuts, the cut of their suits were completely different to what we'd seen. We got to chat with Paul and George, but it was their music that was different. There was no stage or anything, so you could reach out as they were playing. They were on the same level as the dance floor. The next time I saw them was when they were bottom of the bill on the Helen Shapiro tour at the Gaumont. They came back later to the Baths and finally back to the Gaumont again. The thing I remember was the screams were getting louder and louder on each visit. By the time they came that last time, it was absolutely ear-busting. I didn't know how loud girls could yell. I think I've still got a hearing problem from that night!

I had left school and went to work as an apprentice for my father, who was a plumber. We did a lot of work for the Barnsley Brewery Company, who owned the Punch's Hotel, known as 'The Punches'. We'd always be called down there. 'Can you do this, can you do that?' Lots of different things. It was a popular stopping point with pop stars of the day, owing to its proximity to the old A1. Girls used to climb on the flat roof at the back to get on to the fire escape. The staff were always on their toes when pop stars were staying. That November I was working there when they were extending the bedrooms. One of the chambermaids on the previous day said, 'We've got some famous artists staying tomorrow night. It's the Beatles.'

So the following morning I got to work early and waited at the front of the hotel. Two cars came along. Three of the Beatles came out of the front of the hotel with Brian Epstein and a couple of other people. There was a bit of a noise because they were waiting for one person to get out of bed. It was Ringo. They were getting a bit annoyed. Eventually they all came out and I got all their autographs on my copy of the *Twist And Shout* EP I'd brought with me. They were very polite lads and it was quite an experience to meet them. I gave the EP as a Christmas present to my sister-in-law Yvonne. She was about 13 at the time. She took it to a party and at the end of the evening she went to get it and it had gone. So if there's somebody out there in Doncaster who's got a signed copy of the *Twist And Shout* EP, just think where it came from. Back then everyone would buy their records at Fox's. It was on French Gate, smack in the centre of town. They only closed down about ten or fifteen years ago now. I would buy the *NME* from WH Smith, which was located on one of the platforms at the station. A bus inspector used to stand in the middle and blow a whistle at eleven o'clock at night when the last bus left, and basically, after the whistle had gone, there was nobody in town! There were no nightclubs at that time, so if a concert finished early everyone would have had time to wander down to the Old Barrel for a drink. **J**

BILL ROWORTH, TEACHER, BESSECARR, SOUTH YORKSHIRE

WEDNESDAY 11 DECEMBER

The group headed north to Yeadon Airport outside Leeds. They liaised with a police inspector, who drove them on the A64 to Scarborough on the north-east coast of Yorkshire for two performances at 6.25pm and 8.45pm at the 2,150-seater Futurist. They stopped off at the White Lodge Hotel in Filey for lunch and, afterwards, the inspector took them on a detour so he could introduce the group to teenager Barbara Dobson. When they arrived, there was no answer and they headed off to the theatre – unbeknownst to them, the family was at the bottom of the garden. Chimpanzees Susan, Lulu and Jackie and orangutan Charles were driven from Flamingo Park Zoo near Pickering, Yorkshire, for a photo op with the Beatles. The Futurist's manager Mr RW Curtis didn't let them in, despite the protestations of a zoo official, who said, 'They are real Beatle fans.'

The group arrived at 4.30pm, only watched by a handful of fans. They immediately had a cup of tea in their dressing room as an order for food was placed with Jaconelli's snack bar. John, Paul and George had steak, mushrooms, chips and tomatoes – because the meal came with onions, Ringo had eggs, beans and chips instead. John and Paul followed the main course with apple pie and custard, while George had apple pudding and Ringo rice pudding. All four had French bread and butter and tea with plenty of milk. Denis Jaconelli later said, 'We drove it down in a car in wicker baskets. We took it through the crowds of girls and when we got inside, the baskets were full of little bits of paper with names, addresses and telephone numbers on!'

After eating, Ringo wandered onto the stage and launched into an impromptu jazz number on the piano as various members of the press asked the group questions. John was asked, 'What do you think about the rumours you wear wigs?' He replied, 'We have a good giggle about it.' Paul added, 'You can pull one of my hairs out if you don't believe it's my own.' John confessed to not knowing 'a dicky bird about' Scarborough, at which point George chipped in, 'We've heard you have some lovely swimming pools here. It was dark when we arrived so we couldn't see a thing – but I'd like to see the sea. I love the sea when it's rough.'

Between shows, about five hundred fans were squeezed in the passageway leading to the stage door. They broke through a barricade but reinforcements pushed them back. During the group's twenty-five-minute set at the second house, six hundred screaming teens in the stalls surged forward and were only prevented from mounting the stage by a barrier of policemen and theatre staff officials. About twenty girls briefly passed out. Paul told the audience to shut up – 'I can't hear myself think.' Not that anyone heard his plea. At the end of the second show, the curtain was brought down prematurely as five hundred fans stormed the stage. The group quickly escaped through the stage door and climbed into Pete Jaconelli's old Hillman shooting brake. They were driven up Bland's Cliff and through Eastborough Road. Their car waited on standby as a decoy in front of the theatre, where eleven coaches were parked, waiting to take fans back home. The group were driven to the Hylands Hotel in nearby Filey, where they stayed the night.

> ❛ I was 14 at the time, and a huge fan of the Beatles. I was learning to play the guitar, taking regular lessons with Keith Robson in Bridlington, and had a Broadway electric guitar with a 10-watt amplifier, which my aunt and uncle had bought me on hire purchase from the Kay's mail order catalogue for £18. I lived with them in Scarborough, and they bought me the ticket for the show, and took me to Montague Burton in Bridlington to be measured up for a Beatle suit. It was grey, collarless and cost £30, and I only wore it that one night! They also bought me a pair of black Cuban-heeled boots, just like the Beatles wore.
>
> They drove me and my friend, Michael Bastion, to the Futurist. When we got to the top of Blands Cliff, we could see the group standing on the back balcony waving to the crowd. Everyone was going crazy. Our tickets were for the fourth row, to the right of the stage. We couldn't hear a thing, just hundreds of girls screaming. The group had just received Vox 50-watt amplifiers to replace their AC-30 Top Boost amps, but still were not loud enough over the screaming fans. We were hoping to see them after the show, but they drove off up Blands Cliff in a black car. When they came to Scarborough the following year, I couldn't see them because I was in my own group then – Three Plus One – and we were doing a show ourselves that night. Our agent used to promote us as playing 'slick, well rehearsed routines which cover the whole field of dance hall and club entertainment.' Adding, 'They appear well presented, well groomed and sporting real musical talent, spiced with just a touch of humour.' Between January 1964 and 1965, we appeared throughout the north east, supporting the likes of the Searchers, the Nashville Teens, the Swinging Blue Jeans and the Animals. In the late 1990s, we reformed the group as Three Plus One Again, playing '60s and '70s music. After that came to an end, I formed my own group Zippy Weasel. ❜
>
> **JOHN LESSENTIN, SECURITY OPERATIVE, SCARBOROUGH, NORTH YORKSHIRE**

THURSDAY 12 DECEMBER

The front-page headline in *Disc* read 'Beatles First Film Out Next Week!', with word that Pathé News would be releasing newsreels in widescreen Technicolor in cinemas across the country on 22 December. In the paper's latest Top 30 chart, 'I Want To Hold Your Hand' and 'She Loves You' were at numbers 1 and 2 – where they stayed for the rest of the year. The *Twist And Shout* EP was at number 12, *With The Beatles* at number 13, *The Beatles' Hits* EP at number 17 and *The Beatles (No. 1)* EP at number 29. Reader Kevin Tunstall suggested the Beatles be featured on a series of special commemorative postage stamps. 'Miss World has this privilege, why not the Beatles?' he mooted.

The group made the front cover of *NRM* for the second time in five weeks. 'I Want To Hold Your Hand' jumped ten places to number one in the chart, knocking 'She Loves You' down to number 2 (the two records stayed in those positions through the end of the year). After an initial advance order of 940,000 copies, 'I Want To Hold Your Hand' went on to sell 1.5 million copies in the UK and fifteen million worldwide.

It was the ninth UK chart-topper from a Liverpool-based group in the year. The Beatles became the first act to replace itself at number one. Lennon also did this posthumously in 1981, when 'Woman' replaced 'Imagine' at the top.

Dee Wells, in a *Daily Herald* article headlined 'The Beatles Are Good For Girls', wrote about the previous weekend's TV show. 'The young furies in the studio audience (unless my old eyes are failing too) were obviously in the grip of another emotion. Their screams drowned what little noise the beat Beatles could make. They shuddered. They moaned. They rocked. Their mouths hung open. And their eyes glittered like those of so many broody cobras.' The *Daily Mail* launched its Beatle Drive with the announcement, 'We start today. Three thousand Oxford undergraduates, the Beatles – and the Daily Mail – We want to help raise £500,000 in 20 days to complete the "Hunger Million" to save the starving.'

The group set off from the Hylands Hotel, heading south on the A164 for the two-hour drive to the Odeon in Nottingham. Arriving in the city shortly before 4pm, the group liaised with police at their city headquarters. Superintendent Ossie Sutton, who was in charge of 'Operation Beatles', had told the *Evening Post*, 'Security arrangements have been made and we shall have a sufficient number of officers on duty, with an adequate strength in reserve. I expect our youngsters will be like our football fans – good humoured and well behaved.'

The Beatles played two shows at two shows at 6.15pm and 8.30pm. After the second show had ended, the group were whisked away in a Black Maria from St James's Street, where the Austin Princess was parked. A police van picked up their luggage from a side entrance, while their instruments were taken out through the front. PC Terry Lambley recalled the day. 'It was supposed to have been my day off, but with all leave cancelled I was drafted in and ended up carrying the radio – it weighed about five tons and had an aerial that was about 12 feet tall. With all that power it could only just about transmit between the street outside and the dressing room, but it was the height of technology back then. After the shows were over, we drove back to the police station and along with a fellow PC, we followed the group's car from the police station down the London Road over the bridge and past Nottingham Forest's City Ground and the Trent Bridge cricket ground before it headed down the A606 towards Melton Mowbray. When we got to the Melton Road Post Office in West Bridgford, their car stopped and I saw John Lennon dash out and put a letter in the post box. As soon as they got into the countryside we turned tail. That was our job done. It had been quite a night.'

❛ I was educated at the Convent of the Sacred Heart High School in Filey. In the common room at lunch time, we were allowed to have a Dansette record player, where we would jive. I remember jiving to 'Love Me Do', and we played it till it wore out. I was living in Bridlington at the time and went to see the Beatles at the Futurist. A coach trip was organised by the Maurice Thorpe Youth Club. I remember pulling up outside the venue and seeing coaches and huge crowds. There was plenty of pushing and shoving, and people screaming. There was a lot of mayhem going on. I went to the 6.15 show, sitting in seat M14 in the Circle. The ticket and programme cost me 7/6.

We heard the Beatles were staying at the Hylands Hotel, which was across the road from the Convent. We had a very understanding and charming headmistress, Sister Claire. I'm quite sure she had never heard of the group, but we asked if we could go and see them at the hotel. She said it would be all right if we went in numbers. I had been a boarder until I was in the Upper Sixth, and then a day girl, which allowed me more freedom – lessons and exams permitting I couldn't interest anyone else in the Upper Sixth to go with me, so I went with girls from the Lower Sixth. It was arranged we'd go after lunch before afternoon lessons. We assumed when we got to the hotel that the manager would take our autographs books, and say, 'Wait here, girls.' But he went upstairs, and came back down saying the Beatles had said, 'Bring them up!' So off we went. The Beatles were probably thinking, 'Oh, four convent girls, this is going to be fun!' but when we rocked up in our ill-fitted gym slips and Lisle stockings, I think the image was just dispelled straight away.

We were quite expecting to go into a luxury suite, but the room was so 'grotty' (John's word) – surprising considering the Hylands was the smartest hotel in town. The room had five single divans in it and was at the back of the hotel. The Beatles were wearing jeans, and we just thought it was the coolest thing in the world, to meet boys wearing jeans. Anyway, they were polite, but to be fair, Paul was the most welcoming. The others were just chilled out and relaxing. I remember Ringo sprawled out on one bed, reading a magazine, George was in the background, and John emerged through an interconnecting door, which was probably an en-suite loo or something. We were shuffling around, thinking of something intelligent to say, but Paul really put us at our ease. He asked us questions about school and we asked him questions about the gig and their new record and so forth. We asked if they'd mind signing our books, and they said, 'No, not at all.' In those days, you couldn't use anything but a fountain pen at school, so I proffered my Conway Stewart – a birthday gift from my grandparents. We had taken our exercise books, and they signed several pages for the other girls. I still have that pen! I daren't ask Paul for a lock of his hair, so I asked him if there was anything else we could take as a memento, and he took this block of soap off the wash basin in the bedroom. It was that thin hotel soap that is still used today, and he gave it to us. I can't remember if he cut it up for us, or if we cut it up later, but I think he probably cut it as I still have my piece, wrapped in the very loo roll, probably bearing Paul's DNA!

We all shook hands very politely, and scuttled back to school in complete euphoria, and of course all the other girls gathered round. Two of us kept the autographs, and the others sold theirs for chocolate! They swapped them for Mars bars and Kit-Kats – bear in mind they were boarders, and they didn't get an awful lot of food! I kept my Beatles' autographs. The sad thing was, I framed them, and put them up in my bedroom, but of course, being written in fountain pen, over the years they just faded and faded. It got to the point when I thought, if I don't do something about it, they're going to be worthless. To get all four Beatles autographs on one page was quite a thing. I did try and sell them to a company in Liverpool, but when they asked what provenance I had, all I had was my word, and probably a diary entry. As that wasn't sufficient, I hung on to them for a few more years. Eventually I sold them through an auction house called Dee & Atkinson in Driffield, around 2002. Someone paid £1,500 for the ticket and programme, which was just in time to mend the hole in my roof! It made me think of 'I'm fixing a hole where the rain gets in.' **)**

**PAMELA SHAW JOHNSTON, PUBLIC RELATIONS AND MARKETING
EXECUTIVE, BROMPTON-BY-SAWDON, NORTH YORKSHIRE**

FRIDAY 13 DECEMBER

'Want To Hold Your Hand' and 'She Loves You' remained at numbers 1 and 2 in the *NME* singles chart, while *Twist And Shout* was at number 12, *With The Beatles* at number 14, *The Beatles' Hits* at number 17 and *The Beatles (No. 1)* at number 29. Inside the paper, George Martin revealed that Ringo only played tambourine on 'Love Me Do'. It also announced the results of its twelfth annual poll. The Beatles were named World's Outstanding Group, British Vocal Group and won Best Disc of the Year for 'She Loves You'.

'I Want To Hold Your Hand' and 'She Loves You' also remained at numbers 1 and 2 in the *Melody Maker* singles chart, while *Twist And Shout* dropped a place to number 12, *The Beatles' Hits* climbed back up three places to number 14 and *The Beatles (No. 1)* dropped to number 23. Under the headline 'Hands Off – They're Trying To Bash The Beatles', Ray Coleman succinctly made the point that those who complained about police having to guard the group had no problem with a police presence at football matches. Elsewhere in the paper, several artists were asked what they wanted for Christmas. The Beatles responded, 'It depends on the sex of the receiver. We'd buy a country for someone who needs one.' Kenny Lynch's wish was for 'a year's free subscription to the famous hairdresser Vidal Sassoon for the Beatles.'

The group's London solicitor, David Jacobs, said that writs were being served by post to Blackpool Publishers and the Palace Rock Company, seeking an injunction to restrain them from using the name 'The Beatles' or any photographs of goods. The case was expected to come before a Queen's Bench judge shortly thereafter. The *Evening Standard* devoted its front-page headline ('Libel Suit By The Beatles') to the story. Cubbon Brothers immediately announced they would stop selling small cakes decorated with the names of the group. 'We have discontinued the line because of the writ issued by the Beatles last week,' they said. 'They were only a gimmick line and we don't suppose they would have lasted much longer anyway.' One of the more inventive items subject to the injunction were 6" toffee discs costing 1/6. Each packet listed the group's top songs and gave the speed of the record as forty-five licks a minute.

As the first snow of winter fell, variously described as 'a light dusting' to 'blizzard-like', particularly along the coast at Southend and in Eastbourne and Hastings, the group finished their thirty-three-date tour with two concerts at 6.30pm and 8.45pm at the Gaumont in Southampton. Once again, fans had slept overnight to snap up the 4,460 tickets on sale. One happy attendee was Terry Jamieson, whose mother queued all night to buy him tickets. 'She said it was the best night's entertainment she had since the days and nights she had spent in the bomb shelters during the Second World War,' he said.

The Gaumont's manager Ken Watts arranged for the group to change from the Austin Princess to a Ford Consul on the outskirts of town, four hours before the show. A coach was driven to the stage door as a decoy, while the group entered through the front entrance. Eighteen-year-old projectionist Les Acres witnessed a kerfuffle between George and the theatre's 80-something doorman Archie. Paul responded to a reporter asking if he had secretly married Jane Asher, 'I have been out with Jane once or twice, but she is only one of a number of girl friends,' neglecting to mention he was living with the Asher family.

A Beatle decided to make some mischief during the Vernon Girls' set, sitting at the piano with a coat over his head and pulling the microphone away from Jean Owen while she sang 'Tomorrow's Another Day'. After the 8.45pm show, 19-year-old *Evening Echo* journalist James Arlott, son of cricket commentator and writer John Arlott, interviewed the group, before they were driven to the Polygon Hotel, where they stayed the night. An *Echo* Staff Reporter wrote, 'Little girls, near-hysterical, bobbed in their seats as though they were electrocuted, waved giant photos of the Beatles. It sounded like a slaughter house... Saints v Manchester United in the Cup semi-final at Aston Villa had nothing on this... Perhaps somebody ought to strike a medal for unruffled "General" Watts: "For bravery in the face of Beatlemania, over and above the call of duty." The hundred police on duty 'had a fairly easy, if noisy, time of it.'

In the US, CBS Television issued a press release announcing that 'the Beatles, wildly popular quartet of English recording stars, will make their first trip to the United States Feb. 7 for their American television debut on 'The Ed Sullivan Show', Sunday, Feb. 9 and 16'. There were 50,000 ticket applications for 728 tickets and on the day of the first broadcast eight blocks on Broadway were clogged with fans. An estimated 40 per cent of the American population reportedly watched the show.

‘ Southampton was a good place to grow up in the late '50s/early '60s. It was quite multicultural even back then and there were never any problems. Lots of different people came off the ships, no one ever thought about it, they were all just like us as far as we were concerned, so in that way it was quite forward-thinking. I first heard 'Love Me Do' on Radio Luxembourg in October 1962, listening under the bedclothes on my new-fangled Dansette transistor radio. Right away, I thought, 'Wow, this is different.' It was obviously based on Bruce Channel's 'Hey Baby', with the harmonica. I went out and bought it straight away from Spikin's, our local record shop in Woolston. After I bought the single, I'd take my harmonica along to Itchen Grammar School and play 'Love Me Do', and a crowd would gather in the playground! I also bought the *Please Please Me* LP when it came out.

We'd all read about them and talked about the Beatles, and when we found out they were coming to Southampton with Roy Orbison, who I was also a fan of, I just had to get a ticket. My friend Ken Derham and I queued all night. It was that freezing cold winter which had broken all records, and although we didn't have snow being down by the sea, it was a bitter night. I can still picture the place in my mind where we queued at the side of the Gaumont on Commercial Road. The Gaumont was our local cinema, and they used to have Saturday morning shows for children, and local groups would play there as well, so there was a good music scene in Southampton at the time. We had a couple of dance halls in town, but when the big names came, they always played at either the Gaumont or the ABC. We'd skip school and hop on the bus into town from the east side of the river. When we got there in the late afternoon, the queue was already halfway down the building. We had sleeping bags, hot drinks, and sandwiches with us. The atmosphere was great, with everyone passing the time by singing Beatles songs, and other pop songs of the day. Mum came over to relieve us for a couple of hours so we could stretch our legs and replenish ourselves with hot tea and more sandwiches. There was no problem back then letting youngsters out, because it was all rather new, the explosion of rock'n'roll, and the teen movement. We managed to get tickets for the first house, seats about ten rows back in the stalls on Paul McCartney's side, on the left, and they cost 10/6.

When it was announced they were coming again in December '63, I went over to queue again, but this time I couldn't queue overnight, but I got tickets up on the balcony. I had turned 15 that October and by this time I had my Beatles look – I was wearing a black corduroy suit, with a round collar, and the hair was long enough to get into trouble at school! On this occasion, it was just non-stop screaming. You couldn't hear a thing. Of course, at the time, all those acts used to use the house microphones, which were pretty bad, Vox AC-30s, and a T60 bass amp for Paul. I absorbed all of that sort of thing, as I just wanted to be like them, in a group, so I would notice those sorts of things. By then end of '63 I was just getting my first group together, the Ab-Do Men. I was the lead singer and played harmonica. That really set me up for the next ten years. The Beatles had been singing lots of obscure rhythm and blues stuff, unusual stuff that none of us had ever heard of. Everybody else copied them. Every year at the Concorde Club in Southampton, I organise a reunion of local musicians since 2008. We have about four or five hours of original guys from the '60s who are still playing, and we do a charity show. The two experiences seeing the Beatles twice in 1963, sort of shaped my whole career, the next fifty years. ’

DAVID ST JOHN, MUSICIAN AND COMEDIAN, CANNOCK, STAFFORDSHIRE

SATURDAY 14 DECEMBER

The first wave of special pass holders, braving sub-zero temperatures, arrived for the Southern Area Fan Club Convention at Wimbledon Palais in High Street, Merton, south-west London. The first in line was Denise Kett, aged 17, who said, 'I got here at 7am, and I'm frozen. But it's worth it. The Beatles are the best thing since telephones.' At 11.45am, the Palais doors opened, an hour and a half earlier than planned because of the cold weather. Three thousand fans poured into the ballroom. To cope with the deluge, two hundred police had been drafted in for the day from as far afield as Penge and Kennington, along with sixty commissionaires and ten stewards. The day before, all police leave had been cancelled and local hospitals warned to expect a spate of fainting girls.

At 1.30pm, shortly after the group arrived, fan club members got the chance to meet their idols in the Long Bar. They shook hands and signed autographs for the fans, ultimately giving up signing as the line grew too long. As one girl reached them, she lifted her sweater to reveal the word 'Touch'. It seems her invitation was turned down. Paul received a giant four-page Christmas card from Maxine Cornthwaite and Lynn Barry, which took them three months to make. He also received a teddy bear, while Ringo was presented with a bottle of aftershave. A bank clerk from Balham thought the group looked 'terribly tired'. She briefly talked with Ringo, who thought the group would be finished by the end of 1964: 'We're booked months in advance, but it's only a question of time before we fade out.' One girl had a coloured garter round her leg with Jelly Babies tied on; another had a shopping basket full of them.

By 3pm, the seven nurses and two ambulance men of the St John Ambulance Brigade were handling fainting girls, 140 in total, many suffering from hysteria and one from an appendicitis. Many girls were left inconsolable afterwards. At 4pm, the group performed a short set – but not before they threatened to walk out, seeing a 7-foot high steel mesh fences between them and the audience. Girls pressed so hard against the barricade that it started to give way. By five o'clock, arrangements were completely chaotic and Tony Barrow declared 'no photographers, no reporters.' Most of the group's performance was drowned out by screaming girls and shouts from the police, trying in vain to stop fans climbing over the barrier onto the stage. One commissionaire sitting with the group said, 'It was terrible. The girls were absolutely hypnotised by them. Dozens of them were shaking the pop stars' hands and then just completely flaking out.' Another commissionaire, John Fitzmorris, cracked a rib while trying to rescue a fainting girl trapped in crowd. Half a dozen policemen had their uniforms torn. One girl slipped a disc, although at first it was thought she had fractured her spine. Five girls were taken to hospital. One policeman was heard to say, 'Can you ever imagine this lot growing up and having kids of their own? It's incredible, incredible.'

Barrow said, 'The Beatles have been touring all week and they just couldn't take any more,' leaving red pass holders to be turned away. Fans were sent out into the rain, until the doors reopened at 7.30pm for the 9pm performance. Between the shows, 18-year-old Balham girl Lesley Duggan managed to find her way into the group's dressing room – passing herself off as waitress Mrs Brown, the landlady from the Nelson Arms, after persuading Brown to let her commandeer a tea tray and take it into the room. The group left at 9.30pm and headed back to the West End. A reporter from the *Liverpool Daily Post* wrote that 'the screams of the girls were so piercing it seemed that thousands of penny whistles were being blown in unison.'

Lost in the mayhem were the two support groups who valiantly performed in the face of an almost total lack of interest. Geoff Quarterman, lead guitarist of the Hustlers, remembered the unusual booking. 'Unlike any other event we had played at, we had to be there a day before on the Friday to set up our equipment. We set up and had to be back early next day, by which time the congestion outside had increased. Inside, we had to wait for hours, hanging around all afternoon on a side stage next to the main stage. Paul came past once and said hello as he went by. Our bass player, who built our PA equipment and an enormous bass amplifier which we called his coffin, asked Paul if he would like a customised bass amp, to which Paul replied, "I've already got one." Our spot was to last an hour as far as I remember. When we came on, the ballroom was absolutely full of fans waiting for the big moment. We started our act at that time with Larry Williams' 'Slow Down' which the Beatles later put on record. It was in many groups' repertoires. There was no interest at all in what we played, just an atmosphere of restless waiting. Now and then someone clapped out of sympathy, but mainly it was very hard going. Towards the end of our set, our singer Roger announced, 'And now for our last number...' – the rest of the sentence was lost in a deafening roar of approval and applause. At last, we would be getting off the stage! After that the Beatles entered their cage-stage and the audience noise reached jet aircraft level. They started, and as we were very close, more or less in the wings, we could hear what they were playing fairly well. But I doubt if anyone in the audience heard much. They were really good, the harmonies and instrumental parts were perfect. I remember being impressed by 'You Really Got A Hold On Me'. Their set was about half an hour at the most, after which they bowed, downed instruments and dashed backstage where a door opened magically and they tumbled into a waiting car and disappeared into the dark, something like a scene from *A Hard Day's Night*. So that was it, the evening fizzled out, we packed our gear and loaded up our van.'

❛ I was living in a prefab in Melbourn, a small village just south of Cambridge, in the early '6os. My mother worked on munitions at the Rover Aero engine factory in Birmingham during the war and radio programmes such as *Workers' Playtime* were on continuously. So growing up, the radio was on in our house all the time. The first record I bought was *Telstar* by the Tornados but when I first heard the Beatles, that was it – I was hooked. I went to see many groups at the Regal in Cambridge, including the Beatles in November 1963. Until I could drive, the only way to get to town was by bus and the last one left at 9.45 pm! If we went to the cinema we had to go in early to see the end first. I remember when we went to see *A Hard Day's Night* in 1964, we stayed in the cinema and watched it two or three times, which you could do back then. My friend and I queued overnight for the tickets in the alleyway beside the cinema!

I had already become a member of the fan club in 1963 and in November that year I was sent a ticket to go to a fan club get together in London. Because I was only 15, my mum said she'd take me and would go shopping while I was at the concert. We were on the train halfway to King's Cross, when I realised I'd forgotten my ticket. Needless to say, I was very upset. Mum said, 'Never mind. We'll go to the venue and see if we can find the secretary of the fan club, you can tell her your name and she can look you up.' When we got there, the queue was very long, so we went to the front and Mum spoke to a policeman, thinking he would go and speak to someone. But he said, 'Come with us, love' and we thought he was going to find somebody. And he pushed open this door and said, 'In you go.' Mum and I were pushed in and were both allowed to go to the concert. When the get together started, the Beatles were in the bar area sitting behind the counter while everyone filed past them to say 'Hello.' Mum would have been 52 at the time, so when we walked past, John said, 'Hello Mum' and she patted Paul on the head! I wasn't too impressed that they were more interested in her than me – at 15 she seemed old to me. (Now I'm over 60 my view has changed!) I thought, why can't they look at me? They were making jokes and it was a bit like one of their films. We all then went into the ballroom and the boys did a concert for us, which was great but Mum thought it was very loud. Everyone was packed in (it must have been before Health and Safety) so when we left we felt our arms were still clamped to our sides. My bedroom wall was covered in posters, including the famous one of them in old-fashioned bathing suits. One evening, we heard a loud noise and found that the whole lot had fallen down. The sticky tape hadn't been strong enough! **"**

LYNN CATLEY, BRITISH TELECOM DRAUGHTSWOMAN, CAMBRIDGE, CAMBRIDGESHIRE

SUNDAY 15 DECEMBER

A snowstorm caused the Beatles to arrive four hours late to Alpha Studios in Aston for the recording of *Thank Your Lucky Stars - Lucky Stars on Merseyside for Christmas!* The programme also featured hostess Cilla Black, Gerry and the Pacemakers, Billy J. Kramer with the Dakotas, the Searchers, the Breakaways, Tommy Quickly, Janice Nicholls and guest DJ Bob Wooler. The group were met by a police car at the city boundary in Sheldon and driven to the Victoria Road police station, before finally arriving in a police van. The Dakotas had to fill in for them at a rehearsal for the benefit of the cameramen, miming to 'I Want To Hold Your Hand' with Ray Jones playing his bass guitar left handed. Plate-glass windows in

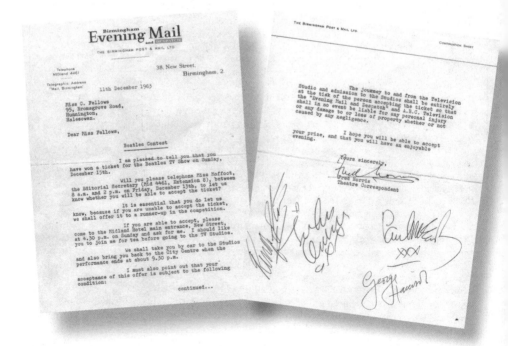

the reception area were boarded up, and fans broke through a police cordon. One small girl succeeded in squeezing past the police into the studio. After gaining Ringo's autograph she left, weeping with joy. Between 300 and 400 teenagers standing outside in constant drizzle kept up a continuous chant of 'We Want The Beatles!' during the recording of the show. George Martin presented the group with two gold discs for 'Twist And Shout' and 'She Loves You' and at the conclusion of their appearance, they were presented with further gold discs for million-plus sales of 'She Loves You' and 'I Want To Hold Your Hand'. The group mimed to 'I Want To Hold Your Hand', 'All My Loving', 'Twist And Shout' and 'She Loves You'.

Teenagers Cherryl Fellows, Carol Ann Young, Patricia Thacker and Mary Hatwell, 43-year-old Yvette Jones and 69-year-old Edward Turner, were winners of a competition in the *Birmingham Evening Mail & Despatch*. They got to meet the group backstage, and saw the dress rehearsal and performance. More than twenty entries for the competition came from people aged over 70, most of whom professed that the Beatles kept them young.

The New York Times reported that the group, 'described as Elvis Presley multiplied by four', would be appearing on *The Ed Sullivan Show*. Listed in the 'News of TV and Radio' section, the newspaper deemed as more noteworthy than a scheduled appearance by former President Harry S. Truman on *Candid Camera* on 29 December and the announcement that CBS-TV would be airing a tribute to Jackie Gleason on 4 January, celebrating his thirty-five years in show business. Writer Val Adams, who said the group would be granting 'England a respite early next year and come here to render musical mayhem', questioned whether Beatlemania would become a fad in the US or millions of viewers would tune in their TV sets.

❛ It is early winter 1963. I am a schoolgirl who has just celebrated her 16th birthday. Quite shy, but interested in horses and pop music, I particularly like the Beatles. In order to support the expensive ownership of my newly acquired horse, I have started babysitting for a couple of families in my village of Romsley. On one such evening, the children fast asleep, the biscuit barrel raided and nothing of interest on television, in the absence of anything else to do I scan the local paper. On the back page a headline shouts at me – 'YOU can meet the BEATLES! – Meet them in person, have tea with them. Have your photograph taken with them. Then see them take part in a televised Merseyside Beat package show.' All I have to do is say

in fifty words why I like them. Babysitting duties complete, I return home, rescue my parents' copy of the paper, go to my room and with pen and paper, set to work. I know that if I am to win this prize, I must tell no one. Complete secrecy is vital! If I confide what I am doing to anyone, the spell will be broken. Knowing nothing of the editing process, I nevertheless write and rewrite the precious fifty words until they cannot, in my opinion, be improved upon. I keep the words under my pillow for a couple of nights until I can do no more. I am bursting with excitement and anticipation. Carefully I write them out for the final time, putting the piece of paper, together with the official coupon, into an envelope. I still remember how I felt when it dropped into the post box. I was with friends and still the secret was kept. And I wait. I have NO DOUBT whatsoever that victory will be mine. So, I stand in the front bar of my parents' pub awaiting the bus for school. I can see it stop at the top of the hill, the journey down allowing me enough time to stroll out to the stop and get on. I have gauged that this should be the day. The post arrives just before the bus. I am handed a typed envelope with a Birmingham franked mark on the front and on the reverse the words *Birmingham Post and Mail*. This is what I've been waiting for! I have omitted the name of the pub, but happily the postman is able to identify that 95 Bromsgrove Road is indeed the Sun. The letter is from Fred Norris, the Theatre Correspondent of the *Birmingham Evening Mail*. It tells me that I have indeed won one of the coveted tickets and implores me to telephone Miss Morfoot on Friday the 13th if I am unable to attend so that another might benefit from the prize. The event warrants a new outfit and a trip to the local town results in the purchase of a white polo neck sweater and a blue pinafore dress with a pleated skirt.

The day arrives. My father drives me the 10 miles or so into Birmingham City Centre. We are to meet our heroes at the Midland Hotel and have tea with them. We are greeted by the jovial Fred Norris, who explains that 'the boys' are running late. The tea and cakes will be consumed with our fellow competition winners. The meeting with our heroes will happen, but later. To a man (and woman), we are almost incapable of swallowing at this point, so the news fazes no one. We are loaded into enormous black cars, fit for prizewinners, and are delivered to Aston on the east side of town, where the ATV studios are located. We are here to see a recording of *Thank Your Lucky Stars* – part of our prize. We are taken onto the stage surrounded by enormous television cameras. After a couple of photos we await the arrival of the Fab Four and in no time, in they bound. There are six winners – an elderly gent, a woman the age of one of our mothers and one girl for each Beatle. We each have a favourite. Paul is mine and joy of joys he walks over to me and puts his arm over my shoulder. MY SHOULDER. What LUCK! Had it been John or George or Ringo, I would have been happy, but this was what dreams are made of. BLISS! BLISS! BLISS! I had never been so happy in my life EVER! Photos are taken to record the event for posterity, not that I will ever forget this moment. Even after all these years I can remember almost every second of it.

One of the other prizewinners an American girl called Carol has come with a felt-tipped pen. 'Will you sign my arm, Paul?' she asks. This strikes me, who has arrived totally unprepared with neither autograph book nor pen, as a very good idea. 'Mine too please' I say and my proffered hand is signed by my hero with his name and three kisses. This is to remain on the back of my hand in ever diminishing size and increasing grubbiness until three weeks later I am obliged to wash it clean. I am relieved at the age of past 70 that tattoos were not the fashion item then that they are today. I fear if that had been the case, my career may have taken a slightly different path if I had chosen to secure the inking in perpetuity. Having no book for autographs, all I have is the letter from the newspaper confirming my right to be there. So in the absence of anything else other than my other limbs, they sign this for me. John, cynical and already a little world-weary; George, quiet, diffident and bemused by the fuss; Ringo, rather like a bouncy puppy, the least good-looking one of the four and my beloved doe-eyed Paul. Like the boy next door, oh how wish he could be my boyfriend!

Photocall over, we are taken to our seats to watch the show. The screaming is overwhelming. They can't hear themselves play. Neither can the audience hear a thing. But aware that this is a recording I bide my time. I wait for a moment of quiet and then I scream my head off. I am later to hear myself, when the TV programme is broadcast – a lone voice in the gap where the rest of the audience took breath. Show over, we are taken upstairs to the studio's VIP lounge. So the promised tea with the Beatles turns neatly into canapes and cocktails, too young to participate in the alcohol. I don't need it anyway. I am already dizzy with the excitement of the occasion. The Beatles are settled on a series of sofas against the back wall. EVERYONE wants a piece of the action. I fight my way to the front and sit at the feet of George, shy diffident George, and whatever words I share with him and he with me are lost in the excitement of the encounter. We are then shipped back to the newspaper offices in the city centre where Fred asks for our reaction to the event. 'Well,' I say, 'you can tell them I will never wash my hand again!' And this provides the opening copy for the article next day. Did it change my life? Yes, in a sense it did. A little. A shy schoolgirl I was suddenly more popular at school, people wanted to be my friend, I was asked out on dates. They could say they were going out with the girl who met the Beatles. Reflected glory! I even got a mention in school assembly. 〕

CHERRYL VINES, AUTHOR AND AFTER-DINNER SPEAKER, STOURBRIDGE, WEST MIDLANDS

MONDAY 16 DECEMBER

The group were once again featured on the front cover of the week's *Mirabelle* with the caption, 'What it feels like to sing before a Queen'. Despite telling the press the previous day that he had no plans to marry Jane Asher, Paul escorted her to the Prince of Wales Theatre to see the new American comedy *Never Too Late*. He paid 25s for each ticket in the dress circle. The couple left during the second intermission after they were recognised and mobbed. It was the first time the pair had been spotted in public. They hailed a taxi and went back to Asher's home. Jane's mother Margaret told the attendant press, 'There was nothing unusual about their being together. They see quite a lot of each other. What was different tonight was that Paul got a break from work

and it gave them the opportunity to go to the theatre. I wouldn't say there was anything extra special about their friendship. Paul is one of Jane's many friends.' Paul concurred, saying, 'I like Jane. I go out with her when I am in London, but I go out with other girls too – in London and on tour.' When asked what he would say if Miss Asher proposed marriage the next year – a Leap Year – he said, 'I'd say don't be daft.' (When it became public knowledge that Paul was living at Wimpole Street, fans began camping outside. Jane's father Richard devised a plan to get him in and out of the house. Paul would climb on to a foot-wide parapet at the back of the house, go through the flat of a retired colonel at number 56, clamber in through the window of the home of Frederick and Rona Shambrook at 10 Browning Mews and finally exit into New Cavendish Street.)

TUESDAY 17 DECEMBER

It was Paul's turn to be featured in *Today*. He admitted that he had a tendency to get more impatient than he used to. Asked to compare the Beatles with other artists, he said, 'Our granny has a wooden leg and so has our kitchen table. Doesn't mean the kitchen table looks like granny!'

Arriving an hour early for the recording of the Christmas edition of *Saturday Club* at the Playhouse Theatre, the group went shopping. They sent Brian Sommerville into Simpsons in nearby Piccadilly to make sure the coast was clear, then headed over and bought some clothes. The three-and-a-half-hour session began at 3pm. They performed 'All My Loving' (the first of four performances on BBC radio), 'This Boy', 'I Want To Hold Your Hand', 'Till There Was You', 'Roll Over Beethoven' and 'She Loves You'. Either side of Paul reading some requests, they also performed a brief pastiche of 'All I Want For Christmas Is A Beatle', titled 'All I Want For Christmas Is A Bottle' and a thirty-second medley combining the titles of 'Love Me Do', 'Please Please Me', 'From Me To You', 'I Want To Hold Your Hand' and 'Rudolph The Red-Nosed Reindeer', over a riff made famous by Duane Eddy's 'Shazam'. Brian Matthew introduced it as a 'muddley – I'm sorry – medley'. The show aired the following Saturday.

Carroll James Jr. became the first disc-jockey to play 'I Want To Hold Your Hand' in the US on Washington station WWDC. He later hosted the Beatles' first US concert in 1964. He invited Marsha Albert, who had alerted him to the record a week earlier, to introduce it on air. She read a few lines of copy James had scrawled on the back of a traffic report. After playing it, James asked the listeners, 'We'd like to know what you think about the record. Don't call. Please write.' His request went unheeded as the station switchboard lit up. He played the record again an hour later and then went on to play it every night that week. In response, Capitol asked the station to stop playing the record before its 13 January release date. After WWDC declined to do so, Capitol hired attorney Walter Hofer to issue a 'cease and desist' order. Not only did the station continue playing the record, but James sent a tape of it to a DJ friend in Chicago, who also began playing it. A St Louis station soon followed suit. Capitol made the wise decision to bring forward the release date to 26 December.

At day's end, Paul got into conversation with Jane and one of her brother's friends, John Dunbar, at the Asher family home. Peter and Gordon Waller returned briefly from performing at the Pickwick Club, before going out again to play chemin de fer at a Soho club. Soon after Paul stood up and said, 'Well, I've had a very tiring day, making lots of people happy. I'm going to bed.'

WEDNESDAY 18 DECEMBER

The group visited the *Daily Express* offices in Fleet Street, but when word got out, they had to escape through a side door and into a waiting car. At 7pm, they began a three-and-a-half-hour recording session at the Paris Studio for their Boxing Day show, now titled, *The Beatles Say From Us To You*. They played 'She Loves You', 'All My Loving', 'Roll Over Beethoven', 'Till There Was You', 'Boys', 'Money', 'I Saw Her Standing There', 'Tie Me Kangaroo Down Sport' with host Rolf Harris ('Cut your hair once a year, boys,' he said. 'Don't ill treat me pet dingo, Ringo.') and 'I Want To Hold Your Hand'. They opened and closed the show with 'From Us To You' – a lyrical rewrite of their number one. Susan Maughan, Jeanie Lambe, Kenny Lynch, Joe Brown and the Bruvvers, the Kenny Salmon Seven and Alan Elsdon's Jazzband with Mick Emery also featured in the programme. Harris remembered his involvement with the show: 'I was sent to interview the Beatles and my hands were shaking so much I could barely flick the switch on the tape recorder. I shoved the mic in John's face and said, "Well, do you like spaghetti then?" Fortunately for me, they all fell about the place. I think they said 'No,' but buoyed by their enthusiasm I pulled out a crumpled song sheet and announced, "I've got something for you boys." I had written a new version of 'Tie Me Kangaroo Down Sport' with a verse for each of them. When I asked them if they'd like to sing it with me, they responded with a deafening, "Yes!"'

The Western Theatre Ballet company's *Mods And Rockers*, featuring the music of Lennon and McCartney and choreographed by Peter Darrell, opened at the Prince Charles Theatre, sharing the space with *Sooty's Christmas Party*, which played twice daily. *The Observer* was ambivalent in its review. 'An honest working face peers out between the party rig and the Beatle wig.' It particularly liked the jazz ballets with their 'wonderful snooty pin-table anti-charm.' The play ran until 11 January 1964.

THURSDAY 19 DECEMBER

The front page of *Disc* featured the group dressed as Father Christmases, accompanied by the greeting 'The Beatles Wish You... A Merry Christmas'. Below it was an ad for Bing Crosby's 'Do You Hear What I Hear?'. 'I Want To Hold Your Hand' and 'She Loves You' remained at the top of the chart, *Twist And Shout* stayed at number 12, *With The Beatles* dropped two places to number 15, *The Beatles' Hits* climbed a place to number 16, and *The Beatles (No. 1)* climbed three places to number 26. Mr D. Arnold, a reader from Newport, the Isle of Wight, was featured in the paper's Post Bag. 'I think the Beatles are being over-plugged. With six records in the charts, the public will become tired of hearing their voices and they will slip into oblivion. The secret is to leave the fans wanting more – and the Beatles should do this.'

The group were once again featured on the front cover of *NRM*. In the paper's last charts of 1963, 'I Want To Hold Your Hand' and 'She Loves You' remained at numbers 1 and 2 respectively. 'I Wanna Be Your Man' climbed two places to number 13, 'I'll Keep You Satisfied' by Billy J. Kramer with the Dakotas

dropped five places to number 16, 'All I Want For Christmas Is A Beatle' climbed three places to number 21, and the Fourmost's 'Hello Little Girl' climbed one place to number 44. The newspaper's year-end chart survey had 'From Me To You' at number one with 801 points, 'She Loves You' at number 2 with 775 points and 'Please Please Me' at number 13 with 603 points. A far cry from the comparable American survey which had the distinctly middle-of-the-road 'I Will Follow Him' by Little Peggy March and 'The End Of The World' by Skeeter Davis at numbers 1 and 2. They headed the Top Artistes poll with 2,299 points, ahead of second place Cliff Richard, with 2,234 points. The headline of the latest edition of *Mersey Beat* trumpeted 'Popularity Poll 1963 Beatles Hat-Trick – They Top Poll For Third Time!'

The Rex North Column in the *Daily Mirror* reported that the most popular Christmas carol in classrooms and schools was, 'We four Beatles of Liverpool are/Paul on a bike and John in a car/George on a scooter, blowing his hooter/Following Ringo Starr,' sung to the tune of 'We Three Kings Of Orient Are'. The group spent most of the day rehearsing for the forthcoming Christmas show and, in the evening, attended EMI's traditional Christmas party at Abbey Road Studios. Helen Shapiro, Alma Cogan, Gerry and the Pacemakers, and many others were also present.

> **❛** I formed the Rebel Rousers in 1957 and we were managed by these two wrestlers, Bob Alexander and Paul Lincoln – Paul used to wrestle under the name of Doctor Death, and had opened the 2i's Coffee Bar the previous year. We initially worked with Joe Meek. He was very difficult to work with. If you said the wrong thing, he could blow off at the slightest little thing. He'd say, 'You know what, pack up all of your stuff, I don't want to do any more with you today,' and so you had to be prepared for that sort of thing. Very temperamental he was. We were one of his house bands and used to back up his other artists. Joe leased our first single, 'You've Got What I Like', to EMI and it was put out on the Parlophone label. When we first approached the label they didn't want to know. It was voted a hit on *Juke Box Jury*, and I was behind  the screen when they all said, 'This is brilliant.' That went out on the Saturday, and on the Monday after, Parlophone rang up and said, 'We've changed our mind, we'd like to sign you direct now,' which didn't go down very well with Joe, as you can imagine.
>
> The first time I saw the Beatles was in Finsbury Park in early '63, but I met them for the first time at EMI's Christmas do that year. They were held each year in Studio one at Abbey Road, and all the acts signed to the label were invited, so it was quite a celebrity turnout. The following year, Brian Epstein signed us to his NEMS label around the same time we had our first hit, 'One Way Love'. That pretty much changed everything for us. Paul had really pushed Brian into coming and listening to us and signing us. The Beatles were the hottest thing, and of course Brian used to play the Beatles off against anyone in his stable. 'If you want the Beatles, you will have to take Cliff Bennett or Billy J. Kramer or Cilla Black,' or whatever. He could play the field. Everyone wanted the Beatles, so they had to take whoever else he said, so we did a lot of radio and TV because of that. The first stage show we did with them was one of Brian's Sunday concerts at the Prince of Wales. In fact, we played there quite a few times.
>
> In 1966, we were one of the Beatles' support acts on their tour of Germany. We were in Essen, at a big sports stadium, and the boys came in, John and Paul, and they said, 'We've written a song with you in mind,' and Paul just went 'La la la la.' Later, Brian said, 'Did the boys play that song to you?' and when we got back we had a two-week tour before going into Abbey Road and recording 'Got To Get You Into My Life', just before the boys brought their own version out on 'Revolver'. We cut a couple more singles, then changed the name of the group to the Cliff Bennett Band and cut a version of 'Back In The U.S.S.R.', as an afterthought really. That group soon split and I formed Toe Fat with two of the Rebel Rousers, who went on to become Chas and Dave. I then quit the music business and went into shipping, but in the past few years I've been back on the road, touring on these oldies packages. **❜**
>
> **CLIFF BENNETT, SINGER, GLASTONBURY, SOMERSET**

FRIDAY **20 DECEMBER**

The front page of the *NME* was taken up with a full-page ad from the six acts in the Epstein camp 'Wishing You All Happy Christmas'. In the paper's Top 30, 'I Want To Hold Your Hand' remained at number one, while 'She Loves You' was knocked down a place by the Dave Clark Five's 'Glad All Over'. *Twist And Shout* was at number 14, *With The Beatles* at number 17 and *The Beatles' Hits* at number 20. The group won the World Vocal Group and British Vocal Group categories in the paper's Poll Winners for 1963. In the World Vocal Group category, they secured 14,666 votes, more than the next twelve acts combined. In the British Vocal Group category, they received 18,623 votes, with the Searchers a distant second with 2,169 votes. In the Best British Disc of the Year category, they took the top four spots with 'She Loves You' (4,721 votes), 'Twist And Shout' (3,333 votes), 'Please Please Me' (2,899 votes) and 'From Me To You' (2,779 votes). The only category they didn't top was British Small Group, where they trailed the Shadows by 10,323 votes to 7,111. John and Paul also managed to both make the World Male Singer, World Musical Personality, British Vocal Personality and British Male Singer categories. The group responded with the message, 'This is John writing, with his hand. I'd like to say a great big thank you on behalf of Paul, George and Ringo (to name but one), but I honestly don't know where to start! Seriously, it's so difficult to try and sum up the tremendous excitement we've felt over the *NME* Poll'.

Proving the insatiable desire for all things Beatles, *Melody Maker* featured Dora Bryan holding four miniature cut-out Beatles on its front cover. 'I Want To Hold Your Hand' and 'She Loves You' remained at numbers 1 and 2 for a third week in the singles chart, while all three EPs dropped – *Twist And Shout* fell down a place to number 13, *The Beatles' Hits* down three places to number 17 and *The Beatles (No. 1)* two places to number 25. The Joe Meek-produced cover version of 'All My Loving' by the Dowlands was released.

The *Daily Mirror* reported on four pupils at St Barnabas School in Woodford Green, Essex, who caused a rumpus when they staged a charity concert impersonating the Beatles. Girls' headmistress Rosina Rutherford said, 'The girls went wild. They didn't stop the noise, even when they were turned out. I was so angry when I heard how the girls had let me down that I cancelled their Christmas party and I'm not sorry. I don't like the Beatles. I've never seen anything like the mob hysteria they spark off.' Fake Beatle Martin Neil said, 'I don't think I would like to be a Beatle in real life. I couldn't stand being screamed at like that.' Their performance raised £9 for charity. On the letters page, Mrs R. L. of Shadwell, Leeds 17 wrote, 'When I heard my first carol singers of the year the other evening I stood, delighted, inside the door as they gave a lovely version of 'We Three Kings'. Then came their rat-tat on the door and I opened it to find three lads with Beatles haircuts, drainpipe trousers and elastic-sided, high-heeled boots.'

The group had their last rehearsal for the Christmas show, where they conducted film and press interviews. *Scene At 6.30 With The Beatles*, a repeat of their appearance with Ken Dodd the previous month featuring the group miming to 'This Boy', aired on Northern ITV.

' St Barnabas School in Woodford Green was a secondary modern school, the building split down the middle – one half girls, one half boys. Everything was separate – the playgrounds, the lessons. The boys part of the school was run by an ex-naval man called Mr. Davidson, who was absolutely brilliant. He wasn't the head, only the deputy, but he wielded the power. The head, Mr Calvert, didn't display much authority, but he didn't need to, he had that in Mr Davidson. Four friends and I were made prefects, which gave us the honour of wearing a yellow enamel badge bearing the word 'Prefect' on our lapels, and various other privileges. There was a prefects' room, where you could have your sandwich lunch, and Mr Davidson would take the new fifth year prefects out for dinner prior to our last full year of school. He was always firm but fair, a figure to be revered. The four of us – myself, Martin Neil, Hayden Bates and Malcolm Smith – were all huge fans of the Beatles. Martin was the first one of us to buy the *Please Please Me* LP, and we all followed suit, listening eagerly on radiograms and Dansettes at our various homes.

On the evening we had dinner with [Deputy Head] Mr Davidson, Martin brought along his LP, which we all listened to. It was a lovely evening which I remember well. It was our joint enthusiasm for the group that made us come up with our fundraising idea. The school chose a charity to support, and the concert was held before each of the Christmas parties – the boys was separate from the girls of course! I was the only one who played a musical instrument, having learned guitar from the age of 10, so the plan was that we would feed the newly released *With The Beatles* LP through the school's PA system, and mime, which worked very well. We had to beg and borrow the instruments, and somebody lent me a famous Lucky Seven guitar. Made by Rosetti, you could buy them from a catalogue for about 12/6 at the time. It was very similar to George Harrison's Gretsch, although not to the aficionado. It had one pick up, and was red, with a white pick-guard. Everyone did a great job of miming, it was quite something!

The first day was the boys' concert followed by their Christmas party. It was busy, but ruly, other than the other boys making the most of taking free shots at the prefects with Jelly Babies. Someone had had the bright idea that bags of Jelly Babies should be handed out. The next day was the girls' concert and party. By this time of course, Beatlemania was in full swing and the girls just went berserk. We were in a storm of Jelly Babies, and they really, really hurt! The hysteria continued, although we managed to complete our 'set', but Mrs Rutherford was not happy. She was the headmistress of the girls' school, and very stern. She didn't stand for any nonsense and was unimpressed by all this wild behaviour. She just went ballistic and announced that the party would not be going ahead, and sent them all home. Word obviously got round about this, because a few days later, we were in the prefects' room and somebody came in and said, 'There's someone outside at the gate who wants to have a chat with you.' We went out, wondering what it was about. It was a lady reporter and a gentleman photographer, and they asked if it was true about the concert, asked some questions, and took some photographs of us. Mrs Rutherford wasn't very happy when the words 'Daily' and 'Mirror' reached her! We never thought any more of it though and broke up for Christmas a few days later.

At the time, I did a paper round, cycling the three miles to collect my bag of papers from a kiosk at WHSmith on Snaresbrook station. I remember going into the kiosk on the morning of 20 December and flicking through the *Daily Mirror* whilst they fetched my bag. I froze – there on page 3 – MOCK BEATLES START A RIOT! To say I was surprised would be an understatement. It was quite a shock. I'm sure there was something about the Berlin Wall on the cover, and there we were on page 3. When I got home I quickly telephoned the others to tell them, and they were all as surprised as I was. Despite Mrs Rutherford's reaction, the tickets for our concert at thruppence each raised £9 for that year's chosen charity. I suppose you can't really blame her. It was a phenomenon that her generation weren't really ready for, just something completely out of their field. **"**

CHARLES BURSTON, SHIP BROKER, WEYBRIDGE, SURREY

SATURDAY 21 DECEMBER

The group left London at 9.30am in the Austin Princess, driven as always by chauffeur Bill Corbett, heading north to Bradford – a four-hour-plus journey. At 10am, the Christmas edition of *Saturday Club* aired, which had been recorded the previous Tuesday. They met up with police at the Shibden Mill Inn near Halifax and were escorted into town. They arrived at New Victoria Street at 3.40pm and within minutes were inside the Gaumont.

At 5.50pm, they switched on the television set installed in their dressing room and watched themselves on *Thank Your Lucky Stars – Lucky Stars on Merseyside for Christmas!*, recorded the previous Sunday. Drum City's Gerry Evans also watched, noticing the 'dwig' of Ludwig had rubbed off Ringo's bass drum – hence John's frequent comment, 'And on the Lu, Ringo'. Evans enlisted Eddie Stokes to repaint the four missing letters.

The evening's show was a preview for the group's forthcoming Christmas season at the Finsbury Park Astoria, with Billy J. Kramer with the Dakotas, Tommy Quickly, Cilla Black, the Fourmost, the Barron Knights with Duke D'Mond, and compère Rolf Harris. For this warm-up show, the group sang 'Roll Over Beethoven', 'All My Loving', 'This Boy', 'I Wanna Be Your Man', 'She Loves You', 'Till There Was You', 'I Want To Hold Your Hand', 'Money' (dedicated to DJ Jimmy Savile, who was in the audience) and 'Twist And Shout'. Sketches written by director Peter Yolland were only incorporated into the Finsbury Park shows. Thirty-two St John Ambulance Brigade attendants were on hand. The Wurlitzer organ console in the orchestra pit, boarded over for safety, served as a means for fans to attempt to scramble onto the stage. One 15-year-old girl told her father, 'We couldn't hear a thing – it was fabulous'.

Following the concert, the group made their getaway from the Gaumont's Thornton Road exit and drove the 70 miles back to Liverpool. Peter Holdsworth in the *Bradford Telegraph & Argus* wrote, 'There were more than six thousand sore throats in Bradford and district yesterday. There would have been a pair of semi-deaf ears, too, had not a kind Press colleague given me some cotton wool plugs. For the big scream which went up on Saturday night would have drowned an artillery barrage. Bradford had never heard anything like it. The cause of it all? Yes, the Beatles... The faces of many of the swaying head-rocking girls had an expression of dervish ecstasy. In contrast one little old lady who had obviously escorted her grandchildren to the show provided a study in perplexed astonishment'.

The *Daily Telegraph* printed a letter by Josephine Terry that suggested a possible explanation for Beatlemania. 'For glandular plus psychological reasons young females like to scream. The Beatles give an opportunity for girls to let go in a manner as free as makes a dog bark when running the first length of his day's "walkie." The *Evening Standard* announced the Cleave Awards for 1963. Maureen Cleave chose 'From Me To You' as her Best Record, although she was less complimentary about 'Do You What To Know A Secret' which she named Most Idiotic Record. 'When he wants to whisper in her ear, he tells her to say the words he wants to hear. Who's doing the whispering, I ask myself,' she wrote. Her general opinion of the group was that they had written and recorded the best songs. 'They have simplified pop music and that's how we like it'.

> ❝ We had set off just after midnight on 1 December to queue for our Beatles tickets. We had our blankets rolled under arms, and something to eat with us. As we walked down Bolton Road, a police car stopped us, and gave us a lift to our other friend's house. We set off and walked the rest of the way into Bradford. It was cold, but we were so excited we didn't feel it. When we got into Bradford you could not queue at first, then they said you could, and I just ran, and was the first girl in queue. As the day went on it got quite bad as you got pushed back and police horses were brought in, and it was raining. I was brought out of the queue, and taken inside, wet, and crying, and thinking I would not get a ticket. But I did, a ticket for the fourth row when I came back out. It was a day I will never forget but it was worth it. I had my ticket.
>
> Then the day came when my dreams were going to come true. I was going to see the Beatles. I remember being excited all day. I went to

meet my friends Pat and Joyce in Bradford. I was carrying a big tube of Jelly Babies. We made our way over to the Gaumont. They were selling posters and papers outside. The excitement was too much, waiting to see them all, but particularly Paul, who was my favourite. They were just amazing. I just screamed, and shouted, just lost in my own dreams, really thinking Paul could just hear me. I did not want it to end, but it did, too soon. I saw them. It was a dream I will never forget. What a memory. I will keep it forever. **]**

COLLEEN HUNT, HOME CARE WORKER, SHIPLEY, WEST YORKSHIRE

SUNDAY 22 DECEMBER

A photograph of the Beatles with Dora Bryan graced the front page of the *Sunday Mirror*, under the heading 'She's Got A Beatle (Beatle Beatle Beatle) For Xmas!', subheaded, 'Sorry, girls – but Dora's grabbed the lot'. The Pathé News documentary *The Beatles Come To Town*, shot on 20 November, opened in cinemas throughout the UK. Over footage of a factory producing Beatle wigs, Bob Danvers-Walker reported: 'Only a year ago the Mersey was no more than a river to most of us, now it's dominating the pop world and on top of it all are the incomparable Beatles. As it takes too long to cultivate the hairstyle they've made popular at any rate starting now you can't achieve it by Christmas you have to settle for a wig. The demand keeps the cutters and all the rest of the factory staff going all out. There's no time to twist and shout or reflect that she loves you, the public's clamouring for Beatles wigs. Wonderful idea for Christmas presents if he or she says please please me. From me to you says Santa Claus and instant Merseybeat hairdo. The only trouble here is how to get them dispatched in time.'

The ten-minute film was selected to launch Pathé's Techniscope Technicolor news in scope dimensions. The film was being shown with Elvis Presley's *Fun At Acapulco*. In the US, ABC-TV also broadcast a segment of the previous month's Ardwick concert.

The group performed the second of two warm-up performances for their Christmas show, this time at the Liverpool Empire. Because of Sunday licensing laws, fans saw a concert-only version of the show, without the sketches which featured when the show came to London. During the show, teenagers stormed the stage. Outside the venue, more than a hundred police prevented fans from charging through the stage door. After the second show, there was a moment of concern when fans heard a dressing-room window opening and two hundred rushed to the stage door. They were kept at bay by police and were persuaded to make their way down Lord Nelson Street and away from the venue. First aid workers treated thirty-six girls, most of whom had fainted with excitement.

EMPIRE LIVERPOOL

THE BEATLES
1st Performance 5-40
SUNDAY
DECEMBER **22**
ROYAL STALLS
10/6
R47
TO BE RETAINED

[I wanted to be a rock'n'roll singer but I couldn't sing. I did a lot of photography and I was taking pictures of a group called the Rave-Ons who said, 'You have a suit and a big mouth, would you be our manager?' Consequently, I was running an entertainments agency in 1963, booking into Southport venues like the Klic Klic Club, Kingsway, Palace Hotel, Floral Hall, Club Django, Glenpark Club, etc. I started importing albums from Ronnie Kellerman, a pen pal in America. Often, an American artist would have a hit in England but, although their single was released here, the album never made it across the Atlantic. I used to tape the tracks then sell the albums to groups who were only too anxious to get new material. The Searchers, Dave Berry, the Dakotas were among my customers.

I got in touch with John Lennon and told him I had these rare American LPs. He said they would be in Southport in October. I told him I lived right across the road from the Floral Hall, on the Promenade, so we arranged for the group to come back to my house after the show. They could have a drink and some supper and I would show them the catalogues. My mother was quite excited at this because, by then, Beatlemania was rife and she would be able to tell all her friends she'd had the Beatles to supper. Sadly, this never happened because that was the very day it was announced that the group would be appearing on the Royal Variety Show, and when I arrived at the theatre, the backstage area was crammed with the world's press and the group then had to be smuggled into the limo by the police.

It was thus that I arranged to go with the Dakotas to the Liverpool Empire on Sunday 22 December, where they were playing at a second Christmas concert headlined by the Beatles. The Dakotas took me to meet the Beatles and I showed them a case full of albums I had taken with me together with catalogues of the latest American releases. Ringo bought a mixture of everything but mostly country and western and little-known gospel albums. Paul didn't buy anything. George selected the more popular singers such as the Coasters and B. B. King, but it was John who was the keenest and most discerning. He was interested in the more obscure R&B artistes like Dr. Feelgood, Inez and Charlie Foxx, Bobby 'Blue' Bland, James Ray and Rufus Thomas. All of them were interested in Tamla Motown material that had not been issued in the UK. John looked at my catalogues and wrote me a list of albums he wanted me to order for him. Later, I cut John's written list up into forty-eight 1-inch squares and sold them for two shillings each to schoolgirls from Trinity Hall who came into Birkdale Library where I was working. Think what that sheet of paper would be worth today – the music that influenced the Beatles, written in John Lennon's handwriting. **⅃**

RON ELLIS, AUTHOR AND JOURNALIST, SOUTHPORT, MERSEYSIDE

MONDAY 23 DECEMBER

*D*isc published three days early, due to Christmas. The group topped the paper's annual Top 30 Artists of 1963 table with 1,803 points, significantly higher than Cliff Richard's 1,155 points. June Harris talked with NEMS press officer Jo Bergman, who spent three days in Paris the previous week to gauge how the French might react to the Beatles. 'French girls are already nutty over the Beatles because they think they look so chic, and in some ways, so French,' she said, 'a lot of them already wear Beatle-type sweaters.'

A psychiatrist analysed the two shows in Bradford in the *Telegraph & Argus*, feeling that 'while the screaming is not harmful, it is not good because taking part in such demonstrations dulls the sensitivity, to some extent, of those taking part.' The *Birmingham Daily Post* published a letter from William Conduit bemoaning the demise of Christian standards. 'Today we have the immoral hysteria manifested by mobs surrounding the Beatles,' he wrote. 'In more notable Christian times we merely had hysterical mobs cheering at public hangings.' Radio Luxembourg's *It's The Beatles* series began at 9pm. The fifteen-part weekly series of fifteen-minute spots was presented by Peter Carver. The station had earlier announced

that the group had won the year's 'Swoon Clubs' pop poll, as well as the Favourite Vocal Group section.

Billboard gave details of the group's February visit to the US and the attendant industry hoopla. Under the headline 'English Lads Stirring Trade', the article said that Beatlemania was such that 'the publicity ruckus stirred so far is of major proportions'. It went on to say that there had been two new developments. 'Capitol Records is rushing to get out its first Beatles' disking by 26 December. But one enterprising jockey, Carroll Baker on Washington's WWCD, with the co-operation of an airline stewardess on BOAC, got hold of an original Parlophone disking from London and has been "laying on the record" all week.'

Paul Russell, Capitol Records' National Merchandising Manager, circulated a memo with details of the label's forthcoming 'Beatle Campaign', hoping that its salesmen would be 'fired up to the maximum degree' for its start. A two-page spread appeared in the following week's edition of *Billboard*, while bulk quantities of a 'Beatle hair-do wig' would be available in January. 'You and each of your sales and promotion staff are to wear the wig during the business day! ... Get these Beatle wigs around properly, and you'll find you're helping to start the Beatle Hair-Do Craze that should be sweeping the country soon.' It was reported that rival pressing plants were producing some half million copies of *Meet The Beatles*, due for release on 20 January 1964.

TUESDAY 24 DECEMBER

*T*oday finished its four-part series written by the group's individual members. George thought it was going to be tough to write the article, but 'having seen the load of old rubbish the other three wrote,' decided it was going to be fairly straightforward. Regarding his musical ambitions for the group, he wrote that he wanted to become 'a really good guitar player' and would 'like to hear John sing in tune'. The *Evening Standard*'s front-page headline read '1963 ... the year of the Beatles' – with the subheading '1963 has been their year. An examination of the heart of the nation at this moment would reveal the word BEATLE engraved upon it'. A Maureen Cleave article revealed that the group had sold close to six million records during the year. Cleave thought that future social historians would look back at 1963 as the year 'the British nursery rhyme was replaced by poems with tri-syllabic titles like 'She Loves You,' 'Please Please Me' and 'Love Me Do." Ringo once again mentioned that owning a hairdressing business was in his future. Journalist Angus McGill loved them because 'like well-bred Victorian children, they are seen and not heard'. *The Beatles* aired on the Light Programme from 10am to noon. *Day By Day* featured an interview with the group conducted by Terry Carroll, airing on Southern TV at 6.05pm. Asked about the forthcoming US trip, Paul said, 'We don't expect too much. We hope for a lot but we don't expect it'. At 9.10pm, ITV broadcast the documentary *Beat City*, a study of the Liverpool phenomenon by Daniel Farson. The show opened with the Beatles singing 'There's A Place'.

The group began 'The Beatles Christmas Show' at the Astoria in Finsbury Park, London. The twice-nightly, sixteen-night run was seen by a hundred thousand people before it ended on 11 January. The group performed a nine-song set and appeared in a series of sketches pre-recorded by Peter Yolland and mimed in performance. They played 'Roll Over Beethoven,' 'All My Loving,' 'This Boy,' 'I Wanna Be Your Man,' 'She Loves You,' 'Till There Was You,' 'I Want To Hold Your Hand,' 'Money' and 'Twist And Shout'. Colin Manley of the Remo Four, who backed Tommy Quickly, recalled that he did not think 'they had any interest in what they were doing. No one could hear what they were playing. It was like being in the birdhouse of a zoo, greatly amplified'. He also noted the group 'fled as fast as they could' after their performance. Cilla Black remembered the first night. 'Everybody else seemed dead nervous and they all wondered why I seemed so confident. I'll tell you what it was – a glass of champagne for courage. And it's worked for me ever since'. During the show's run, many celebrities attended, including the Rolling Stones' Mick Jagger, the Big Three's Johnny Gustafson, actress Fenella Fielding and singer Alma Cogan. Recording engineer Geoff Emerick travelled on top of a double-decker bus to see group – the only occasion he saw them live.

Following the second show, the Liverpudlian contingent of the bill boarded a chartered Viking plane hired by Brian Epstein for £400 from Autair International Airways and flew home to spend Christmas with their families. Chief Air Hostess Sheila Whitworth helped fasten Ringo's seat belt. Epstein also laid on limousines to deliver his stable to their respective doors after they landed shortly after midnight. News leaked out forcing precautions to be taken to cope with the number of fans expected to greet them. An airport spokesman said, 'We hope they will behave themselves'.

' When I was a teenager. I was mad on horse riding and I worked in a stable. I learned how to ride well, and was a member of the Waddon Chase Pony Club. What happened was I bought a guitar – purely by watching our next-door neighbour's television. We didn't have one, so I used to watch *Sunday Night At The London Palladium* at theirs and a bloke called Slim Whitman came on one week, and Lonnie Donegan the next, and I said that's it! I wanted to buy a guitar, so I saved enough money and bought one, and decided that that was what I wanted to do. Another guy in Leighton Buzzard called Tony Osmond decided to form a group, and we called ourselves the Knights of the Round Table, which was very quickly shortened to the Barron Knights so we could fit our name on a poster. We did all the dance halls around Aylesbury, Dunstable, Bedford, Biggleswade, and then we extended up to Yorkshire, then Scotland, and that's where we first heard of the Beatles. We came across a poster that said 'From Liverpool – The Beatles' at the Beach Ballroom in Aberdeen.

We played in areas like Perth, Kilmarnock, Oban, Elgin, Inverness, Invergordon, Buckie, Oban, all the places that had dance halls, we did that circuit several times, just getting paid about £20 a week. It was enough money for petrol and fish and chips at night. We used to eat in the cafe at the Two Red Shoes in Elgin, which was owned by the great Albert Bonici. It was our apprenticeship and was very important for us. It was so important to do the dance halls. Brian Epstein came to see us in a dance hall in Liverpool, I can't remember which one, it was in September 1963, and he said, 'Would you do a Christmas show with the Beatles?' The Beatles were great. McCartney used to come in every night to the dressing room to say, 'Hi. How are you doing?' One night he popped his head round and said, 'Have you met my friend who's on *Sunday Night At The London Palladium* this Sunday? He's never been on TV before.' It was Jimmy Tarbuck.

At those shows, we came on two or three times. The one thing I really remember was that when we'd finished one of our songs, we used to have to drop our guitars and run off stage in a complete black out and the Beatles used to run on and pick up their guitars. One night in the blackout Lennon got hold of Butch [Baker, guitarist], and when the lights went up and all the kids were screaming, there was McCartney with his bass on, Harrison with his guitar, Ringo on his drums, and there was John cuddling Butch! It wasn't a regular part of the show, but it was great, really funny, and a wonderful moment for us.

We recorded at Abbey Road. The Beatles were in Studio Two and we were in Studio One. We were allowed three hours, they had the whole week. Once when we had about half an hour to go, in walked John and Paul. Paul said, 'What are you recording?' and we said something or other. He asked whether we wanted to hear what they were recording. So naturally we said, 'Yeah, but can you hurry up, because we've only got half an hour', and Paul sat at this great big black piano, and played 'Hey Jude'. So we were the first people to hear it. We introduced our piano player Reg Dwight to them. I remember Elton being asked one of his happiest memories. He said when the Barron Knights introduced him to Lennon and McCartney at Abbey Road Studios. We do a concert at the Chelsea Flower Show every year, and it's a great venue for us, like a mini-Hollywood Bowl with a thousand people in front of you. A couple of years ago someone said, 'Oh, a mate of yours is here to see you.' I asked who it was and was told it was Ringo. I went to have a chat with him, but unfortunately as soon as I got there – and we were chatting about old times – along came Sky Television and I said, 'Ringo, all they want is you!' and I disappeared. '

PETER LANGFORD, SINGER/SONGWRITER AND ENTERTAINER, WOBURN, BEDFORDSHIRE

WEDNESDAY 25 DECEMBER

The group enjoyed Christmas Day with their families. Paul had told the *NME* that the group had trudged through the snowy streets of Hamburg the previous Christmas to go to a party. 'We got to the party in the end. But what a let-down!... We found our longed-for Christmas dinner was fish and horse-radish sauce! It was a great, shiny looking carp, with a big eye in the middle, staring right at you. We were dining with some German friends and you can appreciate we didn't want to say anything after their kindness. So we just went ahead and forced it down!'

Top Pops Of 1963, recorded on 7 December, aired on the Light Programme at 6pm. Hosted by Alan Freeman and featuring the Joe Loss Orchestra, Rose Brennan, Ross McManus (Elvis Costello's father), Larry Gretton and Bill Brown. It also featured discs by Cliff Richard, Frank Ifield, Gerry and the Pacemakers and the chart-topping Beatles, as well as an interview the group did at the Liverpool Empire on the same day. Between *Christmas Startime* and *Mr Pickwick*, ITN news aired a clip of the group recorded backstage at the Finsbury Park Astoria on the 20th. Perhaps universal acceptance for the group was still around the corner – *Christmas Swingtime*, starring Cliff Richard and the Shadows alongside more middle of the road fare including Edmund Hockridge and Joan Regan, preceded the Queen's speech in the afternoon, while *Christmas Night With The Stars* featured the likes of the Black and White Minstrels, Russ Conway, Billy Cotton and His Band and Kenneth McKellar.

❛ In hindsight 1963 was a pivotal year in my world. I may have only been 7 years old but it was certainly a year of discovery as three integral parts of my life fell, one by one, into place. First, there was Liverpool Football Club. Merseyside is a hotbed of English soccer and back in '63 I was bitten big-time by the bug. Second, was *Doctor Who!* That bastion of English sci-fi was televised for the first time firing the imagination, and sometimes bringing terror into lives of young lads around the country like myself. Third, I fell in love with 'four lads from Liverpool who shook the world' – the Beatles. Life was never quite the same again. The Beatles were not new to me. Around October 1962, as we settled down to our evening tea, the Granada TV's news magazine show *People And Places* were presenting a Liverpool group just back from Hamburg, Germany. They were the Beatles who were about to release their first single 'Love Me Do'. I'm not quite sure why, but these four unknowns stuck in my head. Maybe it was John Lennon's harmonica playing! More likely, it was something to do with the indefinable magic that made them the greatest, and most successful group, in rock/pop history.

However, another factor might have been my auntie Irene who regularly visited the Cavern Club in Liverpool and raved about these four local lads. Irene was still living with my grandmother and we were regular visitors to their home on Utting Avenue. Music, more specifically pop music, was very much part of each and every visit. I would love to play all her singles and spent many happy hours putting all the records carefully into the correct sleeves! 'Moon River' by Danny Williams was perhaps the first song I fell in love with but one record, above all others, really fired my imagination – 'Apache' by the Shadows. I loved that record and played it endlessly. For me the Shadows were 'it' with their space-age looking guitars and I well recall going to the cinema that year to see *Summer Holiday*. Heaven! I do recall Irene talking more and more about the Beatles after her treks to the Cavern. I liked their records but in my mind they hadn't quite eclipsed 'the Shads' as yet.

In hindsight, a major Beatles milestone came that summer with the release of 'She Loves You' I can vividly recall the enthusiasm of my grandmother, well into her sixties, who loved the 'Yeah, Yeah, Yeahs' in the song. Perhaps that gave a big clue to the undeniable appeal of the Beatles, they were loved by all generations. When Christmas Day arrived that year my sister and I hung up our pillowcases for Father Christmas as was the family tradition. It was a bumper year. Santa had brought me a Scalextric set, a Lego box and my first ever LP record – *With the Beatles*. I have that album to this day and have purchased it again three times since. I also received the Shadows' *Foot Tapper* EP. I have no idea of what happened to that record but I do know from Christmas Day 1963 onwards the Beatles have been a constant presence in my life be it on my turntable, Walkman, Discman and, these days, my iPhone. Looking back, 1963 was such a great year for the Fabs. They came from obscurity, and the unfashionable regions of England, to dominate the charts in the UK and plant the seeds for future American and worldwide domination. For someone like myself they became an intrinsic part of our world and our lives. This is something that will always be and, for me, will never change. Let it be! Yeah, yeah, yeah! ❜

RALPH FERRIGNO, SOCCER COACH, IPSWICH, MASSACHUSETTS, USA

THURSDAY 26 DECEMBER

The 18 December recording of *The Beatles Say From Us To You*, originally titled *Beatle Time*, aired on the Light Programme. The *Radio Times* described it as a show 'that should have the ghosts of Christmas Past, Present, and Future shaking around the Christmas tree'. The Audience Research Department's report of the programme concluded, 'This was definitely family listening. Teenagers, right, left, and centre and across the road had the set on. I found it quite happy and melodious, with plenty of zip. I am quite a fan of the Beatles. To me they are the new "Today," clean and wholesome and gay'. Over the year, the group performed a total of sixty-two different songs on the BBC, including forty-eight cover versions.

'I Want To Hold Your Hand', coupled with 'I Saw Her Standing There', was released on Capitol Records (catalogue number 5112) in the US. Realising the initial order of two hundred thousand singles was not enough, Capitol ordered factories in Scranton and Los Angeles to press the single exclusively. Label promotion and sales staffers were not allowed vacation time. Promotion men hand delivered copies of the single to all the major radio stations before 9am. New York's WMCA began playing the record, soon followed by WABC and WINS. Two hundred and fifty thousand copies were sold in its first three days of release. Unable to keep up with demand, Capitol contracted Columbia and RCA to press more copies of the single.

The group flew back to London to resume 'The Beatles Christmas Show'. First Officer Bill Stewart kept an eye on temporary co-pilot Ringo Starr, who said, 'This is better than a car – and no roundabouts.' Pete Shotton and his wife Beth, Nigel Walley and his wife Pat, and Cynthia Lennon and her mother Lillian Powell also travelled down and saw the second show. Shotton recalled, 'As we approached Finsbury Park, however, the traffic grew so hopeless that I decided to complete the journey on foot. I then found myself engulfed in a scene of utter pandemonium, the like of which I'd never before witnessed. The streets were packed with screaming teenagers and dozens of flustered bobbies vainly attempting to reroute traffic and control the hysterical mob.' After the second show, the Shottons and the Walleys went to John's flat in Emperor's Gate. As the Walleys were leaving at 4am, John jumped over the bonnet of their mini, injuring his ankle in the process.

> ❝ It was almost by accident that I started drumming. I went with a couple of friends to see the film *Blackboard Jungle*, and when 'Rock Around The Clock' came out, they said, 'Why don't we form a rock'n'roll group?' and that's how it all got going. My first drum kit was a bit ragbag. I bought a second-hand snare drum, with a big bass drum over the top and a symbol. I think I paid about £20 for it altogether. That got me started. My career as such began at the 2i's Coffee Bar in Soho, along with Brian Bennett. We were sort of the house drummers if you like, then I played with Johnny Kidd and the Pirates, and the Beat Boys. I'd just come back from doing a tour in Italy with Colin Hicks, Tommy Steele's brother, when Alan Caddy, the guitar player, rang me and said there was an advert in one of the music papers looking for a guitar player for a studio group. He was thinking of applying and asked if I would go along to give him a bit of support. It turns out it was Joe Meek's studio, which

was down the Holloway Road, not far from where I lived in Wood Green. When we got there, Joe asked Alan to play a couple of numbers, and he said, 'Do you mind if my mate plays drums while I play the guitar?' After a couple of numbers, Joe could see that Alan was a fine guitarist, and then said to me, 'Do you want a job as well?' So that was really the start of the Tornados. We also did quite a lot of work in the studio with Joe. The first record we made as the Tornados was called 'Love And Fury', which didn't really do much.

At the time, we were doing a summer season at the Windmill Theatre in Great Yarmouth with Billy [Fury], so we rushed up to London and recorded it that weekend. It was the same weekend that Joe wrote 'Telstar', which we also recorded. It was during that same summer season that we heard 'Telstar' had got to number one. Believe it or not, I was in the toilet at the time and Alan Caddy banged on the door and said, 'Have a look at this!' and shoved the paper under the door! And there it was, at number one. We were the only people on the bill with a number one record, and we were only allowed to play 'Telstar.' Larry Parnes wouldn't let us do anything else, unfortunately. Larry wanted us to go to America with Billy, but over there, he was unheard of. 'Who's Billy Fury?' they would say. Joe had also signed us up to do a tour the following spring, so we never did make it to America, despite being the first British group to get a number one hit in America!

Then of course the Beatles came along, and everybody's career went for a burton! We all suffered because another era had come along. We had known them for a few years before that of course, from playing with Billy up in places like Blackpool and Liverpool. We played with them at the *NME* poll concert in Wembley. They really were every bit as good as everyone had said, but to see them getting ready for the show – well that was really something. They just wandered around, looking as if they couldn't care less. They set up their equipment with the sort of air that said it didn't matter to them whether it was right or wrong. We watched them and thought it'd be a miracle if they ever got through their part of the programme. They were kidding about and joking. But as soon as they started working it was electric. I also went to see their Christmas Show at the Finsbury Park Astoria, but you couldn't hear anything other than screaming. I was a friend of the guy who ran the Odeon cinemas, he was the big white chief, and he invited me along. I was invited backstage and it was good to catch up with them. When we played the summer season in Blackpool the following summer, they came over to see us. I got to know Paul and George quite well. I interviewed them for the *Record Mirror*. I had a weekly column that would start, 'Hi folks, this is Clem from Blackpool.' ❞

CLEM CATTINI, DRUMMER, WINCHCOMBE HILL, LONDON

FRIDAY 27 DECEMBER

"**N**ME Pic. Scoops Beatles New Year Greetings' blasted one of the banner headings on the front page of the new *NME*. On page three, the group wished their fans, 'Yeah! Yeah! Yeah! A healthy, happy and prosperous New Year to all NME readers!' In the final chart of 1963, the group continued to dominate, with 'I Want To Hold Your Hand' at number one, 'She Loves You' at number 4, the Rolling Stones' 'I Wanna Be Your Man' at number 12, the *Twist And Shout* EP at number 13, the *With The Beatles* LP at number 15, Dora Bryan's 'All I Want For Christmas Is A Beatle' at number 16, *The Beatles' Hits* EP at number 20 and Billy J. Kramer with the Dakotas' 'I'll Keep You Satisfied' at number 22. In the year ending points table, the group headed the list with the highest total ever accumulated with 1,741 points, topping Russ Conway's 1959 total of 1,548. Cliff Richard was second in 1963 with 1,323 points. 'She Loves You' picked up the most points with 522, as it had occupied the pole position for eighteen weeks. In the final four weeks of the year, the Beatles accrued 421 points.'

During the day John's ankle grew increasingly painful, so much so that a doctor advised him not to go onstage that night. John ignored the advice. In the *Daily Herald*, Mike Nevard reviewed the Christmas Show – 'Screams barrier beats the Beatles' – 'If you have bought tickets for the Beatles' London Christmas show with the idea of hearing their act – sell up. You'll get a good price on the black market... the eight Beatle numbers were obliterated by a never-ending wall of scream. Only familiarly rhythm patterns which penetrated the squeal barrier identified the songs. Screams used to be triggered off by a phrase (I love you, Hold my hand, Kiss me), a wink or a gesture... The fans just screamed and screamed, and the fact that prevented them from hearing the group did not seem to matter. I suggest that the Beatles save their breath and energy and just stand there.' Ringo's bass drum pedal broke, but Drum City told him they couldn't fix it until Monday. 'Oh well, it doesn't matter, because they can't hear it anyway,' he said. 'It's all just screaming.'

Under the heading 'Seen But Hardly Heard', *The Times* reviewed the show, writing that 'the shrill cries which greet vocal tricks, gestures, or unexpected movements become hysterical as the Beatles begin. Votive offerings are thrown on the stage, and it is impossible to tell how much of the hubbub, which leaves nothing audible but the thudding rhythms, is spontaneous, and how much is ritual observance. The four energetic, unpretentious figures on the stage do nothing to arouse it... What they do counts for little, but no one listens to it; their secret is that they, rather than their work, express the adolescents' idea of themselves.'

The paper's music critic William Mann, although uncredited, hailed Lennon and McCartney as 'the outstanding English composers of 1963.' In an editorial, which Beatle fans probably needed a music dictionary to translate, Mann went on to say 'one gets the impression that they think simultaneously of harmony and melody, so firmly are the major tonic sevenths and ninths built into their tunes, and the flat submediant key switches, so natural is the Aeolian cadence at the end of 'Not A Second Time' (the chord progression which ends Mahler's 'Song Of The Earth').'

‘ I had first heard 'Love Me Do' in the autumn of 1962 when my friend Penny and I went to dance on weekend afternoons at the Lyceum in the Strand, London. I loved that harmonica-driven beat. My school friend Lyn, Penny and I eagerly listened out for the Beatles new records. We just had to see them live. Lyn knew a friend of a friend who was a cleaner at the Lewisham Odeon where the group were due to appear. She was able to get us tickets for BOTH performances! What bliss! When the day came, we were there in the queue for the first performance, feeling happy and smug. The group were just amazing but of course the screams just drowned out the songs. When they sang 'She Loves You' and shook their heads at the 'Yeah Yeahs', we couldn't hold back the screams either. When the performance was over, we were emotionally exhausted and we hoped we might be able to stay in the theatre and just move over to where our seats were for the next performance. But no, the ushers made sure everyone

was out, and we then had to go back outside into the street and queue up for a second time. The second performance we were sitting even nearer the front and it was every bit as magical as the first.

Lyn and I had heard about the Beatles doing a series of Christmas shows at the Finsbury Park Astoria. We must have written off for the tickets immediately, enclosing a postal order, because north London was a foreign land to us and in any event, our parents would not have let us queue outside for tickets. And sure enough, we did receive tickets in the post. We thought wouldn't it be wonderful to meet the boys? Lyn and I read in the *NME* that the Beatles had a tape recorder they used to take round with them in case the muse hit them while on the road, and they could record their songwriting efforts there and then. I had a Philips reel-to-reel four-track tape recorder, and knowing that the Beatles loved fooling around, were brilliant at repartee, and liked the Goons, we hatched an idea to make our own fan tape and send it to them during their Christmas Show stint. We reasoned that it might stand out from the sackloads of fan letters they received, and they may be curious enough to listen to it, and wouldn't it be wonderful if they thought we sounded pretty groovy chicks with a similar sense of humour, and let us come backstage to meet them when we went to see the show. So in my bedroom one day a few days later, we recorded our message; playing snippets of sound effects, speeded up speech and songs, bits from *The Goon Show*, and we rambled on a bit about our lives and made some rather cringe-making jokes. We were really very cheeky! And we managed to fill a fifteen-minute tape. We addressed it to the Beatles at the Astoria, and off it went in the post. Would we ever hear any more? So, after Christmas we braved the wilds of north London. We came out of the tube station to be confronted by a solid block of noisy, excited fans. We just followed on and the Astoria wasn't hard to find. We had not heard anything about our tape. We thought it was probably in a bin somewhere.

Fast forward to April 2013. Out of the blue I received a letter from a researcher on BBC-TV's *The One Show*, asking if I was the Barbara Helmore who had recorded a tape and sent it to the Beatles in 1963! I replied back that I was, gave them Lyn's last known address (we had lost touch in the 1970s), and I was told that a local historian from Great Yarmouth had bought the tape in a car boot sale and, hoping to find the two girls who made it, had contacted the BBC asking for help in tracking us down. The BBC agreed it would make a good story and consequently I was sent up to the Beatles Museum in Liverpool where TV presenter Gloria Hunniford talked to me about the origins of this tape, and then brought on my long-lost friend Lyn and David McDermott, who had found the tape. We were filmed touring round the museum, and then we were brought to stand in front of some gruesome waxworks of the boys. Gloria produced an envelope with a note inside which read 'Hi Lynda and Barbara – thanks very much for your lovely tape, it finally got through, better late than never! Great to hear that you found each other again after all these years – keep enjoying the music. Love, Paul.' The magic of the Beatles' name had worked its magic for us – more than fifty years on! **"**

BARBARA BEZANT, OFFICE WORKER, DOVERCOURT, ESSEX

SATURDAY 28 DECEMBER

Tony Barrow, writing as the 'Disker', looked back at the year in pop in the *Liverpool Echo*. He wrote, 'The Beatles. Any review of the 1963 pop record scene would fall short of its appointed task if it did not open up with those two ultra-meaningful words. Liverpool was always renowned for its Tunnel, its port and its two local football teams. But in 1963 it has become the centre of national attraction as the breeding ground and home base for some of the year's most triumphant chart-toppers. The Beatles have made front-page news headlines on a scale never before achieved by pop stars, and have become a household talking point as well as a recording industry phenomenon.'

The *Daily Mirror* reported that former amateur heavyweight boxer Ray Armstrong had come up with the idea of timing training sessions at a Loughborough gymnasium with Beatles' records, after his trainer Frank Markey lost his stop watch. The *Daily Worker*'s Nina Hibbin reviewed the Beatles' Pathé newsreel, which she described as the funniest film of the seasonal round-up. 'I found myself simply roaring with laughter all through – from the first views of the irrepressible excitement on the faces of the usherettes in a last-minute line-up, to the final swish of the curtain amid a crescendo of squeaks.' The Light Programme's *Saturday Club* played a request from the Beatles – the Miracles' 'I've Been Good To You'. In the evening, the group gave two more performances of 'The Beatles Christmas Show' at the Astoria. Afterwards the Lennons and the Shottons went on a pub and club crawl around London, ending up at the West London Air Terminal cafeteria near their flat in the early hours, where they ate breakfast.

❝ I was working at the Westminster Bank in Hatfield and moonlighting with my own group the Cortinas when the Beatles came to Luton in September. I almost had a nervous breakdown wondering if I would get out in time to see the show. We left the bank when the day's work was done and the books were balanced – Friday was always the busiest day. I was especially worried as there had been some rather late nights recently and a couple of times we hadn't left until 9pm. I rushed around all day probably driving the rest of the staff mad trying to make sure they weren't slacking. I was just too conscientious in those days. I should have called in sick. I eventually got away at 8pm. My two mates were waiting outside and we drove straight to Luton for the 8.45pm performance. We had pretty good seats about fifteen rows from the front and had to endure four other acts before the Beatles. No matter how good they were, there was only one act the audience had come to see. Suddenly the compère, Ted King, announced, 'Ladies and Gentlemen, THE BEATLES!', and there they were. There were no curtains at the Odeon, the group just ran onstage wearing their famous grey collarless suits, plugged in, and went straight into 'Roll Over Beethoven'. The PA system was two small speakers, one each side of the stage and you could just about make out which songs they were singing above the continual screams, but it was fantastic. We drove home from Luton planning when we would see them again.

Well, it didn't turn out to be very long. The following month it was announced they would be playing at the Finsbury Park Astoria. A friend and I managed to get two tickets (7/6d each – 37p in today's money) for the show on 28 December 1963. We took the main line train from Hatfield to Finsbury Park. As we headed down the Seven Sisters Road to the Astoria we saw the pavements were packed with fans waiting to get in. Girls were in a state of hysteria, screaming at every movement from the windows of the Astoria. If a shadow passed a window it must have been a Beatle. The Astoria was an impressive building with a fountain in the entrance hall. At the beginning of the show a large cardboard helicopter was lowered to the stage and one by one each act pretended to climb out and then be introduced by Rolf Harris. Everybody was off except the Beatles and the audience was teased by the helicopter taking off and hovering. Eventually it landed again and out came the Beatles to the loudest screams imaginable. They took part in a series of sketches with their voices on tape that lasted around a couple of minutes each and the crowd just screamed all the way through. And then it was time for their closing spot which included tracks from *With The Beatles*. Once again, it was a great show. So great that two weeks later I managed to get hold of another ticket for Friday 10 January 1964 and saw it all over again. This time I was high up in the balcony and could barely hear a thing over the screaming. ❞

PAUL GRIGGS, MUSICIAN, WELWYN, HERTFORDSHIRE

SUNDAY 29 DECEMBER

The group had the day off, with no Christmas performances. Lionel Crane wrote an in-depth piece titled 'The Mad Mad World Of Beat' in the *Sunday Mirror*. One of his interviewees was Dick James, who described himself as 'one of the luckiest guys in the business'. He described how what he thought was a piece of bad luck turned out to be the opposite. 'I had a song which I liked but all the top artists turned it down. I took it to George Martin who handles all the recording stars for EMI. He told me he was bringing down a Liverpool group called the Beatles, and was going to experiment with them in the studio. He got them to record it twice, but it was no good. Brian Epstein came to see me. He played a record the boys had done called 'Please Please Me'. It knocked me out. I heard some of their other songs, and I thought they were great. Right off, he and I agreed to form a separate company to publish all the Beatles' songs.' At 9pm *It's The Beatles* aired on Radio Luxembourg.

In the US, the *Los Angeles Times* finally jumped on the bandwagon, with a piece titled 'British Beatles Sing Up A Teen-Age Storm' written by Lawrence Malkin. 'Four young men with hair combed down to their eyebrows donned policemen's helmets and greatcoats. They plunged into the crowd of screaming teen-agers and scuffled through, unnoticed in their disguise. The Beatles had made it to safety again. "Beatlemania" is the latest craze of Britain's young, but in this fad for popular singers there seems to be something different about it, and about them... They share a common past and this appears to be the key to their success. All are blitz babies from the back-streets of Liverpool; they are native and unashamed "skouses," as Liverpudlians proudly call themselves... One Beatles fan in his twenties – and there are plenty of them, although they're not frenzied – says he likes the group because they represent "a break with America".'

Flora Lewis, who had already written about the group in the *Washington Post* in late October, wrote another article headlined 'The Golden Bugs', subheaded 'Beetle-Browed Beatle-Bubs Put Boxoffice on Upbeat'. She reported that, 'None of the hundreds of thousands of young Britons who sang 'All I Want For Christmas Is A Beatle' got his wish,' going on to comment that 'Beatle records and photographs have already become a staple – so much a part of the scene that they have made their way into Court Society.' Less complimentary was the *Baltimore Sun*: 'America had better take thought as to how it will deal with the invasion ... Indeed a restrained 'Beatles go home' might be just the thing.' In the *Chicago Tribune*, Donald Freeman opined, 'They look like four of the Three Stooges with a hairy measure of Ish Kabibble, and if they ever submitted to a barber who loves music – snip, snip! – that would be the end of the act.' Even as the year came to an end, Ringo was reiterating that when it was all over, he'd be happy to take his winnings, go back to Liverpool and open a hairdresser's shop.

MONDAY 30 DECEMBER

The *Times* printed 'What Songs The Beatles Sang' on its letters page – 'Sir – Your music critic will have won the thanks of countless parents today with his article on the Beatles. At last this phenomenon has been written about in our newspaper in what we can at least pretend is our language. A swift and very welcome turning of the tables. Yours faithfully, H. J. L. Osbourn, Durrant House, Chiswell Street, EC 1, December 27'. Gordon Rudlin, Oxfam's finance officer, revealed that the organisation was still short of its £1 million end of year target. The Beatles' national appeal fund had fallen short of expectations, in part because the group had only been asking for a basic half-crown donation and each donor received a photograph of the group as a receipt.

To celebrate the group's phenomenally successful year, Dick James hosted a private lunch for them at the Café Royal at 68 Regent Street. Afterwards, the group drove to north London for two further performances of 'The Beatles Christmas Show' at the Astoria. At 9pm, *It's The Beatles* aired on Radio Luxembourg.

A two-page spread appeared in *Billboard*, the start of a major campaign which saw Capitol Records producing 'Be A Beatle Booster' buttons and Beatle wigs for sales staff, DJs and radio station give-aways, 'The Beatles Are Coming' stickers as well as a four-page Beatle issue tabloid newspaper. The magazine's review of 'I Want To Hold Your Hand' described the Beatles as the 'hot British group that has struck gold overseas' and the single as a 'driving rocker with surf on the Thames sound'. *Cash Box* had the single as one of its Picks of the Week, describing it as 'an infectious twist-like thumper that could spread like wildfire here,' by 'the boys behind the expression "Beatlemania," which is sweeping England and currently receiving endless publicity'. A double-page spread headed 'Meet The Beatles', featuring news of their upcoming TV appearances on the *Jack Paar Show* and *The Ed Sullivan Show*, also appeared in the magazine.

❛ In October 1962 I was about to turn 13. My friend who was like a brother to me and three years older had bought 'Love Me Do' the day it was released. He played it to me and asked me what I thought. I said I really liked it and asked who it was as I had never heard of them. I was hooked straight away. My mum wasn't very impressed when the family saw them on TV for the first time. She never forgave him for getting me into them. I started listening to *Pop Go The Beatles* on the Light Programme.

I was in my second year at an all-girls' secondary school. In the autumn term of 1963, our form teacher surprised us by asking who would like to see the Beatles Christmas show. She would arrange everything. The whole class went except one, she was a Cliff Richard fan like I was before I heard and saw the Beatles. When the time came to see the show, there was a thick blanket of snow over the whole country. All I was worried about was the coach being able to get us to London! After leaving Kent on a very cold afternoon, we arrived at the Finsbury Park Astoria and it was packed in the foyer with mainly girls like me. We were up in one of the balconies and I was worried about falling into the stalls the way I was jumping about. Because the Beatles were on last, every time the compère introduced the other acts nobody could hear him because of all the non-stop screaming. The Beatles were fantastic. It was a great show and we all came out crying and exhausted. Our teacher took us all again the following December to see their second Christmas show. By 1965, I was at work so I went with friends to see them that December at the Hammersmith Odeon. I have been a Beatle fanatic since 1962 and still am in retirement. ❜

CATHY HATFIELD, HOUSEWIFE, PRAZE-AN-BREEBLE, CORNWALL

TUESDAY 31 DECEMBER

Oxfam's twenty-day *Daily Mail* Beatle Drive came to a close. Eleven thousand fans sent in donations the day before, bringing the total raised to £491,154. With nearly forty thousand letters still unopened, the campaign target of £500,000 was guaranteed. A spokesman for Henri Selmer, the country's largest suppliers of guitars and other instruments, reported that business had been substantially up during 1963, saying, 'We have been overwhelmed.' Musical and Plastic Industries shipped three quarters of a ton of guitars from the US because of overwhelming demand. Selcol planned to introduce a range of cheap 'Beatle' guitars selling between 10/- and £3. It was subsequently reported that £22 million worth of records were sold in the UK during 1963, £6,250,000 of which was courtesy of the Beatles. Only six years earlier in 1957, total sales had been £8 million.

At some point during the day, John recorded a demo of 'If I Fell', which appeared on the *A Hard Day's Night* LP. The final performance of the year of 'The Beatles Christmas Show' took place at the Astoria – only one show was scheduled because of New Year's celebrations. The group's 4 October appearance on *Ready, Steady, Go!* was repeated as part of an hour-long New Year's Eve special at 11.15pm, titled *Ready, Steady, Go! The New Year Starts Here!* John, George, Ringo and Pete Shotton went looking for John Bloom's New Year's Eve party, but couldn't remember where he lived, so crashed someone else's party instead. Thus ended the Beatles' 1963.

❛ I went to Romford County High grammar school, a couple of bus rides away from home. I bought 'Love Me Do' on 8 January 1963. I'd heard it on the radio over Christmas and went to buy it after school at a record shop in nearby Ardleigh Green. I'd been given a diary for Christmas from an aunt. It was a small diary, with a padlock, and I wrote a whole page in it every day. It was the first year I had kept a diary. I was 15 at the time, and also kept a diary the following year. After that it petered out. The Beatles featured quite a bit in 1963! My second Beatles entry in my diary was on 26 January when they appeared on *Saturday Club*, and then nothing until 20 April when they were on *Thank Your Lucky Stars* with Del Shannon. When John appeared on *Juke Box Jury* later in the year, and it clashed with them being on *Thank Your Lucky Stars* – you had to decide which one you were going to watch.

At the end of May, my friends and I decided to get up early to go and queue for tickets for the Beatles show at Romford Odeon on 16 June. The alarm went off at a quarter to four, and I got up and set off. There weren't any buses at that time in the morning, so I had to walk all the way into the centre of Romford, which must have taken me about three quarters of an hour. When I arrived, there were already several people there, so we weren't right at the front of the queue. The girls at the front had been there since midnight! Lots of my friends then turned up, so it was quite an interesting little morning, as they didn't open the doors until about eleven o'clock. I took quite a few photos of us standing there in the queue, and you can see in the background that the film showing that week was *The Day Of The Triffids*. My father was a Research Chemist for Ilford Films, so I had my own camera, and was always taking photos. It was quite unusual at the time for someone of my age to have a camera. My diary also records that it was Cup Final day that day, and it read 'Manchester United won!'

Whitsun Bank Holiday was 3 June and they were on a radio programme at half past ten in the morning, singing 'I Saw Her Standing There' and 'From Me To You.' I wrote quite a lot of my diary in French, which I was learning at the time. I figured that if my mum got hold of it, she wouldn't be able to understand it! Then on the 16th was the Romford concert. It was the only time I saw them. I wrote a list of the songs that they sang, and then somebody we knew went to the second performance and told us that Ringo sang 'Boys', which he didn't do in the first performance. I made a note of that in my diary. On the 18th was their third *Pop Go The Beatles* programme – and Paul's 21st birthday, of course. Followed three days later by an article about John in the paper saying he'd been in a fight and 'sent his best friend to hospital.' He said, 'I was too drunk to know what I was doing.' On the Sunday, they were on *Easy Beat*, and my diary recalled they sang 'Some Other Guy', 'A Taste of Honey', 'Thank You Girl' and 'From Me To You.' On the 29th, John was on *Juke Box Jury*. 'He said

[Handwritten diary entry:] New Year's Eve!! DECEMBER 31 1963. Tuesday. Last entry for this year – so make it good! Didn't get up till 10.00am! Read papers. Then had brek, then elevenses. Coffee in new mugs + bix. Then played 'old maid' with John + Pete, Or rather, John + Ringo (I was Paul!) I only lost once! Heard 'Pop-Inn' and had own Soup + potato blobs. But then the Fourmost came on Radio, but they wanted 'Andy Pandy' on – so I had to go upstairs + listen. After dins. Have 'Od Maid'. Then took John to shops. Didn't have Beatles book. Posted letter to BBC asking if I could have 'George' from last night! Then I walked round, hoping it would rain cos had umbrella with me. Home. Put new Beatles LP on Tab! Says Billy Fury on Saclock Club. Tea 2.6.46!!! Then went upstairs + made a Beatle-counter to go over bookcase. They saw TV World – last one. Flying! BBC tv centres. Had mixed eye film. Mongolia. Had Fish + Chips! Then queer film about John No Beatles! George Ringo John Paul George Ringo. Happy.

good things like Elvis is sounding like Bing.' On 5 July, we found out that John was married, and we were all very disappointed, especially my friend Marilyn, because she liked John best! On the 18th I read somewhere that there was going to be a Beatles book coming out every month. I wrote, 'Very excited!' I managed to get one, as my friend Marilyn's dad worked in a newsagents, and she was able to get one for me. They sold out very quickly. On the 21st they were on *Easy Beat* again. On the Tuesday, *Pop Go The Beatles* was back again at five o'clock. I also wrote in my diary, 'The Beatles *Twist and Shout* EP is at number 14. Very exciting!'

In August I went off to Girl Guide camp, so not much exciting to report from the diary while I was there. It was somewhere up near Dovercourt in Essex and there was no radio there. On the 8th – 'Got the Beatles book!' My friend sent it to me through the post. Near the end of the month, me, my mum and dad, and my three little brothers – well in fact, two little brothers – the baby was at home with granny – went on holiday to Pontin's in Bracklesham Bay, down by the Isle of Wight. I was really bored, being stuck there with my little brothers, and I got talking to a girl called Linda, and we got quite pally. Anyway, this particular day, I agreed to take my brothers to the beach. We spent the afternoon there, and when I came back, later in the evening, Linda came and found me and said, 'Did you see him? Did you see him?' I said, 'Who?' 'Paul! He was here this afternoon!' It turns out that his cousin was the Entertainments Manager of this Pontins, and of course they had been appearing nearby, and he had popped over to see him. He had been there all afternoon, talking to people, and signing autographs! And where was I? On the beach with my little brothers! So I cried for about three days. To say I was disappointed would be putting it mildly.

On the 24th, they were on *Thank Your Lucky Stars* again. I mentioned that George's hair was very long, and my dad didn't like it. I also watched *Juke Box Jury*, and they played 'She Loves You.' There's nothing in my diary for September until Tuesday the 17th, where it says the radio show had started up again. We finished school at a quarter to four, so provided you got the bus ok, you could be back in time. The following Tuesday was the last one! 'Very good but sad.' On the 26th, I went off and got an enormous poster from *Reveille* magazine. It was about 6-foot square and covered my entire bedroom wall – much to my mother's disgust! On 4 October, they were on *Ready Steady Go*, and the following day they were on *Saturday Club*. It was the show's fifth birthday, and they were having a bit of a celebration. On the 9th, there was a Beatles TV documentary on quite late, I had to fight to be able to stay up! Then came *Sunday Night At The London Palladium*, which was the big show of the week. Des O'Connor was on, and then they were on after him. Bruce Forsyth was the host, and he kept teasing the audience, just because there was so much screaming. My diary then reads, 'I went up to bed, but then somebody yelled the Beatles are on again! I nearly fell down the stairs! Ringo said, "The police tell us not to look out or we'll excite them." So, they must have been looking out the window of somewhere, I don't know what it was about. Perhaps it was on the news. I recall that on the following week's *Sunday Night at the London Palladium*, Bruce Forsyth came on with one of those insect repellent sprays, and was spraying it all over the stage.'

On 3 November, they were on the Ken Dodd show and the following day was the Royal Variety Performance. On the 12th there was an article in the paper saying that Paul had gastric flu. The next day the Beatles documentary was on again. Couldn't have been that late, as that night I went to bed at 9.15. On Saturday the 23rd I joined their fan club! There was a form in *The Beatles Monthly*, which you filled in and sent off with a postal order. It was 5 shillings! There was a Beatles Christmas Card that had just come out as well. My diary says, 'The Beatles popped into *Saturday Club* to talk about all the publicity they were getting.' On 7 December they were on *Juke Box Jury*. 'They were very funny! Ringo's mic didn't work! They did their own show as well.' On Christmas Day, I got *With The Beatles*. I was worried that I wouldn't get it, but I did. On the 30th, there was an interesting story about computers on television and what they could do in the future. One of the things they did was put photographs of famous people into it, and it would say whether they were male or female. They put a picture of George up, and it said he was female! And so, 1963 came to an end. **⟩**

CHRISTINE DANIELS, TEACHER, WICKFORD, ESSEX

DISCREPANCIES, MYTHS & MISTAKES

Over the years much has been written about The Beatles. False memories, made-up stories and poor research have contributed to clouding the picture. Often, once a story takes hold it remains in the ether forever. This section aims to clarify some of these discrepancies, myths and mistakes. This book makes no claim to having the answer to everything. The true circumstances of some of these events will never be known. Hopefully this will provide some clarification.

2 January

As unlikely as it seems that John would have flown from Aberdeen to Liverpool to see Cynthia, there is no doubt that he did. Cynthia's diary entry for January 2nd read, "John home – surprise. Didn't know till 7pm. Flies tomorrow at 5am". Obviously, the time he arrived home means that he flew to Liverpool from Aberdeen not London.

3 January

Many myths have evolved over the years about this visit, perhaps the most ludicrous being that they all jumped into the River Lossie to clean up. It seems highly unlikely they would have done so because it was freezing cold and they had stayed in hotels over the previous two nights. Additionally, according to multiple sources, John arrived with the rest of the group and not on his own, minutes before the show started. How could he have travelled from Aberdeen to Elgin on his own? A 65-mile taxi ride? The likeliest explanation is that after leaving the Gloucester Hotel, they drove north to the airport which is on the road to Elgin and picked John up. In *The Beatles Anthology*, Ringo recalls this show incorrectly. He remembered an L-shaped concert hall, when in fact the ballroom had a dog-leg shape. He said he drove away in his car after the show, but he had not been back to Liverpool after Hamburg and therefore wouldn't have had his car.

4 January

One fan who was at the Dingwall gig said she travelled with the group when they drove up to the Strathpeffer Pavilion after they finished their set to see what all the fuss was about. Anne Gunn's story about them returning to the National Hotel at about ten o'clock would suggest they did not. The author has driven from Dingwall to Strathpeffer and even on a nice day, it's not the easiest of roads to navigate.

5 January

Although driving from Dingwall to Bridge of Allan by way of Aberdeen adds a couple of hours on to the journey, there is no doubt that they did. Hamilton Harwood is insistent that he met them on a Saturday and not the Monday. He had a nine-to-five job at the time and would not have been able to go to JT Forbes on a weekday. The author spoke with several people who live in villages and towns along the A9 and without exception all recall the road being blocked on occasion in January 1963. It has been reported that it was at this concert that the crowd was predominantly male, drunk and threw coins onstage. This story originated from the same person who said they performed 'Please Please Me', 'From Me To You' and 'She Loves You' in succession, despite the fact that two of the songs hadn't been written at this stage.

7 January

John's cousin Stan Parkes tells the story of the time John spent the night with him in Edinburgh when he was due to make a TV appearance in Glasgow. This is probably the only occasion on which it could have happened, meaning Neil Aspinall would have dropped John off in Edinburgh and continued on to Glasgow with the rest of the group. Realising the TV show had to be filmed in Glasgow and not in Edinburgh, Parkes drove John to the studios arriving in the nick of time.

11 January

It has not been possible to confirm the support acts for the Plaza show. It seems the Plazents and the Silhouettes are the most likely.

13 January

In his book *Brian Epstein - The Man Who Made The Beatles*, Ray Coleman wrote that Tony Barrow said Andrew Loog Oldham was on board for 'Love Me Do', which apparently was not the case.

14 January

The date of the first Angus McBean photo session has never been identified, but this is the most likely. The only other possible date would have been two days earlier on their way to Chatham. As that was a Saturday, it is unlikely McBean would have been working that day – and would Epstein have risked booking a photo shoot when they had to drive from Liverpool? The only other possible date is 21 January, but getting from Liverpool by way of Whitchurch, where they were known to have been close to midday, would have meant arriving in the late afternoon, and the shoot apparently was at lunchtime.

17 January

It seems that Earl Royce and the Olympics might have been one of the support groups at the Majestic Ballroom, but it has not been possible to confirm it.

19 January

Helen Shapiro says that they watched themselves on national TV for the first time in her dressing room this night. They were playing in Whitchurch at the time. Two people claim the group went back to their respective houses after the show, but Michael Dale's account seems the more plausible.

27 January

In an article in *Mojo* magazine, Paul recalled driving to the Three Coins on January 23rd (sic) and hearing 'Love Me Do' on the radio for the first time. "I'm down by the ballrooms that we used to play... the Locarno and the Grafton. I was driving right there and it came on the radio, y'know. I remember just wanting to lean out the window and scream at everyone. That's me! Listen to this! This is me!" Obviously, he's confused this with another date, probably in late 1962.

28 January

The group's weekly schedule has them staying at St Margaret's Hotel in Jesmond, but it seems a last-minute change was made and they spent the night at the Imperial Hotel.

29 January

Thelma Pickles wrote in her diary entry for this day that "Paul came back from playing at Middlesbrough". She must have got this confused with Newcastle-upon-Tyne the day before or thought the planned concert in Middlesbrough had gone ahead.

1 February
Some sources have them staying at the Norfolk Hotel in Hagley Road, Birmingham and then making their way to Bradford for the first date of the Helen Shapiro tour.

2 February
Helen Shapiro apparently told author Ray Coleman that John Lennon consoled her on the coach between cities during the tour. "I picked up a copy of the *Melody Maker* and opened it up to a headline 'Is Helen a has been at sixteen'?" The headline appeared in the December 8, 1962 edition of the paper, so it seems Shapiro is mistaken.

11 February
In a BBC documentary about the making of the *Please Please Me* LP, former *NME* journalist Alan Smith recalled suggesting they record 'La Bamba' as their last number. However, George Martin in *Anthology* makes it clear that 'Twist And Shout' was always going to be the last song recorded that day. "I knew that 'Twist And Shout' was a real larynx-tearer and I said, "We're not going to record that until the very end of the day".

12 February
The date of the Valentine photo session at the University of London has never before been determined, but by process of elimination this is the only possible date. The session obviously took place before Ringo had his first Beatle haircut on 25 March. Sid Hayden clearly recalls 'Please Please Me' climbing the charts at the time. The origins of the myth that the Beatles performed at the Azena Ballroom on this date are from an interview with Peter Stringfellow. He had booked the group to perform at the Black Cat, but realising the demand far exceeded the supply, booked the larger Azena Ballroom for a 2 April date. Whether he genuinely forgot those details or wanted to retain the credit for being the first promoter to book them in Sheffield (come April they had made two appearances in the city) will never be known. There's a poster of the '12 February Azena' show, but any eagle-eyed Beatle fan will spot the three errors on the poster.

16 February
The group's weekly schedule had them booked into the Mitre Hotel following the show, but apparently they returned to London instead if David Pearson's article in *Disc* is correct.

21 February
Although billed, it seems Rory Storm and the Hurricanes did not perform.

3 March
Although several sources claim they stayed in digs at Adventure Place, which is close to the Gaumont, it seems strange they did not stay in a hotel.

14 March
Cavern bouncer Paddy Delaney claimed he was drinking with John in the Blue Angel on one of the nights he was absent from the tour. Apparently, John told him he was rejoining the tour in York on Wednesday the 13th, but he was at Abbey Road that morning so he could not have been in Liverpool as claimed. John missed shows in Bedford, York and Wolverhampton. He rejoined the tour in Bristol on the 15th. There is ample evidence that John overdubbed his harmonica part at EMI Studios on the morning of the 13th, so

if he did meet up with Delaney in the Blue Angel, it could only have been on the night of the 13th or more likely the 14th. John also did a joint interview for *Disc* with Gerry Marsden. Once again, it has not been possible to confirm which day of this week it was.

16 March

Ken Brown, formerly a member of the Quarrymen, claimed the group came round to his flat and asked whether he could lend them £20. He said it was the day before the Sheffield concert, which is obviously inaccurate, but it seems unlikely the group would have gone from Broadcasting House to Sheffield by way of his flat – not to mention the fact that they were on a weekly wage at the time.

31 March

It seems that on one occasion the group bumped into Cliff Richard and the Shadows at the Blue Boar service station at the Watford Gap on the M1. This seems to be the most likely date as Cliff was on his way to Coventry, but it has not been possible to confirm this.

6 April

There is a source that says that exuberant fans caused a girl to lose her eye in a melée. There is no reference to this in the local newspaper, so it seems highly unlikely it happened.

10 April

Most sources for John's tie story have 17 April but it was first reported in the *NME* week ending 19 April which means it can't have been on that date.

24 April

There's no proof this was the day they met with Giorgio Gomelsky and Peter Clayton, but again through process of elimination, it seems the most likely.

26 April

Some sources have the group staying in a Shrewsbury hotel after the show, but it has not been possible to confirm this.

28 April–9 May

Some sources have John and Brian Epstein staying at the Manila Hotel. There's a story that while Paul, George and Ringo were in Tenerife they met up with Cliff and the Shadows who were recording in Barcelona. There is no evidence of that happening.

10 May

The story goes that Dick Rowe, when told by George about the Rolling Stones, left the contest immediately and caught a train to London and headed straight over to the Crawdaddy to see them – except they were not playing there that night. Bill Wyman says Rowe saw them at the venue on 5 May, five days before the contest. The next time they played the Crawdaddy was on 12 May. On the 10th, the Stones were in the studio recording 'Come On'. Decca never signed the Rolling Stones directly to the label. They signed a deal with Andrew Loog Oldham and Eric Easton's production company, Impact Sound. Unfortunately, myth and not fact.

11 May

Some sources have the group being smuggled in and out of the venue in a Black Maria dressed as policemen. There is no evidence this happened prior to the Birmingham shows on 10 November.

15 May

Bob Gaudio claims the Beatles came to see the Four Seasons when they played in London in 1963. This was the date of their sole London performance, unfortunately the Beatles were performing in Chester on the night.

1 June

Sean O'Mahony says in *The Beatles Book* that he met the group for the first time on May 21st. It seems he got the date wrong.

10 June

Some sources have the group being escorted back to Liverpool with a car in front and another behind. This seems highly implausible.

12 June

It has been reported widely that Jeffrey Archer staged this concert. He didn't. This concert was in aid of the NSPCC. Archer's involvement came later in the year when he met the group backstage at the Liverpool Odeon and persuaded them to get involved with Oxfam's Christmas campaign.

27 June

There is a photo of Paul in the control room of Abbey Road's Studio Two, where the recording took place between 7pm and 10.30pm. In the morning they rehearsed in Studio Three and it's known Paul was definitely there for that. Paul has always said they finished writing 'She Loves You' one evening, so the only explanation can be is that at some point during the day they went into Studio Two to have the photo taken.

29 June

These two performances in Handsworth and Old Hill have never been reported anywhere before, but too many people – both musicians and fans – recall these two dates. George wrote a letter to his sister Louise from the Albany Hotel in Birmingham on the night, which would imply they were in the area for a reason. Ian Lees, who was a member of the Telstars, recalls sitting on the wall in front of the Holy Trinity Church opposite the Plaza eating fish and chips with John. The only two possible occasions it could have been were 29 June or 5 July. However, it has not been possible to confirm the Telstars being on the bill for either of those shows. Bruce Prochnik's memory of Brian Poole and the Tremeloes' version of 'Twist And Shout' being played on *Juke Box Jury* is probably faulty, unless extra records were played at the recording, but not broadcast.

1 July

It has always been thought that the session at Abbey Road began at 2.30. It's quite clear from Derek Driver's story that it could not have.

5 July

The information on the support acts for these two shows are based on group members' memories, but it's possible they have mixed up some dates.

7 July
There are conflicting opinions as to who the support acts were. A Blackpool historian has Freddie Starr, the Brook Brothers, Terry Young Combo and George Meaton. The author believes the Fourmost were on the bill instead of Freddie Starr.

8 July
This is the date that is most likely for when they got their new Vox amps, but it has not been possible to confirm it.

18 July
Some sources have George making the comment to Brian Epstein.

21 July
Most sources have the group climbing up ladders and scaffolding before their 4 August show in Blackpool. The *Blackpool Evening Gazette* on 22 July ran the story headlined "Beatles Go In By Skylight".

3 August
After the show Bob Wooler reportedly counted up all their appearances at the Cavern and came up with the figure of 292. However, diaries were subsequently destroyed and it is thought some gigs remain undocumented. Mark Lewisohn's total is 274.

18 August
The Horseshoe Pass story has its origins with Tony Bramwell. If it happened this is the only possible occasion. Whoever might have been in the van is a mystery. It seems both Paul and Ringo had their cars with them in Bournemouth – and perhaps George. It has been impossible to confirm how they got their cars in order to drive to Torquay and then on to Bournemouth. The likeliest scenario is that Neil Aspinall drove them back to Liverpool from Llandudno last thing Saturday night or first thing Sunday morning and they then made their separate ways to Torquay during Sunday. So, if the Horseshoe Pass story happened there's a good chance John was the only Beatle travelling in the van that day. Most sources have them recording their appearance on *Lucky Stars – Summer Spin* this day, but it has now been confirmed this happened on 4 August. Although the Kestrels appeared on the poster for the Torquay shows, it seems their place was taken by Rod and Carolyn (listed at the time as Rod and Caralyn).

2 September
Although a date for the plane mishap has never before been revealed, piecing together different newspaper and magazine articles confirms this could have been the only possible one.

5 September
Some sources claim that Freddie Starr and the Midnighters performed instead of the Fourmost and they were listed in the *Somerset County Gazette* prior to the show. However, a subsequent review of the show mentions the Fourmost's performance.

10 September
The participants in this story would have different versions of what happened, with Paul remembering Oldham in the cab and stopping them as they walked down Charing Cross Road, while Stones' bassist Bill Wyman would claim Oldham saw them getting out of a cab outside Leicester Square tube station.

3 October

It has always been thought that George returned from New York on the morning of the 3rd, but if *Disc* journalist Alan Walsh was being truthful about travelling down from Liverpool one early morning, this must have been the date it happened – meaning George came back on the 2nd. A couple of weeks earlier George wrote in *Disc* that he was coming back on the 3rd, but perhaps he changed his mind so he could go home and tell his parents about their visit to see his sister Louise.

7 October

Some sources have Tommy Dene and the Tremors as one of the support acts rather than the Overlanders. According to Donald Stuart, the Tremors' rhythm guitarist, they supported the Beatles in Dundee the following October.

11 October

It is possible that the Black Orchids were also on the bill, but the author has been unable to confirm this.

12 October

The Guardian's Stanley Reynolds said he travelled on the train with them from Liverpool to London. He must have confused it with another occasion. Coverage at the time reported that the group stayed overnight in the North Stafford Hotel and drove to London the following morning. It seems implausible they would head back to Liverpool after the Trentham Gardens show to then take the train the following day. If they did go by train, it seems unlikely they would have arrived an hour late to the Donmar Rehearsal Theatre.

2 November

Clearly, the *Daily Mirror* headline following the opening night of their tour in Cheltenham was not the first time the word "Beatlemania" was used in print. It appeared in *The Observer* on 13 October and was used again in the *Daily Mail* on 24 October and the *Sunday Mirror* and *Sunday People* on 27 October. Others have claimed using the term earlier than this reference, but the author has been unable to vouch for any of those claims.

4 November

Although Princess Margaret has been credited with the line "Slough Slough quick quick Slough", and it was reported thus in the *Daily Telegraph*, apparently the Beatles also used the phrase to the press earlier in the day.

5 November

The "Beatles Siege" headline in the *Daily Sketch* is somewhat of a mystery. The headline in the day's newspaper was "Why Our Super Jet Crashed – Official". The only explanation is that there were different editions printed.

11 November

Peter Prichard was Ed Sullivan's European talent co-ordinator and had taken his American counterpart Jack Babb to see the Beatles during the summer. Prichard had phoned Brian Epstein to tell him that he should try to get the group on the show and offered to negotiate a deal. He did some exploratory work and phoned Sullivan but it was Epstein who made the deal.

28 November

There is a well-documented story reported in the national press that the parents of Elva Jamieson placed an ad in their local newspaper, the *Prescot & Huyton Reporter*, stating that Elva was not going to marry Ringo. The following day Elva was quoted at length saying Ringo was a good friend of her brother David and that he often came to their house. Her parents had placed the ad to dispel rumours that had been rife for weeks. The only problem with this story is that the author has been unable to find any reference to an ad or anything else for that matter in the *Prescot & Huyton Reporter*.

4 December

Both references to George and John come from Michael Braun's book *Love Me Do*. By process of elimination, this date is the most likely, although it is possible it was the following day.

7 December

The Jeffrey Archer quote, he's "a nice enough fella, but the kind of bloke who would bottle your piss and sell it" said to Sheridan Morley in March 1964, has also been credited to George.

10 December

There is a story that after the Doncaster show, the group went to the Scala Club in Sprotbrough, but this has not been possible to confirm.

17 December

There is no confirmed date of Paul's conversation with Jane and John Dunbar. There is a possibility it was the following night, but this seems more likely.

26 December

Pete Shotton has mentioned that he, John, George and Ringo went to a party at John Bloom's, but unable to find it crashed another one instead. The author has been unable to confirm this.

SOURCES

The template for this book is Mark Lewisohn's two seminal books on the subject – *The Complete Beatles Recording Sessions* and *The Complete Beatles Chronicle*. No self-respecting Beatles researcher should contemplate writing on the subject without referencing these two books. Because they have been referred to so often for this book, they have not been listed in this section – they would appear under most dates if they had been.

1 January
Daily Express, Evening Standard, NRM, Record Retailer & Music Industry News, The Times, Tune In (Mark Lewisohn)

2 January
Glasgow Evening Times, Scottish Daily Mail, The Beatles Gear (Andy Babiuk)

3 January
Daily Herald, Disc, Forbes Elgin & Nairn Gazette, New Record Mirror

4 January
Melody Maker, New Musical Express

5 January
Aberdeen Express, Allanwater Herald

6 January
Sunday Pictorial, BBC Radio 2, *The Beatles In Scotland* (Ken McNab)

7 January
Aberdeen Express, The Beatles In Scotland (Ken McNab)

8 January
Daily Mirror

9 January
Liverpool Daily Post, Liverpool Echo

10 January
Billboard, Disc, Evening Standard, Liverpool Echo, Liverpool Daily Post, New Record Mirror, The Beatles Are Coming! (Bruce Spizer)

11 January
Liverpool Echo, Liverpool Daily Post, Melody Maker, Mersey Beat, New Musical Express, New Record Mirror, Record Retailer

SOURCES

12 January
Chatham Observer & Kent Messenger, "The Clock Tower", *Beatles Gear* (Andy Babiuk)

13 January
The Guardian, Liverpool Echo, TV Times, Shout (Philip Norman), *Stoned* (Andrew Loog Oldham)

14 January
Valentine, The Beatles' London (Piet Schreuders)

15 January
Liverpool Daily Post, New Record Mirror

16 January
Liverpool Echo, New Record Mirror, The Beatles – The BBC Archive (Kevin Howlett)

17 January
The Guardian, Liverpool Echo, Liverpool Daily Post, Mersey Beat, New Record Mirror

18 January
Melody Maker, Morecambe Guardian, Morecambe Visitor

19 January
Liverpool Echo, Radio Times

20 January
The Beatles Book, I'll Never Walk Alone (Gerry Marsden with Ray Coleman)

21 January
Boyfriend, Liverpool Echo, Liverpool Daily Post

22 January
Liverpool Echo, Radio Times, The Beatles – The BBC Archive (Kevin Howlett)

23 January
Liverpool Echo, Liverpool Daily Post

24 January
Daily Mirror, Liverpool Echo, Liverpool Daily Post, New Record Mirror, Wrexham Leader, The Beatles And Wales (David Jones)

25 January
Liverpool Echo, Melody Maker, Radio Times, The Beatles – The BBC Archive (Kevin Howlett)

26 January
Liverpool Echo, Radio Times, Sunday Pictorial, The Beatles – The BBC Archive (Kevin Howlett)

27 January
New Musical Express, "The Manchester Musical History Tour" (Phill Gatenby & Craig Gill, *Manchester Beat*)

28 January
Evening Chronicle, The (Newcastle) Journal

29 January
Liverpool Echo, Radio Times, The Beatles – The BBC Archive (Kevin Howlett)

30 January
Liverpool Daily Post, New Record Mirror

31 January
Disc, Liverpool Daily Post, New Record Mirror

1 February
Daily Mail, Melody Maker, New Musical Express, Tamworth Herald

2 February
Bradford Telegraph & Argus, Evening Standard, Liverpool Echo, Melody Maker, New Musical Express, Yorkshire Post, John Winston Lennon (Ray Coleman), *The Beatles Off The Record* (Keith Badman), *Ringo* (Ringo Starr)

3 February
Liverpool Echo, New Record Mirror, The Cavern Club – The Rise of The Beatles and Merseybeat (Spencer Leigh), *McCartney* (Christopher Sandford)

4 February
Liverpool Echo, Liverpool Daily Post, Melody Maker

5 February
Doncaster Free Press, Liverpool Echo, Jon Kelly/Sine Radio

6 February
Bedford Record & Circular, Bedfordshire Times & Advertiser, Stoned (Andrew Loog Oldham)

7 February
Disc, New Record Mirror, The Beatles Are Coming! (Bruce Spizer)

8 February
Daily Mail, Melody Maker, New Musical Express, (Carlisle) *News & Star*

9 February
Northern Echo, R&R, *Sunderland Echo, John Winston Lennon* (Ray Coleman)

10 February
The Beatles Off The Record (Keith Badman)

SOURCES

11 February
The Beatles Book, The True Story of the Beatles (Billy Shepherd), *Tune In* (Mark Lewisohn), *The Beatles Off The Record* (Keith Badman), *The Beatles As Musicians* (Walter Everett), *The Beatles – An Oral History* (David Pritchard & Alan Lysaght)

12 February
Oldham Evening Chronicle, It Won't Be Long (Michael Turner)

13 February
Goole Times, The Beatles And Me (Dean Johnson)

14 February
Disc, Liverpool Echo, Liverpool Daily Post, New Record Mirror, Record Retailer, The Beatles (Hunter Davies), spencerleigh.co.uk

15 February
Melody Maker, New Musical Express

16 February
Rocking In Oxford (Trevor Hayward)

17 February
Disc, TV Times, The Beatles – An Oral History (David Pritchard & Alan Lysaght)

18 February
Liverpool Echo, Widnes Weekly News

19 February
Honey, New Musical Express

20 February
Doncaster Chronicle, New Musical Express, Radio Times, The Beatles – The BBC Archive (Kevin Howlett)

21 February
Disc, Liverpool Echo, New Record Mirror

22 February
Boyfriend, Melody Maker, New Musical Express, Many Years From Now (Barry Miles), *Northern Songs* (Brian Southall with Rupert Perry), "The Manchester Musical History Tour" (Phill Gatenby & Craig Gill, *Manchester Beat*)

23 February
John Winston Lennon (Ray Coleman)

24 February
Coventry Express

25 February
Leigh Chronicle

26 February
Somerset County Gazette, Somerset County Herald

27 February
Yorkshire Evening Press

28 February
Hit Parade, New Musical Express, New Record Mirror, The Mammoth Book of the Beatles (Sean Egan)

1 March
Melody Maker, New Musical Express, Southport Visiter

2 March
Sheffield Star, TV Times, The Music Game (David Hamilton)

3 March
Evening Sentinel, Staffordshire Weekly Sentinel, The True Story of the Beatles (Billy Shepherd)

5 March
Boyfriend, New Musical Express

6 March
Radio Times, The Beatles – The BBC Archive (Kevin Howlett)

7 March
Disc, New Record Mirror, Nottingham Evening Post

8 March
Melody Maker, New Musical Express

9 March
Melody Maker, New Musical Express, "The Anthology", *Beatlemania! – The Beatles UK Tours 1963-1965* (Martin Creasy), *The Beatles* (Hunter Davies)

12 March
Bedford Record & Circular, Bedfordshire Times & Advertiser, Radio Times

13 March
Yorkshire Evening Press, Here, There And Everywhere – My Life Recording The Music Of The Beatles (Geoff Emerick & Howard Massey)

14 March
Disc, (Wolverhampton) *Express & Star, New Record Mirror, Wolverhampton Chronicle, Beatles For Sale* (John Blaney)

SOURCES

15 March
Bristol Evening Post, Melody Maker, New Musical Express

16 March
Disc, Radio Times, Sheffield Star, The Beatles – The BBC Archive (Kevin Howlett)

17 March
Peterborough Evening Telegraph, Peterborough Standard

18 March
Beatlemania! – The Beatles UK Tours 1963-1965 (Martin Creasy)

19 March
Cambridge News, Beatlemania! – The Beatles UK Tours 1963-1965 (Martin Creasy)

20 March
Romford Times

21 March
Croydon Times-Herald, Disc, Mirabelle, New Record Mirror, The Beatles – The BBC Archive (Kevin Howlett)

22 March
Doncaster Chronicle, Melody Maker, New Musical Express

23 March
(Newcastle) *Evening Chronicle, The (Newcastle) Journal*

24 March
New Record Mirror, The Ultimate Beatles Encyclopedia (Bill Harry)

25 March
The Beatles – An Oral History (David Pritchard & Alan Lysaght)

26 March
Mansfield & North Nottinghamshire Chronicle Advertiser

27 March
Northampton Chronicle & Echo, Beatlemania! – The Beatles UK Tours 1963-1965 (Martin Creasy)

28 March
Disc, New Musical Express, New Record Mirror, Radio Times, The Beatles – The BBC Archive (Kevin Howlett), *Beatlemania! – The Beatles UK Tours 1963-1965* (Martin Creasy)

29 March
(Lewisham) *Advertiser & News, Lewisham Journal & Borough News, Melody Maker, New Musical Express, Love Me Do* (Michael Braun)

THE BEATLES 1963 – A YEAR IN THE LIFE

30 March
(Portsmouth) *Evening News, Hampshire Telegraph*

31 March
Leicester Advertiser, Leicester Mercury, Mojo, The Beatles Gear (Andy Babiuk)

1 April
Mirabelle, The Beatles – The BBC Archive (Kevin Howlett)

2 April
Sheffield Star, The Beatles Off The Record (Keith Badman)

3 April
Disc, Radio Times, The Beatles At The BBC (Kevin Howlett)

4 April
Disc, New Record Mirror, The Beatles – The BBC Archive (Kevin Howlett)

5 April
Daily Mail, Melody Maker, Mirabelle, New Musical Express

6 April
Buxton Advertiser, Liverpool Echo, The Stage

7 April
Radio Times, The Beatles – The BBC Archive (Kevin Howlett)

8 April
Mojo, Beatlemania! – The Beatles UK Tours 1963-1965 (Martin Creasy), *A Twist of Lennon* (Cynthia Lennon)

9 April
Kilburn Times, Radio Times, Romeo, TV Times, The Beatles – The BBC Archive (Kevin Howlett), *The Beatles* (Hunter Davies), *Beatlemania! – The Beatles UK Tours 1963-1965* (Martin Creasy)

10 April
Liverpool Echo

11 April
Daily Mirror, Disc, Hit Parade, Melody Maker, Middleton Guardian, New Musical Express, New Record Mirror, Reveille, Lennon (Tim Riley)

12 April
Liverpool Echo, Liverpool Daily Post, New Musical Express, I'll Never Walk Alone (Gerry Marsden with Ray Coleman), *The Cavern* (Spencer Leigh)

508

SOURCES

13 April
The Beatles – The BBC Archive (Kevin Howlett)

14 April
Stone Alone (Bill Wyman with Ray Coleman)

15 April
Shropshire Star, The Beatles (Hunter Davies)

16 April
Daily Mirror, The Beatles – The BBC Archive (Kevin Howlett)

17 April
Luton News & Bedfordshire Advertiser, New Musical Express

18 April
Disc, New Record Mirror, Radio Times, The Beatles – The BBC Archive (Kevin Howlett), *Paul McCartney – A Life* (Peter Ames Carlin), *Stone Alone* (Bill Wyman with Ray Coleman), *John Winston Lennon* (Ray Coleman), *McCartney* (Chris Salewicz)

19 April
Melody Maker, New Musical Express

20 April
TV Times, Discovering Mersey View, Frodsham. An Illustrated History

21 April
IQ, Jewish Chronicle, New Musical Express, The True Story of the Beatles (Billy Shepherd)

22 April
Radio Times

23 April
Southport Visiter

24 April
Disc

25 April
Croydon Advertiser, Croydon Times-Herald, Disc, New Record Mirror

26 April
Melody Maker, New Musical Express

27 April
TV Times

28 April–9 May
Disc, Liverpool Echo, Melody Maker, Mirabelle, New Musical Express, New Record Mirror, Record Retailer, In My Life (Debbie Geller), *The Beatles – An Oral History* (David Pritchard & Alan Lysaght), *John Winston Lennon* (Ray Coleman), *The Man Who Made The Beatles* (Ray Coleman), *The True Story of the Beatles* (Billy Shepherd), *Ringo* (Ringo Starr)

10 May
BBC Archives, *The* (Bootle) *Times, Liverpool Daily Post, Mersey Beat, Melody Maker, New Musical Express, New Record Mirror, The (Liverpool) Times*

11 May
Lancashire Telegraph, Liverpool Echo, Nelson Leader, New Record Mirror

12 May
The Independent, TV Times, Rock & Roll Hall of Fame Museum, *Ringo* (Ringo Starr)

13 May
Disc, Radio Times

14 May
Newcastle Journal, randrlife.co.uk

15 May
Chester Chronicle, Wrexham Leader, The Beatles And Wales (David Jones)

16 May
Disc, New Record Mirror, Radio Times, Sunday Times, The Beatles – The BBC Archive (Kevin Howlett)

17 May
Melody Maker, New Musical Express, The Beatles (Hunter Davies),

18 May
Liverpool Echo, Sunday Times, TV Times, Windsor Slough & Eton Express, Beatlemania! – The Beatles UK Tours 1963-1965 (Martin Creasy)

19 May
Beatles Bible, *Evening Sentinel, New Record Mirror, Stoke City Times, Beatlemania! – The Beatles UK Tours 1963-1965* (Martin Creasy)

20 May
Mirabelle, Southampton Echo, Beatlemania! – The Beatles UK Tours 1963-1965 (Martin Creasy)

21 May
The Beatles – The BBC Archive (Kevin Howlett)

SOURCES

22 May
East Anglian Daily Times, Ipswich Star, Beatlemania! – The Beatles UK Tours 1963-1965 (Martin Creasy)

23 May
Disc, New Record Mirror

24 May
Melody Maker, New Musical Express, New Record Mirror, Walthamstow Guardian, The Beatles – The BBC Archive (Kevin Howlett)

25 May
New Musical Express, Radio Times, Sheffield Telegraph, The Beatles – The BBC Archive (Kevin Howlett)

26 May
New Record Mirror, How They Became The Beatles (Gareth L. Pawlowski)

27 May
Cardiff & Suburban News, Cash Box, South Wales Echo, The Beatles And Wales (David Jones), BBC Radio Wales' "The Dragon's Breath", *The Beatles Are Coming!* (Bruce Spizer)

28 May
Worcester Evening News

29 May
Yorkshire Evening Press

30 May
Daily Express, Disc, The Guardian, Manchester Chronicle, New Record Mirror

31 May
Daily Express, Melody Maker, New Musical Express, Southend Standard

1 June
Balham & Tooting News & Mercury, The Beatles – The BBC Archive (Kevin Howlett), *Stoned* (John McMillian)

2 June
Beatlemania! – The Beatles UK Tours 1963-1965 (Martin Creasy)

3 June
Cash Box, The Guardian, Radio Times

4 June
Birmingham Post, Evening Mail & Despatch, Radio Times, The Beatles – The BBC Archive (Kevin Howlett), *Beatlemania! – The Beatles UK Tours 1963-1965* (Martin Creasy)

THE BEATLES 1963 – A YEAR IN THE LIFE

5 June

Yorkshire Evening News, Yorkshire Evening Post, Northern Songs (Brian Southall with Rupert Perry)

6 June

Disc, Mersey Beat, New Record Mirror, The Beatles – The BBC Archive (Kevin Howlett), *Ringo* (Ringo Starr)

7 June

Glasgow Herald, Melody Maker, New Musical Express, The Beatles In Scotland (Ken McNab), *Beatlemania! – The Beatles UK Tours 1963-1965* (Martin Creasy)

8 June

The (Newcastle) Journal

9 June

Blackburn Times, (Blackburn) *Evening Telegraph*

10 June

Beatles Bible

11 June

Radio Times

12 June

Bilston & Willenhall Times, New Record Mirror, How They Became The Beatles (Gareth L. Pawlowski)

13 June

Disc, Goole Times, New Record Mirror

14 June

Melody Maker, New Musical Express, The Beatles Untold Tales (Howard DeWitt)

15 June

Salisbury Journal, Swindon In The News (John Hudson), BBC Radio Wiltshire, *The Man Who Made The Beatles* (Ray Coleman)

16 June

Romford Recorder, Romford Times, The World At My Feet (Sandie Shaw)

17 June

Marilyn, *The Beatles – The BBC Archive* (Kevin Howlett)

18 June

Prescot & Huyton Reporter, Radio Times, Record Collector, The Beatles Off The Record (Keith Badman), *John Winston Lennon* (Ray Coleman), *Paul McCartney Encyclopedia* (Bill Harry), *The John Lennon Letters* (Hunter Davies), *John Lennon In My Life* (Pete Shotton)

SOURCES

19 June
The Beatles - The BBC Archive (Kevin Howlett), *Fifty Years Adrift* (Derek Taylor), *In My Life* (Debbie Geller)

20 June
Daily Express, Disc, New Record Mirror

21 June
Daily Mirror, Guildford Dragon, Guildford & Godalming Times, Melody Maker, New Musical Express

22 June
Abergavenny Chronicle & Monmouthshire Advertiser, Daily Sketch, The Beatles - The BBC Archive (Kevin Howlett), *The Beatles And Wales* (David Jones)

23 June
Pop Weekly, Radio Times

24 June
Radio Times, The Beatles - The BBC Archive (Kevin Howlett)

25 June
(Middlesbrough) *Evening Gazette, Radio Times*, Stan Laundon

26 June
(Newcastle) *Evening Chronicle, The (Newcastle) Journal*

27 June
Daily Express, Disc, New Record Mirror, Many Years From Now (Barry Miles)

28 June
Melody Maker, New Musical Express, Tune In (Mark Lewisohn)

29 June
Daily Herald, Pop Weekly, Radio Times

30 June
Liverpool Daily Post

1 July
Mojo, The Beatles - An Oral History (David Pritchard & Alan Lysaght), *Here, There And Everywhere - My Life Recording The Music Of The Beatles* (Geoff Emerick & Howard Massey)

2 July
Disc, Melody Maker, The Beatles - The BBC Archive (Kevin Howlett)

3 July
Manchester Chronicle, The Beatles - The BBC Archive (Kevin Howlett)

4 July
Disc, New Musical Express, New Record Mirror, Radio Times, Rolling With The Stones (Bill Wyman)

5 July
Melody Maker, Mirabelle, New Musical Express, The True Story of the Beatles (Billy Shepherd), *1963* (John Lawton)

6 July
Chester Chronicle, Liverpool Echo, Northwich Guardian, Vale Royal Times

7 July
Blackpool Evening Gazette, Disc, Cliff Richard – The Complete Chronicle (Mike Read, Nigel Goodall & Peter Lewry)

8 July
Isle of Thanet Gazette

9 July
Isle of Thanet Gazette

10 July
The Beatles – The BBC Archive (Kevin Howlett)

11 July
Daily Mirror, Disc, Liverpool Echo, New Record Mirror, Record Retailer, The Stage

12 July
Boyfriend, Disc, Melody Maker, New Musical Express

15 July
Birkenhead News & Advertiser, Liverpool Echo, Way Beyond Compare – The Beatles' Recorded Legacy – Volume 1957-1965 (John C. Winn)

16 July
Disc, Radio Times, Record Retailer, The Beatles At The Beeb 62-65 (Kevin Howlett), *The Beatles – The BBC Archive* (Kevin Howlett)

17 July
Disc, The Beatles – The BBC Archive (Kevin Howlett)

18 July
Disc, New Record Mirror, How They Became The Beatles (Gareth L. Pawlowski)

19 July
Melody Maker, New Musical Express, New Record Mirror, Beatles In Wales (David Jones)

SOURCES

20 July
The Times

21 July
Blackpool Evening Gazette, Radio Times, Sunday Mirror, The Beatles Off The Record (Keith Badman)

22 July
New Musical Express, Weston Mercury & Somersetshire Herald

23 July
New Musical Express, Radio Times

24 July
Beatles For Sale (John Blaney)

25 July
Disc, New Record Mirror

26 July
Melody Maker, New Musical Express, Weston Mercury & Somersetshire Herald

27 July
Liverpool Echo

28 July
Great Yarmouth Mercury

29 July
New Musical Express

30 July
Radio Times, The Beatles Gear (Andy Babiuk)

31 July
Nelson Leader, Record Retailer

1 August
The Beatles Book, Disc, Liverpool Daily Post, Mojo, New Record Mirror

2 August
Melody Maker, New Musical Express

3 August
Mojo, New Musical Express, The Beatles Gear (Andy Babiuk), *The Beatles – An Oral History* (David Pritchard & Alan Lysaght), *The Beatles Untold Tales* (Howard DeWitt), *The Cavern* (Spencer Leigh)

4 August
Blackpool Gazette & Herald, Disc

5 August
New Musical Express, Stretford & Urmston Journal

6 August
Liverpool Echo, Radio Times

7 August
Southend Standard

8 August
Daily Mirror, Disc, Guernsey Evening Press, Guernsey Star, New Record Mirror, Record Retailer, The Beatles On Vee-Jay (Bruce Spizer), *The Beatles Are Coming!* (Bruce Spizer)

9 August
Daily Mail, Melody Maker, New Musical Express

11 August
Mersey Beat, New Musical Express

12 August
North Wales Weekly

13 August
Disc, New Musical Express

14 August
Manchester Chronicle

15 August
Disc, Liverpool Echo, New Record Mirror

16 August
Daily Mail, Melody Maker, New Musical Express

17 August
New Musical Express, North Wales Weekly News, The Beatles And Wales (David Jones)

18 August
Herald Express, Paignton News, The Beatles (Hunter Davies), *Magical Mystery Tours - My Life With The Beatles* (Tony Bramwell)

19 August
Bournemouth Evening Echo, Mirabelle, New Musical Express, Bournemouth A Go! Go! (Jon Kremer)

SOURCES

20 August
The Beatles Book, Liverpool Daily Post, Radio Times, Bournemouth A Go! Go! (Jon Kremer), *The Beatles Off The Record* (Keith Badman)

21 August
She, I Me Mine (George Harrison)

22 August
Disc, Melody Maker, Mojo, New Record Mirror, The Beatles – A Private View (Robert Freeman)

23 August
Bournemouth Times, Melody Maker, New Musical Express

24 August
Bournemouth Times, New Record Mirror, Radio Times, The Beatles – The BBC Archive (Kevin Howlett)

26 August
Journal & Guardian, Southport Visiter, Wallasey News

27 August
Radio Times

28 August
Manchester Evening News, New Record Mirror, Cilla (Douglas Thompson), *The Man Who Made The Beatles* (Ray Coleman)

29 August
Disc, New Record Mirror, Southport Visiter

30 August
Melody Maker, Mirabelle, New Musical Express, Radio Times

1 September
Sunday Telegraph

2 September
The Guardian, Mirabelle

3 September
Radio Times

4 September
New Musical Express, Worcester Evening News

5 September
Disc, New Musical Express, New Record Mirror, Somerset County Gazette, Somerset County Herald

6 September
Luton News & Bedfordshire Advertiser, (Luton) *Saturday Telegraph*, *Melody Maker*, *New Musical Express*

7 September
Beatles Bible, *Croydon Advertiser*, *Croydon Times-Herald*, *The Beatles – The BBC Archive* (Kevin Howlett)

8 September
Blackpool Evening Gazette, *New Record Mirror*

9 September
Daily Mirror, *Marilyn*, *Mirabelle*

10 September
Daily Mirror, *Melody Maker*, *Radio Times*, *The Beatles Off The Record* (Keith Badman), *The Beatles – An Oral History* (David Pritchard & Alan Lysaght)

11 September
Daily Mail, *Melody Maker*

12 September
Disc, *New Record Mirror*, *Radio Times*

13 September
Daily Mail, *Melody Maker*, *Nelson Leader*, *New Musical Express*

14 September
Daily Mirror, *Disc*, *New Record Mirror*, *Northwich Guardian*, *Preston Evening Post*

15 September
Daily Express, *Daily Mirror*, *Marilyn*, *New Record Mirror*, *The Observer*, *Sunday Times*

16 September-2 October
Cash Box, *Disc*, *Melody Maker*, *New Musical Express*, *New Record Mirror*, *Radio Times*, Reveille, *The Beatles – An Oral History* (David Pritchard & Alan Lysaght), *The Beatles Are Coming!* (Bruce Spizer), "Magical Mystery Tours" website

3 October
Disc, *New Record Mirror*, *Radio Times*, *The Beatles – The BBC Archive* (Kevin Howlett), *The Beatles At The BBC* (Kevin Howlett)

4 October
Beat Instrumental, *Daily Herald*, *Melody Maker*, *New Musical Express*

5 October
Edinburgh Evening Times, *Glasgow Evening Telegraph*, (Glasgow) *Evening Times*, *Radio Times*

SOURCES

6 October
Belfast Telegraph, Daily Record, (Dundee) *Courier & Advertiser, Fifeshire Advertiser*

7 October
Daily Express, (Dundee) *Courier & Advertiser, Dundee Evening Telegraph, Fife Free Press,* (Glasgow) *Evening Times, Mirabelle,* BBC Radio Scotland

8 October
Dundee Telegraph, Glasgow Herald, The Guardian

9 October
Liverpool Echo, The Observer, Radio Times, Sunday Telegraph, The Beatles – The BBC Archive (Kevin Howlett)

10 October
Disc, Liverpool Daily Post, Liverpool Weekly News, New Record Mirror

11 October
Melody Maker, New Musical Express, Staffordshire Evening Sentinel, Staffordshire Weekly Sentinel, Stone Guardian

12 October
Daily Sketch

13 October
Daily Mirror, Melody Maker, The True Story of the Beatles (Billy Shepherd)

14 October
Bristol Evening Post, Coventry Evening Telegraph, Evening Standard, Portsmouth Evening News

15 October
Daily Express, Southport Journal, Southport Visiter

16 October
The Beatles Book, Disc, The True Story of the Beatles (Billy Shepherd)

17 October
Boyfriend, Disc, Evening Standard, NRM, Here, There And Everywhere – My Life Recording The Music Of The Beatles (Geoff Emerick & Howard Massey)

18 October
Liverpool Daily Post, Melody Maker, New Musical Express

19 October
Buxton Advertiser, Evening Standard

20 October
Birmingham Daily Post, Birmingham Evening Mail & Despatch, Birmingham Planet, Daily Mail, Evening Standard, Leicester Illustrated Chronicle, Liverpool Daily Post, Liverpool Echo, Radio Times, Sunday Mirror, TV Times

21 October
Bournemouth Times, Daily Mail, Daily Sketch

22 October
Daily Sketch, Hornsey Journal, Western Daily Press, Weston Mercury & Somersetshire Herald, Evening News & Star

23 October
Crosby Herald, Daily Sketch, Hull & Yorkshire Times, Yeah! Yeah! Yeah! (Borje Lundberg & Ammi Bohm)

24 October
Bournemouth Evening Echo, Christchurch Herald, Daily Express, Daily Herald, Daily Record, Daily Sketch, Disc, Hampshire Telegraph, Manchester Evening News, New Record Mirror, Our Time, Portsmouth Evening News

25 October
Melody Maker, New Musical Express, Yeah! Yeah! Yeah! (Borje Lundberg & Ammi Bohm)

26 October
Cambridge Independent Press, Cambridge News, Evening Standard, News Of The World, TV Times, Yeah! Yeah! Yeah! (Borje Lundberg & Ammi Bohm)

27 October
(Newcastle) *Evening Chronicle, The* (Newcastle) *Journal, The Northern Echo, Sunday Mirror, Yeah! Yeah! Yeah!* (Borje Lundberg & Ammi Bohm)

28 October
Lincolnshire Standard, The (Newcastle) *Journal, Yeah! Yeah! Yeah!* (Borje Lundberg & Ammi Bohm)

29 October
Daily Herald, Daily Sketch, The (Newcastle) *Journal, Washington Post, Wolverhampton Chronicle, Yeah! Yeah! Yeah!* (Borje Lundberg & Ammi Bohm)

30 October
Daily Express, Daily Telegraph, New Musical Express, The Today, Yeah! Yeah! Yeah! (Borje Lundberg & Ammi Bohm)

31 October
Daily Herald, Daily Sketch, Daily Telegraph, Disc, Liverpool Daily Post, New Record Mirror, The Beatles Yesterday Today And Tomorrow (Anthony Scaduto), *Yeah! Yeah! Yeah!* (Borje Lundberg & Ammi Bohm)

SOURCES

1 November
Cheltenham Chronicle & Gloucestershire Graphic, The Citizen, Daily Express, Disc, Gloucestershire Echo, Melody Maker, New Musical Express, Oxford Mail, John Winston Lennon (Ray Coleman), *Rocking In Oxford* (Trevor Hayward)

2 November
Cheltenham Chronicle, News Of The World, Sheffield Star, Sheffield Telegraph, South Yorkshire Times & Rotherham Express, Sunday People

3 November
Radio Times, Sunday Mirror, Yorkshire Evening News, Yorkshire Post

4 November
Beat Instrumental, The Times, Evening Standard, Liverpool Echo, Mirabelle, The Observer, Record Retailer, The Sphere, The Beatles – The BBC Archive (Kevin Howlett), *The Beatles – The Real Story* (Julius Fast), *A Cellarful Of Noise* (Brian Epstein), *1963* (John Lawton)

5 November
Daily Mirror, Daily Telegraph, Windsor & Slough Advertiser, The Times

6 November
Daily Express, Daily Mirror, Gazette Herald, Northampton Chronicle & Echo, Northampton Evening Telegraph, Northampton Mercury & Herald, Beatlemania! – The Beatles UK Tours 1963–1965, The Real Story of the Beatles UK Tours (Martin Creasy)

7 November
Belfast Telegraph, Disc, (Dublin) *Evening Press,* (Dublin) *Evening Herald, Irish Independent, Irish Telegraph, New Record Mirror, News Letter,* (Dublin) *Sunday Press, The Beatles Film & TV Chronicle 1961-1970* (Jörg Pieper & Volker Path)

8 November
Belfast Telegraph, Evening Herald, (Dublin) *Evening Press, Irish Independent, Irish News, News Letter, The Beatles Irish Concerts* (Colm Keane)

9 November
Belfast Telegraph, (Dublin) *Sunday Press, Beatlemania! – The Beatles UK Tours 1963–1965, The Real Story of the Beatles UK Tours* (Martin Creasy), *A Secret History* (Alastair Taylor), *Yesterday – The Beatles Remembered* (Alastair Taylor)

10 November
Birmingham Evening Mail & Despatch, Birmingham Daily Post, Radio Times, Sunday Mirror, The Beatles – The BBC Archive (Kevin Howlett)

11 November
A Cellarful Of Noise (Brian Epstein), *The Beatles' Story on Capitol Records, Part One* (Bruce Spizer)

12 November
Daily Sketch, Evening Standard, Portsmouth Evening News

13 November
(Bournemouth) Chronicle & Echo, Daily Mirror, Evening Standard, Plymouth Herald, The (Plymouth) Independent, Portsmouth Evening News & Southern Daily Mail, Western Evening Herald, Western Evening News, Western Morning News

14 November
Bristol Evening Post, Disc, Evening Standard, Exeter Express & Echo, New Record Mirror, South Devon Times, Southend Evening Echo, Western Daily Press, Western Morning News

15 November
Bristol Evening Post, Clevedon Mercury, (Exeter) Evening Echo, Melody Maker, New Musical Express, Somerset County Herald, Western Daily Press

16 November
Bournemouth Evening Echo, Bournemouth Times, Christchurch Times, Clevedon Mercury, Swanage Times, Yeah Yeah Yeah: The Beatles and Bournemouth (Nick Churchill)

17 November
Abingdon Herald & Advertiser, Christchurch Herald, News Of The World, Western Daily Press, Yeah Yeah Yeah: The Beatles and Bournemouth (Nick Churchill)

18 November
Cannock Advertiser, Daily Sketch, Disc, New Musical Express, Newsweek, Time, (Wolverhampton) Express & Star, It Was Thirty Years Ago Today (Terence Spencer)

19 November
Wolverhampton Chronicle, (Wolverhampton) Express & Star

20 November
Gorton Reporter, The Independent, Manchester County Express, Manchester County News, Manchester Evening News, Manchester Independent, Radio Times, It Was Thirty Years Ago Today (Terence Spencer)

21 November
Carlisle Journal, Cumberland Evening News, Disc, New Record Mirror, Radio Times, The Beatles (Hunter Davies)

22 November
Evening Gazette, Newcastle Evening Chronicle, Melody Maker, New Musical Express, The (Newcastle) Journal, Northern Daily Mail, Stockton Express, According To Dora (Dora Bryan)

23 November
Consett Chronicle, (Newcastle) Evening Chronicle, The (Newcastle) Journal

SOURCES

24 November
Hull & Kingston Times, Hull Daily Mail, The (Newcastle) Journal, New York Times, News Of The World

25 November
Bradford Telegraph & Argus, TV Times

26 November
Cambridge Independent, Cambridge News, Isle of Ely & Wisbech Advertiser & Pictorial, Our Times, Varsity, Beatlemania! – The Beatles UK Tours 1963-1965 (Martin Creasy), *Love Me Do* (Michael Braun)

27 November
Cambridge News, Daily Mirror, Liverpool Echo, New Musical Express, Northern Echo, Radio Times, Yorkshire Evening Press, The Beatles – The BBC Archive (Kevin Howlett), *Love Me Do* (Michael Braun)

28 November
Daily Express, Disc, Lincolnshire Echo, The (Lincoln) Standard, New Record Mirror, Love Me Do (Michael Braun), *Photograph* (Ringo Starr)

29 November
The Beatles Book, Huddersfield Daily Examiner, Huddersfield Weekly Examiner, Melody Maker, New Musical Express

30 November
Daily Sketch, randrlife.co.uk, *Sunday Mirror, Sunderland Echo*

1 December
Bradford Telegraph & Argus, Daily Mail

2 December
Evening Standard, News Of The World, Portsmouth Evening News, Love Me Do (Michael Braun)

3 December
The Beatles Book, Hampshire Telegraph, News Of The World, Portsmouth Evening News

4 December
Lewisham Borough News, Lewisham Journal, Liverpool Daily Post, Liverpool Echo, Love Me Do (Michael Braun)

5 December
Disc, Merseybeat, New Record Mirror, Reveille

6 December
Daily Herald, Daily Sketch, Melody Maker, New Musical Express, The Times, Love Me Do (Michael Braun)

7 December

Liverpool Daily Post, Liverpool Echo, New Musical Express, Pop Weekly, Radio Times, The Beatles – The BBC Archive (Kevin Howlett), *FAB: An Intimate Life of Paul McCartney* (Howard Sounes), *John Lennon In My Life* (Pete Shotton), *Love Me Do* (Michael Braun)

8 December

Disc, Kentish Times, Lewisham Journal & Borough News, Sunday Mirror, Beatlemania! – The Beatles UK Tours 1963-1965 (Martin Creasy)

9 December

Billboard, Disc, Southend Standard, Southend Star, Beatlemania! – The Beatles UK Tours 1963-1965 (Martin Creasy)

10 December

Cash Box, Doncaster Gazette & Chronicle, The Huffington Post, Beatlemania! – The Beatles UK Tours 1963-1965 (Martin Creasy)

11 December

Scarborough Evening News

12 December

Daily Herald, Daily Mail, Disc, New Record Mirror, Nottingham Evening Post & News, Nottinghamshire Guardian

13 December

Billboard, Daily Herald, Evening Standard, Southern Evening Echo, The Guardian, Melody Maker, New Musical Express, Beatlemania! – The Beatles UK Tours 1963-1965 (Martin Creasy)

14 December

Daily Mirror, Evening Standard, Liverpool Daily Post, Mitcham News & Mercury, Streatham News, Wandsworth Advertiser & News

15 December

Birmingham Evening Mail & Despatch, Birmingham Planet, Birmingham Post, The New York Times

16 December

Mirabelle, The Times

17 December

Today, The Beatles Are Coming! (Bruce Spizer), *The Beatles – The BBC Archive* (Kevin Howlett), *Love Me Do* (Michael Braun)

18 December

Daily Sketch, Liverpool Daily Post, The Observer, The Beatles At The BBC (Kevin Howlett), *The Beatles – The BBC Archive* (Kevin Howlett)

SOURCES

19 December
Daily Mirror, Disc, New Record Mirror

20 December
Daily Mirror, Liverpool Echo, Melody Maker, New Musical Express

21 December
Bradford Telegraph & Argus, Daily Telegraph, Evening Standard, Radio Times

22 December
Daily Express, Liverpool Daily Post, Liverpool Echo, Sunday Mirror

23 December
Billboard, Birmingham Daily Post, Bradford Telegraph & Argus, Disc

24 December
Evening Standard, Liverpool Echo, Mojo, Today, Cilla (Douglas Thompson), *Let's Go Down The Cavern* (Spencer Leigh)

25 December
Radio Times

26 December
Mirabelle, Popular Music and Society, New Record Mirror, Radio Times, The Beatles At The BBC (Kevin Howlett), *John Lennon In My Life* (Pete Shotton)

27 December
Daily Herald, New Musical Express, The Times

28 December
Daily Mirror, Daily Worker, Liverpool Echo, Liverpool Daily Post

29 December
Baltimore Sun, Chicago Tribune, Los Angeles Times, Sunday Mirror, Washington Post

30 December
Billboard, Cash Box, The Times

31 December
Daily Mail, Record Retailer, John Lennon In My Life Co-written by Pete Shotton and Nicholas Schaffner

ACKNOWLEDGEMENTS

First and foremost, my thanks go to Jan Gammie, a friend from my days at Decca and Record Business, who threw herself into the task of spending hours on the phone collecting stories from people who are the backbone of this book. It's probably fair to say she is responsible for the majority of the stories. I'd also like to thank the Gammie clan – Richard, Lottie and Edward, all of whom made some contribution. Thanks also to Luke Crampton and Pete Compton, with whom I spent many happy years past MRIB, who also made invaluable contributions. Mention must be made of people who provided useful information for the book but sadly didn't make the final cut. Many hours were spent at the British Newspaper Library in its old home in Colindale – sadly the victim of the wrecking ball, and the British Library, where the kindness and helpfulness of the staff made this job easier than it otherwise would have been. (The British Library, like the BBC, is one of Britain's greatest institutions – we should all be proud of it.) Thanks also to the good folk at Omnibus – David Barraclough, Greg Morton, David Stock, Imogen Clark, Claire Browne and Debra Geddes. I am also deeply indebted to Mark Lewisohn, who graciously invited me into his home where I spent a day rummaging through his files, unearthing untold gems. When I was reaching a brick wall and thinking I wouldn't be able to finish this project, Mark encouraged me not to give up. I would like to thank my son Christiaan, who made no contribution to the book whatsoever, but reminds me how wonderful it is to be a proud father. Lastly, I would like to thank my darling wife Wellesley, who has helped all along the way. Although her idea of a nice holiday in London probably isn't spending it at Colindale, she nonetheless pored over musty volumes of newspapers from 1963 with unbound enthusiasm.

PHOTO CREDITS

11 January Mirrorpix
11 February Richard Langham
5 April Chris Ware/Getty Images
10 April John Pratt/Getty Images
14 April Western Mail Archive/Mirrorpix
18 April Express/Stringer/Getty Images
21 April V&A Images/Getty Images
24 April Peter Bussey/Getty Images
30 May *Daily Herald*/Mirrorpix
2 June Colin Payne
5 June V&A Images/Getty Images
18 June *Daily Mirror*/Mirrorpix
23 June David Redfern/Getty Images
27 July Mark & Colleen Hayward/Getty Images
7 August *Liverpool Echo*/Mirrorpix
20 August David Evans
27 August Paul Popper/Popperfoto/Getty Images
7 September *Daily Mirror*/Mirrorpix
8 September Terry Fincher/Getty Images
9 September *Daily Mirror*/Mirrorpix
10 September *Daily Mirror*/Mirrorpix
13 September *Daily Mirror*/Mirrorpix
4 October David Redfern/Getty Images
6 October Mirrorpix
13 October Edward Wing/Getty Images
16 October Paul Popper/Popperfoto
19 October *Daily Mirror*/Mirrorpix
20 October Getty Images
23 October *Evening Standard*/Getty Images
25 October David Cooke

30 October Popperfoto/Getty Images
31 October *Daily Mirror*/Mirrorpix
1 November *Daily Mirror*/Mirrorpix
2 November Jo Rees
3 November Mirrorpix/Getty Images
4 November Popperfoto/Getty Images
6 November *Daily Mirror*/Mirrorpix
8 November *Daily Mirror*/Mirrorpix
9 November *Sunday Mirror*/Mirrorpix
12 November Mirrorpix
13 November *Daily Mirror*/Mirrorpix
17 November Coventry Telegraph Archive/Mirrorpix
18 November Keystone
19 November *Birmingham Post & Mail*/Mirrorpix 21 November *Daily Mirror*/Mirrorpix
22 November Mirrorpix
25 November Mirrorpix
7 December Icon & Image/Getty Images
8 December Terry Fincher
9 December Mark & Colleen Hayward/Getty Images
15 December Mirrorpix
16 December Tom King
19 December Mirrorpix
19 December *Evening Standard*/Mirrorpix
23 December Arthur Sidey
26 December Sayle/*Daily Mirror*
27 December *Daily Mirror*/Mirrorpix

All other images are the copyright of their respective storytellers.

MEET THE BEAT

STAR SPECIAL

Number Twelve

AN
INFORMAL
DATE IN
WORDS &
PERSONAL
PICTURES

2'6

INTRODUCED
BY THEMSELVES
Written and
compiled by
TONY BARROW